Communication Yearbook 36

Communication Yearbook 36

Edited by
Charles T. Salmon

international communication association

Published Annually for the
International Communication Association

Routledge
Taylor & Francis Group

NEW YORK AND LONDON

First published 2013
by Routledge
711 Third Avenue, New York, NY 10017

Simultaneously published in the UK
by Routledge
2 Park Square, Milton Park, Abingdon, Oxon OX14 4RN

Routledge is an imprint of the Taylor & Francis Group, an informa business

ISSN: 0147-4642
ISSN: 1556-7429

ISBN: 978-0-415-52548-0 (hbk)
ISBN: 978-0-203-11365-3 (ebk)

Typeset in Times by
EvS Communication Networx, Inc.

Printed and bound in the United States of America by Sheridan Books, Inc. (a Sheridan Group company).

Contents

The International Communication Association

The International Communication Association (ICA) was formed in 1950, bringing together academics and other professionals whose interests focus on human communication. The Association maintains an active membership of more than 4,000 individuals, of whom some two-thirds teach and conduct research in colleges, universities, and schools around the world. Other members are in government, law, medicine, and other professions. The wide professional and geographic distribution of the membership provides the basic strength of the ICA. The Association serves as a meeting ground for sharing research and useful dialogue about communication interests.

Through its divisions and interest groups, publications, annual conferences, and relations with other associations around the world, the ICA promotes the systemic study of communication theories, processes, and skills. In addition to the *Communication Yearbook*, the Association publishes the *Journal of Communication, Human Communication Research, Communication Theory, Journal of Computer-Mediated Communication, Communication, Culture & Critique, A Guide to Publishing in Scholarly Communication Journals*, and the *ICA Newsletter*.

For additional information about the ICA and its activities, visit online at www.icahdq.org or contact Michael L. Haley, Executive Director, International Communication Association, 1500 21st Ave. NW, Washington, DC 20036 USA; phone 202-955-1444; fax 202-955-1448; email ica@icahdq.org.

Editors of the *Communication Yearbook* series:

Communication Law & Policy
Peter J. Humphreys—Div. Chair, *University of Manchester*
Laura Stein—Div. Vice-Chair, *University of Texas – Austin*

Ethnicity and Race in Communication
Roopali Mukherjee—Div. Chair, *CUNY – Queens College*
Miyase Christensen—Div. Vice-Chair, *Karlstad U; Royal Institute of Technology (KTH)*

Feminist Scholarship
Radhika Gajjala—Div. Chair, *Bowling Green State University*
Paula M Gardner—Div. Vice-Chair, *OCAD University*

Global Communication and Social Change
Antonio C. La Pastina—Div. Chair, *Texas A&M University*
Rashmi Luthra—Div. Vice-Chair, *University of Michigan – Dearborn*

Health Communication
Monique Mitchell Turner—Div. Chair, *George Washington University*
Mohan Jyoti Dutta—Div. Vice-Chair, *Purdue University*

Information Systems
Elly A. Konijn—Div. Chair, *VU University – Amsterdam*
Prabu David—Div. Vice-Chair, *Washington State University*

Instructional/Developmental Communication
Rebecca M. Chory—Div. Chair, *West Virginia University*
Brandi N. Frisby—Div. Vice-Chair, *University of Kentucky*

Intercultural Communication
Steve T. Mortenson—Div. Chair, *University of Delaware*
Hee Sun Park—Div. Vice-Chair, *Michigan State University*

Interpersonal Communication
John P. Caughlin—Div. Chair, *University of Illinois, Urbana-Champaign*
Timothy R. Levine—Div. Vice-Chair, *Michigan State University*

Journalism Studies
Frank Esser—Div. Chair, *University of Zurich*
Stephanie L. Craft—Div. Vice-Chair, *University of Missouri*

Language & Social Interaction
Evelyn Y. Ho—Div. Chair, *University of San Francisco*
Theresa R. Castor—Div. Vice-Chair, *University of Wisconsin – Parkside*

Mass Communication
David Tewksbury—Div. Chair, *University of Illinois, Urbana-Champaign*
Rene Weber—Div. Vice-Chair, *University of California – Santa Barbara*

Organizational Communication
Janet Fulk—Div. Chair, *University of Southern California*
Ted Zorn—Div. Vice-Chair, *University of Waikato*

Philosophy of Communication
Laurie Ouellette—Div. Chair, *University of Minnesota*
Amit Pinchevski—Div. Vice-Chair, *Hebrew University*

Political Communication
Yariv Tsfati—Div. Chair, *University of Haifa*
Claes H. De Vreese—Div. Vice-Chair, *University of Amsterdam*

Popular Communication
Paul Frosh—Div. Chair, *Hebrew University of Jerusalem*
Jonathan Alan Gray—Div. Vice-Chair, *University of Wisconsin – Madison*

Public Relations
Juan-Carlos Molleda—Div. Chair, *University of Florida*
Jennifer L. Bartlett—Div. Vice-Chair, *Queensland University of Technology*

Visual Communication
Michael S. Griffin—Div. Chair, *Macalester College*
Jana Holsanova—Div. Vice-Chair, *Lund University*

SPECIAL INTEREST GROUP CHAIRS

Communication History
Jefferson D. Pooley—IG Chair, *Muhlenberg College*
Philip Lodge—IG Vice-Chair, *Edinburgh Napier University*

Environmental Communication
Richard J. Doherty—IG Chair, *University of Illinois – Chicago*

Game Studies
Dmitri Williams—IG Chair, *University of Southern California*

James D. Ivory—IG Vice-Chair, *Virginia Tech*

Gay, Lesbian, Bisexual, & Transgender Studies
Vincent Doyle—IG Chair, *IE University*
Adrienne Shaw—IG Chair, *University of Pittsburgh*

Intergroup Communication
Liz Jones—IG Chair, *Griffith University*

Editor's Introduction

Charles T. Salmon

When I agreed to serve a three-year term as Editor of ICA's *Communication Yearbook* (CY) series in 2009, my goal was to make CY the most international and interdisciplinary of all ICA publications. Our discipline may once have been characterized as a crossroads through which many pass but few tarry, but to the extent that such a characterization was fair at the time, it is no longer fitting. After all, our sprawling and eclectic field has insinuated itself in nearly every crevice of the academic community. Communications is a discipline that virtually knows no bounds, sharing concepts and overlapping research interests with engineering, mathematics, computer science, psychology, economics, sociology, agriculture, medicine, business, education, literature, linguistics, art, and music, to name only a few allied disciplines. Further, the rapid and dynamic growth of communications research and education around the globe has forever altered the intellectual terrain of our field and significantly enriched our repertoire of concepts and theories. This point is much more salient to me now, than three years ago, as I have largely edited one volume in this series from a university known as an iconic pillar of U.S. communications scholarship for more than half a century (Michigan State University); another volume from a fledgling undergraduate communications program in a Middle Eastern high-tech zone (the Interdisciplinary Center in Herzliya, Israel); and a third volume from a respected Asian center of communications research in one of the most culturally diverse cities in the world (Nanyang Technological University, Singapore).

Distinguished contributors to this volume from Australia, China, Germany, Great Britain, Israel, Netherlands, Scotland, Singapore and the United States reflect the global and disciplinary diversity that is redefining our field. Among the thirty-two authors are Honorary Fellows of the American Statistical Association; American Academy for the Advancement of Science; Academy of Social Sciences in Australia; British Academy; British Psychological Society; Society for the Science of Design Studies, Japan; Society of Experimental Social Psychology; International Academy of Social Relations; Society for Risk Analysis; Institute of Mathematical Statistics; International Communication Association; and Midwest Association for Public Opinion Research. I am very pleased to be able to compile this collection of academic insight from such a diverse and august group of international scholars.

Acknowledgments

As I look back across the pages of volumes 34, 35 and now 36 of this series, I must thank a number of colleagues and friends who contributed so much of their time, effort and energy to these works.

Linda Bathgate, Senior Editor at Taylor & Francis, provided unparalleled support throughout the past three years and helped navigate through several challenging issues that arose along the way; Lynn Goeller, of EvS Communication Networx, Inc., provided great advice throughout the production process while exhibiting much-appreciated calm under fire; ICA Executive Director Michael Haley provided strong direction and essential resources; and Sam Luna (ICA), Kayley Hoffman (Taylor & Francis) and Katherine Ghezzi (Taylor & Francis) provided considerable behind-the-scenes support.

Associate editors Cindy Gallois (volumes 34, 35, 36), Christina Holtz-Bacha (volumes 34, 35, 36), Joseph Walther (volumes 34, 35, 36), Guillermo Mastrini (volume 34), Onuora Nwuneli (volume 34), Xinshu Zhao (volume 34) and Nurit Guttman (volume 35), contributed sage advice, wisdom and insight in discussions, reviews and decisions. Editorial assistants Laleah Fernandez (volumes 34, 35, 36), Robin Blom (volume 35) and Su Lin Yeo (volume 36) spent untold hours toiling over manuscripts, corresponding with authors, and filling in where needed through the various stages of the editorial and production processes. Editorial board members, *ad hoc* reviewers and authors from more than twenty countries provided substantial intellectual capital, critique and insight. These three volumes could not have materialized without the dedication and contributions of every person involved.

I would like to give special thanks to the following individuals for going above and beyond the call of duty to spend extra time with authors to help improve their work; for agreeing to write an additional review or to comment on an author's second, third or even fourth draft with nary a complaint; or for demonstrating a willingness to jump into the fray on particularly short notice where needed and when asked: Frank Boster, Isabel Botero, Jane Brown, Sahara Byrne, Kenzie Cameron, Rebecca Chory, Jim Dillard, Sharon Dunwoody, Cindy Gallois, Kathleen Galvin, Nurit Guttman, Jake Harwood, Christina Holtz-Bacha, Steve Lacy, Caryn Medved, Robin Mansell, Ronald Rice, Rajiv Rimal, Dietram Scheufele, Sandi Smith, Joe Walther and Ruth Wodak. To these individuals and the many other dedicated colleagues who contributed to the CY enterprise over the past three years, please accept my sincere gratitude. I hope that the next editor is as fortunate as I have been to be able to work with so many capable, conscientious scholars and good friends.

Communication Yearbook 36

CHAPTER CONTENTS

1 The Dissonant Self

Contributions from Dissonance Theory to a New Agenda for Studying Political Communication

Wolfgang Donsbach and Cornelia Mothes

Dresden University of Technology

Due to technological changes in today's communication environments, the investigation of media use and media effects has become an ever more complex research venture. In order to adequately comprehend the social practices of media users in the age of the Internet, various scholars have recently recommended a new agenda for the future study of political communication. Based on these suggestions, the following paper briefly outlines two research strands of political communication—political polarization and political demobilization—which are currently the focus of significant attention and scientific dispute. In reference to cognitive dissonance theory, we propose one possible strategy for media research to determine future developments of political communication in both research domains by observing citizens' motivational changes in their exposure to political information.

Social communication has reached a whole new level of complexity due to the development of the Internet, a situation that poses new challenges for today's media consumers as well as media researchers. The quantitative growth of communication offers and information services allows citizens to take on a significantly higher level of personal control over their information environment. An individual's attention to public issues and specific media content is increasingly decided by the user's personal communication motives, attitudes, and habitual propensities (cf. Bimber & Davis, 2003; Stroud, 2011; Wirth & Schweiger, 1999). According to Prior (2005), media scholars therefore need to take into account that a person's "media content preferences become the key to understanding the political implications of new media" (p. 587).

Increased user activity within a multifaceted information environment has led to an ongoing academic debate on the implications of the Internet for social life in a democracy (cf. DiMaggio, Hargittai, Neuman, & Robinson, 2001; Mitchelstein & Boczkowski, 2010; Norris, 2001). Optimists expect the Internet to enhance political interest and political discussion because technological developments would make it easier for citizens to exchange information and opinions with a minimum of effort. In this way, even those who until now have had little interest in politics might become more politically involved (e.g., Bucy & Gregson, 2001; Coleman & Gøtze, 2001; Kaid, 2003; Krueger, 2002;

Papacharissi, 2002b; Weber, Loumakis, & Bergman, 2003). For some scholars, through "increasing social connectedness and the sense of community" (Johnson & Kaye, 2003, p. 11), the Internet first and foremost represents an enrichment of public and political life. In contrast to these hopes for a deliberative democracy, critics fear that the Internet could foster the development of "communication ghettoes" (Graber, 2003, p. 153). Pessimists suspect that the Internet will accelerate the process of social fragmentation and will become a threat to public consensus (e.g., Galston, 2003; Gehrau & Goertz, 2010; Holtz-Bacha, 1998; Margolis & Resnick, 2000; Prior, 2005; Putnam, 2000; Zittel, 2004). According to Sunstein (2001), people could "wall themselves off from topics and opinions that they would prefer to avoid" (pp. 201–202). Similarly, Tewksbury (2005) assumes that an increasing fragmentation of information sources "may reduce the likelihood of sustained, widespread attention to political issues" (p. 346).

When speaking about the Internet's potential threat to democracy, two problems of social fragmentation come to the fore: On the one hand, scholars fear an increase of political polarization resulting from a reinforced exposure of media users to attitude-consistent political information (e.g., Iyengar & Hahn, 2009; Sunstein, 2001). On the other hand, scholars show heightened concern about political demobilization in the sense of an alienation of citizens from politics and public affairs (e.g., Prior, 2007; Xenos & Moy, 2007). Both polarization and political demobilization may have serious consequences for political life. A free exchange of contrasting political opinions and a basic interest in politics are seen as fundamental requirements for citizens to comply with their civic duties in a democracy (cf. Dewey, 1927; Habermas, 1962/1989; Mill, 1859/1956). Accordingly, if news audiences know "less about broader subjects" and have "less and less in common with each other" (Davis, 1999, p. 55), the performance of democracy might become severely hampered.

A New Agenda for Communication Research in the Age of the Internet

Media scholars generally agree that today's technological developments have promoted some changes in societal communication. Yet, up to now the consequences of these developments have remained relatively unclear because optimists and pessimists have derived opposing scientific prognoses on the social implications of the Internet. Following recent metatheoretical reviews on communication research (Bennett & Iyengar, 2008; Mitchelstein & Boczkowski, 2010), conflicting scientific perceptions can partly be traced back to the theoretical and methodological orientations of communication research itself. Reflecting on the state of political communication in times of social change, Bennett and Iyengar (2008), who particularly focused on media effects approaches, doubt the actual significance of current research insights in the field of political communication. They claim that contemporary media research provokes "battles over findings" (p. 707) but does not yet provide sufficient explanations for these contradictory findings, thereby impeding a comprehension of political communication in a changing and ever more complex society (pp. 713–716). The authors believe that one reason for this shortcoming is that scholars have rarely made social change itself a constituent part of their theoretical models. Instead, scholars would normally adhere to theories that, under current circumstances, are increasingly losing their explanatory power (pp. 707–713):

> The inevitable result is that the field is adrift theoretically, seldom looking back to see where foundational modern theory needs to be adapted and, in some cases, overthrown, in order to keep pace with the orientations of late modern audiences, and new modes of content production and information delivery. (p. 713)

Mitchelstein and Boczkowski (2010) come to a similar conclusion for online research: Up until now, communication studies have been "characterized by stability rather than change ... because research has usually drawn on traditional theoretical and methodological approaches" (p. 1085). In this way, current research lacks a "programmatic vision of possible directions for future journeys" (p. 1086).

Both research reviews independently point to similar challenges for communication research in the Internet age. Bennett and Iyengar (2008) propose a "new agenda for studying political communication" (p. 713) that pays greater attention to processes of social change in our so-called postmodern era. According to the authors, theoretical approaches, which have formerly been treated separately, would need to be incorporated into comprehensive models that describe and explain broader social "effects of effects" (p. 716) of political communication. When increased self-selection in the use of information is considered, the focus would necessarily be on political content that is actually used by citizens (p. 724). Similarly, Mitchelstein and Boczkowski (2010) emphasize the necessity for an "integrative research agenda" (p. 1093), which connects media effects and media use approaches in a more comprehensive way. The authors point to several methodological and theoretical improvements that are needed in current online research. They urge media scholars to be more rigorous in tracing observed media features back to media users' actual behaviors (p. 1089), to differentiate between "extraordinary" and "ordinary" social practices in online communication (p. 1091), and to overcome the rather artificial distinction between media genres or formats to produce a more detailed analysis of media content that is actually used (p. 1088).

A joint investigation of media use and media effects for depicting developments of political communication requires that existing media approaches be theoretically linked. The motivation of the individual to engage in political communication can be expected to be such a focal linkage point because it acts as both a cause and an effect of a person's communication behavior. As moderators of simple stimulus-response explanations, motivational components had been introduced early into communication studies (e.g., Blumler, 1979; Rubin & Perse, 1987). As a central part of O-S-O-R models, the individual's motivation is still of great relevance for contemporary media effects research (e.g., Eveland, Shah, & Kwak, 2003; McLeod, Kosicki, & McLeod, 1994). In his proposed "*reinforcing spirals* framework" (p. 281), Slater (2007) presents a communication model that moves beyond the often rather linear motivational approaches by considering reciprocal effects of motivation and media use in a cumulative, dynamic process (pp. 282–284):

> Persons engaging in this process should tend toward continued or increased use of that particular media content. This should lead to the maintenance or strengthening of the attitude or behavior in question, leading in turn to continued or increased use of relevant media content. (Slater, 2007, p. 285)

Keeping to Bennett and Iyengar's (2008) terminology, besides the *effects* of media use on the individual's motivation, Slater's model additionally includes the *effects of effects* of media content on subsequent information behavior. On the basis of Slater's assumptions, we can expect the individual's motivation—in being affected by previous information exposure and, again, affecting subsequent exposure—to represent an important connecting link between media *effects* and *effects of effects*. A motivational approach similar to Slater's model was introduced in the early 1980s by two German scholars (Früh & Schönbach, 1982; Schönbach & Früh, 1984). In critical response to the uses and gratifications approach, their "dynamic-transactional model" conceives the media and their users as communication elements that are involved in an ongoing interaction process. Früh and Schönbach point out that the media and their audiences constantly react to each other and can therefore be considered as both causes and effects of one another. The work of Früh and Schönbach has rarely been published or discussed outside of Germany, keeping its academic reputation predominantly confined to the German research landscape (cf. Früh & Schönbach, 2005).

Against the backdrop of Schönbach and Früh's early dynamic-transactional model and more recent theoretical reviews in the field of communication research, three factors appear to be of particular importance for a "new agenda" (Bennett & Iyengar, 2008, p. 713) in the study of political communication in times of social and technological change:

1. In order to make developments in political communication comprehensible—such as political polarization or demobilization—communication processes need to be causally examined in terms of *effects* of political messages on media users and in terms of *effects of effects* of political messages on users' subsequent communication behavior.
2. In order to make changes in political communication traceable to specific information characteristics, a more detailed analysis of actually used communication features is needed.

3. The examination of the individuals' motivation might help to understand the dynamic of political communication as a reciprocal process. As a result and a cause of communication processes, motivational changes might represent an important connecting link between media *effects* and *effects of effects*, thereby conflating media effects and media use research.

With the help of these three methodological components, there surely are many ways for media scholars to describe developments of political communication more comprehensively. Two possible applications will be presented in the following chapter. First, we will provide an overview on developments and contradictory findings in current research on political polarization and demobilization as two highly controversial fields of contemporary media research. Referring back to the social psychological theory of cognitive dissonance (Festinger, 1957), we will then outline how these two developments in political communication might be traced in terms of media *effects* and *effects of effects* on the basis of motivational changes. The theory of cognitive dissonance is of central relevance to both phenomena for three reasons. First, it constitutes the theoretical basis of partisan selective exposure research, which crucially contributes to the current examination of political polarization. Second, we assume that the theory of cognitive dissonance can provide more precise insights into political polarization processes by taking into consideration attitude-polarizing and attitude-depolarizing effects of political messages. Third, the theory might also be useful for the observation of political demobilization. In this context, dissonance theoretical self-concept approaches could be of particular interest because the self-concept, as examined in today's dissonance research, displays numerous similarities with motivational components that have been found to be influential in political contexts, above all the concept of political efficacy.

Polarization of Political Communication

Conflicting Viewpoints on the Severity of Echo Chambers for Deliberation

Selective exposure research has a long research tradition, going back to Lazarsfeld, Berelson, and Gaudet's (1944) as well as Klapper's (1960) influential works on minimal media effects and Festinger's (1957) social psychological assumption that people's striving for cognitive consonance leads them to prefer attitude-consistent over counterattitudinal information. In the early 2000s, selective exposure had lost its importance for media research. Consistency motives were shown to have a significant but only weak impact on people's media use (e.g., D'Alessio & Allen, 2002; Donsbach, 1991). In recent years, particularly in the United States, the number of studies concerning the influence of personal attitudes on content choices has been growing again. A majority of studies finds strong support for selective exposure to attitude-consistent messages in today's information environment (e.g., Bimber & Davis, 2003; Garrett, 2009a; Graf & Aday, 2008; Iyengar & Hahn, 2009; Knobloch-Westerwick & Meng, 2009; Meffert, Chung, Joiner, Waks, & Garst, 2006). Some authors already speak of a "return" (Stroud, 2008, p. 342) or "revival" (Iyengar & Hahn, 2009, p. 20) of the selective exposure phenomenon.

Garrett (2009b, p. 682) attributes the new research boom in the domain of selective exposure to an increasing variety of available information due to the Internet and an increase of news sources with a clear political stance, which could facilitate the avoidance of challenging viewpoints. Recent content analyses seem to support this notion. For instance, a comparison of daily newspapers, online sites of TV channels, and online news aggregators by Maier (2010) revealed a significantly higher amount of opinionated content on the front pages of online news outlets in contrast to offline sources. Additionally, Baum and Groeling (2008) found that political news had a greater chance of becoming top news on Fox News.com and the Daily Kos blog if they were compatible with the editorial line of the medium. Thus, findings on blog use, as presented by Johnson, Bichard, and Zhang (2009), seem unsurprising: More than a half of their online respondents said they would use political blogs that correspond with their own political viewpoints, while only 20% visited blogs with an opposing political stance. With regard to the use of "traditional media," an investigation of homogeneous and heterogeneous media environments by Mutz and Martin (2001) revealed that people in areas with politically colored media outlets less frequently encountered differing viewpoints than people in regions with neutral news sources. More recently, Stroud (2008) demonstrated that a person's political ideology influences the choice of content even more on the Internet than in traditional media, especially if compared to daily newspapers. According to a survey by the Pew Internet & American Life Project, an increase of selective exposure on the Internet holds especially true for young people and users with a high level of interest in political issues: While in 2004 only 22% of the users 18 to 24 years old claimed to use online sources corresponding to their views, in 2008 this number had increased to 44% (Smith, 2009, p. 7).

At the same time, growing economic pressures on media organizations have also caused an increase of politically one-sided "niche news" (Iyengar & Hahn, 2009, p. 21) among offline sources. As for American television, Hamilton (2003) found that the political slant in TV news is closely related to a heightened need for viewer bonding. An economic analysis of Gentzkow and Shapiro (2010) supports this finding for the U.S. newspaper market. Based on their "Economic Model of Slant" (Gentzkow & Shapiro, 2010, p. 48), the authors conclude that "consumer demand responds strongly to the fit between a newspaper's slant and the ideology of potential readers, implying an economic incentive for newspapers to tailor their slant to the ideological predispositions of consumers" (p. 64).

Because of the trend toward political bias in news production as well as news consumption, several media scholars fear that citizens in the sense of a "big sort" (Bishop, 2008) could wall themselves off from politically opposing arguments (e.g., Iyengar & Hahn, 2009; Jamieson & Cappella, 2008; Kull, Ramsey, & Lewis, 2003; Sunstein, 2001). Other scholars object to such a view. Critics particularly question if selective exposure to attitude-consistent information is synonymous with selective avoidance of counterarguments. Although, according to Garrett (2009a, 2009b), individuals show a stronger preference for politically compliant content; an equally strong avoidance of inconsistent information is not proved by selective exposure research. In his representative survey on the evaluation of political candidates of the 2004 presidential campaign, Garrett (2009b) showed that the interest in the election campaign promoted not only attention to positive statements toward the preferred candidate but also increased knowledge about politically challenging statements. Similarly, in a comparison of adolescents' and adults' attention to the 1998 California election campaign, Chaffee, Saphir, Graf, Sandvig, and Hahn (2001) came to the conclusion that "attention to counter-attitudinal political messages is a fairly commonplace and normal behaviour of politically involved citizens, young and old" (p. 260).

Another objection to the threat of political polarization is the assumption that an increasing number of information sources, though promoting a greater selectivity per se, make it even harder for users to select information purposefully according to their preexisting attitudes. Huckfeldt, Mendez, and Osborn (2004) posit that "the likelihood of disagreement grows larger as a citizen's range of contacts increases, and disagreement is likely to be the rule rather than the exception" (p. 68). According to Brundidge (2010, p. 687), the enhanced likelihood of contacts with challenging information is due to a higher inadvertency toward attitude-inconsistent messages within increasingly complex communication environments. Brundidge (2010, p. 696) assumes that the Internet may impede partisan selectivity "by providing a context in which exposure to political difference is likely to occur," particularly due to weakened social boundaries. Online communication studies seem to confirm such a notion: Kim (2011), for instance, found that the use of social networking sites and online political messaging was positively related to contacts with challenging views. In their investigation of online political talk, Wojcieszak and Mutz (2009) showed that particularly when political opinion exchange is not intended to be the main goal of communication, American users of message boards and chat rooms tend to encounter opposite political opinions. The authors concluded that, "because they draw participants for non-political reasons, leisure chat rooms and message boards are natural places for disagreement to occur when political talk comes up" (Wojcieszak & Mutz, 2009, p. 49).

Attitudes in Reinforcing Spirals of Effects and Effects of Effects of Political Information

Findings that currently prove an increase of selective exposure among citizens, and findings that speak against a general tendency of individuals to blind themselves to contrary viewpoints are not mutually exclusive. Yet, both research strands provide opposite prospects with regard to the Internet's impact on the development of deliberation in a democracy. For instance, Iyengar and Hahn (2009, p. 34) state that the audience's shift to attitude-consistent messages may lead to a "less informed and more polarized electorate" (see also Stroud, 2011; Sunstein, 2009). Garrett (2009b) in contrast contends that the "prediction that people take any opportunity to screen out other perspectives seems unnecessarily grave" (p. 695) in the light of empirical evidence against selective avoidance of challenging viewpoints.

The question remains which of these two scientific prognoses on the actual severity of political polarization is closer to the citizens' "ordinary" behavior in technologically and socially changing societies: Do citizens increasingly tend to turn their back on opposing arguments and lose interest in discussing alternative viewpoints, or not? Is there a general threat that democracy will break up into scattered "enclaves" (Sunstein, 2001), which lack a common agenda of goals and interests? Thus, does the stated phenomenon of political polarization become a real jeopardy to democracy or can it rather be considered as an exceptional case that is unlikely to expand over time? In order to make the risk of political polarization scientifically comprehensible, it is necessary to examine polarization in terms of its temporal development on the basis of *effects* and *effects of effects* of political information. For this purpose, we suggest tracing the *societal* process of political polarization on an *individual* level; that is, to consider a person's level of attitudinal polarization as a central "motivational engine" of political information behavior. More precisely, we propose to examine two *reinforcing spirals*, a process of polarization and a process of depolarization of political attitudes.

Attitudinal Polarization.   An attitude is termed polarized if a person holds either extremely favorable or unfavorable views toward an attitude object, which may become more intense over time (cf. Lord, Ross, & Lepper, 1979; Miller, McHoskey, Bane, & Dowd, 1993). In the field of politics, for instance, a polarized attitude is defined as holding extremely positive views toward one political candidate or party while holding equally negative views toward the political opposition (Stroud, 2011, p. 134). Extreme, polarized attitudes have been found to be associated with higher attitude strength, that is, a higher durability and a higher resistance to change (e.g., Krosnick, Boninger, Chuang, Berent, & Carnot, 1993; Krosnick & Petty, 1995; Shrum, 1999).

The relationship between attitude polarization and the use of political messages has been of central interest for media researchers for a long time (e.g., Berelson, Lazarsfeld, & McPhee, 1954; Lord et al., 1979) and attracts renewed attention among today's media scholars. Measuring political attitudes before and after selection behavior, Taber and Lodge (2006), for example, demonstrated that the polarization of attitudes is a function of both selective exposure to consistent information (confirmation bias) and the counterarguing of inconsistent information (disconfirmation bias). The impact of exposure to congenial information on attitude polarization was also shown in field studies. For instance, Druckman and Parkin (2005) examined the effect of the relative media slant of two daily newspapers on readers' comparative candidate evaluations and found that the use of an outlet with a stronger slant was associated with higher positive evaluations of the favored candidate. A panel analysis of Jones (2002) revealed that during the 1990s daily listeners to the conservative talk radio program Rush Limbaugh intensified their identification with the Republican Party and defined themselves as more conservative in 1996 than in the early 1990s. Occasional and nonlisteners of Rush Limbaugh, however, showed no significant change in their political ideology. Considering attitude polarization as an independent variable, a study by Brannon, Tagler, and Eagly (2007) showed that the extremity of one's attitude affects the magnitude of exposure to attitude-compliant content: Subjects estimated attitude-consistent op-ed articles about abortion as significantly more interesting the more they held polarized attitudes toward this issue. The authors concluded that "overcoming the barriers of selective exposure is challenging for communicators" when their audience holds strong and extreme attitudes (Brannon et al., 2007, p. 616).

Previous research in this area had certain limitations with respect to the generalizability of findings. Experimental settings and separate examinations of single media formats gave only limited insight into the actual behavior of recipients within their daily information environment. Furthermore, it was not the focus of previous research to capture the reciprocal process of attitude polarization through selective exposure (media effects) and the increase of selective exposure through attitudinal polarization (media *effects of effects*). A study by Stroud (2008, 2010, 2011) can be seen as an advance in selective exposure research with respect to either previous research limitations. On the basis of cross-sectional and panel data, Stroud analyzed political attitudes both as causes and as results of political information exposure during the 2004 presidential election campaign. In addition to their attitudes, respondents were asked to indicate which newspaper, radio program, television format, and online source they most often refer to for political information. After controlling for a variety of demographic variables and multiple indicators of political involvement, attitude polarization could be confirmed as a function of attention to consistent sources, both on the basis of the two-wave panel analyses and by means of a cross-sectional time series analysis. Analyses on the individual level also proved the existence of some, though weaker, evidence for the assumption that attitude polarization increases attention to attitude-conforming information. With respect to Slater (2007), Stroud concluded that there might be a societal spiral effect, which "could indicate nonlinear growth of both polarization and partisan selective exposure up to a maximum level" (Stroud, 2010, p. 570). With respect to the severity of political polarization as a societal process we can therefore assume that the polarization of people's attitudes increases the polarization of political communication in society.

Besides these detrimental effects of congenial political information for a deliberative democracy, there is some evidence that both exposure to attitude-consistent information and the formation of extreme, strong attitudes may also have positive effects for democracy in that they increase political involvement (e.g., Dilliplane, 2011; Krosnick et al., 1993; Stroud, 2007, 2011; Visser, Krosnick, & Simmons, 2003). That is, people who are surrounded by attitude-consistent arguments may not only become more polarized toward political issues but also more engaged in politics.

Attitudinal Depolarization. In contrast to people with polarized attitudes, people with depolarized attitudes simultaneously hold conflicting favorable and unfavorable views toward an attitude object or—in the realm of politics—equally favorable or unfavorable views toward political opposites such as political contenders (e.g., Binder, Dalrymple, Brossard, & Scheufele, 2009, p. 318; Parsons, 2010, p. 184). The presence of competing considerations of positive and negative elements—as opposed to polarized, extreme viewpoints—is better known as attitude ambivalence (cf. Kaplan, 1972; Krosnick et al., 1993; Kruglanski & Stroebe, 2005; Priester & Petty, 1996). Ambivalence is defined and measured as both a *cognitive* coexistence of negative and positive evaluations of an issue and an *emotional* conflict accompanied by psychological tension and feelings of being torn (e.g., Kaplan, 1972; Newby-Clark, McGregor, & Zanna, 2002; Parsons, 2010; Thompson, Zanna, & Griffin, 1995).

Research in the area of social networks consistently shows that citizens who are surrounded by individuals with challenging political viewpoints have less polarized attitudes than people who discuss politics with like-minded individuals. While homogeneous networks give rise to attitude polarization (e.g., Binder et al., 2009), a person in heterogeneous social networks represents more tolerant political views and names significantly more reasons for stances which oppose his or her own viewpoint (e.g., Huckfeldt et al., 2004; Mutz, 2002a, 2002b, 2006; Mutz & Mondak, 2006; Price, Cappella, & Nir, 2002). These findings imply that citizens who are confronted with opposing views, and thus hold more ambivalent political attitudes, could, in principle, counteract the process of political polarization. On the other hand, social network research assumes that attitude ambivalence due to cross-pressures might reduce political involvement in general. Various studies have shown that people in heterogeneous networks are less interested in politics (Huckfeldt et al., 2004; Parsons, 2010) and less likely to vote (Eveland & Hively, 2009; Mutz 2002b; Parsons, 2010). Similar to the early assumptions of Lazarsfeld and his colleagues (1944), Mutz (2002b, 2006) assumes that cross-pressures might hamper citizens' political involvement in that they make a clear political position more difficult. There is some evidence that inconsistent information exposure promotes a formation of depolarized, ambivalent attitudes (Smith, Fabrigar, MacDougall, & Wiesenthal, 2008), and there is also some support for the notion that ambivalent attitudes, in turn, decrease a person's level of political involvement (Lavine, 2001; Nir, 2005). Other studies, however, even found positive effects of network heterogeneity on political participation (Kwak, Williams, Wang, & Lee, 2005; Scheufele, Hardy, Brossard, Waismel-Manor, & Nisbet, 2006; Scheufele, Nisbet, Brossard, & Nisbet, 2004).

According to Eveland and Hively (2009), contrasting findings regarding the impact of cross-pressures on political engagement, can mainly be traced back to differing operationalizations of the dependent variable and a lack of control variables such as network size or discussion frequency. Another reason for controversial findings in social network research might be that the relationship between information exposure, attitudinal depolarization, and political involvement has been rarely examined in a causal way. A panel analysis by Parsons (2010) provided a more comprehensive view on the *effects* and *effects of effects* of political discussion. His study confirmed a positive impact of exposure to disagreement on attitudinal ambivalence as well as a negative impact of ambivalence on political interest and participation.

With Lipset (1960) we can therefore assume that the "more pressures are brought to bear on individuals or groups which operate in opposing directions, the more likely are prospective voters to withdraw from the situation by 'losing interest' and not making a choice" (p. 211). This assumption is also supported by social psychology research, which proves that ambivalent attitudes due to their "lack of directional guidance" (Ullrich, Schermelleh-Engel, & Böttcher, 2008, p. 775) stimulate a deeper elaboration of information (Hodson, Maio, & Esses, 2001; Maio, Esses, & Bell, 2000) but concurrently reduce the individual's capability to act (Hänze, 2001). Moreover, ambivalence is shown to be negatively associated with the perceived importance to the person of the issue in question (Costarelli & Colloca, 2007; Lavine, Borgida, & Sullivan, 2000), while polarized attitudes have been found to be positively related with attitude importance (Liu & Latané, 1998). Psychologists assume that to discount the relevance of an ambivalent attitude object could be an effective means for individuals to reduce psychological discomfort caused by ambivalence (cf. Costarelli & Colloca, 2007).

Toward a Comprehensive Model of Political Polarization on the Basis of Cognitive Dissonance Theory. In the light of current research findings, we can assume that people who turn to consistent information will develop more polarized attitudes that, in turn, will cause a decrease in contacts with inconsistent information. On the other side, people who are exposed to inconsistent information today, thereby preventing political polarization and its threats to democracy, might be weakened in their political attitudes over time and eventually turn their back on politics. Thus, due to their possible withdrawal from the political sphere, people with ambivalent political attitudes can be assumed to have a large indirect impact on the development of societal polarization processes: Citizens who are exposed to attitude-inconsistent viewpoints might gradually lose their interest in politics, and thus cede the field to citizens with incrementally polarized viewpoints.

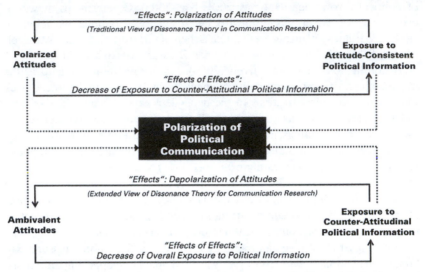

Figure 1.1 Political polarization as a function of attitudinal polarization and depolarization.

In order to determine the danger of political polarization as a societal process, it is therefore needed to consider its individual-level roots; that is, the causes and effects of attitudinal polarization and depolarization as two equivalent motivational processes, which are directly or indirectly contributing to the phenomenon. In other words, political communication research may acquire a more comprehensive view on societal polarization processes through the investigation of a *reinforcing spiral* of attitude polarization and an additional examination of a "reversed" *reinforcing spiral* of attitudinal depolarization (see Figure 1.1).

Due to its expertise in the explanation of causal links between individuals' attitudes and information behavior, selective exposure research seems to be particularly suitable for the examination of these *effects* and *effects of effects* of political information—whereas social network research, with a few exceptions (e.g., Parsons, 2010), is mainly based on correlative analyses and does not primarily deal with causalities between network characteristics and attitude properties. Indeed, current selective exposure research has laid an essential foundation for the explanation of political polarization. Today's research ties the analysis of reduced attention to challenging political viewpoints to explanations which focus on (a) the *effects* of one-sided political content on the polarization of citizens' political attitudes and (b) the *effects of effects* of slanted political information on people's tolerance toward counterattitudinal content in subsequent communication situations.

For the study of attitudinal depolarization, as an equally important process that contributes to political polarization, selective exposure research will need to make two adjustments to its traditional research orientation. First, the analysis of political ambivalence requires a more comprehensive picture of citizens' concrete information environment. For future research it might be useful to track a person's media exposure in a more detailed way; that is, to analyze sources, which have been mentioned by survey participants, not only according to their general partisan leanings (cf. Stroud, 2010, 2011) but also according to their average ratio of consistent and inconsistent messages. In this way, we would be capable of more fine-grained distinctions between different levels of exposure to attitudinal (in-)consistency. Moreover, such an analysis could help to illuminate potential differences and similarities between various information sources and their conjoint—maybe cumulative, maybe moderating—effects on attitude (de-)polarization.

In consideration of social network research findings on attitudinal ambivalence, it might also be necessary for selective exposure research to go beyond the study of rather dissemination-oriented media content and to more rigorously incorporate the examination of political discussions in social networks. Already the influential works by Lazarsfeld and his colleagues have shown that political opinion formation on the basis of media content is significantly moderated by interpersonal communication on politics (Berelson et al., 1954; Lazarsfeld et al., 1944). In the wake of Web 2.0 technologies, the significance of political discussion is once again increasing since interpersonal interaction is spreading to ever-growing social networks (Castells, 2000; De Zúñiga & Valenzuela, 2011; Skoric, Ying, & Ng, 2009; Williams, 2006). Surveys by the Pew Internet & American Life Project, for instance, show that the use of social networking sites and online communities is not only on the rise among teenagers but also among adults with Internet access (Lenhart, Purcell, Smith, & Zickuhr, 2010). During the American presidential campaign in 2008 every fifth Internet user took the opportunity to post comments or questions on the Internet (A. Smith, 2009). According to Meraz (2011), it is therefore important for today's media scholars to "reexamine how pre-existing media theories operate in environments where social influence among and within networks of connected citizens may be high" (p. 108).

Additionally, it seems to become necessary for media scholars to differentiate more purposefully between offline and online social networks. In offline social networks, a person might not be able to incessantly rearrange social ties according to his or her attitudes and beliefs. Thus, the individual might be more likely to encounter uncongenial information in offline networks that, in turn, foster attitudinal ambivalence and its detrimental effects on political participation (cf. Mutz, 2002b, 2006). The Internet, in contrast, undoubtedly facilitates contacts with like-minded others (e.g., Brundidge, 2010). Boyd (2008) points out: "Given the typical friend overlap in most networks, many within those networks hear the same thing over and over until they believe it to be true" (p. 243). Additionally, following Meraz (2011), we can assume that within homogeneous political online groups "elite traditional media's attribute agenda setting power is no longer guaranteed" (p. 120). Thus, political polarization might be a likely result of social practices on the Internet because of a diminishing breadth of information in homogeneous networks. Furthermore, in a recent survey among neo-Nazi online forums, Wojcieszak (2010) has presented evidence that not even dissimilar offline social ties were able to counteract attitudinal polarization resulting from homogeneous online discussions.

From these findings we can infer that, in order to comprehend political polarization, it is increasingly important for selective exposure research to track people's actual media use and their social environment in greater detail. Besides this more content-related requirement, a second adjustment for the analysis of political polarization—as a function of not only attitudinal polarization but also attitudinal depolarization—concerns the theoretical and empirical focus of selective exposure research on the process of attitude bolstering. On the basis of a rather traditional understanding of cognitive dissonance theory, selective exposure research is predominately interested in citizens' use of attitude-consistent information and the stabilization of their preexisting political attitudes. The effects of inconsistent information have so far played a rather subordinate role in selective exposure research. Whenever exposure to counterattitudinal content became the subject of empirical investigation, usually scholars have focused on the individual's striving to bolster existing viewpoints. Concurrently, the same studies show that people are much better able to defend their opinions against inconsistent arguments when they are equipped with solid political knowledge (e.g., Eagly, Kulesa, Brannon, Shaw, & Hutson-Comeaux, 2000; Meffert et al., 2006; Taber & Lodge, 2006). The question of what happens if people do not meet the requirement of political sophistication to bolster their attitudes—for example, when social networks come up with political cross-pressures—deserves more research attention because high levels of political knowledge do not seem to be the norm among the general population (e.g., Delli Carpini & Keeter, 1992).

In order to examine potential attitude-depolarizing effects of political communication, it might be useful for selective exposure research to reconsider its theoretical roots. In contrast to common assumptions, the theory of cognitive dissonance (Festinger, 1957) is not primarily concerned with attitude bolstering but with attitude change in terms of a weakening of formerly held opinions. Although dissonance theory is mainly associated with consistency theories (e.g., Heider, 1946; Newcomb, 1953; Osgood & Tannenbaum, 1955), the special achievement of Festinger was to trace the causes and effects of consistency needs to the interaction between the individual and his or her environment. With reference to Lewin's (1936) cognitive field theory, Festinger considered the occurrence and reduction of cognitive dissonance under the influence of a constant individual need for environmental adaptation. In a posthumously published early statement on dissonance theory, Festinger (1999) posited that "there will be forces acting on the person to have his cognition correspond to reality as he experiences it. The result of this will be that, in general, persons will have a correct picture of the world around them in which they live" (p. 356). With his differentiation of human needs into the pursuit of psychological consistency on the one hand and an adequate adaptation to the environment on the other, Festinger explained human behavior from two opposing motives. Not least for this reason, dissonance theory is considered as a starting point for the study of "social cognition" (Stone, 2001, p. 41) in social psychology. Down to the present day, it is therefore not attitude bolstering but attitude change that dissonance research is primarily interested in. According to Festinger (1957, p. 95), changing one's attitude is the most effective and efficient way for individuals to reduce feelings of dissonance and restore cognitive consonance. Dissonance-related attitude change in terms of attitudinal alleviation is primarily studied within the so-called induced-compliance paradigm, which is still the most widely used and most significant paradigm in dissonance research (cf. Harmon-Jones & Mills, 1999).

A reconsideration of dissonance theory with regard to its assumptions on attitude change might facilitate the assessment of the actual threat of political polarization to deliberative democracy because it allows for an equal scientific treatment of consistent and inconsistent communication environment effects in terms of attitudinal polarization and depolarization. In this way, two sides of political polarization can be taken into consideration, which according to Huckfeldt, Mendez, and Osborn (2004), have a similarly high risk potential for a deliberative democracy:

> If collective deliberation among citizens in a democracy does *not* involve disagreement, its value is fundamentally called into question. At the same time, if disagreement produces politically disabling consequences—if individuals withdraw from political life as a consequence of disagreement—then the democratic potential for a shared process of collective deliberation is similarly undermined. (p. 68)

Political Demobilization in a Widening Communication Environment

Conflicting Viewpoints on the Internet's Potential for Political Mobilization

The increasing alienation of many citizens from the political system in Western democracies has triggered many research activities. According to a study by the Pew Research Center for the People & the Press (2010, p. 44) Americans show less and less interest in news on politics and public affairs. In 2004 there was still a majority of 52% who followed the news "at regular times." Six years later this proportion of the citizens had dropped by 14 percentage points. Instead, the proportion of the people who only got the news "from time to time" had risen from 46 to 57%. Not surprisingly, there are also fewer people who "enjoy keeping up with the news." This drop is particularly pronounced among the younger generation. While in 2008 38% of the respondents 18 to 29 years old said they gazed at the news, this figure had dropped sharply to only 27% in 2010 (Pew, 2010, pp. 43–44). The decreasing news interest seems to be a general characteristic of modern democracies. According to surveys of the Allensbach Institute in Germany the attention and interest of the younger population (30 years and below) has within only 10 years shifted away from politics, the economy, and culture—all areas of "public affairs"—and moved to computer-related topics and fashion (Köcher, 2008).

The logical consequence of this decreasing interest and exposure to the news is generational knowledge gaps. Patterson (2007) has shown by means of day-by-day surveys asking questions about topical news of politics and public affairs that the younger generation just does not get the news as much as the older age groups. This generational knowledge gap applies to hard and soft news. The first author has replicated this methodologically innovative study in Germany. We asked a total of 1,800 respondents over a period of 30 days if they had heard about the most important news events of the previous day. These news items were selected on a daily basis by a panel of editors, political scientists, and communication researchers. The data show a sharp correlation between age and news awareness. Of the respondents 30 years and older two thirds had heard about these top news events. The corresponding figures for respondents 18 to 29 years was 50% and for 14- to 17-year-olds only 39%. Accordingly, knowledge about concrete facts and the historical background of the events had traveled very unevenly to the different age groups (Donsbach, Rentsch, & Walter, 2011).

Assumptions about the (positive or negative) consequences of the Internet for political communication have led to several publications in which authors discuss whether the existence of this new communication ecology might be able to stop or even reverse this trend toward political alienation and disinterest. Does the Internet, and particularly social networks on the Internet, motivate young people to delve into the political sphere and thus lead to a stronger participatory democracy? The empirical evidence so far is not coherent. Some studies show a positive relationship between the degree to which citizens go online and several forms of political participation. For instance, a German study by Vowe, Emmer, and Seifert (2007) was able to show on the basis of a panel survey between 2002 and 2005 that people's exposure to the news increased after they had Internet access. Similarly, a survey by Bakker and De Vreese (2011) conducted among young people in the Netherlands found that exposure to online news not only affected political participation via the web but also in more traditional forms. Quintelier and Vissers (2008) were able to measure an effect of news use via online news media, social networks, and blogs on political participation of people in Belgium. Finally, Drew and Weaver (2006) have shown that already in the 2004 presidential campaign the Internet was a significant predictor of campaign interest and knowledge. Obviously, the Internet increases political interest more than any other news medium, particularly among those users who already have previously shown a higher interest (Johnson & Kaye, 2003). Thus, Weber, Loumakis, and Bergman (2003) conclude that "there may be something about Internet participation that mobilizes citizens into political life" (p. 38), and Johnson and Kaye

(2003) that the "web politically empowers individuals" (p. 28; see also Shah, Cho, Eveland, & Kwak, 2005; Tolbert & McNeal, 2003).

But there are also other voices and findings that are less optimistic about the role of the Internet for a participatory democracy (e.g., Davis, 1999, p. 168; Uslaner, 2004). For instance, Bimber (2001) concluded from his empirical study on the influence of the Internet on political participation that there "is very little to show for this otherwise remarkable technological phenomenon in terms of aggregate political engagement" (p. 64). One main argument against the Internet as a factor for increased political participation and mobilization is the finding that it fosters participation predominantly among those with a prior interest in politics and thus leads to an "increasing participation gap" (e.g., Bimber, 2003; Bonfadelli, 2002; Davis, 1999). For instance, Poindexter and McCombs (2001) have confirmed their finding from the early eighties (McCombs & Poindexter, 1983) about the relationship between the duty to keep informed and exposure to political news. Although there was no significant effect of the duty to keep informed on Internet use in general, people with a higher duty to keep informed were more likely to go to news about the election campaign. Shah, Kwak, and Holbert (2001) found ambivalent results for the effect of Internet use on civil engagement. People who used the Internet primarily for information indeed showed a stronger civil engagement while those who used it primarily for leisure and recreation showed a reverse effect. The authors draw the conclusion that entertainment-driven online content "may not provide much opportunity to connect to the real world" (Shah et al., 2001, p. 155). Xenos and Moy (2007) came to a similar result for active political participation. Based on the 2004 NES surveys in the United States they could show that positive effects of Internet use on political participation are moderated by prior political interest as an intervening variable. The authors hold "that in the political context, Internet use may also be acting to increase extant gaps in participation" (Xenos & Moy, 2007, p. 714). A study by Scheufele and Nisbet (2002) also points into the direction of socially differential effects. The authors showed that those who used the Internet primarily for entertainment content were significantly less informed about politics than respondents who used it for information and news about politics and current affairs. Although most of these studies—due to their nonexperimental designs—fall short of being able to draw conclusive causal relations, their evidence is rather consonant and therefore suggests the existence of such ambivalent effects regarding the Internet.

Thus, if politics is not directly in the radar of a person's primary interests, the likelihood of getting confronted with political information on the Internet is rather small. This assertion seems obvious if not banal, but its consequences for the quality of public discourse might sharply increase. When information channels increase and information content offered to the recipient becomes ever broader, it is more and more unlikely that people seek information that is not directly related to their private spheres of interests—and politics and public affairs are probably the primary candidates for these increasingly neglected areas. Unless it is purposely accessed, such news just gets lost to large parts of the audience in the course of the communication process. This could explain the differential effects reported above.

The counterhypothesis—and the likely explanation for the more positive effects on political participation and engagement—assumes that an increased use of the Internet will also increase the likelihood of getting incidentally confronted with information not searched for and maybe not even wanted. Tewksbury, Weaver, and Maddex (2001) found a positive relationship between the amount that respondents used the Internet and unintentional exposure to news, and, between such incidental news use and knowledge of the news. The authors draw the conclusion that "the World Wide Web of today may provide a public space where a broad cross-section of the population encounters news not purposely but accidentally while going about [its] daily business" (Tewksbury et al., 2001, p. 547). Wojcieszak and Mutz (2009) found a similar result for users of social networks on the Internet. Half of the users of such nonpolitical networks said that they also discuss political and social topics on their platforms: "Even the least politicized online chat rooms and message boards expose visitors to some political discussion ... while socializing or flirting" (Wojcieszak & Mutz, 2009, p. 45).

Although these results have an optimistic flavor concerning mobilization and participation effects of the Internet we cannot ignore the counterhypotheses and results that point in the opposite direction; that is, increasing gaps in information and participation and thus a growing fragmentation of society. Obviously, we have to look deeper into the whole communication process and its mid- and long-term effects. With the more complex and powerful methodological design of a panel study, Prior (2005) came to the conclusion that voting and political knowledge not only was lower among users of entertainment content on the Internet but also significantly decreased over the course of time. The author concluded that the plurality and segmentation of information on the Internet available to these recipients has caused this development of an increasing alienation for the political world (see also the study by Overby and Barth regarding exposure to campaign advertisements; 2009). A more seasoned panel analysis by Jennings and Zeitner (2003) also showed that interest in public affairs is affected by media use. They compared political interest and media use of their respondents between 1982 and 1997. Controlling for the use of other news media, exposure to news on the Internet in 1997 did not correlate with political interest in the first wave in 1982 but significantly with their political interest in 1997. This suggests that prior interest in politics today plays a more important role for exposure than in earlier times.

In Search of a "Motivational Engine" for Political (De-)Mobilization

Thus, questions about the quality of and trends in political communication and deliberative democracy in this new communication environment have to be answered in a very differentiated and often ambivalent way. We just do not know if the Internet leads to a distancing from the political and public world. The majority of the studies depend on cross-sectional designs and correlation analyses. Rarely have studies looked at developments and change over time on an individual basis or used designs that allow clear causal conclusions. The panel studies by Prior (2005), Jennings and Zeitner (2003), or Overby and Barth (2009) are more the exception than the rule in this research field. These studies have investigated the *effects* of the communication ecology in terms of interest and participation in politics. However, how these changes have resulted in subsequent changes in political communication behaviors, thus have led to motivational changes in dealing with politics and public affairs (*effects of effect*), has not been addressed so far. We believe that an analysis of such reciprocal effects would be particularly of interest because possible dysfunctional consequences such as alienation and demobilization can only be assessed when they become themselves the object of investigation; that is, when one investigates the consequences of exposure on motivational changes.

In the field of political polarization this motivational component has been well described through citizens' political attitudes. In the case of (de-)mobilization effects we have first to ask the question as to which motivational components could be of interest for this reciprocal causal process. In a study on causal explanations for information patterns—that did not have political mobilization or demobilization in its primary focus—Strömbäck and Shehata (2010) looked at the role of political interest for exposure. By means of a three-wave panel analysis during the 2006 Swedish elections they investigated how exposure to the news affected the respondents' interest in politics and public affairs, and conversely, how such political interest affected exposure to the news. They found that both variables interact positively; that is, news use amplifies political interest, and political interest amplifies interest in and exposure to the news.

Following these results by Strömbäck and Shehata (2010), we could assume that an individual's political interest could be the motivational component also for the investigation of the *effects* and the *effects of effects* of political (de-)mobilization. However, if we look into the way political interest has been operationalized in studies of political communication we must conclude that this construct would lead to problems of validity and confound results because political interest and interest in the news cannot be sufficiently distinguished. For instance, Strömbäck and Shehata (2010, p. 583) have measured political interest by means of a very broad question: "Generally speaking, how interested are you in politics?" Similar ways of operationalization can be found in the studies by Drew and Weaver (2006, p. 29), Xenos and Moy (2007, p. 710), or Johnson and Kaye (2003, p. 17). Other researchers have operationalized political interest via questions as to what extent respondents follow political affairs (e.g., Jennings & Zeitner, 2003, p. 331; Kenski & Stroud, 2006, p. 180), or, even more directly related to the theoretical construct at hand, on their willingness to learn more about politics (e.g., Lupia & Philpot, 2005, p. 1132). This operational fuzziness, representing a lack of analytical clarity, makes the construct of political interest inappropriate as a motivational component for mobilization and demobilization. It is just too close to the construct of exposure to political news, which is the other main variable in the interdependent relationship between exposure and (de-)mobilization.

Another motivational component relevant for political (de-)mobilization is the construct of political efficacy, which usually means two forms of self-perception of the individual relative to the political system. "Internal efficacy" describes perceptions related to the self and its political role such as the belief that one is able to influence the political process and one's capability to understand the political process in a competent way. For the latter—the ability to understand politics—Kaid, McKinney, and Tedesco (2007) have introduced the subconcept of "political informational efficacy," which is closely related to internal efficacy but solely focuses "on the voter's confidence in his or her own political knowledge and its sufficiency to engage the political process" (p. 1096). "External efficacy" on the other side relates more to perceptions of the political system such as the belief that government and politicians are interested in the people's needs and take these into consideration when making political decisions (cf. Balch, 1974; Converse, 1972; Niemi, Craig, & Mattei, 1991). The construct of political efficacy is closely related to the concept of political trust, here understood as trust in the actions of politicians (cf. Kaid, 2003; Niemi et al., 1991). Both subforms of political efficacy are also closely related to different forms of political participation (e.g., Abramson & Aldrich, 1982; Balch, 1974; Johnson & Kaye, 2003; Kaid et al., 2007; Krueger, 2002; McLeod, Scheufele, & Moy, 1999; Quintelier & Vissers, 2008; Scheufele & Nisbet, 2002; Zhang, Johnson, Seltzer, & Bichard, 2010).

The relationship between political efficacy and the use of political information has received some attention in the research area of Internet and political communication. Some authors have hypothesized that the Internet—as a source of political information and a forum for political participation—might have effects on a person's political efficacy. People just might get the feeling that they have a greater impact on politics because they can contact political figures or organizations directly or communicate with many other citizens in an interactive way via the Internet (e.g., Bucy & Gregson, 2001; Tedesco, 2004). Studies, that have used political efficacy as the dependent variable show a positive correlation with general use of the Internet (Kenski & Stroud, 2006), a negative correlation with the use of entertainment-oriented content (Scheufele & Nisbet, 2002), and a positive interaction effect between the use of online news and political discussions on political efficacy (Nisbet & Scheufele, 2004). Political efficacy also has been investigated as a predictor for the use of political information online. While data based on surveys conducted in the nineties did not yet show a relationship between respondents' degree of self-efficacy and their news use on the Internet (e.g., Bimber, 2001; Jennings & Zeitner, 2003), more recent studies show such a relationship and are interpreted by the authors as an effect of political efficacy on the use of the Internet as a source of (political) information (Krueger, 2002; Leung, 2009) and on political knowledge (Prior, 2005).

So far we have not seen studies that regard political efficacy simultaneously in its role as a cause *and* as an effect of exposure to information on politics and public affairs on the Internet. There is only one study from the early nineties that, evidently, only looks at traditional media. Semetko and Valkenburg (1998) analyzed the reciprocal relationship between internal political efficacy and the use of (German) dailies and television newscasts by means of a three-wave panel analysis. The authors found that exposure to political news leads to a significant increase in political efficacy, while political efficacy had no reverse effect on news use. This leads to the question of whether this finding is still valid when we can assume—following Althaus and Tewksbury (2000, p. 22)—that the patterns of media use as well as the influences of this exposure have changed tremendously as a result of technological changes. A new look at the interdependent relationship between political efficacy and political information use seems necessary for three reasons:

1. According to an online survey by Leung (2009), the construct of political efficacy is closely related to another feature of a person's self-perception, namely "psychological empowerment." Following a concept by Katz (1984), Leung defines this as an individual "process through which people gain mastery or control over their lives, improve strengths and competences and develop proactive behaviors to manage their social affairs" (Leung, 2009, p. 1330). The author can show that both components of political efficacy are related to psychological empowerment.

2. In our postmodern era, an individual's self-image becomes more salient because, following Giddens (1991), the increasingly transient concepts of the self require permanent processes of self-reflection. We can assume that the Internet supplies a platform for creating, finding, developing, and presenting identities and self-images (cf. Christakis & Fowler, 2009; Palfrey & Gasser, 2008; Turkle, 1995). Several studies, some of them using social comparison theory, have shown how individuals use features of the Internet to present themselves in comparison to others or by "borrowing" identities from others (cf. Haferkamp & Krämer, 2011, in press; Jung, Youn, & McClung, 2007; Papacharissi 2002a).

3. Bennett and Iyengar's (2008) concept of political communication as well as the concept of *reinforcing spirals* by Slater (2007) attribute an important role to the individual's identity for the analysis of communication processes. For Bennett and Iyengar (2008), "it is clear we are entering another important turning point not just in communication technologies but in social structure and identity formation that affect the behaviors of audiences" (p. 716). Slater (2007) assumes that "those individuals who identify with a given set of ... beliefs and values (i.e., a shared group or communal identity) will have certain preferred media outlets, and will

selectively attend to content that reflects and shares the values of that social identity group" (p. 290).

Thus, political efficacy might be valuable as a motivational component for analyzing and explaining political (de-)mobilization because it is related to the person's self-image and identity, the latter becoming increasingly salient in interpersonal communication. Not surprisingly, self-image and identity have been investigated primarily in the discipline of social psychology, the discipline in which cognitive dissonance has also played a varying but on average important role (cf. Donsbach, 2009). Therefore, it might be useful to look at the theoretical development and empirical evidence of cognitive dissonance theory as well, and combine them with those in self-perception with the aim of developing a better tool for describing the influence of the Internet on political mobilizing and demobilizing effects of communication processes. If successful, this could lead to a more comprehensive theory going beyond singular approaches that can only control for other factors without integrating them into the explanatory system.

The Self-Concept in Dissonance Research: Possible Implications for Studying Political Demobilization

In a summary of cognitive dissonance theory so far, Cooper (2008) writes: "Questions about how the self affects—and is affected by—what we do and think have moved to the forefront of social psychology" (p. 90). The concept of the self, defined as the individual's most relevant cognitions that are activated in social behavior (e.g., DeMarree, Petty, & Briñol, 2007), has played an important role in revisions of Festinger's (1957) original theory and was part of the criticism of it early on. Frey (1984) mentioned several theories that could more or less replace the explanatory power of cognitive dissonance theory, Bem's (1965) theory of self-perception and Tedeschi's impression management theory (for a summary see Tedeschi, 1984). This shows that cognitive dissonance theory and theories of perceptions of the self have been closely connected from the beginning.

The concept of the self has been discussed as a dependent variable also in Aronson's consistency theory (E. Aronson, 1968, 1969) and in the "new look model" (Cooper & Fazio, 1984; Stone & Cooper, 2001). Both approaches, although taking opposite stands on cognitive dissonance theory, argue that dissonance emerges through an attack on the individual's "self-standards" (Stone & Cooper, 2001, p. 228). Such an attack on the value of the self can happen for two reasons: first, when central expectations of the individual toward his or her own self are jeopardized and finally not met (E. Aronson, 1968, 1999), and second, when the individual faces severe aversive consequences, for instance when following an action central norms of the individual are in question (Cooper, 1999; Cooper & Fazio, 1984; Scher & Cooper, 1989; Stone & Cooper, 2003).

In cognitive dissonance research an attack on the self has been observed in several situations, for instance when the individual scores badly in TAT- or intelligence tests (e.g., Carr & Steele, 2009; Fein & Spencer, 1997; Götz-Marchand, Götz, & Irle, 1974; Steele & Aronson, 1995); in cases of hypocrisy (e.g., E. Aronson, 1999; Fried & Aronson, 1995; Thibodeau & Aronson, 1992); or when the individual has invested unjustified costs to reach a certain goal (e.g., E. Aronson, 1999; E. Aronson & Mills, 1959; Gerard & Mathewson, 1966). Experimental research so far has targeted three components of the self-concept: "because most people have relatively favorable views of themselves, they want to see themselves as (a) competent, (b) moral, and (c) able to predict their own behavior" (E. Aronson, 1999, p. 111). Similarly, Cooper (2008) writes about an "own sense of worthiness, moral rectitude, or competence" (p. 90) that can trigger dissonance as soon as it is attacked. More recent research has shown that such a state of dissonance must not only be caused by the individual's own behavior but also by observing the behavior of others (Cooper & Hogg, 2007; Norton, Monin, Cooper, & Hogg, 2003). Norton et al. (2003) describe this as "vicarious dissonance"; "a type of vicarious discomfort resulting from imagining oneself in the speaker's position" (p. 47).

Comparing the components of the self as applied in cognitive dissonance research with the elements in the construct of political efficacy (see above), two similarities become obvious. First, to see oneself as competent and perceive one's own behavior as rational and meaningful complies in the realm of the political with the subconcept of internal political efficacy and its subconcept of political informational efficacy (e.g., Kaid et al., 2007, p. 1096; Nisbet & Scheufele, 2004, pp. 882–883; Semetko & Valkenburg, 1998, p. 200). Second, the desire to see oneself as a person with moral integrity, or in a vicarious situation, the trust in others that they have this moral integrity finds its parallels in the subconcept of external political efficacy (e.g., Leung, 2009, p. 1335; Scheufele & Nisbet, 2002, p. 70) and the related concept of political trust (e.g., De Vreese & Semetko, 2002, p. 625; Johnson & Kaye, 2003, p. 17; Mutz & Reeves, 2005, p. 14).

Studies by Mutz and colleagues draw the relationship of this area of research to processes of political communication. The authors investigated the influence of civility and incivility in the behavior of political actors in televised debates on the physiological state of arousal of the recipients. Subjects in the experimental condition of uncivilized behavior showed higher degrees of arousal than those in the civilized condition. The authors concluded that "people react to violations of televised face-to-face norms in the same way they would if the violation existed in real life … especially when negative consequences are possible" (Mutz, Reeves, & Wise, 2003, p. 5–6; see also Mutz & Reeves, 2005). Arousal has also been employed in other studies as an indicator for the emergence of dissonance (e.g., Elkin & Leippe, 1986; Harmon-Jones, 2004; Losch & Cacioppo, 1990), so we can assume that dissonance can emerge as a consequence of attacks on the self through media content.

It is then self-affirmation theory (Steele 1988; Steele & Liu, 1981, 1983) that has investigated the individual's strategies to decrease or destroy or terminate an existing state of cognitive dissonance. The theory states that individuals can regain their self-integrity by shifting their attention to those factors of their self-concept that are not involved in the particular dissonance process at hand. Such "affirmational resources" would lead to stabilizing the general or global self-esteem (e.g., J. Aronson, Fried, & Good, 2002; Koole, Smeets, Van Knippenberg, & Dijksterhuis, 1999; Steele, 1988, 1997; Steele, Spencer, & Lynch, 1993; Tesser & Cornell, 1991).

In an extension of the assumptions, J. Aronson, Blanton, and Cooper (1995) have confirmed experimentally that an individual activates these affirmational resources selectively and through disidentification with the currently dissonant component of the self: "when one's behavior or performance in a domain casts negative light on oneself, one can maintain global self-esteem by disidentifying with the domain in question" (J. Aronson, Cohen, & Nail, 1999, p. 142). Recent results by Knobloch-Westerwick and Meng (2011) suggest that these general strategies for dissonance reduction can also be transferred to the world of political communication. In their selective exposure experiment they confronted their subjects with claims by political parties that were either consistent or inconsistent with the subjects' own beliefs. The implicit association tests showed that in the case of inconsistent information subjects disidentified with their favorite party while exposure to consistent information led to an enhancement of the person's political self-esteem.

What does this mean for our assumptions about political mobilization or demobilization? If we see political efficacy as a motivational component of the self-image, we can look at the causes and consequences of political efficacy by applying the evidence from modern cognitive dissonance theory. Attacks on an individual's political efficacy creating dissonance as well as the known strategies for dealing with this dissonance can help us to understand processes of mobilization and demobilization. Self-consistent information can enhance political efficacy and thus lead to a mobilization and participation, while inconsistent information, attacking the concept of the self, can lead to demobilization in the form of an increasing disidentification with the world of politics (see Figure 1.2).

However, for such an analysis it is important and necessary to identify and categorize the concrete nature of communication content that can lead to the above described processes. Thereby it will be of particular interest, and a challenge, to find interindividual and thus more general patterns of constellations between characteristics of the self and characteristics of the messages. This was already a challenge for traditional research on cognitive dissonance (cf. Donsbach, 1991) but becomes even more complicated when the reservoir of cognitions that are potentially relevant for the emergence or dissolution of dissonance is much broader and multidimensional—as is the case with political efficacy.

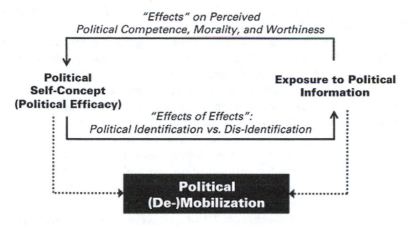

Figure 1.2 Political (De-)Mobilization as a Function of (In-)Consistencies between Political Information and the Political Self-Concept.

On the side of the exposure to messages this implies two strategies for research. First, we must abandon the rather crude distinction between media genres (e.g., Drew & Weaver, 2006; Jennings & Zeitner, 2003; Johnson & Kaye, 2003) and patterns of media use (e.g., Bakker & De Vreese, 2011; Prior, 2005; Quintelier & Vissers, 2008; Scheufele & Nisbet, 2002; Shah et al., 2001). This suggestion does not imply that existing distinctions between information channels and media use patterns should be abandoned. We propose, rather, to reconsider the classification of recipients as representatives of only one of these genres or patterns at a time; in the communication environment of the early 21st century it seems to become more and more unrealistic to expect that a user is primarily motivated by only one media type or one type of media use. Second, we must on an individual basis relate people's political mobilization and participation to the concrete content of the media that they have used. Thus, content analyses have to be a necessary part of such designs. For instance, when we know from prior research that the preference for either information-oriented or entertainment-oriented content significantly correlates with political attitudes and behaviors (e.g., Prior, 2005; Scheufele & Nisbet, 2002; Shah et al., 2001; Xenos & Moy, 2007) it is important to investigate the concrete features of messages that have such effects.

Such research exists so far only for traditional media (e.g., Ansolabehere & Iyengar, 1995; Cappella & Jamieson, 1996, 1997; De Vreese & Semetko, 2002; Kepplinger, 2000; Moy & Pfau, 2000; Mutz & Reeves, 2005; Patterson, 1993; Stroud, Stevens, & Pye, 2011). The distinction between hard and soft news especially has received a great amount of research attention. Researchers identified as peculiar characteristics of political soft news a higher concentration of negative events and conflict and a focus on personal news about political figures rather than news on issues and the political process per se (e.g.,

Cappella & Jamieson, 1996, 1997; Donsbach & Büttner, 2005; Kepplinger & Weißbecker, 1991; Patterson, 1993).

It is contested among today's media scholars whether a theoretical segmentation of media content in soft and hard news is empirically plausible (Boczkowski, 2009; Lehman-Wilzig & Seletzky, 2010; Zelizer, 2004). Furthermore, it is discussed whether soft news has solely detrimental effects on political life (e.g., Bennett, 2003b; Patterson, 2003; Zaller, 2003). Baum (2002), for instance, has shown that soft news programs may also have some potential to catch the attention of less politically interested and knowledgeable citizens (see also Baek & Wojcieszak, 2009). Nonetheless, studies investigating the causal relationship between political alienation and message features such as negativism or strategic reporting, which are known to be generally more often present in soft news formats, have a rather negative impact on political trust, satisfaction, and engagement (Baumgartner & Morris, 2006; Cappella & Jamieson, 1997; De Vreese, 2005; Jackson, 2011; Maurer, 2003; Valentino, Beckmann, & Buhr, 2001).

For traditional media there are studies which combine surveys with content analyses to demonstrate the effects of negative and "game" news (Patterson, 1993) on perceptions of the political process or political figures (e.g., Adriaansen, Van Praag, & De Vreese, 2010; De Vreese, 2005; De Vreese & Semetko, 2002; Kleinnijenhuis, Van Hoof, & Oegema, 2006; Maurer, 2003; Wolling, 1999). In light of the increasing relevance of the Internet for political communication we must also direct our attention to online content and the messages conveyed via interpersonal communication, particularly in social networks. We know that discussions in social networks are not only relevant for political engagement (e.g., Hardy & Scheufele, 2005; Nisbet & Scheufele, 2004; Price & Cappella, 2002) or political knowledge (see, e.g., Eveland, 2004; Robinson & Levy, 1986; Scheufele, 2002), but—in the context of the Internet—often show a more aggressive tenor, which might make attacks on the person's self more likely (e.g., Davis, 1999; Hill & Hughes, 1998).

To reconstruct interpersonal discussions is a challenging empirical endeavor. For rather quantitative features such as discussion frequency and social network size we can draw on a wide range of empirical research that has repeatedly proved the relevance of these features in predicting a person's level of political knowledge, participation, and efficacy (e.g., Eveland & Thomson, 2006; Hardy & Scheufele, 2005; Huckfeldt, Beck, Dalton, & Levine, 1995; Kwak et al., 2005; Moy & Gastil, 2006). Even more insightful, but also more difficult to track, is the qualitative side of political discussion. Here, more empirical research is needed. For the investigation of (de-)mobilization processes we particularly recommend including questions that address the tenor of what is said about politicians and politics when political talk comes up in social networks. Similar to what has been found as effects of negative news in traditional media research, social network studies suggest that expressions of devaluation of or indignation toward political topics might give rise to political demobilization (Eliasoph, 1998; Gamson, 1992; Schmitt-Beck & Mackenrodt,

2010). Political engagement can be encouraged, however, when the individual is surrounded by politically active and interested people (Leighley, 1990; Passy & Giugni, 2001; Verba, Scholzman, & Brady, 1995). Another feature that could be of interest for the examination of potential mobilizing or demobilizing effects of political talk is the existence of "network experts," which might foster an individual's understanding of politics (Ryan, 2010) and thus help to strengthen a person's political self-concept.

When we apply the cognitive dissonance-based construct of political efficacy to the analysis of concrete messages consumed by the recipient we should be able to predict how discrete features of political communication affect the perception of one's political efficacy and, in a second step, reversely affect political interest. So far we can solicit hypotheses only in an indirect manner. For instance, a study by Adriaansen, Van Praag, and De Vreese (2010) shows a negative influence of substantive news on political cynicism among the younger population. At the same time research shows an increase in soft news formats and tabloidization, including political negativism (e.g., Baum, 2003; Bennett, 2003a; Donsbach & Büttner, 2005; Schulz & Zeh, 2005), and the particular attraction of such formats for younger people (e.g., Patterson, 2007; Young & Tisinger, 2006). Based on these findings we could investigate by means of the concepts of self-esteem and political efficacy how far a dwindling contact with hard and substantial political news exacerbates an understanding of the political process, while the individual's perception of this increasing incompetence represents an attack on its political efficacy which finally leads to a disidentification with the political system. Furthermore, we could investigate how a young person's social environment—which due to the Internet might have become enlarged, particularly by weak-tie relationships— may counteract or exacerbate this process (Boase, Horrigan, Wellman, & Rainie, 2006; Ellison, Steinfield, & Lampe, 2007; Williams, 2006). Evidently, such a theory would also enable us to identify those characteristics in political communication content that can lead to an increase in political efficacy and, thus, to counterbalance the processes of demobilization that we have observed.

Summary and Conclusion

The increasing and diversifying activities of citizens in ever more complex information environments require that students of political communication incorporate these changes in their existing theories in order to detect the opportunities and risks of these new communication structures. We have proposed connecting theories of exposure and effects in the form of comprehensive theories that allow us to see the motivation to turn to substantial political news in a reciprocal causal process (Bennett & Iyengar, 2008; Mitchelstein & Boczkowski, 2010; Slater, 2007).

For the investigation of processes of political polarization, that is, an increasing exposure to attitude-consistent messages, research has already taken a promising path by including attitudinal polarization as a motivational component for the citizen's selective exposure behavior. To make our causal models more precise it now seems necessary to further differentiate between attitudinal polarization (and exposure to consistent messages) and attitudinal ambivalence (and exposure to inconsistent messages). The causal examination of the *effects* and *effects of effects* of a confrontation with attitude-consistent political content should thereby be complemented by an equal investigation of inconsistent information. If we can assume that attitude-inconsistent messages, while representing an inevitable requirement for deliberation, give rise to attitudinal ambivalence and a withdrawal from political life, we thus also need to pay attention to the reciprocity of inconsistent messages and attitudinal depolarization as an indirect *reinforcing spiral* of political polarization. Such a theoretical expansion of selective exposure research could shed further light on the societal process of how tendencies of political polarization get amplified. This way, we would be able to examine, if increasingly only those citizens stay politically interested who find their already existing attitudes confirmed by their information environment. Theories of selective exposure can contribute substantially to our conceptualization of these processes. Cognitive dissonance theory is of particular relevance here because its extensive empirical foundation not only explains the bolstering of attitudes but also changes in form of an attenuation of attitudinal positions.

On the other side, cognitive dissonance research might offer something for the explanation of political demobilization. In its modern conception the concept of the self can be a cause and an effect of dissonance. Transferred to the realm of political communication, political efficacy is equivalent to the construct of the self. Thus, we can look at mobilizing and demobilizing effects of political communication in a motivational manner via the self-perception of the individual.

Summing up, we recommend that today's media scholars track serious societal processes such as political polarization and demobilization on the basis of increases and decreases of people's motivation to devote themselves to (certain kinds of) political information. For this purpose, research should consider either motivational direction (i.e., the increase and the decrease) in their temporal evolution and in relation to each other. For instance, if we knew about the development and effects of both attitudinal polarization *and* depolarization in society, we might better understand the actual and prospective pervasiveness of communication enclaves. Similarly, if we possessed more knowledge about citizens' information behavior following from as well as affecting high *and* low political efficacy, we might be capable of better estimating the severity of political demobilization in the age of the Internet.

There can be no question that our suggestions represent only a few out of many possibilities that exist of how to achieve more comprehensive theories in political communication. In our view it is worth examining to what extent our suggestions can be combined with other concepts of *effects* and *effects of effects* to develop even broader and more integrative approaches for a "programmatic vision" (Mitchelstein & Boczkowski, 2010, p. 1086) for future research.

References

Abramson, P. R., & Aldrich, J. H. (1982). The decline of electoral participation in America. *American Political Science Review, 76*, 502–521.

Adriaansen, M. L., Van Praag, P., & De Vreese, C. H. (2010). Substance matters: How news content can reduce political cynicism. *International Journal of Public Opinion Research, 22*, 433–457.

Althaus, S., & Tewksbury, D. (2000). Patterns of Internet and traditional news media use in a networked community. *Political Communication, 17*, 21–45.

Ansolabehere, S., & Iyengar, S. (1995). *Going negative: How political advertisements shrink and polarize the electorate.* New York: Free Press.

Aronson, E. (1968). Dissonance theory: Progress and problems. In R. P. Abelson, E. Aronson, W. J. McGuire, T. M. Newcomb, M. J. Rosenberg, & P. H. Tannenbaum (Eds.), *Theories of cognitive consistency: A sourcebook* (pp. 5–27). Chicago, IL: Rand McNally.

Aronson, E. (1969). The theory of cognitive dissonance: A current perspective. In L. Berkowitz (Ed.), *Advances in experimental social psychology* (Vol. 4, pp. 1–34). New York: Academic Press.

Aronson, E. (1999). Dissonance, hypocrisy, and the self-concept. In E. Harmon-Jones & J. Mills (Eds.), *Cognitive dissonance: Progress on a pivotal theory in social psychology* (pp. 103–126). Washington, DC: American Psychological Association.

Aronson, E., & Mills, J. (1959). The effect of severity of initiation on liking for a group. *Journal of Abnormal and Social Psychology, 59*, 177–181.

Aronson, J., Blanton, H., & Cooper, J. (1995). From dissonance to dis-identification: Selectivity in the self-affirmation process. *Journal of Personality and Social Psychology, 68*, 986–996.

Aronson, J., Cohen, G., & Nail, P. R. (1999). Self-affirmation theory: An update and appraisal. In E. Harmon-Jones & J. Mills (Eds.), *Cognitive dissonance: Progress on a pivotal theory in social psychology* (pp. 127–147). Washington, DC: American Psychological Association.

Aronson, J., Fried, C. B., & Good, C. (2002). Reducing the effects of stereotype threat on African American college students by shaping theories of intelligence. *Journal of Experimental Social Psychology, 38*, 113–125.

Baek, Y. M., & Wojcieszak, M. E. (2009). Don't expect too much! Learning from late-night comedy and knowledge item difficulty. *Communication Research, 36*, 783–809.

Bakker, T. P., & De Vreese, C. H. (2011). *Good news for the future? Young people, Internet use, and political participation.* Retrieved from http://crx.sagepub.com/content/early/2011/01/07/0093650210381738. doi: 10.1177/0093650210381738.

Balch, G. (1974). Multiple indicators in survey research: The concept "sense of political efficacy." *Political Methodology, 1*, 1–43.

Barber, B. R., Mattson, K., & Peterson, J. (1997). *The state of "electronically enhanced democracy": A survey of the Internet.* New Brunswick, NJ: Walt Whitman Center.

Baum, M. A. (2002). Sex, lies, and war: How soft news brings foreign policy to the inattentive public. *American Political Science Review, 96*, 91–109

Baum, M. A. (2003). *Soft news goes to war: Public opinion and American foreign policy in the new media age.* Princeton, NJ: Princeton University Press.

Baum, M. A., & Groeling, T. (2008). New media and the polarization of American political discourse. *Political Communication, 25,* 345–365.

Baumgartner, J., & Morris, J. S. (2006). The Daily Show effect: Candidate evaluations, efficacy, and American youth. *American Politics Research, 34,* 341–367.

Bem, D. J. (1965). An experimental analysis of self-persuasion. *Journal of Experimental Social Psychology, 1,* 199–218.

Bennett, W. L. (2003a). *News: The politics of illusion* (5th ed.). New York: Longman.

Bennett, W. L. (2003b). The burglar alarm that just keeps ringing: A response to Zaller. *Political Communication, 20,* 131–138.

Bennett, W. L., & Iyengar, S. (2008). A new era of minimal effects? The changing foundations of political communication. *Journal of Communication, 58,* 707–713.

Berelson, B. R., Lazarsfeld, P. F., & McPhee, W. N. (1954). *Voting: A study of opinion formation in a presidential campaign.* Chicago, IL: University of Chicago Press.

Bimber, B. (2001). Information and political engagement in America: The search for effects of information technology at the individual level. *Political Research Quarterly, 54,* 53–67.

Bimber, B. (2003). *Information and American democracy: Technology in the evolution of political power.* Cambridge, England: Cambridge University Press.

Bimber, B., & Davis, R. (2003). *Campaigning online: The Internet in U.S. elections.* New York: Oxford University Press.

Binder, A. R., Dalrymple, K. E., Brossard, D., & Scheufele, D. A. (2009). The soul of a polarized democracy: Testing theoretical linkages between talk and attitude extremity during the 2004 presidential election. *Communication Research, 36,* 315–340.

Bishop, B. (2008). *The big sort: Why the clustering of like-minded America is tearing us apart.* Orlando, FL: Houghton Mifflin Harcourt.

Blumler, J. G. (1979). The role of theory in uses and gratifications studies. *Communication Research, 6,* 9–36.

Boase, J., Horrigan, J. B., Wellman, B., & Rainie, L. (2006). *The strength of Internet ties.* Retrieved from http://www.pewinternet.org/~/media//Files/Reports/2006/PIP_Internet_ties.pdf.pdf

Boczkowski, P. J. (2009). Rethinking hard and soft news production: From common ground to divergent paths. *Journal of Communication, 59,* 98–116.

Bonfadelli, H. (2002). The Internet and knowledge gaps: A theoretical and empirical investigation. *European Journal of Communication, 17,* 65–84.

Boyd, D. (2008). Can social network sites enable political action? *International Journal of Media and Cultural Politics, 4,* 241–244.

Brannon, L. A., Tagler, M. J., & Eagly, A. H. (2007). The moderating role of attitude strength in selective exposure to information. *Journal of Experimental Social Psychology, 43,* 611–617.

Brundidge, J. (2010). Encountering "difference" in the contemporary public sphere: The contribution of the Internet to the heterogeneity of political discussion networks. *Journal of Communication, 60,* 680–700.

Bucy, E. P., & Gregson, K. S. (2001). Media participation: A legitimizing mechanism of mass democracy. *New Media & Society, 3,* 359–382.

Cappella, J. N., & Jamieson, K. H. (1996). News frames, political cynicism, and media cynicism. *Annals of the American Academy of Political and Social Science, 546,* 71–85.

Cappella, J. N., & Jamieson, K. H. (1997). *Spiral of cynicism: The press and the public good.* New York: Oxford University Press.

Carr, P. B., & Steele, C. M. (2009). Stereotype threat and inflexible perseverance in problem solving. *Journal of Experimental Social Psychology, 45,* 853–859.

Castells, M. (2000). *The rise of the network society.* Malden, MA: Blackwell.

Chaffee, S. H., Saphir, M. N., Graf, J., Sandvig, C., & Hahn, K. S. (2001). Attention to counter-attitudinal messages in a state election campaign. *Political Communication, 18,* 247–272.

Christakis, N. A., & Fowler, J. H. (2009). *Connected: The surprising power of our social networks and how they shape our lives.* New York: Little, Brown.

Coleman, S., & Gøtze, J. (2001). *Bowling together: Online public engagement in policy deliberation.* London: Hansard Society.

Converse, P. (1972). Change in the American electorate. In A. Campbell & P. E. Converse (Eds.), *The human meaning of social change* (pp. 263–337). New York: Russell Sage Foundation.

Cooper, J. (1999). Unwanted consequences and the self: In search of the motivation for dissonance reduction. In E. Harmon-Jones & J. Mills (Eds.), *Cognitive dissonance: Progress on a pivotal theory in social psychology* (pp. 149–174). Washington, DC: American Psychological Association.

Cooper, J. (2008). *Cognitive dissonance: Fifty years of a classic theory.* London: Sage.

Cooper, J., & Fazio, R. H. (1984). A new look at dissonance theory. In L. Berkowitz (Ed.), *Advances in experimental social psychology* (Vol. 17, pp. 229–266). New York: Academic Press.

Cooper, J., & Hogg, M. A. (2007). Feeling the anguish of others: A theory of vicarious dissonance. In M. P. Zanna (Ed.), *Advances in experimental social psychology* (Vol. 39, pp. 359–403). San Diego, CA: Academic Press.

Costarelli, S., & Colloca, P. (2007). The moderation of ambivalence on attitude—Intention relations as mediated by attitude importance. *European Journal of Social Psychology, 37,* 923–933.

D'Alessio, D., & Allen, M. (2002). Selective exposure and dissonance after decisions. *Psychological Reports, 9,* 527–532.

Davis, R. (1999). *The web of politics: The Internet's impact on the American political system.* New York: Oxford University Press.

Delli Carpini, M. X., & Keeter, S. (1992). The public's knowledge of politics. In J. D. Kennamer (Eds.), *Public opinion, the press, and public policy* (pp. 19–40). Westport, CT: Praeger.

DeMarree, K. G., Petty, R. E., & Briñol, P. (2007). Self and attitude strength parallels: Focus on accessibility. *Social and Personality Psychology Compass, 1,* 441–468.

De Vreese, C. H. (2005). The spiral of cynicism reconsidered. *European Journal of Communication, 20,* 283–301.

De Vreese, C. H., & Semetko, H. A. (2002). Cynical and engaged: Strategic campaign coverage, public opinion, and mobilization in a referendum. *Communication Research, 29,* 615–41.

Dewey, J. (1927). *The public and its problems.* Chicago, IL: Swallow Press.

De Zúñiga, H. G., & Valenzuela, S. (2011). The mediating path to a stronger citizenship: Online and offline networks, weak ties, and civic engagement. *Communication Research, 38,* 397–421.

Dilliplane, S. (2011). All the news you want to hear: The impact of partisan news exposure on political participation. *Public Opinion Quarterly, 75*, 287–316.

DiMaggio, P., Hargittai, E., Neuman, W. R., & Robinson, J. P. (2001). Social implications of the Internet. *Annual Review of Sociology, 27*, 307–336.

Donsbach, W. (1991). Exposure to political content in newspapers: The impact of cognitive dissonance on readers' selectivity. *European Journal of Communication, 6*, 155–186.

Donsbach, W. (2009). Cognitive dissonance theory—Roller coaster career: How communication research adapted the theory of cognitive dissonance. In T. Hartmann (Ed.), *Media choice. A theoretical and empirical overview* (pp. 128–149). New York, London: Routledge.

Donsbach, W., & Büttner, K. (2005). Boulevardisierungstrend in deutschen ernsehnachrichten [Sensationalism in German TV news]. *Publizistik, 50*, 21–38.

Donsbach, W., Rentsch, M., & Walter, C. (2011, May). *Everything but the news: How relevant are the social media for exposure to the news?* Paper presented to the panel "Social Media as News Sources—Empirical Evidence from Four Countries," at the International Communication Association Annual Meeting, Boston, MA.

Drew, D., & Weaver, D. (2006). Voter learning in the 2004 presidential election: Did the media matter? *Journalism & Mass Communication Quarterly, 83*, 25–42.

Druckman, J. N., & Parkin, M. (2005). The impact of media bias: How editorial slant affects voters. *Journal of Politics, 67*, 1030–1049.

Eagly, A. H., Kulesa, P., Brannon, L. A., Shaw, L., & Hutson-Comeaux, S. (2000). Why counterattitudinal messages are as memorable as proattitudinal messages: The importance of active defense against attack. *Personality and Social Psychology Bulletin, 26*, 1392–1408.

Eliasoph, N. (1998). *Avoiding politics: How Americans produce apathy in everyday life.* Cambridge, England: Cambridge University Press.

Elkin, R. A., & Leippe, M. R. (1986). Physiological arousal, dissonance, and attitude change: Evidence for a dissonance-arousal link and a "Don't remind me" effect. *Journal of Personality and Social Psychology, 51*, 55–65.

Ellison, N. B., Steinfield, C., & Lampe, C. (2007). The benefits of Facebook "friends": Social capital and college students use of online social network sites. *Journal of Computer-Mediated Communication, 12*, 1143–1168.

Eveland, W. P. (2004). The effect of political discussion in producing informed citizens: The roles of information, motivation and elaboration. *Political Communication, 21*, 177–194.

Eveland, W. P., & Hively, M. H. (2009). Political discussion frequency, network size, and "heterogeneity" of discussion as predictors of political knowledge and participation. *Journal of Communication, 59*, 205–224.

Eveland, W. P., Shah, D. V., & Kwak, N. (2003). Assessing causality in the cognitive mediation model. *Communication Research, 30*, 359–386.

Eveland, W. P., & Thomson, T. (2006). Is it talking, thinking, or both? A lagged dependent variable model of discussion effects on political knowledge. *Journal of Communication, 56*, 523–542.

Fein, S., & Spencer, S. J. (1997). Prejudice as self-image maintenance: Affirming the self through derogating others. *Journal of Personality and Social Psychology, 73*, 31–44.

Festinger, L. (1957). *A theory of cognitive dissonance.* Stanford, CA: Stanford University Press.

Festinger, L. (1999). Social communication and cognition: A very preliminary and highly tentative draft. In E. Harmon-Jones & J. Mills (Eds.), *Cognitive dissonance: Progress on a pivotal theory in social psychology* (pp. 355–379). Washington, DC: American Psychological Association.

Frey, D. (1984). Die Theorie der kognitiven Dissonanz [The theory of cognitive dissonance]. In D. Frey & M. Irle (Eds.), *Theorien der Sozialpsychologie: Band 1. Kognitive Theorien* (pp. 243–292) [Theories of social psychology: Vol.1. Cognitive theories]. Bern, Switzerland: Huber.

Fried, C. B., & Aronson, E. (1995). Hypocrisy, misattribution, and dissonance reduction. *Personality and Social Psychology Bulletin, 21*, 925–934.

Früh, W., & Schönbach, K. (1982). Der dynamisch-transaktionale Ansatz: Ein neues Paradigma der Medienwirkungen [The dynamic-transactional approach: A new media effects paradigm]. *Publizistik, 27*, 23–40.

Früh, W., & Schönbach, K. (2005). Der dynamisch-transaktionale Ansatz III: Eine Zwischenbilanz [The dynamic-transactional approach III: An interim balance sheet]. *Publizistik, 1*, 4–20.

Galston, W. A. (2003). If political fragmentation is the problem, is the Internet the solution? In D. M. Anderson & M. Cornfield (Eds.), *The civic web: Online politics and democratic values* (pp. 35–44). Lanham, MD: Rowman & Littlefield.

Gamson, W. A. (1992). *Talking politics*. Cambridge, England: Cambridge University Press.

Garrett, R. K. (2009a). Echo chambers online?: Politically motivated selective exposure among Internet news users. *Journal of Computer-Mediated Communication, 14*, 265–285.

Garrett, R. K. (2009b). Politically motivated reinforcement seeking: Reframing the selective exposure debate. *Journal of Communication, 59*, 676–699.

Gehrau, V., & Goertz, L. (2010). Gespräche über Medien unter veränderten medialen Bedingungen [Conversations about the media under changing media conditions]. *Publizistik, 55*, 153–172.

Gentzkow, M., & Shapiro, J. M. (2010). What drives media slant? Evidence from U.S. daily newspapers. *Econometrica, 78*, 35–71.

Gerard, H. B., & Mathewson, G. C. (1966). The effect of severity of initiation on liking for a group: A replication. *Journal of Experimental Social Psychology, 2*, 278–287.

Giddens, A. (1991). *Modernity and self-identity: Self and society in the late modern age*. Stanford, CA: Stanford University Press.

Götz-Marchand, B., Götz, J., & Irle, M. (1974). Preference of dissonance reduction modes as a function of their order, familiarity, and reversibility. *European Journal of Social Psychology, 4*, 201–228.

Graber, D. A. (2003). The media and democracy: Beyond myths and stereotypes. *Annual Review of Political Science, 6*, 139–160.

Graf, J., & Aday, S. (2008). Selective attention to online political information. *Journal of Broadcasting & Electronic Media, 52*, 86–100.

Habermas, J. (1989). *The structural transformation of the public sphere*. Cambridge, MA: MIT Press. (Original work published 1962)

Haferkamp, N., & Krämer, N. C. (2011). Social comparison 2.0: Examining the effects of online profiles on social-networking sites. *Cyberpsychology, Behavior, and Social Networking, 14*, 309–314.

Haferkamp, N., & Krämer, N. C. (in press). Creating a digital self: Impression management and impression formation on social networking sites. In K. Drotner & K. C. Schröder (Eds.), *Digital content creation: Creativity, competence, critique*. New York: Peter Lang.

Hamilton, J. T. (2003). *All the news that's fit to sell: How the market transforms information into news*. Princeton, NJ: Princeton University Press.

Hänze, M. (2001). Ambivalence, conflict, and decision making: Attitudes and feelings in Germany toward NATO's military intervention in the Kosovo war. *European Journal of Social Psychology, 31*, 693–706.

Hardy, B. W., & Scheufele, D. A. (2005). Examining differential gains from Internet use: Comparing the moderating role of talk and online interactions. *Journal of Communication, 55*, 71–84.

Harmon-Jones, E. (2004). Contributions from research on anger and cognitive dissonance to understanding the motivational functions of asymmetrical frontal brain activity. *Biological Psychology, 67*, 51–76.

Harmon-Jones, E., & Mills, J. (1999). An introduction to cognitive dissonance theory and an overview of current perspectives on the theory. In E. Harmon-Jones & J. Mills (Eds.), *Cognitive dissonance: Progress on a pivotal theory in social psychology* (pp. 3–21). Washington, DC: American Psychological Association.

Heider, F. (1946). Attitudes and cognitive organization. *Journal of Psychology, 21*, 107–112.

Hill, K. A., & Hughes, J. E. (1998). *Cyberpolitics: Citizen activism in the age of the Internet*. Lanham, MD: Rowman & Littlefield.

Hodson, G., Maio, G. R., & Esses, V. M. (2001). The role of attitudinal ambivalence in susceptibility to consensus information. *Basic and Applied Social Psychology, 23*, 197–205.

Holtz-Bacha, C. (1998). Fragmentierung der Gesellschaft durch das Internet [Social fragmentation through the Internet]. In W. Gellner & F. von Korff (Eds.), *Demokratie und Internet* (pp. 219–226) [Democracy and the Internet]. Baden-Baden, Germany: Nomos.

Huckfeldt, R., Beck, P. A., Dalton, R. J., & Levine, J. (1995). Political environments, cohesive social groups, and the communication of public opinion. *American Journal of Political Science, 39*, 1025–1054.

Huckfeldt, R., Mendez, J. M., & Osborn, T. (2004). Disagreement, ambivalence, and engagement: The political consequences of heterogeneous networks. *Political Psychology, 25*, 65–95.

Iyengar, S., & Hahn, K. S. (2009). Red media, blue media: Evidence of ideological selectivity in media use. *Journal of Communication, 59*, 19–39.

Jackson, D. (2011). Strategic media, cynical public? Examining the contingent effects of strategic news frames on political cynicism in the United Kingdom. *The International Journal of Press/Politics, 16*, 75–101.

Jamieson, K. H., & Cappella, J. N. (2008). *Echo chamber: Rush Limbaugh and the conservative media establishment*. New York: Oxford University Press.

Jennings, M. K., & Zeitner, V. (2003). Internet use and civic engagement: A longitudinal analysis. *Public Opinion Quarterly, 67*, 311–334.

Johnson, T. J., Bichard, S. L., & Zhang, W. (2009). Communication communities or "CyberGhettos?": A path analysis model examining factors that explain selective exposure to blogs. *Journal of Computer-Mediated Communication, 15*, 60–82.

Johnson, T. J., & Kaye, B. K. (2003). A boost or bust for democracy? How the web influenced political attitudes and behaviors in the 1996 and 2000 presidential elections. *The Harvard International Journal of Press/Politics, 8*, 9–34.

Jones, D. A. (2002). The polarizing effect of new media messages. *International Journal of Public Opinion Research, 14*, 158–174.

Jung, T., Youn, H., & McClung, S. (2007). Motivations and self-presentation strategies on Korean-based "Cyworld" weblog format personal homepages. *Cyberpsychology & Behavior, 10,* 24–31.

Kaid, L. L. (2003). Effects of political information in the 2000 presidential campaign. Comparing traditional television and Internet exposure. *American Behavioral Scientist, 46,* 677–691.

Kaid, L. L., McKinney, M. S., & Tedesco, J. C. (2007). Introduction: Political information efficacy and young voters. *American Behavioral Scientist, 50,* 1093–1111.

Kaplan, K. J. (1972). On the ambivalence–indifference problem in attitude theory and measurement: A suggested modification of the semantic differential technique. *Psychological Bulletin, 77,* 361–372.

Katz, R. (1984). Empowerment and synergy: Expanding the community's healing resources. *Prevention in Human Services, 3,* 201–26.

Kenski, K., & Stroud, N. J. (2006). Connections between Internet use and political efficacy, knowledge, and participation. *Journal of Broadcasting & Electronic Media, 50,* 173–192.

Kepplinger, H. M. (2000). The declining image of the German political elite. *The Harvard International Journal of Press/Politics, 5,* 71–80.

Kepplinger, H. M., & Weißbecker, H. (1991). Negativität als Nachrichtenideologie [Negativity as news ideology]. *Publizistik, 36,* 330–342.

Kim, Y. (2011). The contribution of social network sites to exposure to political difference: The relationships among SNSs, online political messaging, and exposure to cross-cutting perspectives. *Computers in Human Behavior, 27,* 971–977.

Klapper, J. T. (1960). *The effects of mass communication.* Glencoe, IL: The Free Press.

Kleinnijenhuis, J., Van Hoof, A. M. J., & Oegema, D. (2006). Negative news and the sleeper effect of distrust. *The Harvard International Journal of Press/Politics, 7,* 86–104.

Knobloch-Westerwick, S., & Meng, J. (2009). Looking the other way: Selective exposure to attitude-consistent and counterattitudinal political information. *Communication Research, 36,* 426–448.

Knobloch-Westerwick, S., & Meng, J. (2011). Reinforcement of the political self through selective exposure to political messages. *Journal of Communication, 61,* 349–368.

Köcher, R. (2008). *Die junge Generation als Vorhut gesellschaftlicher Veränderungen* [The young generation as a vanguard of social change]. Retrieved from http://www.awa-online.de/praesentationen/awa08_Junge_Generation.pdf

Koole, S., Smeets, K., Van Knippenberg, A., & Dijksterhuis, A. (1999). The cessation of rumination through self-affirmation. *Journal of Personality and Social Psychology, 77,* 111–125.

Krosnick, J. A., Boninger, D. S., Chuang, Y. C., Berent, M. K., & Carnot, C. G. (1993). Attitude strength: One construct or many related constructs? *Journal of Personality and Social Psychology, 65,* 1132–1151.

Krosnick, J. A., & Petty, R. E. (1995). Attitude strength: An overview. In R. E. Petty & J. A. Krosnick (Eds.), *Attitude strength: Antecedents and consequences* (pp. 1–24). Mahwah, NJ: Erlbaum.

Krueger, B. S. (2002). Assessing the potential of Internet political participation in the United States: A resource approach. *American Politics Research, 30*, 476–498.

Kruglanski, A. W., & Stroebe, W. (2005). The influence of beliefs and goals on attitudes: Issues of structure, function, and dynamics. In D. Albarracín, B. T. Johnson, & M. P. Zanna (Eds.), *The handbook of attitudes* (pp. 323–368). Mahwah, NJ: Erlbaum.

Kull, S., Ramsey, C., & Lewis, E. (2003). Misperceptions, the media, and the Iraq war. *Political Science Quarterly, 118*, 569–598.

Kwak, N., Williams, A. E., Wang, X., & Lee, H. (2005). Talking politics and engaging politics: An examination of the interactive relationship between structural features of political talk and discussion engagement. *Communication Research, 32*, 87–111.

Lavine, H. (2001). The electoral consequences of ambivalence toward presidential candidates. *American Journal of Political Science, 45*, 915–929.

Lavine, H., Borgida, E., & Sullivan, J. L. (2000). On the relationship between attitude involvement and attitude accessibility: Toward a cognitive-motivational model of political information processing. *Political Psychology, 21*, 81–106.

Lazarsfeld, P. F., Berelson, B. R., & Gaudet, H. (1944). *The people's choice.* New York: Columbia University Press.

Lehman-Wilzig, S. N., & Seletzky, M. (2010). Hard news, soft news, and "general" news: The necessity and utility of an intermediate classification. *Journalism, 11*, 37–56.

Leighley, J. E. (1990). Social interaction and contextual influences on political participation. *American Politics Quarterly, 18*, 459–475.

Lenhart, A., Purcell, K., Smith, A., & Zickuhr, K. (2010). *Social media and mobile Internet use among teens and young adults.* Retrieved from http://www.pewinternet.org /~/media//Files/Reports/2010/PIP_Social_Media_and_Young_Adults_Report_Final_with_toplines.pdf

Leung, L. (2009). User-generated content on the internet: An examination of gratifications, civic engagement and psychological empowerment. *New Media & Society, 11*, 1327–1347.

Lewin, K. (1936). *Principles of topological psychology.* New York: McGraw-Hill.

Lipset, S. M. (1960). *Political man: The social bases of politics.* Baltimore, MD: Johns Hopkins University Press.

Liu, J. H., & Latané, B. (1998). The catastrophic link between the importance and extremity of political attitudes. *Political Behavior, 20*, 105–126.

Lord, C. G., Ross, L., & Lepper, M. R. (1979). Biased assimilation and attitude polarization: The effects of prior theories on subsequently considered evidence. *Journal of Personality and Social Psychology, 37*, 2098–2109.

Losch, M. E., & Cacioppo, J. T. (1990). Cognitive dissonance may enhance sympathetic tonus, but attitudes are changed to reduce negative affect rather than arousal. *Journal of Experimental Social Psychology, 26*, 289–304.

Lupia, A., & Philpot, T. S. (2005). Views from inside the net: How websites affect young adults' political interest. *The Journal of Politics, 67*, 1122–1142.

Maier, S. (2010). Newspapers offer more news than do major online sites. *Newspaper Research Journal, 31*, 6–19.

Maio, G. R., Esses, V. M., & Bell, D. W. (2000). Examining conflict between components of attitudes: Ambivalence and inconsistency are distinct constructs. *Canadian Journal of Behavioral Science, 32*(2), 71–83.

Margolis, M., & Resnick, D. (2000). *Politics as usual: The cyberspace "revolution."* Thousand Oaks, CA: Sage.

Maurer, M. (2003). *Politikverdrossenheit durch Medienberichte: Eine Paneluntersuchung* [Political apathy through news stories: A panel analysis]. Konstanz, Germany: UVK.

McCombs, M. E., & Poindexter, P. M. (1983). The duty to keep informed: News exposure and civic obligation. *Journal of Communication, 33,* 88–96.

McLeod, J. M., Kosicki, G. M., & McLeod, D. M. (1994). The expanding boundaries of political communication effects. In J. Bryant & D. Zillmann (Eds.), *Media effects: Advances in theory and research* (pp. 123–162). Hillsdale, NJ: Erlbaum.

McLeod, J. M., Scheufele, D. A., & Moy, P. (1999). Community, communication, and participation: The role of mass media and interpersonal discussion in local political participation. *Political Communication, 16,* 315–36.

Meffert, M. F., Chung, S., Joiner, A. J., Waks, L., & Garst, J. (2006). The effects of negativity and motivated information processing during a political campaign. *Journal of Communication, 56,* 27–51.

Meraz, S. (2011). The fight for "how to think": Traditional media, social networks, and issue interpretation. *Journalism, 12,* 107–127.

Mill, J. S. (1956). *On liberty.* Indianapolis, IN: Bobbs–Merrill. (Original work published 1859)

Miller, A. G., McHoskey, J. W., Bane, C. M., & Dowd, T. G. (1993). The attitude polarization phenomenon: Role of response measure, attitude extremity, and behavioral consequences of reported attitude change. *Journal of Personality and Social Psychology, 64,* 561–574.

Mitchelstein, E., & Boczkowski, P. J. (2010). Online news consumption research: An assessment of past work and an agenda for the future. *New Media & Society, 12,* 1085–1102.

Moy, P., & Gastil, J. (2006). Predicting deliberative communication: The impact of discussion networks, media use, and political cognitions. *Political Communication, 23,* 443–460.

Moy, P., & Pfau, M. (2000). *With malice toward all? The media and public confidence in democratic institutions.* Westport, CT: Praeger.

Mutz, D. C. (2002a). Cross-cutting social networks: Testing democratic theory in practice. *American Political Science Review, 96,* 111–126.

Mutz, D. C. (2002b). The consequences of cross-cutting networks for political participation. *American Journal of Political Science, 46,* 838–855.

Mutz, D. C. (2006). *Hearing the other side: Deliberative versus participatory democracy.* New York: Cambridge University.

Mutz, D. C., & Martin, P. S. (2001). Facilitating communication across lines of political difference: The role of mass media. *American Political Science Review, 95,* 97–114.

Mutz, D. C., & Mondak, J. J. (2006). The workplace as a context for cross-cutting political discourse. *Journal of Politics, 68,* 140–55.

Mutz, D. C., & Reeves, B. (2005). The new videomalaise: Effects of televised incivility on political trust. *American Political Science Review, 99,* 1–15.

Mutz, D. C., Reeves, B., & Wise, K. (2003, May). *Exposure to mediated political conflict: Effects of civility of interaction on arousal and memory.* Paper presented at the International Communication Association Annual Meeting, San Diego, CA. doi: ica_proceeding_12070.PDF

Newby-Clark, I. R., McGregor, I., & Zanna, M. P. (2002). Thinking and caring about cognitive inconsistency: When and for whom does attitudinal ambivalence feel uncomfortable? *Journal of Personality and Social Psychology, 82*, 157–166.

Newcomb, T. M. (1953). An approach to the study of communicative acts. *Psychological Review, 60*, 393–404.

Niemi, R. G., Craig, S. C., & Mattei, F. (1991). Measuring internal political efficacy in the 1998 National Election Study. *The American Political Science Review, 85*, 1407–1413.

Nir, L. (2005). Ambivalent social networks and their consequences for participation. *International Journal of Public Opinion Research, 17*, 422–442.

Nisbet, M. C., & Scheufele, D. A. (2004). Political talk as a catalyst for online citizenship. *Journalism & Mass Communication Quarterly, 81*, 877–896.

Norris, P. (2001). *Digital divide: Civic engagement, information poverty, and the Internet worldwide*. New York: Cambridge University Press.

Norton, M. I., Monin, B., Cooper, J., & Hogg, M. A. (2003). Vicarious dissonance: Attitude change from the inconsistency of others. *Journal of Personality and Social Psychology, 85*, 47–62.

Osgood, E. E., & Tannenbaum, P. H. (1955). The principle of congruity in the prediction of attitude change. *Psychological Review, 62*, 42–55.

Overby, L. M., & Barth, J. (2009). The media, the medium, and malaise: Assessing the effects of campaign media exposure with panel data. *Mass Communication and Society, 12*, 271–290.

Palfrey, J., & Gasser, U. (2008). *Born digital: Understanding the first generation of digital natives*. New York: Basic Books.

Papacharissi, Z. (2002a). The presentation of self in virtual life: Characteristics of personal home pages. *Journalism & Mass Communication Quarterly, 79*, 643–660.

Papacharissi, Z. (2002b). The virtual sphere: The Internet as a public sphere. *New Media & Society, 4*, 9–27.

Parsons, B. M. (2010). Social networks and the affective impact of political disagreement. *Political Behavior, 32*, 181–204.

Passy, F., & Giugni, M. (2001). Social networks and individual perceptions: Explaining differential participation in social movements. *Sociological Forum, 16*, 123–153.

Patterson, T. E. (1993). *Out of order*. New York: Knopf.

Patterson, T. E. (2003). The search for a standard: Markets and media. *Political Communication, 20*, 139–143.

Patterson, T. E. (2007). *Young people and news: A report from the Joan Shorenstein Center on the Press, Politics and Public Policy*. Retrieved from http://www.hks.harvard.edu/presspol/research/carnegie-knight/young_people_and_news_2007.pdf

Pew Research Center for the People & the Press. (2010). Americans spending more time following the news. Retrieved from http://people-press.org/files/legacy-pdf/652.pdf

Poindexter, P. M., & McCombs, M. E. (2001). Revisiting the civic duty to keep informed in the new media environment. *Journalism and Mass Communication Quarterly, 78*, 113–126.

Price, V., & Cappella, J. N. (2002). Online deliberation and its influence: The electronic dialogue project in campaign 2000. *IT & Society, 1*, 303–329.

Price, V., Cappella, J. N., & Nir, L. (2002). Does disagreement contribute to more deliberative opinion? *Political Communication, 19*, 97–114.

Priester, J. R., & Petty, R. E. (1996). The gradual threshold model of ambivalence:

Relating positive and negative bases of attitudes to subjective ambivalence. *Journal of Personality and Social Psychology, 71*, 431–449.

Prior, M. (2005). News vs. entertainment: How increasing media choice widens gaps in political knowledge and turnout. *American Journal of Political Science, 49*, 577–592.

Prior, M. (2007). *Post-broadcast democracy: How media choice increases inequality in political involvement and polarizes elections.* New York: Cambridge University Press.

Putnam, R. D. (2000). *Bowling alone: The collapse and revival of American community.* New York: Simon & Schuster.

Quintelier, E., & Vissers, S. (2008). The effect of Internet use on political participation: An analysis of survey results for 16-year-olds in Belgium. *Social Science Computer Review, 26*, 411–427.

Robinson, J. P., & Levy, M. R. (1986). Interpersonal communication and news comprehension. *Public Opinion Quarterly, 50*, 160–175.

Rubin, A. M., & Perse, E. M. (1987). Audience activity and television news gratifications. *Communication Research, 14*, 58–84.

Ryan, J. B. (2010). The effects of network expertise and biases on vote choice. *Political Communication, 27*, 44–58.

Scher, S. J., & Cooper, J. (1989). Motivational basis of dissonance: The singular role of behavioral consequences. *Journal of Personality and Social Psychology, 56*, 899–906.

Scheufele, D. A. (2002). Examining differential gains from mass media and their implications for participatory behavior. *Communication Research, 29*, 46–65.

Scheufele, D. A., Hardy, B. W., Brossard, D., Waismel-Manor, I. S., & Nisbet, E. (2006). Democracy based on difference: Examining the links between structural heterogeneity, heterogeneity of discussion networks, and democratic citizenship. *Journal of Communication, 56*, 728–573.

Scheufele, D. A., & Nisbet, M. C. (2002). Being a citizen online. New opportunities and dead ends. *The Harvard International Journal of Press/Politics, 7*, 55–75.

Scheufele, D. A., Nisbet, M. C., Brossard, D., & Nisbet, E. C. (2004). Social structure and citizenship: Examining the impacts of social setting, network heterogeneity, and informational variables on political participation. *Political Communication, 21*, 315–338.

Schmitt-Beck, R., & Mackenrodt, C. (2010). Social networks and mass media as mobilizers and demobilizers: A study of turnout at a German local election. *Electoral Studies, 29*, 392–404.

Schönbach, K., & Früh, W. (1984). Der dynamisch-transaktionale Ansatz II: Konsequenzen [The dynamic-transactional approach II: Consequences]. *Rundfunk und Fernsehen, 32*, 314–329.

Schulz, W., & Zeh, R. (2005). The changing election coverage of German television. A content analysis: 1990–2002. *Communications, 30*, 385–407.

Semetko, H. A., & Valkenburg, P. M. (1998). The impact of attentiveness on political efficacy: Evidence from a three-year German panel study. *International Journal of Public Opinion Research, 10*, 195–210.

Shah, D. V., Cho, J., Eveland, W. P., & Kwak, N. (2005). Information and expression in a digital age: Modelling Internet effects on civic participation. *Communication Research, 32*, 531–565.

Shah, D. V., Kwak, N., & Holbert, R. L. (2001). "Connecting" and "disconnecting" with civic life: Patterns of Internet use and the production of social capital. *Political Communication, 18,* 141–162.

Shrum, L. J. (1999). The relationship of television viewing with attitude strength and extremity: Implications for the cultivation effect. *Media Psychology, 1,* 3–25.

Skoric, M. M., Ying, D., & Ng, Y. (2009). Bowling online, not alone: Online social capital and political participation in Singapore. *Journal of Computer-Mediated Communication, 14,* 414–433.

Slater, M. D. (2007). Reinforcing spirals: The mutual influence of media selectivity and media effects and their impact on individual behavior and social identity. *Communication Theory, 17,* 281–303.

Smith, A. (2009). *The Internet's role in campaign 2008.* Retrieved from http://www.pewinternet.org/~/media//Files/Reports/2009/The_Internets_Role_in_Campaign_2008.pdf

Smith, S. M., Fabrigar, L. R., MacDougall, B. L., & Wiesenthal, N. L. (2008). The role of amount, cognitive elaboration, and structural consistency of attitude-relevant knowledge in the formation of attitude certainty. *European Journal of Social Psychology, 38,* 280–295.

Steele, C. M. (1988). The psychology of self-affirmation: Sustaining the integrity of the self. In R. F. Baumeister (Ed.), *The self in social psychology: Key readings in social psychology* (pp. 372–390). Philadelphia, PA: Psychology Press.

Steele, C. M. (1997). A threat in the air: How stereotypes shape intellectual identity and performance. *American Psychologist, 52,* 613–629.

Steele, C. M., & Aronson, J. (1995). Stereotype threat and the intellectual test performance of African Americans. *Journal of Personality and Social Psychology, 69,* 797–811.

Steele, C. M., & Liu, T. J. (1981). Making the dissonant act unreflective of self: Dissonance avoidance and the expectancy of a value-affirming response. *Journal of Personality and Social Psychology Bulletin, 7,* 393–397.

Steele, C.M., & Liu, T. J. (1983). Attitude and social cognition. Dissonance processes as self-affirmation. *Journal of Personality and Social Psychology, 45,* 5–19.

Steele, C. M., Spencer, S. J., & Lynch, M. (1993). Self-image resilience and dissonance: The role of affirmational resources. *Journal of Personality and Social Psychology, 64,* 885–896.

Stone, J. (2001). Behavioral discrepancies and construal processes in cognitive dissonance. In G. Moskowitz (Eds.), *Cognitive social psychology: The Princeton Symposium on the legacy and future of social cognition* (pp. 41–58). Mahwah, NJ: Erlbaum.

Stone, J., & Cooper, J. (2001). A self-standards model of cognitive dissonance. *Journal of Experimental Social Psychology, 37,* 228–243.

Stone, J., & Cooper, J. (2003). The effect of self-attribute relevance on how self-esteem moderates attitude change in dissonance processes. *Journal of Experimental Social Psychology, 39,* 508–515.

Strömbäck, J., & Shehata, A. (2010). Media malaise or a virtuous circle? Exploring the causal relationships between news media exposure, political news attention and political interest. *European Journal of Political Research, 49,* 575–597.

Stroud, N. J. (2007). Media effects, selective exposure, and Fahrenheit 9/11. *Political Communication, 24,* 415–432.

Stroud, N. J. (2008). Media use and political predispositions: Revisiting the concept of selective exposure. *Political Behavior, 30*, 341–366.

Stroud, N. J. (2010). Polarization and partisan selective exposure. *Journal of Communication, 60*, 556–576.

Stroud, N. J. (2011). *Niche news: The politics of news choice.* New York: Oxford University Press.

Stroud, N. J., Stevens, M., & Pye, D. (2011). The influence of debate viewing context on political cynicism and strategic interpretations. *American Behavioral Scientist, 55*, 270–283.

Sunstein, C. R. (2001). *Republic.com.* Princeton, NJ: Princeton University Press.

Sunstein, C. R. (2009). *Going to extremes: How like minds unite and divide.* Oxford, England: Oxford University Press.

Taber, C. S., & Lodge, M. (2006). Motivated skepticism in the evaluation of political beliefs. *American Journal of Political Science, 50*, 755–769.

Tedeschi, J. T. (Ed.). (1984). *Impression management theory and social psychological research.* New York: Academic Press.

Tedesco, J. C. (2004). Web interactivity and young adult political efficacy. In A. P. Williams & T. C. Tedesco (Eds.), *The Internet election: Perspectives on the web in campaign 2004* (pp. 187–202). Lanham, MD: Rowman & Littlefield.

Tesser, A., & Cornell, D. P. (1991). On the confluence of self processes. *Journal of Experimental Social Psychology, 27*, 501–526.

Tewksbury, D. (2005). The seeds of audience fragmentation: Specialization in the use of online news sites. *Journal of Broadcasting & Electronic Media, 49*, 332–348.

Tewksbury, D., Weaver, A. J., & Maddex, B. D. (2001). Accidentally informed: incidental news exposure on the world wide web. *Journalism & Mass Communication Quarterly, 78*, 533–554.

Thibodeau, R., & Aronson, E. (1992). Taking a closer look: Reasserting the role of self-concept in dissonance theory. *Personality and Social Psychology Bulletin, 18*, 591–602.

Thompson, M. M., Zanna, M. P., & Griffin, D. W. (1995). Let's not be indifferent about (attitudinal) ambivalence. In R. E. Petty & J. A. Krosnick (Eds.), *Attitude strength: Antecedents and consequences* (pp. 361–386). Mahwah, NJ: Erlbaum.

Tolbert, C. J., & McNeal, R. S. (2003). Unraveling the effects of the Internet on political participation? *Political Research Quarterly, 56*, 175–185.

Turkle, S. (1995). *Life on the screen: Identity in the age of the Internet.* New York: Simon & Schuster.

Ullrich, J., Schermelleh-Engel, K., & Böttcher, B. (2008). The moderator effect that wasn't there: Statistical problems in ambivalence research. *Journal of Personality and Social Psychology, 95*, 774–794.

Uslaner, E. M. (2004). Trust, civic engagement, and the Internet. *Political Communication, 21*, 223–242.

Valentino, N. A., Beckmann, M. N., & Buhr, T. A. (2001). A spiral of cynicism for some: The contingent effects of campaign news frames on participation and confidence in government. *Political Communication, 18*, 347–367.

Verba, S., Scholzman, K. L., & Brady, H. E. (1995). *Voice and equality: Civic voluntarism in American politics.* Cambridge, MA: Harvard University Press.

Visser, P. S., Krosnick, J. A., & Simmons, J. P. (2003). Distinguishing the cognitive and behavioral consequences of attitude importance and certainty: A new approach to testing the common-factor hypothesis. *Journal of Experimental Social Psychology, 39*, 118–141.

Vowe, G., Emmer, M., & Seifert, M. (2007). Abkehr oder Mobilisierung? Zum Einfluss des Internets auf die individuelle politische Kommunikation [Alienation or mobilization? On the Internet's impact on political communication]. In B. Krause, B. Fretwurst, & J. Vogelgesang (Eds.), *Fortschritte der politischen Kommunikationsforschung* (pp. 109–130) [Advances in political communication research]. Wiesbaden, Germany: VS Verlag für Sozialwissenschaften.

Weber, L. M., Loumakis, A., & Bergman, J. (2003). Who participates and why? An analysis of citizens on the Internet and the mass public. *Social Science Computer Review, 21*, 26–42.

Williams, D. (2006). On and off the 'net: Scales for social capital in an online era. *Journal of Computer-Mediated Communication, 11*, 593–628.

Wirth, W., & Schweiger, W. (1999). Selektion neu betrachtet: Auswahlentscheidungen im Internet [Selective exposure reconsidered: Selection decisions on the Internet]. In W. Wirth & W. Schweiger (Eds.), *Selektion im Internet: Empirische Analysen zu einem Schlüsselkonzept* (pp. 43–70) [Selective exposure on the Internet: Empirical analyses of a key concept]. Opladen, Germany: Westdeutscher Verlag.

Wojcieszak, M. E. (2010). "Don't talk to me": Effects of ideologically homogeneous online groups and politically dissimilar offline ties on extremism. *New Media & Society, 12*, 637–655.

Wojcieszak, M. E., & Mutz, D. C. (2009). Online groups and political discourse: Do online discussion spaces facilitate exposure to political disagreement? *Journal of Communication, 59*, 40–56.

Wolling, J. (1999). *Politikverdrossenheit durch Massenmedien? Der Einfluß der Medien auf die Einstellungen der Bürger zur Politik* [Political apathy through mass media? The impact of the media on citizens' attitudes toward politics]. Opladen, Germany: Westdeutscher Verlag.

Xenos, M., & Moy, P. (2007). Direct and differential effects of the Internet on political and civic engagement. *Journal of Communication, 57*, 704–718.

Young, D. G., & Tisinger, R. A. (2006). Dispelling late-night myths: News consumption among late-night comedy viewers and the predictors of exposure to various late-night shows. *Harvard International Journal of Press/Politics, 11*, 113–134.

Zaller, J. R. (2003). A new standard of news quality: Burglar alarms for the monitorial citizen. *Political Communication, 20*, 109–130.

Zelizer, B. (2004). *Taking journalism seriously*. Thousand Oaks, CA: Sage.

Zhang, W., Johnson, T. J., Seltzer, T., & Bichard, S. L. (2010). The revolution will be networked: The influence of social networking sites on political attitudes and behavior. *Social Science Computer Review, 28*, 75–92.

Zittel, T. (2004). Political communication and electronic democracy: American exceptionalism or global trend? In F. Esser & B. Pfetsch (Eds.), *Comparing political communication: Theories, cases, and challenges* (pp. 231–250). Cambridge, England: Cambridge University Press.

2 Commentary
Online News and the Demise of Political Disagreement

Dietram A. Scheufele

University of Wisconsin–Madison

Matthew C. Nisbet

American University

Information processing is never free of partisan biases. We know from decades of research in social psychology, political science, sociology, and communication that our values and ideological predispositions influence how much bias we see in media reports (Vallone, Ross, & Lepper, 1985), how willing or likely we are to attend to particular stories (Donsbach, 1991), and, maybe most importantly, how we interpret seemingly objective pieces of information differentially, depending on our personal value systems (Brossard, Scheufele, Kim, & Lewenstein, 2009; Ho, Brossard, & Scheufele, 2008; Kunda, 1990; Nisbet, 2005).

But why are we concerned about selectivity? In many ways, selectively attending to some messages over others, based on perceptions of source credibility, ideological congruence, or issue-specific interest, is what enables us to efficiently sift through large amounts of information. But as Donsbach and Mothes outline in their chapter, the notion of selectively attending to or discounting information, based on ideological or value-based predispositions, is also directly at odds with normative views of democratic citizenship.

The Nature of Political Discourse and Its Effects on Democratic Citizenship

The notion of a truly deliberative (or civil) society is based on a few key premises (Scheufele, 2011). Among them are two that are particularly relevant for thinking operationally about the issue of selectivity: (a) all possible views and supporting arguments are *expressed*, and (b) participants are willing to *listen* to and engage with arguments that are different from their own. As a result, truly civil deliberations among citizens can be defined as the rational exchange of non-like-minded views (or disagreement).

As is so often the case, however, empirical realities are at odds with these normative ideals. Many of us are simply not used to being confronted on a regular basis with others who hold views that are strongly opposed to our own. Our social networks, that is, the people we are surrounded by in most of our daily activities, tend to be extremely like-minded and homogenous in their demographic and ideological makeup. In the United States, we have always tended to buy houses, socialize, play sports, and discuss politics mostly with people who think and look like us (McPherson, Smith-Lovin, & Cook, 2001), and in recent decades, the political similarity of our social, political, and geographic enclaves has increased appreciably (Abramowitz, 2010; Bishop, 2008). As a result, we are less and less likely to talk to people who hold different views from our own (Mutz, 2002b).

Yet avoiding disagreement may not necessarily be a bad thing. In fact, some researchers have suggested that when we *do* encounter heterogeneity or disagreement in our social networks, it can have detrimental effects on our willingness to participate in the political process. Mutz (2002a), for example, argues that being exposed to non-like-minded partisan information in one's social network can create feelings of ambivalence among voters and consequently promote apathy rather than engagement with the political process.

But exposure to non-like-minded information can also have significant positive effects on democratic citizenship, especially if we conceptualize disagreement in ways that go beyond discussing politics across political party lines or left–right ideology. In a series of studies, for instance, we compared citizens whose discussion networks exposed them to varying levels of disagreement not just by political lines but also by gender, racial, and religious differences (Kim, Scheufele, & Han, 2011; Scheufele, Hardy, Brossard, Waismel-Manor, & Nisbet, 2006; Scheufele, Nisbet, & Brossard 2003; Scheufele, Nisbet, Brossard, & Nisbet, 2004). We were particularly interested in finding out why disagreement matters, and what the effects of people's everyday interactions across social settings such as church, work, and volunteer groups were on their willingness to participate in the political process. The take-away conclusion is consistent across studies: Encountering disagreement in one's social network is a good thing. In many cases, it promotes participation and a number of civically relevant outcomes (McLeod, Scheufele, & Moy, 1999; Scheufele, Hardy et al., 2006; Scheufele, Nisbet et al., 2004).

The End of Disagreement?

When the Internet first began to provide citizens with broad access to virtually infinite amounts of information, commentators heralded online information environments as new commonwealths of information. Many of these commentators expressed the hope that online communication could close informational divides and enable a truly deliberative discourse across all cross-sections of society (for an overview, see Nisbet & Scheufele, 2004; Scheufele & Nisbet, 2002).

Recent reviews have been distinctly more pessimistic, and have suggested that we may in fact be returning to a fractionalized, partisan news environment that will reinforce citizens' existing views through higher levels of selectivity, and ultimately narrow public discourse along partisan lines of disagreement (Bennett & Iyengar, 2008). Donsbach and Mothes's overview in this volume offers a more in-depth look at this idea and explores a set of complementary explanatory models for how these selectivity-based processes may play from an audience perspective.

But given the dynamic nature of online news environments, it may be useful to think about the particular mechanisms or filters that are unique to online information environments and will continue to change the landscape of how we selectively attend to information around us. At the most abstract level, we can distinguish two sets of mechanisms or filters: media-centric ones and audience-centric ones.

Media-Centric Filters

Applying as a filter their professional judgment and expertise, journalists have historically guided audiences toward the issues they deem the most newsworthy and important (White, 1950). Not only would some issues make it into the day's news while others would not, but audiences could rely on experienced professionals organizing these stories by a hierarchy of importance via lead stories and front-page headlines. Downie and Schudson (2009) note that "reporting the news means telling citizens what they would not otherwise know" (p. 8). Empirically, of course, researchers have shown a number of potential distortions in how news items get selected or presented, based on characteristics of the story (Galtung & Ruge, 1965), professional norms and ideologies (Tuchman, 1978), and various external pressures (Gans, 1979). Overall, however, by applying the filter of their professional judgment and expertise, journalists have fulfilled an essential surveillance and agenda-setting function in society.

Yet today with more Americans saying that they get their news on a daily basis from online sources than from local newspapers (Purcell, Rainie, Mitchell, Rosenstiel, & Olmstead, 2010), the presentation, selection, and availability of news is no longer chiefly controlled by journalists. Nor is the primary goal to attract diverse audiences to a hierarchically organized portfolio of coverage defined by an entire broadcast or newspaper edition. Instead, the objective is to lure a combination of habitual and incidental news consumers to specific online stories by way of search engines, aggregators, and social networks. This strategy allows news organizations to maximize page views while also tracking and selling personal information about consumers via third party partners such as Facebook. At least three related trends enable this goal.

1. *Opinionated news and niche audiences*: The proliferation of niche cable channels such as MSNBC and Fox News and highly specialized online information environments such as Huffington Post or The Daily Caller have led to an increasing fractionalization of news choices and audiences. Driven by commercial concerns, much of this fractionalization has occurred along partisan fault lines. Or as Rachel Maddow put it: "Opinion-driven media makes the money that politically neutral media loses" (Maddow, 2010, p. 22). And as more recent research shows, these fragmented news environments have the potential to produce more apathy among some segments of the electorate and more partisan polarization across the population overall (Prior, 2007).

2. *Algorithms as editors*: The increasing shift toward online presentation of news, even among traditional news outlets, has also provided media organizations with new real-time metrics of audience preference and the ability to make decisions about news selection and placement based on these metrics. This use of "algorithms as editors" (Peters, 2010) is not without pitfalls. Increasing the influence that reader preferences have on story selection and placement also increases the likelihood of a spiral of mutual reinforcement. In other words, stories that readers selectively attend to will be placed more prominently on news(paper) websites, which in turn increases the odds of readers finding them in the first place. This makes it easy for readers to select content based on popularity, interest, or political identity; opting out of the professional hierarchy of front page headlines and lead stories that might appear in a printed newspaper or broadcast.

3. *Self-reinforcing search and tagging spirals*: This notion of reinforcing spirals is exacerbated in online search environments where search engine rankings and search suggestions can heavily influence the overall information infrastructure. The process depends not only on the algorithms used by search engines but also on the tagging and optimization strategies pursued by news content providers, aggregators, bloggers, and interest groups (Hindman, 2009). Examining the presentation of scientific information online, Ladwig and colleagues (Ladwig, Anderson, Brossard, Scheufele, & Shaw, 2010), for example, found that the "suggest" function in Google's search results often did not correspond to the online information environment that was available to audiences (based on systematic analyses of the complete population of websites and blogs). As a result, the guidance provided by Google search suggestions is likely to disproportionally drive traffic, regardless of the content available, and create a self-reinforcing spiral that reduces the complexity and diversity of the information that citizens encounter online (Ladwig et al., 2010).

Audience-Centric Filters

Many of these more media-centric filters work in tandem with individual-level behaviors and choices. Prior's (2007) hypotheses about the polarizing effects of increasing channel diversity, for instance, are based heavily on the assumption that individuals actively make choices about the content (news vs. entertainment) that they attend to. But the social texture that is developing in Web 2.0 information environments produces a communication landscape in which at least two *new* modes of audience-centric selectivity are likely to influence news choices.

1. *Automated selectivity*: In online environments, news portals and aggregator sites allow for highly effective *individual* preselection of the information that reaches us. iGoogle, myYahoo, and other news aggregators allow audiences to selectively receive and attend to news items, based on a set of fine-grained filters that can include medium, outlet, content, author, and a host of other predefined criteria. In contrast, visitors to the landing page for online newspapers may be able to skim or skip stories that they disagree with or find boring, but they will have a hard time making a selective choice without at least briefly glancing at the lead or headline. By contrast, portals and other news aggregators will make sure that some stories never even reach our computer screen. Smart phones, tablets, and other portable devices make it easier to skim and select when consuming news, creating further incentives for news organizations to cater to this selectivity in their design of mobile applications.

2. *Networks as filters*: This individual-level set of filters, however, is being complemented by maybe even more effective *social* filters. Based on a series of experiments about online information use patterns in various social settings, Messing and colleagues (Messing, Westwood, & Lelkes, 2011), for example, predict that "social information, and especially personal recommendations, will emerge as the most important explanatory factor shaping both the media environment to which an individual is exposed, and the content that the individual chooses to view" (p. 29). And the notion of networks as selective filters may be more prevalent than we think. Seventy-five percent of online news consumers now say they get news forwarded through e-mail or posts on social networking sites (Purcell et al., 2010); that is, information that is passed along and preselected by people who are very likely to share their worldviews and preferences. And much of this information is not presented in an isolated news environment, similar to traditional newspapers or television broadcasts, but instead is socially contextualized almost immediately by a host of reader comments, Facebook "like" buttons, and indicators of how often a story has been retweeted.

The potential effects of such social-level contextualization on individual news selection are less clear, and two competing hypotheses can be put forth. They map nicely onto the two self-reinforcing spirals that Donsbach and Mothes outline in their essay in this volume.

The first hypothesis suggests that we may be moving toward a society where we are less and less exposed to (and less and less used to) disagreement and viewpoints that are different from our own. Highly like-minded and homophilic networks, in other words, may exacerbate the effects of individual-level selectivity and produce an even more fine-grained filter for incoming information. The result would be a very pronounced spiral of *self-reinforcing attitude polarization* to use Donsbach and Mothes's term. Journalists and other professional groups such as scientists are likely to be part of this attitude polarization because these groups tend to be disproportionately like-minded in their political outlook, are heavier users of online news sources and social media, and face greater demands on their time in managing and using information (Besley & Nisbet, forthcoming; Donsbach, 2004).

A number of recent studies, however, provide some preliminary evidence for a more optimistic hypothesis. It is based on the assumption that friendship networks may often be more politically diverse than the individuals in these networks perceive them to be. In other words: "friends disagree more than they think they do" (Goel, Mason, & Watts, 2010, p. 611). This also means that socially homophilic networks may be characterized by more political diversity than we often assume. Messing et al. (2011), in fact, infer that socially networked information environments can "create at least marginally more cross-cutting exposure to political information" (p. 30) than situations where individuals select news items without additional social cues.

It remains to be seen if these findings are replicated in future work and socially networked information environments can in fact increase exposure to non-like-minded views. If they do, they could produce some of the same beneficial outcomes that we outlined in our work on heterogeneous face-to-face networks (Scheufele, Hardy et al., 2006; Scheufele, Nisbet et al., 2004), or at least reinforce the spirals of depolarization that Donsbach and Mothes outline in their models.

It is clear that communication researchers have only begun to fill in parts of a large grid of research questions which will have to be answered in the near future. It is hoped that the overview provided here and in Donsbach and Mothes's essay will systematize these efforts. Whatever the answers may be that we as a discipline provide, they will have important implications for how we conceptualize and measure communication effects, effectively design online media, educate professionals and the public, and regulate media content and platforms. But more importantly, they will raise normative questions about the future of a media system that is driven by media-centric or audience-centric shifts and no longer provides a commonly shared and professionally defined hierarchy of stories and ideas.

References

Abramowitz, A. (2009). *The disappearing center.* New Haven, CT: Yale University Press.

Bennett, W. L., & Iyengar, S. (2008). A new era of minimal effects? The changing foundations of political communication. *Journal of Communication, 58*(4), 707–731. doi:10.1111/j.1460-2466.2008.00410.x

Besley, J., & Nisbet, M. (forthcoming). How scientists view the public, the media and the political process. *Public Understanding of Science.* doi:10.1177/0963662511418743.

Bishop, B., & Cushing, R. (2008). *The big sort: Why the clustering of like-minded America is tearing us apart.* New York: Houghton Mifflin.

Brossard, D., Scheufele, D. A., Kim, E., & Lewenstein, B. V. (2009). Religiosity as a perceptual filter: Examining processes of opinion formation about nanotechnology. *Public Understanding of Science, 18*(5), 546–558. doi:10.1177/0963662507087304

Donsbach, W. (1991). *Medienwirkung trotz Selektion: Einflussfaktoren auf die Zuwend- ung zu Zeitungsinhalten* [Media effects despite selection: Influences on attention to newspaper content]. Cologne, Germany: Böhlau.

Donsbach, W. (2004). Psychology of news decisions. *Journalism, 5*(2), 131.

Downie, L. & Schudson, M. (2009). The reconstruction of American journalism. *Columbia Journalism Review.* Retrieved February 27, 2012, from http://www.jour-nalism.columbia.edu/system/documents/1/original/Reconstruction_of_Journal-ism.pdf from http://www.cjr.org/reconstruction/the_reconstruction_of_american.php?page=all.

Galtung, J., & Ruge, M. H. (1965). The structure of foreign news. *Journal of Peace Research, 2*(1), 64–91.

Gans, H. (1979). *Deciding what's news.* New York: Pantheon Books.

Goel, S., Mason, W., & Watts, D. J. (2010). Real and perceived attitude agreement in social networks. *Journal of Personality and Social Psychology, 99*(4), 611–621. doi: 10.1037/a0020697

Hindman, M. (2009). *The myth of digital democracy.* Princeton, NJ: Princeton University Press.

Ho, S. S., Brossard, D., & Scheufele, D. A. (2008). Effects of value predispositions, mass media use, and knowledge on public attitudes toward embryonic stem cell research. *International Journal of Public Opinion Research, 20*(2), 171–192.

Kim, E., Scheufele, D. A., & Han, J. Y. (2011). Structure or predisposition? Explor- ing the interaction effect of discussion orientation and discussion heterogeneity on political participation. *Mass Communication & Society, 14*(4), 502–526. doi: 10.1080/15205436.2010.51346

Kunda, Z. (1990). The case for motivated reasoning. *Psychological Bulletin, 108*(3), 480–498. doi: 10.1037/0033-2909.108.3.480

Ladwig, P., Anderson, A. A., Brossard, D., Scheufele, D. A., & Shaw, B. (2010). Narrowing the nano discourse? *Materials Today, 13*(5), 52–54. doi:10.1016/s1369-7021(10)70084-5

Maddow, R. (2010). Theodore H. White Lecture on press and politics [transcript]. *Joan Shorenstein Center on the Press, Politics and Public Policy, Harvard University.* Retrieved from http://www.hks.harvard.edu/presspol/prizes_lectures/th_white_lecture/transcripts/th_white_2010_maddow.pdf

McLeod, J. M., Scheufele, D. A., & Moy, P. (1999). Community, communication, and participation: The role of mass media and interpersonal discussion in local political participation. *Political Communication, 16*(3), 315–336.

McPherson, M., Smith-Lovin, L., & Cook, J. M. (2001). Birds of a feather: Homophily in social networks. *Annual Review of Sociology, 27*(1), 415–444. doi:10.1146/annurev.soc.27.1.415

Messing, S., Westwood, S. J., & Lelkes, Y. (2011). *Online media effects: Social, not political, reinforcement.* Unpublished manuscript, Stanford University. Palo Alto, CA. Retrieved from http://www.stanford.edu/~messing/PopRecSrcNews2.pdf

Mutz, D. C. (2002a). The consequences of cross-cutting networks for political participation. *American Journal of Political Science, 46*(4), 838–855.

Mutz, D. C. (2002b). Cross-cutting social networks: Testing democratic theory in practice. *American Political Science Review, 96*(1), 111–126.

Nisbet, M. C. (2005). The competition for worldviews: Values, information, and public support for stem cell research. *International Journal of Public Opinion Research, 17*(1), 90–112.

Nisbet, M. C. & Scheufele, D. A. (2004). Political talk as a catalyst for online citizenship. *Journalism & Mass Communication Quarterly, 81*(4), 877–896.

Peters, J. W. (2010, July 5). At Yahoo, using searches to steer news coverage, *The New York Times,* p. B1. Retrieved from http://www.nytimes.com/2010/07/05/business/media/05yahoo.html

Prior, M. (2007). *Post-broadcast democracy: How media choice increases inequality in political involvement and polarizes elections.* Cambridge,England: Cambridge University Press.

Purcell, K., Rainie, L., Mitchell, A., Rosenstiel, T., & Olmstead, K. (2010). Understanding the participatory news consumer. *Pew Internet & American Life Project.* Retrieved from http://www.pewInternet.org/Reports/2010/Online-News.aspx

Scheufele, D. A. (2011). *Modern citizenship or policy dead end? Evaluating the need for public participation in science policy making, and why public meetings may not be the answer.* Paper no. R-34 presented at the Joan Shorenstein Center on the Press, Politics and Public Policy Research Paper Series, Harvard University, Cambridge, MA. Retrieved from http://www.hks.harvard.edu/presspol/publications/papers/research_papers/r34_scheufele.pdf

Scheufele, D. A., Hardy, B. W., Brossard, D., Waismel-Manor, I. S., & Nisbet, E. (2006). Democracy based on difference: Examining the links between structural heterogeneity, heterogeneity of discussion networks, and democratic citizenship. *Journal of Communication, 56*(4), 728–753.

Scheufele, D. A., & Nisbet, M. C. (2002). Being a citizen online—New opportunities and dead ends. *Harvard International Journal of Press-Politics, 7*(3), 55–75.

Scheufele, D. A., Nisbet, M. C., & Brossard, D. (2003). Pathways to participation? Religion, communication contexts, and mass media. *International Journal of Public Opinion Research, 15*(3), 300–324.

Scheufele, D. A., Nisbet, M. C., Brossard, D., & Nisbet, E. C. (2004). Social structure and citizenship: Examining the impacts of social setting, network heterogeneity, and informational variables on political participation. *Political Communication, 21*(3), 315–338.

Tuchman, G. (1978). *Making news: A study in the construction of reality.* New York: Free Press.

Vallone, R. P., Ross, L., & Lepper, M. R. (1985). The hostile media phenomenon: Biased perception and perceptions of media bias in coverage of the Beirut massacre. *Journal of Personality and Social Psychology, 59,* 577–585.

White, D. M. (1950). The "gatekeeper": A case study in the selection of news. *Journalism Quarterly, 27*(3), 383–390.

CHAPTER CONTENTS

3 Intergroup Contact
An Integration of Social Psychological and Communication Perspectives

Jake Harwood

University of Arizona

Miles Hewstone

University of Oxford

Yair Amichai-Hamburger

The Interdisciplinary Center, Herzliya

Nicole Tausch

University of St Andrews

This chapter examines the literature on intergroup contact from a communication perspective. The basic idea of intergroup contact theory—that contact between groups reduces prejudice—is presented. Research examining this idea from a communication perspective is described and integrated with the large social-psychological body of work. We focus first on direct, face-to-face contact between members of different groups. We then discuss various forms of indirect contact including vicarious, extended, imagined, and computer-mediated forms of contact. Finally, we present an extended research agenda for the field of communication to contribute to what is fundamentally a communicative event.

The idea that communication between groups results in increased intergroup cooperation and reduced prejudice is intuitive and appealing. If communication facilitates perspective taking, personal insight, and the building of relationships, it should do so across group boundaries, and such communication should result in reductions in both prejudice and intergroup conflict. This idea has spawned a long tradition of research on intergroup contact and prejudicial attitudes which spans psychology, sociology, education, and more recently communication. In this chapter we review the research on contact from an interdisciplinary perspective, emphasizing the work that explicitly considers communication variables, and laying out an agenda for where scholars interested in communication processes can best contribute to future work in this area. As will become clear, our understanding of the effects of contact is at this point clear and conclusive: contact typically has positive effects. The size of those effects is moderated by other variables, and certainly contact is not a panacea in all circumstances, but a strong claim concerning contact's effectiveness is justified. Our knowledge of the *communicative processes* of contact is considerably weaker, and it is more intensive work in this area that we are hoping to stimulate with this chapter.

We start by distinguishing *direct* and *indirect* forms of contact. Although we typically think of intergroup contact as being in the form of face-to-face encounters (i.e., direct contact), this is not exclusively the case. As technology and research have developed, researchers have explored how we experience members of out-groups in alternate, indirect ways (e.g., via virtual communication). We will review the evidence for direct and indirect contact in separate sections, highlighting the overall research evidence, and both moderating and mediating factors. After the review of direct and indirect contact, we examine the evidence for the broad impact of intergroup contact on dependent measures beyond self-report measures of explicit attitudes. Finally, we propose an agenda for communication research on intergroup contact, and draw some conclusions.

Direct Contact

Williams (1947), a sociologist, was the first scholar to systematically expound on the idea that intergroup contact could improve intergroup relations. But it is the Harvard social psychologist Gordon Allport (1954) who is generally credited with being the first scholar to propose details on how members of different groups can be brought together in face-to-face encounters to reduce intergroup hostility. Allport coined the term the *contact hypothesis* (Hewstone & Brown, 1986; Hewstone & Swart, in press), and proposed that contact would be more likely to reduce prejudice and improve intergroup relations if four conditions were met. First, there should be *equal status* among the individuals in the contact situation. Second, the situation should require *cooperation* between groups or offer common goals to both groups. Third, the contact situation should be structured in such a way as to allow the development of *close relationships* with members of the out-group. Finally, contact should be legitimized through *institutional support*.

Allport's (1954) formulation of the contact hypothesis has proven extremely influential and has inspired considerable research that tested and extended its basic principles (Brown & Hewstone, 2005; Dovidio, Gaertner, & Kawakami, 2003; Pettigrew & Tropp, 2006). This work has used diverse research methods (field studies, lab experiments, longitudinal surveys), and has had a profound impact on social policy in many countries (Hewstone, 2009; Tausch, Kenworthy, & Hewstone, 2005). However, the impressive body of research on the contact hypothesis is not without its limitations, which include the reliance on self-report measures of contact as well as on survey studies rather than experiments; these are briefly noted where relevant.

Research Evidence

The prejudice-reducing effect of contact is now well-established, with the most convincing evidence accumulated by Pettigrew and Tropp (2006). Their ground-breaking meta-analysis covered 515 studies (including 713 independent samples), and was based on a total of over 250,000 participants. Summarizing greatly, we highlight here three of their most important findings. First, there was a highly significant negative relationship between contact and prejudice (mean effect size $r = -.22$, $p < .001$), suggesting that contact is an effective tool for reducing prejudice. Second, the effect size in the 134 samples where contact was structured to meet Allport's optimal contact conditions ($r = -.29$, $p < .001$) was significantly greater than in studies that did not ($r = -.20$, $p < .001$). Third, having contact with out-group friends was found to be significantly more predictive of reduced prejudice ($r = -.26$) than was general intergroup contact ($r = -.22$), lending further support to the contention that cross-group friendships are the most effective form of intergroup contact (Hamberger & Hewstone, 1997; Pettigrew, 1997).

Pettigrew and Tropp (2006) also found a number of variables that moderated the size of the contact effect, including contact setting, target group, dependent measure, and majority vs. minority group status. The effect of contact was greater in laboratory and recreational, than in educational and residential settings; for target groups based on sexual-orientation and ethnicity than for those based on physical or mental disability; for affective measures (emotions and feelings) than for cognitive measures (beliefs and stereotypes); and for majority than for minority-status groups. It must be emphasized that these moderation effects qualify the *extent* of the contact effect, not its existence. Across all studies, the baseline effect is that contact is associated with reduced prejudice. Thus, notwithstanding the booster effect of contact involving Allport's four conditions, these factors should be seen as facilitating rather than as necessary conditions (Pettigrew, 1998). We consider theoretically based moderators of direct contact below.

One limitation of the database for this meta-analysis is that many studies are cross-sectional, rather than experimental or longitudinal. In these studies, we cannot be sure whether varying amounts of contact bring about change in intergroup attitudes, or whether people with different prior attitudes differentially seek or avoid out-group contact, or both. Complex modeling techniques can compare both directional effects using cross-sectional data, and sometimes both paths are significant (Tausch et al., 2005); but typically the path from contact to attitudes is somewhat greater than the reverse (Pettigrew, 1998; Powers & Ellison, 1995). Studies have also assessed the effect of contact when people were given *no choice* about participating in intergroup contact; thus prior attitudes could not be driving contact. Pettigrew and Tropp's (2006) meta-analysis reported that no-choice studies yielded the *largest* effect sizes between contact and attitudes.

Notwithstanding these attempts to exploit cross-sectional data, longitudinal designs permit stronger causal interpretations, and show that under certain conditions contact does indeed lead to generalized attitude change. Several impressive longitudinal studies have recently emerged; these studies illuminate contact processes and enhance our confidence in the value of contact as a social intervention (Christ, Hewstone, Tropp, & Wagner, in press; see Christ & Wagner, in press, for methodological issues in longitudinal research). Next, we discuss one prominent longitudinal study.

Levin, van Laar, and Sidanius (2003; Sidanius, Levin, van Laar, & Sears, 2009) collected data from American college students over a period of 5 years. Their results indicate that students reporting less favorable ethnic attitudes (and more intergroup anxiety) in their first year were less likely to have out-group friends (from different racial and ethnic groups) during their second and third years of college—consistent with the argument that prior attitudes determine the extent of intergroup contact. Nevertheless, those students with more out-group friends in years 2 and 3 had more positive attitudes and were less anxious in year 5, even after their prior attitudes, friendships, and a number of relevant background variables were controlled. Notably, both causal paths were equally strong. Given that the relationship between contact and prejudice should be regarded as an ongoing, reciprocal process (Eller & Abrams, 2004), these bidirectional paths are to be expected. What is most crucial in terms of assessing contact as a social intervention, however, is that the path *from* contact *to* out-group attitudes remains statistically significant even after the reverse causal path has been accounted for. This underscores the viable role of contact in improving out-group evaluations overall, notwithstanding the acknowledged evidence for self-selection bias.

Moderators of Direct Contact

As noted above, Pettigrew and Tropp's (2006) meta-analysis reported numerous variables that moderated the overall negative impact of contact on prejudice. In this section we highlight two broad types of variable found to moderate the impact of direct contact on attitudes and other dependent variables: varying levels of categorization during contact, and participant factors as boundary conditions (Tausch & Hewstone, 2010).

Varying Levels of Categorization during Contact. Some theoretical approaches have argued that contact situations should be structured to reduce the salience of available social categories and increase the likelihood of a more interpersonal mode of thinking and behaving (e.g., Brewer & Miller, 1984, 1988; N. Miller, 2002). This would allow those in the intergroup interaction to focus on personal information and individuate out-group members. In contrast, we argue that this approach is limited, because it tends to create positive *interpersonal* relations, rather than changing generalized views of out-groups as a whole. In short, by focusing solely on individuating information, the out-group member would not be seen as an out-group member at all, and thus any positive outcomes that result from the interaction would fail to generalize to other members of the category.

We propose that there are advantages in maintaining intergroup *salience* during contact, so long as some of Allport's key conditions apply (Brown & Hewstone, 2005; Hewstone, 1996). If the contact is arranged so that it takes place between in-group and out-group members who can be regarded as sufficiently typical or representative of their groups, then the positive changes that occur should generalize to the groups as a whole. Experimental and correlational studies now provide extensive evidence for this view (Brown & Hewstone, 2005).

In the experimental studies (e.g., Brown, Vivian, & Hewstone, 1999, Study 1; Van Oudenhoven, Groenewoud, & Hewstone, 1996; Wilder, 1984), researchers have manipulated whether contact under favorable conditions takes place with a member of the relevant target group who is either typical or atypical of the group as a whole. The correlational studies (e.g., Brown et al., 1999, Study 2; Voci & Hewstone, 2003), have been conducted in naturalistic settings where it is generally not possible to manipulate typicality or salience. Thus, this research includes self-report measures of both the quantity and quality of contact that respondents report having with members of an out-group, as well as assessments of subjective group salience or perceived typicality of the out-group person. Moderated regression or similar techniques are then used to test whether the association between contact and intergroup attitude is qualified by group salience (i.e., whether the association between contact and attitudes was greater for respondents who report "high" vs. "low" salience during contact). For example, Harwood, Hewstone, Paolini, and Voci (2005, Study 1) investigated whether grandchildren's attitudes toward older adults were affected by the amount and quality of contact the grandchildren had with the grandparents they saw most frequently. A significant positive effect of contact quality on attitudes emerged when grandchildren were aware of age differences and saw their grandparents as typical of other older people during contact. The effect was weaker when awareness of age and perceived typicality of the grandparent were lower. In other words, group (in this case age) salience moderates the effects of contact on attitudes.

Research on the communication factors that enhance group salience is very limited (e.g., Harwood, 2010; Harwood, Raman, & Hewstone, 2006). Nonetheless, the literature suggests that treating group memberships as a *topic* of discussion, talking about group-related topics, or talking in a style that is (perhaps stereotypically) characteristic of one's group are relatively straightforward communicative manifestations of group salience.

Atypical out-group members are not completely ineffective in influencing attitudes. For example, research has shown that encountering largely atypical out-group members can increase the perceived *variability* of the out-group as a whole (Hamburger, 1994), even if it does not impact central tendencies (Paolini, Hewstone, Rubin, & Pay, 2004).

Participant Factors as Boundary Conditions. One challenge of research on intergroup contact is that the same objective contact conditions can be perceived differently by different people, which affects the success of contact interventions (Tropp, 2008). For example, individual difference variables can influence the effectiveness of contact (Stephan, 1987). Allport (1954) recognized participants' initial level of prejudice as they enter a contact situation as a potential barrier to prejudice reduction. Interacting with out-group members is highly challenging and requires increased self-regulation among highly prejudiced individuals, which can result in impaired executive function (Richeson & Trawalter, 2005; Vorauer & Kumhyr, 2001).

Nonetheless, there is evidence that contact may, apparently paradoxically, be particularly effective for more prejudiced participants. Dhont and Van Hiel (2009), for example, showed that the impact of contact with immigrants on individuals scoring high on right-wing authoritarianism (RWA) and social dominance orientation (SDO) was *greater* than the impact of contact on respondents who scored low on RWA and SDO. Likewise, Hodson (2008) showed that White prison inmates with higher SDO scores reported less in-group bias with increasing direct contact with Black inmates, compared to White inmates scoring lower in SDO. Similarly, Maoz (2003) showed that, although Israeli "hawks" were less motivated to interact with Palestinians and had more negative out-group attitudes before an encounter program than did "doves," they showed greater positive attitude change in response to the intervention. Of course, more prejudiced participants have more room for their attitudes to change, while it is rather difficult to show reduced prejudice among individuals who are unprejudiced to start with.

Turning to group factors, Tropp and Pettigrew's (2005a) meta-analysis showed that the contact–prejudice link was significantly weaker for members of disadvantaged groups ($r = -.18$), than dominant groups ($r = -.23$). They also demonstrated that Allport's (1954) optimal contact conditions did not predict the strength of contact effects among minority group members. Additional findings indicate that personalized contact is less effective for members of minority groups (Bettencourt, Charlton, & Kernahan, 1997; see also Binder et al., 2009; Gómez, Tropp, & Fernández, 2011). These findings suggest that members of disadvantaged groups may construe intergroup interactions in different ways than do members of advantaged groups. In particular, members of disadvantaged groups may be less likely to believe that they have equal status (Robinson & Preston, 1976). They are also more likely to anticipate prejudice and discrimination against them from dominant group members, which may further reduce the effectiveness of contact (Shelton, 2003; Tropp, 2006).

This may be a good moment to acknowledge that not all group contexts are the same. The contact literature sometimes takes a rather homogeneous view of contact effects (i.e., contact with a member of group X has effects on attitudes about group X). However, contact effects actually vary by group and we know relatively little about why that might be (e.g., Pettigrew & Tropp's meta-analysis shows stronger effects for contact with gay people than for contact with elderly people). Perspectives that attend to structural and psychological differences between specific intergroup relations contexts may provide more information about why such differences exist, and could be developed into better understandings of what type of contact works for whom (Fiske, Cuddy, Glick, & Xu, 2002). We would advocate attending to the sociohistorical conflicts between groups to explain some of the variance here. It might also be profitable to examine the degree of communicative "availability" of one group to the other: the extent to which communication is plausible based on both linguistic commonality and cultural similarity in the meaning and purpose of communication might be a significant influence on the potential for communication to solve problems. Some degree of communicative accessibility is undoubtedly essential for meaningful contact; however, in some contexts it is easy to imagine that communicative barriers might be functional in providing attributions for breakdown, and apparent communicative similarity between groups (e.g., a shared language) might mask deeper barriers that cause miscommunication.

Mediators of Direct Contact

A major development since Allport's (1954) pioneering work is that researchers have moved from the mere demonstration that contact works, to the more demanding question of *how* it works. Although the effects of contact may partly be due to mere exposure (i.e., the principle that familiarity fosters liking; Bornstein, 1989), the published research demonstrates that more sophisticated mechanisms are at work. Sufficient evidence on mediators has accrued to merit extensive coverage in a narrative review (Brown & Hewstone, 2005) and a meta-analysis specifically of mediators of contact (Pettigrew & Tropp, 2008). We consider three classes of mediator: cognitive, affective, and communication variables. Within each category, we consider simpler studies of single mediators first, but later introduce more ambitious studies that simultaneously explored both multiple mediators and their interplay with moderating variables.

Cognitive Variables. Allport (1954) suggested that unfavorable out-group attitudes are due to a lack of information about that out-group, and that contact can thus reduce prejudice by providing opportunities to learn about the out-group. *Increased knowledge* can reveal similarities and thus lead to liking (Pettigrew, 1998), and reduces uncertainty about how to interact with others (Stephan & Stephan, 1985). For example, Stephan and Stephan (1984) demonstrated that White Americans' amount of contact with Hispanics increased knowledge about Hispanic culture, which partially mediated the effects of contact on out-group attitudes, although the variance in attitudes explained by gains in knowledge is modest (Eller & Abrams, 2004).

As well as increasing factual knowledge, contact can also teach alternative behaviors toward out-group members (Pettigrew, 1997). This, in turn, can change attitudes by (a) setting new norms for intergroup behavior, and (b) reducing cognitive dissonance (Leippe & Eisenstadt, 1994), which serves to justify attitude-inconsistent behavior. There is empirical support that behavior change partially mediates the relationship between contact and attitudes (Eller & Abrams, 2004).

Gaertner and Dovidio's (2000) common in-group identity model suggests that contact situations could be transformed so that the current in-group and out-group are recategorized into a larger superordinate entity. They provide experimental and field evidence that cognitive representations of intergroup relations mediate contact effects. Several studies using artificial groups have attested to the power of a superordinate categorization to reduce the amount of in-group bias shown, especially in comparison to situations where two group memberships remain salient, but also compared to individualized conditions in which categories are not mentioned and the focus is on provision of individuating information (see Gaertner, Dovidio, & Houlette, 2010, for review). In the field, students at a multiethnic high school who adopt a "school" identity as more important than an ethnic identity demonstrate less bias and more positivity toward ethnic out-groups (Gaertner, Rust, Dovidio, Bachman, & Anastasio, 1996).

Another line of research has shown that repeated, intimate contact causes the out-group to become incorporated into the self-concept (Aron, Aron, Tudor, & Nelson, 1991; Pettigrew, 1997), and that this process leads to more positive out-group attitudes (Eller & Abrams, 2004). There is also evidence that extended contact (discussed later) works through this process.

Affective Variables.   Current work points to affective processes as more pivotal than cognitive processes in contact (Brown & Hewstone, 2005; Pettigrew & Tropp, 2008; Tropp & Pettigrew, 2005b). Contact appears to exert its effect both by reducing negative affect (e.g., anxiety and threat), and by inducing positive affective processes such as empathy.

Intergroup *anxiety* is a negative affective state experienced when anticipating future contact with an out-group member. It stems from the expectation of negative consequences for oneself during intergroup interactions (e.g., embarrassment, rejection), and may be augmented when there are negative out-group stereotypes, a history of intergroup conflict, or a high ratio of out-group to in-group members (Stephan & Stephan, 1985). Anxiety is accompanied by a narrowed cognitive and perceptual focus, and information-processing biases that can undermine positive effects of contact (Wilder & Shapiro, 1989). Intergroup anxiety may lead to the avoidance of contact (Plant & Devine, 2003; Shelton & Richeson, 2005) or, if contact does occur, render the interaction awkward and less enjoyable (e.g., Shelton, 2003). Because this negative affective state is linked to out-group members, it is strongly associated with negative out-group attitudes (Stephan & Stephan, 1985).

Extensive research has shown that successful intergroup contact helps to overcome these apprehensions, and that reduced anxiety is a key mediator in the negative relationship between contact and prejudice (e.g., Islam & Hewstone, 1993; Voci & Hewstone, 2003). Two recent studies have added impressive longitudinal evidence of anxiety as a mediator. Binder et al. (2009) conducted a two-wave study (over approximately 6 months) on minority- and majority-status secondary school children in Belgium, Germany, and England. They explored the relationship between contact (quality and quantity), inter-group anxiety, and two measures of prejudice. They found support for bidirectional paths between contact and prejudice over time, but more pertinent here, they found that intergroup anxiety mediated the contact-prejudice relationship over time. Swart, Hewstone, Christ, and Voci (2011) further extended the analysis, by conducting a three-wave study (over 12 months) of Coloured junior high-school students' attitudes to Whites in South Africa (the term *Coloured* is still widely used in South Africa as an official category and self-reference group; this population has its origins in unions between White, male settlers and local slaves). This study tested, for the first time, the full mediation of the effects of cross-group friendships on three measures of prejudice (attitudes, perceived out-group variability, and negative action tendencies) via the mediators of intergroup anxiety and empathy. Support was found for the bidirectional relationship between contact and the various dependent variables, but full mediation of the relationship between the variables at Time 1 and the variables at Time 3 was only supported from contact at Time 1 to prejudice at Time 3 (via mediators at Time 2). Cross-group friendships decreased prejudice via both reduced intergroup anxiety and increased affective empathy over time.

Intergroup relations are often characterized by perceptions that the out-group poses *a threat to the in-group*. These threats can be realistic and involve conflicting interests (e.g., competition for scarce resources, territory, political or economic power), or they can be symbolic, involving perceived discrepancies in beliefs and values (Stephan & Stephan, 2000). Stephan and Stephan's integrated threat theory argued that both the amount and the nature of inter-group interactions (e.g., whether contact is cooperative or competitive, intimate or superficial) are likely to determine the extent to which the out-group is seen as realistically or symbolically threatening (Stephan, Ybarra, & Morrison, 2009). Tausch, Tam, Hewstone, Kenworthy, and Cairns (2007) demonstrated cross-sectionally, in samples of Catholic and Protestants in Northern Ireland, that reduction in perceived group-level threats significantly mediated the relationship between contact and prejudice reduction, but only for people who identify strongly with their in-group. For low identifiers, reduction in individual-level concerns (i.e., intergroup anxiety) mediated the relationship between contact and prejudice reduction. Thus, this work demonstrates a case of moderated mediation (Muller, Judd, & Yzerbyt, 2005), showing that different mediators can operate for different subgroups.

Al Ramiah, Hewstone, Little, and Lang (under review) provided further evidence that perceived threats mediate the impact of contact on attitudes. In a cross-lagged multigroup field study, they tested a combination of integrated threat theory (Stephan & Stephan, 2000) and intergroup contact theory in Malaysia's three-month National Service Camp program, which aims to promote positive relations between ethnic Malays, Chinese, and Indians. Controlling for initial levels of the constructs, postcamp intergroup contact was negatively associated with perceived threat and positively associated with out-group evaluations, and perceived threat and out-group evaluations were negatively associated. Precamp intergroup contact also positively predicted postcamp out-group evaluations, even in the presence of a strong reciprocal path from precamp out-group evaluations to postcamp intergroup contact. These results speak to the potential of contact for improving intergroup relations in nation-building interventions.

Empathy has both emotional (empathic concern) and cognitive (perspective taking) facets and is associated with positive attitudes and prosocial behavior (Batson et al., 1997; Batson & Ahmad, 2009). A handful of studies have demonstrated that contact positively affects empathy and perspective taking, and that these variables partially mediate contact-prejudice effects (Harwood et al., 2005; Tam, Hewstone, Harwood, Voci, & Kenworthy, 2006). Aberson and Haag (2007) provided further evidence consistent with a three-stage theoretical model in which contact was associated with increased perspective taking, which was associated with more positive views of the out-group, partly by reducing intergroup anxiety.

Communication Variables. Only two distinct communication variables have thus far been investigated as potential mediators of intergroup contact: self-disclosure and communication accommodation. Pettigrew (1997, 1998) identified *self-disclosure* as a central process in cross-group friendship. Self-disclosure is the presentation of significant aspects of oneself to another person, and is important in the development of interpersonal relationships; it may also contribute to more positive attitudes in an intergroup situation. In addition to reducing anxiety for the recipients of disclosures, self-disclosure serves to give the disclosers control of how others see them (Berger & Bradac, 1982). By self-disclosing, disclosers tell others how to understand the way they see themselves, or how to empathize with them. Self-disclosure also promotes relational intimacy and depth (Laurenceau, Barrett, & Pietromonaco, 1998; Reis & Shaver, 1988), which may result in more positive affect toward the out-group if used during intergroup contact. By personalizing an interaction, self-disclosure focuses attention on individuating features of participants, which may reduce stereotyping in a contact situation (Fiske & Neuberg, 1990). Central to the notion of self-disclosure as a mediator is that it establishes mutual trust and detailed knowledge about the other party, which may disconfirm negative attitudes. Finally, self-disclosure is theoretically important because it is typically reciprocal and reciprocated. Self-disclosure is, thus, something that happens at the level of the dyad and hence something that can be seen as a shared activity—a point of connection between individuals building a relationship.

Tam et al. (2006) examined the effects of contact with grandparents on implicit attitudes (measured with the Implicit Association Test; Greenwald,

McGee, & Schwartz, 1998). Implicit attitudes do not require direct report of attitudes, are beyond conscious control, and are less likely to be influenced by social desirability than are explicit measures. Implicit measures are also important because they predict spontaneous behavior better than explicit measures (Dovidio, Kawakami, Johnson, Johnson, & Howard, 1997). This study measured self-disclosure, anxiety, and empathy as mediators at the level of one out-group exemplar (the grandparent with whom participants interacted most regularly). Quantity of contact with older people had a direct, positive effect on young people's implicit attitudes, and positively predicted self-disclosure. In turn, self-disclosure negatively predicted anxiety, and positively predicted empathy; and anxiety negatively predicted explicit attitudes, while empathy positively predicted them (see Soliz, Ribarsky, Harrigan, & Tye-Williams, 2009, for similar effects relating to anxiety and disclosure).

In their research on contact between young White and South Asian students in the United Kingdom, Turner, Hewstone, and Voci (2007, Study 4) also found that self-disclosure significantly mediated the effect of contact on out-group attitudes. Further probing revealed that having Asian friends predicted greater self-disclosure that, in turn, predicted more positive out-group attitudes via increased empathy, self-disclosure importance, and trust. Exemplifying the complex interconnections between a number of these variables, Soliz, Thorson, and Rittenour (2009) demonstrate that self-disclosure enhances the perception of sharing a common group membership with an out-group member—in this particular case, perceptions of sharing a "family" identity within a multiracial family context. Thus, variables that we distinguish as mediators may themselves influence one another.

The second communication variable of interest, *communication accommodation,* was investigated by Harwood et al. (2005, Study 2). They examined five potential mediators of the effect of contact with the most frequently seen grandparent on attitudes toward the elderly: intergroup anxiety, perspective-taking, individuation, self-disclosure, and communication accommodation. The accommodation measure tapped the degree to which young people adapted communicatively to their grandparents, a crucial signal of interpersonal solidarity, the absence of which may signal intergroup differentiation (Shepard, Giles, & LePoire, 2001). When examined separately, three variables proved to be reliable mediators of the effects of contact quality on attitudes: anxiety, perspective-taking, and accommodation. When all significant mediators were entered together, perspective-taking was the only significant mediator. These mediation effects for out-group attitudes were also moderated by group salience, holding only for respondents for whom the young–elderly relationship was above the average in salience. Further analyses showed that the paths affected by group salience were the ones between contact quality and mediators. Contact quality affected perspective-taking more when salience was high rather than low; anxiety was reduced by contact more when group salience was high rather than low; and the link between contact and accommodation was significant only when salience was high.

This study, like that of Tam et al. (2006), measured mediators at the individual, rather than group, level: mediators were tapped in terms of the relationship and interaction with the same grandparent with whom we assessed quality of contact. Both types of mediators are necessary for a complete understanding of the mechanisms behind contact effects (Paolini, Hewstone, Voci, Harwood, & Cairns, 2006). If quality of contact with a specific out-group individual influences general out-group attitudes, then very specific interactional experiences might affect group level mediators and serve as mechanisms for such influence. Experiencing a specific affect, cognition, or behavior in interaction with a particular out-group member (i.e., individual-level mediator) makes it more likely that such a phenomenon might be seen as possible with other out-group members (i.e., group-level mediator). This perception may extend to more general expectations for intergroup contact, and hence the nature of the entire out-group.

Moving away from the specific contact literature, there is considerable work on communication between groups, particularly cultural groups, in the communication discipline (Gudykunst & Mody, 2002). The most relevant of such work for the current article focuses on the variables that make for effective communication between different cultures. This includes consideration of inherent communicative barriers (e.g., different languages, different understandings of the purpose of communication; Ting-Toomey & Oetzel, 2001), varying verbal and nonverbal communication styles across cultural groups (Kim, 2002), and individual differences (e.g., intercultural competence: Deardorff, 2009). This research also examines ways in which psychological constructs such as identity are constructed and maintained in communication (both inter- and intracultural; Abrams, O'Connor, & Giles, 2002). While already described, research on communication accommodation processes is common in the study of intercultural communication, including examinations of how accommodation can emphasize group differences or interpersonal similarities (Gallois, Giles, Jones, Cargile, & Ota, 1995). Perhaps most intriguing at this point in the discussion are ties between accommodation and negative contact (the topic of the next section). Divergent behaviors (those that emphasize in-group identities and distinctiveness from an out-group interlocutor) have distinctly negative consequences for intergroup encounters (Giles, Coupland, & Coupland, 1991) and hence, presumably, for contact's attitudinal outcomes. Such themes tend to be skirted in much contact research. While familiar to many readers of this chapter, brief mention of this huge body of research is warranted to emphasize the ways in which separate literatures might usefully inform one another. Many constructs examined in the intercultural communication literature contribute to positive communication (i.e., contact) between groups, and positivity contributes greatly to desirable effects of contact. Hence, seeking out intercultural communication research will yield sensible (yet novel) hypotheses for contact researchers. As hinted at in the previous paragraph, intercultural communication research can also direct us to some of the pitfalls of intergroup contact, to which we now move.

Negative Contact

Thus far we have reviewed evidence for the impact of positively structured intergroup contact. Relatively little research in the contact paradigm has examined the opposite valence (negative contact). This is understandable given that the framework was developed to promote positive intergroup encounters and thereby reduce prejudice. Nonetheless, awareness that poorly designed or executed contact can have negative effects is essential to real world contact applications as well as our theoretical understanding of the psychological and communicative processes underlying the effect.

One area of current interest is the connection between group salience (which has already been described as facilitating generalization of contact effects), and valence. In spite of its beneficial generalization effects, considerable work now shows that group salience and valence are frequently negatively related (Paolini, Harwood, & Rubin, 2010). Harwood et al. (2006) discuss communicative phenomena that should theoretically be linked to group salience in intergenerational communication, showing that negative behaviors (e.g., painfully detailed disclosures of illness from an older person) indeed predicted group salience, but positive behaviors such as story-telling did not predict salience. Similarly, Soliz, Ribarsky, Harrigan, and Tye-Williams (2009) show that group salience is negatively associated with supportive and accommodative communication.

Building on this work, Paolini et al. (2010) demonstrate a causal link between valence and salience such that negative encounters increase group salience. Paolini et al. elaborate on the slightly disturbing possibility that negative intergroup contact has greater power to influence prejudice than does positive intergroup contact. Paolini et al. note that more work is needed to investigate negative effects of contact and to understand how to jointly enhance salience and positivity. Harwood (2010) presents some preliminary ideas of positive communication strategies that should retain high levels of group salience. For example, group-relevant questions that demonstrate genuine curiosity about the out-group place groups "front and center," while deferring to the out-group member as to the specific content, tone, and detail of the discussion. This contrasts with conversations wherein group memberships either remain implicit (and stereotypes drive the conversation), or where group characteristics are framed as fixed and known by both parties, perhaps in ways that appear constraining or derogatory to the other.

Summary of Research on Direct Contact

Direct contact between groups has been conclusively shown to improve intergroup attitudes (Pettigrew & Tropp, 2006). Its effectiveness is facilitated by, but does not require, Allport's (1954) conditions. Contact is particularly effective under conditions of high group salience, although group salience carries with it some complexities related to valence. The positive effects of contact are mediated by cognitive, affective, and communicative variables, with affective mechanisms receiving the most study and support. Communicative mechanisms have received less research attention overall, but there is great scope for examining novel verbal (e.g., social support, humor) and nonverbal (smiling, backchannels) communicative mechanisms as mediators of the effect of contact. Communicative mediators have the advantage of being potentially easier targets of interventions. Asking people to "be less anxious" in an interaction is less reasonable than suggesting that they "smile more" or "ask questions."

Indirect Contact

Pettigrew (1997) suggested that a reduction in prejudice might be achieved by promoting direct friendship between members of rival groups. As we have seen, there is strong meta-analytic support for this. Unfortunately, however, direct cross-group friendships can only be used as an intervention to reduce prejudice when group members have the opportunity for contact in the first place. If people do not live in the same neighborhood, attend the same school, or occupy the same workplace as out-group members, they are unlikely to develop friendships with them. Given the practical obstacles to direct intergroup contact posed by segregation or outright conflict, recent approaches have investigated the effectiveness of less direct forms of contact. Recently, Dovidio, Eller, and Hewstone (2011) proposed that indirect contact can be conceived in three ways: (a) *extended* contact: learning that an in-group member is friends with an out-group member; (b) *vicarious* contact: observing an in-group member interact with an out-group member; and (c) *imagined* contact: imagining oneself interacting with an out-group member. We will consider the evidence separately for each form of indirect contact, as well as current knowledge regarding moderating and mediating factors. We also examine a fourth form of indirect contact: mediated contact with a real out-group member via computer or other technology. Harwood (2010) discusses in more detail some of the complexities of differentiating forms of indirect contact, and the dimensions on which they differ from direct contact.

"Extended" Contact

The most widely researched of these indirect forms of contact, extended contact, refers to the impact on prejudice of knowing about, or observing, at least one, and preferably more than one, in-group member who has an out-group friend (Wright, Aron, McLaughlin-Volpe, & Ropp, 1997). Pettigrew and Tropp (2006) excluded tests of extended cross-group friendship from their meta-analysis, because they do not involve face-to-face contact. However, this form of contact, which was examined during a relatively recent period, is important and effective in its own right.

Research Evidence of the Impact of Extended Contact.   Wright et al. (1997) provided both correlational and experimental evidence in support of this hypothesis. They showed that respondents—belonging to either majority or minority groups—who knew at least one in-group member with an out-group friend reported weaker out-group prejudice than did respondents without indirect friends; furthermore, the greater the number of members of the in-group who were known to have friends in the out-group, the weaker was the prejudice.

Wright and colleagues (1997) give two reasons why interventions involving extended friendship are more effective and easier to implement than direct friendship. First, to observers of cross-group friendship, the group memberships of those involved are relatively salient (e.g., it is clear that a White child has an Asian friend); in contrast, the observer may be unacquainted with individual characteristics of the out-group member, thus increasing the likelihood that his or her behavior is taken as typical or representative of the group (Hewstone & Lord, 1998). This characteristic of extended contact should facilitate generalization of positive attitudes from the individuals engaged in direct contact to the views of their respective groups (Brown & Hewstone, 2005; Hewstone & Brown, 1986). Second, when one is merely observing another in-group member engaged in contact with an out-group member, any intergroup anxiety felt about interacting with members of that out-group (Stephan & Stephan, 1985) should be lower than when one is involved directly in the contact. Intergroup interactions that go unpunished and have been observed or known about may also change the perceived in-group and out-group norms regarding intergroup interactions. Experimental, quasi-experimental, and correlational studies have provided empirical evidence that people knowing about or observing intergroup friendships show less prejudice than those who do not, even while controlling for direct contact with out-group members (for reviews see Turner, Hewstone, Voci, Paolini, & Christ, 2007; Vonofakou et al., 2008).

Extended contact has also been applied as a quasi-experimental intervention to reduce prejudice among elementary school children (e.g., Cameron, Rutland, Brown, & Douch, 2006; Liebkind & McAllister, 1999). For example, 5- to 10-year-old children who read stories of friendships between nondisabled and disabled children showed more positive attitudes and intended behavior toward disabled children (Cameron & Rutland, 2006). Extended contact using media stimuli (e.g., books) becomes intertwined with forms of *vicarious contact* described later (see Harwood, 2010, for extensive discussion of these distinctions).

Moderators of Extended Contact.   Evidence has accrued for four factors that moderate the impact of extended contact. The negative relationship between extended cross-group friendship and reduced prejudice is consistently stronger for participants with few direct cross-group friends or living in segregated rather than mixed communities (Christ et al., 2010; Dhont & Van Hiel, 2011).

Thus extended contact may be especially useful for those in segregated neighborhoods.

Tausch, Hewstone, Schmid, Hughes, and Cairns (2011) examined the effects of extended contact via different types of *in-group* contacts (neighbors, work colleagues, friends, and family members), showing that extended contact interacted with closeness of in-group relationship in predicting out-group trust. As predicted, extended contact via more intimate in-group relationships (friends and family) was more strongly related to out-group trust than extended contacts via less intimate in-group relations (neighbors and work colleagues). Within each level of intimacy, extended contact was related to out-group trust only at high levels of rated closeness to in-group contacts.

Three recent studies have identified individual differences that moderate the impact of extended contact. Paralleling the earlier evidence that SDO moderated direct contact, Hodson, Harry, and Mitchell (2009) found stronger effects of extended contact on heterosexuals' prejudice toward homosexuals for respondents higher in SDO. Similarly, Dhont and Van Hiel (2011), using a representative Dutch sample, found that participants higher in authoritarianism showed stronger positive effects of extended contact on intergroup attitudes. Again, these effects might partially be explained by regression to the mean for more extreme scorers; however, Dhont and Van Hiel found that the positive effects were mediated by lower feelings of threat and greater trust of out-group members, which reduces the power of the simple regression explanation. Using a different individual difference measure, Sharp, Voci, and Hewstone (2011) found that social comparison moderated the effects of extended contact. White, heterosexual participants with stronger social comparison tendencies exhibited stronger positive extended contact effects involving both Asian and gay target groups, consistent with these authors' contention that social comparison taps into sensitivity to normative forces, a proven mediator of extended contact effects (see below).

Finally, Paolini, Hewstone, and Cairns (2007) tested whether the effectiveness of extended (vs. direct) contact was moderated by the bases (cognitive vs. affective) of prejudice. Dovidio, Brigham, Johnson, and Gaertner (1996) classified close intergroup contact between members of racial groups as an affective experience, because of the inherently affective nature of interpersonal situations. In contrast, Wright et al. (1997) argued that an advantage of extended friendship is that it evokes weaker emotions and makes cognitive aspects of the contact experience more accessible. Attitude change is greater when the bases of the persuasive message match, rather than mismatch, the bases of the attitude (Huskinson & Haddock, 2004). In three cross-sectional studies, Paolini et al. (2007) showed that effects of extended friendship were larger for out-groups generating cognitive than affective responding (the opposite pattern was found for direct friendship effects).

Notwithstanding this evidence of moderators of extended contact, it is noteworthy that whereas group status moderates the effects of both direct (Pettigrew & Tropp, 2006) and imagined contact (Stathi & Crisp, 2008; see below), the effects of extended contact were equally strong for majority and minority groups (Gómez et al., 2011).

Mediators of Extended Contact. When Wright et al. (1997) outlined the extended contact idea, they proposed, but did not test, four mechanisms that might underlie the prejudice-reducing impact of extended cross-group friendship: observing a positive relationship between members of the in-group and the out-group, (a) should involve less anxiety than found in initial direct intergroup encounters (Stephan & Stephan, 1985), (b) should lead to the perception that there are positive in-group norms regarding the out-group, (c) should lead to the perception that there are positive out-group norms about the in-group, and (d) should lead the observer to include the in-group member's out-group friend as part of the observer's self (e.g., Aron et al., 1991; see earlier section on cognitive mechanisms in direct contact). Turner, Hewstone, Voci, and Vonofakou (2008) tested simultaneously the role of all four mechanisms proposed by Wright and colleagues in the context of contact between Whites and South Asians in Britain. Both their studies supported the four mediators proposed by Wright et al. (1997). Other studies have also confirmed that extended contact effects are mediated by reduced anxiety (Paolini, Hewstone, Cairns, & Voci, 2004; but cf. Eller, Abrams, & Zimmermann, 2011; Gómez et al., 2011), stronger in-group norms (De Tezanos-Pinto, Bratt, & Brown, 2010; Gómez et al., 2011), reduced threat and increased trust (Dhont & Van Hiel, 2011), and lower perceived ignorance about the out-group, greater awareness of more positive out-group behavior, and greater inclusion of the other in the self (Eller et al., 2011).

Vicarious Contact

The key distinction between extended and vicarious forms of contact is that vicarious contact typically involves *observing* an out-group member via some form of medium; sometimes the out-group member is interacting with an in-group member, and typically the out-group member is a stranger or even a fictional character. Much of this research is influenced by work on parasocial relationships with media figures; notably the tradition of work stemming from Horton and Wohl (1956). Within this tradition, relationships with media characters can be as "real" and influential in some people's lives as relationships with real people. Hence, intergroup contact with out-group media characters can mirror real contact with real out-group members. As elaborated below, some of the work is also informed by Bandura's (e.g., 2001) social cognitive theory.

Research Evidence of the Impact of Vicarious Contact. Vicarious contact has already been exploited by communication research. Mutz and Goldman's (2010) review shows that television, radio, and the Internet are primary sources of information for people's impressions of other social groups. Encounters with portrayals of out-group members on television, sometimes termed *parasocial* contact (Schiappa, Gregg, & Hewes, 2005), can influence the attitudes of vast numbers of viewers, often without their conscious awareness. Allport himself (1954, pp. 200–202) noted the importance of the mass media in prejudice, but he did not expressly link it to the contact hypothesis. Schiappa et al. point out that people's parasocial contact with (some) out-groups may be much greater than their actual, or even extended contact. As such, one would expect the impact of parasocial contact to be greater in contexts where the opportunities for and actual contact with out-group members are lower (see section on moderators, below).

Schiappa, Gregg, and Hewes (2006) studied correlational responses to viewing of a television show with a prominent gay character. They reported a significant negative association between the level of prejudice towards gay men and viewing frequency. Additional experimental research tested whether people exposed to positive cross-group interactions in television programs would reveal more positive attitudes to the target out-group than participants not exposed to the programs. In three studies, Schiappa et al. (2005) investigated parasocial contact shown in three television programs (two involving viewing parasocial contact with gay men, and one involving parasocial contact with comedian and male transvestite Eddie Izzard). All three studies demonstrated that parasocial contact was associated with lower levels of prejudice.

These results were reinforced by Ortiz and Harwood (2007), who showed comparable effects for both gay–straight and Black–White interactions presented in two television programs. Ortiz and Harwood focus on the viewing of *intergroup relationships* (as opposed to just out-group characters). From a social cognitive theory perspective (Bandura, 2001), they suggest that viewing intergroup relationships allows for modeling (hence learning) of positive intergroup behavior. As such, exposure to a quality intergroup relationship should be more powerful in influencing attitudes than mere exposure to a positive portrayal of an out-group member. The social cognitive theory approach also has implications for moderators of the vicarious contact effect, as elaborated below.

While the preceding research on parasocial contact has involved television, a study by Paluck (2009) has demonstrated that radio too has potential for parasocial contact. In a year-long randomized field experiment in Rwanda she compared the effects of listening to a reconciliation program versus a health program. She showed the impact of norms and empathy experienced vicariously through characters in a peace-building radio soap opera designed by an NGO. Communities exposed to the reconciliation program showed changes in social norms and behaviors relating to trust and cooperation compared to communities who listened to a control radio soap opera.

Negative Effects of Media Exposure.   In contrast to the relatively small body of work on positive media effects from contact theory, there is a substantial body of work that discusses *negative* effects of media on intergroup attitudes.

Very little of this work is framed from a contact theory perspective—again unsurprisingly given the primarily positive goals of contact theory. This research typically describes the media environment via systematic content analysis of group portrayals, demonstrating that the media show minority or low status groups stereotypically and negatively, or else fail to show these groups at all (Mastro, 2010). This work is complemented by either survey or experimental research demonstrating that exposure to negative portrayals has negative consequences for attitudes and behaviors concerning the out-group (Dixon, 2008).

This literature is large and unsuitable for review in the present context (see Mastro, 2010). However, it does complement trends in the contact literature such as an interest in the effects of negative contact (e.g., Paolini et al., 2010). It is consistent with a vicarious contact model (albeit the dark side of that model). The work also raises the intriguing possibility that the media may show in-group and out-group members working together cooperatively to engage in *antisocial* activities, which adds numerous complexities to understanding vicarious contact (Ortiz & Harwood, 2011). Globally, we advocate less mutual ignorance between research on contact and research on negative effects of media's group portrayals. Empirical and theoretical cross-fertilization across these areas would benefit all concerned (e.g., examining positive effects of positive portrayals, while minimizing negative effects using media literacy: Ramasubramanian, 2007). The content analytic side of this research draws attention to a major barrier in expecting mass mediated contact to have positive effects on attitudes. If media portrayals of social groups are largely negative, the most likely effects of exposure to such portrayals will be negative (Brown Givens & Monahan, 2005; Gerbner, Gross, Morgan, & Signorielli, 2002).

Selective Exposure and Perception.   As already described, the traditional literature on intergroup contact has struggled to understand whether correlational data indicate effects *of* contact or selective *seeking* of contact. Similar issues are apparent in the media literature. Harwood (1997, 1999) has noted that people tend to seek out in-group portrayals and at times actively avoid out-group portrayals altogether (Abrams & Giles, 2007; Allen & Bielby, 1979); such preferences are driven by social identity concerns (Harwood & Roy, 2005). Hence, while potentially beneficial media portrayals may exist, we cannot force people to watch them. One means for overcoming this barrier is to diversify casts (e.g., shows with major characters of multiple ages tend to draw a more diverse audience in terms of age; Harwood, 1997). Interestingly, such shows would presumably also feature more portrayals of intergroup contact, a factor that might be meaningful from the social cognitive theory perspective described above as well as extended contact (Ortiz & Harwood, 2007).

Selective perception includes understanding when and for whom specific portrayals have specific effects. Vidmar and Rokeach's (1974) classic study demonstrates that a portrayal of a racist is understood as a parody mocking racism by some viewers, but that highly prejudiced viewers identify with the racist character and have their attitudes reinforced. In other words, media consumers are creative beings who assign meaning to messages in ways that do not necessarily conform to senders' intent (Harwood & Roy, 2005). As such, we must examine media effects as the result of an interaction between content and active viewership based on initial attitudes as well as the many other reasons people have for seeking specific messages (Krcmar & Strizhakova, 2008).

Moderators of Vicarious Contact. Several studies showed an effect parallel to that found by Christ et al. (2010), whereby the impact of extended contact was moderated by the level of direct contact. In Schiappa et al. (2005, 2006) the impact of vicarious contact was stronger for respondents who reported low prior out-group contact. Ortiz and Harwood's (2007) research also provided evidence of moderators. First, and consistent with the authors' social cognitive theory account, contact effects were stronger when viewers identified with the in-group character involved in the intergroup contact (Cohen, 2001). For a straight viewer who identifies with a straight character on television, that straight character's friendship with a gay character will more strongly influence homophobia because the in-group (straight) character is more closely included in the self (Aron et al., 1991; Wright et al., 1997). There are clear links here to the idea underlying extended contact, that *observing* intergroup contact influences attitudes over and above *experiencing* contact. Indeed, some studies of vicarious contact effects frame the results explicitly as *extended* contact effects (Cameron & Rutland, 2006). Second, the effect of vicarious contact is stronger when the out-group character is perceived as more typical of the out-group (see also Joyce & Harwood, in press). This suggests that effects of group typicality operate in similar ways in mass communication and direct contact. Both effects were restricted to the gay–straight televised contact, and were not found for Black–White contact, possibly as a result of the specific television shows used in the study.

Mediators of Vicarious Contact. There has been little research on mediators of vicarious contact. However, Mazziotta, Mummendey, and Wright (2011) found a difference between *viewing* and merely knowing about a positive interaction between an in-group member and an out-group member, and that the two forms of contact involved different underlying processes. They found that vicarious contact had greater impact on attitudes than in control conditions, and that it impacted favorable attitudes via reduced uncertainty and greater feelings of self-efficacy for future interactions involving the self (see also Mallett & Wilson, 2010). Harwood and Vincze (2011) investigated the effects of consuming second-language media in a bilingual context. They found that effects on prejudice were differentially mediated by language-learning motivations, with integrative language learning motivations mediating a classic contact effect, but instrumental motivations not mediating. Integrative motivations focus on learning language to feel more included in the culture and desiring out-group friends; instrumental motivations focus on needing to know the language for work or other instrumental tasks. Given the growth in multilingual media environments, people's use of nonnative language media, including the motivations they seek when using such media, should be a focus of future research (Harwood & Vincze, 2012).

Imagined Contact

Work on extended and vicarious contact demonstrates that the actual experience of contact with out-group members may not be necessary to improve intergroup attitudes. Turner, Crisp, and Lambert (2007) extended this idea still further. Based on work on the effects of mental imagery on social perception, these authors investigated whether simply imagining contact with out-group members could improve intergroup attitudes.

Research Evidence of the Impact of Imagined Contact. The earliest demonstration of an effect of imagined contact that we are aware of comes from Desforges et al. (1997), although their use of the technique was grounded in a desire for experimental control rather than developing a new paradigm for contact interventions. Their research, nonetheless, demonstrated that for an individual to merely imagine working with an out-group member (observed on a video screen) had positive effects. Turner, Crisp, and Lambert (2007) were the first to frame imagined contact as its own paradigm, and to demonstrate that participants who imagined talking to an out-group member showed lower levels of prejudice and viewed the out-group as more variable than did participants who were instructed to just think about an out-group member. Turner and colleagues' work also develops the early Desforges studies by using a pure "imagined" intervention rather than including a supplementary video or other stimuli.

The proponents of imagined contact do not claim that we can imagine away prejudice. Rather, noting that for some out-groups contact can be difficult to orchestrate, and may well involve an element of risk (Corrigan et al., 2002; Schulze & Angermeyer, 2003), Turner, Crisp, and colleagues have suggested that imagined intergroup contact can be *part of* a program for reducing intergroup bias; thus they see it as "an inexpensive and practical means of reducing intergroup anxiety and prejudice that would be useful even where direct contact is very limited" (Turner, Crisp, & Lambert, 2007, p. 439; see also Crisp, Stathi, Turner, & Husnu, 2008). A number of studies have found that imagined contact can reduce intergroup bias and improve both explicit and implicit out-group attitudes (Turner & Crisp, 2010; Turner, Crisp, & Lambert, 2007), enhance intentions to engage in future contact (Crisp & Turner, 2009, in press; Husnu & Crisp, 2010), and even improve attitudes about out-groups not featured in the imagined contact (Harwood, Paolini, Joyce, Rubin, & Arroyo, 2011; for review see Crisp, Husnu, Meleady, Stathi, & Turner, 2010).

Skeptical views and alternate approaches to this paradigm are provided by Bigler and Hughes (2010) and Honeycutt (2010). Honeycutt, in particular, describes links between this research and his more directly communication-related work on "imagined interactions." Honeycutt's work has not explicitly examined intergroup relations or intergroup contact effects, but integration of his imagined interaction work with imagined contact research has great potential. Honeycutt defines and operationalizes specific dimensions of imagined interactions which are immediately applicable to imagined contact. His dimension of "emotional valence" maps onto valence of contact; "discrepancy" connects to issues of whether imagined contact is representative of real world interaction; "variety" pertains to effects on perceived out-group heterogeneity; and "specificity" connects to assessments of vividness (Husnu & Crisp, 2010). In some cases, the two literatures are calling fundamentally similar concepts by different names, and in others the literatures are developing independent constructs that would mutually benefit one another.

Moderators of Imagined Contact.   Stathi and Crisp (2008) are the only researchers, thus far, to have investigated conditions that might moderate the effectiveness of imagined contact. In their first study they found that an ethnic minority was more resistant to the benefits of imagined contact than an ethnic majority (Mestizos and Indigenous people, respectively, in Mexico). The weaker effect of imagined contact for the minority group parallels the pattern for direct contact (Pettigrew & Tropp, 2006; Tropp, 2003), and is consistent with the idea that minority groups tend to experience more anxiety at the thought of intergroup contact than do majorities (Plant & Devine, 2003). In their second experiment, Stathi and Crisp found that in-group identification also moderated the impact of imagined contact. For British students, effects of imagined contact with French students were stronger for participants who did not identify strongly with their national in-group.

Mediators of Imagined Contact.   Consistent with the mediating effect of intergroup anxiety in direct contact and, albeit less consistently, extended contact, Turner, Crisp, and Lambert (2007, Study 3) found that intergroup anxiety mediated the impact of male heterosexual participants' imagined contact with a gay man on their attitudes toward gay people. In a series of three studies on imagined contact with people with schizophrenia, West, Holmes, and Hewstone (2011) demonstrated that a neutral imagined contact task with such a target group can have negative effects, compared to a control condition, and that an enhanced form of imagined contact scenario must be used. When this is done, ensuring that imagined contact is positive, reduced intergroup anxiety mediates more positive attitudes, even toward this challenging group. West et al.'s analyses of participants' descriptions of the imagined interactions in and across all three studies (something not done in previous studies) confirmed that positive and high quality imagined contact is important for reducing prejudice via lowered anxiety.

As the work of Crisp and colleagues has increasingly drawn on other techniques that involve imagery (e.g., therapeutic interventions for anxiety), they have added cognitive mediators to the original affective mediator of intergroup anxiety. Husnu and Crisp (2010, Expt. 2) explored British non-Muslim students' future contact intentions with Muslims. They reported evidence consistent with the existence of two routes from imagery to intentions: a cognitive (i.e., vividness) pathway and an affective (i.e., anxiety) pathway. The impact of imagined contact on behavioral intentions was mediated both by out-group attitudes (preceded by intergroup anxiety) and by the reported vividness of the imagined scenario (consistent with social cognitive research on script availability).

Finally, Crisp and Husnu (2011) found that imagining intergroup contact enhances script availability, that perceivers' metacognitive judgments as to their own tolerance reflect this availability, and these mediate future contact intentions. They also found that imagining intergroup contact from a third-person perspective (i.e., "see the event from an external viewpoint"), compared with a first-person perspective (i.e., "see the event through your own eyes"), enhanced future contact intentions. These authors theorized that imagining contact from a third-person perspective would enhance future contact intentions because it places the (imaginary) spotlight on the self, making a dispositional attribution more likely. Analyses confirmed that the impact on intentions of taking a third-person perspective in the imagined contact task was mediated by the extent to which participants' attributed to themselves a positive orientation toward out-group contact.

Computer-Mediated Contact

Amichai-Hamburger and McKenna (2006) categorize the major challenges in organizing direct face-to-face contact in terms of practicality, anxiety, and generalization. They note that Internet contact ameliorates these problems. *Practicality* refers to the logistical problems encountered when organizing face-to-face contact between rival groups which fulfills all the contact prerequisites, including those prior to the meeting (Pettigrew, 1971; Trew, 1986). Contact over the Internet is far less costly in terms of time, travel, and accommodation than direct contact. It streamlines difficulties in scheduling, and by design provides a "neutral place" in which to hold the encounters. Virtual workgroups show that collaboration through the Internet has proved to be an effective tool worldwide in developing cooperation toward superordinate goals (Spears, Postmes, Lea, & Wolbert, 2002). *Anxiety* has already been discussed, including its tendency to exacerbate stereotype use (Stephan & Stephan, 1985). Online, participants have more control over how they present themselves and their views (e.g., being able to edit comments before presenting them), and presumably feel less threatened by a nonpresent interlocutor, all of which should reduce anxiety (Amichai-Hamburger, 2005). *Generalization* refers to the fact that while many face-to-face contacts are successful on the interpersonal level, participants do not necessarily change their stereotyped view of the out-group as a whole (Hamburger 1994; Hewstone & Brown, 1986). Online, one can quite easily manipulate the degree of individual versus group salience in a given contact situation to achieve a positive generalization from the intergroup contact (Thompson & Nadler, 2002).

Research Evidence of Computer-Mediated Contact Effects.   The use of the Internet in improving intergroup conflict is in its early stages, with much of the focus on Israel and its Arab neighbors. An important example is found in the work of McKenna, Samuel-Azran, and Sutton-Balaban (2009). They opened a blog in which representatives of different communities in the Middle East wrote articles discussing political and cultural issues, and readers commented on the articles. An ethnography of 18 months of activity on the blog showed little impact. This was explained by three factors: fear, insecurity about communicating in English, and an unwillingness to interact with the enemy. There were, however, some examples of shifts in perception among participants from rival sides toward commonly held values, goals, and worldviews, indicating the potential of the medium. In this case the process of change was difficult to measure because there was no examination of the number and the staying power of participants, and it appears that the majority of contributors "came and went."

Mollov (2006) discusses an e-mail-based dialogue between Israeli-Jewish and Palestinian students focusing on the religious practices of Jews and Muslims. Jews and Arabs were paired up and instructed to introduce themselves and describe a Muslim or Jewish holiday, after which they discussed the topic further. Most exchanges were friendly and included significant amounts of information concerning the religious culture of the two holidays. Questionnaires run prior to and following the dialogue revealed an increase in the knowledge of both the Jewish and Palestinian participants concerning the festivities of the two religions, but no change in the mutual perceptions of the two groups. This was attributed to the fact that participants from both groups had held very positive perceptions of the other side *prior to* the dialogue encounter. The project also took place during the year 2000, when the Oslo peace accords were believed to hold great promise for peace.

As is discussed elsewhere in this review, the extent to which people selectively seek contact is apparent in some of this research on computer-mediated contact. This literature is challenged to account for such selective seeking, and to examine ways in which computer-mediated contact can be effectively and meaningfully implemented for those who would not otherwise seek it.

Hoter, Shonfeld, and Ganayem (2009) have been conducting Internet-based courses designed for Arab students, religious and secular Jewish students in nine colleges of education in Israel. Hoter et al. report using the contact hypothesis framework to maximize the effectiveness of the Internet-based contacts they organized. Throughout the project, students were required to record their thoughts on blogs, which were later analyzed by the researchers. At the end of the course, satisfaction levels of the participants were assessed. The last meeting between the students was held as an offline, face-to-face encounter, in which students discussed their experience of the project; this encounter was recorded and reviewed by the organizers. Participants expressed interest in learning about different cultures and religions, and reported high levels of satisfaction.

In November 1999, the Departments of Education in Northern Ireland and the Republic of Ireland established The Dissolving Boundaries project. Its aim was to use Information Communications Technology (ICT) to link schools across the political borders within Ireland (Austin, Abbot, Mulkeen, & Metcalfe, 2003). The objectives of the Dissolving Boundaries project are to use ICT to facilitate valuable curricular work between schools and through a collaborative educational program to increase mutual understanding. The contact hypothesis is used as the theoretical background for the entire project. In the 2003 report, pupils commented explicitly on increased cultural awareness emerging through the project. In response to a question about whether the exchange of information in an online student café had helped them develop friendships, 86% of primary-school aged pupils agreed with this as compared to only 34% of the older students. Austin and Anderson (2008a), reporting on the continuation of the Dissolving Boundaries project, state that 68% of teachers interviewed rated the impact of the program on "North-South understanding" as either "very significant" or "significant," with that number increasing to 75% among primary school teachers. The success of the project is gradual and steady with increasing numbers of schools and upwards of 5,000 children taking part (Austin & Anderson, 2008b).

These studies serve to illustrate that online contact between groups can help to reduce intergroup conflict. The studies differ significantly as to how much they adhere to the stipulations of the contact hypothesis (Amir, 1969). Amichai-Hamburger (2008a) advocated a more structured and supervised intergroup contact. He notes that two of the main obstacles to successful online contact are flaming and lack of commitment. To avoid flaming, he advocates a careful process of choosing the people to participate in the contact and a signed commitment from participants to behave appropriately. The contact itself should be carefully supervised by a social psychologist who places special emphasis on proper conduct. To enhance commitment and motivation, organizers should ensure that the vision of the intergroup contact is a frequent topic of discussion for each group. The group leaders should encourage participants to get actively involved in the online session, rather than observing it from the side. The leader should give group members frequent feedback on their level of involvement in the contact.

Amichai-Hamburger (2008b) advocates supplementary online intergroup contact when face-to-face contact sessions are held infrequently (e.g., due to busy schedules). This is important because there is a danger that the results of successful contact may be lost if the positive dynamic is not maintained. Amichai-Hamburger (2008a) emphasized the importance of the use of a significant superordinate goal. This joint goal should be designed to exploit the special components of the Internet, enabling users to participate in projects across the world without moving out of their own environments (e.g., the task group volunteering in a socially important assignment such as building an AIDS awareness website). The superordinate goal would be chosen according to the abilities and wishes of both groups. Such a project helps to break the us vs. them mindset and allows people to learn about cross-cutting categories and common in-group identities in the setting (Gaertner & Dovidio, 2000). Another component that can lead to the success of the encounter is a "cultural databank." Before actual contact, each group describes its own culture, art, history, and customs, in writing online. This provides a unique firsthand source of information that can help the out-group to prepare more effectively for the contact, and can also be used in real time during contact to avoid cultural misunderstandings (Amichai-Hamburger, 2008a).

As discussed in detail elsewhere (Amichai-Hamburger & Furnham, 2006; Amichai-Hamburger & McKenna, 2006; Harwood, 2010; Walther, 2009), computer-mediated contact offers a productive first step in a continuum of graded contact. As participants become comfortable with contact on the Internet, they can move slowly toward face-to-face contact via stages of increasing media richness and interactivity (e.g., from text, to text with images, to online video and audio, to direct contact). This approach has been supported by the work of McKenna and colleagues (Bargh, McKenna, & Fitzimmons, 2002; McKenna, Green, & Gleason, 2002). They found that people who participate in graded contact like one another more than if they had begun their interaction in person, and experience greater liking and kinship when a face-to-face meeting does take place.

An additional benefit of the online context is that the environment can be designed to address the specific profile of prejudice within the specific intergroup context. Prejudice against different groups may be based on different types of negative affect (e.g., anger, fear, guilt, envy, or disgust: Cottrell & Neuberg, 2005; Glick, 2002; Mackie & Smith, 2002). These emotions yield different kinds of discrimination against the out-group (e.g., prejudice based on fear causes defensive protection of in-group status; Neuberg & Cottrell, 2002). Attempts to reduce prejudice must tackle the relevant affect (e.g., by analyzing its sources and ensuring that the data bank addresses them explicitly, and that the relevant information is conveyed to the out-group). It is evident that, compared with direct contact and other forms of indirect contact, computer-mediated contact is still in its infancy. There are, as yet, no studies identifying moderators and mediators of contact in this form, and this is an important area for future research.

Summary of Research on Indirect Contact and an Integrative Framework

A wide variety of forms of indirect contact exist, each of which lacks certain elements of face-to-face contact (e.g., access to nonverbal cues, personal involvement, a real interlocutor). However, each has specific advantages (e.g., reduced anxiety, asynchronicity, logistical ease). All show promise as routes to reduce prejudice that complement (while not necessarily replacing) face-to-face contact.

In an attempt to synthesize work across various direct and indirect contact literatures into a single framework, Harwood (2010) describes the "contact space." The space is defined by two dimensions, broadly recognizing (a) the degree to which the self is *directly* involved in the contact, and (b) the *richness* of the self's experience of the out-group. The first dimension distinguishes, for instance, direct contact and mediated interpersonal contact (both of which feature the self interacting in some way with an out-group member) from experiences in which the self is an observer (e.g., seeing intergroup contact in the media, or having an in-group friend who has an out-group friend). The second dimension draws on the concept of "richness"—the extent to which the experience of the out-group features multiple cues conveyed through multiple channels (Daft & Lengel, 1984). This dimension distinguishes instances in which someone has a rich experience of an out-group member (e.g., by talking with them face-to-face, or seeing them engage in interactions in the immediate social space) from more impoverished experiences of the out-group (e.g., computer-mediated contact, or merely hearing about intergroup contact). Following our discussion of extended contact, this dimension distinguishes between "knowing about" and "observing" a friend having an out-group friend, a distinction downplayed in the current literature.

Harwood (2010) argues that not only is the contact experience different across the contact space, but that the mediators and moderators of contact vary across the space. For example, the mediating effects of perceived *norms* for intergroup contact are hypothesized to be stronger when the self's involvement in contact is low—seeing other members of the in-group engaging in contact should enhance perceptions that contact is normative more than self engaging in contact; other people's behavior is more central to norms. Harwood also attends to the variety of communicative experiences across the contact space. For instance, he notes that communication *about* contact will be particularly influential in situations where both richness and personal involvement are low. In such contexts, we rely on second-hand accounts of contact (the "knowing about" aspect of extended contact), and as such, what is said *about* contact deserves attention (see van Dijk, 1987). Stewart, Pitts, and Osborne (2011) elaborate on this notion, demonstrating the ways in which the media build group associations using language (e.g., "illegal immigrants" and "Latino immigrants"), and that such descriptions build expectations for negative intergroup contact experiences. More research is required to examine the validity of some of these claims; however, it is clear that contact can occur in many different ways, and that integrative frameworks for this area are required.

What Can Contact Change? Dependent Variables in Intergroup Contact Research

The general aim of contact interventions is to reduce prejudice and improve intergroup relations. Early work on intergroup contact focused primarily on cognitive (e.g., stereotypes) and affective aspects of prejudice, generally finding greater effects on affect than cognition (Tropp & Pettigrew, 2005b). Recent work goes beyond assessing prejudice per se, and examines the effects of contact on attitude strength, implicit associations with out-groups, attitudes toward out-groups not involved in the contact situation, physiological reactions to the out-group, and indices of intergroup reconciliation in settings of conflict.

Attitude Strength

Research shows that *strong* attitudes (attitudes that are held with greater certainty, are more important, more accessible in memory, less ambivalent) are more stable over time, more resistant to change, more likely to influence information processing, and more likely to guide behavior (Krosnick & Petty, 1995). Vonofakou, Hewstone, and Voci (2007) demonstrated that contact with out-group friends was associated with self-reported meta-attitudinally stronger out-group attitudes and more accessible out-group attitudes (derived from a computer-based response-latency procedure). The authors also showed that the effects of contact on attitude strength were mediated by reduced anxiety, showing the broad influence of intergroup anxiety in shaping out-group attitudes. Christ et al. (2010) confirmed, with longitudinal survey data, effects of both direct and extended contact on meta-attitudinal measures of attitude strength.

Implicit Associations

As noted above, studies have explored the effects of contact on implicit bias, resolving any doubts about contact research being overly reliant on self-report measures (Hewstone, Judd, & Sharp, 2011, also show that observer reports validate self-reports of direct contact). Turner, Hewstone, and Voci (2007) found that opportunities for contact with South Asians (e.g., living in mixed neighborhoods, going to mixed schools), but not the number of South Asian friends, predicted more positive implicit associations with the out-group among White British students. The fact that implicit bias was influenced by nonevaluative contact measures rather than evaluative measures, bypassing relevant mediating variables (e.g., anxiety, which predicted explicit attitudes), suggests that the effect on implicit measures may be explained by familiarity with the out-group (see Tam et al., 2006, reported above; but there is also some evidence for mediated effects of contact on implicit measures, see Prestwich, Kenworthy, Wilson, & Kwan-Tat, 2008). Moreover, Aberson and Haag (2007) found that quantity and quality of contact interacted to predict implicit attitudes, indicating that the nature of the environmental associations matters; that is, whether associations or experiences are mostly positive or negative.

"Secondary Transfer Effects" of Intergroup Contact

The potential of contact would be even greater *if* it could be shown that contact effects generalize from experience with one out-group to attitudes toward *other* out-groups (e.g., positive contact between Catholics and Protestants in Northern Ireland generalizes to positive attitudes toward ethnic minorities; Tausch et al., 2010). Far-reaching, or wildly optimistic as this sounds, it is, in fact, the case. Pettigrew (1997, 2009) demonstrated that respondents with an out-group friend from one minority group were more accepting of other out-groups, even groups that were not present in their country (Galinsky & Moskowitz, 2000; Van Laar, Levin, Sinclair, & Sidanius, 2005). Tausch et al. (2010) reported the most extensive, including longitudinal evidence to date, for three phenomena: (a) that secondary-transfer effects occur via a process of attitude generalization (i.e., from attitude towards primary out-group to attitude toward secondary out-group), rather than change of in-group attitude; (b) that they occur while controlling for direct contact with the secondary out-groups; and (c) that they cannot be explained in terms of socially desirable responding. Harwood et al. (2011) demonstrated that secondary transfer effects can also emerge from an experimental manipulation of imagined contact. Their work demonstrates that secondary transfer is strongest to groups that are more similar to the target group.

Physiological Reactions to Out-Group Members

Recent research has explored the physiological responses and neural substrates involved in evaluations of, and responses to, out-groups as a function of contact. This work demonstrated that contact is associated with reduced automatic physiological threat responses to out-group members. For example, Blascovich, Mendes, Hunter, Lickel, and Kowai-Bell (2001) showed that participants with more interracial contact exhibited reduced physiological threat reactions (i.e., responses of the autonomic system like sweating and increased heart rate) during interracial interactions; and Page-Gould, Mendoza-Denton, and Tropp (2008) found that induced cross-group friendships between Latinos/Latinas and Whites led to decreases in cortisol reactivity during intergroup contact.

Findings also suggest that contact can moderate the neural processing of faces of other races. Measuring event-related potentials, Walker, Silvert, Hewstone, and Nobre (2008) showed that differences in Whites' processing of their own vs. other-race faces were reduced with increased self-reported out-group contact, demonstrating the malleability of internal neural responses through external social experiences such as intergroup contact.

Trust and Forgiveness

Research on conflict resolution has stressed the importance of intergroup trust and forgiveness as markers of intergroup reconciliation. Trust facilitates the achievement of mutually beneficial outcomes during negotiations, making it a key concept for research on peace building (Kramer & Carnevale, 2001). Forgiveness, on the other hand, is an emotional state that permits the relationship between the conflicting parties to move forward after a transgression (Cairns, Tam, Hewstone, & Niens, 2005). Studies show that intergroup contact is associated with greater trust and forgiveness, even among respondents who have personally been affected by intergroup violence (e.g., those deeply affected by years of ethnopolitical violence in Northern Ireland; Hewstone, Cairns, Voci, Hamberger, & Niens, 2006; Tam et al., 2007).

An Agenda for Communication Research on Intergroup Contact

The careful reader of our chapter, thus far, may be forgiven for thinking, "Well, these guys have learned a lot about how and when different forms of contact affect prejudice, but I don't seem to have learned much about what happens when members of groups actually interact." This is fair comment. Most social-psychological research, to date, focuses on cognition and affect, and we are all aware just how complex the study of ongoing social interaction can be. We believe that communication scholars can contribute massively to the next wave of contact research on face-to-face interactions between members of different groups. Social psychologists have laid down some markers at least and identified some processes that are likely to be very influential.

Much of our knowledge here comes from the impressive research of three scholars, Shelton, Richeson, and Vorauer (e.g., Shelton & Richeson, 2006; Shelton, Richeson, & Vorauer, 2006), whose approach is founded on taking a relational approach to cross-group social interaction, and to studying meta-perceptions. From a relational perspective, researchers should not only ask participants to evaluate an out-group "target," but also to think about "how the out-group 'target' is likely to evaluate them." This way of studying interracial interactions focuses on the consequences that individuals' beliefs have for their own and their partner's experiences during the interaction.

In metaperception research the focus is, then, on individuals' perceptions of, and feelings about, how others view them (e.g., Whites' perceptions of Blacks' beliefs about Whites: Vorauer & Kumhyr, 2001). Various theoretical approaches– including symbolic interaction theory, attachment theory, and self-verification theory—suggest that individuals do give considerable thought to understanding others' reactions to them (Vorauer, in press). For example, Vorauer, Hunter, Main, and Roy (2000) found that when Whites imagined (Study 1) or anticipated (Study 2) having an interaction with a First Nations (Native American) person, these metastereotypes (i.e., prejudiced, selfish, closed-minded) were activated, as measured by a word fragment completion task and a lexical decision-making task. Research on metaperceptions suggests that the context of an interracial interaction often activates concerns about being judged negatively in both Whites and ethnic minorities.

In the United States, Whites are often concerned with appearing prejudiced (e.g., Dunton & Fazio, 1997; Monin & Miller, 2001; Plant & Devine, 1998), while ethnic minorities are often concerned with being treated negatively because of prejudice during interracial interactions (Crocker, Major, & Steele, 1998; Major, Quinton, & McCoy, 2002; Miller & Myers, 1998). A key contribution of Richeson, Shelton, and Vorauer's research has been to explore how these metaperceptions influence individuals' choosing to avoid interacting with out-group members. Shelton and Richeson (2005, Study 1) showed that Whites and ethnic minorities believe they, as well as their in-group, are more interested in engaging in interracial contact than out-group members are. Both racial groups perceived that they wanted to have more out-group friends and interracial contact than the average out-group student. For example, Whites reported that they wanted to have more contact with Blacks, but that Blacks did not want to have more contact with them.

Shelton and Richeson (2005, Studies 3–5) also examined the extent to which Whites and Blacks make divergent attributions about their own and an out-group member's explanation for avoiding interracial interactions. They predicted that explanations for one's own failure to initiate interracial contact would be grounded in concerns of being rejected because of race, whereas explanations of out-group members' failure to initiate contact would be based in a lack of interest. Results showed that both racial groups believed different psychological states underpinned their own and the out-group members' motivations for not initiating interracial contact. Specifically, Whites and Blacks indicated that fear of rejection because of their race would be a more likely explanation for their own inaction than for the out-group members' inaction. Conversely, both Whites and Blacks indicated that lack of interest would be a more likely explanation for the out-group members' inaction than for their own.

Based on this relational approach, research is increasingly examining minorities' reactions to and impressions of members of majority groups, and vice versa, during intergroup interactions (e.g., Conley, Devine, Rabow, & Evett, 2002; Page-Gould et al., 2008; Pearson et al., 2008; Vorauer & Kumhyr, 2001). A recent review notes that, over the past decade, researchers have focused on physiological (e.g., Page-Gould et al., 2008), behavioral (e.g., Dovidio et al., 2002; Trawalter & Richeson, 2008), cognitive (e.g., Richeson & Trawalter, 2005), and affective (e.g., Pearson et al., 2008) dynamics of intergroup interactions (Richeson & Shelton, 2010). We cannot do justice, here, to the wealth of these researchers' programs, but let us focus on one aspect: the emphasis on affect and arousal (paralleling findings we have reported for anxiety).

Shelton and Richeson propose that affective reactions, such as anxiety, are particularly likely to "leak out" through nonverbal and paraverbal channels.

Consistent with this reasoning, majority-group or nonstigmatized individuals display more nonverbal signs of anxiety and discomfort (e.g., excessive blinking) during intergroup, compared with intragroup, interactions (Dovidio et al., 1997; Trawalter & Richeson, 2008). The display of fewer affiliative behaviors (e.g., nodding, direct eye gaze) during intergroup relative to intragroup interactions may be due to increased negative arousal, not negative attitudes. Specifically, Shelton and Richeson note that interracial interactions can trigger a state of physiological arousal that impedes the fluid behaviors that encourage positive conversation (Mendes, Blascovich, Hunter, Lickel, & Jost, 2007).

It is not easy to overcome these unwanted effects, least of all by trying to. In fact, trying to respond without prejudice can result in paradoxical behavioral outcomes. Richeson et al. (2003), using a sophisticated mix of psychological and neuroscience techniques, reported that Whites who interacted with a Black experimenter showed short-term resource depletion due to temporary negative effects on executive function. The effort required to control the expression of bias during intergroup interactions is cognitively demanding (Richeson & Trawalter, 2005), and, as a consequence, can make individuals behave in ways that are the opposite of how they intend to behave (Apfelbaum, Sommers, & Norton, 2008). For example, Shelton et al. (2006) studied interactions in which Whites discussed race-related topics with a Black partner, hence activating Whites' concerns about appearing prejudiced. In these circumstances, Whites with higher levels of implicit racial bias were rated more engaged (as judged by their interaction partners) than were Whites with lower levels of implicit racial bias. Likewise, avoiding mention of race in interaction (so as to appear nonprejudiced) can backfire and make Whites appear more prejudiced (Apfelbaum et al., 2008).

Building upon this impressive body of findings, we suggest that future work on communication and intergroup contact be organized around three primary themes: content, sequencing, and integrating work on different types of contact.

Content

Broadly, one prerequisite for effective contact is that it be positive. This is obviously an overly broad concept, but retaining it as a touchstone is important. In situations involving intergroup tensions, the *risks* involved in negative contact are substantial in both the short and long term. Many communication variables contribute to this—some already discussed include self-disclosure and accommodative behaviors. Others also deserve more detailed examination in both face-to-face contact and other forms (e.g., virtual contact, which has advantages concerning the storage of data and control of nontextual features of interaction). Using another person's name to address them directly, for example, is a simple communication phenomenon that reveals personal interest and a positive attitude (Li, 1997), but it has not (to our knowledge) been examined as a process variable in contact studies. More sophisticated means exist for examining the content of language and could be used productively. For instance, text analysis software can tap such phenomena as expressions of positive or negative affect (including differentiating anger, sadness, and anxiety), as well as assessing relevant phenomena such as inclusive/exclusive language and use of first person plural pronouns (*we, us*; e.g., Pennebaker & Stone, 2003).

Nonverbal communication has not always received the attention it deserves in this arena. Beyond subtle leakage behaviors described earlier, more basic nonverbal immediacy behaviors offer routes to effective communication (e.g., smiling, forward lean, nodding, open body posture; Dovidio, Kawakami, & Gaertner, 2002). When examining face-to-face contact, such behaviors deserve more attention than they have received. Smiling, for instance, not only generates positive affect in the partner, but also may serve to improve the emotional state of the speaker via intrapersonal self-perception processes (Schnall & Laird, 2003). As part of a broad call to examine communication in contact, we suggest these as manageable and critical areas to provide insight into what goes on during contact.

The social cognitive theory perspective on vicarious contact initially presented by Ortiz and Harwood (2007) has interesting implications for the types of media portrayals that should be the focus of future research on media content and effects. If portrayals of intergroup relationships are important, then we should pay particular attention to such portrayals, examining (at least) the dyadic level of analysis—the majority of current work examining media portrayals focuses on individual characters as the unit of analysis. Research should also contrast intergroup and intragroup portrayals of relationships for characteristics such as intimacy, conflict management, and group salience. Given the extensive evidence that group salience is critical for generalization (Brown & Hewstone, 2005), examinations of media content should also examine how intergroup dyads in the media maintain positive relationships while also demonstrating group salience. For example, in the sitcom *Modern Family* (on the U.S. ABC network), Jay and Gloria are a married couple. Jay is Anglo and Gloria is Hispanic. Gloria's ethnicity is apparent from her marked Spanish accent and frequent plot devices centering on her Colombian heritage. This portrayal should facilitate greater attitude change about Hispanics among Anglo viewers than might be the case either with a less group-salient Hispanic portrayal, or with a character who lacked a close relationship with an Anglo character. A focus on group salience also raises challenges in terms of understanding the subtleties of portrayals, including negotiating the line between group salience and parody (e.g., Gloria's accent and mannerisms may cross the line into reinforcing stereotypes about Latinas).

Sequencing

In a seminal piece, Pettigrew (1998) outlines an ideal order for the development of constructive and positive intergroup relationships. He argues that such relations need to be first personalized, and that later in the relationship elements of group salience and "deeper" issues can be introduced. We would argue that such sequencing notions can be effectively translated to the level of individual interactions. Initial exchanges in any interaction are likely to be influenced by some of the basic affective issues described above—maintaining a positive tone, establishing liking, and identification with the other person. Effective intergroup contact requires establishing this common ground on a microlevel in order to "proceed." Once a positive "base" has been established, however, the most promising interactions will grow in group salience (with its attendant potential for generalization). As has been discussed elsewhere (Paolini et al., 2010), the challenge of balancing group salience and positivity in interaction is a critical one in fully capitalizing on the promise of contact. We suggest that translating Pettigrew's ideas to the microinteractional level offers similar pathways to effective contact: first positivity, then salience. We know of no work that has examined the sequential pattern of intergroup encounters to understand whether the same elements in different order have differential effects. Examining such questions in the context of vicarious or imagined contact would probably be a useful first step in such investigations.

Integrating Work on Different Types of Contact

As described above, recent work on intergroup contact has massively expanded the types of contact being investigated. Most research continues to investigate these types of contact in isolation. Even researchers who look at different types of contact tend to do so in different studies: the primary exception to this rule is researchers in the area of virtual contact who do often compare (or pair) their manipulations with traditional face-to-face conditions. As this work develops, there is a pressing need to establish paradigms wherein types of contact can be compared within a single design. The challenges here are substantial, but such work is the best way to examine whether moderators and mediators differ in their efficacy across types of contact, whether certain types of contact are better suited to specific intergroup contexts, and the like (Harwood, 2010). The challenges are not insurmountable, and Ioannou, Hewstone, Al Ramiah, and Psaltis (2011) have already conducted a series of studies comparing direct, extended, and imagined contact within the same experimental paradigm. Likewise, it would be relatively straightforward to compare a specific media stimulus (e.g., a television show) against an "imagined" contact condition in which the instructions mirror the content of the television show.

There is also tremendous scope for work looking at interactions between various types of contact. Paluck (2010) provides a very interesting illustration of such work, showing how conversations stimulated by a radio talk-show influence attitudes in an extremely tense intergroup context (Democratic Republic of Congo). This work integrates ideas from contact theory with core communication theory (e.g., two-step flow models; Katz & Lazarsfeld, 1955). Similar integrative ideas are apparent in suggestions that specific (generally indirect) forms of contact may serve as gateways or pathways for entry into more direct contact (e.g., Amichai-Hamburger & McKenna, 2006; Crisp & Turner, 2009; Harwood, 2010; Turner, Hewstone, Voci, Paolini, et al., 2007b).

Conclusion

The promise of intergroup contact theory has been fulfilled in many ways. The volume of work produced has demonstrated conclusively that contact works. However, numerous exciting challenges remain for the field. The story is far from told on how we maximize the possibilities for positive outcomes and minimize potential negative effects of contact. Clearly not all contact is positive, and being able to predict when and where contact effects might backfire merits attention. We are also only in the early stages of examining the massive array of *types* of contact, and both theory and data are required to make sense of what even "counts" as contact, how the contact experience differs across such diverse experiences, and how different types of contact can best be used in a temporal sequence. Finally, we are only just beginning to learn what occurs *during* intergroup contact. How do the microdynamics of a contact experience tie into the broader psychological and sociological phenomena that surround it and emerge from it? These are questions that communication scholars are uniquely equipped to answer, and that should be at the core of a subdiscipline of intergroup communication (Giles, Reid, & Harwood, 2010).

References

Aberson, C. L., & Haag, S. C. (2007). Contact, perspective taking, and anxiety as predictors of stereotype endorsement, explicit attitudes, and implicit attitudes. *Group Processes and Intergroup Relations, 10*, 179–201.

Abrams, J., & Giles, H. (2007). Ethnic identity gratifications selection and avoidance by African Americans: A group vitality and social identity gratifications perspective. *Media Psychology, 9*, 115–134.

Abrams, J., O'Connor, J., & Giles, H. (2002). Identity and intergroup communication. In W. B. Gudykunst & B. Mody (Eds.), *Handbook of international and intercultural communication* (2nd ed., pp. 225–240). Thousand Oaks, CA: Sage.

Allen, R. L., & Bielby, W. T. (1979). Blacks' attitudes and behaviors toward television. *Communication Research, 6*, 407–436.

Allport, G. W. (1954). *The nature of prejudice*. Reading, MA: Addison-Wesley.

Al-Ramiah, A., Hewstone, M., Little, T., & Lang, K. (under review). *A longitudinal assessment of intergroup contact and integrated threat theory in the context of a nation-building intervention*. Manuscript under review.

Amichai-Hamburger, Y. (2005). Personality and the Internet. In Y. Amichai-Hamburger (Ed.), *The social net: Human behavior in cyberspace* (pp. 27–55). New York: Oxford University Press.

Amichai-Hamburger, Y. (2008a). Potential and promise of online volunteering. *Computers in Human Behavior, 24*, 544–562.

Amichai-Hamburger, Y. (2008b). Interacting via Internet: Theoretical and practical aspects. In A. Barak (Ed.), *Psychological aspects of cyberspace: Theory, research, applications* (pp. 207–229). Cambridge, England: Cambridge University Press.

Amichai-Hamburger, Y., & Furnham, A. (2006). The positive net. *Computers in Human Behavior, 23,* 1033–1045.

Amichai-Hamburger, Y., & McKenna, K. Y. A. (2006). The contact hypothesis reconsidered: Interacting via the Internet. *Journal of Computer-Mediated Communication, 11,* article 7. Retrieved from http://jcmc.indiana.edu/vol11/issue3/amichai-hamburger.html

Amir, Y. (1969). Contact hypothesis in ethnic relations. *Psychological Bulletin, 71,* 319–342

Apfelbaum, E. P., Sommers, S. R., & Norton, M. I. (2008). Seeing race and seeming racist? Evaluating strategic colorblindness in social interaction. *Journal of Personality and Social Psychology, 95,* 918–932.

Aron, A., Aron, E., Tudor, M., & Nelson, G. (1991). Close relationships as including other in the self. *Journal of Personality and Social Psychology, 60,* 241–253.

Austin, R., Abbot, L., Mulkeen, A., & Metcalfe, N. (2003). Dissolving boundaries: Cross-national co-operation through technology in education. *The Curriculum Journal, 14,* 55–84.

Austin, R., & Anderson, J. (2008a). *E-schooling: Global messages from a small island.* Oxford, England: Routledge.

Austin, R., & Anderson, J. (2008b). Building bridges on-line: Issues of pedagogy and learning outcomes in intercultural education through citizenship. *International Journal of Information Communication and Technology Education, 13,* 86–94.

Bandura, A. (2001). Social cognitive theory of mass communication. *Media Psychology, 3,* 265–299.

Bargh, J. A., McKenna, K., & Fitzimmons, G. M. (2002). Can you see the real me? Activation and expression of the "true self" on the Internet. *Journal of Social Issues, 58,* 33–48.

Batson, C. D., & Ahmad, N. Y. (2009). Using empathy to improve intergroup attitudes and relations. *Social Issues and Policy Review, 3,* 141–177.

Batson, C. D., Polycarpou, M. P., Harmon-Jones, E., Imhoff, H. J., Mitchener, E. C., Bednar, L. L., … Highberger, L. (1997). Empathy and attitudes: Can feeling for a member of a stigmatized group improve feelings toward the group? *Journal of Personality and Social Psychology, 72,* 105–118.

Berger, C. R., & Bradac, J. J. (1982). *Language and social knowledge.* London: Edward Arnold.

Bettencourt, B. A., Charlton, K., & Kernahan, C. (1997). Numerical representation of groups in cooperative settings: Social orientation effects on ingroup bias. *Journal of Experimental Social Psychology, 33,* 630–659.

Bigler, R. S., & Hughes, J. M. (2010). Reasons for skepticism about the efficacy of simulated contact interventions. *American Psychologist, 65,* 131–132.

Binder, J., Zagefka, H., Brown, R., Funke, F., Kessler, T., Mummendey, A., … Leyens, J.-P. (2009). Does contact reduce prejudice or does prejudice reduce contact? A longitudinal test of the contact hypothesis among majority and minority groups in three European countries. *Journal of Personality and Social Psychology, 96,* 843–856.

Blascovich, J., Mendes, W. B., Hunter, S. B., Lickel, B., & Kowai-Bell, N. (2001). Perceiver threat in social interactions with stigmatized others. *Journal of Personality and Social Psychology, 80,* 253–267.

Bornstein, R. F. (1989). Exposure and affect: Overview and meta-analysis of research, 1968–1987. *Psychological Bulletin, 106*, 265–289.

Brewer, M. B., & Miller, N. (1984). Beyond the contact hypothesis: Theoretical perspectives on desegregation. In N. Miller & M. B. Brewer (Eds.), *Groups in contact: The psychology of desegregation* (pp. 281–302). Orlando, FL: Academic Press.

Brewer, M. B., & Miller, N. (1988). Contact and cooperation: when do they work? In P. Katz & D. Taylor (Eds.), *Eliminating racism* (pp. 315–326). New York: Plenum.

Brown Givens, S., & Monahan, J. (2005). Priming Mammies, Jezebels, and other controlling images: An examination of the influence of mediated stereotypes on perceptions of an African American woman. *Media Psychology, 7*, 87–106.

Brown, R., & Hewstone, M. (2005). An integrative theory of intergroup contact. In M. P. Zanna (Ed.), *Advances in experimental social psychology* (Vol. 37, pp. 255–342). San Diego, CA: Elsevier.

Brown, R., Vivian, J., & Hewstone, M. (1999). Changing attitudes through intergroup contact: The effects of group membership salience. *European Journal of Social Psychology, 29*, 741–764.

Cairns, E., Tam, T., Hewstone, M., & Niens, U. (2005). Intergroup forgiveness and intergroup conflict: Northern Ireland, a case study. In E. L. Worthington (Ed.), *Handbook of forgiveness* (pp. 461–476). New York: Brunner/Routledge.

Cameron, L., & Rutland, A. (2006). Extended contact through story reading in school: Reducing children's prejudice toward the disabled. *Journal of Social Issues, 62*, 469–488.

Cameron, L., Rutland, A., Brown, R., & Douch, R. (2006). Changing children's intergroup attitudes towards refugees: Testing different models of extended contact. *Child Development, 77*, 1208–1219.

Christ, O., Hewstone, M., Tausch, N., Voci., A., Wagner, U., Hughes, J., & Cairns, E. (2010). Direct contact as a moderator of extended contact effects: Cross-sectional and longitudinal impact on attitudes and attitude strength. *Personality and Social Psychology Bulletin, 36*, 1662–1674.

Christ, O., Hewstone, M., Tropp, L. R., & Wagner, U. (in press). Longitudinal studies of intergroup contact [Special section]. *British Journal of Social Psychology.*

Christ, O., & Wagner, U. (in press). Methodological issues in the study of intergroup contact: Towards a new wave of research. In G. Hodson & M. Hewstone (Eds.), *Advances in intergroup contact.* New York: Psychology Press.

Cohen, J. (2001). Defining identification: A theoretical look at the identification of audiences with media characters . *Mass Communication and Society, 4*, 245–264.

Conley, T., Devine, P. G., Rabow, J., & Evett, S. R. (2002). Gay men and lesbians' experiences in and expectations for interactions with heterosexuals. *Journal of Homosexuality, 44*, 83–109.

Corrigan, P. W., Rowan, D., Green, A., Lundin, R., River, P., Uphoff-Wasowski, K., … Kubiak, M. A. (2002). Challenging two mental illness stigmas: personal responsibility and dangerousness. *Schizophrenia Bulletin, 28*, 293–310.

Cottrell, C. A., & Neuberg, S. L. (2005). Different emotional reactions to different groups: A sociofunctional threat-based approach to "prejudice." *Journal of Personality and Social Psychology, 88*, 770–789.

Crisp, R. J., & Husnu, S. (2011). Attributional processes underlying imagined contact effects. *Group Processes and Intergroup Relations, 14:* 255–274. doi:10.1177/1368430210390533

Crisp, R. J., Husnu, S., Meleady, R., Stathi, S., & Turner, R. N. (2010). From imagery to intention: A dual route model of imagined contact effects. In W. Stroebe & M. Hewstone (Eds.), *European review of social psychology* (Vol. 21, pp. 188–236). Hove, UK: Psychology Press.

Crisp, R. J., Stathi, S., Turner, R. N., & Husnu, S. (2008). Imagined intergroup contact: Theory, paradigm, and practice. *Personality and Social Psychology Compass, 2,* 1–18.

Crisp, R. J., & Turner, R. N. (2009). Can imagined interactions produce positive perceptions? Reducing prejudice through simulated social contact. *American Psychologist, 64,* 231–240.

Crisp, R. J., & Turner, R. N. (in press). Imagined intergroup contact: Refinements, debates and clarifications. In G. Hodson & M. Hewstone (Eds.), *Advances in intergroup contact.* New York: Psychology Press.

Crocker, J., Major, B., & Steele, C. (1998). Social stigma. In D. Gilbert, S. T., Fiske, & G. Lindzey (Eds.), *Handbook of social psychology* (Vol. 2, pp. 504–553), Boston, MA: McGraw Hill.

Daft, R. L., & Lengel, R. H. (1984). Information richness: A new approach to managerial behavior and organizational design. In L. L. Cummings & B. M. Staw (Eds.), *Research in organizational behavior* (Vol. 6, pp. 191–233). Homewood, IL: JAI Press.

Deardorff, D. K. (Ed.). (2009). *The Sage handbook of intercultural competence.* Thousand Oaks, CA: Sage.

Desforges, D. M., Lord, C. G., Pugh, M. A., Sia, T. L., Scarberry, N. C., & Ratcliff, C. D. (1997). Role of group representativeness in the generalization part of the contact hypothesis. *Basic and Applied Social Psychology, 19,* 183–204. doi: 10.1207/s15324834basp1902_3

De Tezanos-Pinto, P., Bratt, C., & Brown, R. (2010). What will the others think? Ingroup norms as a mediator of the effects of intergroup contact. *British Journal of Social Psychology, 49,* 507–523.

Dhont, K., & Van Hiel, A. (2009). We must not be enemies: Interracial contact and the reduction of prejudice among authoritarians. *Personality and Individual Differences, 46,* 172–177.

Dhont, K., & Van Hiel, A. (2011). Direct contact and authoritarianism as moderators between extended contact and reduced prejudice: Lower threat and greater trust as mediators. *Group Processes and Intergroup Relations, 14,* 223–237. doi: 10.1177/1368430210391121

Dixon, T. (2008). Crime news and racialized beliefs: Understanding the relationship between local news viewing and perceptions of African Americans and crime. *Journal of Communication, 58,* 106–125.

Dovidio, J. F., Brigham, J. C., Johnson, B. T., & Gaertner, S. L. (1996). Stereotyping, prejudice, and discrimination: Another look. In N. Macrae, C. Stangor, & M. Hewstone (Eds.), *Foundations of stereotypes and stereotyping* (pp. 276–319). New York: Guilford.

Dovidio, J. F, Eller, A., & Hewstone, M. (2011). Improving intergroup relations through direct, extended and other forms of indirect contact. *Group Processes and Intergroup Relations, 14,* 147–160.

Dovidio, J. F., Gaertner, S. L., & Kawakami, K. (2003). Intergroup contact: The past, present and future. *Group Processes and Intergroup Relations, 6,* 5–21.

Dovidio, J. F., Kawakami, K., & Gaertner, S. L. (2002). Implicit and explicit prejudice and interracial interaction. *Journal of Personality and Social Psychology, 82,* 62–68. doi: 10.1037/0022-3514.82.1.62

Dovidio, J. F., Kawakami, K., Johnson, C., Johnson, B., & Howard, A. (1997). On the nature of prejudice: Automatic and controlled processes. *Journal of Experimental Social Psychology, 33,* 510–540.

Dunton, B. C., & Fazio, R. H. (1997). An individual difference measure of motivation to control prejudiced reactions. *Personality and Social Psychology Bulletin, 23,* 316–326.

Eller, A., & Abrams, D. (2004). Come together: Longitudinal comparisons of Pettigrew's reformulated intergroup contact model and the common in-group identity model in Anglo-French and Mexican-American contexts. *European Journal of Social Psychology, 34,* 1–28.

Eller, A., Abrams, D., & Zimmerman, A. (2011). Two degrees of separation: A longitudinal study of actual and perceived extended international contact. *Group Processes and Intergroup Relations, 14,* 175–191. doi: 10.1177/1368430210391120

Fiske, S. T., Cuddy, A. J. C., Glick, P., & Xu, J. (2002). A model of (often mixed) stereotype content: Competence and warmth respectively follow from status and competition. *Journal of Personality and Social Psychology, 82,* 878–902

Fiske, S. T., & Neuberg, S. L. (1990). A continuum model of impression formation from category-based to individuating processes: Influences of information and motivation on attention and interpretation. In M. P. Zanna (Ed.), *Advances in experimental social psychology* (pp. 1–74). San Diego, CA: Academic Press.

Gaertner, S. L., & Dovidio, J. F. (2000). *Reducing intergroup bias: The common ingroup identity model.* Philadelphia, PA: Psychology Press.

Gaertner, S. L., Dovidio, J. F., & Houlette, M. A. (2010). Social categorization. In J. F. Dovidio, M. Hewstone, & V. M. Esses (Eds.), *Handbook of prejudice, stereotyping and discrimination* (pp. 526–543). Thousand Oaks, CA: Sage.

Gaertner, S. L., Rust, M. C., Dovidio, J. F., Bachman, B. A., & Anastasio, P. A. (1996). The contact hypothesis: The role of a common in-group identity on reducing intergroup bias among majority and minority group members. In J. L. Nye & A. M. Brower (Eds.), *What's social about social cognition?* (pp. 230–360). Newbury Park, CA: Sage.

Galinsky, A. D., & Moskowitz, G. B. (2000). Perspective-taking: Decreasing stereotype expression, stereotype accessibility, and ingroup favoritism. *Journal of Personality and Social Psychology, 78,* 708–724.

Gallois, C., Giles, H., Jones, E., Cargile, A. C., & Ota, H. (1995). Accommodating intercultural encounters: Elaborations and extensions. In R. L. Wiseman (Ed.), *Intercultural communication theory* (pp. 115–147). Thousand Oaks, CA: Sage.

Gerbner, G., Gross, L., Morgan, M., & Signorielli, N. (2002). Growing up with television: Cultivation processes. In J. Bryant & D. Zillmann (Eds.), *Media effects: Advances in theory and research* (pp. 43–67). Hillsdale, NJ: Erlbaum.

Giles, H., Coupland, N., & Coupland, J. (Eds.) (1991). *Contexts of accommodation.* Cambridge, England: Cambridge University Press.

Giles, H., Reid, S., & Harwood, J. (Eds.). (2010). *The dynamics of intergroup communication.* New York: Peter Lang.

Glick, P. (2002). Sacrificial lambs dressed in wolves' clothing: Envious prejudice, ideology, and the scapegoating of Jews. In L. S. Newman & R. Erber (Eds.), *Understanding genocide: The social psychology of the Holocaust* (pp. 113–142). London: Oxford University Press.

Gómez, A., Tropp, L. R., & Fernández, S. (2011). When extended contact opens the door to future contact: Testing the effects of extended contact on attitudes and inter-group expectancies among majority and minority groups. *Group Processes and Intergroup Relations, 14,* 161–173. doi: 10.1177/1368430210391119

Greenwald, A. G., McGhee, D. E., & Schwartz, J. L. K. (1998). Measuring individual differences in implicit cognition: The Implicit Association Test. *Journal of Person-ality and Social Psychology, 74,* 1464–1480.

Gudykunst, W. B., & Mody, B. (Eds.). (2002). *The handbook of international and intercultural communication* (2nd ed.). Thousand Oaks, CA: Sage.

Hamberger, J., & Hewstone, M. (1997). Inter-ethnic contact as a predictor of blatant and subtle prejudice: Tests of a model in four West European nations. *British Jour-nal of Social Psychology, 36,* 173–190.

Hamburger, Y. (1994). The contact hypothesis reconsidered: Effects of the atypical outgroup member on the outgroup stereotype. *Basic Applied Social Psychology, 15,* 339–358.

Harwood, J. (1997). Viewing age: Lifespan identity and television viewing choices. *Journal of Broadcasting and Electronic Media, 41,* 203–213.

Harwood, J. (1999). Age identification, social identity gratifications, and television viewing. *Journal of Broadcasting and Electronic Media, 43,* 123–136.

Harwood, J. (2010). The contact space: A novel framework for intergroup contact research. *Journal of Language and Social Psychology, 29,* 147–177.

Harwood, J., Hewstone, M., Paolini, S., & Voci, A. (2005). Grandparent–grandchild contact and attitudes towards older adults. *Personality and Social Psychology Bul-letin, 31,* 393–406.

Harwood, J., Paolini, S., Joyce, N., Rubin, M., & Arroyo, A. (2011). Secondary transfer effects from imagined contact: Group similarity affects the generalization gradient. *British Journal of Social Psychology, 50,* 180–189. doi: 10.1348/014466610X524263

Harwood, J., Raman, P., & Hewstone, M. (2006). Communicative predictors of group salience in the intergenerational setting. *Journal of Family Communication, 6,* 181–200.

Harwood, J., & Roy, A. (2005). Social identity theory and mass communication research. In J. Harwood & H. Giles (Eds.), *Intergroup communication: Multiple perspectives* (pp. 189–212). New York: Peter Lang.

Harwood, J., & Vincze, L. (2011). Mediating second language learning and intergroup contact in a bilingual setting. *Journal of Multilingual and Multicultural Develop-ment,* published online.

Harwood, J., & Vincze, L. (2012). *Undermining stereotypes of linguistic groups through mediated intergroup contact.* Unpublished manuscript, University of Arizona.

Hewstone, M. (1996). Contact and categorization: Social psychological interventions to change intergroup relations. In C. N. Macrae, C. Stangor, & M. Hewstone (Eds.), *Stereotypes and stereotyping* (pp. 323–368). New York: Guilford.

Hewstone, M. (2009). Living apart, living together? The role of intergroup contact in social integration. *Proceedings of the British Academy, 162,* 243–300.

Hewstone, M., & Brown, R. (1986). Contact is not enough: An intergroup perspective on the "contact hypothesis." In M. Hewstone & R. Brown (Eds.), *Contact and con-flict in intergroup encounters* (pp. 1–44). Oxford, England: Blackwell.

Hewstone, M., Cairns, E., Voci, A., Hamberger, J., & Niens, U. (2006). Intergroup contact, forgiveness, and experience of "The Troubles" in Northern Ireland. *Journal of Social Issues, 62*, 99–120.

Hewstone, M., Judd, C. M., & Sharp, M. (2011). Do observer ratings validate self-reports of intergroup contact?: A round-robin analysis. *Journal of Experimental Social Psychology, 47*, 599–609.

Hewstone, M., & Lord, C. G. (1998). Changing intergroup cognitions and inter-group behavior: The role of typicality. In C. Sedikides, J. Schopler & C. A. Insko (Eds.), *Intergroup cognition and intergroup behavior* (pp. 367–392). Mahwah, NJ: Erlbaum.

Hewstone, M., & Swart, H. (in press). Fifty-odd years of inter-group contact: From hypothesis to integrated theory. *British Journal of Social Psychology.*

Hodson, G. (2008). Interracial prison contact: The pros for (socially dominant) cons. *British Journal of Social Psychology 47*, 325–351. doi: 10.1348/014466607X231109

Hodson, G., Harry, H., & Mitchell, A. (2009). Independent benefits of contact and friendship on attitudes toward homosexuals among authoritarians and highly iden-tified heterosexuals. *European Journal of Social Psychology, 39*, 509–525.

Honeycutt, J. M. (2010). Imagined interactions. *American Psychologist, 65*, 129–130. doi: 10.1037/a0018052

Horton, D. R., & Wohl, R. (1956). Mass communication and para-social interaction: Observations on intimacy at a distance. *Psychiatry, 19*, 215–229.

Hoter, E., Shonfeld, M., & Ganayem, A. (2009). Information and communication technology (ICT) in the service of multiculturalism. *The International Review of Research in Open and Distance Learning, 10*(2). Retrieved from http://www.irrodl. org/index.php/irrodl/article/view/601/1207

Huskinson, T. L., & Haddock, G. (2004). Individual differences in attitude structure: Variance in the chronic reliance on affective and cognitive information. *Journal of Experimental Social Psychology, 40*, 83–90.

Husnu, S., & Crisp, R. J. (2010). Elaboration enhances the imagined contact effect. *Journal of Experimental Social Psychology, 46*, 943–950.

Ioannou, M. E., Hewstone, M., Al Ramiah, A., & Psaltis, C. (2011). *An experimental paradigm for comparing direct, extended and imagined forms of contact.* Manu-script in preparation, Oxford University, England.

Islam, M. R., & Hewstone, M. (1993). Dimensions of contact as predictors of inter-group anxiety, perceived outgroup variability, and outgroup attitude: An integrative model. *Personality and Social Psychological Bulletin, 19*, 700–710.

Joyce, N., & Harwood, J. (in press). Improving intergroup attitudes through televised vicarious intergroup contact: Social cognitive processing of ingroup and outgroup information. *Communication Research.*

Katz, E., & Lazarsfeld, P. F. (1955). *Personal influence: The part played by people in the flow of mass communications.* New York: Free Press.

Kim, M. S. (2002). *Non-western perspectives on human communication: Implications for theory and practice.* Thousand Oaks, CA: Sage.

Kramer, R. M., & Carnevale, P. J. (2001). Trust and intergroup negotiation. In R. Brown & S. Gaertner (Eds.), *Blackwell handbook of social psychology: Intergroup processes* (pp. 431–450). Oxford, England: Blackwell.

Krcmar, M., & Strizhakova, Y. (2008). Uses and gratifications as media choice. In T. Hartmann (Ed.), *Media choice: A theoretical and empirical overview* (pp. 53–69). New York: Routledge.

Krosnick, J. A., & Petty, R. E. (1995). Attitude strength: An overview. In R. E. Petty & J. A. Krosnick (Eds.), *Attitude strength: Antecedents and consequences* (pp. 1–24). Hillsdale, NJ: Erlbaum.

Laurenceau, J.-P., Barrett, L. F., & Pietromonaco, P. R. (1998). Intimacy as an interpersonal process: The importance of self-disclosure, partner disclosure, and perceived partner responsiveness in interpersonal exchanges. *Journal of Personality and Social Psychology, 74,* 1238–1251.

Leippe, M. R., & Eisenstadt, D. (1994). Generalization of dissonance reduction: Decreasing prejudice through induced compliance. *Journal of Personality and Social Psychology, 67,* 395–413.

Levin, S., van Laar, C., & Sidanius, J. (2003). The effects of ingroup and outgroup friendships on ethnic attitudes in college: A longitudinal study. *Group Processes and Intergroup Relations, 6,* 76–92.

Li, D. C. S. (1997). Borrowed identity: Signaling involvement with a Western name. *Journal of Pragmatics, 28,* 489–513.

Liebkind, K., & McAlister, A. (1999). Extended contact through peer modeling to promote tolerance in Finland. *European Journal of Social Psychology, 29,* 765–780.

Mackie, D. M., & Smith, E. R. (Eds.). (2002). *From prejudice to intergroup emotions: Differentiated reactions to social groups.* Philadelphia, PA: Psychology Press.

Major, B., Quinton, W., & McCoy, S. (2002). Antecedents and consequences of attributions to discrimination: Theoretical and empirical advances. In M. P. Zanna (Ed.), *Advances of Experimental Social Psychology* (Vol. 34, pp. 251–330), New York: Academic Press.

Mallett, R. K., & Wilson, T. D. (2010). Increasing positive intergroup contact. *Journal of Experimental Social Psychology, 46,* 382–387.

Maoz, I. (2003). Peace-building with the hawks: Attitude change of Jewish-Israeli hawks and doves following dialogue encounters with Palestinians. *International Journal of Intercultural Relations, 27,* 701–714.

Mastro, D. (2010). Intergroup communication in the context of traditional media. In H. Giles, S. Reid, & J. Harwood (Eds.), *The dynamics of intergroup communication* (pp. 195–208). New York: Peter Lang.

Mazziotta, A., Mummendey, A., & Wright, S. C. (2011). Vicarious intergroup contact can improve intergroup attitudes and prepare for direct contact. *Group Processes & Intergroup Relations, 14,* 255–274. doi: 10.1177/1368430210390533

McKenna, K. Y. A., Green, A. S., & Gleason, M. (2002). Relationship formation on the Internet: What's the big attraction? *Journal of Social Issues, 58,* 9–31.

McKenna, K. Y. A., Samuel-Azran, T., & Sutton-Balaban, N. (2009). Virtual meetings in the Middle East: implementing the contact hypothesis on the Internet. *The Israeli Journal of Conflict Resolution, 1,* 63–86.

Mendes, W. B., Blascovich, J., Hunter, S., Lickel, B., & Jost, J. T. (2007). Threatened by the unexpected: Challenge and threat during inter-ethnic interactions. *Journal of Personality and Social Psychology, 92,* 698–716.

Miller, C. T., & Myers, A. (1998). Compensating for prejudice: How heavyweight people (and others) control outcomes despite prejudice. In J. K. Swim & C. Stangor (Eds.), *Prejudice: The target's perspective* (pp. 191–218). San Diego, CA: Academic Press.

Miller, N. (2002). Personalization and the promise of contact theory. *Journal of Social Issues, 58,* 387–410.

Mollov, B. (2006, June) *Results of Israeli and Palestinian student interactions in*

CMC: An analysis of attitude changes toward conflicting parties. Paper presented at the annual meeting of the International Communication Association, Dresden, Germany.

Monin, B., & Miller, D. (2001). Moral credentials and the expression of prejudice. *Journal of Personality and Social Psychology, 81,* 33–43.

Muller, D., Judd, C. M., & Yzerbyt, V. T. (2005). When moderation is mediated and mediation is moderated. *Journal of Personality and Social Psychology, 89,* 852–863.

Mutz, D. C., & Goldman, S. K. (2010). Mass media. In J. F. Dovidio, M. Hewstone, P. Glick, & V. Esses (Eds.), *Handbook of prejudice, stereotyping, and discrimination* (pp. 241–258). Thousand Oaks CA: Sage.

Neuberg, S. L., & Cottrell, C. A. (2002). Intergroup emotions: A biocultural approach. In D. M. Mackie & E. R. Smith (Eds.), *From prejudice to intergroup relations: Differentiated reactions to social groups* (pp. 265–283). New York: Psychology Press.

Ortiz, M., & Harwood, J. (2007). A social cognitive approach to intergroup relationships on television. *Journal of Broadcasting and Electronic Media, 51,* 615–631.

Ortiz, M., & Harwood, J. (2011). *Different when it is more than Juan: The subjective group dynamics of intergroup criminality in the news.* Unpublished manuscript, Ohio State University.

Page-Gould, E., Mendoza-Denton, R., & Tropp, L. R. (2008). With a little help from my cross-group friend: Reducing anxiety in intergroup contexts through cross-group friendship. *Journal of Personality and Social Psychology, 95,* 1080–1094.

Paluck, E. L. (2009). Reducing intergroup prejudice and conflict using the media: A field experiment in Rwanda. *Journal of Personality and Social Psychology, 96,* 574–587.

Paluck, E. L. (2010). Is it better not to talk? Group polarization, extended contact, and perspective-taking in eastern Democratic Republic of Congo. *Personality and Social Psychology Bulletin, 36,* 1170–1185.

Paolini, S., Harwood, J., & Rubin, M. (2010). Negative intergroup contact makes group memberships salient: Explaining why intergroup conflict endures. *Personality and Social Psychology Bulletin, 36,* 1723–1738. doi: 10.1177/0146167210388667

Paolini, S., Hewstone, M., & Cairns, E. (2007). Direct and indirect intergroup friendship effects: Testing the moderating role of the affective-cognitive bases of prejudice. *Personality and Social Psychology Bulletin, 33,* 1406–1420.

Paolini, S., Hewstone, M., Cairns, E., & Voci, A. (2004). Effects of direct and indirect cross-group friendships on judgments of Catholics and Protestants in Northern Ireland: The mediating role of an anxiety-reduction mechanism. *Personality and Social Psychology Bulletin, 30,* 770–786.

Paolini, S., Hewstone, M., Rubin, M. & Pay, H. (2004). Increased group dispersion after exposure to one deviant group member: Testing Hamburger's model of member-to-group generalization. *Journal of Experimental Social Psychology, 40,* 569–585.

Paolini, S., Hewstone, M., Voci, A., Harwood, J., & Cairns, E. (2006). Intergroup contact and the promotion of intergroup harmony: The influence of intergroup emotions. In R. Brown & D. Capozza (Eds.), *Social identities: Motivational, emotional, and cultural influences* (pp. 209–238). Hove, England: Psychology Press.

Pearson, A. R., West, T. V., Dovidio, J. F., Powers, S. R., Buck R., & Henning, R. (2008). The fragility of intergroup relations: Divergent effects of delayed audiovisual feedback in intergroup and intragroup interaction. *Psychological Science, 19,* 1272–1279.

Pennebaker, J. W., & Stone, L. D. (2003). Words of wisdom: Language use over the lifespan. *Journal of Personality and Social Psychology, 85,* 291–301.

Pettigrew, T. F. (1971). *Racially separate or together?* New York: McGraw-Hill.

Pettigrew, T. F. (1997). Generalized intergroup contact effects on prejudice. *Personality and Social Psychology Bulletin, 23,* 173–185.

Pettigrew, T. F. (1998). Intergroup contact theory. *Annual Review of Psychology, 49,* 65–85.

Pettigrew, T. F. (2009). Secondary transfer effect of contact: Do intergroup contact effects spread to noncontacted outgroups? *Social Psychology, 40,* 55–65. doi: 10.1027/1864-9335.40.2.55

Pettigrew, T. F., & Tropp, L. R. (2006). A meta-analytical test of the intergroup contact theory. *Journal of Personality and Social Psychology, 90,* 751–783.

Pettigrew, T. F., & Tropp, L. (2008). How does intergroup contact reduce prejudice? Meta-analytic tests of three mediators. *European Journal of Social Psychology, 38,* 922–934.

Plant, E. A. & Devine, P. (1998). Internal and external motivation to respond without prejudice. *Journal of Personality and Social Psychology, 75,* 811–832.

Plant, E. A., & Devine, P. G. (2003). The antecedents and implications of interracial anxiety. *Personality and Social Psychology Bulletin, 29,* 790–801.

Powers, D. A., & Ellison, C. G. (1995). Interracial contact and black racial attitudes: The contact hypothesis and selectivity bias. *Social Forces, 74,* 205–226.

Prestwich, A., Kenworthy, J. B., Wilson, M., & Kwan-Tat, N. (2008). Differential relations between two types of contact and implicit and explicit racial attitudes. *British Journal of Social Psychology, 47,* 575–588.

Ramasubramanian, S. (2007). Media-based strategies to reduce racial stereotypes activated by news stories. *Journalism and Mass Communication Quarterly, 84,* 249–264.

Reis, H. T., & Shaver, P. (1988). Intimacy as an interpersonal process. In S. Duck (Ed.), *Handbook of personal relationships* (pp. 367–389). Chichester, England: Wiley.

Richeson, J. A., Baird, A. A., Gordon, H. L., Heatherton, T. F., Wyland, C. L., Trawalter, S., & Shelton, J. N. (2003). An fMRI investigation of the impact of interracial contact on executive function. *Nature Neuroscience, 6,* 1323–1328.

Richeson, J. A., & Shelton, J. N. (2010). Prejudice in intergroup dyadic interactions. In J. F. Dovidio, M. Hewstone, P. Glick, & V. M. Esses (Eds.), *Handbook of prejudice, stereotyping and discrimination* (pp. 276–293). London: Sage.

Richeson, J. A., & Trawalter, S. (2005). Why do interracial interactions impair executive function? A resource depletion account. *Journal of Personality and Social Psychology, 88,* 934–947.

Robinson, J., & Preston, J. D. (1976). Equal-status contact and modification of racial prejudice: A reexamination of the contact hypothesis. *Social Forces, 54,* 911–924.

Schiappa, E., Gregg, P. B., & Hewes, D. E. (2005). The parasocial contact hypothesis. *Communication Monographs, 72,* 92–115.

Schiappa, E., Gregg, P. B., & Hewes, D. E. (2006). Can one TV show make a difference? *Will & Grace* and the parasocial contact hypothesis. *Journal of Homosexuality, 51,* 15–37.

Schnall, S., & Laird, J. D. (2003). Keep smiling: Enduring effects of facial expressions and postures on emotional experience and memory. *Cognition and Emotion, 17,* 787–797.

Schulze, B., & Angermeyer, M. C. (2003). Subjective experiences of stigma: A focus group study of schizophrenia patients, their relatives, and mental health professionals. *Social Science and Medicine, 56*, 299–312.

Sharp, M., Voci, A., & Hewstone, M. (2011). Individual difference variables as moderators of the effect of extended cross-group friendship on prejudice: Testing the effects of public self-consciousness and social comparison. *Group Processes & Intergroup Relations, 14*, 207–221. doi: 10.1177/1368430210391122

Shelton, J. N. (2003). Interpersonal concerns in social encounters between majority and minority group members. *Group Processes and Intergroup Relations, 6*, 171–185.

Shelton, J. N., & Richeson, J. A. (2005). Pluralistic ignorance and intergroup contact. *Journal of Personality and Social Psychology, 88*, 91–107.

Shelton, J. N., & Richeson, J. A. (2006). Interracial interactions: A relational approach. In M. P. Zanna (Ed.), *Advances in experimental social psychology* (Vol. 38, pp. 121–181). San Diego, CA: Academic Press.

Shelton, J. N., Richeson, J. A., & Vorauer, J. D. (2006). Threatened identities and interethnic interactions. In W. Stroebe & M. Hewstone (Eds.), *European review of social psychology* (Vol. 17, pp. 321–358). Hove, England: Psychology Press.

Shepard, C. A., Giles, H., & LePoire, B. A. (2001). Communication accommodation theory. In W. P. Robinson & H. Giles (Eds.), *The new handbook of language and social psychology* (pp. 33–56). Chichester, England: Wiley.

Sidanius, J., Levin, S., van Laar, C., & Sears, D. O. (2009). *The diversity challenge: Social identity and intergroup relations on the college campus.* New York: Russell Sage Foundation.

Soliz, J., Ribarsky, E., Harrigan, M. M., & Tye-Williams, S. (2009). Perceptions of communication with gay and lesbian family members: Predictors of relational satisfaction and implications for outgroup attitudes. *Communication Quarterly, 58*, 77–95.

Soliz, J., Thorson, A. R., & Rittenour, C. E. (2009). Communicative predictors of relational satisfaction, shared family identity, and ethnic group salience in multiethnic families. *Journal of Marriage and Family, 71*, 819–832.

Spears, R., Postmes, T., Lea, M., & Wolbert, A. (2002). When are net effects gross products? The power of influence and the influence of power in computer-mediated communication. *Journal of Social Issues, 58*, 91–107.

Stathi, S., & Crisp, R. J. (2008). Imagining intergroup contact promotes projection to outgroups. *Journal of Experimental Social Psychology, 44*, 943–957.

Stephan, W. G. (1987). The contact hypothesis in intergroup relations. In C. Hendrick (Ed.), *Group processes and intergroup relations: Review of personality and social psychology* (Vol. 9, pp. 13–40). Newbury Park, CA: Sage.

Stephan, W. G., & Stephan, C. W. (1984). The role of ignorance in intergroup relations. In N. Miller & M. B. Brewer (Eds.), *Groups in contact: The psychology of desegregation* (pp. 229–255). Orlando, FL: Academic Press.

Stephan, W. G., & Stephan, C. W. (1985). Intergroup anxiety. *Journal of Social Issues, 41*, 157–175.

Stephan, W. G., & Stephan, C. W. (2000). An integrated threat theory of prejudice. In S. Oskamp (Ed.), *Reducing prejudice and discrimination* (pp. 23–46). Hillsdale, NJ: Erlbaum.

Stephan, W. G., Ybarra, O., & Morrison, K. R. (2009). Intergroup threat theory. In T. D. Nelson (Ed.), *Handbook of prejudice, stereotyping, and discrimination* (pp. 43–60). New York: Psychology Press.

Stewart, C. O., Pitts, M. J., & Osborne, H. (2011). Mediated intergroup conflict: The discursive construction of "illegal immigrants" in a regional U.S. newspaper. *Journal of Language & Social Psychology, 30,* 8–27. doi: 10.1177/0261927X10387099

Swart, H., Hewstone, M., Christ, O., & Voci, A. (2011). Affective mediators of intergroup contact: A three-wave longitudinal study in South Africa. *Journal of Personality and Social Psychology, Journal of Personality and Social Psychology, 101,* 1221–1238. doi: 10.1037/a0024450

Tam, T., Hewstone, M., Cairns, E., Tausch, N., Maio, G., & Kenworthy, J. B. (2007). The impact of intergroup emotions on forgiveness in Northern Ireland. *Group Processes and Intergroup Relations, 10,* 119–135.

Tam, T., Hewstone, M., Harwood, J., Voci, A., & Kenworthy, J. (2006). Intergroup contact and grandparent-grandchild communication: The effects of self-disclosure on implicit and explicit biases against older people. *Group Processes Intergroup Relations, 9,* 413–429. doi: 10.1177/1368430206064642

Tausch, N., & Hewstone, M. (2010). Intergroup contact and prejudice. In J. F. Dovidio, M. Hewstone, P. Glick, & V. M. Esses (Eds.), *The Sage handbook of prejudice, stereotyping, and discrimination* (pp. 544–560). Newburg Park, CA: Sage.

Tausch, N., Hewstone, M., Kenworthy, J. B., Psaltis, C., Schmid, K., Popan, J. R., & Hughes, J. (2010). Secondary transfer effects of intergroup contact: Alternative accounts and underlying processes. *Journal of Personality and Social Psychology, 99,* 282–302. doi: 10.1037/a0018553

Tausch, N., Hewstone, M., Schmid, K., Hughes, J., & Cairns, E. (2011). Extended contact effects as a function of closeness of relationship with ingroup contacts. *Group Processes and Intergroup Relations, 14,* 239–254. doi: 10.1177/1368430210390534.

Tausch, N., Kenworthy, J., & Hewstone, M. (2005). The contribution of intergroup contact to the reduction of intergroup conflict. In M. Fitzduff & C. E. Stout (Eds.), The *psychology of global conflicts: From war to peace* (Vol. 2, pp. 67–108). New York: Praeger.

Tausch, N., Tam, T., Hewstone, M., Kenworthy, J. B., & Cairns, E. (2007). Individual-level and group-level mediators of contact effects in Northern Ireland: The moderating role of social identification. *British Journal of Social Psychology, 46,* 541–556.

Thompson, L., & Nadler, J. (2002). Negotiating via information technology: Theory and application. *Journal of Social Issues, 58,* 109–124.

Ting-Toomey, S., & Oetzel, J. (2001). *Managing intercultural conflict effectively.* Thousand Oaks, CA: Sage.

Trawalter, S., & Richeson, J. A. (2008). Let's talk about race, Baby! When Whites' and Blacks' interracial contact experiences diverge. *Journal of Experimental Social Psychology, 44,* 1214–1217.

Trew, K. (1986). Catholic–Protestant contact in Northern Ireland. In M. Hewstone & R. J. Brown (Eds.), *Contact and conflict in intergroup encounters* (pp. 93–106). Oxford, England: Blackwell.

Tropp, L. R. (2003). The psychological impact of prejudice: Implications for intergroup contact. *Group Processes and Intergroup Relations, 6,* 131–149.

Tropp, L.R. (2006). Stigma and intergroup contact among members of minority and majority status groups. In S. Levin & C. van Laar (Eds.), *Stigma and group inequality: Social psychological perspectives* (pp. 171–191). Mahwah, NJ: Erlbaum.

Tropp, L. R. (2008). The role of trust in intergroup contact: Its significance and implications for improving relations between groups. In U. Wagner, L. R. Tropp, G.

Finchilescu, & C. Tredoux (Eds.), *Improving intergroup relations* (pp. 91–106). Malden, MA: Blackwell.

Tropp, L. R. & Pettigrew, T. F. (2005a). Relationships between intergroup contact and prejudice among minority and majority status groups. *Psychological Science, 16*, 951–957.

Tropp, L. R., & Pettigrew, T. F. (2005b). Differential relationships between intergroup contact and affective and cognitive dimensions of prejudice. *Personality and Social Psychology Bulletin, 31*, 1145–1158.

Turner, R. N., & Crisp, R. J. (2010). Imagining intergroup contact reduces implicit prejudice. *British Journal of Social Psychology, 49*, 129–142.

Turner, R. N., Crisp, R. J., & Lambert, E. (2007). Imagining intergroup contact can improve intergroup attitudes. *Group Processes and Intergroup Relations, 10*, 427–441.

Turner, R. N., Hewstone, M., & Voci, A. (2007). Reducing explicit and implicit prejudice via direct and extended contact: The mediating role of self-disclosure and intergroup anxiety. *Journal of Personality and Social Psychology, 93*, 369–388.

Turner, R. N., Hewstone, M., Voci, A., Paolini, S., & Christ, O. (2007). Reducing prejudice via direct and extended cross-group friendship. In W. Stroebe & M. Hewstone (Eds.), *European review of social psychology* (Vol. 18, pp. 212–255). Hove, England: Psychology Press.

Turner, R. N., Hewstone, M., Voci, A., & Vonofakou, C. (2008). A test of the extended contact hypothesis: The mediating role of intergroup anxiety, perceived ingroup and outgroup norms, and inclusion of the outgroup in the self. *Journal of Personality and Social Psychology, 95*, 843–860.

van Dijk, T. A. (1987). *Communicating racism: Ethnic prejudice in thought and talk.* Newbury Park, CA: Sage.

Van Laar, C., Levin, S., Sinclair, S., & Sidanius, J. (2005). The effect of university roommate contact on ethnic attitudes and behavior. *Journal of Experimental Social Psychology, 41*, 329–345.

Van Oudenhoven, J. P., Groenewald, J. T., & Hewstone, M. (1996). Cooperation, ethnic salience and generalization of inter ethnic attitudes. *European Journal of Social Psychology, 26*, 649–662.

Vidmar, N., & Rokeach, M. (1974). Archie Bunker's bigotry: A study in selective perception and exposure. *Journal of Communication, 24*, 36–47.

Voci, A., & Hewstone, M. (2003). Intergroup contact and prejudice towards immigrants in Italy: The mediational role of anxiety and the moderational role of group salience. *Group Processes and Intergroup Relations, 6*, 37–54.

Vonofakou, C., Hewstone, M., & Voci, A. (2007). Contact with outgroup friends as a predictor of meta-attitudinal strength and accessibility of attitudes towards gay men. *Journal of Personality and Social Psychology, 92*, 804–820.

Vonofakou, C., Hewstone, M., Voci, A., Paolini, S., Turner, R., Tausch, N., …Cairns, E. (2008). The impact of direct and extended cross-group friendships on improving intergroup relations. In U. Wagner, L. R. Tropp, G. Finchilescu, & C. Tredoux (Eds.), *Improving intergroup relations: Building on the legacy of Thomas F. Pettigrew* (pp. 107–124). Oxford, England: Blackwell.

Vorauer, J. D. (in press). Getting past the self: Understanding and removing evaluative concerns as an obstacle to positive intergroup contact effects. In G. Hodson & M. Hewstone (Eds.), *Advances in intergroup contact.* New York: Psychology Press.

Vorauer, J. D., Hunter, A. J., Main, K. J., & Roy, S. (2000). Meta-stereotype activation: Evidence from indirect measures for specific evaluative concerns experienced by members of dominant groups in intergroup interaction. *Journal of Personality and Social Psychology, 78*, 690–707.

Vorauer, J. D., & Kumhyr, S. M. (2001). Is this about you or me? Self-versus other-directed judgments and feelings in response to intergroup interaction. *Personality and Social Psychology Bulletin, 27*, 706–719.

Walker, P., Silvert, L., Hewstone, M., & Nobre, A. C. (2008). Social contact and other-race face processing in the human brain. *Social Cognitive and Affective Neuroscience, 3*, 16–25.

Walther, J. B. (2009). Computer-mediated communication and virtual groups: Applications to interethnic conflict. *Journal of Applied Communication Research, 37*, 225–238.

West, K., Holmes, E. A., & Hewstone, M. (2011). Enhancing imagined contact to reduce prejudice against people with schizophrenia. *Group Processes and Intergroup Relations, 14*, 407–428.

Wilder, D. A. (1984). Intergroup contact: The typical member and the exception to the rule. *Journal of Experimental Social Psychology, 20*, 177–194.

Wilder, D. A., & Shapiro, P. N. (1989). The role of competition-induced anxiety in limiting the beneficial impact of positive behavior by an out-group member. *Journal of Personality and Social Psychology, 56*, 60–69.

Williams, R. M. (1947). *The reduction of intergroup tensions.* New York: SSRC.

Wright, S. C., Aron, A., McLaughlin-Volpe, T., & Ropp, S. A. (1997). The extended contact effect: Knowledge of cross-group friendships and prejudice. *Journal of Personality and Social Psychology, 73*, 73–90.

4 *Commentary*
Communication and the Contact Hypothesis

Cindy Gallois

University of Queensland

This large and comprehensive paper by Harwood, Hewstone, Amichai-Hamburger, and Tausch, is a very welcome addition to the literature on intergroup communication. The contact hypothesis has been around and actively researched (in recent years, particularly by these researchers and their many colleagues) for more than 50 years in social psychology. Even so, the groundbreaking idea that there are conditions for intergroup contact that ameliorate perceptions across race, gender, generation, and the like, has only recently come under systematic enquiry in communication. Yet intergroup contact is first and foremost a communication phenomenon, and should be studied through the lens of communication. As the authors note, the social-psychological emphasis has inevitably meant that the research focus has been on antecedent conditions for positive contact and the consequences of contact, with far less attention paid to the dynamics of the contact itself (cf. Hornsey, Gallois, & Duck, 2008). There is an opportunity for communication scholars, in both interpersonal and mediated communication, to contribute greatly to our understanding of intergroup contact in terms of the contact hypothesis, an opportunity that has only begun to be realized.

At the same time, the interest within our field in the negative side of contact and intergroup relations is great and increasing, with studies about intergroup perspectives on hate speech, racism (and other isms) in the media, subtle and covert expressions of intergroup conflict—too many to catalogue here. Following the globalization of organizations, media, and the like, there is also great interest in the impact of diversity on team performance, intergroup attitudes, conflict, and reconciliation. This very timely review paper provides an excellent opportunity to bring this literature together with the systematic approach of the contact hypothesis, toward a more comprehensive theory of intergroup contact.

The authors do us a great service by presenting an unusually comprehensive review of the literature on the contact hypothesis, emphasizing more recent work but going right back to the beginning with Allport (1954). Their perspective is interdisciplinary, but wherever they can, the authors draw out the communication process of intergroup contact, and they present most if not all of the communication literature on the contact hypothesis. They move systematically through direct (interpersonal) and indirect (mediated) contact; the latter is especially interesting given the large impact of the mass media. To my knowledge, this is the first review paper to bring in mediated communication so explicitly, through the concepts of extended contact (e.g., through friends having contact that one hears about), vicarious contact, mainly via the mass media (news or entertainment), and imagined contact. This strongly integrative section will be very useful to both researchers and students.

Harwood and his coauthors go on to review the literature on the moderators and mediators of contact (intergroup anxiety, intergroup threat, empathy, identification with a larger or cross-cutting social category), all broadly consistent with their perspective of social identity theory. They link research on the contact hypothesis explicitly to social identity, stressing the important role of typicality of group members, the impact of the sociohistorical context, and the different effects of contact on majority and minority group members. This extension is important, as much of the research on the contact hypothesis has been experimental, focusing on an immediate interaction and its consequences. Most intergroup contact is long-term and uncontrolled, so they point to important research directions. Even so, their conclusion is that these mediators and moderators can enhance or attenuate the impact of positive contact, but do not in general reverse the impact of contact.

This conclusion includes communicative mediators of contact, including self-disclosure and communication accommodation (cf. Giles, 1973; see recent reviews, e.g., Gallois, Ogay, & Giles, 2005). Most communication research on the contact hypothesis involves intergenerational communication, concentrating on younger and older adults, among them elderly relatives (e.g., Tam, Hewstone, Harwood, Voci, & Kenworthy, 2006; but see also Williams & Giles, 1996); much of it has been done by these authors and their colleagues. There is ample room to extend this research to other intergroup contexts. Finally, the authors review the consequences of contact on attitudes, particularly intergroup trust and forgiveness. This research sometimes employs novel methods, such as implicit and physiological measures of attitudes.

Overall, the conclusion that in the right conditions, contact leads to more positive attitudes across groups (even when prior attitudes are controlled for), is robust and compelling. Not only does positive and equal-status contact, as predicted, lead to more positive intergroup perceptions and attitudes, this attitude change tends to generalize to other groups as well. This powerful conclusion has been useful for many years in attempts to reduce intergroup conflict, and this paper finishes with a research agenda to increase the usefulness and reach of the contact hypothesis in the future. The authors show how communication theory can be integrated into research using the parameters of the contact hypothesis, and work can be extended to mediated forms of communication. The section on imagined communication, with its resonance to research on imagined interactions (e.g., Harwood, Paolini, Joyce, Rubin, & Arroyo, 2011;

Honeycutt, 2010) has special potential to be linked to the long tradition of communication research on parasocial relationships.

Of course, there are some things that are not in this paper, but which could easily be integrated into the research directions sketched in it. First, there is a large literature on team diversity, dating at least from the 1990s (e.g., Jackson, May, & Whitney, 1995; Oetzel, 1995). Much of this work concerns heterogeneous virtual teams in the context of business globalization (e.g., DeSanctis & Poole, 1997; Jarvenpaa, Knoll, & Leidner, 1998). Unlike those working on the contact hypothesis, these researchers have tended to find that, while diversity promotes a larger base for ideas, it also produces more conflict and lower levels of satisfaction. To some extent, this research has undermined confidence in diverse work teams. Thus, it would be fruitful to contrast its research paradigm with the contact hypothesis, and to explicate the differences in results, rather than to continue these research paradigms independently of each other.

The area of negative contact would also profit from more integration with the contact hypothesis. It is almost a truism to say that much intergroup contact is negative, and the authors comment on the ease with which negative reports in the media or personal experiences can produce increases in prejudice. Indeed, over the years many people have denigrated the impact of contact because of all the negative examples. Much intergroup contact evolves in neighborhoods, where small resentments and perceived threats can grow into major prejudice and conflict. The emphasis in communication research on mediated communication means that we are flooded with analyses of negative contact. Harwood and his coauthors go some way to explicating the differences between this work and research on the contact hypothesis, but more needs to be done. We need to face up to the impact on our research of our own theoretical positions and values; only then can we really explain the contradictions (and differences) in these research paradigms. Existing research makes it clear that communication accommodation—the sociolinguistic strategies and moves made in conversation and elsewhere—have a large role to play. Indeed, this might be a good opportunity to extend communication accommodation theory further into mediated and indirect communication.

There are some possibilities for extension of communication research that the authors do not mention, but that are compatible with their research agenda. One path concerns the examination of whether intergroup contact is public or private. This variable is related to the typicality of group members, but is not quite the same. A great deal of face-to-face intergroup contact (and, of course, the vast majority of media-based indirect contact) takes place in the public sphere, especially where organisations are involved. For example, in the maternity care sector in Australia (where I do research), there is serious intergroup conflict between obstetricians and midwives, involving prejudice, discrimination, and highly nonaccommodative communication. In private, however, many doctors and midwives work together and communicate very positively, in conditions that meet all the requirements of the contact hypothesis. Individual practitioners engage in complex subtyping in order to carry this off, so that the impact of intergroup prejudice is hard to specify but well worth studying. There are many contexts like this, including those that involve factors like ethnicity, gender, and religion, and which potentially provide key information about intergroup contact.

There is also an opportunity to study the triggers to positive and negative contact in more detail, as well as to elucidate the limiting conditions for positive contact. What are the contexts where positive contact cannot be achieved, and can indirect contact attenuate these contexts? The authors mention these factors, and there is every reason to add them to the agenda. Overall, the authors have challenged us as communication researchers to take on the contact hypothesis and its empirical bases, to compare its methods and its perspectives to our own, and to expand our consideration of intergroup communication. This can only benefit both the contact hypothesis and communication research as a whole.

References

Allport, G. W. (1954). *The nature of prejudice*. Reading, MA: Addison-Wesley.

DeSanctis, G., & Poole, M. S. (1997). Transitions in teamwork in new organizational forms. *Advances in Group Processes, 14,* 157–176. Greenwich, CT: JAI Press.

Gallois, C., Ogay, T., & Giles, H. (2005). Communication accommodation theory: A look back and a look ahead. In W. Gudykunst (Ed.), *Theorizing about intercultural communication* (pp. 121–148). Thousand Oaks, CA: Sage.

Giles, H. (1973). Accent mobility: A model and some data. *Anthropological Linguistics, 15*(2), 87–109.

Harwood, J., Paolini, S., Joyce, N., Rubin, M., & Arroyo, A. (2011). Secondary transfer effects from imagined contact: Group similarity affects the generalization gradient. *British Journal of Social Psychology, 50,* 180–189. doi:10.1348/014466610X524263

Honeycutt, J. M. (2010). Imagined interactions. *American Psychologist, 65,* 129–130. doi:10.1037/a0018052

Hornsey, M. J., Gallois, C., & Duck, J. M. (2008). The intersection of communication and social psychology: Points of contact and points of difference. *Journal of Communication, 58,* 749–766.

Jackson, S. E., May, K. E., & Whitney, K. (1995). Understanding the dynamics of diversity in decision-making teams. In R. A. Guzzo & E. Salas (Eds.), *Team effectiveness and decision making in organizations* (pp. 7–261). San Francisco, CA: Jossey-Bass.

Jarvenpaa, S. L., Knoll, K., & Leidner, D. E. (1998). Is anybody out there? The implications of trust in global virtual teams. *Journal of Management Information Systems, 14*(4), 29–64.

Oetzel, J. G. (1995). Intercultural small groups: An effective decision-making theory. In R. L. Wiseman (Ed.), *Intercultural communication theory* (pp. 247–270). Thousand Oaks, CA: Sage.

Tam, T., Hewstone, M., Harwood, J., Voci, A., & Kenworthy, J. (2006). Intergroup contact and grandparent–grandchild communication: The effects of self-disclosure on implicit and explicit biases against older people. *Group Processes Intergroup Relations, 9*, 413–429. doi:10.1177/1368430206064642

Williams, A., & Giles, H. (1996). Intergenerational conversations: Young adults' retrospective accounts. *Human Communication Research, 23*, 220–250. doi:10.1111/j.1468-2958.1996.tb00393.x

CHAPTER CONTENTS

5 The Relative Persuasiveness of Different Forms of Arguments-From-Consequences

A Review and Integration

Daniel J. O'Keefe

Northwestern University

Research on persuasive communication has explored a great many different message variations as possible influences on persuasive effectiveness, including image-oriented versus product-quality-oriented advertisements for consumer products, arguments based on long-term or short-term consequences of the advocated action, promotion-oriented versus prevention-oriented appeals, gain-framed versus loss-framed appeals, individualist-oriented appeals versus collectivist-oriented appeals, strong versus weak arguments, and variations in fear appeals—with these commonly treated as more or less independent areas of work. This essay argues that these and other lines of research are in fact quite closely related, because all examine variations of a single argument form, argument-from-consequences. Correspondingly, their findings fit together neatly to underwrite several broad generalizations about the relative persuasiveness of different varieties of consequence-based arguments.

Research on persuasive communication has explored a great many different message variations as possible influences on persuasive effectiveness. Among these—and this is not a comprehensive list—are studies concerning image-oriented versus product-quality-oriented advertisements for consumer products, arguments based on long-term or short-term consequences of the advocated action, promotion-oriented versus prevention-oriented appeals, gain-framed versus loss-framed appeals, individualist-oriented appeals versus collectivist-oriented appeals, strong versus weak arguments, and variations in fear appeals.

These different lines of research are commonly treated as more or less independent enterprises. For example, studies of argument quality variations, fear appeals, and image-oriented versus product-quality-oriented ads do not appear to have much to do with each other.

This essay argues that in fact a great many of these different lines of research are quite closely related, and their findings can be seen to fit together neatly. In what follows, the analysis is introduced by identifying a common form of persuasive appeal that has implicitly been the focus of attention in these various different lines of research, namely, consequence-based arguments. The essay then offers four broad empirical generalizations concerning variations of consequence-based arguments. These generalizations fit these apparently unrelated lines of research into a simple but general conceptual housing.

Consequence-Based Arguments

One of the most basic kinds of argument for supporting a recommended action (policy, behavior, etc.) is a conditional that links the advocated action—the antecedent—with some desirable outcome—the consequent. The general abstract form is: "If the advocated action A is undertaken, then desirable consequence D will occur." Sometimes the conditional is expressed relatively explicitly ("If you wear sunscreen, you'll have attractive skin when you're older"; "If our city creates dedicated bicycle lanes, the number of traffic accidents will be reduced"), sometimes not ("My proposed economic program will increase employment"; "This automobile gets great gas mileage"), and sometimes the consequences of not undertaking the advocated action are cited ("If we don't adopt these fiscal measures, the economy will sink into a recession"), but the underlying form of the appeal is the same, namely, an invocation of potential consequences as a basis for justifying a course of action.

Various conceptual treatments of argument varieties have recognized this kind of argument as distinctive. Perelman (1959) called this appeal form a "pragmatic argument," an argument that "consists in estimating an action, or any event, or a rule, or whatever it may be, in terms of its favorable or unfavorable consequences" (p. 18). Walton (1996) labeled it "argument from consequences," describing it as "a species of practical reasoning where a contemplated policy or course of action is positively supported by citing the good consequences of it. In the negative form, a contemplated action is rejected on the grounds that it will have bad consequences" (p. 75). And this argument form is a recognizably familiar kind of justification. For example, Schellens and de Jong (2004) reported that all 20 of the public information brochures they examined invoked arguments from consequences, whereas, for example, only six used authority-based appeals.

Persuasive Effects of Variations in Consequence-Based Arguments

Although not anywhere explicitly acknowledged previously, a good deal of social-scientific persuasion research has addressed the question of the relative persuasiveness of different forms of consequence-based arguments. Taken together, the existing research underwrites four broad generalizations about consequence-based persuasive message variations. The generalizations concern, in turn, comparisons of appeals invoking more and less desirable consequences of compliance with the advocated view, comparisons of appeals invoking more and less undesirable consequences of noncompliance with the advocated view, comparisons of appeals invoking either desirable consequences of compliance or undesirable consequences of noncompliance, and comparisons of appeals invoking more and less likely consequences of compliance or noncompliance.

Comparing More and Less Desirable Consequences of Compliance

One recurring research question in persuasion effects research has—implicitly—been whether the persuasiveness of consequence-based arguments is influenced by the *desirability* of the claimed consequence (or more carefully: whether the persuasiveness of the argument is influenced by the audience's perception of the desirability of the claimed consequence). Abstractly put, the experimental contrast is between arguments of the form: "If advocated action A is undertaken, then *very* desirable consequence D1 will occur," and "If advocated action A is undertaken, then *slightly* desirable consequence D2 will occur."

Now one might think that the answer would be too obvious to bother investigating. *Of course* appeals that invoke more desirable consequences will be more persuasive than those invoking less desirable consequences. However, the overt research question has not been expressed quite this baldly, but instead has been couched in other terms. For example, many studies have examined a question of the form: "Do people who differ with respect to characteristic X differ in their responsiveness to corresponding kinds of persuasive appeals?"—where characteristic X is actually a proxy for variations in what people value. This section first reviews such research concerning four different personal characteristics (self-monitoring, consideration of future consequences, regulatory focus, and individualism-collectivism), and then discusses how elaboration likelihood model "argument quality" variations reflect the same underlying message property.

Self-Monitoring and Consumer Advertising Appeals. Considerable research attention has been given to the role of the personality variable of self-monitoring in influencing the relative persuasiveness of consumer advertising messages that deploy either image-oriented appeals or product-quality-oriented appeals. Self-monitoring refers to the control or regulation (monitoring) of one's self-presentation (see Gangestad & Snyder, 2000, for a useful review). High self-monitors are concerned about the image they project to others, and tailor their conduct to fit the situation at hand. Low self-monitors are less concerned about their projected image, and mold their behavior to fit their attitudes and values rather than external circumstances.

Hence in the realm of consumer products, high self-monitors are likely to stress the image-related aspects of products, whereas low self-monitors are more likely to be concerned with whether the product's intrinsic properties match the person's criteria for such products. Correspondingly, high and low self-monitors are expected to differ in their reactions to different kinds of consumer advertising, and specifically are expected to react differently to appeals emphasizing the image of the product or its users and appeals emphasizing the intrinsic quality of the product (e.g., Snyder & DeBono, 1987).

Consistent with this analysis, across a large number of studies, high self-monitors have been found to react more favorably to image-oriented advertisements than to product-quality-oriented ads, with the opposite effect found for low self-monitors (e.g., DeBono & Packer, 1991; Lennon, Davis, & Fairhurst, 1988; Snyder & DeBono, 1985; Zuckerman, Gioioso, & Tellini, 1988). Parallel differences between high and low self-monitors have been found with related appeal variations outside the realm of consumer advertising (e.g., Lavine & Snyder, 1996).

Although these effects are conventionally described as a matter of high and low self-monitors having different "attitude functions" to which messages are adapted (e.g., DeBono, 1987), a more straightforward account is that these effects reflect differential evaluation of consequences. High and low self-monitors characteristically differ in their evaluations of various outcomes and object attributes; for instance, high self-monitors place a higher value on aspects of self-image presentation. Given this difference in evaluation, it is entirely unsurprising that high self-monitors find image-oriented appeals to be especially persuasive in comparison to appeals emphasizing product attributes that are, in their eyes, not so desirable. That is, product-quality appeals and image-oriented appeals are differentially persuasive to high self-monitors because the appeals invoke differentially desirable consequences. And the same reasoning applies to low self-monitors: they value the sorts of product attributes mentioned in the product-quality-oriented appeals more than they do those mentioned in the image-oriented appeals—and so naturally are more persuaded by the former than by the latter.

So although this research masquerades as a question about the role of a personality variable in attitude function and persuasion, what the research shows is that for a given message recipient, appeals will be more persuasive if they offer the prospect of consequences the recipient finds relatively more desirable than if they offer the prospect of consequences the recipient finds relatively less desirable. Because high and low self-monitors differ in their relative evaluation of image-oriented and product-quality-oriented consequences, appeals that invoke different kinds of consequences correspondingly vary in persuasiveness.[1]

None of this denies the utility of research focused particularly on self-monitoring and persuasive appeals. It is valuable to know that people systematically differ in their relative evaluations of (specifically) the image-oriented characteristics and the product-quality-oriented characteristics of consumer products, and hence that image-oriented advertising and product-quality-oriented advertising will be differentially persuasive depending on the audience's level of self-monitoring.

But what underlies these findings is a rather more general phenomenon, namely, the greater persuasiveness of arguments that emphasize outcomes deemed especially desirable by the audience. At least when it comes to the consequences invoked by the arguments in these studies' messages, self-monitoring variations go proxy for value variations—and hence these effects of self-monitoring variations on the persuasiveness of different appeals can be straightforwardly ascribed to the underlying variation in evaluations.

Consideration of Future Consequences (CFC) and Corresponding Appeal Variations. An example entirely parallel to that of self-monitoring is provided by research concerning the individual-difference variable known as "consideration of future consequences" (CFC; Strathman, Gleicher, Boninger, & Edwards, 1994). As the name suggests, this refers to differences in the degree to which people consider temporally distant (future) as opposed to temporally proximate (immediate) consequences of contemplated behaviors.

Perhaps unsurprisingly, persons differing in CFC respond differently to persuasive messages depending on whether the message's arguments emphasize immediate consequences (more persuasive for those low in CFC) or long-term consequences (more persuasive for those high in CFC). For example, Orbell and Hagger (2006) presented participants with one of two messages describing both positive and negative consequences of participating in a diabetes screening program. Participants low in CFC were more persuaded to participate when the message described short-term positive consequences and long-term negative consequences; participants high in CFC were more persuaded by a message describing short-term negative consequences and long-term positive consequences (similarly, see Orbell & Kyriakaki, 2008).

As with the self-monitoring research, these findings—even if unsurprising—do represent a genuine contribution: such research underscores the importance of persuaders' thinking about whether the consequences they intend to emphasize are long-term or short-term, and how that connects to the audience's likely dispositions. That is, one substantive dimension of variation in consequences is their temporal immediacy, and attending to that dimension may be important for successful persuasion.

But, as with self-monitoring, what underlies these findings is the general phenomenon of heightened persuasiveness of consequence-based arguments that emphasize more desirable consequences of the advocated viewpoint. At least when it comes to the consequences invoked by the arguments in these studies' messages, CFC variations go proxy for value variations—and hence the effects of CFC variations on the persuasiveness of different appeals can be straightforwardly ascribed to the underlying variation in evaluations.

Regulatory Focus and Corresponding Appeal Variations. A third parallel example is provided by research concerning individual differences in "regulatory focus" (Higgins, 1997, 1998). Briefly, regulatory-focus variations reflect broad differences in people's motivational goals, and specifically a difference between a promotion focus, which emphasizes obtaining desirable outcomes (and hence involves a focus on accomplishments, aspirations, etc.), and a prevention focus, which emphasizes avoiding undesirable outcomes (and hence involves a focus on safety, security, etc.). This individual difference obviously affords a possible basis for adaptation of persuasive messages.

Persons differing in regulatory focus respond differently to persuasive messages depending on whether the message's arguments emphasize promotion-oriented outcomes or prevention-oriented outcomes. For example, Cesario, Grant, and Higgins (2004, Study 2, p. 393) presented participants with messages advocating a new after-school program for elementary and high school students, with the supporting arguments invoking consequences expressed either in promotion-oriented ways ("The primary reason for supporting this program is because it will advance children's education and support more children to succeed") or in prevention-oriented ways ("The primary reason for supporting this program is because it will secure children's education and prevent more children from failing"). Perhaps unsurprisingly, participants tended to be more persuaded by appeals that matched their motivational orientation (for a general review of such research, see Lee & Higgins, 2009).

In a way that is similar to research concerning self-monitoring and CFC, this work identifies another substantive dimension of variation in the consequences associated with the advocated behavior, namely, whether the consequences concern prevention or promotion. This finding is useful because it can emphasize to persuaders that, depending on the receiver's regulatory focus, advocates might prefer to emphasize either prevention-related or promotion-related outcomes.

But, as with self-monitoring and CFC, what underlies these findings is the general phenomenon of the greater persuasiveness of arguments-from-consequences that invoke more desirable consequences of the advocated action. At least when it comes to the consequences invoked by the arguments in these studies' messages, regulatory focus variations go proxy for variations in outcome evaluations—and hence the effects of regulatory focus variations on the persuasiveness of different appeals can be straightforwardly ascribed to the underlying variation in evaluations. (For research linking regulatory-focus differences with differences in more abstract personal values, see Leikas, Lonnqvist, Verkasalo, & Lindeman, 2009.)

Individualism-Collectivism and Corresponding Appeal Variations.   A final parallel example is provided by research on "individualism-collectivism," which refers to the degree to which individualist values (e.g., independence) are prioritized as opposed to collectivist values (e.g., interdependence). Although there is variation from person to person in individualism-collectivism, this dimension of difference has commonly been studied as one element of larger cultural orientations (see Hofstede, 1980, 2001). So, for example, Americans are likely to be relatively individualistic whereas Koreans, say, are more likely to be collectivistic. This variation in cultural values obviously affords a possible basis for adaptation of persuasive messages.

Perhaps unsurprisingly, persons from cultures differing in individualism-collectivism respond differently to persuasive messages depending on whether the message's appeals emphasize individualistic or collectivistic outcomes. For example, advertisements for consumer goods are more persuasive for American audiences when the ads emphasize individualistic outcomes ("This watch will help you stand out") rather than collectivistic ones ("This watch will help you fit in"), with the reverse being true for Chinese audiences (e.g., Aaker & Schmitt, 2001; for a review, see Hornikx & O'Keefe, 2009; for an individual-level example of the phenomenon, see van Baaren & Ruivenkamp, 2007). This effect plainly reflects underlying value differences—differences in the evaluation of various attributes of consumer products.

Thus, as with self-monitoring, CFC, and regulatory focus, these effects derive from the general phenomenon of the greater persuasiveness of consequence-based arguments that invoke more desirable consequences of the advocated action. At least when it comes to the consequences invoked by the arguments in these studies' messages, individualism-collectivism variations go proxy for variations in outcome evaluations—and hence these effects of individualism-collectivism variations on the persuasiveness of different appeals can be straightforwardly ascribed to the underlying variation in evaluations.

The Argument Thus Far. To summarize the argument to this point: Consequence-based appeals are more persuasive when they invoke outcomes of the advocated action that are (taken by the audience to be) relatively more desirable than when they invoke outcomes that are not valued so highly. Individuals can vary in their evaluations of consequences of an action, and so matching appeals to the audience's evaluations is important for persuasive success. Individual variations in the evaluation of particular sorts of outcomes can be related to a number of individual-difference variables—self-monitoring, individualistic-collectivistic orientation, regulatory focus, consideration of future consequences—but these all reflect underlying variation in the evaluations of consequences.

Although the individual-difference variables just discussed are perhaps the most studied, other individual differences have been the subject of similar investigation, that is, examination of the relative persuasiveness of appeals designed to match variations in receivers' psychological needs and values as inferred from an individual-difference variable. Studies by Bailis, Fleming, and Segall (2005), Faber, Karlen, and Christenson (1993), Kowert and Homer (1993), and Settle and Mizerski (1974)—examining, respectively, higher versus lower self-concordance, compulsive vs. normal buyers, firstborns versus later-borns, and inner- versus other-directed persons—provide just four examples.

Even where no systematic individual-difference variable is involved, various investigators have confirmed that where audience members differ in their evaluation of consequences, matching appeals to such variation (i.e., emphasizing outcomes thought by the audience to be desirable) can influence persuasive success. For example, Clary, Snyder, Ridge, Miene, and Haugen (1994) obtained importance ratings of various possible reasons for volunteering, and then presented participants with provolunteering messages that varied in the importance of the proffered reasons; messages invoking important reasons were more persuasive than those invoking unimportant reasons. Notably, work based on Fishbein's (1967) expectancy-value model of attitude, especially as embedded in the theory of reasoned action and its successors (e.g., Ajzen, 1991; Fishbein & Ajzen, 2010), has explicitly emphasized the utility of designing persuasive messages based on the audience's perception of the relative desirability of various consequences (e.g., Cappella, Yzer, & Fishbein, 2003; Fishbein & Yzer, 2003).[2]

So what might seem on the surface to be a crazy quilt of isolated research findings—about self-monitoring, regulatory focus, and so forth—in fact represents the repeated confirmation of a fundamental truth about what makes consequence-based arguments persuasive: Arguments-from-consequences are more persuasive to the extent that they emphasize how the advocated view yields outcomes thought by the audience to be relatively more (rather than less) desirable.

Argument Quality Variations in Elaboration Likelihood Model Research.   The research discussed to this point has focused on differences between people. The general idea has been that persons differ on some variable (e.g., self-monitoring), and that persuasive appeals matched to the audience's level of that variable will be more persuasive than mismatched appeals. But (the argument has been) these variables are all associated with systematic underlying variation in the evaluation of the consequences of the advocated action, and what makes a persuasive appeal matched or mismatched is whether the appeal emphasizes relatively more desirable consequences (matched) or relatively less desirable ones (mismatched).

However, the same basic phenomenon can be detected in an area of persuasion research not involving individual differences, namely, the effects of variation in (what has been called) "argument quality" or "argument strength." Argument-quality variations have figured prominently in research on Petty and Cacioppo's well-known elaboration likelihood model of persuasion (ELM; Petty & Cacioppo, 1986).

ELM researchers have used variations in argument quality as a device for assessing the degree to which message recipients closely attended to message contents. For example, Petty, Cacioppo, and Goldman (1981) varied argument quality, source expertise, and the audience's involvement with the persuasive issue (i.e., the personal relevance of the issue). Under conditions of low involvement, the persuasiveness of the message was more influenced by variations in expertise than by variations in argument quality; under conditions of high involvement, the reverse pattern obtained. The implication is that under conditions of higher involvement, audiences were more closely processing the message and so were more attentive to argument quality variations.

In such ELM research, "argument quality" has been defined in terms of persuasive effects. That is, a high-quality argument is one that, in pretesting, is relatively more persuasive (compared to a low-quality argument) under conditions of high elaboration (close message processing). The question of what makes those high-quality arguments more persuasive has not been of much interest to ELM researchers. From the perspective of ELM researchers, argument quality variations have been used "primarily as a methodological tool to examine whether some other variable increases or decreases message scrutiny, not to examine the determinants of argument cogency per se" (Petty & Wegener, 1998, p. 352).

But other researchers have naturally been concerned to identify the "active ingredient" in these ELM manipulations. There is now good evidence that the key element in ELM argument quality variations is variation in the evaluation of the consequences invoked by the arguments (Areni & Lutz, 1988; Hustinx, van Enschot, & Hoeken, 2007; van Enschot-van Dijk, Hustinx, & Hoeken, 2003; see also Johnson, Smith-McLallen, Killeya, & Levin, 2004). That is, the "argument quality" variations used in ELM research reflect underlying variations in the desirability of claimed consequences—the "strong argument" messages used consequence-based arguments with highly desirable outcomes, whereas the "weak argument" messages used consequence-based arguments with less desirable outcomes. Small wonder, then, that the strong arguments should turn out generally to be more persuasive than the weak arguments (Park, Levine, Westermann, Orfgen, & Foregger, 2007, p. 94).[3]

To illustrate this point concretely: One much-studied message topic in ELM research has been a proposal to mandate university senior comprehensive examinations as a graduation requirement. In studies with undergraduates as research participants, the "strong argument" messages used arguments such as "with mandatory senior comprehensive exams at our university, graduates would have better employment opportunities and higher starting salaries," whereas the "weak argument" messages had arguments such as "with mandatory senior comprehensive exams at our university, enrollment would increase" (see Petty & Cacioppo, 1986, pp. 54–59, for other examples of such arguments). It's not surprising that, at least under conditions of relatively close attention to message content, the "strong argument" messages would be more persuasive than the "weak argument" messages, because the messages almost certainly varied in the perceived desirability of the claimed outcomes.

So here is yet another empirical confirmation of the general point that consequence-based arguments become more persuasive with greater perceived desirability of the claimed consequences of the advocated view. Argument quality research offers a slightly different kind of evidentiary support than that represented by the previously discussed individual-difference research (self-monitoring and so on), because here there is likely to have been relative uniformity across audience members in the comparative evaluations of the consequences under discussion. That is, among the undergraduate message recipients in the ELM studies, there was presumably general agreement that, for example, enhanced employment opportunities is a more desirable outcome than is increased university enrollment, whereas the individual-difference studies focused on circumstances in which study participants varied in their evaluations. (Of course, in those individual-difference studies, evaluations would be relatively homogeneous within a given condition, such as among high self-monitors.)

Summary: Variation in the Desirability of the Consequences of the Advocated Action.   The effects observed in a number of distinct lines of persuasion research appear to all be driven by one fundamental underlying phenomenon, namely, that the persuasiveness of consequence-based arguments is influenced by the desirability of the depicted consequences of the advocated view: As the desirability of those consequences increases, the persuasiveness of the arguments is enhanced. This commonality has not been so apparent as it might have been, perhaps because persuasion researchers have not been as attentive as they might to the argumentative structure of the appeals used in their experimental messages. But once it is seen that these various lines of research all involve arguments based on consequences, and once it is seen that the experimental messages vary with respect to the desirability of the consequences invoked, then it becomes apparent that one basic process gives rise to all these apparently unrelated effects.

Indeed, this may justifiably be thought of as perhaps the single best supported empirical generalization about persuasion that can be described to date. Findings from a variety of different lines of research—self-monitoring, consideration of future consequences, regulatory focus, individualism-collectivism, argument quality—all buttress the conclusion that consequence-based arguments emphasizing relatively more desirable consequences of the advocated action are likely to be more persuasive than are arguments emphasizing relatively less desirable consequences.

Comparing More and Less Undesirable Consequences of Noncompliance

The just-discussed appeal variation involves variations in the consequent of a conditional in which the antecedent was adoption of the communicator's recommendation ("If advocated action A is undertaken"). But a parallel appeal variation can be identified in which the antecedent is a failure to adopt the recommended action ("If advocated action A is *not* undertaken") and the *undesirability* of the consequence varies. Abstractly put, the contrast here is between arguments of the form: "If advocated action A is not undertaken, then *very* undesirable consequence U1 will occur"; and "If advocated action A is not undertaken, then *slightly* undesirable consequence U2 will occur." And the research question is: which of these will be more persuasive?

Again, one might think the answer too obvious to merit study. *Of course* appeals that invoke very undesirable consequences will be more persuasive than those invoking mildly undesirable consequences. Nonetheless, this turns out to have been the object of considerable empirical research—but, as above, the research question has not been stated quite this plainly.

The work of interest here is research on "fear appeals," which are messages that invoke the specter of undesirable consequences from failing to follow the communicator's recommendations. Fear appeal research has addressed a number of different questions concerning the invocation of fear-arousing consequences as a means of persuasion, but one substantial line of work in this area has implicitly addressed the appeal variation of interest here. Specifically, considerable research has manipulated fear-arousal messages so as to vary the depicted undesirability of the consequences. In theoretical frameworks such as protection motivation theory (Rogers & Prentice-Dunn, 1997), this is represented as variation in "threat severity." For example, Block and Keller (1998, p. 1596) compared safer-sex messages that described the possible consequences of failing to adopt the advocated behaviors either as "AIDS-related cancers, dementia, and even death" (relatively high severity) or as "genital discharge, sores, and mild pain" (relatively low severity).

Perhaps unsurprisingly, the general research finding has been that threats perceived as more severe (i.e., more undesirable) make for more effective persuasive appeals than do threats perceived as less severe (less undesirable); see the meta-analytic reviews of de Hoog, Stroebe, and de Wit (2007), Floyd, Prentice-Dunn, and Rogers (2000), and Witte and Allen (2000). Expressed in terms of consequence-based arguments, the appropriate generalization is that appeals invoking consequences of noncompliance are more persuasive when the invoked consequences are relatively more undesirable than when the consequences are relatively less undesirable.

Interlude: Variation in the Evaluative Extremity of Consequences

Two variations of consequence-based arguments have been considered thus far, one where the consequences of adopting the advocated action differ in their desirability, the other where the consequences of not adopting the advocated action differ in their undesirability. But these two variations can plainly be housed together. Abstractly put, these comparisons consider variations in the extremity of evaluation of claimed outcomes. Unsurprisingly, consequences that are evaluated more extremely (more desirable consequences of adopting the advocated action, or more undesirable consequences of failing to adopt the advocated action) make for more persuasive appeals than do consequences that are less extremely evaluated.

Thus, as with self-monitoring, CFC, regulatory focus, individualism-collectivism, and argument quality, what produces the observed fear appeal threat-severity effects is the general phenomenon of the greater persuasiveness of consequence-based arguments that invoke more extremely evaluated consequences. Variations in perceived threat severity plainly represent variations in the evaluative extremity of potential outcomes—and hence these effects of variations in depicted threat severity can be straightforwardly ascribed to the underlying variation in evaluations.

Any persuasive circumstance that permits identification of systematic

variation across individuals in the extremity of the evaluation of consequences is one that permits corresponding adaptation of persuasive appeals.
If people of kind X and people of kind Y generally vary in their evaluation
of possible outcomes, then a persuader will want to craft different appeals
to type X audiences and to type Y audiences (as suggested by research on
self-monitoring, consideration of future consequences, regulatory focus, and
individualism-collectivism).

Similarly, any persuasive circumstance in which there is relative uniformity
(in a given audience) of the evaluation of particular consequences is a circumstance that permits corresponding construction of appeals in ways likely
to maximize the chances of persuasive success. When describing the consequences of adoption of the advocated course of action, advocates will naturally
want to emphasize those consequences the audience thinks most desirable (as
suggested by research on ELM research on argument quality). When describing the consequences of failing to adopt the advocated action, advocates will
naturally want to emphasize those consequences the audience thinks most
undesirable (as suggested by fear appeal research).

But, as will be apparent by now, the underlying phenomenon is exactly
the same in all these different lines of research. That may not have been easy
to see without closely considering the underlying argumentative structure
of these appeals—but once seen, the common thread is obvious: Persuasion
researchers have confirmed, over and over again, that the persuasiveness of
consequence-based arguments is affected by the evaluative extremity of the
depicted consequences.

To be sure, this generalization is in some ways of rather limited utility for
message designers. Although it may be true that it will generally be more persuasive to invoke evaluatively more extreme consequences, this principle does
not help a message designer identify exactly *which* consequences to emphasize
in a given persuasive circumstance. And identifying such consequences can
potentially be quite challenging. For example, some fear appeal research has
suggested that the threat of death will not always be more fearful than other
threats, and that different audiences find different threats fearful (e.g., Henley & Donovan, 2003; Murray-Johnson et al., 2001; Robertson, O'Neill, &
Wixom, 1972).

In that sense, the research to date adds something beyond this broad generalization, because it identifies various substantively different kinds of outcomes
whose evaluations might vary. To express this in terms of message design: A
persuader can, in addition to thinking abstractly about the audience's perceived
desirability of various consequences, also think concretely about some more
specific substantive aspects of the contemplated arguments. For example: Do
the contemplated appeals mostly emphasize long-term rather than short-term
consequences, and are consequences of that sort likely to appeal to the audience? Do the contemplated appeals mostly emphasize promotion-oriented
rather than prevention-oriented consequences, and are consequences of that
sort likely to appeal to the audience? And so forth.

Still, what makes these substantive variations of interest is that they correspond to underlying systematic differences in evaluation of consequences. That is, these particular substantive variations are manifestations of a more general and fundamental phenomenon. For that reason, message designers would be well-served by beginning with the larger organizing question ("What consequences will this audience find especially desirable or undesirable?") rather than with a raft of more specific questions about this or that particular substantive variation.

Comparing Desirable Consequences of Compliance and Undesirable Consequences of Noncompliance

Given the two forms of consequence-based argument already discussed—one based on the desirable consequences of compliance and one based on the undesirable consequences of noncompliance—one might naturally wonder whether there is any general difference in persuasiveness *between* these two forms. As it happens, the research literature on persuasion contains considerable research comparing consequences-of-compliance appeals (with the abstract form "If the advocated action A is undertaken, then desirable consequence D will occur") and consequences-of-noncompliance appeals ("If the advocated action A is not undertaken, then undesirable consequence U will occur").

This message variation is commonly labeled as the difference between "gain-framed" appeals (invoking the advantages of performing the advocated action) and "loss-framed" appeals (invoking the disadvantages of not performing the advocated action). For example, in Meyerowitz and Chaiken's (1987) classic study of breast self-examination (BSE) behavior, the gain-framed message included appeals such as: "Research shows that women who do BSE have an increased chance of finding a tumor in the early, more treatable stage of the disease," whereas the parallel appeal in the loss-framed message was: "Research shows that women who do not do BSE have a decreased chance of finding a tumor in the early, more treatable stage of the disease" (p. 504). Similarly, in McCaul, Johnson, and Rothman's (2002, p. 626) study of messages advocating getting flu shots, one message described consequences of getting a flu shot such as: "You will be less likely to get the flu this fall" and "If you do get the flu, you will probably not be as sick" (the gain-framed message), where the other described consequences of not getting a flu shot such as: "You will be more likely to get the flu this fall" and "If you do get the flu, you will probably be more sick" (the loss-framed message). These experimental manipulations straightforwardly compare appeals emphasizing desirable outcomes of adopting the advocated action and appeals emphasizing parallel undesirable outcomes of failing to adopt the advocated action.

In retrospect, perhaps the labels "gain-framed" and "loss-framed" for these message types were not quite as transparent as one might have liked. For example, "compliance-focused" (instead of "gain-framed") and "noncompliance-focused" (instead of "loss-framed") might have drawn attention to how the antecedents of these appeals vary, rather than the consequences. But "gain-framed" and "loss-framed" are too well-established in the research literature to suppose that any alternative terminology will have much purchase.

For two reasons, invoking undesirable consequences of noncompliance (loss framing) might be expected to generally be more persuasive than invoking desirable consequences of compliance (gain framing). One is the phenomenon of negativity bias, the generally greater impact of and sensitivity to negative information as compared to otherwise-equivalent positive information (for a review, see Cacioppo, Gardner, & Berntson, 1997). The other is the phenomenon of loss aversion, the general preference for avoiding losses as opposed to obtaining gains (e.g., Kahneman, Knetsch, & Thaler, 1990; Kahneman & Tversky, 1979). These two well-established psychological phenomena suggest there should be a natural persuasive advantage for appeals emphasizing the undesirable consequences of noncompliance (i.e., loss-framed appeals).

But it appears that there is no such general difference in persuasiveness between appeals invoking desirable consequences of compliance and appeals invoking parallel undesirable consequences of noncompliance. O'Keefe and Jensen's (2006) meta-analysis found no statistically significant difference in the persuasiveness of gain-framed and loss-framed appeals. Research on gain-framed and loss-framed appeals thus has turned to the question of whether some moderating factor might be at work, such that under some circumstances appealing to the desirable consequences of compliance will be more persuasive, whereas in other situations an appeal to the undesirable consequences of noncompliance will be more effective. Two particular moderators are of interest here: the nature of the advocated action (and specifically a contrast between disease detection and disease prevention) and the receiver's regulatory focus (a contrast between promotion and prevention orientations).

Disease Detection/Prevention as a Moderator.   The leading suggested moderator has been whether the advocated action is a disease prevention behavior (such as wearing sunscreen), for which appeals to desirable consequences of compliance are hypothesized to have an advantage, or a disease detection behavior (such as skin examinations), for which appeals to undesirable consequences of noncompliance are expected to be more persuasive (e.g., Salovey, Schneider, & Apanovitch, 2002; Salovey & Wegener, 2003). The empirical evidence in hand, however, does not seem to fit this picture: The two appeal forms do not significantly differ in persuasiveness for most disease prevention behaviors (O'Keefe & Jensen, 2007) or for most disease detection behaviors (O'Keefe & Jensen, 2009).

Regulatory Focus as a Moderator.   More recently, a second potential moderator of gain-loss message framing effects has been proposed: the receiver's regulatory focus. As discussed above, regulatory-focus variations concern the broad motivational differences between a promotion focus (which empha-sizes obtaining desirable outcomes) and a prevention focus (which emphasizes avoiding undesirable outcomes). This individual-difference variable is similar to approach–avoidance motivation (BAS/BIS; Carver & White, 1984), which suggests that individuals vary in their general sensitivity to reward (desirable outcome) or punishment (undesirable outcome) cues. Several investigators have hypothesized that promotion-oriented (approach-oriented) individuals should be more persuaded by gain-framed appeals than by loss-framed appeals, with the reverse pattern holding for prevention-oriented (avoidance-oriented) indi-viduals (e.g., Jeong et al., 2011; Latimer, Salovey, & Rothman, 2007).

The evidence bearing on this hypothesis is unfortunately flawed by virtue of a confusion about the nature of gain-framed and loss-framed appeals. Gain- and loss-framed appeals are conditional arguments that vary in the *antecedent*, that is, whether the antecedent is compliance (gain-framed) or noncompliance (loss-framed).[4] By contrast, regulatory focus variations are relevant to varia-tions in the substantive *consequences* invoked, and specifically whether the consequences are promotion-oriented or prevention-oriented.

Hence the interplay of gain-loss variations (different kinds of antecedents) and regulatory focus variations (different kinds of consequents) yields four possible appeal types: (a) gain-framed appeals that emphasize prevention con-sequences (e.g., "if you exercise, you'll reduce your risk of a stroke"); (b) gain-framed appeals that emphasize promotion consequences (e.g., "if you exercise, you'll have more energy"); (c) loss-framed appeals that emphasize prevention consequences (e.g., "if you don't exercise, you're missing out on a great way of reducing your stroke risk"); and (d) loss-framed appeals that emphasize pro-motion consequences (e.g., "if you don't exercise, you're missing out on a great way of increasing your energy").

Unfortunately, research examining the role of regulatory-focus variations in gain-loss framing effects has not always isolated the effect of gain-loss framing variations (antecedent variations); it has often confounded antecedent-related variations (compliance vs. noncompliance) and consequent-related variations (promotion vs. prevention consequences). As an illustration, consider Jeong et al.'s (2011) study, in which participants varying in approach/avoidance (BAS/BIS) motivation were presented with gain-framed and loss-framed messages advocating charitable donations. For example, one gain-framed appeal was: "The library at Jefferson University is in need of funding. With funds, it will be able to stay open longer hours for student use and expand the book collection." An example of a loss-framed appeal was: "The cafeteria at Lincoln University is in need of funding. Without funds, it will have to cut down on menu items and increase food prices." Jeong et al. (2011) found that approach-oriented (BAS) participants rated gain-framed appeals as more effective, and indicated willingness to donate more money in response to such appeals; avoidance-oriented (BIS) participants, on the other hand, rated loss-framed appeals as more effective and were more favorably influenced by such appeals.

Notice that Jeong et al.'s (2011) gain-framed and loss-framed appeals differed not only in the antecedent of the appeal (compliance or noncompliance), but also in the consequent of the appeal—how the consequences were described. In the gain-framed appeal, the consequences were described in terms of improvement relative to the status quo ("stay open longer hours"), whereas in the loss-framed appeal the consequences were described in terms of disimprovement relative to the status quo ("cut down on menu items"). To see the relevance of this point, consider that these are not the only ways in which the consequences might have been phrased. For example, the gain-framed appeal could have been worded as follows: "The library at Jefferson University is in need of funding. With funds, it will be able to avoid reducing library hours and avoid having to reduce the book collection." This would still be a gain-framed appeal, that is, an appeal focused on the desirable consequences of compliance—but with the consequences described in terms of preventing (avoiding) disimprovements rather than in terms of promoting (approaching) improvements.

As a similar example: Sherman, Mann, and Updegraff (2006) found that approach-oriented participants were more persuaded by a gain-framed appeal advocating flossing than by a loss-framed appeal, with the reverse result obtained for avoidance-oriented participants—but the gain-framed and loss-framed appeals differed in the consequences invoked. The gain-framed message was entitled: "Great Breath, Healthy Gums Only a Floss Away," which suggests a focus on promotion-oriented consequences of compliance. But the loss-framed message was entitled: "Floss Now and Avoid Bad Breath and Gum Disease"—a title that emphasizes prevention-oriented consequences (and, not incidentally, is phrased in terms of the consequences of compliance).

At best, then, the research evidence is ambiguous about the role of regulatory focus in gain-loss framing effects. Because the research designs have not consistently distinguished antecedent variations and consequent variations, the observed differences in persuasiveness cannot be unequivocally attributed to the antecedent variation (the gain-loss framing manipulation).

But, as perhaps is obvious, it is much more plausible that the observed effects were driven by the variation in consequences than by any variation in antecedents. In Jeong et al.'s (2011) study, for instance, for promotion-oriented persons, a gain-framed appeal emphasizing promotion consequences was more persuasive than a loss-framed appeal emphasizing prevention consequences—but the active ingredient producing such a difference was surely the kind of consequence involved, not the kind of antecedent. Few studies appear to have carefully distinguished consequence variation (i.e., whether the outcomes are promotion-focused or prevention-focused) and antecedent variation (i.e., whether the message was compliance-focused or noncompliance focused). But what limited empirical evidence exists indicates that persons differing in regulatory-focus-related motivations are not differentially persuaded by compliance-focused and noncompliance-focused appeals (i.e., are not influenced by whether the appeals are gain-framed or loss-framed) but rather—across such appeal variations—are differentially persuaded by whether the substantive consequences invoked match their motivational orientation (Chang, 2010, Experiment 2).

In sum, it is unlikely that regulatory-focus variations will yield systematic differences in persuasiveness between compliance-focused and noncompliance-focused appeals independent of the kinds of consequences invoked. Regulatory-focus variations do not map easily onto the contrast between compliance-focused (gain-framed) and noncompliance-focused (loss-framed) appeals. But regulatory-focus variations do map easily onto a contrast between promotion-oriented consequences and prevention-oriented consequences—with, as the empirical evidence suggests, corresponding differences in the persuasiveness of appeals emphasizing these different consequences.

Summary. Two variables have been commonly suggested as possible moderators of gain-loss message framing effects, one concerning the kind of behavior advocated (disease prevention vs. disease detection), the other concerning the kind of message recipient involved (promotion-oriented vs. prevention-oriented). But there is not good evidence for either hypothesis (and for the former, there is good evidence to the contrary). There may be some other yet unconfirmed moderating factor at work that will permit identification of systematic differences in the relative persuasiveness of these two kinds of consequence-based appeals, but at present, the clear generalization to be drawn is that invoking desirable consequences of compliance is in general neither more nor less persuasive than invoking parallel undesirable consequences of noncompliance.

Comparing More and Less Likely Consequences

Just as it seems ordinary and rational that the assessment of alternatives (products, courses of action, etc.) should be affected by the *desirability* of the associated consequences, so it seems similarly sensible that such assessments should be affected by the perceived *likelihood* of those consequences. For example, given two courses of action with equally positively evaluated consequences, the action more likely to produce those consequences should presumably be preferred. Correspondingly, one would expect that—parallel to the effects observed for variations in the desirability of consequences invoked by persuasive messages—variations in the depicted likelihood of consequences should show similar patterns of differential persuasiveness. So, for example, greater persuasion should be observed (ceteris paribus) when outcomes are described as highly likely than when those same outcomes are described as only somewhat likely.

However, the relevant research evidence is surprisingly unclear on this score. In fact, the most appropriate conclusion at present seems to be this: Variations in the depicted likelihood of consequences may not dependably produce corresponding differences in persuasive effects.

At least some research does support the expectation that variation in depicted likelihood will produce corresponding variations in persuasive effectiveness. Specifically, some meta-analyses of fear-appeal research have concluded that variations in depicted threat vulnerability produce the expected effects on persuasive outcomes: As the threatened consequences are depicted as more likely to occur, there is correspondingly greater persuasion. Witte and Allen's (2000) meta-analysis found such a relationship for each of three different persuasive outcomes (attitudes, intentions, and behaviors); a similar conclusion was reached by the more limited meta-analytic review of Floyd, Prentice-Dunn, and Rogers (2000). Curiously, de Hoog et al.'s (2007) meta-analysis found similar results for effects on intentions and behaviors, but not on attitudes. Still, the general pattern in fear appeal research seems to suggest that variation in the depicted likelihood of consequences produces corresponding variation in persuasive effects.

But this pattern of results is not consistent with two other bodies of research. First, a surprisingly large number of other studies—studies that are generally not included in meta-analytic reviews of fear appeal research—have reported that messages varying in the depicted likelihood of consequences did not differentially influence persuasive outcomes, but messages varying in the desirability of depicted outcomes did correspondingly vary in persuasiveness. For example, Hass, Bagley, and Rogers (1975) found that variation in the depicted undesirability of an energy crisis created corresponding variations in intentions to conserve energy (the more undesirable an energy crisis was depicted to be, the greater conservation intentions were), but variation in the depicted likelihood of an energy crisis did not differentially affect intentions. In Wogalter and Barlow's (1990, Experiment 1) study of the perceived safety of consumer products, participants received messages varying in the depicted likelihood and depicted severity of injury; variation in depicted severity had corresponding effects on hazard perceptions (products with high-severity warnings were perceived as more hazardous than those with low-severity warnings), but variation in the depicted likelihood of consequences did not affect hazard perceptions. In a series of studies, Smith-McLallen (2005) manipulated both likelihood information and desirability information, finding that attitudes were more influenced by variations in the desirability of the claimed consequences than by variations in the likelihood of those consequences' occurrence. From a related set of studies, Johnson et al. (2004) concluded that "persuasion is more about suggesting good rather than bad *consequences* (valence) for the message recipient than it is about creating impeccably logical—a.k.a. truthful or likely—arguments" (p. 216); as Levin, Nichols, and Johnson (2000, p. 183) put it, "arguments that were positive in valence but not particularly likely were just as persuasive as arguments that were both good and likely." Relatedly, Lipkus, Green, and Marcus (2003) found that whether participants received or did not receive information about the severity of colorectal cancer significantly affected screening behavior in the expected way (those receiving severity information were more likely to subsequently be screened), but receiving or not receiving information about the likelihood of colon cancer (incidence and risk factors) did not have corresponding effects.

Taken together, these studies obviously suggest complications for a simple, neat picture in which variations in the depicted likelihood of consequences straightforwardly produce corresponding variations in persuasive effects. It may be that some moderating factor is at work, such that under some circumstances (but not others), messages depicting highly likely consequences will generally be more persuasive than messages depicting less likely consequences. But these studies make it plain that, at least for the moment, the direct research evidence is rather more clouded than one might have expected.

The other body of research that casts doubt on the expected role of likelihood-related appeal variations is work aimed at identifying predictors of attitude (and related assessments). For example, Fishbein's (1967) expectancy-value model of attitude (see, similarly, Fishbein & Ajzen, 2010, pp. 96–125) proposes that attitudes are a multiplicative function of belief evaluation (the perceived desirability of each associated salient belief) and belief strength (the perceived likelihood of each belief).

But research has raised significant questions about whether likelihood judgments influence attitudes in the ways one would expect (and hence indirectly has created doubt about whether messages aimed at influencing likelihood judgments would have much effect on attitudes). In particular, several studies have suggested that the apparent contribution of belief-strength scores to attitude prediction is an artifact of using standardized lists of beliefs. When a respondent assesses only his or her unique individualized set of beliefs, only belief evaluation (not belief likelihood) contributes to the prediction of attitudes (e.g., Cronen & Conville, 1975; Eagly, Mladinic, & Otto, 1994). In a similar vein, several studies of product safety judgments have found that evaluative perceptions are much more powerful than likelihood perceptions, with the latter often not making a significant contribution: "people do not readily use injury likelihood in their judgments of product safety" (Young, Brelsford, & Wogalter, 1990, p. 503; similarly, see Wogalter, Brelsford, Desaulniers, & Laughery, 1991; Wogalter, Young, Brelsford, & Barlow, 1999).

These results naturally cast some doubt on the potential persuasiveness of appeals emphasizing the likelihood of consequences. If likelihood judgments do not significantly affect attitudes and similar assessments, then perhaps it should not be surprising that studies of likelihood-related appeal variations should not have consistently found the expected effects on persuasive outcomes.

In short, although it might be plausible to have supposed that likelihood-related appeal variations would straightforwardly produce corresponding variations in persuasive effectiveness, the research evidence in hand offers a much murkier picture. Where persuaders deploy consequence-based appeals, it may be more important to emphasize the valence (desirability or undesirability) of the consequences than to emphasize their likelihood.

Conclusion

A great many seemingly-unrelated lines of persuasion research can be seen to be quite closely connected conceptually, by virtue of involving variations in features of consequence-based arguments. And the substantial accumulated empirical evidence concerning these variations can be summarized in four broad generalizations: (a) appeals invoking the consequences of adopting the advocated action are more persuasive when the invoked consequences are relatively more desirable than when the consequences are relatively less desirable; (b) appeals invoking the consequences of failing to adopt the advocated action are more persuasive when the invoked consequences are relatively more undesirable than when the consequences are relatively less undesirable; (c) there is no general difference in persuasiveness between appeals invoking desirable consequences of compliance and appeals invoking parallel undesirable consequences of noncompliance; and (d) appeals depicting the consequences as relatively more likely may not be dependably more persuasive than appeals depicting those consequences as relatively less likely.

Future investigation might extend this sort of analysis by considering how other aspects of consequence-based appeals might influence persuasive outcomes. For example, one might examine the persuasiveness of messages invoking both desirable consequences of compliance and undesirable consequences of noncompliance, as compared to that of messages invoking only one of these elements. Two existing research lines bear on this matter. One is the study of "mixed-frame" messages in gain-loss message framing research (e.g., Latimer et al., 2008; similarly, see Treiber, 1986; Wilson, Wallston, & King, 1990); these messages deploy appeals invoking both the desirable consequences of compliance and the undesirable consequences of noncompliance (i.e., both "gain-framed" and "loss-framed" appeals). The other is investigations of certain fear-appeal variations. The canonical form of a fear appeal contains two message components, one emphasizing undesirable consequences of noncompliance (the message material meant to arouse fear) and one emphasizing the desirable consequences of the advocated action (message material meant to convey the effectiveness of the recommended action); this combination of message components is conceptually the equivalent of "mixed-frame" messages. Some fear-appeal research designs have compared the persuasiveness of messages containing both components and messages containing only one (e.g., Simonson, Aegerter, Berry, Kloock, & Stone, 1987, Study 4; Tanner, Hunt, & Eppright, 1991). The question to be addressed—and a careful review of relevant research is not in hand—is whether messages discussing both the desirable consequences of compliance and the undesirable consequences of noncompliance will in general, or in specifiable circumstances, differ in persuasiveness from messages discussing only one of these.

In sum: Although not widely appreciated, research on the relative persuasiveness of a number of message variations has implicitly compared different forms of consequence-based arguments. Recognition of this common focus permits the identification of several broad generalizations about consequence-based arguments, and provides a promising larger conceptual framework for housing other research questions concerning persuasion.

Notes

1. The conception and assessment of self-monitoring has not been without controversy, especially concerning the construct's multidimensionality (e.g., Briggs & Cheek, 1988; Briggs, Cheek, & Buss, 1980; Gangestad & Snyder, 2000; Lennox & Wolfe, 1984; Snyder & Gangestad, 1986). But even if simple conceptualizations of the structure of self-monitoring are defective, the empirical relationship of interest here—between self-monitoring scores and differential responsiveness to image-oriented and quality-oriented appeals—is quite secure. Some intimations to the contrary (e.g., Slama & Singley, 1996) are based on vote-counting summaries in which nonsignificant effects are counted as disconfirmations, but, as pointed out by DeBono (2006), the direction of effect has actually been remarkably consistent across a large number of studies. Indeed, one way of reading the present argument is to say that one doesn't need the apparatus of "self-monitoring" to explain that empirical result; all one needs is the recognition that self-monitoring scores—whatever else they might do—tap into differences in evaluations of consumer product attributes.
2. As a reader pointed out, another way of framing the present argument is to house it within the theoretical framework of the theory of planned behavior and its successors. In that framework, the proximal determinants of attitudes are persons' salient beliefs about the behavior (and specifically, the desirability and strength of those beliefs). These beliefs can be influenced by a great many different "background factors," including individual factors (e.g., personality variations) and social factors (e.g., cultural variation). But the effects of all such background factors are obtained through their effects on more proximal factors (Fishbein & Ajzen, 2010, pp. 24–25). The present argument that, for example, self-monitoring and individual-collectivism have their effects because of their systematic relationships to variations in consequence evaluation can plainly be fitted neatly within such a framework.
3. Keller and Lehmann's (2008) review did not find argument strength (or fear) to be significantly related to health-related intentions, but these conclusions are suspect. Keller and Lehmann's (2008) review was not based on experimental (randomized trial) data concerning specifically the independent variables of interest. For example, a study in which all the messages had strong arguments had its results included in the analysis of the effects of strong-argument messages. So Keller and Lehmann's conclusions about a given message variable were not based exclusively on experiments in which levels of that variable were manipulated. In fact, they reported, "we had relatively few manipulated levels for many of the variables" (p. 120). There are, of course, very good and familiar reasons to prefer conclusions based on randomized trials ("this experiment compared the effectiveness of one-sided and two-sided messages and found...") over those based on observational studies ("in this study all the messages were two-sided, and people were really persuaded, so therefore..."). Correspondingly, there are good reasons to prefer meta-analytic conclusions based exclusively

on randomized trial data, such as Witte and Allen's (2000) meta-analysis, over those based largely on observational studies, such as Keller and Lehmann's (2008) report.

4. Because the appeals are intended to persuade, different *valences* of consequences are of course invoked: compliance is depicted as yielding advantages (desirable consequences) and noncompliance is depicted as yielding disadvantages (undesirable consequences). But the *content* of the consequences is free to vary otherwise.

References

Aaker, J. L., & Schmitt, B. (2001). Culture-dependent assimilation and differentiation of the self: Preferences for consumption symbols in the United States and China. *Journal of Cross-Cultural Psychology, 32*, 561–576. doi:10.1177/0022022101032005003

Ajzen, I. (1991). The theory of planned behavior. *Organizational Behavior and Human Decision Processes, 50*, 179–211. doi:10.1016/0749-5978(91)90020-T

Areni, C. S., & Lutz, R. J. (1988). The role of argument quality in the elaboration likelihood model. *Advances in Consumer Research, 15*, 197–203.

Bailis, D. S., Fleming, J. A., & Segall, A. (2005). Self-determination and functional persuasion to encourage physical activity. *Psychology & Health, 20*, 691–708. doi:10.1080/14768320500051359

Block, L. G., & Keller, P. A. (1998). Beyond protection motivation: An integrative theory of health appeals. *Journal of Applied Social Psychology, 28*, 1584–1608. doi:10.1111/j.1559-1816.1998.tb01691.x

Briggs, S. R., & Cheek, J. M. (1988). On the nature of self-monitoring: Problems with assessment, problems with validity. *Journal of Personality and Social Psychology, 54*, 663–678. doi:10.1037/0022-3514.54.4.663

Briggs, S. R., Cheek, J. M., & Buss, A. H. (1980). An analysis of the self-monitoring scale. *Journal of Personality and Social Psychology, 38*, 679–686. doi:10.1037/0022-3514.38.4.679

Cacioppo, J. T., Gardner, W. L., & Berntson, G. G. (1997). Beyond bipolar conceptualizations and measures: The case of attitudes and evaluative space. *Personality and Social Psychology Review, 1*, 3–25.

Cappella, J. N., Yzer, M., & Fishbein, M. (2003). Using beliefs about positive and negative consequences as the basis for designing message interventions for lowering risky behavior. In D. Romer (Ed.), *Reducing adolescent risk* (pp. 210–219). Thousand Oaks, CA: Sage.

Carver, C. S., & White, T. L. (1984). Behavioral inhibition, behavioral activation, and affective responses to impending reward and punishment: The BIS/BAS scales. *Journal of Personality and Social Psychology, 67*, 319–333. doi:10.1037/0022-3514.67.2.319

Cesario, J., Grant, H., & Higgins, E. T. (2004). Regulatory fit and persuasion: Transfer from "feeling right." *Journal of Personality and Social Psychology, 86*, 388–404. doi:10.1037/0022-3514.86.3.388

Chang, C. (2010). Message framing and interpersonal orientation at cultural and individual levels: Involvement as a moderator. *International Journal of Advertising, 29*, 765–794. doi:10.2501/S0265048710201452

Clary, E. G., Snyder, M., Ridge, R. D., Miene, P. K., & Haugen, J. A. (1994). Matching messages to motives in persuasion: A functional approach to promoting volunteerism.

Journal of Applied Social Psychology, 24, 1129–1149. doi:10.1111/j.1559-1816.1994. tb01548.x

Cronen, V. E., & Conville, R. L. (1975). Fishbein's conception of belief strength: A theoretical, methodological, and experimental critique. *Speech Monographs, 42*, 143–150.

DeBono, K. G. (1987). Investigating the social-adjustive and value-expressive functions of attitudes: Implications for persuasion processes. *Journal of Personality and Social Psychology, 52*, 279–287. doi:10.1037/0022-3514.52.2.279

DeBono, K. G. (2006). Self-monitoring and consumer psychology. *Journal of Personality, 74*, 715–737. doi:10.1111/j.1467-6494.2006.00390.x

DeBono, K. G., & Packer, M. (1991). The effects of advertising appeal on perceptions of product quality. *Personality and Social Psychology Bulletin, 17*, 194–200. doi: 10.1177/014616729101700212

de Hoog, N., Stroebe, W., & de Wit, J. (2007). The impact of vulnerability to and severity of a health risk on processing and acceptance of fear-arousing communications: A meta-analysis. *Review of General Psychology, 11*, 258–285. doi: 10.1037/1089-2680.11.3.258

Eagly, A. H., Mladinic, A., & Otto, S. (1994). Cognitive and affective bases of attitudes toward social groups and social policies. *Journal of Experimental Social Psychology, 30*, 113–137. doi:10.1006/jesp.1994.1006

Faber, R. J., Karlen, S., & Christenson, G. A. (1993). Differential preference for advertising appeals among compulsive and non-compulsive buyers. In E. Thorson (Ed.), *Proceedings of the 1993 conference of the American Academy of Advertising* (pp. 216–224). Columbia, MO: American Academy of Advertising.

Fishbein, M. (1967). A behavior theory approach to the relations between beliefs about an object and the attitude toward the object. In M. Fishbein (Ed.), *Readings in attitude theory and measurement* (pp. 389–400). New York: Wiley.

Fishbein, M., & Ajzen, I. (2010). *Predicting and changing behavior: The reasoned action approach.* New York: Psychology Press.

Fishbein, M., & Yzer, M. C. (2003). Using theory to design effective health behavior interventions. *Communication Theory, 13*, 164–183. doi:10.1111/j.1468-2885.2003. tb00287.x

Floyd, D. L., Prentice-Dunn, S., & Rogers, R. W. (2000). A meta-analysis of research on protection motivation theory. *Journal of Applied Social Psychology, 30*, 407–429. doi:10.1111/j.1559-1816.2000.tb02323.x

Gangestad, S. W., & Snyder, M. (2000). Self-monitoring: Appraisal and reappraisal. *Psychological Bulletin, 126*, 530–555. doi: 10.1037/0033-2909.126.4.530

Hass, J. W., Bagley, G. S., & Rogers, R. W. (1975). Coping with the energy crisis: Effects of fear appeals upon attitudes toward energy consumption. *Journal of Applied Psychology, 60*, 754–756. doi:10.1037/0021-9010.60.6.754

Henley, N., & Donovan, R. J. (2003). Young people's response to death threat appeals: Do they really feel immortal? *Health Education Research, 18*, 1–14. doi:10.1093/her/18.1.1

Higgins, E. T. (1997). Beyond pleasure and pain. *American Psychologist, 52*, 1280–1300. doi:10.1037/0003-066X.52.12.1280

Higgins, E. T. (1998). Promotion and prevention: Regulatory focus as a motivational principle. *Advances in Experimental Social Psychology, 30*, 1–46.

Hofstede, G. (1980). *Culture's consequences: International differences in work-related values.* Beverly Hills, CA: Sage.

Hofstede, G. (2001). *Culture's consequences: Comparing values, behaviors, institutions, and organizations across nations* (2nd ed.). Thousand Oaks, CA: Sage.

Hornikx, J., & O'Keefe, D. J. (2009). Adapting consumer advertising appeals to cultural values: A meta-analytic review of effects on persuasiveness and ad liking. *Communication Yearbook, 33*, 39–71.

Hustinx, L., van Enschot, R., & Hoeken, H. (2007). Argument quality in the elaboration likelihood model: An empirical study of strong and weak arguments in a persuasive message. In F. H. van Eemeren, J. A. Blair, C. A. Willard, & B. Garssen (Eds.), *Proceedings of the Sixth Conference of the International Society for the Study of Argumentation* (pp. 651–657). Amsterdam, the Netherlands: Sic Sat.

Jeong, E. S., Shi, Y., Baazova, A., Chiu, C., Nahai, A., Moons, W. G., & Taylor, S. E. (2011). The relation of approach/avoidance motivation and message framing to the effectiveness of charitable appeals. *Social Influence, 6*, 15–21. doi: 10.1080/15298868.2010.524369

Johnson, B. T., Smith-McLallen, A., Killeya, L. A., & Levin, K. D. (2004). Truth or consequences: Overcoming resistance to persuasion with positive thinking. In E. S. Knowles & J. A. Linn (Eds.), *Resistance and persuasion* (pp. 215–233). Mahwah, NJ: Erlbaum.

Kahneman, D., Knetsch, J. L., & Thaler, R. H. (1990). Experimental tests of the endowment effect and the Coase theorem. *Journal of Political Economy, 98*, 1325–1348.

Kahneman, D., & Tversky, A. (1979). Prospect theory: An analysis of decision under risk. *Econometrica, 47*, 263–291.

Keller, P. A., & Lehmann, D. R. (2008). Designing effective health communications: A meta-analysis. *Journal of Public Policy and Marketing, 27*, 117–130. doi:10.1509/jppm.27.2.117

Kowert, D. W., & Homer, P. M. (1993). Targeting consumers through birth order: A match-up hypothesis explanation. In E. Thorson (Ed.), *Proceedings of the 1993 conference of the American Academy of Advertising* (pp. 225–235). Columbia, MO: American Academy of Advertising.

Latimer, A. E., Rench, T. A., Rivers, S. E., Katulak, N. A., Materese, S. A., Cadmus, L., … Salovey, P. (2008). Promoting participation in physical activity using framed messages: An application of prospect theory. *British Journal of Health Psychology, 13*, 659–681. doi:10.1348/135910707X246186

Latimer, A. E., Salovey, P., & Rothman, A. J. (2007). The effectiveness of gain-framed messages for encouraging disease prevention behavior: Is all hope lost? *Journal of Health Communication, 12*, 645–649. doi:10.1080/10810730701619695

Lavine, H., & Snyder, M. (1996). Cognitive processing and the functional matching effect in persuasion: The mediating role of subjective perceptions of message quality. *Journal of Experimental Social Psychology, 32*, 580–604. doi:10.1006/jesp.1996.0026

Lee, A. Y., & Higgins, E. T. (2009). The persuasive power of regulatory fit. In M. Wanke (Ed.), *The social psychology of consumer behavior* (pp. 319–333). New York: Psychology Press.

Leikas, S., Lonnqvist, J.-E., Verkasalo, M., & Lindeman, M. (2009). Regulatory focus systems and personal values. *European Journal of Social Psychology, 39*, 415–429. doi:10.1002/ejsp.547

Lennon, S. J., Davis, L. L., & Fairhurst, A. (1988). Evaluations of apparel advertising as a function of self-monitoring. *Perceptual and Motor Skills, 66*, 987–996.

Lennox, R. D., & Wolfe, R. N. (1984). Revision of the self-monitoring scale. *Journal of Personality and Social Psychology, 46*, 1349–1364. doi:10.1037/0022-3514.46.6.1349

Levin, K. D., Nichols, D. R., & Johnson, B. T. (2000). Involvement and persuasion: Attitude functions for the motivated processor. In G. R. Maio & J. M. Olson (Eds.), *Why we evaluate: Functions of attitudes* (pp. 163–194). Mahwah, NJ: Erlbaum.

Lipkus, I. M., Green, L. G., & Marcus, A. (2003). Manipulating perceptions of colorectal cancer threat: Implications for screening intentions and behaviors. *Journal of Health Communication, 8*, 213–228. doi:10.1080/10810730390196499

McCaul, K. D., Johnson, R. J., & Rothman, A. J. (2002). The effects of framing and action instructions on whether older adults obtain flu shots. *Health Psychology, 21*, 624–628. doi:10.1037/0278-6133.21.6.624

Meyerowitz, B. E., & Chaiken, S. (1987). The effect of message framing on breast self-examination attitudes, intentions, and behavior. *Journal of Personality and Social Psychology, 52*, 500–510. doi:10.1037/0022-3514.52.3.500

Murray-Johnson, L., Witte, K., Liu, W.-Y., Hubbell, A. P., Sampson, J., & Morrison, K. (2001). Addressing cultural orientations in fear appeals: Promoting AIDS-protective behaviors among Mexican immigrant and African American adolescents and American and Taiwanese college students. *Journal of Health Communication, 6*, 335–358. doi:10.1080/108107301317140823

O'Keefe, D. J., & Jensen, J. D. (2006). The advantages of compliance or the disadvantages of noncompliance? A meta-analytic review of the relative persuasive effectiveness of gain-framed and loss-framed messages. *Communication Yearbook, 30*, 1–43.

O'Keefe, D. J., & Jensen, J. D. (2007). The relative persuasiveness of gain-framed and loss-framed messages for encouraging disease prevention behaviors: A meta-analytic review. *Journal of Health Communication, 12*, 623–644. doi: 10.1080/10810730701615198

O'Keefe, D. J., & Jensen, J. D. (2009). The relative persuasiveness of gain-framed and loss-framed messages for encouraging disease detection behaviors: A meta-analytic review. *Journal of Communication, 59*, 296–316. doi: 10.1111/j.1460-2466.2009.01417.x

Orbell, S., & Hagger, M. (2006). Temporal framing and the decision to take part in Type 2 diabetes screening: Effects of individual differences in consideration of future consequences on persuasion. *Health Psychology, 25*, 537–548. doi: 10.1037/0278-6133.25.4.537

Orbell, S., & Kyriakaki, M. (2008). Temporal framing and persuasion to adopt preventive health behavior: Moderating effects of individual differences in consideration of future consequences on sunscreen use. *Health Psychology, 27*, 770–779. doi: 10.1037/0278-6133.27.6.770

Park, H. S., Levine, T. R., Westermann, C. Y. K., Orfgen, T., & Foregger, S. (2007). The effects of argument quality and involvement type on attitude formation and attitude change: A test of dual-process and social judgment predictions. *Human Communication Research, 33*, 81–102. doi:10.1111/j.1468-2958.2007.00290.x

Perelman, C. (1959). Pragmatic arguments. *Philosophy, 34*, 18–27. www.jstor.org/stable/3748617

Petty, R. E., & Cacioppo, J. T. (1986). *Communication and persuasion: Central and peripheral routes to attitude change.* New York: Springer-Verlag.

Petty, R. E., Cacioppo, J. T., & Goldman, R. (1981). Personal involvement as a determinant of argument-based persuasion. *Journal of Personality and Social Psychology, 41*, 847–855. doi:10.1037/0022-3514.41.5.847

Petty, R. E., & Wegener, D. T. (1998). Attitude change: Multiple roles for persuasion variables. In D. T. Gilbert, S. T. Fiske, & G. Lindzey (Eds.), *Handbook of social psychology* (4th ed., Vol. 1, pp. 323–390). Boston, MA: McGraw-Hill.

Robertson, L. S., O'Neill, B., & Wixom, C. W. (1972). Factors associated with observed safety belt use. *Journal of Health and Social Behavior, 13*, 18–24. www.jstor.org/stable/2136969

Rogers, R. W., & Prentice-Dunn, S. (1997). Protection motivation theory. In D. Gochman (Ed.), *Handbook of health behavior research: Vol. 1. Personal and social determinants* (pp. 113–132). New York: Plenum.

Salovey, P., Schneider, T. R., & Apanovitch, A. M. (2002). Message framing in the prevention and early detection of illness. In J. P. Dillard & M. Pfau (Eds.), *The persuasion handbook: Developments in theory and practice* (pp. 391–406). Thousand Oaks, CA: Sage.

Salovey, P., & Wegener, D. T. (2003). Communicating about health: Message framing, persuasion, and health behavior. In J. Suls & K. Wallston (Eds.), *Social psychology foundations of health and illness* (pp. 54–81). Oxford, England: Blackwell.

Schellens, P. J., & de Jong, M. (2004). Argumentation schemes in persuasive brochures. *Argumentation, 18*, 295–323. doi:10.1023/B:ARGU.0000046707.68172.35

Settle, R. B., & Mizerski, R. (1974). Differential response to objective and social information in advertisements. In T. V. Greer (Ed.), *1973 combined proceedings: Increasing marketing productivity and conceptual and methodological foundations of marketing* (pp. 250–255). Chicago, IL: American Marketing Association.

Sherman, D. K., Mann, T., & Updegraff, J. A. (2006). Approach/avoidance orientation, message framing, and health behavior: Understanding the congruency effect. *Motivation and Emotion, 30*, 165–169. doi:10.1007/s11031-006-9001-5

Simonson, M. R., Aegerter, R., Berry, T., Kloock, T., & Stone, R. (1987). Four studies dealing with mediated persuasive messages, attitudes, and learning styles. *Educational Communication and Technology Journal, 35*, 31–41. www.jstor.org/stable/30218209

Slama, M. E., & Singley, R. B. (1996). Self-monitoring and value-expressive vs. utilitarian ad effectiveness: Why the mixed findings? *Journal of Current Issues and Research in Advertising, 18*(2), 39–52.

Smith-McLallen, A. (2005). *Is it true? (When) does it matter? The roles of likelihood and desirability in argument judgments and attitudes* (Doctoral dissertation). Retrieved from UMI. (UMI No. AAT-3187759)

Snyder, M., & DeBono, K. G. (1985). Appeals to image and claims about quality: Understanding the psychology of advertising. *Journal of Personality and Social Psychology, 49*, 586–597. doi:10.1037/0022-3514.49.3.586

Snyder, M., & DeBono, K. G. (1987). A functional approach to attitudes and persuasion. In M. P. Zanna, J. M. Olson, & C. P. Herman (Eds.), *Social influence: The Ontario symposium* (Vol. 5, pp. 107–125). Hillsdale, NJ: Erlbaum.

Snyder, M., & Gangestad, S. (1986). On the nature of self-monitoring: Matters of assessment, matters of validity. *Journal of Personality and Social Psychology, 51*, 125–139. doi:10.1037/0022-3514.51.1.125

Strathman, A., Gleicher, F., Boninger, D. S., & Edwards, C. S. (1994). The consideration of future consequences: Weighing immediate and distant outcomes of behavior. *Journal of Personality and Social Psychology, 66*, 742–752. doi: 10.1037/0022-3514.66.4.742

Tanner, J. F., Jr., Hunt, J. B., & Eppright, D. R. (1991). The protection motivation model: A normative model of fear appeals. *Journal of Marketing, 55*(3), 36–45. www.jstor.org/stable/1252146

Treiber, F. A. (1986). A comparison of the positive and negative consequences approaches upon car restraint usage. *Journal of Pediatric Psychology, 11*, 15–24.

van Baaren, R. B., & Ruivenkamp, M. (2007). Self-construal and values expressed in advertising. *Social Influence, 2*, 136–144. doi:10.1080/15534510701279722

van Enschot-van Dijk, R., Hustinx, L., & Hoeken, H. (2003). The concept of argument quality in the elaboration likelihood model: A normative and empirical approach to Petty and Cacioppo's "strong" and "weak" arguments. In F. H. van Eemeren, J. A. Blair, C. A. Willard, & A. F. Snoeck Henkemans (Eds.), *Anyone who has a view: Theoretical contributions to the study of argumentation* (pp. 319–335). Amsterdam, the Netherlands: Kluwer.

Walton, D. N. (1996). *Argumentation schemes for presumptive reasoning.* Mahwah, NJ: Erlbaum.

Wilson, D. K., Wallston, K. A., & King, J. E. (1990). Effects of contract framing, motivation to quit, and self-efficacy on smoking reduction. *Journal of Applied Psychology, 20*, 531–547.

Witte, K., & Allen, M. (2000). A meta-analysis of fear appeals: Implications for effective public health campaigns. *Health Education and Behavior, 27*, 591–615. doi: 10.1177/109019810002700506

Wogalter, M. S., & Barlow, T. (1990). Injury severity and likelihood in warnings. In *Proceedings of the Human Factors Society 34th Annual Meeting* (pp. 580–583). Santa Monica, CA: Human Factors Society.

Wogalter, M. S., Brelsford, J. W., Desaulniers, D. R., & Laughery, K. R. (1991). Consumer product warnings: The role of hazard perception. *Journal of Safety Research, 22*, 71–82. doi:10.1016/0022-4375(91)90015-N

Wogalter, M. S., Young, S. L., Brelsford, J. W., & Barlow, T. (1999). The relative contributions of injury severity and likelihood information on hazard-risk judgments and warning compliance. *Journal of Safety Research, 30*, 151–163. doi:10.1016/ S0022-4375(99)00010-9

Young, S. L., Brelsford, J. W., & Wogalter, M. S. (1990). Judgments of hazard, risk, and danger: Do they differ? In *Proceedings of the Human Factors Society 34th Annual Meeting* (pp. 503–507). Santa Monica, CA: Human Factors Society.

Zuckerman, M., Gioioso, C., & Tellini, S. (1988). Control orientation, self-monitoring, and preference for image versus quality approach to advertising. *Journal of Research in Personality, 22*, 89–100. doi:10.1016/0092-6566(88)90026-8

6 Commentary
What Makes Arguments-From-Consequences Convincing?

Hans Hoeken

Radboud University, Nijmegen

There is no doubt that the question of what makes an argument convincing merits the attention of scholars interested in persuasion. O'Keefe's review is an important step toward finding the beginning of an answer. Below, I will specify some of its implications for future research as well as for the practice of designing tailored communication.

Implications for Research on Persuasion

Arguments are employed to support the acceptance of a claim. Schellens and De Jong (2004) argue that depending on the type of claim, different types of argument are relevant. Consequence-based arguments typically support claims about the (relative) desirability of a line of action—you should buy this phone (instead of that one), vote for our candidate (instead of theirs), and eat more fruit (instead of hamburgers)—by pointing out the desirable consequences of performing the propagated behavior (or the undesirable consequences of choosing the alternative). O'Keefe shows that there is considerable evidence that people are susceptible to the extent to which the consequences referred to in the argument are perceived as desirable.

This conclusion describes a causal relation between a characteristic of the argument and its convincingness and can therefore be considered a mechanistic explanation of what makes a consequence-based argument strong. The review also enables a second kind of explanation, namely a purposive one. In the "rational analysis" program, cognitive phenomena are explained by the purpose they serve (Chater & Oaksford, 1999). Methodologically, rational analysis starts with specifying the cognitive system's goals, charting the environment in which it has to function, making some (minimal) assumptions about the system's computational limitations, and developing a (normative) model that describes the optimal functioning of the system given the environment and its computational limitations. Next, the data of actual people performing those tasks are compared to the standards set by the normative model. Hahn and Oaksford (2006) call for a rational analysis approach to the concept of argument strength. They argue that a normative model of argument strength provides a standard against which human performance can be compared and that the results of such a comparison provide a research agenda including questions of where and why people's performance may fall short.

O'Keefe's review provides an excellent starting point for a rational analysis approach. When people are confronted with (consequence-based) arguments, their goal is to assess the extent to which the argument provides support for the acceptability of the advocated claim. This claim is, as noted above, typically about the relative desirability of a certain action (compared to its alternatives). In other words, assessing the quality of an argument serves the purpose of making optimal choices between alternatives. Within the literature on rational decision making, normative models for this task have been proposed. The expected utility model of decision making (e.g., Baron, 2000) appears a logical candidate in this respect. According to this model, the alternative that most likely will have the most desirable consequences should be preferred. Translating this model to the concept of argument strength leads to the conclusion that a strong argument should make it highly probable that the propagated action has a highly desirable outcome. In argumentation theory, these same criteria have been proposed to distinguish strong consequence-based arguments from weak ones (e.g., Reinard, 1991, pp. 89–90). In conclusion, the most convincing arguments should be the ones referring to consequences that are both highly probable and highly desirable.

In his review, O'Keefe concludes that "perhaps the single best-supported empirical generalization about persuasion" is "that consequence-based arguments emphasizing relatively more desirable consequences of the advocated action are likely to be more persuasive than are arguments emphasizing relatively less desirable consequences" (p. 118). Thus, people do exactly what normative models would advise them to. Research within the argument quality tradition shows that arguments considered to be strong typically refer to more desirable consequences than those arguments perceived of as weak. Even stronger evidence for the claim that people act according to normative standards is to be found in studies showing that the desirability of a consequence may depend on individual preferences. The fact, for instance, that high self-monitors consider image-oriented consequences more convincing than product-quality consequences reveals that they use their own goals and values to assess a consequence's desirability (as would be advised by normative models of decision making). Finally, people appear to be rather insensitive to framing effects. Pointing out the parallel desirable consequences of compliance does not yield a more convincing argument compared to pointing out the undesirable consequences of noncompliance. Again, from a normative point of view, that is exactly the kind of insensitiveness people should display.

Whereas people's behavior with respect to differences in the consequence's desirability of the argument meets the standard set by rational decision models, it appears to fall short when it comes to people's susceptibility to differences in the probability part of the argument. O'Keefe finds no evidence that appealing to the likelihood of consequences yields a reliable persuasive advantage. The difference in impact of the desirability and the probability components of consequence-based arguments has been demonstrated in studies in which the probability and the desirability of the consequences were manipulated independently (Hustinx, Van Enschot, & Hoeken, 2007; Johnson, Smith-McLallen, Killeya, & Levi, 2004). Whereas the desirability manipulation did influence the messages' persuasiveness, the probability manipulation did not, leading Johnson et al. (2004, p. 229) to conclude that "valence matters more than likelihood."

From a rational analysis perspective, the question of why people deal with desirability and probability in a different way is interesting. Taking a closer look at the manipulation of a consequence's desirability may provide a clue as to where to look for an answer. O'Keefe discusses examples related to the implementation of a senior comprehensive exam. The strong argument refers to the consequence that "undergraduates would have better employment opportunities and higher salaries" whereas the weak one states that "enrollment would increase." With the possible exception of university administrators, most people do not have to think twice to detect a difference in desirability between those consequences. In fact, Mercier and Sperber (2011) would go as far as to say that people do not have to (consciously) think at all to reach that conclusion. They would consider the conclusion to be an "intuitive belief"; that is, a belief held without awareness of the reasons for holding it. Assessing the probability that the implementation of the comprehensive exam is likely to increase job opportunities and salaries, however, appears to require conscious reasoning and possibly additional information on why this consequence is expected to occur. This difference may explain why people find it much easier to distinguish desirable from less desirable consequences than to distinguish likely from less likely consequences (Areni & Lutz, 1988) and why message designers feel the need to provide additional evidence to support a claim about a consequence's probability much more often than to provide such support for the claim about its desirability (Hornikx, Starren, & Hoeken, 2003).

O'Keefe clearly shows that people meet normative standards when responding to the desirability component of consequence-based argument but fail to do so when responding to the probability component. This difference may be the result of people's ability to assess a consequence's desirability without much (or any) conscious reasoning, whereas conscious effort and/or additional information is required to assess its probability. A different explanation could be that people are unable to evaluate evidence in support of probability claims. However, Hoeken and Hustinx (2009) have shown that people can evaluate such information in a normatively adequate way. A logical next step would be to study the persuasiveness of consequence-based arguments in which consequences are not instantly recognized as desirable or undesirable but that can be categorized as such if the supporting evidence is processed. In the period before Al Gore, reference to the "thinning of the ozone layer" may have not been regarded immediately as an undesirable consequence by most people. In such a case, evidence may be required to influence people's perception of the consequence's desirability. Hoeken, Timmers, and Schellens (in press) show that people possess the relevant tools to assess such supporting evidence. The question is whether the desirability of consequences has a different impact on the persuasion process if it needs to be consciously inferred than if it is automatically recognized.

Implications for Tailored Message Design

O'Keefe states that the lesson that more desirable consequences have more impact on the persuasion process is of limited use for message designers because it does not address the question of *which* consequences to emphasize given a certain topic, a certain goal, and a certain target audience. The strategy proposed by Ajzen and Fishbein (1980) to have target audience members list consequences of the targeted behavior is probably still the best advice to compile a list of potential arguments. On this list, there can be short-term and long-term consequences, user-image or product-use consequences, consequences that help the audience to stand out of the crowd or that may help them to blend in, and consequences referring to the prevention of problems or the promotion of success. O'Keefe has shown that the desirability of these consequences depends on an individual's personality characteristics, such as, respectively, their consideration of future consequences, the level of self-monitoring, the person's position on the individualism-collectivism dimension, and his or her regulatory focus.

Information on the interaction between consequence characteristics and personality variables is of great value to message designers who aim to tailor messages to the target audience. Kreuter, Strecher, and Glassman (1999) define tailored materials as ones that are "intended to reach one specific person, are based on characteristics that are unique to that person, are related to the outcome of interest, and have been derived from an individual assessment" (p. 276). Noar, Benac, and Harris (2007) conducted a meta-analysis on tailored print health communication interventions and reported an effect ($r = .074$) of tailoring on behavior change. This relatively modest effect size suggests that tailoring may be an effective strategy but that there is also room for improvement.

Tailoring the message by selecting consequences that are specifically desirable to the target audience may be an important step forward in tailored communication. O'Keefe shows that desirability matters to a message's persuasiveness and that the perception of a consequence's desirability may depend on the audience's personality. Furthermore, attitudes based upon an evaluation of arguments are more stable and better predictors of the subsequent behavior (Petty, Haugtvedt, & Smith, 1995, p. 108). Thus it seems logical to assume that messages containing consequences tailored to an individual's characteristics are more effective in producing stable behavior change. Identifying personality characteristics that lead to differences in the perceived desirability of consequences helps message designers to select which personality characteristics they need to assess in order to tailor the message to an individual.

Conclusion

Fishbein and Ajzen (1981) noted that our lack of knowledge on what constitutes a strong argument "is probably the most serious problem in communication and persuasion research" (p. 351). Almost 30 years later, and despite several calls to address the issue, the same authors complained that "we don't at this point have a good, validated method to assess an argument's strength or validity" (Fishbein & Ajzen, 2010, p. 344). To be sure, O'Keefe does not resolve this issue, neither does he claim to do so. However, by employing the concept of consequence-based arguments as a lens to take a close look at seemingly unrelated lines of research, he elegantly shows that for this frequently used type of argument, we may know quite a lot about what makes them convincing: The more the consequence is perceived as desirable, the more acceptable the conclusion is. I hope to have shown that this finding opens up interesting venues for future research as well as contribute to the improvement of tailored communication.

References

Ajzen, I., & Fishbein, M. (1980). *Understanding attitudes and predicting social behavior.* Englewood Cliffs, NJ: Prentice-Hall.

Areni, C. S., & Lutz, R. J. (1988). The role of argument quality in the elaboration likelihood model. In M. J. Houston (Ed.), *Advances in consumer research* (Vol. 15, pp. 197–203,). Provo, UT: Association for Communication Research.

Baron, J. (2000). *Thinking and deciding* (3rd ed.). Cambridge, England: Cambridge University Press.

Chater, N., & Oaksford, M. (1999). Ten years of the rational analysis of cognition. *Trends in Cognitive Sciences, 3,* 57–65. doi:10.1016/S1364-6613(98)01273-X

Fishbein, M., & Ajzen, I. (1981). Acceptance, yielding, and impact: Cognitive processes in persuasion. In R. E. Petty, T. Ostrom, & T. Brock (Eds.), *Cognitive responses in persuasion* (pp. 339–359). Hillsdale, NJ: Erlbaum.

Fishbein, M., & Ajzen, I. (2010). *Predicting and changing behavior: The reasoned action approach.* New York: Taylor & Francis.

Hahn, U., & Oaksford, M. (2006). A normative theory of argument strength. *Informal Logic, 26,* 1–24.

Hoeken, H., & Hustinx, L. (2009). When is statistical evidence superior to anecdotal evidence? The role of argument type. *Human Communication Research, 35,* 491–510. doi:10.1111/j.1468-2958.2009.01360.x

Hoeken, H., Timmers, R., & Schellens, P. J. (in press). Arguing about desirable consequences: What constitutes a convincing argument? *Thinking and Reasoning,*

Hornikx, J., Starren, M., & Hoeken, H. (2003). Cultural influence on the relative occurrence of evidence types. In F. H. van Eemeren, J. A. Blair, C. A. Willard, & A. F. Snoeck Henkemans (Eds.), *Proceedings of the Fifth Conference of the International Society for the Study of Argumentation* (pp. 531–536). Amsterdam, the Netherlands: Sic Sat.

Hustinx, L., Van Enschot, R., & Hoeken, H. (2007). Argument quality in the Elaboration Likelihood Model: An empirical study of strong and weak arguments in a persuasive message. In F. H. van Eemeren, J. A. Blair, C. A. Willard, & B. Garssen

(Eds.), *Proceedings of the Sixth Conference of the International Society for the Study of Argumentation* (pp. 651–657). Amsterdam, the Netherlands: Sic Sat.

Johnson, B. T., Smith-McLallen, A., Killeya, L. A., & Levin, K. D. (2004). Truth or consequences: Overcoming resistance with positive thinking. In E. S. Knowles & J. A. Linn (Eds.), *Resistance and persuasion* (pp. 215–233). Mahwah, NJ: Erlbaum.

Kreuter, M., Strecher, V., & Glassman, B. (1999). One size does not fit all: The case for tailoring print materials. *Annals of Behavioral Medicine, 41,* 53–62. doi:M. 10.1007/BF02895958

Mercier, H., & Sperber, D. (2011). Why do humans reason? Arguments for an argumentative theory. *Behavioral and Brain Sciences, 34,* 57–11. doi:10.1017/S0140525X10000968

Noar, S. M., Benac, C. N., & Harris, M. (2007). Does tailoring matter? Meta-analytic review of tailored print health behavior change interventions. *Psychological Bulletin, 133,* 673–693. doi:10.1037/0033-2909.133.4.673

Petty, R. E., Haugtvedt, C. P., & Smith, S. M. (1995). Elaboration as a determinant of attitude strength: Creating attitudes that are persistent, resistant, and predictive of behavior. In R. E. Petty & J. A. Krosnick (Eds.), *Attitude strength: Antecedents and consequences* (pp. 93–130). Mahwah, NJ: Erlbaum.

Reinard, J. C. (1991). *Foundations of argument: Effective communication for critical thinking.* Dubuque, IA: Brown.

Schellens, P. J., & Jong, M. D. T. (2004). Argumentation schemes in persuasive brochures. *Argumentation, 18,* 295–323. doi:10.1023/B:ARGU.0000046707.68172.35

CHAPTER CONTENTS

7   Social Media Use in Organizations

Exploring the Affordances of Visibility, Editability, Persistence, and Association

Jeffrey W. Treem and Paul M. Leonardi

Northwestern University

The use of social media technologies—such as blogs, wikis, social networking sites, social tagging, and microblogging—is proliferating at an incredible pace. One area of increasing adoption is organizational settings where managers hope that these new technologies will help improve important organizational processes. However, scholarship has largely failed to explain if and how uses of social media in organizations differ from existing forms of computer-mediated communication. In this chapter, we argue that social media are of important consequence to organizational communication processes because they afford behaviors that were difficult or impossible to achieve in combination before these new technologies entered the workplace. Our review of previous studies of social media use in organizations uncovered four relatively consistent affordances enabled by these new technologies: Visibility, persistence, editability, and association. We suggest that the activation of some combination of these affordances could influence many of the processes commonly studied by organizational communication theorists. To illustrate this point, we theorize several ways through which these four social media affordances may alter socialization, knowledge sharing, and power processes in organizations.

R ecently, numerous commentators have suggested that social media technologies—blogs, wikis, social networking sites (SNS), microblogs, or social tagging[1] tools—may facilitate communication practices in organizations that differ from those associated with traditional computer-mediated communication (CMC) technologies like e-mail, teleconferencing, intranets, decision-support systems, and instant messaging (Grudin, 2006; McAfee, 2006; Steinhuser, Smolnik, & Hoppe, 2011). In addition to the scholarly literature on the role of social media use in organizations, the business press has issued a number of bold proclamations such as: "Social media will change your business" (Baker & Green, 2008) and asked such daring questions as: "Can social apps kill enterprise software?" (DuBois, 2010). Whether or not one believes or discounts such statements, social media adoption within organizations is occurring at a rapid pace. According to a survey by global consulting firm McKinsey, 65% of companies reported the use of Web 2.0 technologies in their organizations (Bughin & Chui, 2010). Forrester Research predicts that corporate spending on enterprise social media will reach more than $4.6 billion annually by 2013 (Young et al., 2008).

Yet despite the increased adoption of social media by firms, the implications of these new technologies for organizational processes are not yet well understood by communication researchers. Scholars have suggested that social media adoption *in organizations*[2] is outpacing empirical understanding of the use of these technologies and our theories about why they may alter various organizational processes (Raeth, Smolnik, Urbach, & Zimmer, 2009). Because the implications of social media use in organizations are not well understood, we use this chapter to accomplish three primary tasks. First, we explore the emerging body of research on the use of social media use in organizations for evidence that social media constitute a set of communication technologies that are distinct in their implications for organizational processes from traditional CMC technologies. We find that scholars treat social media as a new class of technologies that may alter organizational dynamics in profound ways. Given this finding, our second task is to explicate the distinct ways social media merge with ongoing communicative processes that occur within and constitute organizations. We employ an "affordance approach" that allows us to organize findings reported in empirical studies into four categories describing consistent ways organizational members use the material features of social media technologies to accomplish their work. Using this categorization we then commence our third task, which is to draw implications for how the use of social media within organizations may affect particular organizational processes that are of great interest to communication researchers.

Defining Social Media: Toward an Affordance Approach

What Are Social Media?[3]

To address the question of whether social media technologies are distinct from other forms of CMC commonly used in today's organizations it is helpful to briefly trace the history of social media technologies. The first known use of the term *social media* in print is believed to have occurred in 1997, when then-AOL executive Ted Leonsis commented that organizations needed to provide consumers with "social media, places where they can be entertained, communicate, and participate in a social environment" (Bercovici, 2010). The first publicly popular SNS, SixDegrees.com, which let users create online personal profiles and lists of friends, was launched that same year (boyd & Ellison, 2007). During the following decade, a number of other popular social media technologies such as the blogging platforms LiveJournal and Blogger (both in 1999), the wiki-based encyclopedia Wikipedia (2001), the social bookmarking service Delicious (2003, formerly del.icio.us), the SNSs MySpace (2003) and Facebook (2004), and the microblogging service Twitter (2004) made their debuts. As adoption of these technologies grew, social media moved quickly from the domain of the tech-savvy to the mainstream (Shirky, 2008). The Pew

Internet and American Life Project has reported that 61% of adults (18 years and older) have used SNSs and 32% have read a blog (Zickuhr, 2010).

As social media have begun to enter popular consciousness, some scholars have treated them as just another genre of CMC (Herring, 2004), while others have attempted to define social media, broadly, as a distinct category of technologies. Following the latter strategy, Kaplan and Haenlein (2010), for example, refer to social media as "Internet-based applications that build on the ideological and technological foundations of Web 2.0, and that allow the creation and exchange of User Generated Content" (p. 62). In lieu of providing a clear definition of social media, the default approach in many academic writings has been to define the term *social media* by pointing toward the types of technologies that people recognize, implicitly, as social media (e.g., blogs, wikis, SNSs, social tagging, etc.).

However, a referential approach to a definition of social media focuses people's attention on what the technology itself does (or does not do) instead of the ways the technology becomes mutually constituted with the organizational context in which it is embedded (Leonardi, 2009). Moreover, studies that focus on the features of specific technologies in organizations provide limited insight into why use of a technology produced particular effects (Nass & Mason, 1990). In sum, many studies of social media use provide insights about a specific tool, in a particular organizational context, but they do not develop theory about the consequences of social media use for organizing. Current definitions of social media are either too application-focused, preventing generalization across contexts, or too broad, obscuring the ways the technology may influence behaviors. To aid theory development around social media use in organizations this paper eschews a definition of social media based on features, and considers the *affordances* they offer users.

An Affordance Approach

In an effort to explain how animals perceive their environments, James Gibson (1986), a perceptual psychologist, argued that an object like a rock could be used very differently by distinct animals because each animal perceived a particular set of activities for which the rock would be useful. He suggested that animals perceived not what an object is, but rather what kinds of uses it affords and called such perceptions of an object's utility an "affordance." In Gibson's formulation, people do not interact with an object prior to or without perceiving what the object is good for. As he suggests, the physical features of an object exist apart from the people who use them, but those features are infused with meaning "relative to the posture and behavior of the animal being considered" (pp. 127–128). Although the features of an object are common to each person who encounters them, the affordances of that artifact are not. Affordances are unique to the particular ways in which an actor, or a set of actors, perceives and uses the object. To this end, Gibson (1986) offers an explanation of the relationship between materiality and affordances:

> The psychologists assume that objects are composed of their qualities ... color, texture, composition, size shape and features of shape, mass, elasticity, rigidity, and mobility.... But I now suggest that what we perceive when we look at objects are their affordances, not their qualities. We can discriminate the dimensions of difference if required to do so in an experiment, but what the object affords us is what we normally pay attention to. (p. 134)

Because the material out of which an object is made can provide multiple affordances, it is possible that one object can produce multiple outcomes.

Scholars who study the relationship between new technologies and social practices have found great utility in the affordance concept because it helps to explain why people using the same technology may engage in similar or disparate communication and work practices. Since Gibson's formulation of the notion of affordance, some scholars have used the concept to explore the ways in which new technologies can be better designed (Gaver, 1991; Norman, 1990), while others have used it to explore the dynamics of technologically occasioned social change (Orlikowski & Barley, 2001; Zammutto, Griffith, Majchrzak, Dougherty, & Faraj, 2007).

Today, the most nuanced writings on the relationship between technology and organizational change emphasize the relational character of affordances. In this view, affordances are not exclusively properties of people or of artifacts—they are constituted in relationships between people and the materiality of the things with which they come in contact. "Materiality" here refers to the features of a technological artifact—whether that artifact is a piece of hardware or software. In this formulation, materiality exists independent of people, but affordances do not. Because people come to materiality with diverse goals, they perceive a technology as affording distinct possibilities for action. In the relational view, affordances of an artifact can change across different contexts even though its materiality does not. Similarly, people may perceive that an artifact offers no affordances for action, perceiving instead that it constrains their ability to carry out their goals. Building on this relational approach, Leonardi and Barley (2008) and Leonardi (2011) argued that the affordances of one technology are often the same or similar across diverse organizational settings because the material features of the technology place limits on the kinds of interpretations people can form of it and the uses to which it can be put.

As several recent studies of technology use in organizations have noted (Hutchby, 2001; Leonardi, 2010; Markus & Silver, 2008), using a relational approach to affordances to explain how a new technology merges with an existing organizational system is useful for theory in at least four ways. First, focusing on affordances that arise as individuals begin to use features of a new technology helps explain consistency of effects within and across organizations while avoiding deterministic images of technologically induced organizational change. Second, focusing on the relationship between a user and a technology's material features avoids privileging social determinism in explaining organizational changes and ignoring the properties of the technology itself. Third, focusing on affordances, rather than exclusively on either material features or social practice, develops theories of sociomaterial dynamics, as opposed to theories of specific technologies (which may soon become obsolete anyway) or theories of organizations that ignore the empirical reality that most all practice is bound up with the use of particular technologies (Orlikowski, 2007). Finally, an affordance approach encourages the researcher to look at communicative actions enabled by the relationship between an organizational context and a technology's functionality. In other words, it is agnostic to particular features of a technology and, instead, asks what combinations of material features allow people to do things that were difficult or impossible to do without the technology (Leonardi, 2011). For example, IBM's SNS SocialBlue (formerly Beehive) has an "About You" feature through which individuals can decide to enter information that will be displayed to other users as part of the employee's profile on the site (DiMicco et al., 2008). Following an affordance approach, the existence of the "About You" feature is not important in and of itself. Rather, it is only important insomuch as it affords people the ability to communicate in new ways. From an affordance approach, the researcher would ask, "what does the 'About You' feature afford people the opportunity to do?" and then he or she would examine the features of other social media to discover whether those other technologies have a feature (that is perhaps different from the "About You" feature in SocialBlue) that affords the same type of communicative behavior.

We argue that defining social media by describing what kinds of behaviors they typically afford across various organizations is one way researchers can transcend the particularities of any technology or its features, and focus on communicative outcomes. Moreover, defining social media by enumerating its affordances may allow for a nuanced understanding of when, why, and how social media occasion change in organizational practice.

Organizational Affordances of Social Media Use

To explore the affordances of social media use for organizational communication we reviewed the literature for any studies that mentioned "social media," "Web 2.0," "enterprise 2.0," or "social software" *in organizations.*[1] Our decision to focus on social media use in organizations, as opposed to social media use generally, was informed by research suggesting that people's perception of the utility of a technology is formed differently when that technology is used in the workplace rather than outside of it (O'Mahony & Barley, 1999; Wellman et al., 1996). Consequently, our goal was to assemble a wide array of studies that examined use of social media within organizations. We believed that this strategy would highlight affordances of social media use in organizations, as opposed to social media use elsewhere, and enable tentative generalizations about the effects of social media on core organizational communication processes.

Not surprisingly, given that these technologies are only just beginning to proliferate throughout organizations, we found few articles in communication journals that addressed our issue of interest. To expand the pool of empirical studies, we cast our net wider to include work from the areas of Human-Computer Interaction (HCI), Computer-Supported Cooperative Work (CSCW), and System Sciences. All of these disciplines explicitly address issues of organizational communication, though often from the standpoint of designing (as opposed to using) technology to facilitate particular outcomes. We restricted our review to papers that focused on one or more of the following five technologies that are commonly classified as "social media": wikis, SNSs, blogs, social tagging applications, and microblogs. Once a relevant article was identified, we reviewed the articles cited by that work to identify additional material. This process was repeated until no new literature was revealed.

We reviewed this set of studies with two specific questions in mind: (a) What affordances commonly emerged from social media use in organizations? (b) How did these social media affordances differ from those enabled by other forms of organizational CMC technologies? To answer the first question, we used a two-stage inductive coding scheme. In the first stage, we examined each paper to determine what new affordances the technology enabled that users did not experience before its introduction. We sorted papers with similar affordances into categories and revised those categories as we read more papers. Categorization was not mutually exclusive in that papers could be placed in multiple categories. Four distinct affordances emerged from this stage of analysis: visibility, persistence, editability, and association. In the second stage, we examined all papers within each category to enumerate a list of the specific technology features that interacted with the organizational context to produce that affordance. We followed the same process of comparison and recategorization that we conducted in the first stage. The resulting lists of features for the four affordances can be found in Tables 7.2 to 7.5.

To answer the second question, we created Table 7.1, which lists the five types of social media that were the focus of our analysis as well as a list of traditional (nonsocial media) CMC technologies—this list of nonsocial Media CMC was compiled using examples taken from Culnan and Markus (1987) and Rice and Gattiker (2001). In this table we also provide examples of types of popular forms of social media and traditional CMC applications used outside of and within (enterprise applications) organizations. We then ranked each of these types of technologies based on the degree (high to low) to which they enable each of the four affordances uncovered in our review. As the table shows, more traditional forms of organizational CMC enable some of these affordances, but lack a consistent high distribution of these affordances across the four categories. For example, e-mail certainly affords editability because users can carefully craft messages prior to sending, and the medium has high persistence for individual users who can save, store, and search through their own messages. However, e-mail does not afford much visibility into other's communications, as the messages a person receives are limited to those addresses

Table 7.1 Comparison of Affordances Across across Social Media and Bbetween Social Media and other Organizational CMCs

| Technology | Example Applications | | Affordances | | | |
	Public	Organization	Visibility	Editability	Persistence	Association
SOCIAL MEDIA						
Wikis	Wikipedia	Socialtext, MediaWiki	High	High	High	High
Social Networking Applications (SNA)	Facebook	IBM's Social Blue Sales Force's Chatter	High	High	High	High
Blogs	Wordpress, Blogger,	Most can be installed in organization	High	High	High	High
Social Tagging	Delicious	IBM's Dogear; PARC's SparTag	High	High	High	High
Microblogging	Twitter	Yammer	High	High	High	High
OTHER ORGANIZATIONAL CMC						
Instant Messaging (can be recorded, but rarely is)	AOL Instant Messenger, GChat	Jabber	Low	Med.	Low	Low
E-mail	Hotmail, Gmail	Outlook Exchange	Low-High	High	High	Low
Teleconferencing (can be recorded)	Skype	Webex	Low	Med.	Med.	Med.
Shared Database	Dropbox	Microsoft Access/ Sharepoint	Low-High	Med.	High	Low

indicated by the message's sender. Social media, by contrast, rate uniformly high on their ability to foster these four affordances. We argue that in combination, visibility, persistence, editability, and association are four affordances that help to characterize what is new and, quite possibly, consequential about social media for organizational communication processes.

In the following sections we review each of these affordances individually. For each affordance we first briefly discuss how the concept has been addressed in communication technology scholarship (not solely in regards to organizational social media). We then review the literature to exhibit how use of the features of social media creates these specific affordances in organizational contexts.

Visibility

The papers in our sample suggested that social media afford users the ability to make their behaviors, knowledge, preferences, and communication network connections that were once invisible (or at least very hard to see) visible to others in the organization. Our notion of visibility is tied to the amount of effort people must expend to locate information. As research shows, if people perceive that information is difficult to access, or they do not know what information exists for them to access, they will likely not seek it out (Brown & Duguid, 2001). In this regard, information about people's work behaviors, tasks, knowledge, or whatever else, though it may be theoretically available for people to uncover, may be, for all intents and purposes, invisible. Additionally, individuals may be functionally *invisible* to others because even those colocated may not have domain knowledge to understand the work practice of someone form a different specialty (Cross, Borgatti, & Parker, 2003; Nardi & Engeström, 1999).

If social media technologies enable people to easily and effortlessly *see* information about someone else, we say that the technology was used to make that person's knowledge visible. Bregman and Haythornthwaite (2001) note that visibility "refers to the means, methods, and opportunities for presentation; in our usage it primarily addresses the speakers' concerns with the presentation of self" (p. 5). Whether through posts, comments, status updates, votes, friending, revisions, or pictures, contributions to social media are visible to all who have access to the system. Scholars have noted that social media's ability to provide increased visibility into both behaviors and information separates them from other technologies and creates unique consequences (boyd, 2010; Grudin, 2006). Other forms of CMC common in organizations, such as e-mail or instant messaging, make information visible, but not in the communal manner afforded by social media.

Table 7.2 provides an overview of which features of various social media were found by authors to afford visibility when the organizational need arose.

Below, we outline three types of information or actions that are made visible through the use of social media in organizations: (a) work behavior, (b) metaknowledge, and (c) organizational activity streams.

Table 7.2 Social Media Features Affording Visibility

Social Media Technology	Features Affording Visibility	Illustration in Literature
Wikis	• Displays text and graphic content contributions • List of edits to entries • Notification when changes have been made • to entries Personal Profiles	(Danis & Singer, 2008; Holtzblatt et al., 2010; Kosonen & Kianto, 2009)
Social Networking Sites	• Status updates • Pushes activity to connections • Lists of "friends" or connections • Personal Profiles • Visible in Search Engines • Allows comments and opinion expression (e.g., the "like button") on content • Recommender algorithm shows similar others	(DiMicco et al., 2009; Farzan et al., 2008; Holtzblatt & Tierney, 2011)
Blogs	• Content publishing consisting of text, video or audio • Pushes content to subscribers • Personal Profiles A • llows comments on content • Entries indexed by search enginesInbound links	(Brzozowski et al., 2009; Efimova & Grudin, 2007; Farrell et al., 2008; Wattal et al., 2009; Yardi et al., 2009)
Social Tagging	• Content publishing consisting of comments and descriptions of entries • Displays number of people who bookmarked same content • Pushes content to subscribers • Shows others with similar entries	(Damianos et al., 2007; Millen & Feinberg, 2006; Muller et al., 2006; Pan & Millen, 2008; Thom-Santelli & Muller, 2007)
Microblogging	• Content publishing consisting of text or hyperlinks (limited in number of characters) • Pushes content to subscribers • Shows subscribers and those to whom user subscribes • Personal profiles, indexed by search engines	(Schondienst et al., 2011; Zhang et al., 2010; Zhao & Rosson, 2009)

Work Behavior.   One of the most common and basic features of social media is that they present content communally, which means contributions can be easily located and viewed by other employees. Efimova and Grudin (2008) interviewed 34 employee bloggers at Microsoft regarding the reasons why individuals maintained organizational blogs and how they perceived readership.

Bloggers interviewed felt the ability to self-publish content allowed employees to more easily communicate directly about work. The authors concluded that "In employee weblogs, ideas that were previously unarticulated or hidden in personal archives become visible, interlinked, and searchable" (p. 11). Farrell, Kellogg, and Thomas (2008) reviewed studies on the use of internal blogs, wikis, social tagging, and SNS at IBM[4] and also concluded that social media helped people communicate and share work across organizational boundaries. Specifically, they noted how comments on blogs could result in far-reaching organizational conversations and that the iterative nature of wiki contributions could sustain and share communication.

The affordance of visibility was also found in organizational microblog use. Zhang, Qu, Cody, and Wu (2010) studied use of the microblogging tool Yammer by 458 employees inside a Fortune 500 company. The researchers manually coded 300 Yammer messages and found the most commonly shared material was internal company news. They commented that the communal nature of the tool afforded employees "a place to publish their local news at the corporate level, which was close to impossible to do previously" (p. 126). Social tagging applications served a similar function of publicizing behavioral information to the organization. Pan and Millen (2008) conducted a year-long field study of social tagging at a large, multinational company to understand how the tool was used by different work groups. Results suggested that bookmarks reflected the respective goals of business units. The research-focused group tagged more external, trend-focused bookmarks while headquarters and software development employees tagged more internal material. The research-ers noted "the very act of creating a bookmark is an explicit indicator of the utility or value of the internet and intranet information resource" (p. 9).

Users of social media in organizations sometimes recognized the visibility of their work behavior afforded by the use of the technology, and were strate-gic in presenting themselves to others. For example, in their analysis of wiki use over 20 months at an industrial research organization, Danis and Singer (2008) found that workers recognized that posting information to a wiki might provide stakeholders (such as funders) access to works-in-progress. Because employees wanted to be seen as competent, and viewed wiki contributions as "official" communication, workers often documented with other less vis-ible media—like access-controlled project repositories—that did not permit outsiders to see content (Danis & Singer, 2008, p. 7). Similarly, Holtzblatt, Damianos, and Weiss (2010) interviewed 26 wiki users at MITRE, a technol-ogy research organization, and found that individuals were, "uncomfortable sharing documents that were still in a draft state" and instead kept unfinished content in personal repositories such as hard drives and e-mail systems (p. 4667). These examples of wiki use and nonuse indicate that the features of the technology, in this case communal publication of material, afforded workers ways to make communication more or less visible.

Many employees valued the visibility of communication possible through social media. Thom-Santelli and Muller (2007) interviewed 40 users of IBM's dogear social tagging tool regarding the motivations behind the tags chosen. Results indicated that employees found the visibility of the social media useful for attracting the attention of specific organizational audiences. In another study conducted at a large communication technology company, Kosonen and Kianto (2009) held two group interviews to examine how employees were using wikis to manage information. Employees noted that the open nature of social media encouraged informal collaboration and supported knowledge sharing among workers. Many employees liked that the "open-source ideology" afforded by social media opened communication and eliminated decisions regarding who to include, a choice workers faced when using other CMCs (p. 27). Work by Damianos, Cuomo, Griffith, Hirst, and Smallwood (2007), who studied the introduction of a social tagging system at MITRE, and research by Millen and Feinberg (2006), which examined 8 months use of the dogear tool at IBM, revealed that despite options to keep tags private, the overwhelming majority of users chose to make information publicly available to others. Public tags could be used both to find desired information and to direct others' attention to specific content.

Metaknowledge. The visibility of social media can also provide metaknowledge about the type of people in the organization and what they may know. As one example, DiMicco, Geyer, Millen, Dugan, and Brownholtz (2009) reviewed three months of activity by 285 IBM employees on a internal SNS named Beehive and interviewed nine participants to determine how individuals used the tool. Beehive let employees create profile pages that contained photos, corporate directory information, and a summary of content contributed by the individual. Findings showed employees used the visible information contributed to learn more about the backgrounds, interests, and activities of coworkers (DiMicco et al, 2009). In another instance, Muller, Ehrlich, and Farrell (2006) investigated user behaviors at IBM following the implementation of a prototype technology that allowed workers to supplement corporate directory information with tags that would be visible to others. Usage data found that 79% of users tagged content about themselves and for more than half (51%) of users this constituted their only tagging activity. The authors noted that although this form of overt self-presentation could be seen as selfish, it might also help inform others of skills available for potential collaborations (Muller et al., 2006).

Shami, Ehrlich, Gay, and Hancock (2009) surveyed 67 users of an expertise locater system in a global technology company and found that employees were more likely to contact users of social media for information. Workers felt social media users were both more knowledgeable in particular domains and were more likely to respond to inquiries. John and Seligman (2006) discussed how collaborative tags may be used to identify experts in an organization and demonstrated how this information could be integrated into a communication system at the business communication company Avaya. The researchers noted that an underlying premise of their approach to expertise identification was that tags "may be presumed to be representative of user interests and expertise" (p. 1). This ability to advertise one's areas of knowledge may promote social media use in organizations. Schondienst, Krasnova, Gunther, and Riehle (2011) asked survey respondents familiar with microblogging to imagine a "Twitter-like" tool was in use at their place of work, and collected responses regarding expected behaviors and outcomes. Data from 82 individuals found that workers who believed microblogging use could increase one's reputation were the most likely to post material or follow others' contributions.

Organizational Activity Streams.   Social media afford individuals the ability to see information related to the status of ongoing activities in the organization. Zhao and Rosson (2009) interviewed 11 Twitter users at a large IT company and asked how microblogging might influence organizational communication. Respondents felt microblogging could assist in "keeping a pulse on what is going on in others' minds" by providing access to streams of comments from individuals across the organization (p. 249). In another study, Brzozowski (2009) reviewed the use of social media tools at HP and described the design of a tool that used contributions to blogs, wikis, and social tagging tools to help identify novel and popular organizational content. He commented that employees viewed social media content in the company as "a way to orient themselves in the organization" (p. 7).

   The ability to see coworker activity through social media use also influenced decisions to actively communicate. To examine what influenced blog adoption in organizations, Wattal, Racherla, and Mandviwalla (2009) examined log data from 2,667 employees at a multinational electronics corporation. The study found that blog use by one's manager and others in one's office was associated with a greater likelihood of individual blog use. Blog participation can also be influenced by the knowledge one has about the viewers of contributed material. Yardi, Golder, and Brzozowski (2009) analyzed a year of log data on an internal blog server at a global technology company and interviewed 96 employee bloggers of various activity levels. Workers expected posting material to social media to provide increased social recognition in the organization, and lack of recognition deterred continued participation. In a related study conducted at the same organization, analysis of log data revealed that blog authors published more frequently if they saw they received many comments on prior posts (a visible form of information), but the number of actual clicks on one's blog (not visible) had no effect (Brzozowski, Sandholm, & Hogg, 2009).

   Farzan et al. (2008) studied the implementation of an incentive system in IBM's Beehive SNS that was designed to motivate contributions of photographs, lists, comments, and profile updates by providing points and labels to users for adding information. An experiment comparing employee SNS use in the incentive condition against that of those in a nonincentive condition found the visible incentives increased contributions. Additionally, interviews with six employees in the incentive condition found that users monitored and compared their standing relative to coworkers.

Persistence

Communication is persistent if it remains accessible in the same form as the original display after the actor has finished his or her presentation (Bregman & Haythornthwaite, 2001; Donath, Karahalios, & Viegas, 1999). This affordance of persistence has also been referred to as "reviewability" (Clark & Brennan, 1991), "recordability" (Hancock, Toma, & Ellison, 2007), or "permanence" (Whittaker, 2003). When a poster to a blog or SNS logs out, that information remains available to users and does not expire or disappear. In technologies such as instant messaging or video-conferencing, the conversation is normally bound in time, and a record of the interaction does not exist beyond what participants remember. Because social media enable conversations that persist past the time of their initial posts, communicative acts can have consequences long past the initial point of presentation. For example, an individual who is given an assignment during a teleconference or over an instant message conversation may later find another coworker claims responsibility for the task, and have few means by which to clarify the dispute. However, if tasks are assigned via a team wiki, a communal record persists that is difficult to discount. As Erickson and Kellogg (2000) noted, "persistence opens the door to a variety of new uses and practices: persistent conversations may be searched, browsed, replayed, annotated, visualized, restructured, and recontextualized, with what are likely to be profound impacts on personal, social, and institutional practices" (p. 68). Table 7.3 provides an overview of which material features of various social media were shown to afford persistence.

Persistence can aid in the development of common ground in communicative settings, which has been shown to aid the transmission of complex ideas (Clark & Brennan, 1991). Having a record of previous communication can allow presentations of information to be properly contextualized and provide people with the time to better understand conversations (Gergle, Millen, Kraut, & Fussell, 2004; McCarthy, Miles, & Monk, 1991). If a worker is confused about the directions a manager gives over an instant messaging system he or she has little recourse except to ask the manager to clarify. Alternatively, if a manager gives directions using a microblog tool the individual could review the original communication in hopes of gaining understanding. Or, because the information remains over time, another user could later see the original communication and contribute with further useful information.

In what follows, we summarize three ways in which the literature shows how the affordance of persistence affects organizational action: (a) sustaining knowledge over time, (b) creating robust forms of communication, and (c) growing content.

Table 7.3 Social Media Features Affording Persistence

Social Media Technology	Features Affording Persistence	Illustration in Literature
Wikis	• History of activity and discussion recorded • Entries indexed by search engines	(Ding et al., 2007; Giordano, 2007; Grudin & Poole, 2010; Holtzblatt et al., 2010; Kane & Fichman, 2009; Majchrzak et al., 2006; Poole & Grudin, 2010; Rober & Cooper, 2011; Wagner, 2004; White & Lutters, 2007)
Social Networking Sites	• Profiles indexed by search engines • Allows catalogs of photos • Displays past activity of individuals on site	(DiMicco et al., 2009; Geyer et al., 2008; Mejova et al., 2011)
Blogs	• Links to past content • Entries indexed by search engine • Reverse chronological format provides timeline of content	(Huh et al., 2007; Jackson et al., 2007; Kolari et al., 2007)
Social Tagging	• Catalogs history of bookmarking activity • Profiles indexed by search engines • Contributions searchable	(Millen & Feinberg, 2006; M. Muller, 2007a, 2007b)
Microblogging	• Catalog of entries • Profiles indexed by search engines	(Gunther et al., 2009; Riemer & Richter, 2010)

Sustaining Knowledge Over Time.   The persistence of content created and stored in social media allows the knowledge individuals contribute to the technology to develop and remain available over time. Majchrzak, Wagner, and Yates (2006) conducted a survey of 168 corporate wiki users to investigate if wikis are sustainable in organizations, what benefits the tool might provide, and if there were different types of content contributors. Respondents reported that wikis could remain active over the course of months, and wikis that persisted saw increased participation over time. Kolari et al. (2007) examined internal blogs at IBM over a three-year period to explore the network structure of blog communication that developed inside the organization. Analysis of the degree of distribution of blog users and their respective posts showed that participation created a scale-free network in which a minority of contributors garnered the majority of attention. One implication of this network formation is that even if a moderate number of blogs or bloggers ceased activity in the network it would not significantly affect the ability of users to connect to information of interest on others' blogs. Jackson, Yates, and Orlikowski

(2007) also studied internal blog use by exploring participation in a global IT company. The authors analyzed usage statistics, interviewing heavy and non-blog-users, and conducted a web-based survey of different types of blog users identified through use (heavy, medium, and low). Survey results indicated that high blog use was not required in order for organizational members to perceive value from the information available (Jackson et al., 2007).

Research indicates that wikis, even more so than other social media tools, have afforded individuals the opportunity to work over long stretches of time in an asynchronous, collaborative, and distributed manner. In their case study of wiki use at MITRE, Holtzblatt et al., (2010) noted that wikis afforded individuals the means to independently add to tables and lists over time, providing a distinct advantage to the existing document-based method where workers modify the content of previous contributors. Additionally, Kane and Fichman (2009) reviewed attempts to utilize wikis in academic settings and found individuals were willing to use the technology to share and reuse current materials but were reluctant to engage in discussion about content. White and Lutters (2007) conducted phone interviews with seven individuals regarded as champions of wiki use at their respective organizations and concluded that wikis are effective as "a flexible knowledge repository" (p. 2). Similarly, in tracing the role of wikis relative to other knowledge management technologies, Wagner (2004) noted wikis can be particularly effective in ad hoc work—like addressing an organizational crisis—because they can generate information incrementally, and in a centralized form that is historically indexed. For example Majchrzak, Jarvenpaa, and Hollingshead (2007) documented how the use of a wiki in the wake of Hurricane Katrina allowed individuals across the world to quickly contribute and coordinate information regarding rescue and recovery efforts. Only 4 days after the hurricane the wiki was being accessed more than 1 million times a day and hosted information related to finding missing people, assisting relocation efforts, and locating government assistance.

Creating Robust Forms of Communication. When information and communications are persistent, content can be reused and reanalyzed over time to help refine it and make it more useful and robust. By "robust" we mean how difficult it is to destroy, compromise, or abandon content. In their review of social media use at IBM, Farrell et al. (2008) argued that the technologies could create a more "socially resilient enterprise" because "tracking and recording various interactions allows the possibility of *analyzing* interactions over time to improve their effectiveness and efficiency" (p. 3). In a specific example, Millen and Feinberg (2006) conducted an eight-month field study at IBM of how workers searched for information on the dogear social bookmarking tool. Usage data indicated that workers nearly universally viewed existing tags when searching for information, and commonly reused tags or consulted other individuals' lists of tags. Keeping existing tags and lists available to subsequent users of the social media made reuse easier and increased the likelihood that material would be popularized through ongoing use.

Social media also afford reuse of organizational content. Mejova, Schepper, Bergman, and Lu (2011) examined instances of presentation reuse in an internal file repository at IBM to explore why people would choose to reuse an existing file. Results indicated that workers were significantly more likely to reuse a presentation created by an employee that they had friended on the internal SNS tool. The reuse of content in social media also supported the formation of tighter relationships within organizations. In a set of related studies at IBM, researchers concluded that the use of social tags in the company's social bookmarking system, over time, coincided with the formation of communities of practice (Muller, 2007a, 2007b). These emergent communities of practice aided organizational learning by creating pools of knowledge that could be held and displayed in social media. Similarly, in an investigation of the use of lists on a SNS inside of IBM, users interviewed by Geyer et al. (2008) mentioned the lists operated as a template for other workers looking to contribute information to the site.

Further, unlike other technologies used for organizational knowledge management, social media may not require tremendous investment or maintenance by organizational officials. Rober and Cooper (2011) presented a case study of the development of JPL Wired, a Wikipedia-like resource inside NASA's Jet Propulsion Laboratory (JPL). After tracing the genesis and evolution of the tool, the authors asserted that the wikis were a "bottom-up" form of media that was heavily sustained by lower-level employees. Additionally, the researchers noted that the ability to easily capture and keep employee-contributed information in social media was particularly attractive to new and early career employees. Organizational newcomers could access the wiki instead of having to ask colleagues basic questions such as where to find office supplies or what were nearby places to eat (Rober & Cooper, 2011). In their study of blog use at a large IT company, Jackson et al. (2007) also found newer workers used the social media to gain access to an established community of information and resources.

Growing Content.   The nearly limitless space afforded by social media such as blogs and wikis facilitates the growth of communication through the addition of posts and pages. Huh, Bellamy, Jones, Thomas, and Erickson (2007) interviewed 14 internal bloggers at IBM and found one use of the technology was as repositories for knowledge that employees brought in from outside the organization. Poole and Grudin (2010) conducted interviews and online discussions at a large software company in an attempt to categorize types of organizational wikis. One way people used wikis was as a personal information management tool for storing materials, which allowed for the ongoing addition of relevant information. Riemer and Richter (2010) conducted a case study of microblog use at the German software company Communardo, using text analysis and seven interviews to determine if participation could be separated into different genres of use. Analysis found that organizational microbloggers who recognized that social media could hold information for future use occasionally used the tool to record knowledge such as login identifications and meeting minutes. Though this practice was not common, the authors found that users appropriating the technology for the purpose of information storage knew information would be indexed by search engines and could be easily called upon later.

One consequence of this seemingly unlimited storage is that the content embedded in social media tools can become unwieldy over time. In discussing the use of wikis in IBM's research group, Ding, Danis, Erickson, and Kellogg (2007) noted that maintenance quickly became an issue, and Grudin and Poole (2010) found that most wikis at the software company they studied were quickly abandoned. Giordano (2007) chronicled efforts among public-health oriented nonprofits in London to use wikis for shared learning and discovered the clutter of content caused users to "trip over" entries and discouraged use (p. 271). However, social media also provide individuals with the means to find content with filters and search tools. Gunther, Krasnova, Riehle, and Schoendienst (2009) conducted four focus groups aimed at gathering individuals' perceptions about microblogging in the workplace and building a model of adoption of the technology. Comments indicated that though some individuals were concerned with being overwhelmed by information, others felt microblogging, by allowing users to control who and what information streams they follow, could be a useful tool with which to manage content.

Editability

Editability refers to the fact the individuals can spend a good deal of time and effort crafting and recrafting a communicative act before it is viewed by others (Walther, 1993). Dennis, Fuller, and Valacich (2008) describe a similar affordance, rehearsability, that they assert enables a sender to compose a message with the exact meaning that he or she intends. Editability is a function of two aspects of an interaction: communication formed in isolation from others, and asynchronicity. A speaker need not worry about regulating nonverbal cues or involuntary reactions when using an asynchronous CMC; instead, they can focus on the form of the message they hope to convey. When communicating through a teleconferencing technology people can view the physical displays and reactions of counterparts. But when using social media tools, users need not worry about nonverbal cues.

Editability can also refer to the ability of an individual to modify or revise content they have already communicated (Rice, 1987), including straightforward acts such as editing a spelling error or deleting content. For example, an individual who includes a typographical error in an e-mail can do little to fix this mistake, and anyone viewing that e-mail will see the error. Users of a wiki, blog, or SNS can correct errors they identify and later viewers may never know a mistake occurred. Thus, the communicator retains some degree of control over content after the original communicative display. In Table 7.4, we

Table 7.4 Social Media Features Affording Editability

Social Media Technology	Features Affording Editability	Illustration in Literature
Wikis	• Asynchronous text-based entries • Previous history of edits available • Revisions permissible	(Arazy et al., 2009; Danis & Singer, 2008; Giordano, 2007; Grudin & Poole, 2010; Hasan & Pfaff, 2006; Holtzblatt et al., 2010; Yates et al., 2010)
Social Networking Sites	• Asynchronous text-based entries • Revision of own content on site permissible • Content contributions of others on individual's site can be deleted	(Dugan et al., 2008; Farzan et al., 2008)
Blogs	• Asynchronous text-based entries • Revision of content on own site permissible	(Huh et al., 2007)
Social Tagging	• Asynchronous text-based entries • Revision of content on own site permissible • Previous entries of others recommended for potential re-use	(Farrell et al., 2007; Muller et al., 2006; Thom-Santelli et al., 2008)
Microblogging	• Asynchronous text-based entries • Contributions on own site can be deleted	(Riemer & Richter, 2010)

indicate which material features of various social media were shown to afford editability.

By offering individuals the time to craft and compose messages, editability allows for more purposeful communication that may aid with message fidelity and comprehension. Dennis, Fuller, and Valacich (2008) argue that low synchronicity in a communication medium is particularly useful when the organization's goal is to convey information, or share knowledge that was previously unknown. Additionally, editability allows communicators to take into consideration the context in which their message is likely to be viewed (or later, after it was made, view the actual context in which it was viewed) and tailor their ideas accordingly.

In the sections below, we summarize three ways in which the literature suggests that the affordance of editability is used to shape behavior: (a) regulating personal expressions, (b) targeting content, and (c) improving information quality.

Regulating Personal Expressions.   The editability of content entered into social media allows users to strategically manipulate the ways that personal information is shared with others. For example, as discussed earlier, IBM's SNS contained an "About You" feature that allowed people to determine what information they wanted displayed to others in their personal profiles. Dugan et al. (2008) reviewed usage of the SNS over eight months and found that the percentage of users taking advantage of the free-form "About You" feature was higher than rates for other content categories such as lists, photographs, or comments. Furthermore, results from Farzan et al.'s (2008) experiment regarding incentives for SNS participation at IBM suggested many users patterned contributions in a way that would increase recognition from others and garner rewards. Similarly, studies examining social tagging at IBM found that organizational members used the ability to dictate labels as a form of impression management (Muller, Ehrlich, & Farrell, 2006) and "observed that most people tended to be extremely aware of tagging as a social activity. People think about how others will react to the tags they give" (Farrell, Lau, Wilcox, Nusser, & Muller, 2007, p. 99).

Targeting Content.   Studies indicated that users of social media often tailor messages for specific audiences. Because they have a high level of editorial control, communicators using social media can time when they present information and reshape messages based on the perceived responses from audiences. For example, research on the use of wikis in organizations revealed that individuals are reluctant to share works in progress and that they use the technology to control when particular audiences can view material by strategically timing when they contribute (Danis & Singer, 2008; Giordano, 2007; Holtzblatt et al., 2010). In their study of wiki implementation at a software company, Grudin and Poole (2010) found that users took advantage of the ability to control contributions and commented that users "created content to share information opportunistically" (p. 4). Similarly, interviews with organizational bloggers at IBM by Huh et al. (2007) indicated that participants often had an audience in mind when sharing knowledge and provided information they thought would appeal to potential viewers. Although social media can share information widely, the editability afforded by technology provides users with greater control of how content is viewed by others.

Improving Information Quality.   Social media allows employees to edit, revise, and alter organizational content long after the time it is first displayed. A survey by Arazy, Gellatly, Soobaek, and Patterson (2009) of 919 wiki users at IBM found that users valued the technology's flexibility and the "change control" offered, including the maintenance of revisions (p. 62). Workers at a research organization who were interviewed by Danis and Singer (2008) reported that the ability to review and edit content was fundamental to the perceived value of the technology resulting in greater collaboration and a more valuable end product.

Hasan and Pfaff (2006) examined four cases of wiki implementation in organizations in an effort to investigate the opportunities for knowledge sharing presented by the technology. The authors concluded that because it was so easy to publish and maintain content on wikis, novices—not just technical experts—would likely use social media to contribute domain specific information. Research by Yates, Wagner, and Majchrzak (2010), which explored content changes that organizational members made to wiki pages found that some people in the organization assumed responsibility for editing and integrating wiki content, and that willingness to assume this role was not related to one's position in a company. By affording the open-editing of content, wikis provided individuals with a way to take control over the contributions provided by others in a way not available through other CMCs. Thom-Santelli, Muller, and Millen (2008) interviewed 33 users of a social tagging system at IBM and found participants anticipated how others would find information and shaped contributions accordingly. Riemer and Richter (2010) coded the text of microblogging contributions in a German software provider and found that workers often shared messages in order to coordinate ongoing or future activities. By enabling participants to carefully craft communication, the editability afforded by social media provided individuals with the opportunity to revise, reshape, and coordinate content more easily than with existing CMCs.

Association

Associations are established connections between individuals, between individuals and content, or between an actor and a presentation. Associations in social media exist in two forms. The first type of association, of a person to another individual, is most commonly referred to as a social tie. A social tie is best expressed through one's friends on a SNS, following a microblogger, or subscribing to another's tags. This type of association indicates an explicit relationship, albeit of no discernible strength, between two people. Over e-mail, unless someone is included on a communication exchange, there is little information displayed regarding whom individuals communicate with and what the nature of a relationship may entail. boyd & Ellison (2007) argue that a focus on relations is one of the defining characteristics of SNSs. As they noted, "What makes social network sites unique is not that they allow individuals to meet strangers, but rather that they enable users to articulate and make visible their social networks" (p. 211). The other form of association is of an individual to a piece of information. Exemplars of this form of association are a wiki contribution, a blog contribution, or the tagging of an article. The association displayed here is of an individual with a piece of information that they have either created or recognized. Alternatively, a database system that houses documents may not display who contributed specific information, and even if it does it would only be revealed to those who interact with that material. Table 7.5 indicates which material features of various social media were shown to afford association.

Table 7.5 Social Media Features Affording Association

Social Media Technology	Features Affording Association	Illustration in Literature
Wikis	• List of editors for each entry • List of privileges, rights and contributions in profiles	(Ding et al., 2007)
Social Networking Sites	• Relations to others displayed (e.g., Friends) • Comments and opinion (e.g., "Like" Button) on entries • Activity of related others displayed on page	(Chen et al, 2009; Daly et al., 2010; DiMicco, Geyer, et al., 2009; DiMicco, Millen, et al., 2008; Farzan et al., 2009; Ferron, et al., 2010; Freyne et al., 2010; Steinfield et al., 2009; Wu et al., 2010)
Blogs	• Links to other blogs (both on page and in entries) • Identifies commenters with links to profiles or personal sites	(Dugan et al., 2010; Jackson et al., 2007)
Social Tagging	• List of individuals who bookmarked same content • Displays individuals of whom user has subscribed to receive content (e.g., fans) • Shows topic to which user has subscription to receive content	(Millen & Feinberg, 2006; Thom-Santelli, Cosley & Gay, 2010; Thom-Santelli, Muller, & Millen, 2008)
Microblogging	• Displays those to whom user receives and sends content (e.g., followers and following) • Use of tags to show reuse of content or directed messages (e.g., @) • Use of tags to show contribution to topic (e.g., #)	(Ehrlich & Shami, 2010; Zhang et al., 2010)

Although associations are most often conceptualized as actor-initiated (e.g., friending someone on Facebook), social media differ from other forms of CMC in that recommendations for additional association are often provided by the technology itself (e.g., Facebook suggesting people you may know or the prompting of related bookmark tags on Delicious). Numerous social media applications such as SNSs and social tagging use algorithms to recommend content and associations to users based on patterns of use or contributed information.

The associations of people to other people, people to content, or content to content afforded by social media have potential implications for both users and potential audiences. First, research has shown that relationships formed through a variety of CMC media can provide individuals with a form of social capital (Blanchard & Horan, 1998; DiMaggio, Hargittai, Neuman, &

Robinson, 2001; Wellman, Haase, Witte, & Hampton, 2001). Contrary to some arguments that online communication would isolate users, this line of research has shown that the connectivity afforded by CMC can create a bridge between individuals, supplement existing relationships, and help build a greater sense of community. Specific to social media use (but not in an organizational setting), Ellison, Steinfield, and Lampe (2007) found that use of the SNS Facebook provided college students with increased social capital among peers. Social media afford a number of different associations through both active connections and those suggested through the features of the technology.

Below, we outline three outcomes that the literature suggests arise when social media afford association with other individuals or content: (a) supporting social connection, (b) access to relevant information, and (c) enabling emergent connection.

Supporting Social Connection.   Social media afford individuals a way to make associations more explicit. One way in which this explicitness is achieved is through the signaling of relationships with others. For example Thom-Santelli et al. (2008) classified different types of social tagging practices in a large technology organization based on interviews with users and found that workers are often "concerned with using tags to articulate social connections to others in the group" (p. 1042). Additionally, interviews with and log data from users of an SNS inside of IBM revealed that employees used the technology to establish associations with individuals about whom they knew little, and, unlike in nonorganizational contexts, there was less SNS activity among close, colocated colleagues (DiMicco, Geyer, et al., 2009; DiMicco, Millen, et al., 2008).

The ability to forge new associations between people and content through social media influenced the development of social capital in organizations. Steinfield, DiMicco, Ellison, and Lampe (2009) surveyed users of a SNS at IBM regarding use of the technology and social capital and found that increased usage of the tool was correlated with increased social capital among new and existing relationships. Subsequently Wu, DiMicco, and Millen (2010) surveyed IBM SNS users regarding their perceived personal and professional closeness to coworkers. The study looked at the relationship between perceived closeness and behaviors on the SNS site such as viewing a coworker's page, contributing content, or friending others. The results of a regression analysis found that explicit friendship connections, recommendations of content to another person, and time spent viewing another's content were all associated with closeness between coworkers. Ferron, Frassoni, Massa, Napolitano, and Setti (2010) also studied the issue of organizational SNS use and social capital. The researchers surveyed more than 300 employees at an Italian research institute and found workers with SNS access reported significantly higher levels of social capital than those without SNS access.

Beyond increasing social capital of individual users, the use of social media and its support for associations may facilitate the creation of a larger community to support employees. Jackson et al.'s (2007) interviews of bloggers at a large technology company found that users viewed participation as a way to associate with others in the organization, become a part of a community, and build personal networks. Even in organizational microblog use, where associations are not labeled as friendship connections, use may help individuals feel closer to the rest of the company. Ehrlich and Shami (2010) analyzed the messages of 34 IBM employees using an internal microblogging tool, and interviewed 25 of the identified users in order to examine the purposes for participation. The study concluded that use of the technology, particularly among distributed workers, helped individuals feel closer to the rest of the company by providing an ongoing sense of what was happening. Social media increased social connections by facilitating easy affiliation and interactions among users.

Access to Relevant Information.   In addition to the creation of person-to-person ties, individuals also established explicit associations with the content found in social media. For example interviews with wiki users at IBM by Ding et al. (2007) revealed that the use of keywords and tags in entries served as a way for users to view the explicit connections among projects (2007). In another instance of social media use, Millen and Feinberg (2006) examined the social tagging behaviors of IBM employees and found that nearly all individuals using a social tagging application looked at the tags or bookmarks of other individuals at some point. Thus associations should not be thought of merely as existing ties, but also pointers to potential relationships between content.

Associations to information can also benefit the organization by allowing existing experts to share knowledge. Thom-Santelli, Cosley, and Gay (2010) studied the implementation of a social tagging system at a museum gallery, comparing the tagging behaviors of 15 novices with those of 15 experts. Results indicated that experts contributed more content to the system and were more likely to down-vote the tags of novices, causing the researchers to conclude that the tool afforded experts a chance to act in a manner that reaffirmed their superior knowledge. By making explicit associations regarding the source, quality, and usefulness of information, social media may improve content use in organizations.

Enabling Emergent Connection.   In addition to supporting the active, purposeful creation of actor-initiated connections, features such as rankings and recommendations in social media afforded emergent forms of associations and suggested ways to improve existing associations or initiate new ones. For example Zhang et al. (2010) studied the use of the microblog tool Yammer at a global Fortune 500 company, coding 300 random messages, interviewing 18 users, and conducting a survey with 160 employee responses. More than half of users responding to the survey indicated the microblog tool helped them connect with strangers. The researchers suggested that a feature recommending people to follow on the microblog tool may facilitate connections, though in this particular case that feature was not widely used. In another study of recommender systems in organizational social media Freyne, Berkovsky, Daly, and Geyer (2010) extracted log data on instances when IBM SNS users clicked on information in the activity stream of friends' behaviors. Then, offline, the researchers entered in the activity stream information, applied an algorithm to help identify information that would be relevant to the user, and compared the results to the user's actual clicks. Results suggested that the use of algorithms to process content on an organizational SNS could help personalize news delivered to users and prevent information overload. Showing how social media can match users with helpful content, Dugan, Geyer, and Millen (2010) studied reactions to an application at IBM that matched blog authors with topics of interest. Analysis found that the feature resulted in increased blog traffic and interactivity among users.

These emergent associations generated by social media tools are unique in that single uses of the technology afford additional opportunities for relevant interaction with people and content. In other words, the tools helped people develop associations to others or information beyond the intentions of the original communicative act. For example, Farzan, DiMicco, and Brownholtz (2009) implemented a rating system in IBM's SNS Beehive that allowed selected users to promote content to others by applying a visible badge to content that indicates material of interest to another user. This feature was effective in getting workers to view more diverse sources of information. Additionally, research by Shami et al. (2009) on the use of social media to identify expertise in IBM found that individuals were more likely to contact others active in social media at the company because users not only signaled expertise but also that they may be more likely to respond to inquiries. It is important to note that though recommender systems have been shown to be effective in increasing connections among organizational SNS users, different forms of recommendation systems may make certain associations easier to form, more salient, and more likely to be accepted by individuals. In related studies, researchers found that implementation of four different friend recommender systems in the SNS at IBM all expanded friend networks in different ways (Chen, Geyer, Dugan, Muller, & Guy, 2009), and concluded that organizations might want to try different algorithms to support connections in order to find a way to support desired associations (Daly, Geyer, & Millen, 2010).

Implications of Social Media Affordances for Organizational Communication Processes

As we have demonstrated in the previous section, the use of social media across various organizational contexts seems to result in at least four relatively constant affordances for organizational communication: a high degree of visibility, persistence, editability, and association. Given the prevalence of these affordances in the current body of research on social media use in organizations (see Tables 7.2 to 7.5 for summary), we argue that communication scholars should take seriously these affordances in their theorizing about various communicative processes that occur within and constitute organizations. Certainly, other CMC technologies have features that are used to produce occasions of these four affordances. A database system entry may have the same visibility of a blog post, a worker may carefully craft an e-mail just as she would a wiki entry, an employee may record and look back through an instant message conversation just like a microblog thread, and viewing a teleconference could provide similar insights in association as seeing one's friend list on an SNS. However, we argue that social media differ in that they afford *all* of these four communicative outcomes simultaneously, and consistently in an organizational setting. The potential presence of all four of these affordances may offer users greater flexibility in the ways that they employ these communication technologies and enact behaviors with them, which in turn could influence organizational communication processes.

In the following section we conduct a thought exercise by considering how these four social media affordances might alter three processes that have, historically, been of great theoretical concern to organizational communication scholars: socialization, information sharing, and power relations. These three processes were chosen because, as we will discuss, researchers have already recognized, either implicitly or explicitly, that the four social media affordances identified are relevant to these areas of organizational communication theory. By no means do we attempt an exhaustive theoretical exposition of how social media affordances alter the dynamics of these three communication processes, nor do we claim that these are the only constructs affected by social media use. Rather, we use this thought exercise to show the usefulness of the affordance typology established above for integrating social media research into existing organizational communication concerns. In conducting this thought exercise, we raise a number of potential research questions that scholars might explore when examining the implications of social media affordances for each of these three processes (Tables 7.6 to 7.8). As these potential research questions reveal, there are many ways in which social media use in organizations may alter dynamics important to organizational processes. Although intended only to be examples of the utility of adopting an affordance approach, our application of visibility, persistence, editability, and association makes it clear that seemingly stable scholarly knowledge may become more volatile as social media enter into organizational practice. We hope that the exercise conducted below, and the potential research questions it inspires, will seed ideas for research that focuses specifically on how social media use is implicated in the accomplishment of organizational communication.

Socialization

Research on socialization has a long history in the field of organizational communication (Feldman, 1976; Jablin, 1984; Miller & Jablin, 1991; Stohl, 1986; Van Maanen & Schein, 1979). Communication is the primary avenue through which individuals manage the uncertainty related to entering a new organizational setting (Jablin, 2001), and research has shown that socialization outcomes can be influenced by the medium through which organizational messages are communicated (Wesson & Gogus, 2005). As Flanagin and Waldeck (2004) noted about the increase in communication technologies available to organizations, "in addition to understanding the dynamics of traditional socialization, researchers must examine how advanced technologies alter the nature and content of socialization-related communication" (p. 138). We consider the ways in which social media affordances might affect processes related to three of the most commonly discussed topics related to socialization (a) people processing tactics, (b) information seeking, and (c) relationship formation. Table 7.6 highlights some key research questions that should be explored to understand how the affordances of visibility, persistence, editability, and association affect these three processes.

People Processing Tactics.   In a seminal discussion of socialization tactics, Van Maanen and Schein (1979) developed a framework for the dimensions of organizational people processing. They noted that tactics used by organizations could be divided into two main categories: (a) Custodial people processing tactics designed in a formal, singular form aimed at providing a uniform experience for workers, or (b) an innovative approach offering flexible, informal tactics aimed at supporting individual experiences. The principle guiding the choice of people processing dimensions was that an organization's socialization strategy should match the context of the job an individual is entering. However, the visibility afforded by social media may undermine organizational efforts to provide a distinct socialization strategy. For instance, because social media used in organizations have been demonstrated to support widespread informal communication, even among people who do not know each other personally (Zhao & Rosson, 2009), social media use may undermine formal socialization efforts based on strict control of information doled out to employees. Similarly, the persistence afforded by social media, which offers employees the ability to view and search records of communication, may conflict with organizational efforts to structure the timing of information given to employees. Both the visibility and persistence of information may result in diverse socialization experiences for employees and allow greater choice regarding the material that employees access or encounter.

Information Seeking.   Organizational entry is a time of great uncertainty for employees as they seek information about roles, norms, and appropriate behaviors (Van Maanen & Schein, 1979). Employees use a variety of communication tactics to gather information during organizational entry (Miller & Jablin, 1991) and the usefulness of information for socialization is closely related to the communication technology people use to find it (Flanagin & Waldeck, 2004). Therefore, it is important to consider how social media might afford individuals novel ways to seek information. For instance, the persistence

Table 7.6 Potential Research Questions Exploring the Relationship between Social Media Affordances and Organizational Socialization Processes

Affordances	Research Areas in Organizational Socialization		
	People Processing Tactics	Information Seeking	Relationship Formation
Visibility	Does the increase in visibility afforded by social media undermine formal socialization efforts?	How does the visibility afforded by social media affect decisions to seek information from others?	Will newcomers form relationships more or less quickly with individuals who post content similar to them than they will with those who do not?
Persistence	Under what conditions will the persistence afforded by social media use result in individualized versus collective socialization experiences?	Does the persistence afforded by social media use result in less active information seeking?	If new entrants to the organization find content posted by someone in the past, will they assume that the poster is still working in this content area and try to form relationships with him or her?
Editability	In an attempt to influence new members, will long-tenured organizational members edit old content to re-create organizational histories?	When looking to reduce uncertainty about organizational norms, how will information providers edit messages that are intended for select newcomers but that are disseminated to all organizational members?	Under what conditions and how will individuals edit their self-presentations to build relationships with others in the organization and what effects will the recognition that others are doing such editing have throughout the organization?
Association	Under what conditions does the development of online relationships with experienced organizational members undermine managerial socialization tactics?	If content is associated with someone whom an individual trusts, will that individual continue to seek out information, or stop because of a belief believes that his or her trusted friend has the "right" answer?	Does the increase in association afforded by social media use result in larger organizational networks?

of content, over time, may be attractive to organizational newcomers hoping to learn about the company and access information that preceded their arrival (Jackson et al., 2007). Indeed, research at IBM found that both early career employees and workers distant from the organization's headquarters used the company's SNS more heavily than others for acculturation activities like learning about issues surrounding culture and values (Thom-Santelli, Millen, & Gergle, 2011). Alternatively, the visibility afforded by social media use may result in more efficient information seeking by allowing access to more knowledge sources. An example of this occurred at IBM where researchers found that users of a microblogging platform felt they were able to find quality information more quickly than through other forms of communication (Ehrlich & Shami, 2010).

The persistence and visibility of social media can also afford information seeking that does not require direct, interpersonal social interaction. The ability for a person to seek information passively through social media extends arguments by Ramirez, Walther, Burgoon, and Sunnafrank (2002) that forms of CMC, "liberate communicators to seek information in new and unique ways. Contrary to some widely held beliefs about the nature of [technology] as a tool that constrains behavior, we contend that it frees communicators to pursue information in qualitatively significant ways" (pp. 218–219). These affordances create a qualitatively different experience because social media users can decide how visible they want their information seeking behaviors to be to others. Indeed, although social media use is most commonly associated with content contributions, studies in organizations have recognized the presence of lurkers who view content without making their presence visible to other users—a finding that holds for SNS (Farzan et al., 2008), blogs (IP & Wagner, 2008), and microblogging (Zhang et al., 2010). Because many individuals are likely to never contribute actively to an online community (Takahashi, Fujimoto, & Yamasaki, 2003), the visibility and persistence afforded by social media allow more individuals to access the information provided by heavy users (Jackson et al., 2007). Research has shown that decisions by organizational newcomers to seek information are influenced by the perceived difficulty in obtaining the information (Morrison & Vancouver, 2000). The mix of active and passive information seeking strategies afforded by social media may shift perceptions of information accessibility and future research should examine how this change might alter socialization processes and outcomes.

Relationship Formation.   The associations afforded by social media can be a powerful way for employees, particularly newcomers, to establish relationships with others in an organization. Social media offer workers the opportunity to find individuals with similar interests, or discover potential mentors, particularly when they do not know others personally. For example, a social networking application might afford the means for an association with an employee at a different location with similar interests (DiMicco et al., 2008). Also, the lightweight nature of the associations, which are often accomplished through a simple click of a computer mouse, may, in turn, facilitate the formation of a wider organizational network.

The associations afforded by social media use can also exercise a form of social influence that restricts the type of relationships formed. As one example, research on internal blogging at a large, multinational company found that managerial use was strongly related to the level of participation by employees (Wattal et al., 2009). Employees using social media may feel the need to replicate the associations made by senior employees or peers in a business unit, creating a more insular network of connections. Individuals may also want to use social media to display connections with known experts or highly regarded others, regardless of whether they intend to interact with these individuals. Thus the associations afforded by social media may promote symbolic associations that give the appearance of diversity or prestige through relationships.

Knowledge Sharing

Many organizational communication researchers are interested in the processes by which people create and transfer knowledge within and across organizational boundaries (Argote, Ingram, Levine, & Moreland, 2000; Brown & Duguid, 1998; Carlile, 2004; Cramton, 2001; Leonardi & Bailey, 2008). We consider how the affordances enabled by social media use may affect four processes that organizational communication researchers argue are central to effective knowledge sharing in organizations: (a) capturing tacit knowledge, (b) motivating knowledge contributions, (c) overcoming organizational boundaries, and (d) identifying expertise. Table 7.7 outlines a number of important research questions that arise when we consider the ways in which the affordances of visibility, persistence, editability, and association create opportunities for and constrain the knowledge sharing processes detailed below.

Capturing Tacit Knowledge One of the paramount challenges faced by organizations is how to capture and learn from the tacit knowledge held by workers (Nonaka, 1994). The visibility afforded by social media allows workers to present personal information in a publicly available setting such that they can surface many of the nuanced aspects of tasks, routines, and know-how. A case study of participation on IBM's BlogCentral platform found that blogs were used to express individuals' tacit knowledge (Huh et al., 2007). The blogs were useful for capturing tacit knowledge because talking about one's tasks in a public forum forced individuals to work hard to articulate how they conducted tasks. In essence, the visibility of the medium afforded people the opportunity to turn their tacit knowledge into explicit knowledge because they knew others were watching their actions and wanted to appear competent. However, Huh et al. also noted that users often had an audience in mind when sharing knowledge, which implies that users took advantage of the affordance of editability when communicating. If one of the leading motivations to participate in social media use in organizations is to gain recognition in an

Table 7.7 Potential Research Questions Exploring the Relationship between Social Media Affordances and Organizational Knowledge Sharing Processes

| Affordances | Research Areas in Organizational Knowledge Sharing | | | |
	Capturing Tacit Knowledge	Motivating Knowledge Contributions	Overcoming Organizational Boundaries	Identifying Expertise
Visibility	To what extent does the visible knowledge afforded by social media use reflect the tacit knowledge of workers?	Does the increase in visibility afforded by social media encourage or deter contributions of knowledge?	Does mere visibility of the activities of others through social media result in a greater understanding of other work groups?	Will organizational social media result in more accurate identifications of experts?
Persistence	Does an accumulation of poor conversions of tacit into explicit knowledge encourage or deter individuals from trying conversions yet again?	Is there a point of saturation for social media use such that large quantities of content deter further contributions?	Does the discovery of old content used by individuals from across a boundary build positive affect such that individuals are motivated to try to build mutual understanding in the here-and-now?	Can the mining of old documents (either quantitatively or qualitatively) shed light on who is and who is not an expert and can this knowledge shift current-day interactions?
Editability	Can the requirement to enter knowledge into a social media tool compel individuals to carefully articulate tacit processes such that they become explicit?	Under what conditions do individuals revise their old knowledge contributions? What effects do these revisions have on organizational learning?	As individuals from other parts of the organization find the need for information contained in social media tools that does not address their concerns, will they edit this information to align with their needs and, consequently, produce more generalized organizational knowledge?	Does the editable nature of self-presentation allow people to be deceptive about their true knowledge and, hence, alter others' perceptions of where expertise lies in the organization?
Association	Do systems that recommend associations between people or between people and content create connections that enable individuals to convert tacit into explicit knowledge?	Do associations afforded by social media use support social or task-oriented communication?	How can social media use facilitate more working relationships beyond one's existing group?	How can organizational social media use best create and support communities of expertise?

organization (DiMicco et al., 2008; Yardi, Golder, & Brzozowski, 2009) then it stands to reason that users may craft messages in ways that present them as knowledgeable even if it is not an accurate reflection of their knowledge. Future research should consider how the editability of social media influences perceptions of individuals' knowledge and whether this matches actual knowledge.

Motivating Knowledge Contributions. Traditional examinations of communal information technologies have treated decisions for individuals to contribute as discretionary (Connolly & Thorn, 1990; Kalman, Monge, Fulk, & Heino, 2002) and have been largely concerned with how to motivate users to contribute individually held knowledge (Beenen et al., 2004; Cress, Kimmerle, & Hesse, 2006). This concern is similar in much of the research on social media use in organizations, in which scholars discuss a desire amongst progenitors of these technologies to generate the greatest volume of participation and contributions possible (DiMicco et al., 2008; Dugan et al., 2010; Farzan et al., 2008). However, Yardi et al. (2009) note that internal corporate blogs create a paradox in that the goal is for employees to contribute knowledge, but the more knowledge that it is contributed the harder it is to find any specific piece of information. The persistence of content in social media means that there may come a point of diminishing returns where knowledge contributions produce more noise than value. Because research on social media in organizations is largely based on initial adoption, future work should explore whether the growth of content alters motivations to contribute knowledge.

Additionally, associations afforded by social media may do little to actually contribute to task-related knowledge contributions or organizational goals. Mirzaee, Iverson, and Khan (2008) concluded in their study of social tagging that although social media facilitated exploration of knowledge within the organization, it was not likely to be relied on in task-specific situations. One reason that social media may not be seen as valuable in task situations is that communications are often more relationally or personally oriented. For example, Zhao and Rosson (2009) interviewed organizational microbloggers and found that the medium was largely used to promote informal communication. Given the ways that social media support relations, motivating contributions may merely increase social exchanges and not necessarily increase organizational knowledge.

Overcoming Organizational Boundaries.   Information and communication technologies, such as social media, are commonly viewed as a means to organize knowledge and place it in a form accessible to other organizational members (Flanagin, 2002). However, individuals often have trouble understanding communications from other organizational members because they have different vocabularies and situated understandings of work (Bechky, 2003; Cramton, 2001). This issue has been identified as a problem with social tagging systems in organizations—empirical research shows tremendous disparity in tagging terms used across applications and individuals, even within a single firm (Muller, 2007b). One way that social media use can addresses this issue is through the affordance of visibility—social media makes the activities of other individuals and work groups more visible, which helps individuals make connections with people or content that facilitate their own interests. Another way that social media use may help individuals overcome organizational boundaries is through easy associations that encourage workers to explore new relationships. For example, a study by Green, Contractor, and Yao (2006) showed how a social networking application with algorithms to make emergent associations between people and user-generated content spurred cross-boundary interactions and knowledge sharing in environmental engineering and hydrological science research. This increased collaboration occurred because once users learned that others were interested in similar topics to them, individuals were more willing to work to overcome cross-boundary differences and understand one another, even if they did not share a common store of domain knowledge. Additionally, at IBM, the implementation of a feature in an internal SNS that allowed users to recommend content to others resulted in more diverse exposure to the activities of organizational members (Farzan et al., 2009). Future studies should consider the ways that social media can be used to help overcome organizational boundaries.

Identifying Expertise.   The ability to accurately identify the expertise of organizational members allows managers to assign individuals to appropriate organizational tasks and, as research suggests, improve group performance (Brandon & Hollingshead, 2004). The visibility afforded by social media use is one way that individuals can recognize the expertise of others, particularly those with whom they have had little or no interaction (Shami et al., 2009). For example, organizational social tagging is able to leverage the personal act of bookmarking in a way that also shares knowledge with others (Pan & Millen, 2008). Associations also aid in the ability to recognize expertise. Social media bring similar content and activities together, creating communities of knowledgeable individuals (Muller, 2007b) and one's ratings of another's content can be used to signal or assert expertise in work groups (Thom-Santelli et al., 2010). In sum, individuals not only look to visible content, but also to associations in order to develop attributions of expertise.

Power

The processes of managerial power enactment, and resistance to it, have occupied a great deal of organizational communication scholars' attention since the early 1990s. Some scholars take a resource dependency view of power, exploring the asymmetry in distribution of organizational resources (e.g., knowledge, information, money, social capital) and the power dependencies they create (Conrad, 1983; Pfeffer & Davis-Blake, 1987; Scott, 2004), while others have adopted a critical-cultural stance on power, arguing that power is exercised through the enactment and perpetuation of organizational discourse that privileges the interests of some and marginalizes the voices of others (Deetz, 1992; Deetz & Mumby, 1985; Mumby & Stohl, 1991). Across these two perspectives, three processes are often discussed in the relationship between power and organizational communication: (a) resource dependencies, (b) discursive construction, and (c) surveillance. Table 7.8 lists potential research questions that fall at the intersection of these three power processes and the affordances of visibility, persistence, editability, and association.

Resource Dependency.   The knowledge contained in social media is a potential source of power for individuals in organizations. By making information visible to others in the organization, individuals may be able to subtly signal that they possess knowledge. If that knowledge is then perceived as valuable, it can be a source of power that can result in increased influence in decision making (Pfeffer & Salancik, 1974). Research on social media has revealed that visibility can both consolidate and distribute power. Individuals who garner increased attention may become influential figures (Efimova & Grudin, 2007). Alternatively, the ability of any employee to make him- or herself visible through social media may have a democratizing effect on knowledge contributions (Hasan & Pfaff, 2006). As an example of the inclusive potential of technology, the addition of social media to the innovation process at MITRE, the research and technology organization, resulted in more comments on proposals from a wider group of employees (Holtzblatt & Tierney, 2011). Additional research should explore the conditions under which social media use creates a more inclusive or exclusive knowledge environment.

Another way that individuals may become less dependent on others in an organization is through the ease of associations made through social media use. Unencumbered by time and space, workers in organizations can use social media to expand their networks and build social capital across boundaries (Ferron et al., 2010; Steinfield et al., 2009). These associations can provide access to thought leaders that would be otherwise difficult to obtain, thus reducing or eliminating the role of gatekeepers who controlled access to these individuals (Ehrlich & Shami, 2010). Moreover, the use of social media allows individuals to develop weak ties and create a more robust organizational network (DiMicco et al., 2008). Employees using social media, particularly those in less powerful organizational positions, may be able to use the ease of associations to garner social resources.

Participation in Discursive Construction.   Organizational scholars operating in the critical-cultural tradition have developed a perspective that views power as constituted by discursive formations created and reproduced in practice (Mumby, 1987). Social media, by facilitating visible text, can be viewed as an inherently discursive space where individuals are able to put forth arguments and engage in public deliberation. In such studies, researchers are interested in how everyday talk (*d*iscourse with a small *d*) shapes and sustains broader

Table 7.8 Potential Research Questions Exploring the Relationship between Social Media Affordances and Organizational Power Processes

| Affordances | Research Areas in Organizational Power Processes | | |
	Resource Dependency	Participation in Discourse Construction	Surveillance
Visibility	When others can see who uses social media and who does not, does increased social media use result in an increase in perceived power in the organization?	Can the increase in visibility afforded by social media facilitate more diverse participation in Discourse construction?	Does the increase in visibility afforded by social media use result in more monitoring of colleagues?
Persistence	Does the documentation of past dependencies that are revealed through the persistence of older organizational documents have an imprinting affect on one's ability to exercise or enact dependencies today?	Does old content that persists in social media platforms continue to shape Discourse in organizations even if the content's proponents are no longer with the organization?	How do organizations use social media to monitor employees over time?
Editability	Can individuals present content in such a way so as to highlight or obscure critical dependencies on others? If so, can dependencies be controlled through strategic content editing?	Are there conditions under which organizational members might revise past documents to re-shape people's memories of the dominant organizational Discourse? If so, do such changes actually work?	If people feel that others are watching them through social media use, what will it take for them to begin to strategically edit their self-presentation and what consequences will this strategic editing have for communication processes throughout the organization?
Association	Does the association afforded by social media use result in less dependency on senior employees who are normally sought because rank is a proxy for power/status/knowledge?	How can organizations motivate individuals to consider new forms of discourse?	Does a system that suggests associations between people or between people and content lead to more or less surveillance than a system that does not suggest associations?

ideologies (*Discourse* with a big *D*) and how powerful actors marginalize the contributions of other forms of *discourse* so as to maintain their positions of power (Alvesson & Deetz, 1999). Studies of social media in organizations have noted that the visibility of content is seen as an effective way for employees to get a feel for what is happening in an organization (Brzozowski, 2009; Jackson et al., 2007; Zhao & Rosson, 2009). Individuals or groups in the organization who are able to shape *Discourse* and participation in this space will wield power over the narrative around how the social media ought to be used and, in so doing, will perhaps be able to control the larger *Discourse* that controls perception in the organization. However, the visible, informal nature of social media participation may encourage open communication that may make it difficult for any individual to dominate discourse (Kosonen & Kianto, 2009; Zhao & Rosson, 2009).

Additionally, the associations afforded by social media may exert normative pressure for conformity around Discourse. Individuals may use the medium to coalesce support for the existing organizational discourse and the persistence of social media may increase inertia to maintain the status quo. For example, minority voices may be discouraged from communicating because lack of attention from management deters participation in social media (Yardi et al., 2009). Evidence also suggests that absent explicit incentives to encounter diverse content, individuals using SNS in organizations may restrict views to material in their own network (Farzan et al., 2009).

Surveillance.   Scholars have long recognized that technology offered management new ways to monitor workers (Attewell, 1987). Social media, by making the practices and contributions of employees more visible, may increase surveillance of workers. Visible participation via communications technology carries with it a form of accountability on the part of the communicator (Brown & Lightfoot, 2002). Research suggests that workers may recognize the accountability of participation, with findings showing that individuals who used social media in organizations were reluctant to contribute works-in-progress because they knew contributions would be viewed by others (Giordano, 2007; Holtzblatt et al., 2010). Research should explore the processes by which individuals monitor the social media activity of coworkers.

Additionally, the persistence of social media makes surveillance activities easier as information is stored, aggregated, and searchable. At one global IT organization studied, the communications department monitored the activity of internal bloggers to identify any emerging issues or inaccuracies (Jackson et al., 2007). Surveillance also emerges from the associations afforded by social media. This form of surveillance is built into social media through subscriptions such as notification of when an edit has been made on a wiki, or when a blog author has constructed a new post. For instance, when users logged on to the SNS site at IBM they were shown a list of activities in which all of their connections had recently engaged, and the site updated users as statuses change (DiMicco et al., 2008). In sum, social media creates a record of activity that may be used for a variety of surveillance purposes by managers and peers.

Conclusion

In this chapter, we have argued that social media are of important consequence to organizational communication processes precisely because they afford new types of behaviors that were previously difficult or impossible to achieve before these new technologies entered the workplace. Our review of existing studies of social media use in organizations uncovered four relatively consistent affordances enabled by these new technologies: visibility, persistence, editability, and association. We suggested that these four affordances could bring substantial changes to the way that many of the processes, which are core to concerns of organizational communication theorists, are carried out in organizational contexts. To illustrate this point, we engaged in a thought exercise in which we explored what consequences these four social media affordances might have on socialization, information sharing, and power processes in organizations.

Clearly, the study of social media use in organizations is in its infancy. We urge scholars to move forward cautiously. The academic landscape is littered with many studies of *new* communication technologies that are now outdated because their authors focused on particular technologies, exploring what consequences the use of those technologies had on social and organizational dynamics. With the swift development of new communication technologies the particular social media we use today are not likely to be the ones we use in the future. We have argued, herein, that an affordance approach, which focuses attention not on any particular technology, but on the types of communicative practices that various features afford, is much more likely to have staying power because it builds theory about the relationship between technology and communication without foregrounding one concept or the other. Much empirical study is needed on the role that social media affordances play in organizational processes if communication research is to remain important, timely, and applicable. We offer this chapter as an early effort to encourage organizational researchers to undertake this important task and we hope that within it are some bold ideas and provocations that help researchers decide how and where to begin.

Notes

1. Social tagging in organizations has also been commonly referred to as social bookmarking (e.g., Damianos, Cuomo, Griffith, Hirst, & Smallwood, 2007; Pan & Millen, 2008). We use the term *social tagging* to refer to technologies that allow users to apply tags or labels to a variety of online content, not just websites.
2. We recognize that there is a wealth of communication research on social media use in a variety of contexts (e.g., political communication or among college students; Ellison, Steinfield, & Lampe, 2007). Our intent is not to discount the con-

tributions or findings of these studies, but rather to argue that the affordances of social media may have consequences unique to organizational settings.

3. The technologies that constitute social media are often recognized in the literature as Web 2.0 (e.g., Chong & Xie, 2011; Fuchs-Kittowski, Klassen, Faust, & Einhaus, 2009; Scholz, 2008; Stocker, Dosinger, Saaed, & Wagner, 2007; Tredinnick, 2006) or social software (e.g., Raeth et al., 2009; Steinhuser et al., 2011; Warr, 2008). For the sake of consistency we use the term *social media* throughout this paper.

4. We recognize, and regret, that a disproportionate number of studies included in this review are the result of research conducted at IBM and involving that organization's employees. At this point, researchers at IBM are the most active in publishing work related to social media use in organizations, in part because it is related to the development of the company's products. Wherever possible we tried to include studies from other organizations. It is our hope that future research will consider social media use in more diverse organizational contexts.

References

Alvesson, M., & Deetz, S. (1999). Critical theory and postmodernism: Approaches to organizational studies. In S. Clegg & C. Hardy (Eds.), *Studying organization: Theory and method* (pp. 185–211). London: Sage.

Arazy, O., Gellatly, I., Soobaek, J., & Patterson, R. (2009). Wiki deployment in corporate settings. *IEEE Technology and Society Magazine, 28*(2), 57–64. doi:10.1109/MTS.2009.932804

Argote, L., Ingram, P., Levine, J. M., & Moreland, R. L. (2000). Knowledge transfer in organizations: Learning from the experience of others. *Organizational Behavior and Human Decision Processes 82*, 1–8. doi: 10.1006/obhd.2000.2883

Attewell, P. (1987). Big brother and the sweatshop: Computer surveillance in the automated office. *Sociological Theory, 5*, 87–100.

Baker, S., & Green, H. (2008, February 20). Social media will change your business. *BusinessWeek*. Retrieved from http://www.businessweek.com

Bechky, B. (2003). Sharing meaning across occupational communities: The transformation of understanding on the production floor. *Organization Science, 17*, 99–120. doi:10.1287/orsc.14.3.312.15162

Beenen, G., Ling, K., Wang, X., Chang, K., Frankowski, D., Resnick, P., & Kraut, R. E. (2004). Using social psychology to motivate contributions to online communities. *Proceedings of the 2004 Conference on Computer Supported Cooperative Work* (pp. 212–221). New York: ACM. doi:10.1145/1031607.1031642

Bercovici, J. (2010, December 9). Who coined "social media"? Web pioneers compete for credit. Retrieved from http://blogs.forbes.com/jeffbercovici/2010/12/09/who-coined-social-media-web-pioneers-compete-for-credit/

Blanchard, A., & Horan, T. (1998). Virtual communities and social capital. *Social Science Computer Review, 16*(3), 293–307. doi:10.1177/089443939801600306

boyd, d. m. (2010). Social network sites as networked publics: Affordances, dynamics and implications. In Z. Papacharissi (Ed.), *A networked self: Identity, community, and culture on social network sites* (pp. 39–58). New York: Routledge.

boyd, d. m., & Ellison, N. B. (2007). Social network sites: Definition, history, and scholarship. *Journal of Computer-Mediated Communication, 13*, 210–230. doi: 10.1111/j.1083-6101.2007.00393.x

Brandon, D. P., & Hollingshead, A. B. (2004). Transactive memory systems in organizations: Matching tasks, expertise, and people. *Organization Science, 15*, 633–644. doi:10.1287/orsc.1040.0069

Bregman, A., & Haythornthwaite, C. (2001). Radicals of presentation in persistent conversation. *Proceedings of the 34th Annual Hawaii International Conference on System Sciences.* Los Alamitos, CA: IEEE Computer Society Press. doi:10.1109/HICSS.2001.926499

Brown, J. S., & Duguid, P. (1998). Organizing knowledge. *California Management Review, 40*(3), 90–111.

Brown, J. S., & Duguid, P. (2001). Knowledge and organization: A social-practice perspective. *Organization Science, 12*, 198–213. doi:10.1287/orsc.12.2.198.10116

Brown, S. D., & Lightfoot, G. (2002). Presence, absence, and accountability: E-mail and the mediation of organizational memory. In S. Woolgar (Ed.), *Virtual society? Technology, cyberbole, reality* (pp. 209–229). Oxford, England: Oxford University Press.

Brzozowski, M., Sandholm, T., & Hogg, T. (2009). Effects of feedback and peer pressure on contributions to enterprise social media. *Proceedings of the 2009 International Conference on Supporting Group Work* (pp. 61–70). New York: ACM. doi: 10.1145/1531674.1531684

Brzozowski, M. J. (2009). WaterCooler: Exploring an organization through enterprise social media. *Proceedings of the 2009 International Conference on Supporting Group Work* (pp. 219–228). New York: ACM. doi:10.1145/1531674.1531706

Bughin, J., & Chui, M. (2010, December). The rise of the networked enterprise: Web 2.0 finds its payday. *McKinsey Quarterly.* Retrieved from http://www.mckinsey-quarterly.com

Carlile, P. R. (2004). Transferring, translating, and transforming: An integrative framework for managing knowledge across boundaries. *Organization Science, 15*, 555–568. doi:10.1287/orsc.1040.0094

Chen, J., Geyer, W., Dugan, C., Muller, M., & Guy, I. (2009). Make new friends, but keep the old: Recommending people on social networking sites. *Proceedings of the 27th International Conference on Human Factors in Computing Systems* (pp. 201–210). New York: ACM. doi:10.1145/1518701.1518735

Chong, E., & Xie, B. (2011). The use of theory in social studies of Web 2.0. *Proceedings of the 44th Annual Hawaii International Conference on System Sciences.* Los Alamitos, CA: IEEE Computer Society Press. doi:10.1109/HICSS.2011.436

Clark, H. H., & Brennan, S. E. (1991). Grounding in communication. In L. B. Resnick, J. M. Levine, & S. D. Teasley (Eds.), *Perspectives on socially shared cognition* (pp. 127–149). Washington, DC.: American Psychological Association.

Connolly, T., & Thorn, B. K. (1990). Discretionary databases: Theory, data, and implications. In J. Fulk & C. W. Steinfield (Eds.), *Organizations and communication technology* (pp. 219–233). Newbury Park, CA: Sage.

Conrad, C. (1983). Organizational power: Faces and symbolic forms. In L. Putnam & M. Pacanowsky (Eds.), *Communication and organizations: An interpretive perspective* (pp. 173–194). London: Sage.

Cramton, C. D. (2001). The mutual knowledge problem and its consequences for dispersed collaboration. *Organization Science, 12*, 346–371. doi:10.1287/orsc.12.3.346.10098

Cress, U., Kimmerle, J., & Hesse, F. W. (2006). Information exchange with shared databases as a social dilemma: The effect of metaknowledge, bonus systems, and costs. *Communication Research, 33,* 370–390. doi:10.1177/0093650206291481

Cross, R., Borgatti, S. P., & Parker, G. (2003). Making invisible work visible: Using social network analysis to support strategic collaboration. *California Management Review, 44,* 35–46.

Culnan, M. J., & Markus, M. L. (1987). Information technologies. In F. M. Jablin, L. L. Putnam, K. H. Roberts & L. W. Porter (Eds.), *Handbook of organizational communication: An interdisciplinary perspective* (pp. 420–443). Newbury Park, CA: Sage.

Daft, R. L., & Lengel, R. H. (1986). Organizational information requirements, media richness and structural design. *Management Science, 32,* 554–571. doi:10.1287/mnsc.32.5.554

Daly, E. M., Geyer, W., & Millen, D. R. (2010). The network effects of recommending social connections. *Proceedings of the Fourth Conference on Recommender Systems* (pp. 301–304). New York: ACM. doi:10.1145/1864708.1864772

Damianos, L. E., Cuomo, D., Griffith, J., Hirst, D. M., & Smallwood, J. (2007). Exploring the adoption, utility, and social influences of social bookmarking in a corporate environment. *Proceedings of the 40th Annual Hawaii International Conference on Systems Sciences.* Los Alamitos, CA: IEEE Computer Society Press. doi:10.1109/HICSS.2007.219

Danis, C., & Singer, D. (2008). A wiki instance in the enterprise: Opportunities, concerns and reality. *Proceedings of the 2008 Conference on Computer Supported Cooperative Work* (pp. 495–504). New York: ACM. doi:0.1145/1460563.1460642

Deetz, S. (1992). *Democracy in an age of corporate colonization: Developments in communication and the politics of everyday life.* Albany, NY: SUNY Press.

Deetz, S., & Mumby, D. (1985). Metaphors, information, and power. In B. D. Ruben (Ed.), *Information and behavior* (Vol. 1, pp. 369–386). New Brunswick, NJ: Transaction Press.

Dennis, A. R., Fuller, R. M., & Valacich, J. S. (2008). Media, tasks, and communication processes: A theory of media synchronicity. *MIS Quarterly, 32,* 575–600.

DiMaggio, P., Hargittai, E., Neuman, W. R., & Robinson, J. P. (2001). Social implications of the Internet. *Annual Review of Sociology, 27,* 307–336. doi:10.1146/annurev.soc.27.1.307

DiMicco, J., Geyer, W., Millen, D. R., Dugan, C., & Brownholtz, B. (2009). People sensemaking and relationship building on an enterprise social networking site. *Proceedings of the 42nd Annual Hawaii International Conference on System Sciences.* Los Alamitos, CA: IEEE Computer Society Press. doi:10.1109/HICSS.2009.343

DiMicco, J., Millen, D. R., Geyer, W., Dugan, C., Brownholtz, B., & Muller, M. (2008). Motivations for social networking at work. *Proceedings of the 2008 Conference on Computer Supported Cooperative Work* (pp. 711–720). New York: ACM. doi: 10.1145/1460563.1460674

Ding, X., Danis, C., Erickson, T., & Kellogg, W. A. (2007). Visualizing an enterprise wiki. *Proceedings of CHI '07 Extended Abstracts on Human Factors in Computing Systems* (pp. 2189–2194). New York: ACM. doi:10.1145/1240866.1240978

Donath, J., Karahalios, K., & Viegas, F. (1999). Visualizing conversation. *Journal of Computer-Mediated Communication, 4*(4). doi:10.1111/j.1083-6101.1999.tb00107.x

DuBois, S. (2010, November 1). Can social apps kill enterprise software?, *CNNMoney.* Retrieved from http://tech.fortune.cnn.com

Dugan, C., Geyer, W., & Millen, D. R. (2010). Lessons learned from Blog Muse: Audience-based inspiration for bloggers. *Proceedings of the 28th International Conference on Human Factors in Computing Systems* (pp. 1965–1974). New York: ACM. doi:10.1145/1753326.1753623

Dugan, C., Geyer, W., Muller, M., DiMicco, J., Brownholtz, B., & Millen, D. R. (2008). It's all "about you": Diversity in online profiles. *Proceedings of the 2008 Conference on Computer Supported Cooperative Work* (pp. 703–706). New York: ACM. doi:10.1145/1460563.1460672

Efimova, L. (2004). Discovering the iceberg of knowledge work: A weblog case. *Proceedings of the Fifth European Conference on Organisational Knowledge, Learning and Capabilities (OKLC 2004)*. Innsbruck, Austria: University of Innsbruck.

Efimova, L., & Grudin, J. (2007). Crossing boundaries: A case study of employee blogging. *Proceedings of the 40th Annual Hawaii International Conference on System Sciences*. Los Alamitos, CA: IEEE Computer Society Press. doi:10.1109/HICSS.2007.159

Efimova, L., & Grudin, J. (2008). Crossing boundaries: Digital literacy in enterprises. In C. Lankshear & M. Knobel (Eds.), *Digital literacies* (pp. 203–226). New York, NY: Peter Lang.

Ehrlich, K., Lin, C.-Y., & Griffiths-Fisher, V. (2007). Searching for experts in the enterprise: Combining text and social network analysis. *Proceedings of the 2007 International Conference on Supporting Group Work* (pp. 117–126). New York: ACM. doi:10.1145/1316624.1316642

Ehrlich, K., & Shami, N. S. (2010). Microblogging inside and outside the workplace. *Proceedings of the Fourth International Conference on Weblogs and Social Media* (pp. 42–49). Menlo Park, CA: AAAI Press.

Ellison, N., Steinfield, C., & Lampe, C. (2007). The benefits of Facebook "friends": Social capital and college students' use of online social network sites. *Journal of Computer-Mediated Communication, 12*, 1143–1168. doi:10.1111/j.1083-6101.2007.00367.x

Erickson, T., & Kellogg, W. (2000). Social translucence: An approach to designing systems that support social processes. *ACM Transactions on Computer–Human Interaction, 7*, 59–83. doi:10.1145/344949.345004

Farrell, R. G., Kellogg, W., & Thomas, J. C. (2008, November). *The participatory web and the socially resilient enterprise*. Paper presented at the What to Expect from Enterprise 3.0: Adapting Web 2.0 to Corporate Reality workshop at the 2008 Conference on Computer Supported Cooperative Work, San Diego, CA.

Farrell, S., Lau, T., Wilcox, E., Nusser, S., & Muller, M. (2007). Socially augmenting employee profiles with people-tagging. *Proceedings of the 20th Annual Symposium on User Interface Software and Technology* (pp. 91–100). New York: ACM. doi: 10.1145/1294211.1294228

Farzan, R., DiMicco, J., Millen, D. R., Brownholtz, B., Geyer, W., & Dugan, C. (2008). Results from deploying a participation incentive mechanism within the enterprise. *Proceedings of the Twenty-Sixth Annual SIGCHI Conference on Human factors in Computing Systems* (pp. 563–572). New York: ACM. doi:10.1145/1357054.1357145

Farzan, R., DiMicco, J. M., & Brownholtz, B. (2009). Spreading the honey: A system for maintaining an online community. *Proceedings of the 2009 International Conference on Supporting Group Work* (pp. 31–40). New York: ACM. doi: 10.1145/1531674.1531680

Feldman, D. C. (1976). A practical program for employee socialization. *Organizational Dynamics, 5*, 64–80. doi:10.1016/0090-2616(76)90055-3

Ferron, M., Frassoni, M., Massa, P., Napolitano, M., & Setti, D. (2010). An empirical analysis on social capital and Enterprise 2.0 participation in a research institute. *Proceedings of the 2010 International Conference on Advances in Social Networks Analysis and Mining* (pp. 391–392). Los Alamitos, CA: IEEE Computer Society Press. doi:10.1109/asonam.2010.68

Flanagin, A. J. (2002). The elusive benefits of the technological support of knowledge management. *Management Communication Quarterly, 16*, 242–248. doi: 10.1177/089331802237237

Flanagin, A. J., & Waldeck, J. H. (2004). Technology use and organizational newcomer socialization. *Journal of Business Communication, 41*, 137–165. doi: 10.1177/0021943604263290

Freyne, J., Berkovsky, S., Daly, E. M., & Geyer, W. (2010). Social networking feeds: Recommending items of interest.*Proceedings of the Fourth Conference on Recommender Systems* (pp. 111–118). New York: ACM. doi:10.1145/1864708.1864766

Fuchs-Kittowski, F., Klassen, N., Faust, D., & Einhaus, J. (2009, September). *A comparative study on the use of Web 2.0 in enterprises.* Paper presented at I-KNOW '09 and I-SEMANTICS '09, Graz, Austria.

Gaver, W. (1991). Technology affordances. *Proceedings of SIGCHI Conference on Human Factors in Computing Systems* (pp. 79–84). New York: ACM. doi: 10.1145/108844.108856

Gergle, D., Millen, D., Kraut, R., & Fussell, S. (2004). Persistence matters: Making the most of chat in tightly-coupled work. *Proceedings of the SIGCHI Conference on Human Factors in Computing Systems* (pp. 431–438). New York: ACM. doi: 10.1145/985692.985747

Geyer, W., Dugan, C., DiMicco, J., Millen, D. R., Brownholtz, B., & Muller, M. (2008). Use and reuse of shared lists as a social content type. *Proceedings of the Twenty-Sixth Annual SIGCHI Conference on Human factors in Computing Systems* (pp. 1545–1554). New York: ACM. doi:10.1145/1357054.1357296

Gibson, J. J. (1986). *The ecological approach to visual perception.* Mahwah, NJ: Erlbaum.

Giordano, R. (2007). An investigation of the use of a wiki to support knowledge exchange in public health. *Proceedings of the 2007 International Conference on Supporting Group Work* (pp. 269–272). New York: ACM. doi:10.1145/1316624.1316664

Green, H. D., Contractor, N., & Yao, Y. (2006, December). C-IKNOW: *Cyberinfrastructure knowledge networks on the web: A social network enabled recommender system for locating resources in cyberinfrastructures.* Paper presented at the American Geophysical Union, San Francisco, CA.

Grudin, J. (2006). Enterprise knowledge management and emerging technologies. *Proceedings of the 39th Annual Hawaii International Conference on System Sciences.* Los Alamitos, CA: IEEE Computer Society Press. doi:10.1109/HICSS.2006.156

Grudin, J., & Poole, E. S. (2010). Wikis at work: Success factors and challenges for sustainability of enterprise Wikis. *Proceedings of the 6th International Symposium on Wikis and Open Collaboration.* New York: ACM. doi:10.1145/1832772.1832780

Gunther, O., Krasnova, H., Riehle, D., & Schoendienst, V. (2009). Modeling microblogging adoption in the enterprise. *AMCIS 2009 Proceedings.* Retrieved from http://aisel.aisnet.org/amcis2009/544/

Hancock, J. T., Toma, C., & Ellison, N. B. (2007). The truth about lying in online dating profiles. *Proceedings of the SIGCHI Conference on Human Factors in Computing Systems* (pp. 449–452). New York: ACM. doi:10.1145/1240624.1240697

Hargittai, E., Gallo, J., & Kane, M. (2008). Cross-ideological discussions among conservative and liberal bloggers. *Public Choice, 134*(1), 67–86. doi:10.1007/s11127-007-9201-x

Hasan, H., & Pfaff, C. (2006). *Emergent conversational technologies that are democratising information systems in organisations: The case of the corporate wiki.* Faculty of Commerce–Papers, *University of Wollongong.* Retrieved from http://works.bepress.com/hhasan/14

Herring, S. (2004). Slouching toward the ordinary: Current trends in computer-mediated communication. *New Media and Society, 6,* 26–36. doi:10.1177/1461444804039906

Holtzblatt, L., & Tierney, M. L. (2011). Measuring the effectiveness of social media on an innovation process. *Proceedings of the 2011 Annual Conference Extended Abstracts on Human Factors in Computing Systems* (pp. 697–712). New York: ACM. doi:10.1145/1979742.1979669

Holtzblatt, L. J., Damianos, L. E., & Weiss, D. (2010). Factors impeding wiki use in the enterprise: A case study. *Proceedings of the 28th International Conference Extended Abstracts on Human Factors in Computing Systems* (pp. 4661–4676). New York: ACM. doi:10.1145/1753846.1754208

Huh, J., Bellamy, R., Jones, L., Thomas, J. C., & Erickson, T. (2007). BlogCentral: The role of internal blogs at work. *Proceedings of CHI '07 Extended Abstracts on Human Factors in Computing Systems* (pp. 2113–2116). doi:10.1145/1240866.1241022

Hutchby, I. (2001). Technologies, texts and affordances. *Sociology, 35,* 441–456.

IP, R. K. F., & Wagner, C. (2008). Weblogging: A study of social computing and its impact on organizations. *Decision Support Systems, 45,* 242–250. doi:10.1016/j.dss.2007.02.004

Jablin, F. M. (1984). Assimilating new members into organizations. In R. N.Bostrom (Ed.), *Communication yearbook* (Vol. 8, pp. 594–626). Beverly Hills, CA: Sage.

Jablin, F. M. (2001). Organizational entry, assimilation, and disengagement/exit. In F. M. Jablin & L. L. Putnam (Eds.), *The new handbook of organizational communication* (pp. 732–818). Thousand Oaks, CA: Sage.

Jackson, A., Yates, J., & Orlikowski, W. (2007). Corporate blogging: Building community through persistent digital talk. *Proceedings of the 40th Annual Hawaii International Conference on System Sciences.* Los Alamitos, CA: IEEE Computer Society Press. doi:10.1109/HICSS.2007.155

John, A., & Seligmann, D. (2006). Collaborative tagging and expertise in the enterprise. *Proceedings of the 15th International Conference on World Wide Web.* New York: ACM. doi:10.1.1.134.296

Kalman, M. E., Monge, P., Fulk, J., & Heino, R. (2002). Motivations to resolve communication dilemmas in database-mediated collaboration. *Communication Research, 29,* 125–154. doi:10.1177/0093650202029002002

Kane, G. C., & Fichman, R. G. (2009). The shoemaker's children: Using wikis for information systems teaching, research, and publication. *MIS Quarterly, 33,* 1–22.

Kaplan, A. M., & Haenlein, M. (2010, January–February). Users of the world, unite! The challenges and opportunities of social media. *Business Horizons, 53,* 59–68. doi:10.1016/j.bushor.2009.09.003

Kolari, P., Finin, T., Lyons, K., Yesha, Y., Yesha, Y., Perelgut, S., & Hawkins, J. (2007). On the structure, properties and utility of internal corporate blogs. *Proceedings of the International Conference on Weblogs and Social Media.* Menlo Park, CA: AAAI Press.

Kosonen, M., & Kianto, A. (2009). Applying wikis to managing knowledge—A sociotechnical approach. *Knowledge and Process Management, 16*, 23–29. doi:10.1002/kpm.322

Leonardi, P. M. (2009). Crossing the implementation line: The mutual constitution of technology and organizing across development and use activities. *Communication Theory, 19*, 277–309.

Leonardi, P. M. (2010). Digital materiality? How artifacts without matter, matter. *First Monday, 15*(6). Retrieved from http://firstmonday.org

Leonardi, P. M. (2011). When flexible routines meet flexible technologies: Affordance, constraint, and the imbrication of human and material agencies. *MIS Quarterly, 35*, 147–167.

Leonardi, P. M., & Bailey, D. E. (2008). Transformational technologies and the creation of new work practices: Making implicit knowledge explicit in task-based offshoring. *MIS Quarterly, 32*, 411–436.

Leonardi, P. M., & Barley, S. R. (2008). Materiality and change: Challenges to building better theory about technology and organizing. *Information and Organization, 18*, 159–176. doi:10.1016/j.infoandorg.2008.03.001

Majchrzak, A., Jarvenpaa, S. L., & Hollingshead, A. B. (2007). Coordinating expertise among emergent groups responding to disasters. *Organization Science, 18*, 147–161. doi:10.1287/orsc.1060.0228

Majchrzak, A., Rice, R. E., Malhotra, A., King, N., & Ba, S. L. (2000). Technology adaptation: The case of a computer-supported inter-organizational virtual team. *MIS Quarterly, 24*, 569–600.

Majchrzak, A., Wagner, C., & Yates, D. (2006). Corporate wiki users: Results of a survey. *Proceedings of the 2006 International Symposium on Wikis* (pp. 99–104). New York: ACM. doi:10.1145/1149453.1149472

Markus, M. L., & Silver, M. S. (2008). A foundation for the study of IT effects: A new look at DeSanctis and Poole's concepts of structural features and spirit. *Journal of the Association for Information Systems, 9*, 609–632.

McAfee, A. (2006). Enterprise 2.0: The dawn of emergent collaboration. *MIT Sloan Management Review, 47*(3), 19–28.

McCarthy, J. C., Miles, V. C., & Monk, A. F. (1991). An experimental study of common ground in text-based communication. *Proceedings of the SIGCHI Conference on Human Factors in Computing Systems: Reaching Through Technology* (pp. 209–215). New York: ACM. doi:10.1145/108844.108890

Mejova, Y., Schepper, K. D., Bergman, L., & Lu, J. (2011). Reuse in the wild: An empirical and ethnographic study of organizational content reuse. *Proceedings of the 2011 Annual Conference on Human factors in Computing Systems* (pp. 2877–2886). New York: ACM. doi:10.1145/1978942.1979370

Millen, D. R., & Feinberg, J. (2006). Using social tagging to improve social navigation. *Proceedings of the Workshop on the Social Navigation and Community-Based Adaption Technologies.* Dublin, Ireland: Springer. Retrieved from http://www.sis.pitt.edu/~paws/SNC_BAT06/proceedings.html

Miller, V. D., & Jablin, F. M. (1991). Information seeking during organizational entry: Influences, tactics, and a model of the process. *The Academy of Management Review, 16*, 92–120. doi:10.2307/258608

Mirzaee, V., Iverson, L., & Khan, S. (2008, November). *Implications of integrating social tagging into a task oriented application.* Poster presented at the 2008 Conference on Computer Supported Cooperative Work.

Morrison, E. W., & Vancouver, J. B. (2000). Within-person analysis of information seeking: The effects of perceived costs and benefits. *Journal of Management, 26*, 119–137. doi: 10.1177/014920630002600101

Muller, M. (2007a). Comparing tagging vocabularies among four enterprise tag-based services. *Proceedings of the 2007 international Conference on Supporting Group Work* (pp. 341–350). New York: ACM. doi:10.1145/1316624.1316676

Muller, M. (2007b). *When similar tags do describe similar things: Evidence of communities among user* (Technical Report No. 07-05). Cambridge, MA: IBM Watson Research Center.

Muller, M. J., Ehrlich, K., & Farrell, S. (2006). *Social tagging and self-tagging for impression management* (Technical Report No. 06-02). Cambridge, MA: IBM Watson Research Center.

Mumby, D. K. (1987). The political function of narrative in organizations. *Communication Monographs, 54*, 113–127. doi:10.1080/03637758709390221

Mumby, D. K., & Stohl, C. (1991). Power and discourse in organization studies: Absence and the dialectic of control. *Discourse & Society, 2*, 313–332. doi: 10.1177/0957926591002003004

Nardi, B. A., & Engeström, Y. (1999). A web on the wind: The structure of invisible work. *Computer Supported Cooperative Work, 8*, 1–8. doi:10.1023/A:1008694621289

Nass, C., & Mason, L. (1990). On the study of technology and task: A variable-based approach. In J. Fulk & C. Steinfield (Eds.), *Organizations and communication technology* (pp. 46–67). Newbury Park, CA: Sage.

Nonaka, I. (1994). A dynamic theory of organizational knowledge creation. *Organization Science, 5*, 14–37. doi:10.1287/orsc.5.1.14

Norman, D. A. (1990). *The design of everyday things.* New York: Doubleday.

O'Mahony, S., & Barley, S. R. (1999). Do telecommunications technologies affect work and organizations? The state of our knowledge. In B. Staw & R. Sutton (Eds.), *Research in organizational behavior* (Vol. 21, pp. 125–161). Greenwich, CT: JAI Press.

Orlikowski, W. J. (2007). Sociomaterial practices: Exploring technology at work. *Organization Studies, 28*, 1435–1448. doi:10.1177/0170840607081138

Orlikowski, W. J., & Barley, S. R. (2001). Technology and institutions: What information systems research and organization studies can learn from each other. *MIS Quarterly, 25*, 145–165.

Pan, Y. X., & Millen, D. R. (2008). Information sharing and patterns of social interaction in an enterprise social bookmarking service. *Proceedings of the 41st Annual Hawaii International Conference on System Sciences.* Los Alamitos, CA: IEEE Computer Society Press. doi:10.1109/HICSS.2008.202

Pfeffer, J., & Davis-Blake, A. (1987). Understanding organizational wage structures: A resource dependence approach. *Academy of Management Journal, 30*, 437–455.

Pfeffer, J., & Salancik, G. R. (1974). Organizational decision making as a political process: The case of a university budget. *Administrative Science Quarterly, 19*, 135–151.

Poole, E. S., & Grudin, J. (2010). A taxonomy of wiki genres in enterprise settings. *Proceedings of the 6th International Symposium on Wikis and Open Collaboration.* New York: ACM. doi:10.1145/1832772.1832792

Raeth, P., Smolnik, S., Urbach, N., & Zimmer, C. (2009). Towards assessing the success of social software in corporate environments. *AMCIS 2009 Proceedings.* Retrieved from http://aisel.aisnet.org/amcis2009/662

Ramirez, A., Walther, J. B., Burgoon, J. K., & Sunnafrank, M. (2002). Information-seeking strategies, uncertainty, and computer-mediated communication: Toward a conceptual model. *Human Communication Research, 28,* 213–228. doi:10.1111/j.1468-2958.2002.tb00804.x

Rice, R. E. (1987). Computer-mediated communication and organizational innovation. *Journal of Communication, 37*(4), 65–94. doi:10.1111/j.1460-2466.1987.tb01009.x

Rice, R. E., & Gattiker, U. (2001). New media and organizational structuring In F. M. Jablin & L. L. Putnam (Eds.), *The new handbook of organizational communication: Advances in theory, research, and methods* (pp. 544–581). Thousand Oaks, CA: Sage.

Riemer, K., & Richter, A. (2010). Tweet inside: Microblogging in a corporate context. *BLED 2010 Proceedings.* Retrieved from http://aisel.aisnet.org/bled2010/41/

Rober, M. B., & Cooper, L. P. (2011). Capturing knowledge via an "Intrapedia": A case study. *Proceedings of the 44th Annual Hawaii International Conference on System Sciences.* Los Alamitos, CA: IEEE Computer Society Press. doi:10.1109/hicss.2011.94

Scholz, T. (2008). Market ideology and the myths of Web 2.0. *First Monday, 13*(3). Retrieved from http://firstmonday.org/

Schondienst, V., Krasnova, H., Gunther, O., & Riehle, D. (2011). Micro-blogging adoption in the enterprise: An empirical analysis. *Proceedings of the 10th International Conference on Wirtschaftsinformatik.* Retrieved from http://aisel.aisnet. org/wi2011/22

Scott, W. R. (2004). Reflections on a half-century of organizational sociology. *Annual Review of Sociology, 30,* 1–21. doi:10.1146/annurev.soc.30.012703.110644

Shami, N. S., Ehrlich, K., Gay, G., & Hancock, J. T. (2009). Making sense of strangers' expertise from signals in digital artifacts. *Proceedings of the 27th International Conference on Human Factors in Computing Systems* (pp. 69–78). New York: ACM. doi:10.1145/1518701.1518713

Shirky, C. (2008). *Here comes everybody.* New York: Penguin.

Steinfield, C., DiMicco, J. M., Ellison, N. B., & Lampe, C. (2009). Bowling online: Social networking and social capital within the organization. *Proceedings of the Fourth International Conference on Communities and Technologies* (pp. 245–254). New York: ACM. doi:10.1145/1556460.1556496

Steinhuser, M., Smolnik, S., & Hoppe, U. (2011). Towards a measurement model of corporate social software success—Evidences from an exploratory multiple case study. *Proceedings of the 44th Annual Hawaii International Conference on System Sciences.* Los Alamitos, CA: IEEE Computer Society Press. doi:10.1109/hicss.2011.447

Stocker, A., Dosinger, G., Saaed, A., & Wagner, C. (2007, September). *The three pillars of, "corporate Web 2.0": A model for definition.* Paper presented at I-MEDIA, '07 and I-SEMANTICS ,'07, Graz, Austria.

Stohl, C. (1986). The role of memorable messages in the process of organizational socialization. *Communication Quarterly, 34,* 231–249. doi: 10.1080/01463378609369638 *Proceedings of the 2008 Conference on Computer Supported Cooperative Work* (pp. 649–658). New York: ACM. doi:10.1145/1460563.1460664

Takahashi, M., Fujimoto, M., & Yamasaki, N. (2003). The active lurker: Influence of an in-house online community on its outside environment. *Proceedings of the 2003 International Conference on Supporting Group Work* (pp. 1–10). New York: ACM. doi:10.1145/958160.958162

Thom-Santelli, J., Cosley, D., & Gay, G. (2010). What do you know?: Experts, novices and territoriality in collaborative systems. *Proceedings of the 28th International Conference on Human Factors in Computing Systems* (pp. 1685–1694). New York: ACM. doi:10.1145/1753326.1753578

Thom-Santelli, J., Millen, D. R., & Gergle, D. (2011). Organizational acculturation and social networking. *Proceedings of the 2011 Conference on Computer Supported Cooperative Work* (pp. 313–316). New York: ACM. doi:10.1145/1958824.1958871

Thom-Santelli, J., Muller, M. J., & Millen, D. R. (2008). Social tagging roles: Publishers, evangelists, leaders. *Proceeding of the Twenty-Sixth Annual SIGCHI Conference on Human Factors in Computing Systems* (pp. 1041–1044). New York: ACM. doi:10.1145/1357054.1357215

Tredinnick, L. (2006). Web 2.0 and business. *Business Information Review, 23*, 228–234. doi:10.1177/0266382106072239

Van Maanen, J., & Schein, E. H. (1979). Towards a theory of organizational socialization. In J. Van Maanen (Ed.), *Research in organizational behavior* (Vol. 1, pp. 209–264). Greenwich, CT: JAI Press.

Wagner, C. (2004). Wiki: A technology for conversational knowledge management and group collaboration. *Communications of the Association for Information Systems, 13*, 265–289. Retrieved from http://aisel.aisnet.org/cais/vol13/iss1/19

Walther, J. B. (1993). Impression development in computer-mediated interaction. *Western Journal of Communication, 57*, 381–398. doi:10.1080/10570319309374463

Walther, J. B., Van Der Heide, B., Hamel, L. M., & Shulman, H. C. (2009). Self-generated versus other-generated statements and impressions in computer-mediated communication. *Communication Research, 36*, 229–253. doi:10.1177/0093650208330251

Warr, W. A. (2008). Social software: Fun and games, or business tools? *Journal of Information Science, 34*, 591–604. doi:10.1177/0165551508092259

Wattal, S., Racherla, P., & Mandviwalla, M. (2009). Employee adoption of corporate blogs: A quantitative analysis. *Proceedings of the 42nd Annual Hawaii International Conference on System Sciences*. Los Alamitos, CA: IEEE Computer Society Press. doi:10.1109/HICSS.2009.188

Wellman, B., Haase, A. Q., Witte, J., & Hampton, K. (2001). Does the internet increase, decrease, or supplement social capital? Social networks, participation, and community commitment. *American Behavioral Scientist, 45*, 436–455. doi:10.1177/00027640121957286

Wellman, B., Salaff, J., Dimitrova, D., Garton, L., Gulia, M., & Haythornthwaite, C. (1996). Computer networks as social networks: Collaborative work, telework, and virtual community. *Annual Review of Sociology, 22*, 213–238. doi:10.1146/annurev.soc.22.1.213

Wesson, M. J., & Gogus, C. I. (2005). Shaking hands with a computer: An examination of two methods of organizational newcomer orientation. *Journal of Applied Psychology, 90*, 1018–1026. doi:10.1037/0021-9010.90.5.1018

White, K. F., & Lutters, W. G. (2007). Midweight collaborative remembering: Wikis in the workplace. *Proceedings of the 2007 Symposium on Computer Human Interaction for the Management of Information Technology*. New York: ACM. doi:10.1145/1234772.1234793

Whittaker, S. (2003). Theories and methods in mediated communication. In A. C. Graesser, M. A. Gernsbacher & S. R. Goldman (Eds.), *Handbook of discourse processes* (pp. 243–286). Mahwah, NJ: Erlbaum.

Wu, A., DiMicco, J. M., & Millen, D. R. (2010). Detecting professional versus personal closeness using an enterprise social network site. *Proceedings of the 28th Interna-*

tional Conference on Human Factors in Computing Systems (pp. 1955–1964). New York: ACM. doi:10.1145/1753326.1753622

Yardi, S., Golder, S. A., & Brzozowski, M. (2009). Blogging at work and the corporate attention economy. *Proceedings of the 27th International Conference on Human Factor in Computing Systems* (pp. 2071–2080). New York: ACM. doi: 10.1145/1518701.1519016

Yates, D., Wagner, C., & Majchrzak, A. (2010). Factors affecting shapers of organizational wikis. *Journal of the American Society for Information Science and Technology, 61*, 543–554. doi:10.1002/asi.21266

Young, G. O., Brown, E. G., Keitt, T., Owyang, J. K., Koplowitz, R., & Shey, H. (2008, April 20). *Global Enterprise Web 2.0 market forecast: 2007 to 2013*. Retrieved from http://www.forrester.com/rb/research

Zammutto, R. G., Griffith, T. L., Majchrzak, A., Dougherty, D. J., & Faraj, S. (2007). Information technology and the changing fabric of organization. *Organization Science, 18*, 749–762. doi:10.1287/orsc.1070.0307

Zhang, J., Qu, Y., Cody, J., & Wu, Y. (2010). A case study of micro-blogging in the enterprise: use, value, and related issues. *Proceedings of the 28th International Conference on Human Factors in Computing Systems* (pp. 123–132). New York: ACM. doi:10.1145/1753326.1753346

Zhao, D., & Rosson, M. B. (2009). How and why people Twitter: The role that microblogging plays in informal communication at work. *Proceedings of the 2009 International Conference on Supporting Group Work* (pp. 243–252). New York: ACM. doi:10.1145/1531674.1531710

Zickuhr, K. (2010). *Generations 2010*. Pew Internet and American Life Project. Retrieved from http://pewinternet.org/Reports/2010/Generations-2010.aspx

8 *Commentary*
Affordances, Effects, and Technology Errors

Joseph B. Walther

Michigan State University

Treem and Leonardi's "Social Media Use in Organizations" is an innovative effort to identify characteristics of communication technologies and how those characteristics shape the uses to which they are put in context. Whereas the intersection of the specific technologies (relatively new, so-called social media) and the context (organizations) is unique, the work joins a long line of efforts to offer such a general framework (e.g., Eveland, 2003). The focus on affordances offers a middle-ground path through the growing forest on the use of social media. On the one hand, affordances help us focus on technology characteristics that invite users to employ the technologies in certain ways. Following this approach, Treem and Leonardi broadly review ways which, according to the authors of primary studies, various features of new technological systems led users to appropriate them in a variety of organizational settings. On the other hand, the authors avoid discussing these uses, and the possible outcomes of these uses, as "effects" of technologies or of technological features. This approach allows them to dodge a degree of determinism (which seems to have become a devil term) in characterizing how communication technologies work. In this light, their essay tends to weigh in on the side of how users experience and adapt social media rather than linking features to outcomes or effects.

Although the effects of media on communication processes and outcomes has a long history in communication research, a focus on effects seems to be especially troublesome and problematized in social media and new communication technology research. Yet the field may benefit from renewed focus on effects of social media, for epistemological reasons as well as substantive ones. That is, by focusing on the question of effects, researchers have to ask difficult questions about what their research has shown and what their research methods either reveal or conceal with regard to the kinds of claims they might make from their investigations.

The study of communication technology effects has become quite complicated. Social media and traditional computer-mediated communication technologies have become embedded in the social and organizational lives of so many people. As a result, researchers face a daunting question of how to isolate or even trace the causal influences of technology factors that lead to various outcomes, without considering a variety of unarticulated users' goals and users' implicit theories of media, as well as contextual features, that complicate the relationships of affordances to effects. All this occurs in a sociotechnical environment in which any given user may be hopping from application to application for reasons researchers have yet to understand and users themselves simply intuit (Baym, Zhang, Kunkel, Ledbetter, & Lin, 2007).

One consequence of this seems to have been a greater reliance on descriptive research—surveys, case studies, and correlational studies focusing on users' characteristics and their activities with various communication systems—that acknowledge the potential uniqueness of usages from sample to sample and setting to setting. Another feature of these approaches is that they generally do not concern themselves with comparisons outside of the system they study. Although they are not experimental in nature, these approaches do not entail some kind of comparison condition, for example, to similar organizations that do not adopt certain media, or to organizations that adopt different media or media with different affordances, or to what people do with older forms of CMC or with older forms of communication, not to mention offline communication of almost any sort (such as the that old standby in organizational communication research, the "water cooler conversation").

Research requires such comparisons in order for theoretical thinking to progress. Although Treem and Leonardi suggest that a focus on affordances lends itself to the development of theory, affordances (or any other approach) can only do so if they provide a stable basis for comparisons. When affordance X is enabled by technological attributes, and users appropriate it in Y manner, and it leads to Z effects across settings (not idiosyncratically but systematically), then theoretical generalizations can be made. These kinds of comparisons may ultimately be what research needs to organize its findings and to infer support for propositions.

Another danger we see in the lack of comparisons in much social media research comes from the potential to reach conclusions that are "false positives" or "false negatives" with respect to the influence of technology on behaviors (Walther, 2011). A "Type I Technology Error" occurs when we conclude that certain behaviors result from various qualities of media, yet without comparison to offline behavior that may exhibit similar patterns, such conclusions are fallacious. We see claims that may be Type I Technology Errors with respect to deception in online settings, where no offline comparison is made (see DeAndrea, Tong, Liang, Levine, & Walther, in press). Research concludes that in online interaction work partners develop more trust for one another when their linguistic styles converge, noting that in online discourse language cues are more salient because nonverbal cues are absent. When such conclusions do not take into consideration the wealth of theoretical and empirical findings on language convergence in negotiation and other offline settings for accommodation (e.g., Donohue & Roberto, 1993), such conclusions may be Type I Technology errors. The chance of these types of errors appears to be becoming more and more common, as research increasingly relies on exclusively online samples, or uses case study approaches no matter how statistically sophisticated they may be.

A Type II Technology Error occurs when evidence from a computational environment leads to claims about universal behavior, but technological artifacts affected data in such a way that should limit generalization to technological contexts. Although this type of universalistic claim is less often asserted, it is not without precedent. Very recent work, for example, employed linguistic analyses of 509 million Twitter messages from 2.4 million individuals around the world, from which researchers concluded that people's moods systematically vary in different phases of the workday and work week (Golder & Macy, 2011). Although the authors recognized limitations of lexical analysis techniques and a lack of demographic and occupational backgrounds "that may influence how much people sleep" (which affects moods; p. 1881), they did not comment on the potential influence of Twitter, Twitter culture, restriction to English, or other similar technologically contextual factors that may suggest limited generalizability of these results despite the massive sample size.

These alarms about overreaching empirical conclusions should not be taken as a recommendation not to seek out causal relationships and bona fide effects of communication technologies, or to focus only on users' self-reported experiences, or conduct in-depth case studies. Rather, these issues caution us to be both broad in method and conservative in conclusions, to do more comparisons and remain tentative until having done so, and to dig deeper past techno-phenomenological results. The developing research on Facebook and social capital provides a good example of advancing precision and meaningfulness of effects. Early research established correlations among the intensity of an individual's Facebook use—including the number of one's Facebook friends—and scores on a self-report measure of social capital (theoretically, the ability to share and synthesize resources among members of a social network). More friends, more Facebook, more social capital (Ellison, Steinfield, & Lampe, 2007): This line of research has moved past simple correlations toward efforts that show a sequential relationship between Facebook use and social capital (Steinfield, Ellison, & Lampe, 2008), and that it is not all Facebook friends, but actual friends (those with a preexisting relationship of more than a passing nature) that contribute to social capital (Ellison, Vitak, Gray, & Lampe, 2011). What this represents is movement from a gross phenomenology of sociology, where only in a certain technological setting can one have upwards of a few hundred people one calls a friend (unlike offline relationships), to something in which a technology offers affordances that facilitate dynamics that exist by the nature of actual friendship, whether online or offline. Even more recent steps have situated the phenomenon back in the field of communication, as Ellison, Vitak, et al. (2011) identified specific communication behaviors that occur in Facebook (as they may elsewhere) such as offering condolence, congratulations, etc., that are linked to relational maintenance and capital. The phenomenology of Facebook is giving way to a communication-centric view where the affordances of visibility, editability, and association—as Treem and Leonardi posit—facilitate basic relationship messages in ways that theorists of both traditional and new communication can readily understand. Extant theory from relationships research can help predict and explain effects.

Other approaches wait in the wings. For instance, the social influence theory of technology selection (Fulk, Schmitz, & Steinfield, 1990) can be applied to the question of how affordances come to be perceived and adopted. Adaptive structuration theory (Poole & DeSanctis, 1992) can help to understand how affordances are appropriated by different groups of users. There are many other robust frameworks on which to draw. Ultimately these avenues to the regularities and comparisons among and between communication with and without technologies can help us organize and understand the affordances, applications, and effects of continually emerging media.

References

Baym, N. K., Zhang, Y. B., Kunkel, A., Ledbetter, A., & Lin, M.-C. (2007). Relational quality and media use in interpersonal relationships. *New Media & Society, 9*, 735–752.

DeAndrea, D. C., Tong, S. T., Liang, Y., Levine, T. R., & Walther, J. B. (in press). When do people misrepresent themselves to others? The effects of social desirability, accountability, and ground truth on deceptive self-presentations. *Journal of Communication.*

Donohue, W. A., & Roberto, A. J. (1993). Relational development as negotiated order in hostage negotiation. *Human Communication Research, 20*, 175–198.

Ellison, N., Steinfield, C., & Lampe, C. (2007). The benefits of Facebook "friends": Exploring the relationship between college students' use of online social networks and social capital. *Journal of Computer-Mediated Communication 12*(3). Retrieved from http://jcmc.indiana.edu/vol12/issue4/ellison.html

Ellison, N., Vitak, J., Gray, R., Lampe, C., & Brooks, B. (2011, September). *Cultivating social resources on Facebook: Signals of relational investment and their role in social capital processes.* Paper presented at the Oxford Internet Institute "A Decade in Internet Time" Symposium, Oxford, England.

Eveland, W. P. Jr. (2003) A mix of attributes approach to the study of media effects and new communication technologies. *Journal of Communication, 53*, 395–410.

Fulk, J., Schmitz, J., & Steinfield, C. W. (1990). A social influence model of technology use. In J. Fulk & C. W. Steinfield (Eds.), *Organizations and communication technology* (pp. 117–140). Newbury Park, CA: Sage.

Golder, S. A., & Macy, M. W. (2011). Diurnal and seasonal mood vary with work, sleep, and day length across cultures. *Science, 333*, 1878–1881.

Poole, M. S., & DeSanctis, G. (1992). Microlevel structuration in computer-supported decision making. *Human Communication Research, 19*, 5–49.

Steinfield, C., Ellison, N., & Lampe, C. (2008). Social capital, self-esteem, and use of online social network sites: A longitudinal analysis. *Journal of Applied Developmental Psychology, 29*, 434–445.

Walther, J. B. (2011). Theories of computer-mediated communication and interpersonal relations. In M. L. Knapp & J. A. Daly (Eds.), *The handbook of interpersonal communication* (4th ed., pp. 443–479). Thousand Oaks, CA: Sage.

CHAPTER CONTENTS

9 Reconsidering the Concept of Workplace Flexibility

Is Adaptability a Better Solution?

Karen K. Myers, Bernadette M. Gailliard, and Linda L. Putnam

University of California, Santa Barbara

Flexibility is a key issue in organizational life, especially because organizations rely on work from remote locations and create policies to accommodate work–life balance. Most existing research examines workplace flexibility in primarily the individual or the organizational domain. Views of communication in these domains typically embrace transmission or transaction assumptions without concern for how organizational discourses shape the enactment of flexibility. This paper argues that workplace flexibility emerges from the intersection among the discourses linked to four domains: organizational policies and arrangements; workplace norms and practices; worker–supervisor relationships; and an individual's sense of agency. We contend that the discourses rooted in and across these domains introduce contradictions that come from an organizational logic that perpetuates a competition between work and life. In this logic, the burden of workplace flexibility is placed on individual workers who must make choices about whether to ignore or rebuke normative organizational practices. Rather than placing the onus on individuals, we argue that organizations need to adopt a new philosophy grounded in a discourse of adaptability, one that both workers and employers embrace. The discourse of adaptability supersedes workplace flexibility and transforms workers' needs and the organization's objectives into a system of worker autonomy that incorporates fluidity in achieving both personal and organizational goals.

Until recently, American workers were a homogenous group. In the 1950s, 56% of the U.S. workforce consisted of White males who were the sole provider for their families (Bailyn, Drago, & Kochan, 2001). Because the wives of the workers assumed primary responsibility for caring for the home and children, the men were enabled (and required) to focus their time and attention on their work. Today's workforce is anything but homogenous, with a broad range of responsibilities and roles. Women comprise more than half of today's workforce (U.S. Bureau of Labor Statistics, 2011). Many workers are single parents or part of a dual-income family in which both parents work outside the home. They also have other obligations that include caring for elderly family members, participation in community politics and events, and tending to their own spiritual and health-related needs. Working individuals strive for ways to balance life demands, such as caring for family, maintaining a home, and incorporating other interests, into their busy lives. Given a finite amount of time and energy, work–life balance refers to the ways that individuals attempt to manage (or juggle) the various roles in their lives (Cowan & Hoffman, 2007).

Many organizations recognize that human capital, in the form of talented and dedicated workers, is their single most important strategic resource (Delaney & Huselid, 1996; Huselid & Becker, 1995). To protect this valuable resource, organizations look for ways to retain employees and to provide them with opportunities for balancing their work and personal lives. Workers who experience work–life conflict are less focused, more likely to call in sick, less productive, and more likely to leave the organization (Richman, Civian, Shannon, Hill, & Brennan, 2008). On this basis, over the past two decades many organizations have implemented workplace flexibility initiatives to help members achieve work–life balance.

Workplace flexibility refers to what organizations and employees do to develop an environment that aids in balancing the stresses and demands of work with life commitments (Kirby, Golden, Medved, Jorgenson, & Buzzanell, 2003). It entails the degree of variability or fixed nature of a job, how much autonomy an employee has at work, and norms about what is and is not negotiable (Hill, Jacob, et al., 2008). It is more than the existence of policies; it is the way arrangements regarding time, structure, and nature of work interface with and socially construct variability, autonomy, and fluidity of work. Examples of workplace flexibility initiatives include family leave, compressed workweeks, and opportunities to telecommute.

Despite positive outcomes, efforts to make workplace flexibility initiatives fundamental to core employment systems have not been entirely successful. These initiatives remain marginalized rather than mainstream, and thus, lead to mixed messages about using them (Kirby, 2000). These messages simultaneously enable employees to manage work and personal life while they increase work intensity and perpetuate stereotypes of the ideal worker.

Researchers in a variety of disciplines have examined workplace flexibility, particularly studies that center on maternity leave policies and negotiations (Buzzanell & Liu, 2007; Kirby & Krone, 2002; Miller, Jablin, Casey, Lamphear-Van Horn, & Ethington, 1996); telecommuting and use of technology (Broadfoot, 2001; Fonner & Roloff, 2010; Golden & Geisler, 2006); scheduling (Bohen & Viveros-Long, 1981; Hyman, Scholarios, & Baldry, 2005; Kirby, Wieland, & McBride, 2006); and facilitating work–family balance (Brewer, 2000; Buzzanell et al., 2005; Golden & Geisler, 2006; Weisberg & Buckler, 1994). Despite this attention, these literatures that attempt to provide better understanding of workplace flexibility situate it in a particular frame that shapes the contours of the construct. Research findings highlight contradictions between the intended use of policies and what actually occurs in implementing them. Organizational members often experience these con-traditions as dilemmas or mixed messages that create more stress, frustration, and work–life conflict than existed prior to enacting workplace flexibility policies (Breaugh & Frye, 2008; Gajendran & Harrison, 2007; Kirby, 2000; Kirby & Krone, 2002).

Contributing to the dilemma is the way that various organizational domains enter into, and often compete, in the enactment of workplace flexibility. Narrowly focused policies and practices limit an organization's ability to deliver on the flexibility promise. Supervisors have a large influence on the ways policies are enacted in their department. Likewise, workers are limited by their ability to navigate flexibility negotiations effectively. These complexities inhibit practice as well as the development of a coherent understanding of workplace flexibility. Multiple and varied definitions of this construct exist in the literature. Scholars need to sharpen these definitions and further theorize about the nature and limitations of workplace flexibility.

Thus, this paper has three primary goals. First, we situate the construct of workplace flexibility in the literature on four organizational domains: organizational structures, workplace norms and practices, supervisor–worker relationships, and worker agency. We examine the role that communication plays in understanding workplace flexibility within these domains and we highlight contradictions that surface among them. Second, we unpack and critique the organizational logic of workplace flexibility that perpetuates a competition between work and life. Organizations offer opportunities for flextime, job sharing, telecommuting, and flexible use of personal days as ways to address work–life conflict; however, organizations also cast flexibility as a benefit rather than a right and convey mixed messages about the use of these accommodations. Through revealing how these contradictions arise, how they cross domains, how they are perpetuated, and how they feed into notions of the ideal worker, we uncover alternative ways to manage the work–life dialectic that are aimed at transcending the oppositional push-pulls rather than integrating or balancing them. Finally, we call for breaking this logic, altering organizational cultures, and moving away from administering systems of universal practices toward an adaptive system that accommodates the diverse needs of workers and the changing needs of organizations. We introduce the concept of adaptability through describing its philosophy and practices, providing examples of its use, pointing out challenges that this approach faces, and discussing ways that research on it can alter workplace flexibility.

Defining and Broadening the Scope of Workplace Flexibility

Workplace flexibility is a part of the work–life balance and work–family conflict literatures that focus on how individuals construct, manage, and negotiate boundaries, individual identities, and relationships across the work, family, and community spheres (Clark, 2000; Golden & Geisler, 2006; Golden, Kirby, & Jorgenson, 2006). These literatures address managerial and organizational perspectives, family issues, gender concerns, and identity work in multiple and conflicting roles. Other initiatives, such as balancing home and family needs or providing community support programs, also address work–life balance, but our focus centers on organizational initiatives to deal with work–life conflict. Theorizing about workplace flexibility contributes to the broad work–life literatures and to conceptions of the ideal worker. Rooted in organizational voice, this construct encompasses the material constraints of time-place, issues of flexible work policies, managerial appropriation of these policies, and the social construction of worker identities within these accommodations.

Most studies generally locate workplace flexibility either at the organizational or the individual level. At the organizational level, corporations offer policies and programs that provide opportunities for employees to modify the timing, location, or structure of work (Hall & Richter, 1988; Nesbit, 2005). Some scholars locate workplace flexibility only at this level—as the way an organization creates flexible arrangements for work. At the individual level, however, employees interpret these policies, collect insights about how the company views using them, and make inferences as to how using the policies will impact their careers. From an employee's perspective, workplace flexibility involves individual agency or the degree to which an employee feels able to make choices about his or her professional life, particularly about where, when, and how long work is performed (e.g., Buzzanell & Lucas, 2006; Buzzanell et al., 2005). Agency, in this sense, refers to the capacity, condition, or ability to act in making choices about flexible work arrangements. In general, organizations often place the responsibility for attaining flexibility on the individual (e.g., Gottlieb, Kelloway, & Barham, 1998; Moe & Shandy, 2010), thus making flexibility primarily a matter of agency.

However, examining multiple levels of analysis is central to understanding the logics that underlie workplace flexibility. Communication around flexible accommodations functions simultaneously at the organizational, workgroup, supervisor–subordinate, and individual levels and encompasses macrosocietal presumptions of gender, race, and class that penetrate organizations (Kirby & Krone, 2002; Kirby et al., 2006). Yet, most research projects only examine one or two of these levels. Specifically, at the organizational level, structures and policies foster discursive practices that influence how workplace flexibility is defined and enacted. Organizational policies and arrangements refer to developing flexible schedules, job assignments, and work location. Workplace norms and practices encompass values and beliefs that underlie expectations for acceptable and unacceptable use of the policies. Within the supervisor–worker domain, the strength of the relationship, supervisor supportiveness, and use of performance standards affect how workplace flexibility is negotiated. Lastly, worker agency relates to how individual characteristics influence perceptions of accessibility and ability to engage in negotiations about workplace flexibility issues. For example, discourses about gender, class, and race; and the rights and privileges of certain positions influence an individual's likelihood of using workplace flexibility arrangements.

Crossing multiple levels of analysis reveals how enactments and social constructions of workplace flexibility operate in contradictory and inconsistent ways. These inconsistencies become embedded in a logic rooted in conceptions of the ideal worker, norms and expectations for collegial behaviors, and societal conceptions of work and life. Even though societal discourses impinge on this construct, this essay situates workplace flexibility primarily within the organizational context. Thus, this paper does not examine issues related to gender roles, cultural support, community support, family networks, and socioeconomic status, to name a few. Other scholars have explored these relationships and revealed complex interfaces between societal and organizational domains (e.g., Ashcraft, 2006; Golden et al., 2006; Medved, 2009; Tracy & Rivera, 2010). We, in turn, center on multiple levels within the organizational arena, and seek to understand the contradictions that enable and constrain flexible workplace practices and suggest alternatives to transcend these dualities and move to a system of adaptability.

A Discursive Approach to Workplace Flexibility

A discursive perspective examines how workplace flexibility is produced through various discourses that create and influence the organizational culture across multiple organizational levels (Ainsworth & Hardy, 2004; Ashcraft, 2006). These discourses embody beliefs, norms, values, traditions, and practices that shape organizational structures, influence interpretations of policies and practices, and infuse everyday communication (Kossek, Lewis & Hammer, 2010; Tracy & Rivera, 2010). Through these daily interactions, individuals (re)create, resist, conform, and reform the enactment of workplace flexibility.

This approach differs from much of the existing literature in two important ways. First, a majority of the research examines workplace flexibility from a unidimensional perspective, treating the construct as rooted either completely in organizational structure or completely in individual agency. When rooted in structure, workplace flexibility becomes synonymous with organizational policies about the timing and location of work; for example, flextime, part-time work, or telecommuting (e.g., Brewer, 2000; Broadfoot et al., 2008; Costa, Sartori, & Akerstedt, 2006; Cowan & Hoffman, 2007; Guest, 2002; Jenkins, 2004). The role of communication is virtually nonexistent and managers serve as conduits for transmitting information about the policies. When researchers foreground the organizational policies and arrangements, other domains are overlooked and contradictions arise from different ways that workplace flexibility is enacted.

When workplace flexibility is rooted in individual agency, communication plays a central role, but flexibility becomes an interpersonal negotiation in that employees receive a "greater scope for arranging their own schedules and working practices, albeit within the parameters set by others" (Alvesson & Willmott, 2002, p. 624), such as supervisors (Buzzanell & Liu, 2007), coworkers (Hyman et al., 2005), or even family members (Carlson, Kacmar, &

Williams, 2000). While researchers gain insights about the ways that employees negotiate idiosyncratic arrangements (Hornung, Rousseau, & Glaser, 2008), these studies typically ignore how other domains outside of supervisor–worker relationships and individual agency impinge on, inhibit, and recast these negotiations.

A second contribution of the discursive approach is the ability to expand studies of workplace flexibility beyond the work–home dichotomy. In the late 1970s when research on flexible workplaces began, the discourse concentrated on improving employees' "quality of life" by reducing the mental and physical strain of work. Organizations were containers in which flexibility was negotiated through penetrating the boundary between work and life. In the 1980s, after the passage of the Family Medical Leave Act (FMLA), the discourses changed. With added governmental regulations linked to family leaves, the organizational discourse shifted to integrating work and family, despite years of separation between the two domains (Eaton, 2003). Thus, research now focuses on understanding how employees can achieve workplace flexibility while decreasing work–family conflict (Clark, 2000; Cowan & Hoffman, 2007; Donald & Linington, 2008; Guest, 2002). Initiatives, such as "family-friendly policies" and "family supportive programs," aim to foster effective management of the two roles—worker and family member (Adams & Jex, 1999; Grover & Crocker, 1995; Kossek & Ozeki, 1998).

Focusing only on the work–family relationship, however, limits the roles that individuals play. An individual might be a volunteer, a student, a part-time time employee, a church member, and an athlete in addition to being a parent and a worker. By limiting flexibility to the work and family domains, other discourses become marginalized. Thus, another shift, currently underway, is the move from work–family policies to work–life arrangements. Expanding the discourse beyond family to "life" recognizes that employees need to be supported in all areas outside of work. The new work–life discourse adds to the complexity and the contradictions that surface in implementing workplace flexibility. Namely, a certain discourse may be beneficial for some groups of employees while detrimental to others. For example, Hylmö (2004) finds that men are more likely to engage in telecommuting than women, but they do so without invoking the same family discourses that women use when they work from home. Such findings beg the questions: What domains draw on these discourses and how do they create contradictions that lead to ironic outcomes in enacting flexible workplace arrangements?

Examining the communication across multiple organizational domains brings these contradictions to the forefront and reveals the inherent complexity of workplace flexibility and the difficulty of negotiating it amid competing organizational discourses. The communication around flexibility also raises a concern about the underlying message threaded through the domains, one that places the responsibility for enacting flexibility on the individual. Thus, we utilize the discursive approach to reexamine the promise of workplace flexibility and to explore options for reconceptualizing this construct through an alternative organizational philosophy that embraces adaptability as a way to meet the needs of individuals and organizations.

Locating Workplace Flexibility

Organizational Structure: Policies and Arrangements

Organizational structure situates workplace flexibility at the organizational level and contends that it surfaces through developing policies that allow for variability in time/schedule arrangements, job assignments, and location of work. The overall presumption is that employees can manage the emotional strain between work and life through using flextime, flexplace, job sharing, part-time work, and personal leaves. This literature, however, indicates that the opposite often prevails; that is, control over time/schedule often leads to increased hours and less flexibility and telecommuting creates stress through multitasking demands and long hours needed to meet task deadlines. The logic that underlies this level of analysis is that work–life programs are "add-ons" to an employee's benefit system, one that fails to examine the organizational culture or daily interactions that shape the nature of these accommodations.

The first contradiction that arises from the organizational structure literature is that the policies should improve work–life balance. However, research shows that the existence of formal policies does not necessarily lead to fewer hours of work—even though employees' perceptions of these flexibility arrangements improve their attitudes, morale, and commitment (Gottlieb et al., 1998; Kirby et al., 2006). For example, although Adams and Jex (1999) show that control over time/schedule yields less family conflict, the type of control moderates these findings. The more workers set their own goals and priorities, the more they are committed, and ironically, the less flexible they feel. In addition, professionals who control their own hours and shifts have schedule flexibility, but they are often on call when they are not at work; thus they experience long and uneven hours (Hyman et al., 2005). Sennett (1998) describes this inverse relationship as the "corrosive" effects of flexible work, in that autonomy in work settings often leads to less work–life balance through increasing work hours.

Another contradiction arises in the ways that the use of flextime policies can stigmatize employees. For some employers, taking advantage of flexible time/schedules may signal low commitment to the job or not being serious about work (Bailyn, 1993; Perlow, 1997). To avoid being seen as "unprofessional," employees may conceal their actual reasons for flex schedules. As an example, female engineers in Jorgenson's (2000) study used excuses like 5:00 p.m. traffic congestion and business obligations to justify leaving work early for family commitments. Their explanations focused on maintaining their professional reputations and avoiding the stigma linked to flexschedules. Thus, the ways that policies become stigmatized may shape how employees view them; namely, flexibility gets processed as constraints.

In like manner, policies regarding personal and maternity leaves, part of the repertoire of these workplace flexibility initiatives, are often seen as rigid rather than flexible. Employees often have difficulty obtaining information about such policies (Buzzanell & Liu, 2007). Some employees believe that organizations want to avoid discussing leaves to prevent setting precedents or dealing with special cases, such as time off for doctor appointments or extended leaves. Furthermore, requests for maternity leaves often entail extended paperwork and rules that deter the use of these policies (Liu & Buzzanell, 2004). These bureaucratic hassles lead some employees to refer to them as "rigid policies" related to flexible leaves.

A fourth contradiction surrounding these policies centers on simultaneously encouraging and discouraging the use of them. Companies that offer maternity leaves may expect their most ambitious workers to forego them (Kirby & Krone, 2002; Rapoport & Bailyn, 1996). To retain opportunities for career advancement, some women accommodate and work during their maternity leaves (Buzzanell & Lucas, 2006). In an effort to avoid being labeled, "mommy track" or a "working mother," they claim a primary orientation to their careers, even when they are on personal or maternity leave. Some women who take a maternity leave feel slighted when they are not considered for advancement because they have a young baby (Buzzanell & Lucas, 2006). Thus, companies provide flexible leave policies, but often keep them buried, create bureaucratic hurdles, and discourage career-oriented professionals from using them. Overall, flexible workplace arrangements might exist but employees who use them feel compelled to work longer and harder (Buzzanell & Lucas, 2006; Hymlö, 2004). In addition, flextime practices and leaves of absence may carry stigmas that discourage employees from using them or stymie an individual's organizational advancement.

Workloads often lead to a contradiction between a variable-sum and a fixed-sum view of one's job; that is, if one person gets a flexible arrangement the other employees get more work. This view of flexible work assignments leads to decreased rather than increased workplace flexibility. For example, some employees treat maternity leaves as increasing tasks for others, causing scheduling difficulties, and creating problems in meeting project deadlines (Liu & Buzzanell, 2004). For some women, their workloads increase after they return from maternity leave, a situation that results in decreased workplace flexibility (Buzzanell & Liu, 2007).

Task deadlines also create contradictions between freedom and constraint in using flexible work arrangements. Specifically, workers may experience freedom in the content, location, and timing of their work but incur constraints through firm deadlines, coordination requirements, and pay schedules; thus, limiting actual workplace flexibility. Autonomy may allow workers to be their own bosses and give them flexibility over how, when, and where they do their work, but strategically, their schedules may be constrained by employers' deadlines and billing schedules (Broadfoot, 2001).

Location of work or flexplace, another type of flexible work arrangement, increases fluid use of time and space, but often at the expense of isolation or sacrificed opportunities for advancement. Telecommuting is a type of flexible work arrangement in which employees complete most of their tasks away from central offices (Hylmö, 2004). It provides high levels of autonomy and control because workers can be their own bosses (Edley, 2004). Employees who telecommute are able to work around children's schedules and have more contacts with friends and family. For this flexibility, however, some teleworkers believe that they sacrifice opportunities for supervisors' and coworkers' interactions, ones that might lead to advancement in an organization (Edley, 2004; Voydanoff, 2005).

In particular, Frank and Lowe (2003) found that individuals in the accounting industry who varied their schedules, but worked in the central office were seen as more competent in handling challenging job responsibilities and more likely to be promoted in a standard time frame than were individuals who telecommuted. Similarly, Gajendran and Harrison's (2007) meta-analysis of research on the link between telecommunication and job satisfaction revealed that telework yielded the benefits of managing the interface between home and work and higher job control and autonomy, but often at the expense of isolation and relational impoverishment.

In contrast, Fonner and Roloff (2010) found that spending less than 50% of a week in a collocated office added flexibility, aided in balancing work and personal roles, and lowered stress from interruptions and organizational politics. Similarly, Gajendran and Harrison (2007) observed that information exchange adequacy, not the amount of time engaged in face-to-face interaction, was the primary factor in how telework affected workplace relationships. Their study found that teleworkers were able to filter and avoid information overload and stress, while allowing them to retain important connections to the office network. Hence, the research is inconclusive as to whether telecommuting reduces opportunities for advancement, leads to isolation, hinders workplace relationships, and reduces work–life conflict. More research is needed to tease out the inconsistencies in these studies.

Telecommuting may not promote work–life balance for other reasons. Telecommuters often feel as if they have to work harder and longer than they do in the office to account for their hours during the day, especially if they are billing by the hour (Hylmö, 2004). Thus, when paid work takes place at home, workers often feel schizophrenic; they are torn between work and family and stressed by the demands of multitasking. Flexibility, then, becomes a justification for allowing work to spill over into nonwork hours (Hill, Hawkins, & Miller, 1996; Hill, Martinson, Ferris, & Baker, 2004). However, teleworkers who enact a fixed schedule with structured work time at home seem able to reduce the stress between work and family (Voydanoff, 2005).

Overall, in the literatures on organizational structure, work arrangements are the keys to instantiating workplace flexibility. Specifically, flexibility becomes housed in the opportunities that employers provide for flextime, official leaves, variable job assignments, and telecommuting. Researchers typically adopt an organizational rather than an individual perspective and presume that individuals have equal access to these arrangements.

In general, workplace flexibility resides in a delicate balance between the existence of policies and practices, the control over schedules, and the stigmas attached to using these benefits. This delicate balance often leads to contradictions in that autonomy over time and schedule often fosters increasing work hours rather than reducing them. In addition, employees who use these initiatives often feel added stress from the demands of multitasking, meeting deadlines, and conforming to the image of the ideal worker. Moreover, organizations simultaneously encourage and discourage employees from using these policies through implementing bureaucratic hurdles, setting implicit standards of professionalism, and holding fixed-sum attitudes about workloads. This literature also relegates communication to transmitting information about policies or to implementing particular practices. Policies become a way to promote a company's image rather than how workers develop flexibility in their daily routines. This literature typically fails to address how communication constitutes workplace arrangements, the socially constructed meanings of these policies, and the interplay between workgroup norms and the use of flexible arrangements.

Workplace Norms and Practices

Workgroup norms and practices exert a strong effect on an employee's use of flexible arrangements, but only a few studies locate workplace flexibility at the workgroup level of analysis. However, this domain is critical for understanding the norms and expectations of acceptable practices. Even if an organization promotes workplace flexibility policies or programs, employees are less likely to use them if coworkers devalue them, view them as inequitable, or see them as gendered (Moe & Shandy, 2010).

Inconsistencies arise when coworkers treat workplace flexibility as "time away from work" and employees feel that they have to work harder to compensate for using the policies. Specifically, Kirby and Krone (2002) found: "[i]n the discourse about work-family policies at Regulatory Alliance, the examiners continually compared themselves to each other in terms of benefits they were or were not able to use" (p. 59). One participant felt negative tension from coworkers because she utilized family leave policies. She asks, "Does it make them happier if I'm on annual leave rather than if I'm on sick leave [under the family leave policy ... There's no reason to compare" (p. 68). This type of critical judgment stems from perceptions of injustice when some workers are permitted to take time off, forcing their colleagues to cover for them in their absence.

When these negative attitudes emerge in recurring patterns, it can create toxic environments through discourses known as sludge and black sludge (Ressler & Thompson, 2008). The term *sludge* depicts negative comments that coworkers make to reinforce ideas about how work gets done. Sludge most typically includes negative judgments about how colleagues are not pulling their own weight. Black sludge may be even more toxic as the term depicts hostile workgroup discourse in which coworkers hinder one another from using work–life initiatives. The implicit message is that work–life arrangements disrupt the workflow and create inequities in the workplace. This message reinforces values of meritocracy and images of the ideal worker as someone who should refrain from using flexible arrangements.

Companies also foster mixed messages between their public images and the norms that they convey implicitly. Specifically, Mescher, Benschop, and Doorewaard (2010) examined workplace flexibility policies on 24 websites of companies that were purported to be highly supportive of work–life balance. They found that companies proudly publicized their policies, but cast them as extras or as special benefits rather than as rights that employees should have. When workplace flexibility policies are seen as benefits, managers and coworkers rely on norms rooted in meritocracy and beliefs that the ideal worker does not need these extras. Thus, coworkers, managers, and employees typically accept these dominant workplace norms as powerful and as inevitable (Mescher et al., 2010), a practice that creates an environment in which the policies exist but employees do not use them (Kirby & Krone, 2002).

This literature fills an important gap in the research on workplace flexibility. Specifically, it houses this concept in workgroup values and beliefs as well as socially constructed meanings about these routines. Yet, it continues to position individuals as the source of adhering to or violating workplace norms, choosing whether to work extra hours to compensate for using these policies, and interpreting how these policies will affect workplace relationships. Communication gains a constitutive role in that socially constructed meanings become central to understanding the symbolic nature of flexible benefits. Most studies, however, presume these meanings are pervasive and difficult to change. This presumption stems from the discourses of the ideal worker, meritocracy, and equality that underlie assumptions about how work should be done. Moreover, it limits the ways that micropractices and daily interactions create, maintain, or change cultural norms. Thus, understanding the concept of workplace flexibility needs to encompass supervisor–subordinate relationships and the agency that individuals feel regarding whether or not to use these policies.

Supervisor–Worker Relationships

At the dyadic level, supervisors are often the key to making work schedules flexible, communicating positive attitudes and values about work–life accommodations, allowing workers to integrate nonwork concerns into work domains and negotiate the use of flexible arrangements (Clark, 2000; Kirby et al., 2006; Kirchmeyer, 1995). Yet, issues of fairness, equal access, and demands on productivity often create contradictions in supervisors' support of flexible work arrangements. In their efforts to be fair and to accomplish work in traditional ways, supervisors may send mixed messages about workplace flexibility (Kirby, 2000). Specifically, they may support and not support these policies for different reasons. Moreover, the quality of relationships are pivotal to effective supervisor–employee negotiations about flexible accommodations; thus, some employees are positive about the use of these policies, while others see their supervisors as working against them. These inconsistencies suggest that the logic of workplace flexibility is idiosyncratic—often giving supervisors the final say in supporting and implementing flexible policies.

Supervisors are key sources of flexibility through supporting or denying requests for workplace arrangements (Buzzanell & Liu, 2007; Cowan & Hoffman, 2007; Kirby, 2000). Workers who feel that they can openly communicate with their supervisors also believe they can negotiate about flexibility issues (Ashforth, Kreiner, & Fugate, 2000; Breaugh & Frye, 2008; Fairhurst, 1993; Miller, Johnson, Hart, & Peterson, 1999). Supervisors' support also mediates some potentially negative social effects of telecommuting (Gajendran & Harrison, 2007). Yet, a supervisor's attitude, perceptions of fairness, and willingness to negotiate, send mixed messages as to whether employees should use these policies. Specifically, Bohen and Viveros-Long's study (1981) compared workers who used flextime policies to those who did not. Employees reported that their supervisors' attitudes were the most significant predictors of users and nonusers of flextime. While many supervisors encouraged employees to use these arrangements, others were irritated by workers who were not available when they were needed. In a study that compared managerial levels, CEOs held less positive attitudes toward telework than did HR managers who adhered to occupational norms about such practices (Peters & Heusinkveld, 2010); hence, individuals at higher levels in the organization may impinge on a manager's attitudes about using flexible workplace arrangements.

Supervisors' attitudes also create contradictions in the ways that they handle issues of fairness. Some supervisors employ a philosophy of "always fair." They may distribute privileges equally, for example, by offering flexibility to workers with children as well as to those who are not parents. However, to maintain productivity, supervisors cannot offer flexible arrangements to all employees simultaneously. In peak production times, supervisors must decide who will receive flexible arrangements and who will be denied. While making decisions on a case-by-case basis is potentially valuable, such arrangements can exacerbate favoritism and create mixed messages about the use of these policies (Graen & Scandura, 1987; Graen & Uhl-Bien, 1995).

The use of maternity leaves provides an excellent example of how supervisors send mixed messages about the use of flexible workplace arrangements. Buzzanell and Liu (2007) found that supervisor–employee negotiations varied considerably and were influenced by whether workers perceived that they could reach agreements on the condition and timing of their leaves. Women who had good relationships with their bosses and were optimistic about their negotiations often received favorable pregnancy leaves while those who were not optimistic felt that their supervisors worked against providing them with flexibility. The optimistic women felt as if they were valuable contributors who could not easily be replaced while the less optimistic women felt their supervisors held personal and social biases that made it difficult for them to talk about flexibility issues (Buzzanell & Liu, 2007).

Some of these inconsistencies in managerial attitudes toward implementing flexible work–life arrangements occur because of how the managerial domain intersects with other organizational domains. Supervisors' attitudes often relate to institutional concerns and pressures related to costs and productivity. In particular, managers may fear that offering increased autonomy and flexible schedules will disrupt work flows and be more costly to the organization (Kirby et al., 2006). They may be unwilling to let employees work part-time or share jobs because they believe fixed costs would increase if two part-time workers are needed to cover the job that one full-time employee formerly held (Weisberg & Buckler, 1994). In effect, although an organization may officially promote workplace flexibility, supervisors often feel pressured to meet stringent deadlines and thus get caught in conveying inconsistent messages about flexible arrangements (Kirby, 2000).

Supervisors' pressures along with workplace norms also directly affect their communications and negotiations with employees, especially about maternity leaves. For instance, many of the women in Buzzanell and Liu's (2007) study felt their supervisors would not make compromises regarding pregnancy complications. Moreover, pregnant women who wanted to advance in their organizations often accommodated their supervisors' concerns through sacrificing their personal and family commitments because they feared negative evaluations from their supervisors (Liu & Buzzanell, 2004). Knowing this, employees skewed their communication with supervisors to emphasize perceived shared values. These adaptations reinforce the belief that individuals should be committed to either their work or their families and should use these policies in ways to serve the organization.

Furthermore, supervisors shape the social meanings of workplace flexibility policies through their performance evaluations of employees. These evaluations can convey contradictory messages when supervisors evaluate work based on the amount of time an employee is in the office, despite supporting the use of organization-wide flexibility policies. To address problems with these mixed messages, researchers suggest that supervisors need to be evaluated based on their effectiveness in implementing these work–life initiatives as opposed to the company's images of ideal workers (Hammer & Barbara, 1997; Hammer, Kossek, Yragui, Bodner, & Hansen, 2009).

In summary, supervisor–subordinate relationships are a focal point for unraveling contradictions and inconsistencies in using workplace flexibility. A supervisor's supportiveness directly influences the degree to which employees can negotiate and use flexible arrangements. When supervisors believe that work–life initiatives decrease productivity and increase costs, flexibility may be denied. These findings suggest that supervisors often have the final say in making flexible arrangements available to individual employees; hence, access to flexibility may hinge on personal relationships or on an employee's sense of agency in negotiating with supervisors and coworkers.

Worker Agency

At the individual level, worker agency refers to the degree of access to and empowerment that an individual feels in negotiating and using flexible arrangements. Perceptions of access are linked to norms and expectations about who should or should not use these initiatives while empowerment draws on notions of self-efficacy or an individual's view of his or her ability to negotiate these arrangements. Within existing literatures, when workplace flexibility is rooted in agency the assumption is that workers have unlimited access and empowerment because flexibility policies are universally available to all employees. However, research shows that the social constructions of both access and empowerment are closely tied to organizational positions and societal discourses regarding gender, race, and class that create inconsistencies in how policies are administered. That is, an employee's sense of agency when engaging in flexibility negotiations is influenced by his or her position (Ciulla, 2000), gender (Kirby & Krone, 2002), race (Bell & Nkomo, 2001), and other individual characteristics.

Workers receive vastly different, and often contradictory, messages about workplace flexibility, depending on their organizational position (Ciulla, 2000). In many organizations, a two-tiered structure presumes that professional workers have more competencies and add more value to an organization than do lower level employees. This presumption makes professionals entitled to more autonomy over their work schedules (Brewer, 2000; Hyman et al., 2005; Miller et al., 1996). Entry- and lower-level employees (e.g., service workers), in turn, are required to perform their jobs on location and are subject to continuous observation and stringent controls; hence, these employees lack access to flexible arrangements because they often feel tied to their places of work and to inflexible schedules in comparison with managers and professional staff. They may also feel less empowered to engage in negotiations for flexible arrangements because of their lack of education, few employment alternatives, and the relative ease with which entry-and lower-level workers can be replaced.

Thus, organizations often send contradictory messages to employees based on their professional versus entry-level positions. Professional employees generally work with clear project deadlines but considerable control over when, where, and how the work gets done. Entry-level employees, however, enjoy little operational autonomy and their job performance is monitored on a daily basis, if not continuously (Hantrais, 1993). While the professional position may appear more flexible, ironically, the institutional norms that dictate commitment to customers and organizations often constrain these individuals, especially executives who are expected to prioritize their work above their family and personal lives. In this sense, both professional and entry-level employees experience constraint and inflexibility in using work–life initiatives (Hill et al., 2004).

When considering the micropractices of negotiating flexibility, worker agency is closely tied to gendered expectations that create differential and inconsistent perceptions of access and empowerment in using flexible accommodations. It is well known that women are more likely than men to use parental leave policies (Buzzanell & Liu, 2007; Kirby & Krone, 2002) and to seek flexible ways of combining paid work and family care (Jurik, 1998). Coworkers also sympathize with women who take maternity leaves while they question men's need for paternity leaves (Kirby et al., 2003). Due to gendered expectations about who should provide parental care, women are perceived to have more agency (via access norms) to negotiate flexible arrangements regarding parental leave than are men.

This inconsistency leads men to use informal, nonpublic channels to take advantage of flexible work options in order to meet family needs. So, if a father with flextime changes his schedule, it may not occur to his coworkers that he is doing it to meet family responsibilities (Kirby et al., 2003). These practices may support individual agency, but they also perpetuate gendered organizational structures and inconsistent practices that allow men to have the agency to negotiate flexibility without being penalized for taking parental leaves (Kirby & Krone, 2002). Women, in contrast, typically draw on family-related discourses to negotiate flexible work arrangements (like maternity leaves) and thus face a contradiction in that they are supported but seen as less dedicated to their jobs than are employees who do not take such leaves. For instance, even though a woman may feel supported in taking a maternity leave, she simultaneously receives mixed messages about the potential long-term disadvantage in advancement, compensation, and organizational equity.

According to Moe and Shandy (2010), women who feel supported also fear the repercussions of violating the norms associated with the ideal worker, so they attempt to minimize interference of family obligations with work commitments. A national survey of highly educated women reaffirms that the communication that women often receive results in contradictory messages regarding the use of flexible policies. Even when employers offered flexible work opportunities, tacit rules prevented women from taking advantage of them. Only 4 out of 10 women whose firms offered telecommuting options felt they could use them. Even though 91% of the women at high levels of corporate leadership believed that they had flexibility at work, only 24% felt that they could invoke family reasons as a basis for rejecting a work opportunity, without harming their career trajectory (Moe & Shandy, 2010). These findings underscore the micropractices within organizations that influence a worker's sense of agency to negotiate workplace flexibility while ironically perpetuating gendered occupations and organizational hierarchies (Medved, 2009).

Class issues also intersect with organizational position and gender to highlight inconsistencies in who does and who does not have access to flexible workplace arrangements. Specifically, working-class employees often lack the option to choose nonstandard organizational arrangements, and must subvert the system to gain access to flexibility. For example, Hyman and colleagues (2005) found that clerical workers with low pay, low status positions, and high organizational control were primarily women (with family demands) who felt unable to engage in formal negotiations to make their jobs more flexible. Hence, they used shift swapping and other informal arrangements to achieve workplace flexibility. In contrast, managers, who were primarily men in high paying, professional positions were able to negotiate workplace flexibility through maintaining variable hours and working from home.

Likewise, Jenkins (2004) found that working-class women held a disproportionate number of part-time jobs, earned lower wages, and received less occupational training, and thus had limited opportunities to negotiate for increased salaries and job promotions. Such issues restrict access to flexibility even further because part-time workers often are seen as less committed, less motivated, and by extension, less viable for advancement (Hill et al., 2004). Full-time workers forget that part-time employees gain their workplace flexibility through an economic sacrifice; that is, they receive a disproportionate decrease in salary while tacitly being held to the same performance standards of full-time employees (Kirby & Krone, 2002; Weisberg & Buckler, 1994). Also, ironically, part-time employees may appear to have workplace flexibility due to working fewer hours, but their hours are often very inflexible and are scheduled around the needs and availability of full-time employees.

Race has the potential to influence one's agency in negotiating flexibility in ways similar to class, but it is typically overlooked in studies of flexible work arrangements (Kirby et al., 2003). Studies outside of the work–life literatures have shown that organizational leaders sometimes set low targets for advancing people of color (e.g., Bell & Nkomo, 2001). This practice limits an employee's agency through lack of access to the professional and managerial positions that include flexible options (such as autonomy and control of schedules). They also may feel less empowered to negotiate workplace flexibility due to questions about the fairness of policies, the degree of autonomy and control they actually have, or the extent to which flexibility negotiations are based on racial expectations (L. Parker & Allen, 2001).

The primary contradiction that extends from this domain is that flexible workplace arrangements are touted as being universal or available to all employees, but the expectations for using them and the perceived accessibility to them may vary by position, gender, class, and race. The logic that underlies worker agency is that the individual must decide if flexible arrangements, as defined by the organization, are appropriate, discriminatory, or (dis)advantageous for her or his personal and professional life. This logic is deeply rooted in individualism, that is, in the belief that an employee must decide if and how work–life balance is attained.

Contradictions also occur in relation to empowerment or the degree to which employees feel able to negotiate their multiple roles and identities. A major flaw in most workplace flexibility literature is that an individual is primarily characterized as either a worker or family member (usually a parent). Yet, all individuals occupy multiple identities at any given time and the relationships among identities change in various contexts; thus, creating inconsistencies in the need for and enactment of flexible workplace arrangements. Tracy and Trethewey's (2005) discussion of the crystallized self highlights the multidimensional nature of identity and calls attention to how these identities overlap and intersect at work, home, and the spaces in between. Interactions in the "third spaces" (Oldenburg, 1999), beyond the locales of work and home, certainly impact interactions at work, yet there is little attention to these relationships (Trethewey, Tracy, & Alberts, 2006).

Also, varied needs shape an individual's sense of agency and become salient at different points in one's life. For example, parenting, age, and responsibilities outside the home influence needs for work–life accommodations and one's sense of empowerment in attaining them. Specifically, married women with more than three young children often do not feel the benefits of flexible work arrangements (Pitt-Catsouphes & Matz-Costa, 2008). Working part-time does not necessarily lighten the family time demands and may increase the multitude of pressures. These women are more likely to experience home-related conflicts than women who are employed full time, suggesting that women with part-time jobs often experience family role-overload (Greenhaus & Beutell, 1985). Also, older employees have different needs for flexibility as they develop more responsibilities outside of work. Research reveals that, particularly for workers over age 45, increased workplace flexibility can benefit both employees and organizations since it is a strong predictor of engagement (Pitt-Catsouphes & Matz-Costa, 2008). Therefore, older employees who perceive high levels of flexibility are able to manage multiple obligations.

An employee's responsibilities outside of the organization, particularly with family and other social groups can also influence his or her need for and empowerment in negotiating flexible arrangements (Grzywacz, Carlson, & Shulkin, 2008). When individuals have a supportive or self-sufficient family unit, they may feel less need to negotiate flexibility. For instance, African American women have formed communities of fictive kin (Stack, 1974) that help balance work and family demands (P. S. Parker, 2003). Based on this extended network, women are able to meet their family needs without necessarily sacrificing time at work. Conversely, single parents may face many issues with workplace flexibility due to their lack of available contingencies, especially in situations outside normal work routines (Kirby et al., 2003).

In addition, the types of goals that individuals have may impact their need for and use of flexible arrangements. Shapiro and colleagues (Shapiro, Ingols, O'Neill, & Blake-Beard, 2009) found that managerial women made different decisions about flexible work arrangements based on three types of career goals: contemporary goals (e.g., doing work that they're passionate about); balance goals (e.g., having time for personal relationships); and success goals (e.g., progressing to top leadership positions). Their findings demonstrate that as balance goals become more important, women use flexible work arrangements, but when success goals become more important, women used fewer flexible work arrangements.

The inconsistency that arises from this literature is that universal policies about workplace flexibility promote a one-size fits all approach. Clearly, the demands of children, elderly parents, religious commitments, social organizations, and personal goals outside of work operate in conjunction with the needs for workplace flexibility. These demands also shape perceptions of empowerment; the tendency to enter into negotiations; or the fear of relinquishing advancement opportunities, compensation, or autonomy for using these arrangements. The logic is that the individual must decide and negotiate the optimal balance, yet based on organizational position, gender, class, and race, the employee often feels constrained in both access to and use of policies.

Locating Workplace Flexibility in Organizational Discourse

Most theory and research about workplace flexibility begins, and sometimes ends, by examining structural elements, such as policies regarding flextime, personal leaves, flexplace, workloads, and part-time work. Although the existence of rules, policies, and practices is important, the interface of other organizational domains is critical for implementing flexibility initiatives. Our review demonstrates that workplace flexibility is derived from discursive processes rooted in four key domains: organizational structure, workplace norms and practices, supervisor–worker relationships, and a worker's sense of agency. The overlap among these domains implies that the discourses in one arena affect the meanings and practices regarding flexibility in the others. For any employee, workplace flexibility emerges from an intersection of these domains; thus, it is not emanating solely from the organizational policies or the supervisory relationships. Moreover, the degree of flexibility may differ from employee to employee based on his or her workplace relationships or sense of worker agency. In addition, societal discourses also influence how workplace flexibility surfaces across and within each of the domains.

As the literature suggests, the meaning systems within organizations introduce an array of contradictions and mixed messages about flexible workplaces both within and across domains. Specifically, using flexible arrangements often increases rather than decreases work hours, job stress, and work–life conflict. In addition, the negative stigma associated with these policies has consequences for employee evaluation and advancement. Organizational values of meritocracy and views of the ideal worker instantiate norms about "time away from work" and feelings of guilt that lead to not using the policies or to working harder to compensate for use of them.

Concerns for fairness, productivity deadlines, and work disruption often lead supervisors to encourage and discourage employees from using these arrangements simultaneously. In addition, implementation of these policies is tied directly to effective supervisor–subordinate relationships. Finally, the establishment of company-wide policies conveys messages that all employees are able to use them when organizational position, gender, class, and race directly impinge on access to arrangements. Workers may feel disempowered and disadvantaged in using flexible accommodations because of micropractices of negotiating flexibility and the need for these arrangements at different times in employees' lives. Regardless of the progress that organizations have made in providing work–life initiatives, these discourses inherently place the burden for attaining workplace flexibility on individual workers who must make choices about whether they are capable, able, and willing to rebuke the norms of the ideal worker to carve out flexibility to attain work–life balance.

Adaptability—An Alternative to Workplace Flexibility

Although scholars champion workplace flexibility as a solution to work–life balance (Hill, Hawkins, Ferris, & Weitzman, 2001; McNall, Masuda, & Nicklin, 2010), this review suggests that workplace flexibility often leads to contradictory and ironic outcomes; hence, it is not a panacea for work–life conflict. Specifically, flexibility in one domain can create constraints in another and flexible arrangements can produce more rather than less work–life conflict and additional burdens on the individual worker. These findings suggest an inherent problem with failing to integrate flexibility across domains and continuing to rely on the individual worker to implement it. Thus, organizations need a radical alternative or another way of conceptualizing the goals of workplace flexibility.

As previously noted, the lives of contemporary workers are characterized by multiple work–life roles and diverse needs; thus, employees need organizational situations that accommodate their lives as whole individuals—both inside and outside the workplace. At the same time, organizations are not fully benefiting from the workplace initiatives that they offer. When workers feel marginalized for using flexible arrangements, productivity, job satisfaction, and organizational commitment are likely to fail (Kirby et al., 2003). Rather than offering ways to fix flexibility policies, we propose to replace them with programs and practices that emphasize adaptability (Burud & Tumolo, 2004).

Adaptability refers to the ways that organizations and workers mutually adapt to each other's changing needs to benefit both the individuals and the institutions (McNall et al., 2010). This approach is not simply a set of benefits or alternative arrangements, but an organizational philosophy rooted in changing cultures and attitudes of organizational members (Burud & Tumolo, 2004). Underlying the philosophy is an attitude of caring shared by workers and organizational leaders that must permeate the discourse in all four organizational domains. These attitudes underlie a set of beliefs that encourage organizational members to: (a) value and foster strong relationships with various stakeholders (including workers and customers), (b) emphasize goals and objectives that focus on long-term organizational outcomes and sustainability, and (c) provide continuous improvement of operations.

Adaptability requires a shared commitment from workers as well as employers. To become adaptable, organizations must evaluate and restructure operations, policies, and most importantly, relationships with employees. Management makes a commitment to value and invest in people, and workers must invest in the well-being of the organization. This philosophy of adaptability must infuse employee training, workplace practices, norms for coworker relationships, and performance evaluations. To accomplish this goal, organizations must reevaluate and revise major baseline practices. Specifically, organizations must replace traditional notions of the ideal worker, methods of determining workloads, and means of evaluating worker performance.

To compare the two approaches, workplace flexibility may offer some level of schedule flexibility, but workplace norms and managerial attitudes continue to uphold ideals which presume that workers prioritize work above other commitments. Supervisors determine workloads and tasks are performed under management's supervision. Performance evaluations and compensation are based on multiple factors, including employees' abilities to meet managerial expectations.

In contrast, an adaptability system involves workers in setting expectations for performances. Compensation is tied to output and performance assessment relies on new methods. These practices enable individuals to select work projects that fit their life rather than adapting their life to fit their work, a process similar to what Roberts (2008) calls "customization" or a way of tailoring workplace arrangements to individuals' lives at a particular point in time. When workers commit to performing a specified level of output, it is up to them to achieve that level of productivity by whatever means necessary as long as the end results are satisfactory to the relevant stakeholders. This freedom enables workers to press hard for a deadline one week, but relax their schedule and build in more personal time the next week.

Adaptability practices, such as customized workloads and output-based performance, are rooted in fundamentally different principles than is workplace flexibility. Specifically, workplace flexibility focuses on organizational policies and norms that allow employees to negotiate the timing and location of work while adaptability centers on restructuring organizational cultures and values in ways that benefit the long-term goals of both the worker and the organization. Adaptability focuses on the relationships among the organization, its workers, and its clients rather than on adopting universal policies. With an adaptability philosophy, stakeholders coordinate schedules, compensation, performance evaluation, new employee selection, and other organizational processes based on long-term perspectives. Flexible work arrangements become embedded in the system as ways of accomplishing work rather than surfacing as added benefits that employees must negotiate. As a result, organizations enter into a partnership with their employees, one that supports employees' professional and private lives. See Table 9.1 for a comparison of workplace flexibility and adaptability principles, practices, and results.

We contend that the philosophy and practices of adaptability supersede workplace flexibility by transforming workers' needs and organizational

Table 9.1 Comparison of Workplace Flexibility and Adaptability

	Workplace Flexibility	Adaptability
Principles	• Employees manage work–life balance through organizational policies • Most organizational policies are standardized and universal • Flexibility is negotiated around organizational goals related to cost and productivity	• Value strong relationships among organization, workers, and clients • Mutual commitment of organizational leaders and workers • Invest in the long-term outcomes and sustainability of workers and the organization • Continuous improvement of operations
Practices	• Organizational policies for flextime, flexplace, job sharing, part-time work, and personal leaves • Work–life programs are part of the employee benefit system • Work–life programs primarily focus on managing family demands • Employees work to meet strict project deadlines • Informal trade-offs are common for meeting personal obligations • Flexibility arrangements usually negotiated with the supervisor • Workgroup norms dictate individual use of flexibility policies • Performance evaluations often related to norms about hours worked and/or presence	• Organizational policies are not designed to govern flexibility arrangements • Customized career paths; individuals select projects, tasks, and opportunities in line with personal goals • Deadlines are negotiated among employee, supervisor, and client and adjusted as necessary • Employees trusted to work autonomously • Cross training employees in multiple roles • Performance evaluations based on outputs agreed upon by employee and supervisor • Compensation is commensurate with output
Results	• Flexibility is seen as a benefit, not a right • Organization often controls the extent of an employee's flexibility • Can lead to rigid policies • Flexibility negotiations can be idiosyncratic • Supervisors give mixed messages about using flexibility policies • Can promote deception related to reasons for policy use • Individual flexibility is often tied to the workgroup's reciprocity or good will • Often results in increased work hours	• Organization supports workers professionally and in their private lives • Work fits into life rather than life fitting into work • Negotiations of flexible arrangements are expected and honored • Strives for increased productivity • Reduced costs because of space sharing and decreased turnover • Employees control their schedules, workload, and work location

(continued)

Table 9.1 Continued

Workplace Flexibility	Adaptability
• Frequently leads to increased satisfaction, contingent on perceived control over work schedules • Utilizing flexibility policies may hinder career advancement • Many flexibility policies are not easily applied to all positions and employee conditions • Perpetuates the ideal worker stereotype	• Work fits the needs of the organization, employee, and client • Organizations attract and retain the best talent

objectives—factors that often are at odds with each other—into shared goals that benefit both. From an employee's perspective, an adaptability philosophy facilitates task completion with much greater autonomy than does workplace flexibility. Workers have the freedom to perform tasks in remote locations at various times, when prudent to do so. Unlike flexibility initiatives, this freedom is built into the system rather than an employee having to negotiate it with a supervisor. In an adaptability system, employees, supervisors, and clients periodically negotiate deadlines and adjust to personal and organizational needs as they arise. These adjustments allow employees to meet planned and unplanned personal demands of family and other obligations. Some workers may opt for a reduced work position, while others select a more demanding role with related compensation. Although responsibilities, workloads, and compensation are not equal, they are equitable because employees' salaries are based on their outputs and their abilities to meet mutually-defined objectives.

Adaptability, although not a panacea for work–life issues, has the potential to transcend the inevitable contradictions in traditional workplace flexibility. By infusing adaptability into the work process itself, flexible arrangements become a given. They are not benefits or extras but rather part of doing the work. The model of an ideal worker shifts away from criteria such as long work hours, face time at the office, and privileging work over family, and focuses instead on productivity and negotiating client, worker, and organizational needs. Adaptability at the individual level becomes part and parcel of achieving organization level goals.

As an illustration, one company that employs many elements of this philosophy is U.S.-based consulting firm Deloitte LLP, a subsidiary of Deloitte Touche Tohmatsu based in the United Kingdom. Over the past decade, Deloitte has prioritized making the workplace supportive and agile for both workers and business practices (Deloitte, 2010a). Their "Workplace of Tomorrow" initiative sets forth a philosophy that is supportive of the contemporary workforce, work–life accommodation, and the need for cost effectiveness. The philosophy extends to *all* stakeholders because adaptability programs affect clients as well as organizational members. When the firm acquires a new client, employees meet with a representative of the organization to collaborate on work arrangements and to incorporate the client's temporal and seasonal needs into employee constraints.

The company fosters adaptive space–time work arrangements to enable workers to perform in remote locations, to adjust their schedules to suit employee needs, and to save commuting time through traveling at less congested times of the day. Management expects variable work arrangements, including telework and flexschedules, and focuses on the work that is done (Deloitte, 2010c). They de-couple performance from physical presence at work and receive cost savings through fostering the use of shared work space.

They also enable their employees to perform work autonomously—another key feature of an adaptable organization. Deloitte facilitates autonomous work by promoting communication and collaboration through technology and through using distance management practices. In this less structured environment, employees can choose to work primarily from home or other locations. The company also expects employees to adapt to work hours and schedules outside the traditional workweek. Thus, even in situations that might otherwise prevent workers from commuting, employees work from their homes. An adaptability philosophy, then, requires both the employee and the organization to engage in a give-and-take process to make work happen.

Both workers and management are trained to focus on results-based goals that fundamentally change the way that work is performed and evaluated. This process involves evaluating and continuously reevaluating operations and talents (Deloitte, 2010c). In addition, workers are given opportunities to develop new job skills through cross-training and customizing career paths, such as accelerating toward leadership positions or slowing down to accommodate other aspects of their personal lives (Deloitte, 2010b). With an emphasis on adaptation, coworkers are less likely to perceive issues of inequality because all employees have similar choices; that is, to stay in their current roles, retrain, slow down, or accelerate career advancement. Negotiations about leaves, flexible work arrangements, and advancements are not necessary because these options are expected practices for everyone. Thus, one of the fundamental principles of Deloitte's culture of adaptation is "the ability to fit life into work and work into life while growing professionally" (Deloitte, 2010a).

Top managers at Deloitte confirm that its adaptive philosophy saves them money, but most importantly, it improves the organization's productivity and enables them to attract and retain the best talent (Deloitte, 2010b). As evidence, Deloitte reported higher employee morale, improvements in workers' perceptions of career–life fit, a stronger focus on productivity, and an improved retention rate than it did prior to altering its work culture (Deloitte, 2010c). Their efforts have received external recognition as well. Recently, the *Working Mother* website listed Deloitte as one of the top 100 places to work ("Working

Mother Best 100 Companies," 2010), and it was also rated as a "Best Place to Launch a Career" (*Bloomberg Business Week*, 2009).

As the Deloitte example illustrates, an adaptability philosophy aligns with the needs of a contemporary workforce. Adaptive organizations enable employees to achieve personal satisfaction and fulfillment while simultaneously allowing them to meet other nonwork demands. In effect, mutual commitment, which is the foundation of adaptability, infuses the four organizational domains. Rather than each domain acting as a constraining force on the other, the domains work together to facilitate adaptability for the organization and the workers.

Although challenges exist in this new system, initial results suggest that adaptive organizations foster a more fulfilled workforce than does workplace flexibility alone. Several organizations are now operating under adaptive or adaptive-like philosophies including DuPont (science-based research and products), First Tennessee National Corporation (banking), Ernst & Young (accounting), Baxter International (medical products and services), and SAS (software). Early indicators suggest that organizations that operate under this philosophy reduce costs and build long-term commitments with employees. As DuPont Vice President of Diversity and Worklife and President of the North American Region, Willie C. Martin, commented: "When people feel that all of who they are is valued, they produce more" (Burud & Tumolo, 2004, p. 283).

In effect, a philosophy of adaptability offers many advantages to an organization. First, empirical studies demonstrate that organizations that invest in their members and reward members based on results increase the company's overall productivity (Becker & Huselid, 1998, 2010). Second, adaptable workplaces can reduce costs. One cost reduction is related to workspace—when many members work off-site, workspaces can be reconfigured to allow for space-sharing. Another cost savings is related to maintaining productivity when workers cannot make it to the office due to health issues, family needs, and poor weather. When members are able to work from their homes, productivity remains possible, even if roads are snow-filled or if employees must stay home with young children. A third savings is reduced turnover costs. Specifically, organizations that embrace an adaptive philosophy report significant drops in turnover (Deloitte, 2010a). A benefit for both employees and organizations is that when employees perceive that they have control over their schedules, locations in which they perform work, and choices about how much they want to work, they demonstrate increased job satisfaction (Clark, 2000; McNall et al., 2010), less stress and burnout, and lower work–life conflict (Grzywacz et al., 2008; Hill et al., 2008).

Even though adaptability has the potential to transcend the contradictions that typify workplace flexibility, this approach, like other work–life programs, has its limitations. A first shortcoming is that it requires organizational change and changing an organization's culture is very difficult because of the engrained schemas that members hold of work practices and reward systems (Kuhn & Corman, 2003; Lewis, 2000). Workers are accustomed to traditional performance evaluation systems and they may not appreciate the ramifications of reward-based outputs linked to organizational needs. In addition, employees may continue to watch out for their own best interests which could make them less willing to attend to other stakeholders in an unselfish manner. Modifying these schemas and associated behaviors is difficult, even when individuals see the value in making changes (Covin & Kilmann, 1990).

Second, even when an adaptability philosophy prevails, organizational members (workers and supervisors) may fall back on old attitudes and behaviors about ideal workers (Fairhurst, 1993). Supervisors could pressure workers into a more traditional office schedule with long hours and restrictive control. Employees could revert to comparing workloads and hours worked and making judgments about coworkers (Lewis, 2000). These negative evaluations undermine the philosophy of adaptability and limit its success.

A third potential issue may arise if organizational members are not committed to the long-term goals of the company. Workers may lack identification with the organization (Cheney, 1983), or they may expect to leave the organization in the near future. Without commitment, workers could adopt a self-interested bias and ask for adaptation but offer little themselves. A final concern for many organizations is how to develop an equitable means of compensation in situations where tasks vary greatly in complexity, desirability, and hours necessary to complete the work. Management and workers must collaborate to create a reward system that is deemed fair and effective for all organizational members (Huselid & Becker, 2000). Overall, these issues need to be addressed to enhance the implementation of an adaptable philosophy and support its success.

Using an Adaptability Perspective: Research Guidelines

Unlike workplace flexibility and work–life balance studies, research conducted within an adaptability lens would not focus on the use and implementation of organizational policies, on workers' ability to negotiate flexibility, or on consequences associated with variable schedules and workloads. Instead, research would examine communication that reflects how organizations and workers value one another, are willing to adapt, and have embraced long-term commitments. Research projects on adaptable organizations should center on four key concerns. First, researchers would start by determining whether a philosophy of adaptability exists in the organization. This could be assessed in several ways. Researchers could review the organization's mission statement and objectives. Do these documents reflect a commitment to adaptability values and foster strong relationships with employees? Do they value their workers as whole individuals with lives outside of the workplace? Are they focused on continual improvement of operations with an eye toward making work more adaptable? It is important to note that some practices commonly associated with adaptability such as teleworking and nontraditional work schedules, are also part of workplace flexibility initiatives, but without changing the organization's culture and values or restructuring the ways in which work is accomplished and evaluated. Hence, the values are critical for a philosophy of adaptation.

Second, researchers should focus on work–life issues and not on work–family policies. Adaptability scholars argue that families are not the only reason that workers need balance in their lives (Burud & Tumolo, 2004). Workers can structure their personal and professional lives based on their individual needs. Adaptability researchers would critique practices that enable some workers to utilize special benefits, while others cannot. They would argue that adaptable work arrangements should be available to everyone and that organizations should not be in the business of evaluating who deserves work–life balance and who does not.

Third, an adaptability perspective would examine workplace discourse to understand the overall attitude that workers have toward their coworkers, particularly in their use of nontraditional schedules. These attitudes are important because the success of adaptability depends on workers' willingness to adjust, and at times, compromise to facilitate their coworkers' needs. Negative attitudes and behaviors result in detrimental consequences for everyone and deter cooperative actions that make adaptability accessible.

Research on adaptability, similar to that on workplace flexibility, would examine equity of policies, but would also inquire about the widespread use of customized schedules, leaves, and career paths. The more equitable programs should surface in organizational discourses about working remotely, operating autonomously, and customizing schedules to provide long-term mutual advantages for workers and organizations.

Fourth, an adaptability perspective would interrogate the relationship between workers and management. Whereas many flexibility-based programs place the onus of obtaining flexibility on individuals, in an adaptability perspective, management must create situations that make adaptability possible. Managers who embrace an adaptability philosophy design work flow to cover workloads when individuals take leave or when workers opt for part-time work. With an adaptive perspective, scholars would further probe whether telecommuting is part of organizations' adaptive philosophy or merely a stand-alone practice. This information could help scholars decipher how telecommuting and other work–life initiatives could strengthen relationships between workers and management and increase productivity. In addition, adaptability-focused research would not focus on reasons or needs for flexible schedules or locations. Issues of dishonesty and accountability become transformed through emphasizing productivity outcomes. The discourse focuses on outcomes and long-term objectives, if work goals are not met.

Overall, research aimed at studying adaptability in organizations should center on the philosophy, values, and workplace relationships that make questions of access to and availability of flexible arrangements a non-issue. Scholars could focus on the attitudes of workers and the relationships between coworkers and management that enact values of support, equity, and goal accomplishment that permeate this perspective.

Directions for Future Research

We argue that traditional approaches to workplace flexibility lead to contradictions that limit the use, implementation, and social meanings surrounding flexibility practices. We also demonstrate how these contradictions are rooted in organizational conceptions of the ideal worker and a value of individualism, and become manifested in mixed messages that foster a competition between work and life priorities. Finally, we propose adaptability as an alternative to workplace flexibility because it transforms these initiatives from a benefit that some employees use to a standard operating practice used by everyone. This approach offers options that are not present in workplace flexibility, but adaptability is not a panacea and will likely produce its own set of issues. That said, we are unaware of empirical studies that examine whether an adaptability philosophy produces the outcomes that it promises. Hence, we provide some guidelines for how scholars might examine this approach.

First, future studies should investigate organizations that have implemented adaptability workplace programs. These studies might compare adaptability and workplace flexibility practices at several levels. At the organizational level, how do adaptable practices affect productivity? How do adaptable practices affect operations and customer satisfaction? At the workgroup level, how does an adaptability philosophy relate to workplace discourse and worker relationships? Are colleagues willing to be adaptive to one another's needs? At the dyadic level, how does implementing an adaptive philosophy affect the relationships between supervisors and workers? At the individual level, how satisfied are workers with adaptability culture and practices? To assess the success of this approach, researchers could study relevant organizational factors before and after an adaptability orientation is introduced. Studies could also investigate workers' commitment to the long-term viability of the organization—one of the key goals of an adaptability philosophy.

Second, researchers need to explore the various ways that organizations have addressed the contradictions that arise from flexibility initiatives. If they implemented an adaptability philosophy, or elements of it, how did they manage that transition to a new adaptability orientation? Are organizations able to implement certain elements of the philosophy successfully and to disregard others? What can be learned from their experiences?

Third, because adaptive workplaces do not rely on hours spent at the office as the primary measure of workers' contributions, researchers should explore how organizations assess and reward worker outputs. Reward programs may be easy to develop for some tasks. For example, compensating workers who make a product based on their output is perfectly reasonable. However, some tasks are not easy to quantify. What is an appropriate and equitable way to reward employees who work on difficult projects? An examination of various methods that organizations use could reveal best practices.

Finally, as we have done, scholars need to review and critique workplace flexibility studies. How does flexibility in one organizational domain create tensions in another? How could previous flexibility studies be reinterpreted through the lens of adaptability?

Implications and Conclusion

This paper has implications for the research and practice of workplace flexibility. First, it interrogates research on workplace flexibility and argues that this construct is discursively constituted, symbolically created, and enacted simultaneously within organizational structures, workplace norms and practices, supervisor–worker relationships, and worker agency. Moreover, what counts as flexibility and how it is enacted varies across these four domains.

Second, the role of flexibility in each of the organizational domains is complex and overlapping. For example, telework does not ensure workplace flexibility if individuals feel they must adhere to organizationally prescribed deadlines that keep them working around the clock. Likewise, schedule flexibility does not ensure work–life balance when time away from the office is spent responding to e-mails or on conference calls. Thus, policies do not ensure workplace flexibility any more than a lack of structure mandates rigidity. Overall, then, when viewed in isolation, flexibility in one domain can create potentially negative effects in other domains (Kelliher & Anderson, 2010).

Moreover, the research reveals that the enactment of workplace flexibility in each of these four domains creates contradictions and tensions. Thus, when organizations offer policies for flexible arrangements, workplace norms and practices may inhibit the use of them. Conversely, when supervisors support work–life flexibility, policies may prohibit their implementation, or norms may discourage workers from using them. These tensions place considerable pressure on the individual worker who must negotiate flexible arrangements that are often at odds with accepted organizational traditions. Only employees with a strong sense of agency seem likely to push for policy changes, alter workplace norms, and negotiate flexible work arrangements with their supervisors. Those employees also run the risk of jeopardizing career advancement or upsetting coworkers.

An alternative approach to work–life balance stems from a fundamentally different organizational philosophy—one that makes adaptability a major goal for the workplace. Adopting an adaptability philosophy has produced promising results for companies like Deloitte (Burud & Tumolo, 2004). Adaptability is a philosophy that makes flexible arrangements part of the job rather than an employee benefit. It embraces flexibility as embedded in job design and customizes arrangements to fit an individual's life at a particular point in time.

In contrast, most organizations adopt flexible work–life policies to establish an image of a family-friendly firm or as a response to governmental regulatory agencies. What is missing in implementing flexibility policies are changes in workplace norms and attitudes (Kossek et al., 2010). Adaptability emerges only when the discourses surrounding the use of these policies change and worker productivity becomes tied to results rather than to time at work. This change necessitates altering workplace culture in ways that value the whole person, not simply the bottom line (Hill et al., 2008). Managers of companies that embrace adaptability as a corporate philosophy indicate "that they have had to find a way to make the new way of working *the expected way of working* [emphasis added]" (Roberts, 2008, p. 6).

Society, organizations, and individuals need to understand the contradictory messages that emanate from the myth of the ideal worker that governs workplace practices (Bailyn, 2006). To this end, organizations must acknowledge that employees are individuals with demanding lives outside of the workplace. The next stage of workplace flexibility needs to bring work–life initiatives out of the margins and to support employees who do not conform to the model of the *ideal worker*, but who prioritize other aspects of their lives over work (Towers, Duxbury, Higgins, & Thomas, 2006). This stage requires a new discourse that can mainstream work–life considerations into an organization's ongoing business practices (Kossek et al., 2010). Work–life issues need to be integrated with other organizational functions, such as human resources, compensation, career and performance management, and organizational development. Workers, too, must embrace new views of their own personal lives and their relationships to organizational needs. For this system to work, employees and organizations must join together to ensure the long-term viability of the company and the workers.

Finally, the construct of workplace flexibility will continue to attract the interest of management, organizations, and researchers. This paper aims to foster thoughtful reflection in two ways. First, workplace flexibility permeates several domains simultaneously, thus, merely providing for it in one domain will not necessarily ensure its viability in another one. Second, organizations need a new perspective on workplace flexibility, one that is adaptive to diverse needs of workers and to the long-term and changing needs of organizations. When these changes occur, organizations may reap the benefits of not only establishing policies, but embracing the true aim of workplace flexibility.

References

Adams, G. A., & Jex, S. M. (1999). Relationships between time management, control, work–family conflict, and strain. *Journal of Occupational Health Psychology, 4*, 72–77. doi:10.1037/1076-8998.4.1.72

Ainsworth, S., & Hardy, C. (2004). Discourse and identities. In D. Grant, C. Hardy, C. Oswick, & L. L. Putnam (Eds.), *The Sage handbook of organizational discourse* (pp. 153–173). Thousand Oaks, CA: Sage.

Alvesson, M., & Willmott, H. (2002). Identity regulation as organizational control:

Producing the appropriate individual. *Journal of Management Studies, 39*(5), 619–644. doi:10.1111/1467-6486.00305

Ashcraft, K. L. (2006). Back to work: Sights/sites of difference in gender and organizational communication studies. In B. J. Cow & J. T. Wood (Eds.), *The Sage handbook on gender and communication* (pp. 97–122). Thousand Oaks, CA: Sage.

Ashforth, B., Kreiner, G., & Fugate, M. (2000). All in a day's work: Boundaries and micro role transitions. *Academy of Management Review, 25*(3), 472–491. doi:10.2307/259305

Bailyn, L. (1993). *Breaking the mold: Women, men, and time in the new corporate world.* New York: Free Press.

Bailyn, L. (2006). *Breaking the mold: Redesigning work for productive and satisfying lives.* Ithaca, NY: Cornell University Press.

Bailyn, L., Drago, R., & Kochan, T. (2001). *Integrating work and family life: A holistic approach.* Boston, MA: Alfred P. Sloan Foundation Work–Family Policy Network.

Becker, B. E., & Huselid, M. A. (1998). High performance work systems and firm performance: A synthesis of research and managerial implications. *Research in Personnel and Human Resources Management, 16*, 53–101.

Becker, B. E., & Huselid, M. A. (2010). SHRM and job design: Narrowing the divide. *Journal of Organizational Behavior, 31*, 379–388. doi:10.1002/job.640

Bell, E. L., & Nkomo, S. (2001). *Our separate ways: Black and White women and the struggle for professional identity.* Boston, MA: Harvard Business School Press.

Bloomberg Business Week. (2009). Best place to launch a career. Retrieved from http://www.businessweek.com/careers/first_jobs/2009/1.htm

Bohen, H. H., & Viveros-Long, A. M. (1981). *Balancing jobs and family life: Do flexible working schedules help?* Philadelphia, PA: Temple University Press.

Breaugh, J. A., & Frye, N. K. (2008). Work–family conflict: The importance of family-friendly employment practices and family-supportive supervisors. *Journal of Business Psychology, 22*, 345–353. doi:10.1007/s10869-008-9081-1

Brewer, A. M. (2000). Work design for flexible work scheduling: Barriers and gender implications. *Gender, Work, and Organization, 7*, 33–44. doi:10.1111/1468-0432.00091

Broadfoot, K. J. (2001). When the cat's away, do the mice play?: Control/autonomy in the virtual workplace. *Management Communication Quarterly, 15*(1), 110–114. doi:10.1177/0893318901151006

Broadfoot, K. J., Carlone, D., Medved, C. E., Aakhus, M., Gabor, E., & Taylor, K. (2008). Meaning/ful work and organizational communication: Questioning boundaries, positionalities, and engagements. *Management Communication Quarterly, 22*(1), 152–161. doi:10.1177/0893318908318267

Burud, S., & Tumolo, M. (2004). *Leveraging the new human capital: Adaptive strategies, results achieved, and stories of transformation.* Mountain View, CA: Davies-Black.

Buzzanell, P. M., & Liu, M. (2007). It's "give and take": Maternity leave as a conflict management process. *Human Relations, 60*(3), 453–495. doi:10.1177/0018726707076688

Buzzanell, P. M., & Lucas, K. (2006). Gendered stories of career: Unfolding discourses of time, space, and identity. In B. J. Dow & J. T. Wood (Eds), *The Sage handbook on gender and communication* (pp. 161–178). Thousand Oaks, CA: Sage.

Buzzanell, P. M., Meisenbach, R., Remke, R., Liu, M., Bowers, V., & Conn, C. (2005). The good working mother: Managerial women's sensemaking and feelings about work–family issues. *Communication Studies, 56*(3), 261–285. doi:10.1080/10510970500181389

Carlson, D. S., Kacmar, K. M., & Williams, L. J. (2000). Construction and initial validation of a multidimensional measure of work–family conflict. *Journal of Vocational Behavior, 56*(2), 249–276. doi:10.1006/jvbe.1999.1713

Cheney, G. (1983). On the various and changing meanings of organizational membership: A field study of organizational identification. *Communication Monographs, 50*, 342–362.

Ciulla, J. B. (2000). *The working life: The promise and betrayal of modern work.* New York: Times Books.

Clark, S. (2000). Work/family border theory: A new theory of work/family balance. *Human Relations, 53*(6), 747–770. doi:10.1177/0018726700536001

Costa, G., Sartori, S., & Akerstedt, T. (2006). Influence of flexibility and variability of working hours on health and well-being. *Chronobiology International, 23*(6), 1125–1137. doi:10.1080/07420520601087491

Covin, T. J., & Kilmann, R. H. (1990). Participant perceptions of positive and negative influences on large-scale change. *Group and Organizational Studies, 15*, 233–248. doi:10.1177/105960119001500207

Cowan, R., & Hoffman, M. F. (2007). The flexible organization: How contemporary employees construct the work/life border. *Qualitative Research Reports in Communication, 8*, 37–44. doi:10.1080/17459430701617895

Delaney, J. T., & Huselid, M. A. (1996). The impact of human resource management practices on perceptions of organizational performance. *Academy of Management Journal, 39*, 949–969. doi:10.2307/256718

Deloitte (2010a). Deloitte achieves 100 percent rating on human rights campaign's 2011 corporate equality index (CEI) for fifth consecutive year. Retrieved from https://www.deloitte.com/view/en_US/us/press/Press-Releases/ab3736c825bcc210Vgn-VCM1000001a56f00aRCRD.htm

Deloitte (2010b). Federal workplace flexibility. Retrieved from https://www.deloitte.com/view/en_US/us/Industries/US-federal-government/f8e215c16e9f9210VgnVC-M100000ba42f00aRCRD.htm

Deloitte, (2010c). Preparing for the workplace of tomorrow: Why change now? Retrieved from https://www.deloitte.com/view/en_US/us/Industries/US-federal-government/c8f28bd2d7c92210VgnVCM200000bb42f00aRCRD.htm

Donald, F., & Linington, J. (2008). Work/family border theory and gender role orientation in male managers. *South African Journal of Psychology, 38*(4), 659–671.

Eaton, S. C. (2003). If you can use them: Flexibility policies, organizational commitment, and perceived performance. *Industrial Relations, 42*, 145–167. doi:10.1111/1468-232X.00285

Edley, P. (2004). Entrepreneurial mothers' balance of work and family. In P. M. Buzzanell, H. Sterk, & L. Turner (Eds.), *Gender in applied communication contexts* (pp. 255–273). Thousand Oaks, CA: Sage.

Fairhurst, G. T. (1993). The leader-member exchange patterns of women leaders in industry: A discourse analysis. *Communication Monographs, 60*, 321–351. doi: 10.1080/03637759309376316

Fonner, K. L., & Roloff, M. E. (2010). Why teleworkers are more satisfied with their jobs than are office-based workers: When less contact is beneficial. *Journal of Applied Communication Research, 38*, 336–361. doi:10.1080/00909882.2010.513998

Frank, K. E., & Lowe, D. J. (2003). An examination of alternative work arrangements in a private accounting practice. *Accounting Horizons, 17*, 139–151. doi:10.2308/acch.2003.17.2.139

Gajendran, R. S., & Harrison, D. A. (2007). The good, the bad, and the unknown about telecommuting: Meta-analysis of psychological mediators and individual consequences. *Journal of Applied Psychology, 92*, 1524–1531. doi:10.1037/0021-9010.92.6.1524

Golden, A. G., & Geisler, C. (2006). Flexible work, time, and technology: Ideological dilemmas of managing work–life interrelationships using personal digital assistants. *Electronic Journal of Communication/La Revue Electronique de Communication, 16*(3–4). Retrieved from http://www.cios.org/www/ejcmain.htm

Golden, A. G., Kirby, E. L., & Jorgenson, J. (2006). Work–life research from both sides now: An integrative perspective for organizational and family communication. In C. S. Beck (Ed.), *Communication yearbook* (Vol. 30, pp. 142–195). Mahwah, NJ: Erlbaum. doi:10.1207/s15567419cy3001_4

Gottlieb, B. H., Kelloway, E. K., & Barham, E. (1998). *Flexible work arrangements: Managing the work–family boundary*. Chichester, England: Wiley.

Graen, G. B., & Scandura, T. (1987.) Toward a psychology of dyadic organizing. In B. Staw & L. L. Cummings (Eds.), *Research in organizational behavior* (Vol. 9, pp. 175–208). Greenwich, CT: JAI.

Graen, G. B., & Uhl-Bien, M. (1995). Relationship-based approach to leadership: Development of a leader-member exchange (LMX) theory of leadership over 25 years—Applying a multi-level multi-domain perspective. *Leadership Quarterly, 6*, 219–247. doi:10.1016/1048-9843(95)90036-5

Greenhaus, J. H., & Beutell, N. J. (1985). Sources and conflict between work and family roles. *The Academy of Management Review, 10*(1), 76–88. doi:10.2307/258214

Grover, S. L., & Crooker, K. J. (1995). Who appreciates family-responsive human resource policies: The impact of family friendly policies on the organizational attachment of parents and non-parents. *Personnel Psychology, 48*, 271–288. doi:10.1111/j.1744-6570.1995.tb01757.x

Grzywacz, J. G., Carlson, D. S., & Shulkin, S. (2008). Schedule flexibility and stress: Linking formal flexible arrangements and perceived flexibility to employee health. *Community, Work & Family, 11*(2), 199–214. doi:10.1080/13668800802024652

Guest, D. (2002). Perspectives on the study of work–life balance. *Social Science Information, 41*(2), 255–279. doi:10.1177/0539018402041002005

Hall, D. T., & Richter, J. (1988). Balancing work life and home life: What can organizations do to help? *The Academy of Management Executive, 11*(3), 213–223.

Hammer, L. B., & Barbara, K. M. (1997). Toward an integration of alternative work schedules and human resource systems. *Human Resource Planning, 20*(2), 28–36.

Hammer, L. B., Kossek, E. E., Yragui, N., Bodner, T., & Hansen, G. (2009). Development and validation of a multi-dimensional scale of family supportive supervisor behaviors (FSSB). *Journal of Management, 35*(4), 837–856. doi:10.1177/0149206308328510

Hantrais, L. (1993). The gender of time in professional occupations. *Time & Society, 2*(2), 139–157. doi:10.1177/0961463X93002002001

Hill, E. J., Hawkins, A. J., Ferris, M., & Weitzman, M. (2001). Finding an extra day a week: The positive influence of perceived job flexibility on work and family life balance. *Human Relations, 50*, 49–58. doi:10.1111/j.1741-3729.2001.00049.x

Hill, E. J., Hawkins, A. J., & Miller, B. C. (1996). Work and family in the virtual office: Perceived influences of mobile telework. *Family Relations, 45,* 293–301. doi:10.2307/585501

Hill, E. J., Jacob, J. I., Shannon, L. L., Brennan, R. T., Blanchard, V. L., & Martinengo, G. (2008). Exploring the relationship of workplace flexibility, gender, life stage to family-to-work conflict, and stress and burnout. *Community, Work & Family, 11,* 165–181. doi:10.1080/13668800802027564

Hill, E. J., Martinson, V. K., Ferris, M., & Baker, R. Z. (2004). Beyond the mommy track: The influence of new-concept part-time work for professional women on work and family. *Journal of Family and Economic Issues, 25,* 121–136. doi:10.1023/B:JEEI.0000016726.06264.91

Hornung, S., Rousseau, D. M., & Glaser, J. (2008). Creating flexible work arrangements through idiosyncratic deals. *Journal of Applied Psychology, 93,* 655–664. doi:10.1037/0021-9010.93.3.655

Huselid, M. A., & Becker, B. E. (1995). *Strategic impact of high performance work systems.* New Brunswick, NJ: School of Management and Labor Relations, Rutgers University.

Huselid, M. A., & Becker, B. E. (2000). Comment on measurement error in research on human resources and firm performance: How much error is there and how does it influence effect size estimates? *Personnel Psychology, 53,* 835–854.

Hylmö, A. (2004). Women, men, and changing organizations: An organizational culture examination of gendered experiences of telecommuting. In P. M. Buzzanell, H. Sterk, & L. Turner (Eds.), *Gender in applied communication contexts* (pp. 47–68). Thousand Oaks, CA: Sage.

Hyman, J., Scholarios, D., & Baldry, C. (2005). Getting on or getting by: Employee flexibility and coping strategies for home and work. *Work, Employment and Society, 19*(4), 705–725. doi:10.1177/0950017005058055

Jenkins, S. (2004). Restructuring flexibility: Case studies of part-time female workers in six-work places. *Gender, Work, and Organization, 11,* 306–333. doi:10.1111/j.1468-0432.2004.00233.x

Jorgenson, J. (2000). Interpreting the intersections of work and family: Frame conflicts in women's work. *The Electronic Journal of Communication/La revue électronique de communication, 10*(3-4). Retrieved from http://www.cios.org/EJCPUBLIC/010/3/010317.html

Jurik, N. C. (1998). Getting away and getting by: The experiences of self-employed homeworkers. *Work and Occupation, 25,* 7–35. doi:10.1177/0730888498025001002

Kelliher, C., & Anderson, D. (2010). Doing more with less? Flexible working practices and the intensification of work. *Human Relations, 63*(1), 83–106. doi:10.1177/0018726709349199

Kirby, E. L. (2000). Should I do as you say or do as you do? Mixed messages about work and family. *The Electronic Journal of Communication/La revue électronique de communication, 10*(3–4). Retrieved from http://www.cios.org/www/ejcmain.htm

Kirby, E. L., Golden, A. G., Medved, C. E., Jorgenson, J., & Buzzanell, P. M. (2003). An organizational communication challenge to the discourse of work and family research: From problematics to empowerment. In P. Kalbfleisch (Ed.), *Communication yearbook* (Vol. 27, pp. 1–44). Mahwah, NJ: Erlbaum. doi: 10.1207/s15567419cy2701_1

Kirby, E. L., & Krone, K. (2002). "The policy exists but you can't really use it": Communication and the structuration of work–family policies. *Journal of Applied Communication Research, 30,* 50–77. doi:10.1080/00909880216577

Kirby, E. L., Wieland, S. M., & McBride, M. C. (2006). Work/life conflict. In J. G. Oetzel & S. Ting-Toomey (Eds.), *The Sage handbook of conflict and communication* (pp. 327–357). Thousand Oaks, CA: Sage.

Kirchmeyer, C. (1995). Managing the work–nonwork boundary: An assessment of organizational responses. *Human Relations, 48,* 515–536. doi:10.1177/001872679504800504

Kossek, E. E., Lewis, S., & Hammer, L. B. (2010). Work–life incentives and organizational change: Overcoming mixed messages to move from the margin to the mainstream. *Human Relations, 63*(1), 3–19. doi:10.1177/0018726709352385

Kossek, E. E., & Ozeki, C. (1998). Work–family conflict, policies, and the job–life satisfaction relationship: A review and directions for organizational behavior–human resources research. *Journal of Applied Psychology, 83*(2), 139–149. doi:10.1037/0021-9010.83.2.139

Kuhn, T., & Corman, S. R. (2003). The emergence of homogeneity and heterogeneity in knowledge structures during planned organizational change. *Communication Monographs, 70,* 198–229. doi:10.1080/0363775032000167406

Lewis, L. K. (2000). "Blindsided by the one" and "I saw that one coming": The relative anticipation and occurrence of the communication problems and other problems in implementers' hindsight. *Journal of Applied Communication Research, 28,* 44–67. doi:10.1080/00909880009365553

Liu, M., & Buzzanell, P. M. (2004). Negotiating maternity leave expectations: Perceived tensions between ethics and justice of care. *Journal of Business Communication, 41*(4), 323–349. doi:10.1177/0021943604268174

McNall, L. A., Masuda, A. D., & Nicklin, J. M. (2010). Flexible work arrangements, job satisfaction, and turnover intentions: The mediating role of work-to-family enrichment. *Journal of Psychology, 144*(1), 61–81. doi:10.1080/00223980903356073

Medved, C. E. (2009). Crossing and transforming occupational and household gendered divisions of labor: Reviewing literatures and deconstructing divisions. In C. S. Beck (Ed.), *Communication yearbook* (Vol. 33, pp. 301–341). Mahwah, NJ: Erlbaum.

Mescher, S., Benschop, Y., & Doorewaard, H. (2010). Representations of work–life balance support. *Human Relations, 63,* 21–39. doi:10.1177/0018726709349197

Miller, V. D., Jablin, F. M., Casey, M. K., Lamphear-Van Horn, M., & Ethington, C. (1996). The maternity leave as a role negotiation process. *Journal of Managerial Issues, 8,* 286–309.

Miller, V. D., Johnson, J. R., Hart, Z., & Peterson, D. L. (1999). A test of antecedents and outcomes of employee role negotiation ability. *Journal of Applied Communication Research, 27*(1), 24–48. doi:10.1080/00909889909365522

Moe, K., & Shandy, D. (2010). *Glass ceilings & 100-hour couples: What the opt-out phenomenon can teach us about work and family.* Athens, GA: University of Georgia Press.

Nesbit, P. L. (2005). HRM and the flexible firm: Do firms with "high performance" work cultures utilize peripheral work arrangements? *International Journal of Employment Studies, 13*(2), 1–17.

Oldenburg, R. (1999). *The great good place.* New York: Marlowe.

Parker, L., & Allen, T. D. (2001). Work/family benefits: Variables related to employees' fairness perception. *Journal of Vocational Behavior, 58,* 453–468. doi:10.1006/jvbe.2000.1773

Parker, P. S. (2003). Control, power, and resistance within raced, gendered, and classed work contexts: The case of African American women. In P. J. Kalbfleisch (Ed.), *Communication yearbook* (Vol. 27, pp. 257–291). Mahwah, NJ: Erlbaum. doi:10.1207/s15567419cy2701_9

Perlow, L. A. (1997). *Finding time: How corporations, individuals and families can benefit from new work practices.* Ithaca, NY: ILR Press.

Peters, P., & Heusinkveld, S. (2010). Institutional explanations for managers' attitudes toward teleworking. *Human Relations, 63*(1), 107–135. doi:10.1177/0018726709336025

Pitt-Catsouphes, M., & Matz-Costa, C. (2008). The multi-generational workforce: Workplace flexibility and engagement. *Community, Work & Family, 11,* 215–229. doi:10.1080/13668800802021906

Rapoport, R., & Bailyn, L. (1996). *Relinking life and work: Toward a better future.* New York: Ford Foundation.

Ressler, C., & Thompson, J. (2008). *Why work sucks and how to fix it.* New York: Portfolio.

Richman, A., Civian, J., Shannon, L. L., Hill, E. J., & Brennan, R. 2008. The relationship of perceived flexibility, supportive work–life policies, and use of formal flexible arrangements and occasional flexibility to employee engagement and expected retention. *Community, Work and Family, 11,* 183–197. doi:10.1080/13668800802050350

Roberts, E. (2008). Time and work balance: The roles of "temporal customization" and "life temporality." *Gender, Work and Organization, 15,* 430–453. doi:10.1111/j.1468-0432.2008.00412.x

Sennett, R. (1998). *The corrosion of character.* New York: Norton.

Shapiro, M., Ingols, C., O'Neill, R., & Blake-Beard, S. (2009). Making sense of women as career self-agents: Implications for human resource development. *Human Resource Development Quarterly, 20*(4), 477–501. doi:10.1002/hrdq.20030

Stack, C. B. (1974). *All our kin: Strategies for survival in a Black community.* New York: Harper & Row.

Towers, I., Duxbury, L., Higgins, C., & Thomas, J. (2006). Time thieves and space invaders: Technology, work and the organization. *Journal of Organizational Change Management, 19*(5), 593–618. doi:10.1108/09534810610686076

Tracy, S. J., & Rivera, K. D. (2010). Endorsing equity and applauding stay-at-home moms: How male voices on work–life reveal aversive sexism and flickers of transformation. *Management Communication Quarterly, 24*(1), 3–43. doi:10.1177/0893318909352248

Tracy, S. J., & Trethewey, A. (2005). Fracturing the real- self ↔ fake-self dichotomy: Moving toward crystallized organizational identities. *Communication Theory, 15,* 168–195. doi: 10.1093/ct/15.2.168

Trethewey, A., Tracy, S. J., & Alberts, J. K. (2006). Crystallizing frames for work–life. *Electronic Journal of Communication/La revue électronique de Communication, 16.* Retrieved from http://www.cios.org/EJCPUBLIC/016/3/01636.HTML

U.S. Bureau of Labor Statistics. (2011, March). Women at work. Retrieved from http://www.bls.gov/spotlight/2011/women/

Voydanoff, P. (2005). Consequences of boundary-spanning demands and resources for work-to-family conflict and perceived stress. *Journal of Occupational Health Psychology, 10*(4), 491–503. doi:10.1037/1076-8998.10.4.491

Weisberg, A. C., & Buckler, C. A. (1994). *Everything a working mother needs to know about pregnancy rights, maternity leave, and making her career work for her.* New York: Doubleday.

Working mother best 100 companies. (2010). Retrieved from http://www.working-mother.com/node/3836/list

10 *Commentary*

Enhancing Our Understanding of Work–Life Balance from a Communication Perspective

Isabel C. Botero

Aarhus University

Shifts in labor market demographics, increasing work hours, workloads distributed on 24-7 operating systems, changes in pace and intensity of work, and the escalating financial, market, and job insecurity from the global economy have prompted scholars and practitioners to focus on work–life balance as an increasingly important area of research in organizational studies (Kossek & Distelberg, 2009). The idea of understanding what organizations do to help employees deal with balancing life and work issues and how employees perceive these actions has intrigued scholars from a variety of research areas. Early work on work–life balance examined how employee access and use of workplace support initiatives reduced work–family conflict (Goff, Mount, & Jamison, 1990; Kossek & Nichol, 1992). In recent years, this focus has shifted to understanding other forms of workplace support such as flexibility at work (Christensen & Schneider, 2011), supervisor support in work–family issues (Hammer, Kossek, Yragui, Bodner, & Hanson, 2009; Kossek, Pichler, Bodner, & Hammer, 2011), positive work–family organizational climate (Allen, 2001), and organizational support (Kossek et al., 2011).

In the communication discipline, the interest in work–life balance issues has focused on communication challenges for organizations and employees as they manage the need for work and for life spheres (May & Zorn, 2001). From my reading of the literature, most of the research about work–life balance issues in communication can be summarized from a message point of view. That is, as communication scholars we are interested in understanding:

- What are the messages that organizations are providing about work–life balance issues? (e.g., what are the policies that organizations have and choose to communicate about work–life balance?)
- Who are the organizational members that communicate the organization's messages about work–life balance issues? (e.g., who is communicating to the employee information about work–life balance issues? Is it the manager, supervisor, or HR representative?)
- How are messages about work–life balance being communicated? (e.g., how are organizations providing information about work–life balance policies and approaches of the organization?)

- How are employees evaluating these messages? (i.e., what do employees think about what the organizations say regarding work–life balance?), and, finally,
- How do all these factors interact to influence the behaviors of employees? (i.e., how do employees use all of these communication cues to determine what they should do to manage work and life issues?)

In the last 10 years, there has been an increase in the amount of communication research focusing on work–family issues. This research has come from multiple approaches and provided different points of view for analyzing work–life balance. Although our understanding of work–life issues has increased, there are still important considerations that need to be taken into account when exploring work–life balance from a communication point of view. In the remaining parts of this article, I would like to focus on three such considerations.

The Meaning of Work–Life Balance

The first issue pertains to our understanding of the meaning of work–life balance and factors that may affect our interpretation of this meaning. The way in which each person defines balance will affect how he or she interprets and reacts to communication about work–life balance. The notion of "balance" is defined as: (a) state of equilibrium or equal distribution, (b) something used to produce equilibrium, (c) mental steadiness or emotional stability, (d) a state of bodily equilibrium, and (e) instrument for determining weight, typically by equilibrium of a bar at the center of a scale (webster-dictionary.org, n.d.). Given the notion of balance as equilibrium, one primitive conceptualization of work–life balance might consist of equal time devoted to both "work" and "life." Yet such a simplistic bifurcation ignores the reality that balance is defined by individuals in psychological rather than statistical terms. What constitutes adequate "balance" in one's life is heavily influenced by factors such as the level of identification one has with one's job, the satisfaction that one derives from one's work, and the level of identification one has with non-work-related pursuits. In other words, individuals highly devoted to their careers may define adequate balance as having the ability to devote as much time to their work as possible, whereas individuals for whom work is a necessity to be tolerated rather than embraced may define adequate balance as working just enough to get by.

Given the importance of how each individual views work–life balance, two areas of research need to be explored. First, communication researchers should explore the full range of individual and contextual factors that influence views of what constitutes an adequate work–life balance. Second, researchers should study how these same individual and contextual factors mediate employees' interpretations and reactions to organizational messages about work–life issues.

Gender and Work–Life Balance

A second important consideration when exploring work–life balance from a communication approach is the importance of including both men's and women's perspectives about work–life balance. Previous research on work–life balance issues in the communication field has been primarily led by scholars who focus on gender as part of their work and largely on women in particular (Buzzanell, Sterk, & Turner, 2004; Golden, Kirby, & Jorgensen, 2006; Kirby, Golden, Medved, Jorgenson, & Buzzanell, 2003). This focus on the female's perspective is problematic because it ignores the possibility of men taking a primary role in family care, and it also tends to present work-life more narrowly as a "work–family" issue. Although some research is starting to incorporate the male's point of view (Tracy & Rivera, 2010), the perceptions of men have been greatly ignored in communication research about work–life balance. Thus, one way in which we can enhance our understanding of work–life balance issues from a communication point of view could be to explore how gender affects the interpretation of organizational messages about work–life balance. This understanding can help organizations understand how to frame their messages to be more effective, and could also help in understanding what topics about work–life balance issues are more important for men and which are more important for women.

Individual vs. Organizational Responsibility

The third important issue that needs to be considered when exploring work–life balance from a communication perspective is the locus of responsibility for work–life balance. Considerable research in communication has focused on what information organizations provide about work–life balance policies, how these policies are enacted, and how individuals interpret, use, and react to the information presented by the organization. Implicit in this research is an apparent normative expectation that organizations bear a greater share of the responsibility for promoting work–life balance, and that the role of the employee is primarily to receive information. Yet if we consider communication as a two-way process, the individual also has a role and responsibility in this communication process. Thus, to advance our knowledge, we need to better understand the role of the employee in the negotiation of meaning and interpretation of information about work–life balance that is communicated in the organizational context. Additionally, it would also be important to understand what the individual could communicate to the organization during the recruitment and socialization process that would enable two-way communication practices between individuals and organizations. Some topics that could be explored as part of this approach could include where people learn and create expectations about work–life balance issues, how the educational system teaches individuals about work–life balance issues, and how cultural contexts impact the expectations and interpretation of information about work–life balance issues.

Based on these three important considerations, I think that the chapter on "Reconsidering the Concept of Workplace Flexibility: Is Adaptability a Better Solution?" is an important contribution to our understanding of work–life balance issues from a communication perspective. The authors integrate the notion that work–life balance comes from individual perceptions of what balance means; it is not a topic that focuses on females only; and it introduces some ideas about the role of the individual in the communication process of work–life balance issues.

As organizations continue to change and the interests and demographics of their employees continue to become more diverse, understanding work–life balance issues will be of increasing importance to scholars and practitioners. The most important contribution that communication scholarship can offer in this area is a better understanding of what are the communication roles and responsibilities of both employees and organizations to enable work–life balance to occur, and how the substance of what employees and organizations communicate can affect the enactment of work–life balance. Although we have a strong foundation, there are still many areas to explore.

References

Allen T. D. (2001). Family-supportive work environments: The role of organizational perceptions. *Journal of Vocational Behavior, 58*, 41–435. doi:10.1006/jvbe.2000.1774

Buzzanell, P. M., Sterk, H., & Turner, L. (2004). *Gender in applied communication contexts*. Thousand Oaks, CA: Sage.

Christensen, K., & Scheneider, B. (2011). Making a case for workplace flexibility. *The Annals of the American Academy of Political and Social Science, 638*, 6–20. doi:10.1177/0002716211417245

Goff J., Mount M. K., & Jamison R. L. (1990). Employer supported childcare, work–family conflict, and absenteeism: A field study. *Personnel Psychology, 43*, 793–809. doi:10.1111/j.1744-6570.1990.tb00683.x

Golden, A. G., Kirby, E. L., & Jorgenson, J. (2006). Work–life research from both sides now: An integrative perspective for organizational and family communication. In C. S. Beck (Ed.), *Communication yearbook* (Vol. 30, pp. 142–195). Mahwah, NJ: Erlbaum. doi:10.1207/s15567419cy3001_4

Hammer, L., Kossek, E. E., Yragui, N., Bodner, T., & Hansen, G. (2009). Development and validation of a multi-dimensional scale of family supportive supervisor behaviors (FSSB). *Journal of Management, 35*, 83–856. doi:10.1177/0149206308328510

Kirby, E. L., Golden, A. G., Medved, C. E., Jorgenson, J., & Buzzanell, P. M. (2003). An organizational communication challenge to the discourse of work and family research: From problematics to empowerment. In P. Kalbfleisch (Ed.), *Communication yearbook* (Vol. 27, pp. 1–44). Mahwah, NJ: Erlbaum. doi:10.1207/s15567419cy2701_1

Kossek, E. E., & Distelberg B. (2009). Work and family employment policy for a transformed work force: Trends and themes. In N. Crouter & A. Booth (Eds.), *Work–life policies* (pp. 3–51). Washington, DC: Urban Institute Press.

Kossek, E. E., & Nichol V. (1992). The effects of employer-sponsored child care on employee attitudes and performance. *Personnel Psychology, 45*(3), 485–509.

Kossek, E. E., Pichler, S., Bodner, T., & Hammer, L. B. (2011). Workplace social support and work–family conflict: A meta-analysis clarifying the influence of general and work–family–specific supervisor and organizational support. *Personnel Psychology, 64,* 289–313. doi:10.1111/j.1744-6570.2011.01211.x

May, S. K., & Zorn, T. E. Jr. (2001) Forum introduction. *Management Communication Quarterly, 15,* 100–102. doi: 10.1177/0893318901151004

Tracy, S. J. & Rivera, K. D. (2010). Endorsing equity and applauding stay-at-home moms: How male voices on work–life reveal aversive sexism and flickers of transformation. *Management Communication Quarterly, 24,* 3–43. doi: 10.1177/0893318909352248

Webster-dictionary.org. (n.d.). Retrieved from http://www.webster-dictionary.org/definition/balance

CHAPTER CONTENTS

11 Constructionist Social Problems Theory

Joel Best

University of Delaware

Social constructionist approaches have transformed the sociology of social problems by shifting the analytic focus from social conditions to the processes by which issues come to public attention. The social problems process typically involves a series of stages: claimsmaking (involving various figures, including activists and experts, as claimsmakers); media coverage; public reactions; policymaking; the social problems work of implementing policy; and policy outcomes. At each of these stages, individuals reconstruct the troubling condition to reflect their cultural and structural circumstances, so that social problems and social policies can be understood as products of continually shifting arguments and interpretations, emerging through interactions between those making claims and their audiences. Scholars of communications may find the literature on social problems theory useful in their own research.

The growth of the professoriate, higher expectations for faculty research productivity, and the explosion in the numbers of journals and other outlets for publication have fostered a boom in scholarly publishing that makes it increasingly difficult to stay abreast of developments outside one's discipline, even one's specialty. One consequence is the development of parallel literatures in different sectors of the academy. This essay is an effort to bring recent thinking about the sociology of social problems to the attention of scholars in communication who may find this literature of interest. No doubt some of these ideas already have parallels in the communication literature, others may seem more novel. Because I am attempting to draw attention to an approach in another discipline, I have cited few works by scholars in communication. I have no doubt that recent work in communication might helpfully inform the research of sociologists of social problems.

Defining Social Problems

Sociologists assumed ownership of the field of social problems in the early 20th century (Schwartz, 1997). The term had originated a few decades earlier as a singular noun: *the* social problem was the relationship between capital and labor in newly industrialized societies. However, people soon began to speak of various, plural social problems: poverty, vice, and so on. Courses in social pathology or social problems became a standard sociology offering for undergraduates; the typical course examined a different social problem each week (Reinhardt, 1929).

Almost as soon as those courses began being offered, critics questioned whether social problem was a useful concept. The definition of social problem seemed vague and commonsensical: it was understood as being some sort of social condition that, well, was a problem, in that it harmed society. Undergraduates might have found that definition satisfactory, but the critics had their doubts: "The phrase ... is one of those much used popular expressions which turn out to be incapable of exact definition" (Case, 1924, p. 268; see also Fuller & Myers, 1941; Waller, 1936).

There were two major reasons why it was difficult to define social problem. First, the term was routinely applied to quite diverse phenomena, ranging from issues affecting individuals (e.g., suicide, mental illness) to global challenges (e.g., overpopulation, climate change). Because these phenomena had little in common, definitions that sought to encompass all of them necessarily had to be vague. Second, assessments of whether particular conditions ought to be considered social problems displayed a nasty tendency to shift. Conditions once considered serious problems (e.g., divorce, interracial marriage) might come to be seen as acceptable, even as phenomena once taken for granted as normal might be redefined as serious problems (e.g., discrimination against women or homosexuals). Even when a condition continued to be considered a problem, ideas about what sort of problem it might be could change: for instance, drinking alcohol went from being considered a moral problem (drunkenness), to a crime problem (during Prohibition), to a disease that afflicted only some drinkers (alcoholism) (Gusfield, 1967). If time made a difference, so did space: a practice that is routine, nearly universal in one country (e.g., female genital cutting in Egypt), may be considered a terrible problem by the standards of other nations (Boyle, Songora, & Foss, 2001).

In other words, it is very difficult to articulate the objective qualities of a social condition that make it a social problem. Consider how standards for judging racial or gender discrimination have shifted over the course of American history. Or consider the increasingly accepted equal-rights campaigns mounted by gays and lesbians, and by the disabled, as well as the more controversial calls for fat acceptance and claims that discrimination disadvantages those who are too tall or too short, or who fail to meet (or exceed!) social expectations for physical attractiveness. How can we hope to articulate objective standards for defining when some form of discrimination should be considered a social problem, when we know that these judgments have varied wildly across time and space?

One consequence of these definitional difficulties is that, while many sociology departments offered courses called "Social Problems," sociologists rarely used social problem as a concept in their analyses. This led to Spector and Kitsuse's (1977) declaration: "There is no adequate definition of social problems within sociology, and there is not and never has been a sociology of social problems" (p. 1).

Social Problems as Social Processes

Although critics had long challenged the usefulness of defining social problems as harmful social conditions, it was not until the 1970s that a coherent theoretical alternative emerged. Both Herbert Blumer (1971) and Malcolm
Spector and John I. Kitsuse (1977) offered new models that conceptualized
social problems as social processes. Spector and Kitsuse's analysis would
become more influential; they defined social problems as "the activities of
individuals or groups making assertions of grievances and claims with respect
to some putative conditions" (p. 75). This was a radical redefinition. In this
view, analysts need not identify social conditions that have particular objective
qualities that make them social problems; those are merely putative conditions,
alleged to be problematic. Rather, social problems are activities—processes
of alleging, asserting, claiming. Studying social problems requires focusing
analytic attention on those processes.

The recent publication of Berger and Luckmann's (1966) of *The Social
Construction of Reality: A Treatise in the Sociology of Knowledge* had encouraged sociologists to examine how phenomena were socially constructed, that
is, to explore the processes by which people assigned meaning to their worlds.
Berger and Luckmann's basic argument was that human thought depended
on language, and that language was both created and passed along by people,
so that both childhood and adult socialization involved acquiring particular
words, and thereby categories for classifying and understanding the world.
Reality—what people understood to be real, the categories they used to classify the world—was, then, a product of social activity, of the process of social
construction. Sociologists quickly began to apply this abstract framework to
specific sectors of society, to examine how different sorts of knowledge were
created, or constructed. Book titles from the 1970s reveal the dissemination of
constructionist language to studies of news: *Making News: A Study in the Construction of Reality* (Tuchman, 1978); science, *Laboratory Life: The Social
Construction of Scientific Facts* (Latour & Woolgar, 1979); and deviance,
Deviance and Respectability: The Social Construction of Moral Meanings
(Douglas, 1970). Soon, the term spread to other disciplines, sometimes taking
on very different meanings, which in turn led to a theoretical literature comparing schools of constructionist thought (e.g., Hacking, 1999; S. Harris, 2010;
Holstein & Gubrium, 2008; for reviews on constructionism in communication
research, Bartesaghi & Castor, 2008; Foster & Bochner, 2008).

Thus, it was no accident that Spector and Kitsuse titled their book *Constructing Social Problems*. That volume introduced other terms that would
be adopted by sociologists seeking to understand social problems as social
processes. Spector and Kitsuse had defined social problems as "activities of
individuals or groups making ... claims," and analysts began to explore the
nature of *claims*, the people—the claimsmakers—who made those claims, and
the process of *claimsmaking*. This vocabulary redirected analysts' attention.
Instead of trying to dissect the nature of some problematic social condition,
analysts refocused on who was making claims about that condition, and what
the outcomes of that claimsmaking process might be.

By the end of the 1970s, sociologists began publishing case studies that traced the emergence or construction of particular social problems, such as child abuse (Pfohl, 1977) and rape (Rose, 1977). Obviously, these analysts were not claiming that these were previously unknown social conditions, but rather that recent claims had framed these topics in new ways: in the former case, new terms—first *battered child syndrome* and then *child abuse*—had supplanted older ways of understanding the issue (such as cruelty to children); while in the latter case, the feminist movement had challenged older notions of rape as a sex crime, and redefined it in terms of violence and sexual power. These new conceptions could be linked to campaigns by particular activists and other actors to change public understandings of these issues, so that ideas about social conditions could no longer be taken for granted, and were instead transformed into something for analysts to understand. The social construction of social problems was no longer an abstract theoretical approach; it offered a program for doing research.

Theoretical Confusion

Almost as soon as the constructionist approach began to be adopted for the study of social problems, critics raised two objections. The first critique, vulgar constructionism, involved a fundamental misunderstanding of the idea of social construction, although the second, ontological gerrymandering, came from within the constructionist camp, and initially proved more troubling.

Vulgar constructionism equates social construction with fanciful thinking. Constructionists sometimes illustrate their perspective by pointing to claims that strike many people as dubious; for example, that witches bedeviled 17th-century Salem, or that UFOs have abducted millions of contemporary Americans. These examples are useful for understanding the nature of social construction because they lay the process bare: they reveal that people can construct even nonexistent phenomena—or at least phenomena for which claims lack what many consider convincing evidence—as social problems. The problem is that it is easy to learn the wrong lessons from these examples. Thus, a vulgar constructionist draws a distinction between UFO abduction (viewed as merely a social construction) and, say, poverty (considered a real social condition); in this view, the language of social construction should be confined to the analysis of what are viewed as irrational concerns—collective delusions, mass hysteria, moral panics, and the like.

This is not a useful way of thinking about social construction; it is far too constricted. All social problems are socially constructed. Take poverty. It can be understood in many different ways. There are debates about the causes of poverty, ranging from explanations that blame the poor's deficiencies (e.g., laziness, a culture of poverty, etc.), to those that fault society's failings (e.g., insufficient economic opportunities, lack of commitment to social justice). These competing conceptions in turn lead to all sorts of policies designed to eliminate poverty, such as the 19th-century English Poor Laws, LBJ's War on Poverty, and 1990s welfare reform; there is, for instance, a large academic literature on where the "poverty line" ought to be set. No one questions the reality that some people are poor. But how we think about poverty at a given historical moment is shaped by the various claims we encounter and those we choose to accept; that is, poverty is socially constructed, and not just poverty, but rape, HIV-AIDS, and whatever other issues may strike one as fundamental and all too real, are social constructions.

The second criticism, *ontological gerrymandering*, came from within constructionism. Less than 10 years after the publication of *Constructing Social Problems*, Steve Woolgar (himself a prominent constructionist sociologist of science) and Dorothy Pawluch (1985a) published a critique of the emerging constructionist literature on social problems. They argued that constructionist analyses were flawed by a serious internal contradiction. On the one hand, constructionists called into question the assumptions the people they studied made about social conditions; constructionists argued that all reality was socially constructed. On the other hand, Woolgar and Pawluch noted that constructionists themselves seemed to make assumptions about what was and wasn't real. They illustrated this critique by noting that, while discussing changing definitions of marijuana, Spector and Kitsuse (1977) noted: "The nature of marijuana remained constant" (p. 43). Woolgar and Pawluch (1985a) pounced: "The key assertion is that the actual character of a substance (marijuana), condition, or behavior remained constant" (p. 217). In other words, didn't Spector and Kitsuse, and by extension every constructionist analyst, need to make assumptions about the nature of underlying reality in order to argue that changing claims about any social problem were interesting?

At first, the critique of ontological gerrymandering seemed to threaten the constructionist enterprise, and a self-absorbed theoretical literature emerged in response. Some analysts, notably John Kitsuse, took the argument to be well founded, and argued that analysts needed to police their work to avoid lapses into realism (Ibarra & Kitsuse, 1993). Advocates of this position, who came to be characterized as *strict constructionists*, initially found it easy criticize others' work, but it soon became apparent that their position required retreating from studying social life into abstraction. Thus, Woolgar and Pawluch (1985b) recommended that constructionists "move beyond constructivism" to examine the nature of sociological inquiry, although they conceded that this "will not contribute ... to our understanding of the world as we have traditionally conceived that pursuit" (p. 162). Other strict constructionists recommended abstract theorizing (Ibarra & Kitsuse, 1993):

> Our position is that developing a general theory of social problems discourse is a much more coherent way of proceeding than, for example, the development of a series of discrete theories on the social construction of X, Y, and Z. To develop a theory about condition X when the ontological status of X is suspended results in "ontological gerrymandering" ..., which is to say flawed theory. (p. 33)

Neither self-examination nor abstraction proved workable. Even the most abstract theory had to be presented using language, and those words inevitably brought realistic assumptions into the analysis. Moreover, strict construction seemed to forbid analysts from doing any empirical analysis, from studying the processes by which particular social problems came to public attention.

The alternative came to be characterized as *contextual constructionism* (J. Best, 1995). Here, analysts sought to locate claims within their larger social context. Return for a moment to Spector and Kitsuse's remark that the nature of marijuana had not changed before the federal government passed the Marijuana Tax Act of 1937. This can be seen, to be sure, as an assumption, but it is the sort of background assumption necessary to all sorts of science: chemists assume that oxygen has the same properties across time, just as astronomers assume that Mars remains in the same orbit. The point is not that marijuana was actually unchanged during the 1930s, but rather that no one suggested that the drug had changed, even though some claimsmakers began to argue that it should be considered problematic and be banned. It is the redefinition of marijuana's social significance, not some change in its chemical properties or biological effects that is at issue. Contextual constructionists try to understand such redefinitions by locating them in their social context; for example, by considering the circumstances that led the Federal Bureau of Narcotics to promote a federal law against marijuana.

For the most part, the debate over ontological gerrymandering has faded, while the constructionist literature on social problems has expanded. The simplistic models offered in early theoretical statements of the problem have been fleshed out, and analysts have concentrated on empirical studies of various stages within the social problems process. The purposes of organizing this review, we can think of this process as involving six stages: claimsmaking, media coverage, public reactions, policymaking, social problems work, and policy outcomes (J. Best, 2008). At each of these stages, actors construct the nature and meaning of social problems.

Claimsmaking

The social problems process always begins with a claim, with someone arguing that some social condition is harmful and needs to be addressed. The nature of both claims and claimsmakers shapes the social problems process.

The Rhetoric of Claimsmaking

Claimsmaking is an inherently persuasive activity, and can be analyzed as a form of rhetoric (Gusfield, 1981; Ibarra & Kitsuse, 1993). Toulmin (1958) proposed that all arguments involve grounds, warrants, and conclusions. Although his intent was to examine general properties of arguments, I adopt his concepts to explore some specific aspects of social problems claims (J. Best, 1990).

Grounds. The grounds for claims identify the nature of the problem. Grounds reflect the social context from which they emerge; what count as reasonable, relevant grounds will vary from society to society across time and space. A theocratic society may define most social problems in terms of sin; while a society which grants medical professionals considerable authority may characterize many social problems as diseases. In contemporary America, key types of grounds statements include:

- *Typifying examples.* Social problems claims often begin with an example, a terrible case that illustrates the problem (Johnson, 1995). Thus, a claimsmaker may describe a particular abused child to reveal the nature of child abuse. Usually, these cases are chosen for their melodramatic qualities; they demonstrate the problem's seriousness. The examples used to typify problems usually are not especially typical: child abuse may be typified using an example of terrible violence ending in the child's death, although the largest category of child abuse cases involves neglect, rather than physical abuse.
- *Names.* Claimsmakers often couple a typifying example with a name for the problem (e.g., a toddler being beaten to death illustrates the battered child syndrome or child abuse). While some terms, such as rape, may be centuries old, others may have been coined more recently by the claimsmakers, such as marital rape or date rape. Adopting a new name is one way to focus fresh attention on particular claims; it can distinguish the claimsmakers and their cause from their predecessors' constructions of a problem (Placier, 1996).
- *Definitions.* Coupling a typifying example to a name often circumvents the need for a precise definition of the problem (J. Best, 1990). Claimsmakers tend to prefer broad, vague definitions. A broader definition encompasses more cases, meaning that the problem can be understood to be larger and therefore more pressing. Moreover, broad definitions are inclusive, so that more people can be understood as affected by the problem. Claimsmakers may insist that arguing about definitions diverts attention from the urgent need to address the issue.
- *Statistics.* Claimsmakers often offer numbers in an effort to estimate the size of the problem (J. Best, 2001a, 2004). In a culture that grants authority to science, measurements are rhetorically powerful ways of assuring listeners that the claimsmakers have the facts on their side. In practice, efforts to draw attention to some neglected social problem are unlikely to have access to reliable data; a common byproduct of neglect is that people haven't bothered to keep careful track of the condition. This means that claimsmakers often present figures that are little more than estimates or best guesses. Because they themselves believe that the problem is large and demands attention, and because bigger numbers imply that a problem is more serious, those estimates tend to exaggerate the problem's scope. Of course, broad definitions support larger estimates.

- *Orientations.* Claimsmakers often have particular professional or ideological world views that shape the grounds of their claims. Medicalization refers to the process of defining particular phenomena as medical problems, to be understood using a medical vocabulary (disease, symptom, treatment, etc.). As the prestige and authority of medical professionals rose during the 20th century, more and more claims defined various social problems as medical matters (Conrad, 2007). Similarly, the rise of feminism has made it easy to construct social problems from that perspective, invoking its own specialized vocabulary (e.g., sexism, patriarchy, etc.) (Dunn, 2010). Orientations may be taken for granted and therefore difficult to recognize, until we consider the very different language and assumptions claimsmakers have brought to bear across time and space; for example, the prominence of religious claims in Puritan New England or contemporary Iran.
- *Scope.* In addition to statistics estimating a problem's size, claims often insist that a problem is increasing, that it strikes randomly, than it affects everyone, and so on (J. Best, 1999). Characterizing a problem as a wave, epidemic, or growing threat serves to make the issue seem more serious or urgent.
- *Cultural resources.* Claims almost inevitably draw upon a set of existing concepts, ideas, plot lines, or other cultural elements (J. Best, 1999). For instance, the idea of conspiracy is familiar, and it is easy for claimsmakers to draw upon that idea, to argue that a conspiracy is at work without having to explain what conspiracies are, how they operate, and so on. Because audiences have extensive cultural knowledge, claimsmakers can usually choose which cultural resources to invoke. Very often, different audiences—who may be distinguished by age, race, class, religion, or other social variables—respond to different constructions.

Warrants.   While grounds statements describe a social condition, warrants explain why that condition should be considered a problem. Warrants invoke values and emotions. Political scientists distinguish between valence issues around which there is general consensus (e.g., opposition to child pornography) and position issues about which there is public debate (e.g., abortion) (Nelson, 1984). In claims about valence issues, warrants are often implicit, in that the relevant values may seem so self-evident to any culturally competent member of society, that they can go unspoken. In contrast, claims regarding position issues are more likely to articulate their warrants.

Any culture offers a set of values that can be incorporated into warrants. Thus, contemporary Americans are likely to agree that they value equality, freedom, justice, and so on. However, warrants grounded in widely held values are not necessarily persuasive for at least two reasons. First, different values can have contradictory implications: a perfectly egalitarian society may not be all that free, just as a perfectly free society may not be all that egalitarian, so that opponents may argue that different values deserve primacy (e.g., political conservatives are more likely to invoke liberty, and liberals to invoke equality). Second, social problems claims must operationalize abstract values, and this can allow people taking opposite sides in a debate to invoke the same values. Thus, both proponents and opponents of affirmative action will argue that they favor equality (albeit defined in different ways), just as both pro- and anti-abortion advocates speak of rights: a woman's right to choose vs. the unborn child's right to life. Values are often cloaked in emotional appeals, and tap into cultural resources about melodrama (Loseke, 2003, 2009). Thus, children and women may be defined as innocents vulnerable to victimization and deserving protection, threatened by villains who embody the social problem (Best, 1990; Davis, 2005; Dunn, 2010). Like values, emotional appeals must be operationalized, and opponents may invoke the same emotions (e.g., both proponents and opponents of the death penalty justify their position as leading to closure; Berns, 2011). When social problems become the subject of dispute, the warrants in claims may become contentious.

Conclusions.   Finally, every claim features *conclusions*. If grounds identify the nature of the problem, and if warrants explain why something needs to be done, conclusions suggest a course of action. During the early stages of a claimsmaking campaign, the conclusions may involve little more than general calls to raise awareness, to recognize the existence of the problem. After a campaign has become established, the conclusions may include specific policy proposals. Effective claimsmaking rhetoric persuades audiences to adopt the concerns voiced by the claimsmakers.

Claimsmaking as Social Interaction

Claimsmaking is a form of social interaction, in which claimsmakers try to attract and convince audiences. Not all claims are successful; many fall on deaf ears. Claimsmaking occurs in a *social problems marketplace*, wherein many claims compete for public attention; that is, there are lots of claimants trying to arouse concern for their various causes, too many for them all to be heard (Benford & Hunt, 2003; J. Best, 1990; Hilgartner & Bosk, 1988). This marketplace can be subdivided into many arenas, each with its own culture (standards for evaluating claims and claimants) and social structure (forums, audiences, distribution of resources, and so on) that shape the prospects for any claim being heard and validated. Claimsmakers must attend to the feedback, or lack of response, from their audiences, and consider revising their claims so as to attract a better response. If one version of a claim elicits a disappointing reaction, the claimsmaker may have better luck with a reworked version.

Even claims that are successful need to be changed. Relying on the same message becomes predictable and boring over time, and claimsmakers need to refresh their arguments to continue to hold their audience's attention. Moreover, successful claims have the potential to expand. Because definitions of social problems tend to be vague, while typifying examples tend to be extreme, the problem's full domain may be unclear and, once a problem achieves public recognition, it is often possible to expand that domain. Thus, initial claims about child abuse focused on brutal, physical violence against infants and toddlers; however, once people became familiar with the term *child abuse*, the term began to be applied to other forms of injury (such as neglect, emotional abuse, and sexual abuse) against young people of all ages (J. Best, 1990). Once the term *child abuse* became widely known and accepted, advocates of a wide variety of causes argued that their concerns—including spanking, circumcision, smoking during pregnancy, and not placing children in car seats—also constituted child abuse. Such *domain expansion* is common.

In addition, successful claims may provide a conceptual platform upon which to construct parallel social problems. Once a name for a social problem gains widespread acceptance, claimsmakers for other causes may adopt similar names, and argue that theirs is an analogous problem. For instance, the success of *child abuse* as a term inspired claimsmakers to characterize other problems as forms of abuse (e.g., elder abuse and wife abuse); similarly, the familiarity of claims about drug addiction encouraged claimsmakers to speak of food addiction and sex addiction, while the attention given to road rage led to claims about air rage and desk rage (J. Best & Furedi, 2001).

Successful claims may also inspire opposition in the form of counterclaims. These may argue that what has been claimed to be a social problem should not be considered problematic (e.g., the pro-choice movement countering claims by the pro-life movement calling for a ban on abortion, by arguing that abortion should be legally available). In other cases, counterclaimsmakers may agree that something is a problem, but characterize the nature of that problem or the best way to solve the problem in very different ways (e.g., disputes between advocates favoring radical or moderate approaches to address some social problem). Locating claims in context requires identifying the claimsmakers.

Social Movements as Claimsmakers

Who makes claims? The obvious answer is social activists, and there is a very large literature on the sociology of social movements (Snow, Soule, & Kriesi, 2004). Sociologists distinguish between social movements, that is, general causes advancing social changes (e.g., the environmental movement), and the various social movement organizations (SMOs) that form that movement (e.g., the Sierra Club, Greenpeace; McCarthy & Zald, 1977). Various sociological theories address different aspects of social movements. Three that are particularly relevant to studies of social problems are the framing, resource mobilization, and opportunity perspectives.

Framing.   Studies of framing and social movements parallel constructionist analyses of claimsmaking rhetoric. Social movements can be understood as being engaged in persuasion, in attempting to attract new members to the cause, to persuade the media to publicize the movement, and to convince policymakers to adopt the movement's goals (Benford & Snow, 2000). Analysts term the language chosen to achieve these goals as a *frame*, in that it offers a framework for thinking about an issue (on sociological conceptions of frames; see Goffman, 1974). Social movement scholars argue that frames can be subdivided into *diagnostic frames* (which analyze the need for change), *motivational frames* (which justify taking action), and *prognostic frames* (which recommend courses of action); these concepts closely parallel Toulmin's grounds, warrants, and conclusions (Benford & Hunt, 1992).

Recruiting members to join a movement involves *frame alignment*, that is, new adherents must be persuaded to alter their individual understandings of the world—their personal frames—to align them with the movement's frame (Snow, Rochford, Worden, & Benford, 1986). Such transformations vary in difficulty: *frame bridging* (convincing people already allied with similar causes to join one's movement) is relatively easy; *frame amplification* argues that the movement is consistent with widely held values; *frame extension* requires the movement to modify its rhetoric in order to make the cause more attractive to prospective adherents; while *frame transformation* (convincing individuals to understand and adopt an unfamiliar frame presented by movement) is the most challenging. Effective frames often incorporate emotional appeals to attract and hold members (Gould, 2009; Whittier, 2009).

Beyond the interaction between a movement's advocates and those they hope to recruit, movement frames find themselves competing with one another. Different SMOs within a social movement may promote rival frames (e.g., radical vs. moderate), and movements may be divided by *frame disputes* (Benford, 1993; Lofland, 1993). Moreover, movements encounter direct opposition from *countermovements* that advance their own *counterframes*; in turn, activists may respond to their rivals and their opponents by *reframing* their issues (Benford & Hunt, 2003). Like the study of claims, the analysis of social movement frames directs attention to rhetoric. (There is a parallel literature on social movement rhetoric from communication scholars; e.g., Stevens & Malesh [2009].)

Resource Mobilization.   Movements require resources: they must attract adherents who will invest time in movement activities, acquire enough funds to cover expenses, and so on (McCarthy & Zald, 1977). The supply of available resources is finite, and different movements and the SMOs within particular movements find themselves competing for these resources. That is, an individual who decides to contribute time or money to a given SMO is less able to also contribute to another cause. This means that SMOs that are theoretically allied in a single social movement must compete with one another for the scarce resources they require. Thus, in advancing a particular frame, an SMO is not merely trying to help nonmembers understand and join the larger movement in general; its frame also seeks to advance the specific SMO's prospects, to get people to see things their way and join their SMO. Ideological disputes often divide movements, with radicals pushing for faster, more dramatic changes, and moderates calling for slower, less disruptive progress. These debates reflect, not just disagreements about goals and strategies, but an underlying competition to mobilize scarce resources.

Whereas traditional mass movements depended upon their ability to mobilize large numbers of people (e.g., to participate in demonstrations), contemporary movements concentrate on fundraising. Increasingly, direct mail solicitations are being replaced through Internet campaigns, using e-mail, websites, and social networking (Eaton, 2010). Studies of resource mobilization focus on the practical concerns of managing a social movement.

Opportunities.   In addition to studying framing and resource mobilization, social movement scholars examine shifting opportunities for—the timing of—movement successes. These are often subdivided into *political opportunities* (periods when the composition and strength of the state make it easier for a movement's claims to be advanced) and *cultural opportunities* (periods when it is easier to get audiences to attend to a particular claim; Meyer, 2004). Events—such as an election that puts a new party in power, or a news story that draws attention to a particular social condition—can make it harder to easier for a movement's claims to be heard. Shifting opportunities lead movements to alter frames (Whittier, 2009), and when opportunities are especially scarce, movements may enter periods of *abeyance* and wait for more promising conditions to emerge (Taylor, 1989).

Movements can influence opportunities by devising new ways of drawing attention to their campaigns (McAdam, 1983). *Tactical innovation* involves revising movement tactics in order to keep the cause newsworthy or to find new ways to pressure the movement's opposition. Just as SMOs need to adjust their frames to attract new adherents, they need to alter their tactics to take advantage of opportunities.

Experts as Claimsmakers

A second broad category of claimsmakers includes experts of various sorts—people deemed to have special authority to promote claims. Authority is, of course, socially constructed; in some societies, religious authorities' judgments may outweigh those of scientists, while the reverse may be true in other societies. In the contemporary United States, those with considerable authority include physicians and other medical professionals, scientists, and political and legal authorities.

Medical and Scientific Expertise.   Medicine's authority grew during the 20th century, thanks to professionalization and more effective treatments. As the century went on, a host of social problems were medicalized; that is, defined as diseases or disorders that manifested symptoms and could be treated (Conrad, 2007). This medical language gained widespread acceptance, so that it came to be adopted by claimsmakers who were not medical professionals. Thus, people whose drinking caused family or work problems—once considered a moral problem and termed drunkards—have been redefined as suffering from the disease of alcoholism, even though Alcoholics Anonymous, the most visible, active proponent of medicalizing excessive drinking, is not based in the medical professions (Appleton, 1995; Gusfield, 1967).

Medicalization constructs what might otherwise be viewed as products of lifestyle choices, moral judgments, or reactions to crises as ailments to be diagnosed and treated. Like other claimsmakers, medical rhetoric defines problems broadly (e.g., obesity or any drinking during pregnancy increase health risks; E. M. Armstrong, 2003; Saguy & Gruys, 2010). It finds the causes of social problems in the patients' genetic, biological, or psychological makeup, rather than in societal circumstances (e.g., searching for a "gay gene," rather than focusing on societal constructions of sexuality, or focusing on individual traumatic responses, rather than the warfare or other events that led to the trauma; Fassin & Rechtman, 2009; Shostak, Conrad, & Horwitz, 2008). Assessments of responsibility for problems are shifted then by medical assessments, even as they constrict discussions of solutions. Sociological studies of medicalization are paralleled by communication scholars' analyses of medical rhetoric (e.g., Keränan, 2010; Segal, 2005).

The nature of medical expertise evolves over time: in the first half of the 20th century, medical claims often adopted a psychoanalytic framework; following World War II, psychiatry adopted more scientific rhetoric and drug-based treatment (Horwitz, 2002). By the beginning of the 21st century, claims were increasingly *biomedicalized*, as developments in genetics encouraged claims that portrayed social problems as the products of particular genes, and as a growing range of psychological and behavioral problems were viewed as somatic in origin and treatable through prescription drugs (Clarke, Shim, Mamo, Fosket, & Fishman, 2003).

Like medicine, the authority granted to science increased during the 20th century. Paralleling the respect granted to the remarkable discoveries and innovations derived from developments in physics, chemistry, and other natural sciences, popular appreciation for the results of social scientific research also rose. Science, like all forms of knowledge, is socially constructed, and sociologists have been interested in the processes by which scientific findings emerge (Fine, 2007; Gusfield, 1981; Latour & Woolgar, 1979). However, when scientists act as claimsmakers, they additionally argue that scientific findings can be used to identify social problems, assess their characteristics, and recommend policy responses—again, there is a parallel communications literature on rhetoric and science (e.g., Harris, 1997).

This is not a straightforward process; policymakers' responses do not necessarily respond to scientific claims, and scientists' recommendations do not necessarily address the issues faced by policymakers (Pielke, 2007). Medical and scientific claims may inspire counterclaims. Often these may involve researchers whose findings contradict those of the claimsmakers, or critics may challenge the claimsmakers' research as flawed. Still other opposition draws a distinction between research findings and the promotion of particular policy. In contentious political debates, the relevance of scientific knowledge may be disputed. Thus, scientists' warnings about the inevitability of earthquakes have been constrained by their inability to forecast when these events might occur (Stallings, 1995). Similarly, the general consensus among climate scientists that global temperatures are rising does not translate into agreement about appropriate policies (McCright & Dunlap, 2003; Ungar, 1998). Still, whereas social problems claims 100 years ago were likely to be rooted in moralistic terms, by the century's end, claimsmakers were likely to be called upon to support their assertions with empirical evidence derived from medical or scientific research.

Political and Legal Expertise.   Law, government, and politics also are authoritative arenas in contemporary society. Elected and appointed officials often promote new social policies. Especially prominent figures, such as presidents and presidential candidates can command news coverage and become claimsmakers by drawing attention to their particular causes (Callaghan & Schnell, 2005). Other claimsmakers are much less visible. Government agencies may promote social problems; the U.S. Children's Bureau was instrumental in funding the research that drew attention to child abuse (Nelson, 1984). Similarly, private organizations, such as foundations and think tanks, seek not only to raise awareness about particular issues, but to shape the methods policymakers choose when trying to address social problems (Bartley, 2007; Weidenbaum, 2009). Legal scholars address some of the same issues. Often, these political and legal actors represent ideological positions, so that they offer liberal, conservative, feminist, or libertarian constructions of social problems. Still, in many instances, they are understood to have a sort of expertise that can direct social policy (Tetlock, 2005).

Ownership

Successful claimsmakers can become associated with their causes, to the degree that they acquire *ownership* of an issue (Gusfield, 1981). That is, their constructions are widely understood to be authoritative, they find it easier to command an audience, with the result that others may seek them out to comment on particular events. Ownership conveys considerable advantages; rather than struggling to be heard in the cacophony of the social problems marketplace, a problem's owners can concentrate on revising their claims to keep them fresh and compelling, so that their adherents, the media, the public, and policymakers will continue to attend to their views.

Media Coverage

Claimsmaking launches the social problems process; in many cases, media coverage forms the second stage. Although well-placed *insider claimsmak-*

ers may be able to present their claims directly to policymakers, many claims begin with *outsider claimsmakers*, who depend upon coverage in the mass media to publicize to their concerns, and to thereby attract attention among members of the public as well as policymakers (Benford & Hunt, 2003; J. Best, 1990   ). Many familiar forms of claimsmaking, such as holding a press conference or staging a demonstration, are designed to generate media coverage.

Of course, such coverage is hardly automatic. Within the social problems marketplace, claimsmakers promoting many different causes compete to gain the attention of reporters. Those reporters and their editors operate under their own constraints: they have limited resources, such as limited budgets, limited staff, deadlines, and limited amounts of broadcast time or newspaper space. The people who do news work, who produce the news, inevitably find themselves making choices, whether to cover one story and not another, to highlight these elements and not those (Davies, 2008; Gans, 1979; Tuchman, 1978). The news is always selective, never complete.

Geography plays a role. Not only are news media likely to concentrate on covering stories that seem relevant to and likely to interest their audiences, but claimsmakers find it easier to attract coverage in locales where there is a large media presence (Davies, 2008). New York, Los Angeles, and Washington all have heavy concentrations of news workers, and claims launched in those cities seem more likely to attract broad media attention. Similarly, because Columbine High School was located outside a large city (Denver), and because it took some hours to evacuate the building, the media were able to arrive on the scene and provide dramatic live coverage that focused attention on the incident (Filler, 2000).

Studies of journalists focus on the bases for these choices: the values (such as objectivity) and the social arrangements (such as a news organization's allocation of personnel) that give shape to the news. These factors affect which social problems claims receive attention, and savvy claimsmakers understand the constraints on journalists and work to tailor their claims to maximize their chances of receiving coverage, even as those in the media try to avoid being manipulated by their sources (Sobieraj, 2011). Typically, the media translate and transform the claimsmakers' *primary claims* into *secondary claims*; that is, claims must be reconstructed to fit the media's constraints (J. Best, 1990). Thus, overtly ideological elements (e.g., feminist claims denouncing violence against women as a manifestation of patriarchal domination) may be reworked into more objective language, while lengthy claims may be condensed. Even trimmed and diluted, claimsmaking plays a key role in shaping media coverage; media may cover news about social conditions without framing them as *social problems* unless claimsmakers construct those conditions as problematic (R. Best, 2010).

This transformation is important, because most members of the public encounter claims via media coverage. Activists are likely to be passionate about their causes, and their thinking may be guided by a particular ideology, but news workers may invoke the value of objectivity to cut emotional and ideological elements from claims. Although with valence issues, claimsmakers may be able to argue that there should be a general social consensus regarding their issue, so that only their position needs to be covered (the voices of child pornographers are unlikely to be aired in media coverage), position issues are understood to be subjects of debate, which typically means that the media construct two opposing sides which, for reasons of objectivity, must both be heard (thus, issues such as abortion or gun control are understood as subjects of contention, not consensus).

The result is that coverage of social issues tends to create packages of ideas and symbols. Thus, Gamson and Modigliani (1989) argue that coverage of nuclear power framed that issue in terms of a few positions, each with its own spokespeople, slogans, favored policies, iconic symbols, and so on. Nichols (1997) notes that these packages are often shaped by landmark narratives; that is, particular instances that the media treats as emblematic of a larger problem. New events are interpreted within the existing frameworks of the available packages. It takes remarkably little time for breaking news to be packaged; Monahan (2010) describes how the initial confusion about the meaning of airplanes striking the World Trade Center within hours became packaged as terrorist acts in a "war" that required a military response.

Media packages can construct social problems as crises through frequent coverage and emotionally charged presentations emphasizing dangers to the larger society. Claims about some new phenomenon, such as a type of crime or drug use, can be presented in terms that parallel coverage of earlier problems. Thus, media coverage of *crime waves* usually suggests that some sort of crime has been rising, although criminologists tend to view these as waves in media attention, rather than increases of criminal activity (Sacco, 2005). Similarly, sociologists speak of *drug scares* created when the media warn about the spread of some new form of drug abuse (Jenkins, 1999). Both crime waves and drug scares can be subsumed within the more general category of *moral panics*, a term used to highlight the media's role in arousing concern about social issues (Goode & Ben-Yehuda, 2009). Such intensified coverage soon fades, because, as their name suggests, the news media constantly require new topics, and coverage tends to follow an issue-attention cycle: it may increase rapidly in response to newsworthy events or claimsmakers' efforts to bring attention to an issue, but it then declines when the story no longer seems to offer new aspects and news workers fear that their audience is becoming bored by the topic (A. Downs, 1972).

The news media's role has evolved as their role in promoting claims has changed. The rise of electronic media, from broadcast media, to cable and satellite television, to web-based media, has changed how the public acquires news. The broad, general audiences for print journalism and network news broadcasts have declined, even as news outlets have proliferated, resulting in the audience being divided into segments that are more homogeneous in terms of age, ethnicity, political ideology, and so on (Davies, 2008; Turow, 1997).

The Internet offers new platforms for claimsmaking, such as blogs (Maratea, 2008). Still, in this changing environment, some fundamental organizational problems remain: many claimsmakers compete to be heard, and while the Internet offers a platform for a virtually infinite number of claims, it remains difficult to attract broad attention for any given claim. Bloggers depend on having their claims picked up and brought to the attention of larger audiences by more popular websites or the mainstream media, even as claimsmakers who have ownership of social problems continue to find it easier to attract coverage (Amenta, Caren, Olasky, & Stobaugh, 2009).

Although discussions of media influence tend to focus on the news media, similar processes shape the treatment of social problems claims in popular culture, both those forms defined as pure entertainment and the various hybrid forms of infotainment. Popular culture tends to be formulaic and melodramatic. Social problems claims often serve as topics for popular culture, but they are once again reworked to fit the constraints of each genre's formula (Berns, 2004; J. Best, 1990). Thus, claims about missing children, sexual abuse, and stalking all inspired detective novels, but with the villains portrayed as wealthy, powerful figures, strong enough to offer the dramatic challenge to the hero required by the formulaic struggle between good and evil. Popular culture reconstructs social problems claims to match its own conventions.

Similar transformations characterize infotainment's treatment of social problems. For instance, talk shows tend to focus on individual psychological problems; because they focus on private troubles, rather than public issues, these shows lack a sociological imagination (Lowney, 1999). Thus, each program depicts the experiences and emotional reactions of individuals who are presented as typifying some social problem (e.g., the problem of sexual abuse is explored by examining how particular victims deal with this experience); typically, expert understanding of the issue is represented by some sort of psychologist, who again draws attention to the way the problem affects individuals, and the ways those individuals must learn to cope with these effects. While this psychological frame is consistent with the theme of individualism that runs through American culture, the programs often reconstruct social problems in very different terms from those used by the primary claimsmakers who may have emphasized social arrangements as causes, and social reforms as solutions.

In other words, both news and entertainment media reconstruct social problems, adapting primary claims to fit the media's contentions. Because most people become aware of claims and claimsmakers through media coverage, these reconstructions are consequential.

Public Reactions

Some discussions of public opinion seem to assume that the public's understanding of social issues reflects media coverage, but this is too simple. Just as claimsmakers must revise their claims until they find frames that seem to resonate with audiences, and just as the media rework those claims to fit their own constraints, members of the public play an active role in reconstructing social problems.

There is a tendency to equate public opinion with responses to large-scale, sample surveys such as the Gallup Poll or the General Social Survey. In some cases, these data do seem to reveal long-term trends, such as larger percentages of respondents expressing tolerance for homosexuals. However, the limitations of public opinion surveys are well-known (Bishop, 2005). Changes in how questions are worded or the order in which questions are asked can affect the results, as can the sampling methods chosen. More importantly, even the most carefully designed surveys tend to condense understandings of complex issues into simple forced-choice responses to a question or two, so that the reported findings reduce what may be complex, nuanced views to simple categories, to implying, for instance, that people are either pro-choice or pro-life. Moreover, even when public opinion polls seem to show widespread public concern, as in the case of surveys that report broad support for gun control, these attitudes may not translate into effective social movements that influence policymaking (Goss, 2006).

While surveys are the leading sociological research method, there are other, more nuanced means of studying public attitudes. These sacrifice generalizability (responses to well-designed sample survey questions should reflect the proportions of the general population holding those views), in order to gain a richer understanding of the views of some people. Thus, when researchers organize discussion groups or focus groups that give people opportunities to talk about particular issues, and then study their discourse, the picture becomes considerably more complex. For instance, Sasson (1995) conducted focus groups about crime, and identified three themes that ranged through the discussions: faulty system arguments focused on the failures of the criminal justice system to effectively respond to crime; social breakdown arguments suggested that crime was an outgrowth of declining moral consensus; while blocked opportunity arguments viewed crime as a byproduct of society's failure to provide better chances. While some participants adopted only one of these positions, others shifted perspectives at different points in the discussions. Sasson further noted that focus-group participants drew upon information they'd acquired from the media, but also upon popular wisdom (aphorisms and so on), as well as their own personal experiences. Similarly, Polletta and Lee (2006) examined how discussants used storytelling rather than direct arguments to make points in online discussion groups. In other words, members of the public also reconstruct social problems, by reworking the claims they encounter—whether through direct exposure to claimsmakers, or via media exposure—to create their own definitions of what ought to be considered social problems and how they ought to be understood and addressed.

Here, it is useful to examine research on rumors, contemporary legends, and joke cycles (Donovan, 2004; Dundes, 1987; Fine, Campion-Vincent, & Heath, 2005; Fine & Ellis, 2010). While, at first glance, these may not seem to be a part of serious discourse, they are often means by which ordinary people comment on current social problems. While claimsmaking may inspire folklore (e.g., when missing children are in the news, legends about child-kidnappings flourish), the public reconstructs these issues to fit the requirement of folklore genres. For stories or jokes to spread, they must make enough of an impression on those who hear them that they are remembered and considered worthy of being repeated. Memorable stories are relevant: when the Grimm brothers collected early 19th-century folktales, the plots often involved people venturing into the woods and encountering witches, talking wolves, or other dangers; today, such stories have been relocated in shopping malls, and the villains are no longer magical figures, but rather gang members, kidnappers, and other criminals. A compelling tale—such as the danger of drink spiking—may gain broad public acceptance, even when authorities dismiss it (Burgess, Donovan & Moore, 2009). Similarly, newsworthy catastrophes, such as the devastation caused by Hurricane Katrina—become the subject of jokes. Moreover, memorable stories cause emotional reactions; thus, many contemporary legends have disgusting elements (Heath, Bell, & Sternberg, 2001). Such folklore can be seen as further reworking social problems claims about gangs or disasters in new, dramatic forms that allow ordinary individuals to express anxieties and attitudes. Public opinion—how people think about social problems—is far more complex than the condensed reactions summarized by pollsters.

Policymaking

When claimsmakers construct social problems, they call for something to be done, for someone to devise a solution to the problem, usually in the form of a new or altered social policy. Although there is a tendency to envision social policies as laws enacted by legislative bodies, policies emerge within all sorts of organizational settings; new policies come from religious bodies and educational institutions, from government bureaucracies and social service agencies, and so on. There are numerous studies of such policymaking; often they are concerned with the culture and social organization of the policymakers.

For students of the social problems process, the most striking feature of policymaking is that it involves yet another reconstruction of the social problem in question. The policy proposals advanced in the primary claims of claimsmakers are often too diffuse or too ideological to be deemed workable proposals by policymakers. Similarly, the policy recommendations relayed by the media, like the sense of the public expectations conveyed by opinion polls, tend to be too simplistic. Policymakers are likely to be aware of the views of at least some claimsmakers, media outlets, and members of the public, but this knowledge is insufficient to generate policy.

The political scientist John Kingdon (1984) offered a model for how Congress produces bills that can help understand policymaking. Kingdon used the metaphor of three streams; when those streams came together in a confluence, new legislation was a likely outcome. His first stream involved problem recognition; it is the constructions of claimsmakers that draw attention to an issue. The second is the policy proposal stream. Social policies can be—and certainly federal laws passed by Congress inevitably are—complex, elaborate productions; it usually takes time to develop detailed proposals to deal with all of the details. However, Washington is filled with lobbyists, think tanks, and other proposal-generating entities that often have draft proposals ready. The third stream is political: successful legislation depends upon developing a coalition of actors who agree to join forces behind a particular policy proposal. When a confluence of problem, proposal, and politics does occur, the resulting policy is likely to morph into a very different form than the original claimsmakers envisioned. While Kingdon developed this model to describe how Congress works, it seems applicable to other sorts of policymaking bodies: the body must recognize the problem; agree on a particular policy proposal, and gain enough support and approval within the body to establish that proposal as a policy.

Political sociologists focus particularly on the social organization of policymaking. Legislators must make policy on a wide range of topics—far too many for any individual to acquire a deep understanding of the details of all the issues at question. Policy domains (Burstein, 1991) emerge as one solution to this problem. Individuals—legislators, but also staff members, experts, lobbyists, and others particularly concerned with a given issue—tend to interact with one another; the assessments of these more knowledgeable individuals often guide those who have less familiarity with a topic. Legislators encounter claims from social movements and other claimsmakers, from the media and the public, and from lobbyists and other interested parties, all of whom hope to influence the policymaking process (Burstein, 2006; Burstein & Hirsch, 2007; Burstein & Linton, 2002). In addition, political considerations come into play, such as the positions of one's political party and the possibility of logrolling (reaching compromise through exchanged favors). The effects of all these factors are anything but straightforward: for instance, political contributions offer increased access to legislators, but there is only weak evidence that contributions translate directly into votes on particular bills; similarly, legislators pay some attention to public opinion, but there are no polls measuring the public's attitudes toward many issues upon which legislators vote.

Making policy requires reconstructing the problem and its solution. Policymakers must present *causal stories* that explain the nature of the problem, its causes, and how the policy should improve matters (Stone, 1989). They identify *target populations* who in some way embody the problem, and who should be affected by the policy (Schneider & Ingram, 1993, 2005). Over time, policymakers' constructions of policy issues evolve to reflect changes in social conditions, and particularly in the claims being used to construct the social problems the policy is intended to address (Burstein & Bricher, 1997). The need to justify policy choices can be seen in case studies of policymaking making (e.g., Jenness & Grattet, 2001; Staller, 2006).

Policymakers, then, must offer their own constructions of the problem—

its nature, its causes, and the best way to address it. While social problems rhetoric often makes grand promises, policy is necessarily practical, in that it is intended to affect how society can address, perhaps even solve, social problems.

Social Problems Work

Once they have been devised, social policies must be implemented. Social problems work involves the day-to-day application of social problems constructions. At one level, this can occur in everyday life (S. Harris, 2006; Loseke, 2003). Popular culture and public information campaigns disseminate particular constructions of social problems, encouraging the public to view alcoholism as a disease, to be alert for warning signs of eating disorders, to understand the risks of binge drinking, and so on. Before these campaigns, individuals' difficulties might be understood in idiosyncratic terms ("He's under a lot of pressure and needs to relax, so he drinks," "That's just her personality," etc.), now their acquaintances and family members may discuss whether the behavior in question is an *instance* of some larger social problem, such as alcoholism or mental illness. Such applications of available social problems categories constitute everyday social problems work, and these discussions may lead to calling in specialist social problems workers.

Much social problems work is done by professionals, people working in criminal justice, medicine, education, or social services. These are difficult roles because their occupants are subject to multiple, often competing expectations. Popular culture often idealizes this sort of social problems work by portraying police officers, physicians, and even teachers as heroic figures in fictionalized dramas. Policymakers try to specify the ways in which social problems work should proceed. In addition, there may be oversight from professional associations or supervisors in bureaucracies, and of course social problems workers find themselves interacting with the subjects of their work, and perhaps with others who are witnessing what is happening. The result is that a social problems worker, such as a police officer stopping a suspicious individual on the street, is trying to choose a course of action, while feeling pressures from all sorts of other people.

This means that the practical implementation of social policy can seem rather different from the abstract plan of action constructed by policymakers, so that social problems work becomes yet another stage at which social problems are reconstructed. Consider shelters for battered women. The feminist claimsmakers who called for the establishment of these shelters constructed domestic violence as a form of sexual domination, yet the legislators who fund these shelters are likely to define the issue as less about politics (i.e., women's powerlessness) than about a need for social services, so that the shelters wind up being staffed by individuals whose training may emphasize a therapeutic, rather than a feminist framework (Loseke, 1992; Mann, 2000). Moreover, the women who seek refuge in these shelters have their own, personal interpretations of their situations. Even as they flee violence, they may argue that the violence in question is a product of specific circumstances ("He sometimes drinks too much"). It becomes the shelter workers' job to help these women reconstruct the meaning of their lives, to understand that their particular circumstances can be classified as instances of the larger problem of domestic violence, and that they need to reinterpret their own behavior, as well as the behavior of their abusers, in those terms. Shelter workers discover that many of their clients resist these reinterpretations, just as many individuals whose drinking has caused trouble in their lives resist redefining themselves as alcoholics, and so on. Subjects are likely to view their interactions with social problems workers as dehumanizing, in that the specific, unique aspect of their circumstances are defined as irrelevant, and they find themselves classified as cases of some larger social problem.

There are many case studies of social interaction involving social problems workers and their subjects, including research on policing (e.g., Dabney, 2010; Meehan, 2000); prosecutors and courtrooms (Frohman, 1998; Holstein, 1993; Mackinem & Higgins, 2008); corrections (Fox, 1999); medicine (Maynard, 2003; Waitzkin, 1991); psychotherapy (Miller, 1997); and social welfare agencies (Miller, 1991). These reveal that social problems work is tricky, in that it requires balancing societal, institutional, and bureaucratic expectations, while negotiating with subjects to redefine their lives in terms of policymakers' constructions of social problems.

Policy Outcomes

Policy implementation does not end the social problems process. There are typically assessments and evaluations of the policy's workings and its effects. These may range from individuals recounting their first-hand experiences with social problems workers or commentators giving their impressions of how things are going, to much more formal efforts by evaluation researchers or blue-ribbon commissions. Critics may argue that a policy is insufficient (i.e., that it doesn't do enough), excessive (i.e., that it goes too far), or misguided (i.e., because the problem or the policy intended to address that problem have been framed in the wrong way). Institutions such as colleges may find their policies criticized from several sources at once, including students, faculty, parents, and the media (Sloan & Fisher, 2011). These critiques may come from various people: social problems workers may act as owners of the policies and propose various reforms to make them more effective (Dobbin, 2009); activists with different political ideologies may offer their assessments, which often reflect how closely the policy coincided with their constructions of the problem (Noy, 2009); policymakers (especially those who were unhappy with the policies when they were put into place) may decide to revisit the issue (Oberlander, 2003); or court rulings and legal scholarship may question a policy's legitimacy (D. Downs, 1996; Malloy, 2010).

Critiques about policy outcomes may adopt a range of rhetorical devices, from moral appeals to formal efforts to measure a policy's impact using evaluation research. The various critics frame their critiques in terms of their own perspectives and interests: those who favored the adoption of the existing policy (or who now benefit from its workings) are likely to argue that is insufficient; those who opposed the policy (or find themselves disadvantaged by its effects) are likely to claim that it is excessive or misguided. In other words, the policy and the social problem it was intended to address are reconstructed yet again. Often, this leads to a new set of claims that may relaunch another social problems process, so that social problems are best understood less as a linear process that starts with claims and ends with policy outcomes, than as a cycle in which claims lead to outcomes that inspire new claims.

This cycle is fundamentally constructionist and interactive. Individuals at every stage in the social problems process—claimsmakers, media workers, members of the public, policymakers, social problems workers, and those commenting on policy outcomes—must make sense of the social problem. Social problems are not constructed so much as they are continually reconstructed by different actors with their own concerns and constraints. An activist may be especially concerned with linking a social problem to a broader ideological framework, whereas a journalist may view those ideological elements as irrelevant, while trying to work with constraints of meeting a deadline and keeping a report within a particular word limit, even as a legislator may be worried about crafting a bill that can garner enough votes to gain passage yet withstand legal challenges once it is enacted, and a social problems worker will be particularly concerned with the practical considerations for implementing a policy. In each case, actors incorporate their own perspectives and situations in seeking to understand the problem and then convey their understanding—their construction—to others.

Moreover, the process is interactive, in that actors discover that some constructions don't produce the results they seek. Some claims inevitably fail to attract attention in the crowded, competitive social problems marketplace. In general, these failed claims need to be reworked, revised to be more effective, and often, this involves compromises. Vegetarian activists, who tend to be motivated by ethical considerations, discover that it is easier to attract new adherents by emphasizing health and ecological considerations, and downplaying moral issues; similarly, a legislator may include or exclude particular items in a bill solely to attract sufficient support to produce a majority vote. As a result, the histories of many social problems reveal constant, ongoing claimsmaking, as soon as one campaign leads to a new policy, new claims may emerge, framing the issue in different terms and calling for policy reform.

The Social Construction of Social Problems in its Larger Context

Because constructionist studies of social problems originated in late 20th-century American sociology, and because case studies became the accepted method for developing the perspective, the largest share of the constructionist literature that has emerged consists of cases studies of events in the contemporary United States. However, researchers have begun to extend the constructionist model across time (through historical studies) and space (through comparative research).

Constructionist Analyses of Historical Cases

The constructionist framework is useful for exploring historical topics. Social movements of the past (such as the campaign for Prohibition) or short-lived episodes of concern (such as crime waves or the Salem witch trials) can be analyzed in terms of claimsmaking, media coverage, and policymaking. The histories of social problems feature shifting constructions—new categories, new rationales for new policies, and so on (e.g., Trent, 1994). Although the conceptual vocabulary is somewhat different, this application of the constructionist framework is not that different from traditional historical analysis.

Social problems claims often feature historical elements; they incorporate collective memories about the problem's causes, or about earlier policies. These recollections are inevitably selective: they convert the past into a coherent story, highlighting some elements, even as others fall out of memory (E. A. Armstrong & Crage, 2006; Fine & McDonnell, 2007). These collective memories evolve over time, so that the past is constantly reconstructed to identify its relevance to present concerns (e.g., Kubal, 2008).

Moreover, there are more complex patterns. At different periods in American history, social movement activity has been more or less common (Goldstone, 1980). The decades immediately preceding the Civil War were marked, not just by abolitionist claims and counterclaims defending slavery, but by the first American social movement for women's rights, an active temperance campaign, anti-Irish rioting, and a wave of new religions. Similarly, the late-19th and early-20th centuries featured: intense opposition to the new immigration from Southern and Eastern Europe; the Prohibition movement; an anti-Black terror campaign in the South and an antilynching movement in the North; and the movement for women's suffrage. A third great wave of social movement activity began in the 1960s and continues—the civil rights movement, the feminist movement, the gay and lesbian movement, a new anti-immigration movement, the War on Drugs, and so on. Two patterns instantly become visible: it seems to be easier to mount claimsmaking campaigns in some eras than in others; and many of the same themes—especially race, gender, immigration, and drugs—seem to recur in each era.

Understanding why there seem to be waves of more and less intense claimsmaking draws attention to societal conditions. Obviously, the periods of intense ferment were periods of considerable social change, including significant developments in the media used to publicize claims. But this explanation ignores that fact that significant changes have been occurring throughout virtually all of American history, and that media have continued to expand almost constantly. What is noticeable is that serious societal disruptions—the Civil

War, both World Wars, and the Great Depression—diverted attention from most social problems claimsmaking.

Another historical pattern deserves attention: concern about particular social problems tends to wax and wane. For instance, urban gangs were the subjects of considerable concern in the late 1920s and early 1930s, in the 1950s, and again in the late 1980s and early 1990s. Similar wavelike patterns are apparent in the histories of other social problems, including child molestation and cults (Jenkins, 1998, 2000). There is no strong evidence that these waves of concern reflect real fluctuations in, say, the level of gang activity; rather, they seem to be waves of attention. This pattern may be the result of the issue–attention cycle, in that successful claimsmaking campaigns attract considerable attention, but then enthusiasm declines once it becomes evident that whatever policy changes resulted from the campaign, while they may have reduced the problem, they have failed to eradicate it (A. Downs, 1972).

Constructionist Comparisons among Nations

A second sort of comparison is geographic, rather than temporal. Constructions of social problems emerge in particular places and reflect the culture and social structures of those locales. Even cities in the same country may construct a problem differently (Bogard, 2003). However, most analysts focus on differences in how problems are constructed in different nations (Benson & Saguy, 2005; Boyle, Songora, & Foss, 2001; Burgess, 2004; Ferree, Gamson, Gerhards, & Rucht, 2002; Lee, 2003; Saguy, 2003; Saguy & Gruys, 2010; Saguy, Gruys, & Gong, 2010). Typically, these studies use cultural or structural differences among nations—cultural resources, the relative influence of different institutions, policymaking arrangements, and so on—to explain differences in how some social problem is constructed or a policy is devised and implemented.

Thanks to globalization, these national constructions are increasingly linked. Mass media, the Internet, and interlocking social networks make it easy for news about claims and policies to spread across national boundaries (J. Best, 2001b). Through this process of diffusion, some elements may be copied, even as others are altered to reflect conditions in other societies. Thus, Lee (2003) describes campaigns to construct postabortion syndrome as a social problem encountered very different institutional obstacles in the United States and Britain, while Burgess (2004) notes that Americans and Europeans fixed on very different interpretations of the risks of cell phones. In general, claims spread more easily when the countries involved share language and culture (e.g., the United States and Canada), whereas problems and policies are likely to undergo substantial reconstruction when the members of the nations involved define themselves as quite different from one another (e.g., the United States and France) (Benson & Saguy, 2005; Saguy, 2003; Saguy, Gruys, & Gong, 2010).

In addition, globalization encourages the emergence of claimsmaking about conditions in other countries, even when those conditions may not be defined as social problems by most people in the countries affected (Agustín, 2007; Boyle, Songora, & Foss, 2001). These campaigns may enlist the claimsmakers' governments to put diplomatic pressure on the target countries, or those countries may be pressed to ratify and enact international treaties directed at the social problems, or nongovernmental agencies may press for reforms. Some of these campaigns may target practices within other countries (e.g., female genital cutting); others may define the movement of goods or people across borders as social problems.

Social Problems as a Complex System

I have argued that social problems need to be viewed as a social process, rather than as social conditions. The model that I have used to organize this essay identifies six stages in this process: claimsmaking, media coverage, public reactions, policymaking, social problems work, and policy outcomes. However, this linear model oversimplifies the process. Not all social problems pass through all of these stages, or in this order; well-connected insider claimsmakers may be able to bypass the media and the public, and present their claims directly to policymakers, for instance. The entire process may be circular, as debates over policy outcomes may launch a new claimsmaking campaign. At each stage, individuals—often in disputes with rivals and opponents—are actively constructing and reconstructing the meaning of the social problem; they are also affected by feedback, as reactions to claims shape what they want to say next.

In other words, social problems are profoundly interactive, affected by timing, location, and social context. Social problems constitute a complex system, in which processes develop in unexpected ways (Watts, 2011). The study of the sociology of social problems has just begun.

Afterword

Obviously, sociologists are hardly the only ones who study what many now call social problems, and I suspect that most researchers in other disciplines, like most sociologists, are interested in studying the nature, causes, and remedies for particular problems. However, it is sociologists, and particularly constructionist sociologists, who have made the most concerted effort to devise a general framework for understanding social problems as a general phenomenon.

Viewing social problems as a process requires thinking about a host of topics—including rhetoric, social movements, expertise, mass media, public opinion, folklore, policymaking, professions, and policy evaluation—that are studied by researchers in other disciplines. While much of this work adopts very different theoretical assumptions, the diffusion of the idea of social construction has led to constructionist literatures in other disciplines, such as political science and social work. My own sense is that much of this work has received little or no attention from sociologists.

I do not presume, therefore, that the ideas of constructionist sociologists of social problems have no parallels in the communications literature. Nor do I assume that all communications scholars are completely unfamiliar with what the constructionists have done. Rather, I have written an overview of this literature because I am confident that it touches upon what I imagine to be the concerns of communications scholars at various points, and because, knowing how difficult it is for someone specializing in this area to keep abreast of developments, I assume that at least some of this material will be unfamiliar to virtually all this essay's readers. Toward this end, I have tried to survey a broad range of constructionist work, and I have made a special effort to draw attention to relatively recent sources.

References

Agustín, L. M. (2007). *Sex at the margins: Migration, labour markets and the rescue industry.* London: Zed.

Amenta, E., Caren, N., Olasky, S. J., & Stobaugh, J. E. (2009). All the movements fit to print: Who, what, when, where, and why SMO families appeared in the New York Times in the twentieth century. *American Sociological Review, 74,* 636–656.

Appleton, L. M. (1995). Rethinking medicalization: Alcoholism and anomalies. In J. Best (Ed.), *Images of issues: Typifying contemporary social problem* (2nd ed., pp. 59–80). Hawthorne, NY: Aldine de Gruyter.

Armstrong, E. A., & Crage, S. M. (2006). Movements and memory: The making of the Stonewall myth. *American Sociological Review, 71,* 724–751.

Armstrong, E. M. (2003). *Conceiving risk, bearing responsibility: Fetal alcohol syndrome and the diagnosis of moral disorder.* Baltimore, MD: Johns Hopkins University Press.

Bartesaghi, M., & Castor, T. (2008). Social construction in communication: Re-constituting the conversation. *Communication Yearbook* (Vol. 32, pp. 3–39). Mahwah, NJ: Erlbaum.

Bartley, T. (2007). How foundations shape social movements: The construction of an organizational field and the rise of forest certification. *Social Problems, 54,* 229–254.

Benford, R. D. (1993). Frame disputes within the nuclear disarmament movement. *Social Forces, 71,* 677–701.

Benford, R. D., & Hunt, S. A. (1992). Dramaturgy and social movements: The social construction and communication of power. *Sociological Inquiry, 62,* 36–55.

Benford, R. D., & Hunt, S. A. (2003). Interactional dynamics in public problems marketplaces: Movements and the counterframing and reframing of public problems. In J. A. Holstein & G. Miller (Eds.), *Challenges and choices: Constructionist perspectives on social problems* (pp. 153–186). Hawthorne, NY: Aldine de Gruyter.

Benford, R. D., & Snow, D. A. (2000). Framing processes and social movements: An overview and assessment. *Annual Review of Sociology, 26,* 611–639.

Benson, R., & Saguy, A. C. (2005). Constructing social problems in an age of globalization: A French–American comparison. *American Sociological Review, 70,* 233–259.

Berger, P. L., & Luckmann, T. (1966). *The social construction of reality: A treatise in the sociology of knowledge.* Garden City, NY: Doubleday.

Berns, N. (2004). *Framing the victim: Domestic violence, media, and social problems.* Hawthorne, NY: Aldine de Gruyter.

Berns, N. (2011). *Closure: The rush to end grief and what it costs us.* Philadelphia, PA: Temple University Press.

Best, J. (1990). *Threatened children: Rhetoric and concern about child-victims.* Chicago, IL: University of Chicago Press.

Best, J. (Ed.). (1995). *Images of issues: Typifying contemporary social problems* (2nd ed.). Hawthorne, NY: Aldine de Gruyter.

Best, J. (1999). *Random violence: How we talk about new crimes and new victims.* Berkeley: University of California Press.

Best, J. (2001a). *Damned lies and statistics: Untangling numbers from the media, politicians, and activists.* Berkeley: University of California Press.

Best, J. (Ed.). (2001b). *How claims spread: Cross-national diffusion of social problems.* Hawthorne, NY: Aldine de Gruyter.

Best, J. (2004). *More damned lies and statistics: How numbers confuse public issues.* Berkeley: University of California Press.

Best, J. (2008). *Social problems.* New York: Norton.

Best, J., & Furedi, F. (2001). The evolution of road rage in Britain and the United States. In J. Best (Ed.), *How claims spread: Cross-national diffusion of social problems* (pp. 107–127). Hawthorne, NY: Aldine de Gruyter.

Best, R. (2010). Situation or social problem: The influence of events on media coverage of homelessness. *Social Problems, 57,* 74–91.

Bishop, G. F. (2005). *The illusion of public opinion: Fact and artifact in American public opinion polls.* Lanham, MD: Rowman & Littlefield.

Blumer, H. (1971). Social problems as collective behavior. *Social Problems, 18,* 298–306.

Bogard, C. J. (2003). *Seasons such as these: How homelessness took shape in America.* Hawthorne, NY: Aldine de Gruyter.

Boyle, E. H., Songora, F., & Foss, G. (2001). International discourse and local politics: Anti-female-genital-cutting laws in Egypt, Tanzania, and the United States. *Social Problems, 48,* 524–544.

Burgess, A. (2004). *Cellular phones, public fears, and a culture of precaution.* Cambridge, England: Cambridge University Press.

Burgess, A., Donovan, P., & Moore, S. E. H. (2009). Embodying uncertainty: Understanding heightened risk perception of drink "spiking." *British Journal of Criminology, 49,* 848–862.

Burstein, P. (1991). Policy domains: Organization, culture, and policy outcomes. *Annual Review of Sociology, 17,* 327–350.

Burstein, P. (2006). Why estimates of the impact of public opinion on public policy are too high: Empirical and theoretical implications. *Social Forces, 84,* 2273–2289.

Burstein, P., & Bricher, M. (1997). Problem definition and public policy: Congressional committees confront work, family, and gender, 1945–1990. *Social Forces, 75,* 135–169.

Burstein, P., & Hirsch, C. E. (2007). Interest organizations, information, and policy innovation in the U.S. Congress. *Sociological Forum, 22,* 174–199.

Burstein, P., & Linton, A. (2002). The impact of political parties, interest groups, and social movement organizations on public policy: Some recent evidence and theoretical concerns. *Social Forces, 81,* 380–408

Callaghan, K., & Schnell, F., (Eds.). (2005). *Framing American politics.* Pittsburgh, PA: University of Pittsburgh Press.

Case, C. M. (1924). What is a social problem? *Journal of Applied Sociology, 8,* 268–273.

Clarke, A. E., Shim, J. K., Mamo, L., Fosket, J. R., & Fishman, J. R. (2003). Biomedicalization: Technoscientific transformations of health, illness, and U.S. biomedicine. *American Sociological Review, 68,* 161–194.

Conrad, P. (2007). *The medicalization of society: On the transformation of human conditions into treatable disorders.* Baltimore, MD: Johns Hopkins University Press.

Dabney, D. (2010). Observations regarding key operational realities in a Compstat model of policing. *Justice Quarterly, 27,* 28–51.

Davies, N. (2008). *Flat earth news.* London: Vintage.

Davis, J. E. (2005). *Accounts of innocence: Sexual abuse, trauma, and the self.* Chicago, IL: University of Chicago Press.

Dobbin, F. (2009). *Inventing equal opportunity.* Princeton, NJ: Princeton University Press.

Donovan, P. (2004). *No way of knowing: Crime, urban legends, and the internet.* New York: Routledge.

Douglas, J. D. (Ed.). (1970). *Deviance and respectability: The social construction of moral meanings.* New York: Basic Books.

Downs, A. (1972). Up and down with ecology—The "issue-attention cycle." *Public Interest, 28,* 38–50.

Downs, D. A. (1996). *More than victims: Battered women, the syndrome society, and the law.* Chicago, IL: University of Chicago Press.

Dundes, A. (1987). *Cracking jokes.* Berkeley, CA: Ten Speed Press.

Dunn, J. (2010). *Judging victims: Why we stigmatize survivors and how they reclaim respect.* Boulder, CO: Lynne Rienner.

Eaton, M. (2010). Manufacturing community in an online activist organization. *Information, Communication & Society, 13,* 174–192.

Fassin, D., & Rechtman, R. (2009). *The empire of trauma: An inquiry into the condition of victimhood.* Princeton, NJ: Princeton University Press.

Ferree, M. M., Gamson, W. A., Gerhards, J., & Rucht, D. (2002). *Shaping abortion discourse: Democracy and the public sphere in Germany and the United States.* New York: Cambridge University Press.

Filler, D. M. (2000). Random violence and the transformation of the juvenile justice debate. *Virginia Law Review, 86,* 1095–1125.

Fine, G. A. (2007). *Authors of the storm: Meteorologists and the culture of prediction.* Chicago, IL: University of Chicago Press.

Fine, G. A., Campion-Vincent, V., & Heath, C. (Eds.). (2005). *Rumor mills: The social impact of rumor and legend.* New Brunswick, NJ: Aldine Transaction.

Fine, G. A., & Ellis, B. (2010). *The global grapevine: Why rumors of terrorism, immigration, and trade matter.* New York: Oxford University Press.

Fine, G. A., & McDonnell, T. (2007). Erasing the brown scare: Referential afterlife and the power of memory templates. *Social Problems, 54,* 170–187.

Foster, E., & Bochner, A. P. (2008). Social constructionist perspectives in communication research. In J. A. Holstein & J. F. Gubrium (Eds.), *Handbook of constructionist research* (pp. 85–106). New York: Guilford.

Fox, K. J. (1999). Changing violent minds: Discursive correction and resistance in the cognitive treatment of violent offenders in prison. *Social Problems, 46,* 88–103.

Frohmann, L. (1998). Constituting power in sexual assault cases: Prosecutorial strategies for victim management. *Social Problems, 45,* 393–407.

Fuller, R. C., & Myers, R. R. (1941). Some aspects of a theory of social problems. *American Sociological Review, 6,* 24–32.

Gamson, W. A., & Modigliani, A. (1989). Media discourse and public opinion on nuclear power: A constructionist approach. *American Journal of Sociology, 95,* 1–37.

Gans, H. J. (1979). *Deciding what's news.* New York: Pantheon.

Goffman, E. (1974). *Frame analysis: An essay on the organization of experience.* New York: Harper & Row.

Goldstone, J. A. (1980). The weakness of organization. *American Journal of Sociology, 85,* 1017–1042.

Goode, E., & Ben-Yehuda, N. (2009). *Moral panics: The social construction of deviance* (2nd ed.). New York: Wiley-Blackwell.

Goss, K. A. (2006). *Disarmed: The missing movement for gun control in America.* Princeton, NJ: Princeton University Press.

Gould, D. B. (2009). *Moving politics: Emotion and ACT UP's fight against AIDS.* Chicago, IL: University of Chicago Press.

Gusfield, J. R. (1967). Moral passage: The symbolic process in public designations of deviance. *Social Problems, 15,* 175–188.

Gusfield, J. R. (1981). *The culture of public problems: Drinking-driving and the symbolic order.* Chicago, IL: University of Chicago Press.

Hacking, I. (1999). *The social construction of what?* Cambridge, MA: Harvard University Press.

Harris, R. A. (Ed.). (1997). *Landmark essays on rhetoric of science.* Mahwah, NJ: Erlbaum.

Harris, S. R. (2006). *The meanings of marital equality.* Albany, NY: SUNY Press.

Harris, S. R. (2010). *What is constructionism? Navigating its use in sociology.* Boulder, CO: Lynne Rienner.

Heath, C., Bell, C., & Sternberg, E. (2001). Emotional selection in memes: The case of urban legends. *Journal of Personality and Social Psychology, 81,* 1028–1041.

Hilgartner, S., & Bosk, C. L. (1988). The rise and fall of social problems. *American Journal of Sociology, 94,* 53–78.

Holstein, J. A. (1993). *Court-ordered insanity: Interpretive practice and involuntary commitment.* Hawthorne, NY: Aldine de Gruyter.

Holstein, J. A., & Gubrium, J. F. (Eds.). (2008). *Handbook of constructionist research.* New York: Guilford.

Horwitz, A. V. (2002). *Creating mental illness.* Chicago, IL: University of Chicago Press.

Ibarra, P. R., & Kitsuse, J. I. (1993). Vernacular constituents of moral discourse: An interactionist proposal for the study of social problems. In J. A. Holstein & G. Miller (Eds.), *Reconsidering social constructionism: Debates in social problems theory* (pp. 5–23). Hawthorne, NY: Aldine de Gruyter.

Jenkins, P. (1998). *Moral panic: Changing concepts of the child molester in modern America.* New Haven, CT: Yale University Press.

Jenkins, P. (1999). *Synthetic panics: The symbolic politics of designer drugs.* New York: New York University Press.

Jenkins, P. (2000). *Mystics and messiahs: Cults and new religions in American history.* New York: Oxford University Press.

Jenness, V., & Grattet, R. (2001). *Making hate a crime: From social movement to law enforcement.* New York: Russell Sage Foundation.

Johnson, J. M. (1995). Horror stories and the construction of child abuse. In J. Best (Ed.), *Images of issues: Typifying contemporary social problems* (2nd ed., pp. 17–31). Hawthorne, NY: Aldine de Gruyter.

Keränan, L. (2010). *Scientific characters: Rhetoric, Politics, and trust in breast cancer research.* Tuscaloosa: University of Alabama Press.

Kingdon, J. W. (1984). *Agendas, alternatives, and public policies.* New York: HarperCollins.

Kubal, T. (2008). *Cultural movements and collective memory: Christopher Columbus and the rewriting of the national origin myth.* New York: Palgrave Macmillan.

Latour, B., & Woolgar, S. (1979). *Laboratory life: The social construction of scientific facts.* Beverly Hills, CA: Sage.

Lee, E. (2003). *Abortion, motherhood, and mental health: Medicalizing reproduction in the United States and Great Britain.* Hawthorne, NY: Aldine de Gruyter.

Lofland, J. (1993). *Polite protesters: The American peace movement of the 1980s.* Syracuse, NY: Syracuse University Press.

Loseke, D. R. (1992). *The battered woman and shelters: The social construction of wife abuse.* Albany, NY: SUNY Press.

Loseke, D. R. (2003). *Thinking about social problems* (2nd ed.). Hawthorne, NY: Aldine de Gruyter.

Loseke, D. R. (2009). Examining emotion as discourse: Emotion codes and presidential speeches justifying war. *Sociological Quarterly, 50,* 497–524.

Lowney, K. S. (1999). *Baring our souls: TV talks shows and the religion of recovery.* Hawthorne, NY: Aldine de Gruyter.

Mackinem, M. B., & Higgins, P. (2008). *Drug court: Constructing the moral identity of drug offenders.* Springfield, IL: Thomas.

Malloy, T. F. (2010). The social construction of regulation: Lessons from the war against command and control. *Buffalo Law Review, 58,* 267–355.

Mann, R. M. (2000). *Who owns domestic abuse? The local politics of a social problem.* Toronto, Canada: University of Toronto Press.

Maratea, R. (2008). The e-rise and fall of social problems: The blogosphere as a public arena. *Social Problems, 55,* 139–160.

Maynard, D. W. (2003). *Bad news, good news: Conversational order in everyday talk and clinical settings.* Chicago, IL: University of Chicago Press.

McAdam, D. (1983). Tactical innovation and the pace of insurgency. *American Sociological Review, 48,* 735–754.

McCarthy, J. D., & Zald, M. N. (1977). Resource mobilization and social movements. *American Journal of Sociology, 82,* 1212–1241.

McCright, A. M., & Dunlap, R. E. (2003). Defeating Kyoto: The conservative movement's impact of U.S. climate change policy. *Social Problems, 50,* 348–373.

Meehan, A. J. (2000). The organizational career of gang statistics: The politics of policing gangs. *Sociological Quarterly, 41,* 337–370.

Meyer, D. S. (2004). Protest and political opportunities. *Annual Review of Sociology, 30,* 479–506.

Miller, G. (1991). *Enforcing the work ethic: Rhetoric and everyday life in a work incentive program.* Albany, NY: SUNY Press.

Miller, G. (1997). *Becoming miracle workers: Language and meaning in brief therapy.* Hawthorne, NY: Aldine de Gruyter.

Monahan, B. A. (2010). *The shock of the news: Media coverage and the making of 9/11.* New York: New York University Press.

Nelson, B. J. (1984). *Making an issue of child abuse: Political agenda setting for social problems.* Chicago, IL: University of Chicago Press.

Nichols, L. T. (1997). Social problems as landmark narratives: Bank of Boston, mass media and "money laundering." *Social Problems, 44,* 324–341.

Noy, D. (2009). When framing fails: Ideas, influence, and resources in San Francisco's homeless policy field. *Social Problems, 56,* 223–242.

Oberlander, J. (2003). *The political life of Medicare.* Chicago, IL: University of Chicago Press.

Pfohl, S. J. (1977). The "discovery" of child abuse. *Social Problems, 24,* 310–323.

Pielke, R. A., Jr. (2007). *The honest broker: Making sense of science in policy and politics.* New York: Cambridge University Press.

Placier, M. (1996). The cycle of student labels in education: The cases of culturally deprived/disadvantaged and at risk. *Educational Administration Quarterly, 32,* 236–270.

Polletta, F., & Lee, J. (2006). Is telling stories good for democracy?: Rhetoric in public deliberation after 9/11. *American Sociological Review, 71,* 699–723.

Reinhardt, J. M. (1929). Trends in the teaching of "social problems" in colleges and universities in the United States. *Social Forces, 7,* 379–384.

Rose, V. McN. (1977). Rape as a social problem: A byproduct of the feminist movement. *Social Problems, 25,* 75–89.

Sacco, V. (2005). When crime waves. Thousand Oaks, CA: Sage.

Saguy, A. C. (2003). *What is sexual harassment? From Capitol Hill to the Sorbonne.* Berkeley: University of California Press.

Saguy, A. C., & Gruys, K. (2010). Morality and health: Constructions of overweight and eating disorders. *Social Problems, 57,* 231–250.

Saguy, A. C., Gruys, K., & Gong, S. (2010). Social problem construction and national context: News reporting on "overweight" and "obesity" in the United States and France. *Social Problems, 57,* 586–610.

Sasson, T. (1995). *Crime talk: How citizens construct a social problem.* Hawthorne, NY: Aldine de Gruyter.

Schneider, A. L., & Ingram, H. M. (1993). Social constructions of target populations: Implications for politics and policy. *American Political Science Review, 87,* 334–347.

Schneider, A. L., & Ingram, H. M. (Eds.). (2005). *Deserving and entitled: Social constructions and public policy.* Albany, NY: SUNY Press.

Schwartz, H. (1997). On the origin of the phrase "social problems." *Social Problems, 44,* 276–296.

Segal, J. Z. (2005.). *Health and the rhetoric of medicine.* Carbondale: Southern Illinois University Press.

Shostak, S., Conrad, P., & Horwitz, A. V. (2008). Sequencing and its consequences: Path dependence and the relationships between genetics and medicalization. *American Journal of Sociology, 114,* S287–S316.

Sloan, J. J. III, & Fisher, B. S. (2011). *The dark side of the ivory tower: Campus crime as a social problem.* New York: Cambridge University Press.

Snow, D. A., Rochford, E. B. Jr., Worden, S. K., &. Benford, R. D. (1986). Frame alignment processes, micromobilization, and movement participation. *American Sociological Review, 51,* 464–481.

Snow, D. A., Soule, S. A., & Kriese, H. (Eds.). (2004). *The Blackwell companion to social movements.* Malden, MA: Blackwell.

Sobieraj, S. (2011). *Soundbitten: The perils of media-centered political activism.* New York: New York University Press.

Spector, M., & Kitsuse, J. I. (1977). *Constructing social problems.* Menlo Park, CA: Cummings.

Staller, K. M. (2006). *Runaways: How the sixties counterculture shaped today's policies and practices.* New York: Columbia University Press.

Stallings, R. A. (1995). *Promoting risk: Constructing the earthquake threat.* Hawthorne, NY: Aldine de Gruyter.

Stevens, S. McK., & Malesh, P. (Eds.). (2009). *Active voices: Composing a rhetoric of social movements.* Albany, NY: SUNY Press.

Stone, D. A. (1989). Causal stories and the formation of policy agendas. *Political Science Quarterly, 104,* 281–300.

Taylor, V. (1989). Social movement continuity: The women's movement in abeyance. *American Sociological Review, 54,* 761–775.

Tetlock, P. E. (2005). *Expert political judgment: How good is it? How can we know?* Princeton, NJ: Princeton University Press.

Toulmin, S. E. (1958). *The uses of argument.* Cambridge, England: Cambridge University Press.

Trent, J. W., Jr. (1994). *Inventing the feeble mind: A history of mental retardation in the United States.* Berkeley: University of California Press.

Tuchman, G. (1978). *Making news: A study in the construction of reality.* New York: Free Press.

Turow, J. (1997). *Breaking up America: Advertisers and the new media world.* Chicago, IL: University of Chicago Press.

Ungar, S. (1998). Bringing the issue back in: Comparing the marketability of the ozone hole and global warming. *Social Problems, 45,* 510–527.

Waitzkin, H. (1991). *The politics of medical encounters: How patients and doctors deal with social problems.* New Haven, CT: Yale University Press.

Waller, W. (1936). Social problems and the mores. *American Sociological Review, 1,* 922–933.

Watts, D. J. (2011). *Everything is obvious*: *Once you know the answer.* New York: Crown Business.

Weidenbaum, M. (2009). *The competition of ideas: The world of Washington think tanks.* New Brunswick, NJ: Transaction.

Whittier, N. (2009). *The politics of child sexual abuse: Emotion, social movements, and the state.* New York: Oxford University Press.

Woolgar, S., & Pawluch, D. (1985a). Ontological gerrymandering: The anatomy of social problems explanations. *Social Problems, 32*(3), 214–227.

Woolgar, S., & Pawluch, D. (1985b). How shall we move beyond constructivism? *Social Problems, 33*(2), 159–162.

12 *Commentary*
The Industrial Construction of Audiences in Mass Media Industries
Notes toward a Research Agenda

Joseph Turow

University of Pennsylvania

Joel Best's article sketches ways that researchers have adopted social constructionism to illuminate important dynamics among individuals and institutions. One topic Best does not describe is the usefulness of taking a constructionist perspective with respect to media audiences. That is the aim of this contribution. It starts by noting that for many years studies of U.S. media industries have implicitly or explicitly suggested that media practitioners fundamentally *create* their audiences. It explores implications of this suggestion as well as the need for new ways to think about the media system's audience constructions as the 21st century unfolds.

During the past several decades many academics who have explored the processes through which media organizations create content have commented on the ways in which industry practitioners consider their audiences. Through much of the 1970s and sometimes beyond, the idea that audiences are constructs was typically implicit, embedded in the findings. The researchers often underscored the cognitive as well as physical distance of media workers (typically content producers) from the people who engage with the workers' creations. Reflecting this idea in a historical comment focusing on journalism studies, InCheol Min (2004) notes "Mass communication researchers (Atkin, Burgoon, & Burgoon, 1983; Darnton, 1990; Gaunt, 1990; Schlesinger, 1978) argued that professional mass communicators do not really know their actual audiences. Schlesinger (1978: 107) stated that 'total audience remains an abstraction, made real on occasion by letters or telephone calls, encounters of a random kind in public places, or perhaps more structured ones such as conversations with liftmen, barmen and taxi-drivers'" (p. 452).

The researchers agree on the difficulty of grasping the "real" audience, but they split over the importance of audience conceptions for the creation process. Some contended that the significance and nature of mass communication are determined in large part by notions which the practitioners hold of their audiences (e.g., Bauer, 1966; Pool & Schulman, 1959; Riley & Riley, 1951).

Another group of academics (e.g., Breed, 1952; Gieber, 1956) tended to minimize the importance of the audience to producers of mass media content. This was Herbert Gans's (1979) view, when he commented that, "Although they [i.e., national news magazine and network television journalists he studied] had a vague image of the audience, they paid little attention to it; instead, they filmed and wrote for their superiors and for themselves, assuming ... that what interested them would interest the audience" (p. 230).

As Min suggests, journalism researchers were dominant among media scholars who wrote about the difficulty practitioners had of grasping the audience. But Muriel Cantor (1971) took a similar tack in her study of Hollywood television producers during the 1960s. She found that not only did those practitioners not have specific knowledge of viewers' likes and dislikes, viewers were collectively not the most important "audience" for those key figures in the creation of television programs. Instead, the key audience figures were the network executives whom the producers had to convince to green-light their ideas and provide the cash to help them move the shows forward. Reflecting this conclusion, Gaye Tuchman (1974) asserted regarding "the TV establishment" that "All available research indicates that the influence of the audience is, at most, indirect" (p. 4).

From around the 1980s onward, writers on media organizations were more likely than in earlier years to take an explicitly constructionist perspective regarding the audience. For example, while investigating the role "children" play in the children's book industry of the mid-1970s, I noted that they are a "constructed audience" (Turow 1982, p. 97; see also Turow, 1978a, 1978b). I argued that the varied constructions I found of children were the result of different reward systems in the relationships between different sets of publishers and book outlets (stores and libraries). Similarly, writing about the major U.S. television networks, Ien Ang (1991) suggested that television executives reflect their industry's constraints when they construct, and try to control, their audience. And James Ettema and Charles Whitney (1994) edited a book around the proposition that a "fundamental task of communicator studies ... is to explain how mass communication organizations, understood to be components of industry systems, manage the processes of audiencemaking" (p. 5).

None of the authors in the Ettema and Whitney volume mentioned the Internet. That should not be too surprising because it was only in the year of the book's publication (1994) that the Netscape company released the first widely popular graphical web browser. Its ease of use marked the beginning of a revolution in the ways billions of people around the world learn about, access, create, and share various forms of news, entertainment, education, and advertising. In the ensuing years, researchers from across academia have struggled to understand the implications of the online world and the digital technologies connected to it. Built into their work is a new debate about the power of people whom academics have historically called the audience but who now receive a variety of appellations depending on the writer's point of view.

Nicholas Negroponte's 1995 book *Being Digital* grabbed an early influential position in the discussion. Negroponte headed the Massachusetts Institute of Technology's Media Lab, a hothouse for computer-based inventions supported by major corporations. He enthused about how communication technologies of the early 21st century would give all of us power to define ourselves; they would allow us to become the captains of our own attention, to focus our interests on what we value. "Your telephone won't ring indiscriminately," he wrote. "It will receive, sort, and perhaps respond to your incoming calls like a well-trained English butler" (Negroponte, 1995, p. 6).

The idea that individuals would reign over their media destinies in the 21st century got a lot of traction, pro and con. An important book to trumpet the idea positively from economic and legal standpoints was Yochai Benkler's *The Wealth of Networks* (2006). It forecast that the technological openness and flexibility of the Internet would allow individuals unprecedented opportunities to collaborate outside of traditional business frameworks toward the creation of an astonishing new world. He and others (e.g., Jenkins, 2006; Shirky, 2010) argued that the new technologies provided people with previously unheard of levels of power to follow personal interests or collective interests that would benefit society. In contrast to this celebratory view, Cass Sunstein took a negative slant in his book *Republic.com* and in related writings. To Sunstein (2007), the ability to customize news sites by topic, to skip unpalatable topics, and to find comfort in like-minded ideological blogs meant that people can live in idea cocoons of their own making, or of their making in collaboration with people who agree with them—what Sunstein called "cyber-polarization."

The word *audience* is probably not the best term to describe the role that thinkers in the tradition of Negroponte, Benkler, Sunstein, Jenkins, and Shirky saw for the digitally enabled. They would likely note the word privileges *consumption* over *production* in an environment very much involved in both, often at the same time. That some academics prefer *users, producers*, and similar terms indicates how important the awareness of individuals' power in the digital world is to them. The basic point is quite reasonable. Digital technologies *are* providing more people than ever with the tools to be media makers and so to reach out to more people than ever. Similarly clear in the new media landscape is the proposition that individuals are captains of their own interpretations and increasingly use them as starting points to create culturally exciting or politically dangerous worlds of understanding for themselves and others.

Yet these contentions, and those of others about digital-powers-to-the-people, beg important questions that the proponents of such views almost never raise: How broad and deep is this power by individuals and volunteer networks of collaborators compared to the large institutional brokers of cultural and political power in society? Is the new individual or group autonomy the central force that will shape the way Americans and others learn about the world and realize opportunities to benefit from it, or will other emerging factors be more important, more decisive?

A growing stream of academic writing argues that despite these changes the hub of power in the emerging digital environment is comprised not of interconnected individuals but of interconnected corporations that often exercise their clout by encouraging people to think that they—the people—are shaping the media. These writers see the liberational experiences that Jenkins and others have mentioned as actual components of strategies for exploitation. Detlev Zwick, Sanyek Bonsu, and Arib Darmody (2008), for example, argue that media executives

> have begun to realize the benefit of providing individuals with places for playful production of their own consumption experiences, a fact demonstrated by the popularity of numerous massively multiplayer online role-playing games (MMOGs), open-source and hacker cultures, and fan communities.... Always on the lookout for new ideas, products, and services to market, managers are seeking ways to appropriate, control, and valorize the creativity of the common. (p. 174)

Similarly, Mark Andrejevic (2007) highlights various forms of corporate digital surveillance in an attempt to counter what he calls "the ongoing attempt to equate new media technologies with the promise of empowerment, individuation, and creative control" (p. 17).

Andrejevic (2007) argues bluntly that reality shows and user-generated content sites such as Facebook are direct examples of free labor in the interest of corporate profits. Other views try to accommodate both individual interests and corporate power. Tiziana Terranova (2004), for example, allows for the complexity of the situation. She emphasizes that in blogs, Facebook, YouTube, MySpace, and so many other places in the digital economy, the free labor of consumers "is simultaneously voluntarily given and unwaged, enjoyed and exploited" (p. 73). Jose Van Dijck (2009) pushes this understanding even further, arguing for "user agency as a complex concept involving not only his cultural role as a facilitator of civic engagement and participation, but also his economic meaning as a producer, consumer, and data provider, as well as the user's volatile position in the labour market" (p. 55).

Implicit in all these attempts to push back against a view of the autonomous media participant is the idea that firms in the new media space construct them based on the firms' needs—and that these constructions have profound social consequences. Recent work that I conducted on transformations in the advertising industry as a result of the digital revolution (Turow, 2011) carries this idea forward. I studied the new media-buying system. It is comprised of organizations that decide which people advertisers should target and what media they should use to do it. Fundamentally, media-buying is a business based on the industrial construction of audiences. I found that while some writers believe the digital-media world is rooted in empowering the audience and respecting it, the media-buying system exhibits a fundamental lack of audience respect even as its practitioners use rhetorics of consumer power to hide it. None of this denies the spaces for independence of individual and group action that Jenkins, Negroponte, Benkler, Shirky, Sunstein, and others identify in the new environment. My research made clear, though, that these spaces are channeled by industry logics shaped by new media-buying mindsets. These constraints speak directly to whether, when, and how items are presented to particular audiences for attention. Increasingly, I argue, it is the media-buying system that is the prime mover in the emerging digital world.

I fully expect some will disagree. I hope they will concur, though, that social constructionism in the context of research on media-industry structures and outcomes can help address questions about the relative power and position of different actors in the new media system. One new challenge is to understand the "audience" imaginings of those in the audience who participate in the production process. Comparisons of ways paid practitioners and unpaid *producers* (bloggers, tweeters, website creators, video makers, app makers, Facebook contributors) think about the audiences they need/want to reach and the constraints they note in trying to reach them may provide new slants on notions of *professional* and *amateur*. Such explorations might also add insights to policy discussions about such hot-button issues as privacy and data-management as well as to academic theories regarding the creation of news, entertainment, and advertising. Comparisons of how producers construct themselves and their contributions with the ways a site's executives construct them and their contributions can illuminate the extent and nature of tensions coursing through new production-of-culture fields. The same can be said of comparisons of ways that producers construct media executives and their contributions with the ways the executives see themselves and their mandates. Using the lens Joel Best has described nicely, these and other broad approaches to *audience* can open fascinating windows into the struggles that are forming the digital-media environment in which we live.

References

Andrejevic, M. (2007). *iSpy*. Lawrence: University Press of Kansas.

Ang, I. (1991). *Desperately seeking the audience*. London: Routledge.

Atkin, C. K., Burgoon, J. K., & Burgoon, M. (1983). How journalists perceive the reading audience. *Newspaper Research Journal 4*, 51–63.

Bauer, R. A. (1966). *Social indicators*. Cambridge, MA: MIT Press.

Benkler, Y. (2006). *The wealth of networks: How social production transforms markets and freedom*. New Haven, CT: Yale University Press.

Breed, W. (1952). *The newspaperman, news, and society*. New York: Arno Press.

Cantor, M. G. (1971). *The Hollywood TV producer, his work and his audience*. New York: Basic Books.

Darnton, R. (1990). *The kiss of the Lamourette: Reflections in cultural history*. New York: Norton.

Ettema, J. S., & Whitney, D. C. (1994). *Audiencemaking: How the media create the audience*. Thousand Oaks, CA: Sage.

Gans, H. J. (1979). *Deciding what's news: A study of CBS Evening News, NBC Nightly News, Newsweek, and Time*. New York: Pantheon Books.

Gaunt, P. (1990). *Choosing the news: The profit factor in news selection*. New York: Greenwood.

Gieber, W. (1956). Across the desk: A study of 16 telegraph editors. *Journalism Quarterly 33*, 423–432.

Jenkins, H. (2006). *Convergence culture: Where old and new media collide*. New York: New York University Press.

Min, I. (2004). Perceptions of the audience by the alternative press producers: A case study of the Texas Observer. *Media, Culture & Society 26*(3), 450–458.

Negroponte, N. (1995). *Being digital*. New York: Knopf.

Pool, I., & Shulman, I. (1959). Newsmen's fantasies, audiences, and newswriting. *Public Opinion Quarterly 23*(2), 145–58.

Riley, M. W., & Riley, J. W. (1951). A sociological approach to communications research. *Public Opinion Quarterly, 15*(3), 445–460.

Schlesinger, P. (1978) *Putting "reality" together*. London: Constable.

Shirky, C. (2010). *Cognitive surplus: Creativity and generosity in a connected age*. New York: Penguin Press.

Sunstein, C. R. (2007). *Republic.com 2.0*. Princeton, NJ: Princeton University Press.

Terranova, T. (2004). *Network culture: Politics for the information age*. Ann Arbor, MI: Pluto Press.

Tuchman, G. (1974). *The TV establishment; programming for power and profit*. Englewood Cliffs, NJ: Prentice Hall.

Turow, J. (1978a). *Getting books to children: An exploration of publisher–market relations*. Chicago, IL: American Library Association.

Turow, J. (1978b). The impact of differing orientations of librarians on the process of children's book selection: A case study of library tensions. *Library Quarterly 48*(3), 276–292.

Turow, J. (1982). The role of "the audience" in publishing children's books. *Journal of Popular Culture 16*(2), 90–99.

Turow, J. (2011). *The daily you: How the new advertising industry is defining your identity and your worth*. New Haven, CT: Yale University Press.

Van Dijck, J. (2009). Users like you? Theorizing agency in user-generated content. *Media, Culture & Society, 31*(1), 41–58.

Zwick, D., Bonsu, S. K., & Darmody, A. (2008). Putting consumers to work. *Journal of Consumer Culture, 8*(2), 163–196.

CHAPTER CONTENTS

13 Alcohol, Advertising, Media, and Consumption among Children, Teenagers, and Young Adults

Anders Hansen and Barrie Gunter

University of Leicester

While much research on the roles of mediated communication in relation to alcohol consumption, drinking practices, and alcohol-related issues has traditionally focused on alcohol advertising and related types of alcohol promotion, recent decades have witnessed a growing recognition that research attention needs to be given to the wider media and symbolic environment, through which norms and values associated with the use and abuse of alcohol are communicated. We start by reviewing the growing body of research which has examined the extent, distribution across media and genres, and the substance of media messages about alcohol and drinking in advertising and entertainment media content. We then review the research evidence on how young people's learning about alcohol, beliefs about alcohol, and alcohol consumption practices are informed or influenced by alcohol advertising/promotion and by the types of media representations of alcohol identified in the first part of our review. Key approaches and frameworks for analyzing the role and influence of media representations of alcohol on young people's alcohol-related beliefs and practices are examined before considering the role of communication research evidence in relation to (political) questions about the regulation/restriction of alcohol promotion and images in the media. The review demonstrates that significant progress has been made in recent decades toward mapping the contours of the mediated message environment regarding alcohol, and hence, toward identifying where potential effects or influences of media messages about alcohol may or are likely to occur. Our review of research approaches and research evidence on the impact of mediated messages about alcohol on (young) people's beliefs, perception, and behavior regarding alcohol and its uses confirms the complex theoretical, conceptual, and methodological challenges which continue to confront research on media influence/effects. Research evidence in this field has thus established significant and extensive correlations between exposure to media messages and alcohol consumption and beliefs, but has generally failed to demonstrate causality. We conclude by noting areas for improvement in the approaches and measures deployed in research on the influence of media messages about alcohol, and by delineating the areas revealed by the review as areas that in particular would merit further and intensified research attention; for example, notably communication (promotional or other kinds) about alcohol in the new media environment.

Concern about the role played by excessive alcohol consumption in relation to a wide range of social and health related problems in society is neither recent nor new, but such concerns have been growing considerably in the last few decades (British Medical Association, 2008; Hastings & Angus, 2009; Martinic & Measham, 2008). This is evidenced amongst other things in increased media and public attention to alcohol-related "issues" (Gunter, Hansen, & Touri, 2010; Plant & Plant, 2006), but most particularly, it is evident in both the growth and increasing diversification since the 1980s in research on all aspects of mediated communication about alcohol and its role or influence on beliefs and behavior regarding alcohol.

Resonant of the particular foci that have characterized research and public controversy in relation to other areas of legal substance use and abuse, particularly smoking and tobacco, much of the concern about alcohol has traditionally focused on the role of advertising and related forms of promotion (Hastings & Angus, 2009). Advertising and other forms of marketing communication continue to be a prominent focus for research and public concern, but it has also long since been recognized that attention needs to be given to the wider symbolic environment through which norms and values associated with the use and abuse of alcohol are communicated (Martinic & Measham, 2008).

Since the late 1970s numerous studies have examined the portrayal of alcohol and drinking across a broad variety of media (television, film, radio, newspapers, popular music, literature, and more recently, the Internet) and media genres (advertising, persuasive communication campaigns, television drama, situation comedy, news, feature films, cartoons and animated films, radio music, and talk shows, etc.). Hence not all depictions of alcohol consumption are contained within sales messages; alcohol also features in drama and other entertainment content and is discussed in the news.

It is important, in setting the scene, to explain which areas of research literature we will cover and those that we will not. First of all, while we differentiate between "marketing" and "nonmarketing" depictions of alcohol products and their use, our review of marketing-related evidence will focus on that deriving from research into mass media advertising (e.g., in film, television, and print media). "Marketing" can also refer to promotional activities connected with brand image establishment and sales that include direct mail shots to households, point-of-sale premium offers, product displays, and packaging features. Research on these activities will not be covered here.

Second, research into nonmarketing content effects will focus on mainstream media content and its alleged "effects" or more often its associative links with self-reported alcohol consumption. There is a body of research that has examined the way alcohol issues are reported and represented in the news, but these studies are more usually concerned with positioning alcohol consumption as a social problem than demonstrations of its consumption (or encouragement to consume) (Hansen & Gunter, 2007).

Our primary interest here is centered on research that has attempted to demonstrate the potential or actual impact of alcohol-related depictions in dramatic narratives. This has sometimes been investigated by attempting to measure reported exposure to specific categories of media entertainment content, although many studies have obtained broad estimates of overall claimed levels of consumption of specific media (e.g., total amount of TV watching). The rapid penetration of the Internet and third generation mobile telephones has established these platforms as increasingly important advertising media. Research into their role in the context of alcohol advertising has been very limited, but some reference is made to early observations about the way these technologies are being used here.

Third, in examining the "impact" of alcohol advertising or media portrayals a distinction is often made in marketing research between macrolevel (econometric) investigations of statistical relationships between advertising campaigns and total volumes of consumption or sales and microlevel investigations of whether consumption at the level of the individual consumer is affected by his or her personal advertising exposure history. This review will focus on research concerning microlevel assessments of relationships between reported exposure to alcohol advertising and reported consumption of alcohol (or alcohol-related dispositions) for the individual consumer.

Fourth, since most of the concern about alcohol misuse and most of the research on this subject has focused on young people, this is also where our review will be situated. In this respect, "young people" can be taken to mean children, teenagers, and young adults up to their mid-20s.

It is one thing to recognize that excessive alcohol consumption is a social problem; identifying its causes is another. In debates about the genesis of alcohol consumption and the factors that could encourage potentially damaging levels of consumption, the advertising practices of alcohol manufacturers and distributors have come under fire along with examples of irresponsible consumption depicted in the mass media (Fisher & Cook, 1995; Hastings, Anderson, Cook, & Gordon, 2005; Hastings, MacKintosh, & Aitken, 1992; Mathios, Avery, Bisogni, & Shanahan, 1998; Pitt, Forrest, Hughes, & Bellis, 2003).

One key point that has repeatedly been made (e.g., Hansen, 1995; Hastings & Angus, 2009; Montonen, 1996; Strasburger et al., 2010; Wallack, Breed, & Cruz, 1987) over the last few decades is the imbalance between the communicative resources deployed in the service of alcohol promotion compared with those aimed at educating about the potential dangers associated with the use and abuse of alcohol, resulting in a symbolic message environment that is significantly skewed toward increasing consumption at the expense of messages urging moderation or abstinence. As Strasburger et al. (2010) succinctly put it:

> Although parents, schools, and the federal government are trying to get children and teenagers to "just say no" to drugs, more than $25 billion worth of cigarette, alcohol, and prescription drug advertising is effectively working to get them to "just say yes" to smoking, drinking, and other drugs.... The result is that young people receive mixed messages about

substance use, and the media contribute significantly to the risk that young people will engage in substance use. (p. 791)

Given the increasingly media-saturated and mediated nature of our social environment, it is perhaps little wonder that research has had difficulty, as we shall see later in this chapter, in demonstrating simple linear effects between alcohol advertising and alcohol consumption-related beliefs and behavior. Rather, as many have argued and as the diversification of research on "alcohol and the media" shown in this review testifies to, it is necessary to consider how images, messages, and values communicated about alcohol and drinking resonate with, reflect, and in turn inform wider symbolic and cultural values and notions regarding the (acceptable) use of alcohol.

Our aim in this chapter, thus, is to review how, since the late 1970s, research has contributed to our understanding of the role of media and mediated images of alcohol and alcohol consumption in relation to real and perceived problems associated with alcohol consumption in society. We begin by examining research on the ways in which alcohol has been presented, focusing first on the deliberate promotion of alcohol through advertising and marketing. We then review research that has sought to address the wider symbolic message environments of images of alcohol and drinking in film and broadcast entertainment content. Finally, we review research that examines the ways in which media messages about alcohol impact on public belief, perception, and behavior with regard to alcohol and drinking.

Mediated Representations of Alcohol

Promoting Alcohol

The promotion of alcohol and alcohol consumption through advertising, sponsorship, and other marketing practices is but one component of the wider symbolic and mediated environment through which images, beliefs, and ideas about alcohol and its uses are generated, circulated, and sustained in society. Given the deliberately conspicuous and intentionally persuasive nature of alcohol advertising and promotion, it is, however, not surprising that this has been the predominant focus of much of the research on media and alcohol over the last several decades. Later in this review we shall discuss the research evidence on how alcohol advertising and promotion influences public beliefs and behavior regarding alcohol and alcohol consumption, but first we focus on research that has examined the extent and nature of alcohol advertising and promotion.

Research on the extent and nature of alcohol advertising and promotion has focused variously on the amount of expenditure by the alcohol industry; on the volume of alcohol advertising; on the placement/distribution of alcohol advertising across different types of media; on "exposure" statistics detailing how much alcohol advertising audiences for different media are exposed to; and, perhaps most prolifically, on the content or messages about alcohol and drinking communicated through alcohol advertising. In very general terms, the conclusions and concerns emanating from this considerable body of research focus on the very significant and increasing sums of money channeled into the promotion of alcohol, the sophisticated and strategic use of different media and different forms of promotion, the extent to which younger audiences—particularly those who are below the legal age for alcohol consumption—are exposed to promotional messages, and the extent to which idealized positive and "normalizing" messages about alcohol and drinking dominate at the expense of messages highlighting the potentially adverse social and health effects associated with alcohol.

Expenditure and Exposure.   The amount of money spent by the alcohol industry on advertising and marketing of alcohol is impressive and significant by any standard of comparison (Grube, 2004; Hastings & Angus, 2009; Jernigan, 2010), but particularly, as frequently noted by researchers, when compared with expenditure on health promotion marketing and advertising. Hastings and Angus (2009, p. 14) thus note that the total spent in Britain on alcohol advertising on television, radio, in the press, outdoors, and in movie theaters increased overall from £167 million (U.S.$263 million) in 2002 to £194 million (U.S.$306 million) in 2006, but that these figures need to be seen in the context of an estimated overall annual expenditure by the alcohol industry of approximately £800 million (U.S.$1262 million) on all marketing communications as a whole (Hastings & Angus, 2009, p. 15). They further point to this as part of a wider global trend for marketing expenditure to shift away from traditional forms of direct advertising in the print and broadcast media to other types of promotional activity such as "sponsorship, competitions, special promotions and an increased focus on new media online and via mobile phones" (Hastings & Angus, 2009, p. 16).

There is a growing body of research that focuses on the placement of alcohol advertising in particular media and examines the extent to which young people are particularly targeted or exposed to alcohol advertising and other forms of alcohol marketing promotions. Snyder, Milici, Mitchell, and Proctor (2000), for example, note that a large proportion of beer advertising appears in televised weekend sports programming and during prime-time television programming, both of which have a sizable audience below the legal drinking age. An earlier study in the United Kingdom (Barton & Godfrey, 1988) similarly found alcohol advertising on television to be prominent overall (12% of advertising in their sample), prominently positioned within advertising breaks (occurring in first position 56% of the time), longer than other product commercials, and to occur with greatest intensity between 6 p.m. and 7 p.m. when children make up a significant proportion of the audience.

While the study of the extent and positioning of alcohol advertising across different media does not directly investigate the impact that such advertising may have on media audiences, including younger audiences, it helps in identifying where potential effects may occur. This level of analysis is important in view of evidence that indicates widespread and repeated exposure of young people to alcohol advertising, especially on television (Center on Alcohol Marketing and Youth [CAMY], 2002; Fielder, Donovan, & Ouschan, 2009; Grube, 1993; Winter, Donovan, & Fielder, 2008), but also   on radio (CAMY, 2007) and in magazines: see Montes-Santiago, Muniz, and Bazlomba (2007) on magazine advertising in Spain; Garfield, Chung, and Rathouz (2003); Siegel et al. (2008) on magazine advertising in the United States; and Donovan, Donovan, Howat, & Weller (2007) on magazine advertising in Australia. It has been reported in the United States that viewers aged 12 to 20 years are likely to see more alcohol advertising than older viewers given the types of programs in which such advertising most often occurs (CAMY, 2004).

Research published in the United States by the Center on Alcohol Marketing and Youth (CAMY) has been used to reinforce the accusation that alcohol advertisers deliberately target young people. The placement of alcohol advertisements on radio (CAMY, 2007) and in magazines was found to target broadcasts and publications widely consumed by the youth market. This was reported to be true especially in the case of advertisements for beer and distilled spirits (CAMY, 2003, 2005). One study found evidence that "the number of alcohol advertisements in magazines increases significantly with the proportion of youth readers, even after controlling for young adult readership. Our results indicate that youths are disproportionately exposed to alcohol advertising and that reducing youth exposure to alcohol advertising remains an important public policy concern" (Siegel et al., 2008, p. 482). More recently, research by CAMY found that a pledge in 2003 by leading alcohol manufacturers to significantly reduce the amount of alcohol advertising placed in magazines with a sizable underage readership resulted in a 48% decline between 2001 and 2008 in youth exposure to alcohol advertising: "Alcohol advertising placed in publications with under 21 audiences greater than 30% fell to almost nothing by 2008" (CAMY, 2010b, p. 1).

In sharp contrast, the continued importance of television as an advertising medium for the alcohol industry is emphasized by recent research showing that youth's (aged 12–20 years) "exposure to alcohol advertising on US television increased 71% between 2001 and 2009" (CAMY, 2010a, p. 1). The research further notes that this increase was driven by the rise of distilled spirits advertising on cable television and that "youth exposure to all distilled spirits TV advertising was 30 times greater in 2009 than in 2001" (CAMY, 2010a, p. 1). The report concludes that the U.S. alcohol industry and trade associations' commitment in 2003 to advertise only when the underage audience made up less than 30% of the television audience, had been wholly ineffective in reducing underage exposure to alcohol advertising on television in both absolute and relative terms.

Fielder, Donovan, and Ouschan (2009) examined exposure levels in relation to alcohol advertising on Australian metropolitan free-to-air television. They found that overall children (0–12 years) were exposed to one-third the level of mature adults (defined as 25+ years), but there were considerable variations between cities. In two metropolitan markets, underage teens (13–17 years) thus had higher rates of exposure than young adults (18–24 years). The study also found that the "30 highest exposed advertisements contained at least one element known to appeal to children and underage youth, with 23 containing two or more such elements" (p. 1157). On the basis of these findings, the authors argue that the self-regulating system governing alcohol advertising in Australia "does not protect children and youth from exposure to alcohol advertising, much of which contains elements appealing to these groups" (p. 1157).

Despite apparent recent reductions in underage exposure to magazine alcohol advertising, the overall picture that emerges from research and longitudinal monitoring in the United States, Australia, and elsewhere is one of high and increasing levels of alcohol advertising in media which reach young audiences below 21 years of age. The evidence also suggests that voluntary restrictions have not been successful in relation to television alcohol advertising. Evidence of the increased exposure of younger audiences to alcohol advertising and related promotion is particularly relevant in the light of the conclusions reached by a recent comprehensive review of research on the impact of alcohol advertising, namely that "exposure to media and commercial communications on alcohol is associated with the likelihood that adolescents will start to drink alcohol, and with increased drinking amongst baseline drinkers" (Anderson, de Bruijn, Angus, Gordon, & Hastings, 2009, p. 229; see also Nunez-Smith et al., 2010, whose comprehensive review reached similar conclusions).

The Messages of Alcohol Advertising.   In addition to the research reviewed above on alcohol advertising expenditure and alcohol advertising exposure across different media, a major focus of research since the late 1970s has been the actual content and messages of alcohol advertising. Drawing predominantly on the method of content analysis, and on the theoretical frameworks of social learning theory and cultivation analysis, numerous studies have examined the characters (including their demographic profiles), themes, social contexts, types of alcohol, social and gender values, and other content dimensions portrayed and communicated in alcohol advertising.

Early studies of magazine and television alcohol advertising in the United States (Atkin & Block, 1981; Breed & DeFoe, 1979; Finn & Strickland, 1982; Neuendorf, 1985; Postman, Nystrom, Strate, & Weingartner, 1987; Strickland & Finn, 1984) found alcohol advertising to be not only prominent, but perhaps more significantly to persistently link alcohol consumption with having fun with friends, relaxation, humor, and with "valued personal attributes such as sociability, elegance, and physical attractiveness and with desirable outcomes such as success, relaxation, romance, and adventure" (Grube, 2004, p. 604).

Research since the early 1990s has confirmed similar findings, showing, inter alia, that alcohol advertising tends to portray alcohol consumption in glamorous, luxurious, and highly pleasurable settings and to associate alcohol consumption with social and sexual success (Grube, 1993; Madden & Grube,

1994). Content studies of alcohol advertising show this to be characterized by the prominence of "lifestyle themes associating alcohol consumption with long-term wealth and success, then social approval among friends or acquaintances, relaxation, purely hedonistic pleasure, exotic travel and experiences, individualism and selfish experiences, and finally sexual success" (Gunter, Hansen, & Touri, 2010, p. 32).

Studies of alcohol advertising on television in New Zealand (Hill, 1999; Trottman, Wyllie, & Casswell, 1994) and in Brazil (Pinsky & Silva, 1999) have similarly found much emphasis on themes of masculinity (including success with the opposite sex), camaraderie and humor, following or taking part in sports, conformity, and relaxation. In their study of Brazilian television advertising, Pinsky and Silva (1999) also found themes of national symbolism to be prominent, and they found no advertisements containing moderation messages, while a small proportion of advertisements contained appeals that promoted excessive drinking.

A study of beverage advertising in popular magazines and television in the United States in 1999–2000 (Austin & Hust, 2005) concluded that alcohol advertisements emphasized sexual and social stereotypes and lacked diversity. Research in the UK has found alcohol advertising in magazines aimed at women and men respectively to generally promote a discourse of "drinking as normality" while also being clearly gender-differentiated in the sense that women's and men's drinks and drinking behaviors are portrayed in line with pronounced gender stereotypes (Lyons, Dalton, & Hoy, 2006).

Research from the United States found that the most common themes associated with alcohol advertising broadcast within televised sports programs were humor, friendship, surreal fantasy, and love/sex/romance. Less common themes were escape/adventure and success/achievement. Few advertisements focused on product quality and very few exhibited moderate drinking themes (Zwarun & Farrar, 2005). Given the prominence of alcohol advertising images across different media, associating alcohol with themes such as the ones identified above (including masculinity, relaxation, friendship and camaraderie, humor, love/sex/romance, etc.)—many, maybe most, of which appeal to young people—it is not difficult to conceive the potential roots of the impact of advertising on early adoption of alcohol consumption.

Alcohol Promotion in New Media. While alcohol advertising in the established media of cinema, print, and broadcasting is in many countries relatively firmly regulated, new media such as the Internet and mobile phones have proved rather more resistant to regulatory controls. The promotion of alcohol on the Internet comes in a variety of forms, including advertising and linking of alcohol brand names with more generalized entertainment and information content. Websites are often produced or sponsored by alcohol manufacturers and link alcohol brands with interactive games, music, and online social networks designed to have special appeal to the youth market (Anderson, 2007).

Research by CAMY (2004b) shows that, despite age verification screens and similar blockers or filters positioned at the front of websites, significant numbers of children and teenagers are attracted to and access branded alcohol websites because of the games, entertainment, interactive content, and fun downloads that are available there. Due to the deliberately interactive design of websites, users easily become "marketers, engaging in 'viral' marketing that makes them inadvertent promoters of the brand to their friends by sending branded e-cards and the like" (Jernigan, 2010, p. 70).

Gunter et al. (2010) similarly reference work in Australia (G. Roberts, 2002) and New Zealand (Borell, Gregory, & Kaiwai, 2005) that examines the features and promotional strategies of websites maintained by alcohol companies. These Internet sites were found to utilize a number of attributes that could be expected to have youth appeal. Color schemes, music, video material, download options, and interactive games featured among other attributes as core elements. Controls over entry to the sites were found to be minimal and could be easily circumvented by underage users. Featured prominently were competitions, many of which had sexual and sporting themes. A number of campaigns depicted young attractive females. In some instances, these models were depicted at or in association with sports events. These alcoholic brand websites often formed part of a mixed media marketing strategy that embraced a wide range of marketing devices that included advertising in mass media, sponsorship of (usually sporting) events, and merchandising.

In a review, Jernigan (2010) further points to mobile phones as a "new frontier for alcohol marketing." While little systematic research exists into alcohol marketing via mobile phones, the increasing convergence of digital technologies, resulting in enhanced cross-platform availability and delivery of alcohol advertising and associated marketing, is a field ripe for study and monitoring if we wish to begin to understand the modern ecology of marketing communication in its multifaceted forms.

Alcohol in Entertainment

While alcohol advertising and promotion provide perhaps the most obtrusive and obvious images and messages about alcohol in the public sphere, it has been recognized since the 1970s that advertising of alcohol draws on, engages with, and plays into a wider symbolic environment that is itself redolent with mediated images of alcohol and drinking. Since the late 1970s much research has thus focused on studying the portrayal of alcohol in popular television entertainment programming, notably television drama serials (soaps) and series, while a significant but less prolific body of research has also emerged regarding the portrayal of alcohol and drinking in other genres and media, such as film (Cook & Lewington, 1979; Denzin, 1991; D. F. Roberts, Henriksen, & Christenson, 1999; Stern, 2005); radio (Pitt et al., 2003; Daykin et al., 2009); popular music lyrics (Cruz, 1988; Herd, 2005); popular fiction (Cellucci & Larsen, 1995; Greenman, 2000); and music videos (Beullens & Van den

Bulck, 2008; DuRant et al., 1997; Robinson, Chen, & Killen, 1998; J. Van den Bulck & Beullens, 2005). Given the rapid growth and popularity of the Internet, mobile phones, and related new media technologies in the last 10 to 15 years, it is perhaps surprising that only a small number of studies (e.g. Moreno et al., 2010) have so far focused on how these media contribute to the articulation and circulation of alcohol-related images, representations, and messages.

Film.   Research on Hollywood films has demonstrated the relatively consistent prominence of alcohol depiction in popular films since the 1940s (McIntosh, Smith, Bazzini, & Mills, 1998). Everett, Schnuth, and Tribble (1998), in an analysis of top grossing American films from 1985 to 1995, found that 96% of films contained references to alcohol use, while Roberts, Henriksen, and Christenson (1999) found 93% of the 200 most popular movie rentals in 1996 and 1997 included depictions of alcohol use. According to these studies, negative consequences associated with alcohol consumption are infrequently shown, and when alcohol is depicted, "pro-use" statements are more than twice as frequent as "anti-use" statements (D. F. Roberts & Christenson, 2000). Drinkers are shown as more socially and sexually successful than nondrinkers, though also as more aggressive at times. Alcohol consumption in films is essentially depicted as normal and unproblematic (McIntosh et al., 1998).

In a content analysis of top grossing "teen-centered" films from 1999, 2000, and 2001, Stern (2005) found that two-fifths of teen characters were depicted as drinking alcohol. Few differences were found between drinkers and nondrinkers in terms of physical attractiveness, socioeconomic status, gender, or virtuousness, and drinkers were rarely shown refusing offers to drink, regretting drinking, or indeed suffering any consequences—negative or otherwise—from alcohol consumption. Stern (2005) concludes that the overall message conveyed in films targeted toward a predominantly teen audience is that alcohol consumption in this age group is common, mostly risk-free, and appropriate for anyone.

Broadcast Entertainment.   Since the late 1970s, a considerable number of studies have analyzed the portrayal of alcohol and drinking in television programs. These studies have shown that portrayals of alcohol and drinking feature prominently in television entertainment programming and with considerable regularity during peak-time television when young people can be expected to be numerically present in the audience (Breed & DeFoe, 1981; Cafiso, Goodstadt, Garlington, & Sheppard, 1982). Studies in the early 1980s in the United States and in the United Kingdom found alcohol depictions in approximately two-thirds of prime-time television entertainment programs (Hansen, 1986; Wallack, Breed, & Cruz, 1987), while studies focusing particularly on the most watched drama serials or soaps found 86% of them to contain visual or verbal references to alcohol (Furnham, Ingle, Gunter, & McClelland, 1997).

Using the method of content analysis and deploying similar units of analysis, a range of studies conducted since the early 1980s have provided evidence that shows overall increases in the prevalence and prominence of alcohol portrayal in television programming. Christenson, Henrikson, and Roberts (2000) thus found that 77% of prime-time television programming in the United States during the 1998–1999 season contained references to alcohol, while 71% depicted actual alcohol use. In a study examining alcohol-related references across news, drama, and soaps on peak-time broadcasts during one week of terrestrial television output, Hansen (2003) found that references to alcoholic drinks and consumption occurred in 85% of programs analyzed. Visual scenes of alcohol consumption were far more prevalent in soap operas (10.6 per hour) than in either drama episodes (4.3 per hour) or news (1.9 per hour). Comparisons of the soap opera data of Hansen (1986) and Furnham et al. (1997) showed that the rate of visual references had increased to 10.6 per hour in 2003 compared with 9.3 per hour in 1994–1995 and 5.8 per hour in 1984. Alcohol drinking scenes rose from 3.9 per hour in 1984 to 6.4 in 1994–1995 to 7.0 in 2003.

Analyses of television portrayal of alcohol have largely agreed also on the nature of such depictions: alcohol consumption in television programming is presented in a predominantly positive light. Alcohol consumption is predominantly used as a visual signifier of celebration or merely of pleasant and convivial social interaction. Alcoholic intoxication is seen as fun and often displayed in a humorous context, although depictions showing alcohol consumption as a coping mechanism that could be used by someone when under pressure or stressed also occur (Atkin & Block, 1981; Breed, DeFoe, & Wallack, 1984; Hanneman & McEwan, 1976; H. Van Den Bulck, Simons, & Van Gorp, 2008).

Alcohol consumption on television has tended to be shown as an activity that is largely free of adverse consequences (Grube, 1993; Hansen, 1986; Mathios et al., 1998). Portrayal of problematic drinking or the association of alcohol consumption with accidents, illness, or antisocial behavior is infrequent. These studies have found little evidence of the portrayal of underage drinking: drinking characters tend to be male, middle class, and middle aged (e.g., Furnham et al., 1997).

Studies in the UK (Coyne & Ahmed, 2009), New Zealand (McGee, Ketchel, & Reeder, 2007), and the United States (Russell & Russell, 2009) have added further confirmation to the general pattern of findings regarding television entertainment portrayal of alcohol and drinking. In a study of soap operas on British television, Coyne and Ahmed (2009) found that more than 90% of soap opera episodes depicted alcohol-related acts, with an average of 7.65 acts per episode. Assuming that most soap opera episodes are approximately 30 minutes in duration, this figure would indicate a potential further increase in the steady increase identified by Hansen (2003) in the rate of alcohol acts per hour of soap opera programming since the 1980s.

A study of alcohol imagery on New Zealand television (McGee, Ketchel, &

Reeder, 2007) found similarly high rates of alcohol depictions, with an average of one alcohol-related scene every 9 minutes. Confirming patterns identified in previous studies, McGee et al. (2007) also noted that much alcohol imagery was incidental to storylines while scenes depicting uncritical imagery outnumbered scenes showing possible adverse health consequences of drinking by 12 to 1.

Russell and Russell (2009) reported a comprehensive content analysis of alcohol messages in U.S. prime-time television series. Their study monitored 144 unique episodes broadcast over a 10-week period during 2004. Like the British studies discussed earlier, they found alcohol portrayal to have become more prevalent: while data for the late 1990s (Christenson, Henriksen, & Roberts, 2000) showed that just over three-quarters of prime-time television programs contained references to alcohol, Russell and Russell (2009) found every program in their sample to contain references to alcohol.

While numerous studies have noted that film and television programs portray both positive and negative images of alcohol and drinking, albeit with a distinct emphasis on positive images, the study by Russell and Russell (2009) is particularly noteworthy for showing that positive and negative portrayals are qualitatively different. Thus negative messages tend to be foregrounded and central to the narrative, while positive messages are invariably communicated as part of the "normal" background. This finding adds further ammunition to the argument (e.g., Hansen, 1988; Lyons et al., 2006; Wallack, Breed, & Cruz, 1987) that television tends to naturalize alcohol consumption as the unproblematic and positive norm, while treating problem drinking, alcoholism, and negative outcomes associated with alcohol consumption as "exceptional."

Although the evidence regarding alcohol and drinking-related messages on radio is extremely limited when compared with television, it is clear from what little evidence there is from U.S. studies (CAMY, 2007) and in the UK (Daykin et al., 2009; Pitt et al., 2003) that radio may be a potentially important and significant source of perceptions and beliefs about alcohol and its use and abuse in society. Not only do these studies show that alcohol references are prominent in programs aimed at and attracting a predominantly younger audience, but they also indicate how popular radio chat (including with audience members who phone in and with celebrities of various sorts) often draws on, and in turn perpetuates and reinforces, deep-seated cultural assumptions that stress drunkenness and excessive drinking as fun and amiable/sociable behavior.

In summary, numerous studies conducted since the late 1970s have demonstrated that alcohol and drinking images are prevalent throughout popular media entertainment content such as mass movies and television soap opera and drama series. There is also a growing body of evidence that the frequency of alcohol images in popular television drama serials/series has increased steadily over the last three decades since researchers first started monitoring them in the early 1980s. The main findings of these studies show, amongst other things, that the portrayal of alcohol and drinking feature prominently in entertainment media and that drinking is on the whole associated with pleasant social interaction; that there is comparatively little portrayal of the negative consequences associated with drinking; and that drinking is frequently portrayed in the context of attractive situations and milieux and as a necessary component of "having a good time."

Mediated Representations and Learning about Alcohol

This section will cover research evidence that explores how mediated representations of alcohol—both marketing and nonmarketing messages—might play a part in socializing young people to consume alcohol. Relationships between exposure to marketing and nonmarketing depictions of alcohol and reported consumption will be examined in the final section of this chapter. This section is concerned with the "messages" about alcohol and its consumption that people, especially the young and impressionable, acquire, as a consequence of exposure to alcohol themes in marketing and nonmarketing content.

One reason for presenting this evidence separately from research on behavioral effects is that it concerns "prebehavioral" responses linked to beliefs and attitudes about alcohol and its consumption. A number of influential psychological theories about the effectiveness of marketing and advertising have highlighted the importance of cognitive-level influences that often underpin orientations toward product "brands" and associated promotional messages and can then mediate their behavioral impact (see Rucker, Petty, & Priester, 2007). Equally, with nonmarketing content, its influences must be contextualized in relation to established cultural, cognitive-level scripts and codes associated with alcohol consumption (Martinic & Measham, 2008). A number of important questions are addressed here. Can mediated representations impart lessons about the benefits associated with alcohol consumption? Do they make excessive drinking appear to be the norm? Do young people acquire impressions about alcohol brands through promotional messages about alcohol? Is this learning significant in turn because it may lay down the foundations for the onset of alcohol consumption and future patterns of alcohol use?

Although concern about alcohol and young people centers ultimately on consumption—notably the occurrence of bouts of excessive drinking or chronic abuse over time—it is important to understand why this behavior occurs at all. In this context, researchers have asked questions about young people's orientations toward alcoholic drinks in terms of what they think and feel about drinking alcohol. Alcohol consumption does not occur in a social vacuum and understanding how it is perceived by people, young or old, has to be informed by established sociocultural behavioral patterns and norms related to alcoholic drinks (Martinic & Measham, 2008).

Children can be exposed to alcohol from an early age and in this regard the orientations of their parents and other influential people in their lives are important role models (Fisher & Cook, 1995; Kuther & Higgins-D'Alessandro, 2003). Parents may introduce children to alcohol (Wilks, Callan, & Austin, 1989), but as they enter adolescence peer groups become more significant sources of influence and serve in particular as a source of encouragement of underage consumption (Connolly, Casswell, Zhang, & Silva, 1992). In addition, mass mediated depictions and promotions of alcohol consumption have been identified as important sources of influence in relation to attitudes toward alcohol consumption and awareness of branded products. Here, both marketing and nonmarketing representations of alcohol have been hypothesized to play a part. In essence, youngsters can learn about alcohol by watching dramatic portrayals of its consumption in movie theaters and television programs and through exposure to alcohol product advertising (Gunter, Hansen, & Touri, 2010).

Most attention has been fixed on alcohol advertising and especially that occurring in audio-visual media such as film and television. There are other aspects of alcohol marketing, however, that have also come under fire including promotions in retail outlets and bars. These often include special pricing offers which are more often considered as direct enticements to the young to consume alcohol to excess (Hastings et al., 2005; Hastings & Angus, 2009).

Brand awareness has often been taken as starter evidence that children have been socialized early in acceptance of alcohol. Before they have reached their teens, children have demonstrated the ability to recognize alcohol brands (Aitken, 1989; Aitken, Eadie, Leathar, McNeill, & Scott, 1988; Wyllie, Zhang, & Casswell, 1998). Children also learn to associate specific attributes with alcohol brands demonstrating that there is some degree of brand image learning from advertising (Leiber, 1998). Critics who have called for tighter restrictions over alcohol marketing have sometimes inferred that branding is a critical causal factor that draws in young people and encourages their first consumption of alcohol (Hastings & Angus, 2009; Hastings, MacIntosh, & Aitken, 19925). Yet many marketing theories have defined the value of brands only in relation to established product class consumers (see Hoeffler & Keller, 2003; Keller, 2007; Naik, 2007). So far, none of the research that has indicated brand awareness among young people has yielded compelling evidence that this cognitive-level response drives the onset of alcohol consumption.

Mediated representations of alcohol consumption occur in nonmarketing as well as marketing settings (Anderson, 2007). Portrayals of alcohol consumption in movies and TV programs often occur alongside advertisements for alcoholic beverages and could potentially have independent or combined effects on young people who are exposed to them. There has been some evidence indicative of relationships between general media consumption and alcohol consumption, but it is less clear as to whether alcohol portrayals specifically have exerted a causal influence in this context.

Much of the research has relied on self-report measures of alcohol and media consumption. Media consumption measures have sometimes been further informed by parallel evidence of the amount of alcohol-related content identified in media for which exposure frequencies have been measured. Much of this evidence has been theoretically informed by cultivation analysis perspectives that have traditionally made assumptions about levels of exposure to specific categories of media portrayal (usually on television) from relatively crude measures of exposure. Hence, typical findings have indicated that greater reported TV viewing or viewing of specified program genres were associated with a greater propensity for teenagers to consume alcohol (Andsager, Austin, & Pinkleton, 2002; Austin & Leili, 1994; Austin, Pinkleton, & Fujioka, 2000). Norwegian research reported that teenagers' propensity to watch imported U.S. TV programs, known via separate content analysis evidence to contain scenes of alcohol consumption, did display a greater likelihood of their consuming alcohol. Advertising of most alcoholic beverages in Norway is banned (Thomsen & Rekve, 2006).

Research from the United States has reported statistical relationships between teenagers' self-reported TV viewing patterns, attitudes, and beliefs about alcohol consumption, and actual consumption. Interest in drinking alcohol was associated with holding positive expectations about the social effects of using alcohol. This attitudinal disposition was not surprisingly associated with the likelihood of actual consumption, and all these orientations toward alcohol displayed a weak statistical relationship with watching late-night TV programs (Austin, Pinkleton, & Fukioka, 2000). Different explanations can be explored for such findings. It is possible that teenagers who stay up later watching television are also exposed to more advertisements for alcohol, if they occur in concentration at that time. However, it is equally possible that youngsters who drink more while underage generally have greater freedom from parental control, stay up later (and not just to watch television), and engage in late-night social interactions that involve the consumption of alcohol.

Initial learning about alcohol consumption begins at an early age. Preteen-age children can demonstrate an awareness of alcohol brands and a sense of whether drinking alcohol is normative behavior (Hastings & Angus, 2009). There are many different factors that contribute to this early learning, but mediated representations of alcohol are among them. What is not always clear from empirical research is the level of importance that can be attached to alcohol advertising and media portrayals when placed alongside environmental, social, and cultural factors in young people's lives.

Mediated Representations and Their Acceptance by Young People

From their early learning about alcohol, children and teenagers can develop psychological dispositions toward it that provide the foundation of their own eventual consumption. These dispositions become established within and are shaped by prevailing cultural and social contexts within which early socialization takes place (Nahoum-Grappe, 2008). To determine whether this developmental process follows through, we need to consider empirical evidence that examines further how mediated messages about alcohol are taken on board by child, teenage, and young adult consumers. How do young people react to promotional messages about alcohol? Do favorable responses toward media messages about alcohol underpin possible onset of drinking or condition future patterns of consumption? Can negative reactions to mediated messages about alcohol have the reverse effect?

Alcohol advertising has long been regarded as having a significant influence over the way consumers feel about alcoholic drinks (see Gunter et al., 2010). In the past, many promotional campaigns have linked alcoholic brands to specific and highly attractive lifestyles. A common practice has been to portray young people in this advertising and to play on themes—in particular general social popularity, success with the opposite sex, and having a good time—that resonate vibrantly with young consumers (Wallack, Cassady, & Grube, 1990). The objective of this type of campaigning is to draw in the attention and psychological involvement of young people so that they identify personally with the brand through the lifestyle attributes it represents and come to see the consumption of the brand as a signifier of the social image they would like to project to others about themselves (Aaker, 1996).

The process of the alcohol brand as an "extension of self" begins with the emergence of an early awareness of such brands. This awareness has been measured among preteenage children (Aitken, Eadie et al., 1988; Aitken, Leathar, & Scott, 1988; Waiters, Treno, & Grube, 2001). Attention to alcohol advertisements, which is associated with brand awareness, was also found to be greater among early onset drinkers (Aitken, 1989). Disentangling the direction of causality in respect of this relationship has proven to be difficult. However, among children who were nondrinkers, one study reported that those who anticipated that they might drink when older displayed greater liking of alcohol advertisements than did those who claimed to be committed abstainers (Unger, Johnson, & Rohrbach, 1995).

Evidence has emerged over many years that children and adolescents often nominate alcohol advertisements as being among their favorites, especially on television (Hastings, MacKintosh, & Aitken, 1992; Nash, Pine, & Messer, 2009). This may have as much to do with the generic entertaining nature of the narrative themes of these advertisements, such as the amount of humor they contain, as to whether young consumers are psychologically attracted to alcohol (Cragg, 2004; Nash, Pine, & Lutz, 2002; Neuendorf, 1985; Waiters et al., 2001). A number of brands, such as Budweiser and Smirnov Ice, have run very popular campaigns that gained widespread consumer awareness because of their distinctive characterizations and catchphrases (e.g., the Budweiser frogs and "Whassup" campaigns) and which struck a particular chord with children and teenagers, whether they were drinkers or not (Chen, Grube, Bersamin, Waiters, & Keefe, 2005).

The association of celebrities with alcoholic products can attract the attention of young consumers and enhance recall and recognition of brands (Atkin & Block, 1981; Lieberman & Orlandi, 1987). Children's liking of alcohol advertisements can also be enhanced by positioning them close to popular entertainment, such as major sporting events (Phillipson & Jones, 2007). The presence of animated characters in alcohol advertisements is another factor that resonates successfully with children and teenagers (Collins, Ellickson,

McCaffrey, & Hambarsoomians, 2005). Some production features appeal to specific consumer subgroups rather than others. Thus, girls may be drawn more to alcohol advertisements with feminine themes (Aitken, 1989).

The attribute effects of alcohol advertisements evolve in terms of their effectiveness among young consumers as the latter progress through different stages of psychological development. Once they have entered their teens, young consumers become more sensitive to lifestyle fashions and trends. When these factors are effectively deployed in alcohol advertising, they can enhance the extent to which young people identify with the promotional message and the brand (Austin & Knauss, 2000). This process can begin even among pre-teenage children. Those who were better at identifying alcohol advertisements were also more likely to hold positive opinions about drinking (Cragg, 2004; Wallack, Cassady & Grube, 1990).

There is further evidence that media depictions of alcohol consumption, for example, based on portrayals of characters that drink in films and television programs can impact alcohol-related socialization of children and teenagers. This finding should be no surprise given evidence we have already reviewed that showed drinking scenes have characterized popular TV drama serials for many years (Furnham et al., 1997; Hansen, 1986, 2003; Wallack, Breed, & Cruz, 1987). Preteenage boys have been shown to display more positive opinions about alcohol consumption after watching a program that portrayed characters drinking, though there was no clear evidence that such exposure led to an increased likelihood of drinking onset (Kotch, Coulter, & Lipsitz, 1986).

Movies shown in movie theaters, and that contain prominent alcohol consumption, have also been found to be associated with a tendency of teenage viewers to consume alcohol (Hanewinkel, Tanski, & Sargent, 2007). Over time, exposure to movies that depict alcohol consumption was linked among teenagers to the onset of drinking (Hanewinkel & Sargent, 2009). These survey studies can at best demonstrate degrees of association between self-reported exposure to media and alcohol consumption. Causality demonstrations require an interventionist methodology. So far, however, experimental studies of the impact of alcohol portrayals in films and programs have produced only limited evidence of direct effects of exposure on alcohol consumption (Kotch et al., 1986; Rychtarik, Fairbank, Allen, Foy, & Drabman 1983; Sobell, Sobell, Riley, et al., 1986).

Children and teenagers can display a progressively more detailed and sophisticated awareness of alcohol brands as they grow older. Initial interest in alcohol can become established before their teenage years and advertising has been found to play a part in cultivating both that awareness and wider beliefs and attitudes concerning alcohol consumption. Alcohol advertisements can be popular among children and teenagers, but this should not invariably be seen as a signal that they are about to start drinking. Nevertheless, regular exposure to mediated alcohol marketing could create a familiarity with alcohol that can in turn condition a positive mental disposition toward consumption. Media depictions of alcohol use might add to advertising influences, but the evidence so far on the specific influences of this content remains ambiguous.

Alcohol Advertising, Media Depictions, and Reported Consumption Levels

This section turns to claims that alcohol advertising and media portrayals of alcohol consumption can directly or indirectly influence young people's consumption of alcohol (i.e., children, teenagers, and young adults up to their mid-20s). Alcohol consumption can be influenced by a broad range of psychological, social, and cultural factors. The empirical evidence accumulated so far has identified a mix of nonmediated and mediated variables that can trigger and shape interest in alcoholic beverages and their consumption (Gunter et al., 2010; Martinic & Measham, 2008). These factors come into play during childhood long before legal consumption age, at the point when early interest in alcohol emerges.

In this context, we examine mediated influences that have been hypothesized to flow from advertising and media portrayals. In terms of approaches to understanding whether these mediated representations of alcohol can influence alcohol consumption, research has been dominated by survey methodologies and supplemented by a relatively modest number of experimental studies and some qualitative research. The limitations of these methodologies in relation to demonstrating causal links between media exposure and behavior are well known. Surveys in general can only demonstrate associational relationships between variables and are reliant on self-report evidence from respondents that can be problematic, especially when attempting accurately to measure behavioral frequencies. Longitudinal designs, when skillfully executed and resourced, can provide firmer indications of possible trigger effects of mediated portrayals in relation to target behaviors, but never control for all potentially relevant extraneous variables.

Experiments are designed to execute direct analysis of causal-effect relationships, but in their efforts to control or filter out all potentially influential causal agents other than those being manipulated, must create such artificial conditions for media exposure and behavioral observation that they lack ecological validity and may yield findings that have meaning only within the confines of the experimental setting. If experiments are moved out into the field, in an effort to enhance ecological validity, they must relinquish some control over extraneous variables and hence some of the limitations associated with surveys begin to surface. All these generic limitations serve as caveats we must always bear in mind when reviewing empirical evidence about the effects of mediated depictions of alcohol consumption on actual consumption of alcohol.

The seriousness of the potential impact of advertising messages about alcohol on its eventual consumption by children and teenagers has been emphasized by concerns raised by authoritative organizations such as the World Health Organization. It has adopted an unequivocal stance that alcohol advertising can promote positive attitudes and beliefs about alcohol among children and teenagers and encourages young people to consume alcoholic beverages (Babor et al., 2003).

Three key theoretical models underpin this thinking. The first is that regular exposure to alcohol advertising can cultivate beliefs that alcohol consumption is normative behavior. This can therefore create a mind-set among children and teenagers that: "If everyone else is doing it, why shouldn't I?" One could generalize from this position further and argue that if nonmarketing mediated portrayals of alcohol consumption (e.g., in films and TV programs) represent a regular part of a young person's media diet, and also present a positive impression of drinking, the normative belief cultivation effect could be further reinforced.

A second possibility is that mediated depictions of alcohol consumption, whether in marketing or nonmarketing settings, that display consumption by attractive characters, might encourage direct emulation or imitation by young observers, especially if alcohol consumption is associated with specific "rewards," such as an affluent lifestyle and social or sexual success.

A further potential outcome is that regular exposure to alcohol depictions in the media could provide constant reminders to young people about alcohol consumption and serve as cognitive primers that continually bring the idea of drinking into consciousness. According to some theorists, the more often young people think about drinking, the more likely they are to consume (Hastings et al., 2005; Krank & Kreklewetz, 2003; Krank, Wall, Lai, Wekerle, & Johnson, 2003).

Survey Studies

Survey studies can be divided into those conducted on a one-off basis and those that use repeat waves over time with the same panel of respondents. Both types of surveys have yielded evidence of significant statistical relationships between self-reported exposure to alcohol advertising and intended future or reported current alcohol consumption (Atkin & Block, 1984; Atkin, Neuendorf, & McDermott, 1983; Connolly et al., 1994; Ellickson, Collins, Hambarsoomians, & McCaffrey, 2005; Grube, 1993; Robinson, Chen, & Killen, 1998).

Survey studies can be differentiated by the age group studied, with different investigations focusing variously on preteenage, teenage, or early adulthood samples. With preteenage samples, alcohol consumption levels tend to be very low and so a more meaningful question for this age group is whether they intend to drink alcohol in the future. This intention is no guarantee that consumption will eventually occur, nor does denial of intention to drink mean that the young respondent will not change their mind later on. Nevertheless this measure has some significance as a signifier of early emergence of an interest in alcohol and has been found to provide a meaningful indicator of future drinking (Christiansen, Roehling, Smith, & Goldman, 1989).

One survey study with 11- and 12-year-olds in northern California found that a range of social environment factors and media and marketing variables exhibited direct and indirect links to drinking intention. Parental drinking, peer approval, and positive beliefs about alcohol exhibited the most direct predictive links to drinking intention. Knowledge of brands, product-related slogans, and advertisements had no direct predictive links to intention to consume alcohol, but advertising awareness did seem to contribute to positive beliefs about alcohol and these in turn were directly linked to expected future consumption (Grube, 1993).

One early series of studies reported that propensity to drink alcohol among American youngsters aged 12 to 18 years was associated with reported heavy exposure to alcohol advertising (Atkin & Block, 1984). The same research project was extended to include respondents up to age 22 years and found that problem drinking was associated with regular exposure to alcohol advertising (Atkin, Neuendorf, & McDermott, 1983). The findings from this research program have not been universally accepted. One critic challenged the robustness of the sampling and argued that the sample contained a strong bias toward drinkers (Strickland, 1984). In a separate and parallel series of surveys with samples aged 12 to 18 years, the same author reported no overall significant relationships between reported exposure to alcohol advertising and alcohol consumption. However, teenagers who claimed that they used advertisements to make social comparisons between themselves and actors in the promotions did display a significant statistical relationship between advertising exposure and their own propensity to consume alcohol (Strickland, 1981, 1982, 1983, 1984).

Later research from the United Kingdom found that social and marketing factors were both related to young people's alcohol consumption habits, but whereas social factors were more powerfully linked to volume of consumption, advertising effects appeared to be restricted to impact upon level of consumption of specific types of alcoholic beverage, most particularly, cider and alcopops (Gunter, Hansen, & Touri, 2009).

Longitudinal studies have been conducted to track whether there are links over time between patterns of exposure to alcohol advertising and the onset of teenage drinking (Anderson et al., 2009; Ellickson et al., 2005). The importance of these studies is that they acknowledge that the effects of alcohol advertising might build cumulatively over time (Casswell, 2004). These studies have also generally measured a number of other social factors known to influence the onset of alcohol consumption. In the process, they have revealed that both mediated and nonmediated variables can underpin the onset of youth alcohol consumption. Some statistical evidence surfaced that advertising effects persisted even after controls were implemented for nonmediated variables, such as parent, family, and peer group influences (Ellickson et al., 2005).

In a wide-ranging review of research about alcohol advertising and consumption from longitudinal studies, Anderson et al. (2009) concluded that there was evidence that early onset of alcohol consumption was linked to exposure to alcohol advertising. Close inspection of the 16 studies reviewed here revealed that the relationship between these variables was often quite weak and its veracity undermined by methodological weaknesses concerning the measurement of advertising exposure. One illustration of this last point derived from a survey of young U.S. teenagers that derived exposure to alcohol advertising from claims of TV watching based on lists of program titles (Stacy, Zogg, Unger, & Dent, 2004). In essence, there was no direct measurement of exposure to alcohol advertising on TV here.

Although discovery of direct links between reported exposure to alcohol advertising and consumption onset among children and teenagers has been problematic, some researchers have explored the possibility that the link is less direct and operates through a mediating variable of recall of advertisements. Pursuing this line of argument, some studies have found that ability to recall alcohol advertisements and alcohol brands displayed statistical links to alcohol consumption (Henriksen, Feighery, Schleicher, & Fortmann, 2008; Stacy et al., 2004). Young adults who expressed greater liking for alcohol advertisements also exhibited heavier drinking tendencies (Wyllie, Zhang & Casswell, 1998). In another chain of influence, evidence has emerged among young people that exposure to alcohol advertisements is associated with greater liking of alcohol products and that the latter reaction in term is linked to drinking behavior (Unger, Schuster, Zogg, Dent, & Stacy, 2003).

Most survey research into the effects of advertising on alcohol consumption has relied upon self-report measures of advertising exposure. One U.S. longitudinal study departed from this convention by also including market level data on advertising expenditure. Snyder, Milici, Slater, Sun, and Strizhakova (2006) constructed a nationwide panel of respondents aged 15 to 26 years at the outset and surveyed the participants four times over 21 months. Growth in drinking over time was found to be steepest not only among respondents who recalled most advertising exposure but also among those who resided in markets that experienced the greatest levels of expenditure on alcohol advertising. The latter effect was most pronounced for the older respondents.

Longitudinal research that comprised two surveys conducted 2 years apart among 12- to 15-year-olds in Scotland found that the youngsters' awareness of and involvement with different kinds of alcohol marketing (advertising, sponsorship, associated merchandising, point of sale display, and packaging) in the first wave predicted uptake of alcohol consumption and frequency of consumption in the second wave. This statistically significant relationship persisted after controls for other social variables were introduced (Gordon, MacKintosh, & Moodie, 2010).

Recent reviews of longitudinal research have reached conflicting conclusions about whether there is compelling evidence for effects of alcohol advertising on drinking behavior among young people that emerge over time. Smith and Foxcroft (2009) excluded experimental studies, one-off surveys, and time series studies and focused on surveys that constructed panels that were interviewed on two or more occasions and which evaluated a range of advertising formats and behavioral outcome measures. Seven studies were selected for inclusion following extensive screening of research literature: Connolly et al. (1994), Ellicksen et al. (2005), Robinson et al. (1998), Stacy, Zogg, Unger, & Dent (2004), J. Van Den Bulck & Beullens (2005), Snyder, Milici, et al. (2006), and Sargent, Wills, Stoolmiller, Gibson, & Gibbons (2006).

Three of these studies (Ellicksen et al., 2005; Robinson et al., 1998; Sargent et al., 2006) were identified as showing significant degrees of association between onset of alcohol consumption among adolescents who were nondrinkers at the start and level of exposure to alcohol advertising. In two cases (Stacy et al., 2004; J. Van den Bulck & Beullen, 2005), exposure to TV or music videos (and by proxy to advertising they carried) or to alcohol advertising were related to amount of alcohol consumption over time. The reviewers conceded that although these findings were indicative of links between exposure to alcohol advertising and drinking onset or amount of drinking in adolescence, they did not prove causality and provided no explanation for these relationships.

A subsequent wide-ranging critique of longitudinal research that covered 20 studies of alcohol advertising and its effects upon young people concluded that evidence for causality between advertising exposure and consumption was questionable. Key weaknesses centered on measurement of advertising exposure and message reception, sample biases across survey waves, and effectiveness of controls for extraneous variables (Nelson, 2010b).

Experimental Studies

Findings from experimental studies have generally been restricted to demonstrations of whether exposure to alcohol advertising can have an immediate or short-term influence over choice of beverage. Experiments have so far provided few insights into the role played by mediated depictions of alcohol in triggering the onset of alcohol consumption among children and teenagers (Kohn & Smart, 1984; McCarty & Ewing, 1983; Sobell, Sobell, Riley, et al., 1986). Hence, experiments have found that inviting participants to engage directly with specific drinks by evaluating advertisements can produce a priming effect steering their choices toward advertised products in a choice test run immediately after exposure (e.g., Brown, 1978). Furthermore, exposure to advertisements for beer (in the case of young men and wine in the case of young women) via TV that were embedded in other program material encouraged more drinking in a controlled environment compared with conditions in which no alcohol advertisements were shown (Kohn & Smart, 1984, 1987).

Another study combined alcohol advertising and depictions of alcohol consumption in adjacent programming. In this instance, American college students were invited to evaluate programs they were shown and experimental conditions were manipulated for different groups of participants to vary exposure to alcohol-containing material. After the experiment, the participants were invited to take part in a different exercise which they were told was unconnected to the first. In this exercise, they evaluated an alcoholic beverage and could as part of that process consume it. No evidence emerged that the amount of alcohol consumed in this exercise differed significantly between students on the basis of their prior viewing experience (Sobell, Sobell, Riley, et al., 1986).

In a follow-up investigation, Sobell, Sobell, Toneatoo, and Leo (1993) used a similar alcohol representations exposure design but then questioned participants both before exposure and afterwards about their drinking behavior. The only result of significance and relevance here was that those who confessed before exposure to being heavy drinkers reported subsequently that they experienced a lowered resistance to drinking heavily again if they had been exposed to alcohol promoting messages.

A slightly different twist was adopted by another experimental study in which participants were divided up according to whether they saw alcohol advertisements or not and whether or not they had been allowed to drink alcohol prior to advertising exposure. During an interval in the study, all participants were given an opportunity to drink alcohol. Breath test comparisons for these groups showed higher levels of alcohol in the blood of those who had seen an alcohol advertisement earlier. The data can be challenged on the grounds that breath test results are not always reliable indicators of alcohol consumed, because individuals can vary in levels of tolerance for alcohol. In addition, group level results could have been unduly influenced by one or two heavy drinkers and this factor was not controlled (McCarty & Ewing, 1983).

In a field test, participants were exposed to alcohol advertisements as part of an evaluation test and were retested 6 to 12 weeks later via telephone. No differences in levels of alcohol consumption were found contingent upon whether or not they had evaluated advertisements for alcohol products earlier (Kohn, Smart, & Ogborne, 1984).

In a design that again manipulated controlled exposure to alcohol advertisements, no effect was found on the degree to which preteens and early teens expressed an intention to drink in the future (Lipsitz, Brake, Vincent, & Winters, 1993).

Some experimental studies have focused on nonmarketing alcohol representations including depictions of consumption in TV programs. These studies were conducted among preteenage and early teenage children and hence may have a more significant bearing on the role that such depictions could play in triggering an early interest in alcohol. One study found that preteenagers were more likely to choose to serve alcohol to an adult in a pictured scene as an appropriate behavior after having earlier watched a program that featured alcohol consumption (Rychtarik et al., 1983).

A similar design was used with preteenage children who, after exposure to videos depicting alcohol consumption scenes, were asked for their attitudes toward drinking. There were more positive and fewer negative opinions among children who had watched videos with alcohol consumption than among those who had not (Kotch et al., 1986).

Further evidence has emerged from experimental research that exposure to alcohol advertisements could give rise to indirect rather than direct effects upon drinking-related behavior. In particular, these messages could trigger internalized attitudes toward drinking that in turn activate high risk dispositions such as driving while under the influence of alcohol (Goodall & Slater, 2010).

Qualitative Studies

Through the use of qualitative research methods, there have been attempts made to understand how children respond to alcohol advertising. These methods are not equipped to test causal hypotheses but can be useful to determine the significance of advertising for young people alongside other social factors related to alcohol consumption. This type of research has indicated that young people below legal drinking age do notice advertising for alcoholic beverages and discuss promotions as well as drinking in general among their friends. These discourses allow youngsters to explore the social importance of alcohol consumption among their peer groups and to gauge attitudes toward it. Focus group research has demonstrated that exposure to alcohol advertising can induce positive emotional reactions to advertised brands among teenagers (Jones & Donovan, 2001). It is difficult to determine from qualitative evidence what specific impact exposure to alcohol advertising has upon the onset of drinking, but it is apparent that young people draw upon what they see in promotional campaigns for alcoholic products in their conversations about drinking with their friends (Cragg, 2004).

Further qualitative research consisted of focus group interviews with teenagers and young adults in their early 20s in seven countries (Brazil, China, Italy, Nigeria, Russia, South Africa, and Scotland). The research revealed that alcohol and its consumption was defined by a variety of different cultural values and contexts that shaped how much drinking took place and the settings in which this typically occurred. No evidence emerged, however, that alcohol advertising or other forms of alcohol marketing was identified by young drinkers as a factor that influenced their orientations toward alcohol (Martinic & Measham, 2008).

The evidence reviewed in this section has revealed that children and teenagers not only display an interest in alcohol marketing but that it is also linked to their recall of alcohol brands and their attitudes toward those brands and alcohol consumption. What is less certain is whether brand awareness and recall of advertisements are causal agents that drive the onset of alcohol consumption. Some correlational evidence surfaced from longitudinal surveys, but methodological weaknesses in the way drinking behavior and alcohol exposure were measured undermine the credibility of their findings. Direct attempts to demonstrate causal relations between advertising exposure and subsequent drinking behavior via controlled experiments have yielded no clear evidence of behavioral effects and were, in any case, not equipped to prove any hypotheses by the impact of alcohol advertising on the onset of alcohol consumption. Evidence concerning the hypothesized impact of nonmarketing mediated representations of alcohol consumption is also equivocal largely for the same methodological limitations that blight research into alcohol advertising effects.

What is also apparent is that if alcohol advertising does ultimately influence consumption, this process is more likely to be indirect than direct, operating via brand awareness and liking, or even via internalized cognitions about alcohol and its consumption. Even then, more work is needed to clarify the potency of such influences alongside the effects of nonmediated social and environmental factors. Some writers have argued strongly that when parental and peer group factors are taken into account, the influence of advertising exposure on alcohol consumption among young people is seriously weakened (Kinard & Webster, 2010).

Should Alcohol Advertising and Other Media Depictions of Its Use Be More Tightly Controlled?

There are ongoing concerns about underage drinking and abuse of alcohol (Foxcroft, Ireland, Lister-Sharp, Lowe, & Breen, 2003; Roche, 2003). These concerns are reinforced by statements from the World Health Organization (WHO) that confirm national statistics about the prevalence of underage alcohol consumption and excessive consumption. In turn, the WHO has called for countries around the world to review and tighten up their regulatory controls over the sale, distribution, and pricing of alcohol products and the way they are advertised (WHO, 1995, 2004). Concerns about underage drinking have been echoed by medical authorities that have highlighted the short-term and longer-term health risks associated with early onset of alcohol consumption and regular consumption to excess by young people. Among the solutions highlighted here is to place further restrictions on the way alcoholic products can be distributed and promoted (British Medical Association, 2008).

Governments have responded by tightening up licensing laws and encouraging regulators to review codes of practice relating to alcohol marketing. These actions have met with mixed success. Much depends on how far-reaching they are. The introduction of restrictions on the way alcoholic beverages can be advertised will have little impact if vendors are permitted to adopt competitive pricing practices that bring the cost of drinking within a range young people can afford. Furthermore, some retailers have treated alcohol as a loss leader to draw customers in and this can encourage teenagers to buy in bulk to fuel heavy drinking sessions. Social experiments with extended drinking hours are believed to pull drunks off the streets, but may instead have increased rates of excessive consumption and of other associated social problems (Chitritzhs & Stockwell, 2002; Plant & Plant, 2006).

The alcohol industry has attempted to circumvent the implementation of tighter legislated restrictions on their marketing activities by engaging in self-regulation. They publish their own advertising and marketing codes of practice, often resonating closely with those operated by national regulators. Independent observations have criticized the effectiveness of self-regulation by industry (Hill & Casswell, 2004; G. Roberts, 2002; Saunders & Yap, 1991).

Concerns about the abuse and misuse of alcohol by young people, even before they reach adulthood, derive from the prevalence of alcohol-related illnesses and social disturbances. It would be wrong, however, to presume that because such negative social outcomes can derive from irresponsible consumption of alcohol that any media depictions or promotions of alcohol must also be labeled as inherently bad. Ultimately, whether mediated representations of alcohol represent a problem in their own right must be judged according to whether robust empirical evidence exists to demonstrate unequivocally that they play a significant part in causing such behavior.

As the review of evidence provided in this chapter has indicated, research findings are not always clear cut. Empirical research, for example, about the impact of advertising and portrayals of alcohol use in the media has been dogged with methodological limitations in part linked to the intrinsic limitations of specific methods to demonstrate causality and in part to a failure on the part of researchers to build in adequate controls for the effects on drinking onset of nonmediated variables present in the social environments of young people. Such criticisms are not unique to research into the effects of alcohol-related advertising or media reports or portrayals. Nevertheless, they are particularly important in this context where the existing evidence is cited to support arguments for tighter restrictions to be placed on the marketing practices of legitimate businesses.

There is another issue that requires disentangling. Concern about alcohol consumption has frequently been grounded in an observation, or more often an assumption, that this behavior is on the rise. Closer inspection of relevant statistics reveals that this is not always true (Measham, 2007). Drinking trends have always fluctuated over time and it is important to be cognisant of such behavior patterns in deciding whether recent trends reflect a significant social change or part of a conventionally fluctuating cycle. Alcohol consumption has been observed to rise over different periods of time across the 19th and 20th centuries and during the earlier phases of this cycle mediated representations of alcohol were virtually absent (Plant & Plant, 2006).

Average levels of alcohol consumption among children, teenagers, and young adults may have flat-lined in many developed countries, but increased rates of drinking to excess, in order to get drunk, have been observed. In the UK, for instance, drinking to get drunk has become culturally accepted as an appropriate behavior to adopt among teenagers and adults in their early 20s (Talbot & Crabbe, 2008). The success of a social event is often defined by the young in terms of how drunk they got (Engineer, Phillips, Thompson, & Nichols, 2003). Such abuse of alcohol does pose serious health risks for young people (Bonomo, Bowes, Coffey, Carlin, & Patton, 2004; Wells, Horwood, & Ferguson, 2004). The attitudes displayed by young people regarding such behavior signal that health concerns rarely feature in their thinking. Alcohol marketers meanwhile have been accused of deliberately targeting young people with new products designed especially to appeal to this market category (Barnard & Forsyth, 1998; Measham & Brain, 2005). By making drinking more intrinsically appealing by creating products that appeal in particular to the taste preferences of underage drinkers (i.e., sweet tasting beverages with high alcohol content), underage drinking has been encouraged (Hastings & Angus, 2009).

It is not just the manufacture of specific products targeted at the taste bud preferences of the young that is at issue here. In many countries, medical authorities have accused alcohol manufacturers of using advertising themes that are known to appeal to the young (usually referring here to those below the legal drinking age), regardless of the type of product (Fortin & Rempel, 2005). Pressure has then been brought to bear on advertising regulators to introduce more restrictive codes of practice across all the major advertising media.

Many recent alcohol advertising code changes in this context have outlawed the use of themes such as social and sexual success, links with sport and the use of very young looking actors. These changes have been informed by research findings that allegedly showed these factors to promote the attention of children and teenagers to alcohol advertisements (Gunter et al., 2010; Hastings & Angus, 2009;). For some critics, these code reviews have not gone far enough (Hastings & Angus, 2009). It has been claimed, for example, that there are many other attributes not always covered by codes of practice for which research evidence has identified youth appeals (Nash, Pine, & Lutz, 2000). Restrictions can also target the media location of alcohol advertising to reduce the likelihood of youth exposure. This action is not based on precise empirical evidence, however. A magazine, for instance, might be primarily targeted at a young adult readership aged 21 and over, but still attract readers aged under 18 (Nelson, 2005). In addition, thematic restrictions may apply to one medium and not to another. So, the use of themes of social and sexual success may be restricted for advertising on television, but this regulation may not apply in the case of the Internet (Carroll & Donovan, 2002).

In the context of the effectiveness of advertising restrictions in relation to children and teenagers, it is important not to forget that youth traditionally rebel against authority especially when it places restrictions on their freedom to choose. This psychological reactance has been observed to influence people's behavior in a range of contexts (see Bushman & Stack, 1996; Krcmar & Cantor, 1997). For young people, underage alcohol consumption is psychologically wrapped up with a broader rebelliousness (Cragg, 2004). In relation to the sale of alcohol, previous attempts at restrictive social engineering in the form of prohibition failed to stop people from drinking and encouraged an active black market in production and consumption (Hall, 2010). This observation in respect of alcohol advertising restrictions has been reinforced by analysis of alcohol advertising bans across 17 developed countries that indicated no reduction in consumption levels following the introduction of such bans (Nelson, 2010a).

Evidence has emerged among teenagers themselves that the effectiveness of code of practice restrictions has begun to bite. In one analysis, young people in the UK continued to like alcohol advertisements, but in 2007 fewer felt that these promotions were aimed specifically at them compared with in 2005 (Ofcom, 2007). Despite this observation, other audits have detected code of practice violations in print and televised advertising of alcohol (Advertising Standards Association (ASA), 2007; Donovan et al., 2007). Other studies found broad compliance with code of practice rule changes in respect of television advertising of alcohol, though there was some additional evidence that the spirit if not the letter of the law was being stretched by some advertisers (Gunter et al., 2008).

Conclusion

The task of providing clear-cut research evidence on the effects of mediated depictions of alcohol and drinking on public beliefs, perception, attitudes, and behavior in relation to alcohol and alcohol consumption will continue to present a challenge to researchers, in this as in so many other areas of research concerned with the role of media and communication in society. Our review shows, however, that much has been achieved over the last three decades in terms of advancing our understanding of the role played by mediated representations of alcohol. Our cultural and symbolic environment is saturated with images of alcohol and drinking that are largely positive, showing alcohol as a normal, unproblematic, and integral part of successful lifestyles and pleasant social interaction, while much less frequently drawing attention to the potential problems associated with excessive drinking.

The cumulative research evidence moreover shows that symbolic and mediated representations of alcohol and drinking are not a simple or neutral "reflection" of social and cultural values associated with drinking, but are of course subject to the continuous and active influence and manipulation by a wide range of diverse and often directly opposed interests representing different social, political, and business agendas. The sheer social, cultural, and symbolic pervasiveness of alcohol makes it difficult to disentangle the contribution of individual media representations to public beliefs and practices with regard to alcohol and drinking—whether in alcohol advertising, wider forms of marketing, news media reports, or entertainment media portrayals.

Our review of research shows that significant headway has been made in terms of mapping the extent and nature of mediated representations of alcohol, not just in advertising, but importantly, in the much wider media environment, including in entertainment media content. Considerable progress has been made also in terms of providing a more nuanced and differentiated understanding of how and where alcohol-related (mediated) messages appear, and which population groups are targeted or exposed to these messages. In other words, significant progress has been made toward mapping the contours of the mediated message environment regarding alcohol and, hence, toward identifying where potential effects or influences of media messages about alcohol may or are likely to occur. Our review of research approaches and research evidence on the impact of mediated messages about alcohol on (young) people's beliefs, perception, and behavior regarding alcohol and its uses confirms the complex theoretical, conceptual, and methodological challenges which continue to confront research on media influence/effects: particularly, the review confirms, that research evidence has established significant and extensive correlations between exposure to media messages and alcohol consumption and beliefs, but has generally failed to demonstrate causality.

Our review has identified a number of areas and issues that will merit further development, improvement, and research attention, and we finish by listing these:

- The increasing convergence of older (print and broadcast media) and newer media (online communication, the Internet, mobile phone technologies) brings significant changes and opportunities/possibilities to the ways in which messages, information, values, and meanings associated with alcohol and its uses are constructed, manipulated, and communicated. Research urgently needs to begin to catch up with the fast-paced changes that are already taking place in this regard. This would include research on, for example, the ways that companies and advertisers utilize the new media environment for marketing and promotion; exposure to and interaction with new media environments and communication about alcohol; alcohol-related messages and communication in social media such as MySpace and Facebook.
- Under the banner of "new media" we also need better understanding of how young people engage with new technologies and their use as promotional tools involving qualitative and observational research techniques. This is essential to distinguish between the different forms of engagement with alcohol products that are feasible via these technologies so that they can be effectively represented in multivariate research designed to understand their particular role, alongside other potential causal factors, in shaping alcohol-related habits
- Better (systematic, consistent, and regular) monitoring of alcohol promotion and marketing across different media and genres, including monitoring of adherence to relevant voluntary or statutory codes regarding the extent/content of alcohol-messages and the target/actual audiences for such media, genres, and messages.
- More comprehensive survey research is needed into the influence of alcohol advertising and media-related portrayals on the onset of drinking. This means surveys that undergo extensive pretesting to ensure that a more comprehensive range of potential causal factors in relation to the onset of drinking—social, psychological, and mediated variables—are identified and effectively measured. Measures should be constructed to permit complex multivariate modeling.
- Better theoretically informed research that includes effective measurement of cognitive and affective measures of reactions to alcohol advertisements and media portrayals and of how these prebehavioral response measures mediate eventual behavioral responding.

References

Aaker, D. (1996). Measuring brand equity across products and markets. *California Management Review, 38*(3), 102–120.

Advertising Standards Authority. (2007). *Alcohol advertising survey 2007.* London: Advertising Standards Authority (ASA).

Aitken, P. P. (1989). Television alcohol commercials and under-age drinking. *International Journal of Advertising, 8*, 133–150.

Aitken, P. P., Eadie, D. R., Leathar, D. S., McNeill, R. E. J., & Scott, A. C. (1988). Television advertisements for alcoholic drinks do reinforce underage drinking. *British Journal of Addiction, 83*(12), 1399–1419.

Aitken, P. P., Leathar, D. S., & Scott, A. C. (1988). Ten- to sixteen-year-olds' perceptions of advertisements for alcoholic drinks. *Alcohol and Alcoholism, 23*(6), 491–500.

Anderson, P. (2007). *The impact of alcohol advertising: ELSA project report on the evidence to strengthen regulation to protect young people.* Utrecht, the Netherlands: National Foundation for Alcohol Prevention.

Anderson, P., de Bruijn, A., Angus, K., Gordon, R., & Hastings, G. (2009). Impact of alcohol advertising and media exposure on adolescent alcohol use: A systematic review of longitudinal studies. *Alcohol and Alcoholism, 44*(3), 229–243. doi: 10.1093/alcalc/agn115

Andsager, J. L., Austin, E. W., & Pinkleton, B. E. (2002). Gender as a variable in interpretation of alcohol-related messages. *Communication Research, 29*(3), 246–269.

Atkin, C., & Block, M. (1981). *Content and effects of alcohol advertising: Report submitted to the Bureau of Alcohol, Tobacco and Firearms.* Springfield, VA: U.S. National Technical Information Service.

Atkin, C., & Block, M. (1984). The effects of alcohol advertising. In T. C. Kinnear (Ed.), *Advances in consumer research* (Vol. 11, pp. 689–693). Provo, UT: Association for Consumer Research.

Atkin, C. K., Neuendorf, K., & McDermott, S. (1983). The role of alcohol advertising in excessive and hazardous drinking. *Journal of Drug Education, 13*(4), 313–325.

Austin, E. W., & Hust, S. J. T. (2005). Targeting adolescents? The content and frequency of alcoholic and nonalcoholic beverage ads in magazine and video formats—November 1999–April 2000. *Journal of Health Communication, 10*(8), 769–785. doi:10.1080/10810730500326757

Austin, E. W., & Knaus, C. (2000). Predicting the potential for risky behavior among those "too young" to drink as the result of appealing advertising. *Journal of Health Communication, 5*, 13–27.

Austin, E. W., & Meili, H. K. (1994). Effects of interpretations of televised alcohol portrayals on children's alcohol beliefs. *Journal of Broadcasting & Electronic Media, 38*(4), 417–435.

Austin, E. W., Pinkleton, B. E., & Fujioka, Y. (2000). The role of interpretation processes and parental discussion in the media's effects on adolescents' use of alcohol. *Pediatrics, 105*(2), 343–349.

Babor, T., Caetano, R., Casswell, S., Edwards, G., Giesbrecht, N., Graham, K. (2003). *Alcohol: No ordinary commodity: Research and public policy.* New York: Oxford University Press.

Barnard, M., & Forsyth, A. J. M. (1998). Alcopops and under-age drinking: Changing trends in drink preference. *Health Education, 6*, 208–212.

Barton, R., & Godfrey, S. (1988). Un-health promotion—Results of a survey of alcohol promotion on television. *British Medical Journal, 296*(6636), 1593–1594.

Beullens, K., & Van den Bulck, J. (2008). News, music videos and action movie exposure and adolescents' intentions to take risks in traffic. *Accident Analysis and Prevention, 40*(1), 349–356. doi:10.1016/j.aap.2007.07.002

Bonomo, Y. A., Bowes, G., Coffey, C., Carlin, J. B., & Patton, G. C. (2004). Teenage drinking and the onset of alcohol dependence: A cohort study over seven years. *Addiction, 99*(12), 1520–1528. doi:10.1111/j.1360-0443.2004.00846.x

Borell, S., Gregory, M., & Kaiwai, H. (2005). *"If Snoop Dogg was selling it, I'd probably buy it": Alcohol marketing and youth voices.* Paper presented at the ALAC Working Together conference, Auckland, New Zealand

Breed, W., & DeFoe, J. R. (1979). Themes in magazine alcohol advertisements: a critique. *Journal of Drug Issues, 9,* 511–522.

Breed, W., & DeFoe, J. R. (1981). The portrayal of the drinking process on prime-time television. *Journal of Communication, 31*(1), 58–67.

Breed, W., DeFoe, J. R., & Wallack, L. (1984). Drinking in the mass media—A 9-year project. *Journal of Drug Issues, 14*(4), 655–664.

British Medical Association. (2008, February). *Alcohol misuse: Tackling the UK epidemic.* London: BMA Board of Science.

Brown, R. A. (1978). Educating young people about alcohol use in New Zealand: Whose side are we on? *British Journal of Alcohol and Alcoholism, 13,* 199–204.

Bushman, B. J., & Stack, A. D. (1996). Forbidden fruit versus tainted fruit: Effects of warning labels on attraction to television violence. *Journal of Experimental Psychology-Applied, 2*(3), 207–226. doi:10.1037//1076-898x.2.3.207

Cafiso, J., Goodstadt, M. S., Garlington, W. K., & Sheppard, M. A. (1982). Television portrayal of alcohol and other beverages. *Journal of Studies on Alcohol, 43*(11), 1232–1243.

Carroll, T. E., & Donovan, R. J. (2002). Alcohol marketing on the internet: New challenges for harm reduction. *Drug and Alcohol Review, 21*(1), 83–91.

Casswell, S. (2004). Alcohol brands in young people's everyday lives: New developments in marketing. *Alcohol and Alcoholism, 39*(6), 471–476.

Cellucci, T., & Larsen, R. (1995). Alcohol education via American literature. *Journal of Alcohol and Drug Education, 40*(3), 65–73.

Center on Alcohol Marketing and Youth (CAMY). (2002). Television: Alcohol's Vast Adland. Washington, DC: Center on Alcohol Marketing and Youth.

Center on Alcohol Marketing and Youth (CAMY). (2003). Youth Exposure to Radio Advertising for Alcohol: United States, Summer 2003. Washington, DC: Center on Alcohol Marketing and Youth.

Center on Alcohol Marketing and Youth (CAMY). (2004). *Clicking with kids: Alcohol marketing and youth on the Internet.* Washington, DC: Author.

Center on Alcohol Marketing and Youth. CAMY. (2005). Youth Overexposed: Alcohol Advertising in Magazines, 2001 to 2003. Retrieved from http://www.camy.org/research/mag0405/mag0405.pdf

Center on Alcohol Marketing and Youth (CAMY). (2007). *Youth exposure to alcohol advertising on radio 2006.* Washington, DC: Author.

Center on Alcohol Marketing and Youth (CAMY). (2010a). *Youth exposure to alcohol advertising on television, 2001–2009.* Washington, DC: Author.

Center on Alcohol Marketing and Youth (CAMY). (2010b). *Youth exposure to alcohol advertising in national magazines, 2001–2008.* Washington, DC: Author.

Chen, M. J., Grube, J. W., Bersamin, M., Waiters, E., & Keefe, D. B. (2005). Alcohol advertising: What makes it attractive to youth? *Journal of Health Communication, 10*(6), 553–565.

Chikritzhs, T., & Stockwell, T. (2002). The impact of later trading hours for Australian public houses (hotels) on levels of violence. *Journal of Studies on Alcohol, 63*(5), 591–599.

Christenson, P. G., Henriksen, L., & Roberts, D. F. (2000). *Substance use in popular prime-time television.* Washington, DC: Office of National Drug Control Policy.

Christiansen, B. A., Roehling, P. V., Smith, G. T., & Goldman, M. S. (1989). Using alcohol expectancies to predict adolescent drinking behavior after one year. *Journal of Consulting and Clinical Psychology, 57*(1), 93–99. doi:10.1037//0022-006x.57.1.93

Collins, R. L., Ellickson, P. L., McCaffrey, D. F., & Hambarsoomians, K. (2005). Saturated in beer: Awareness of beer advertising in late childhood and adolescence. *Journal of Adolescent Health, 37*(1), 29–36.

Connolly, G. M., Casswell, S., Zhang, J. F., & Silva, P. A. (1994). Alcohol in the mass-media and drinking by adolescents—A longitudinal-study. *Addiction, 89*(10), 1255–1263.

Cook, J., & Lewington, M. (Eds.). (1979). *Images of alcoholism.* London: British Film Institute.

Coyne, S. M., & Ahmed, T. (2009). Fancy a pint? Alcohol use and smoking in soap operas. *Addiction Research & Theory, 17*(4), 345–359. doi:10.1080/16066350801902459

Cragg, A. (2004). *Alcohol advertising and young people* (Research report for the Independent Television Commission and Ofcom, British Board of Film Classification, and Advertising Standards Authority). London: Cragg, Ross, Dawson.

Cruz, J. D. (1988). Booze and blues: Alcohol and black popular music, 1920–1930. *Contemporary Drug Problems, 15*(2), 149–186.

Daykin, N., Irwin, R., Kimberlee, R., Orme, J., Plant, M., & McCarron, L. (2009). Alcohol, young people and the media: A study of radio output in six radio stations in England. *Journal of Public Health, 31*(1), 105–112. doi: 10.1093/pubmed/fdn114

Denzin, N. K. (1991). *Hollywood shot by shot: Alcoholism in American cinema.* New York: Aldine de Gruyter.

Donovan, K., Donovan, R., Howat, P., & Weller, N. (2007). Magazine alcohol advertising compliance with the Australian Alcoholic Beverages Advertising Code. *Drug and Alcohol Review, 26*(1), 73–81. doi:10.1080/09595230601037026

DuRant, R. H., Rome, E. S., Rich, M., Allred, E., Emans, S. J., & Woods, E. R. (1997). Tobacco and alcohol use behaviors portrayed in music videos: A content analysis. *American Journal of Public Health, 87*(7), 1131–1135.

Ellickson, P. L., Collins, R. L., Hambarsoomians, K., & McCaffrey, D. F. (2005). Does alcohol advertising promote adolescent drinking? Results from a longitudinal assessment. *Addiction, 100*(2), 235–246.

Engineer, R., Phillips, A., Thompson, J., & Nichols, J. (2003, February). *Drunk and disorderly: A qualitative study of binge drinking among 18- 24-year-olds* (Home Office Research Study, Vol. 262). London: Home Office Research, Development and Statistics Directorate.

Everett, S. A., Schnuth, R. L., & Tribble, J. L. (1998). Tobacco and alcohol use in top-grossing American films. *Journal of Community Health, 23*(4), 317–324.

Fielder, L., Donovan, R. J., & Ouschan, R. (2009). Exposure of children and adolescents to alcohol advertising on Australian metropolitan free-to-air television. *Addiction, 104*(7), 1157–1165. doi10.1111/j.1360-0443.2009.02592.x

Finn, T. A., & Strickland, D. E. (1982a). A content-analysis of beverage alcohol advertising. Part 2. Television advertising. *Journal of Studies on Alcohol, 43*(9), 964–989.

Fisher, J. C., & Cook, P. A. (1995). *Advertising, alcohol consumption, and mortality: An empirical investigation.* Westport, CT: Greenwood.

Fortin, R. B., & Rempel, B. (2005). *The effectiveness of regulating alcohol advertising: Policies and public health.* Toronto, Canada: Association to Reduce Alcohol Promotion in Ontario.

Foxcroft, D. R., Ireland, D., Lister-Sharp, D. J., Lowe, G., & Breen, R. (2003). Longer-term primary prevention for alcohol misuse in young people: A systematic review. *Addiction, 98*(4), 397–411. doi:10.1046/j.1360-0443.2003.00355.x

Furnham, A., Ingle, H., Gunter, B., & McClelland, A. (1997). A content analysis of alcohol portrayal and drinking in British television soap operas. *Health Education Research, 12*(4), 519–529.

Garfield, C. F., Chung, P. J., & Rathouz, P. J. (2003). Alcohol advertising in magazines and adolescent readership. *Journal of the American Medical Association, 289*(18), 2424–2429.

Goodall, C. E., & Slater, M. D. (2010). Automatically activated attitudes as mechanisms for message effects: The case of alcohol advertisements. *Communication Research, 37*(5), 620–643. doi:10.1177/0093650210374011

Gordon, R., MacKintosh, A. M., & Moodie, C. (2010). The impact of alcohol marketing on youth drinking behavior: A two-stage cohort study. *Alcohol and Alcoholism, 45*(5), 470–480. doi:10.1093/alcalc/agq047

Greenman, D. J. (2000). Alcohol, comedy, and ghosts in Dickens's early short fiction. *Dickens Quarterly, 17*(1), 3–13.

Grube, J. W. (1993). Alcohol portrayals and alcohol advertising on television. *Alcohol Health and Research World, 17*(1), 61–66.

Grube, J. W. (2004). Alcohol in the media: drinking portrayals, alcohol advertising, and alcohol consumption among youth. In R. J. Bonnie & M. O'Connell (Eds.), *Reducing underage drinking: A collective responsibility* (pp. 597–624). Washington, DC: National Academy Press.

Gunter, B., Hansen, A., & Touri, M. (2008). *The representation and reception of meaning in alcohol advertising and young people's drinking* (Report for the Alcohol Education and Research Council). London: Alcohol Education and Research Council.

Gunter, B., Hansen, A., & Touri, M. (2009). Alcohol Advertising and Young People's Drinking. *Young Consumers, 10*(1), 4–16.

Gunter, B., Hansen, A., & Touri, M. (2010). *Alcohol advertising and young people's drinking: Representation, reception and regulation.* Basingstoke, England: Palgrave Macmillan.

Hall, W. (2010). What are the policy lessons of National Alcohol Prohibition in the United States, 1920–1933? *Addiction, 105*(7), 1164–1173. doi:10.1111/j.1360-0443.2010.02926.x

Hanewinkel, R., & Sargent, J. D. (2009). Longitudinal study of exposure to entertainment media and alcohol use among German adolescents. *Pediatrics, 123*(3), 989–995. doi:10.1542/peds.2008-1465

Hanewinkel, R., Tanski, S. E., & Sargent, J. D. (2007). Exposure to alcohol use in motion pictures and teen drinking in Germany. *International Journal of Epidemiology, 36,* 1068–1077. doi:10.1093/ije/dym128

Hanneman, G. J., & McEwen, W. J. (1976). The use and abuse of drugs: An analysis of mass media content. In R. E. Ostman (Ed.), *Communication research and drug education* (Vol. 3, pp. 65–88). London: Sage.

Hansen, A. (1986). The portrayal of alcohol on television. *Health Education Journal, 45*(3), 127–131.

Hansen, A. (1988). The contents and effects of television images of alcohol: Towards a framework of analysis. *Contemporary Drug Problems, 15*(2), 249–279.

Hansen, A. (1995). Viewers' interpretation of television images of alcohol. In S. E. Martin (Ed.), *The effects of the mass media on the use and abuse of alcohol* (pp. 151–156). Bethesda, MD: National Institutes of Health.

Hansen, A. (2003). *The portrayal of alcohol and alcohol consumption in television news and drama programs* (Research Report for Alcohol Concern). University of Leicester, Leicester, England.

Hansen, A., & Gunter, B. (2007). Constructing public and political discourse on alcohol issues: Towards a framework for analysis. *Alcohol and Alcoholism, 42*(2), 150–157.

Hastings, G., Anderson, S., Cooke, E., & Gordon, R. (2005). Alcohol marketing and young people's drinking: A review of the research. *Journal of Public Health Policy, 26*(3), 296–311.

Hastings, G., & Angus, K. (2009). *Under the influence—The damaging effect of alcohol marketing on young people.* London: British Medical Association.

Hastings, G. B., MacKintosh, A. M., & Aitken, P. P. (1992). Is alcohol advertising reaching the people it shouldn't reach? *Health Education Journal, 51*(1), 38–42.

Henriksen, L., Feighery, E. C., Schleicher, N. C., & Fortmann, S. P. (2008). Receptivity to alcohol marketing predicts initiation of alcohol use. *Journal of Adolescent Health, 42*(1), 28–35. doi:10.1016/j.jadohealth.2007.07.005

Herd, D. (2005). Changes in the prevalence of alcohol use in rap song lyrics, 1979–97. *Addiction, 100*(9), 1258–1269. doi:10.1111/j.1360-0443.2005.01192.x

Hill, L. (1999). What it means to be a Lion Red Man: Alcohol advertising and kiwi masculinity. *Women's Studies Journal, 15*(1), 65–85.

Hill, L., & Casswell, S. (2004). Alcohol advertising and sponsorship: Commercial freedom or control in the public interest? In N. Heather & T. Stockwell (Eds.), *The essential handbook of treatment and prevention of alcohol problems* (pp. 339–359). Chichester, England: Wiley-Blackwell.

Hoeffler, S., & Keller, K. L. (2003). The marketing advantages of strong brands. *The Journal of Brand Management, 10*(6), 421–445.

Jernigan, D. H. (2010). The extent of global alcohol marketing and its impact on youth. *Contemporary Drug Problems, 37*(1), 57–89.

Jones, S. C., & Donovan, R. J. (2001). Messages in alcohol advertising targeted to youth. *Australian and New Zealand Journal of Public Health, 25*(2), 126–131.

Keller, K. L. (2007). Advertising and brand equity. In G. J. Tellis & T. Ambler (Eds.), *The Sage handbook of advertising* (pp. 54–70). London: Sage.

Kinard, B. R., & Webster, C. (2010). The effects of advertising, social influences, and self-efficacy on adolescent tobacco use and alcohol consumption. *Journal of Consumer Affairs, 44*(1), 24–43.

Kohn, P. M., & Smart, R. G. (1984). The impact of television advertising on alcohol-consumption—An experiment. *Journal of Studies on Alcohol, 45*(4), 295–301.

Kohn, P. M., & Smart, R. G. (1987). Wine, women, suspiciousness and advertising. *Journal of Studies on Alcohol, 48*(2), 161–166.

Kohn, P. M., Smart, R. G., & Ogborne, A. C. (1984). Effects of two kinds of alcohol advertising on subsequent consumption. *Journal of Advertising, 13*(1), 34–40.

Kotch, J. B., Coulter, M. L., & Lipsitz, A. (1986). Does televised drinking influence children's attitudes toward alcohol. *Addictive Behaviors, 11*(1), 67–70. doi: 10.1016/0306-4603(86)90012-2

Krank, M. D., & Kreklewestz, K. L. (2003). *Exposure to alcohol advertising increases implicit alcohol cognitions in adolescents.* Fort Lauderdale, FL: Research Society on Alcoholism.

Krank, M. D., Wall, A. M., Lai, D., Wekerle, C., & Johnson, T. (2003). *Implicit and explicit cognitions predict alcohol use, abuse and intentions in young adolescents.* Fort Lauderdale, FL: Research Society on Alcoholism.

Krcmar, M., & Cantor, M. (1997). The role of television advisories and ratings in parent–child discussion of television viewing choices. *Journal of Broadcasting and Electronic Media, 41*(3), 393–411.

Kuther, T. L., & Higgins-D'Alessandro, A. (2003). Attitudinal and normative predictors of alcohol use by older adolescents and young adults. *Journal of Drug Education, 33*(1), 71–90.

Leiber, L. (1998). *Commercial and character slogan recall by children aged 9 to 11 years: Budweiser frogs versus Bugs Bunny.* Berkeley, CA: Center on Alcohol Advertising.

Lieberman, L. R., & Orlandi, M. A. (1987). Alcohol advertising and adolescent drinking. *Alcohol Health and Research World, 12*(1), 30–43.

Lipsitz, A., Brake, G., Vincent, E. J., & Winters, M. (1993). Another round for the brewers: Television ads and children's alcohol expectancies. *Journal of Applied Social Psychology, 23*(6), 439–450.

Lyons, A. C., Dalton, S. I., & Hoy, A. (2006). "Hardcore drinking" portrayals of alcohol consumption in young women's and men's magazines. *Journal of Health Psychology, 11*(2), 223–232. doi: 10.1177/1359105306061183

Madden, P. A., & Grube, J. W. (1994). The frequency and nature of alcohol and tobacco advertising in televised sports, 1990 through 1992. *American Journal of Public Health, 84*(2), 293–297.

Martinic, M., & Measham, F. (Eds.). (2008). *Swimming with crocodiles: The culture of extreme drinking.* London: Routledge.

Mathios, A., Avery, R., Bisogni, C., & Shanahan, J. (1998). Alcohol portrayal on prime-time television: Manifest and latent messages. *Journal of Studies on Alcohol, 59*(3), 305–310.

McCarty, D., & Ewing, J. A. (1983). Alcohol consumption while viewing alcoholic beverage advertising. *The International Journal of Addictions, 18*(7), 1011–1018.

McGee, R., Ketchel, J., & Reeder, A. I. (2007). Alcohol imagery on New Zealand television. *Substance Abuse Treatment Prevention and Policy, 2*(6), 1–6. doi: 10.1186/1747-597x-2-6

McIntosh, W. D., Smith, S. M., Bazzini, D. G., & Mills, P. S. (1998). Alcohol in the movies: Characteristics of drinkers and non-drinkers in films from 1940 to 1989. *Journal of Applied Social Psychology, 29*, 1191–1199.

Measham, F. (2007). The turning tides of intoxication: Young people's drinking in Britain in the 2000s. *Health Education, 108*(3), 207–222.

Measham, F., & Brain, K. (2005). "Binge" drinking, British alcohol policy and the new culture of intoxication. *Crime, Media, Culture: An International Journal, 1*(3), 263–284.

Montes-Santiago, J., Muniz, M. L. A., & Bazlomba, A. (2007). Alcohol advertising in written mass media in Spain. *Anales De Medicina Interna, 24*(3), 109–112.

Montonen, M. (1996). *Alcohol and the media* (WHO Regional Publication Series, Vol. 62). Helsinki, Finland: World Health Organization.

Moreno, M. A., Briner, L. R., Williams, A., Brockman, L., Walker, L., & Christakis, D. A. (2010). A content analysis of displayed alcohol references on a social networking web site. *Journal of Adolescent Health, 47*(2), 168–175. doi: 10.1016/j.jadohealth.2010.01.001

Nahoum-Grappe, V. (2008). Beyond boundaries: Youth and the dream of the extreme. In M. Martinic & F. Measham (Eds.), *Swimming with crocodiles: The culture of extreme drinking* (pp. 37–52). London: Routledge.

Naik, P. A. (2007). Integrated marketing communications: Provenance, practice and principles. In G. J. Tellis & T. Ambler (Eds.), *The Sage handbook of advertising* (pp. 35–53). London: Sage.

Nash, A., Pine, K., & Lutz, R. J. (2000). *TV alcohol advertising and children—A longitudinal study: Analysis of the first data collection.* Paper presented at the British Psychological Society Development Conference, Brighton, England.

Nash, A. S., Pine, K. J., & Messer, D. J. (2009). Television alcohol advertising: Do children really mean what they say? *British Journal of Developmental Psychology, 27,* 85–104. doi:10.1348/026151008x349470

Nelson, J. P. (2005). Beer advertising and marketing update: Structure, conduct, and social costs. *Review of Industrial Organization, 26*(3), 269–306.

Nelson, J. P. (2010a). Alcohol advertising bans, consumption and control policies in seventeen OECD countries, 1975–2000. *Applied Economics, 42*(7), 803–823. doi: 10.1080/00036840701720952

Nelson, J. P. (2010b). What is learned from longitudinal studies of advertising and youth drinking and smoking? A critical assessment. *International Journal of Environmental Research and Public Health, 7*(3), 870–926. doi:10.3390/ijerph7030870

Neuendorf, K. A. (1985). Alcohol advertising and media portrayals. *The Journal of the Institute for Socioeconomic Studies, 10*(2), 67–78.

Nunez-Smith, M., Wolf, E., Huang, H. M., Chen, P. G., Lee, L., & Emanuel, E. J. (2010). Media exposure and tobacco, illicit drugs, and alcohol use among children and adolescents: A systematic review. *Substance Abuse, 31*(3), 174–192. doi: 10.1080/08897077.2010.495648

Ofcom. (2007, November). *Young people and alcohol advertising: An investigation of alcohol advertising following changes to the Advertising Code.* London: Office of Communications and Advertising Standards Authority.

Phillipson, L., & Jones, S. C. (2007). *Awareness of alcohol advertising among children who watch televised sports.* Paper presented at the Proceedings of the Australian and New Zealand Marketing Academy (ANZMAC) Conference.

Pinsky, I., & Silva, M. T. A. (1999). A frequency and content analysis of alcohol advertising on Brazilian television. *Journal of Studies on Alcohol, 60*(3), 394–399.

Pitt, G., Forrest, D., Hughes, K., & Bellis, M. A. (2003). *Young people's exposure to alcohol: The role of radio and television.* Liverpool, England: John Moores University.

Plant, M., & Plant, M. (2006). *Binge Britain: Alcohol and the national response.* Oxford, England: Oxford University Press.

Postman, N., Nystrom, C., Strate, L., & Weingartner, C. (1987). *Myths, men and beer: An analysis of beer commercials on broadcast television, 1987.* Falls Church, VA: AAA Foundation for Traffic Safety.

Roberts, D. F., & Christenson, P. G. (2000). *"Here's looking at you, kid": Alcohol, drugs and tobacco in entertainment media*. Washington, DC: The Henry J. Kaiser Family Foundation.

Roberts, D. F., Henriksen, L., & Christenson, P. G. (1999). *Substance use in popular movies and music*. Washington, DC: Office of National Drug Control Policy.

Roberts, G. (2002). *Analysis of alcohol promotion and advertising*. Melbourne, Australia: Center for Youth Drug Studies.

Robinson, T. N., Chen, H. L., & Killen, J. D. (1998). Television and music video exposure and risk of adolescent alcohol use. *Pediatrics, 102*(5), E541–E546.

Roche, A. (2003). Alcohol advertising and promotion. *Of Substance: The National Magazine on Alcohol, Tobacco and Other Drugs, 1*(1), 3–4.

Rucker, D. D., Petty, R. E., & Priester, J. R. (2007). Understanding advertising effectiveness from a psychological perspective: The importance of attitudes and attitude strength. In G. J. Tellis & T. Ambler (Eds.), *The Sage handbook of advertising* (pp. 73–88). London: Sage.

Russell, C. A., & Russell, D. W. (2009). Alcohol messages in prime-time television series. *Journal of Consumer Affairs, 43*(1), 108–128. doi:10.1111/j.1745-6606.2008.01129.x

Rychtarik, R. G., Fairbank, J. A., Allen, C. M., Foy, D. W., & Drabman, R. S. (1983). Alcohol-use in television programming—Effects on children's behavior. *Addictive Behaviors, 8*(1), 19–22.

Sargent, J. D., Wills, T. A., Stoolmiller, M., Gibson, J., & Gibbons, F. X. (2006). Alcohol use in motion pictures and its relation with early-onset teen drinking. *Journal of Studies on Alcohol, 67*(1), 54–65.

Saunders, B., & Yap, E. (1991). Do our guardians need guarding? An examination of the Australian system of self-regulation of alcohol advertising. *Drug and Alcohol Review, 10*(1), 15–27. doi:10.1080/09595239100185031

Siegel, M., King, C., Ostroff, J., Ross, C., Dixon, K., & Jernigan, D. H. (2008). Comment-alcohol advertising in magazines and youth readership: Are youths disproportionately exposed? *Contemporary Economic Policy, 26*(3), 482–492. doi: 10.1111/j.1465-7287.2007.00088.x

Smith, L. A., & Foxcroft, D. R. (2009). The effect of alcohol advertising, marketing and portrayal on drinking behavior in young people: systematic review of prospective cohort studies. *BMC Public Health, 9*(1), 51–61.

Snyder, L. B., Milici, F. F., Mitchell, E. W., & Proctor, D. C. B. (2000). Media, product differences and seasonality in alcohol advertising in 1997. *Journal of Studies on Alcohol, 61*(6), 896–906.

Snyder, L. B., Milici, F. F., Slater, M., Sun, H., & Strizhakova, Y. (2006). Effects of alcohol advertising exposure on drinking among youth. *Archives of Pediatrics and Adolescent Medicine, 160*(1), 18–24.

Sobell, L. C., Sobell, M. B., Riley, D. M., Klajner, F., Leo, G. I., & Pavan, D. (1986). Effect of television programming and advertising on alcohol- consumption in normal drinkers. *Journal of Studies on Alcohol, 47*(4), 333–340.

Sobell, L. C., Sobell, M. B., Toneatto, T., & Leo, G. I. (1993). Severely dependent alcohol abusers may be vulnerable to alcohol cues in television programs. *Journal of Studies on Alcohol, 54*(1), 85–91.

Stacy, A. W., Zogg, J. B., Unger, J. B., & Dent, C. W. (2004). Exposure to televised alcohol ads and subsequent adolescent alcohol use. *American Journal of Health Behavior, 28*(6), 498–509.

Stern, S. R. (2005). Messages from teens on the big screen: Smoking, drinking, and drug use in teen-centered films. *Journal of Health Communication, 10*(4), 331–346.

Strasburger, V. C., Fuld, G. L., Mulligan, D. A., Altmann, T. R., Brown, A., & Christakis, D. A. (2010). Policy statement—Children, adolescents, substance abuse, and the media. *Pediatrics, 126*(4), 791–799. doi:10.1542/peds.2010-1635

Strickland, D. E. (1981, September). *The advertising regulation issue: Some empirical evidence concerning advertising exposure and teenage consumption patterns.* Paper presented at the conference on Control Issues in Alcohol Abuse Prevention, Charleston, South Carolina.

Strickland, D. E. (1982). Alcohol advertising: Orientations and influence. *International Journal of Advertising, 1,* 307–319.

Strickland, D. E. (1983). Advertising exposure, alcohol consumption and misuse of alcohol. In M. Grant, M. Plant, & A. Williams (Eds.), *Economics and alcohol: Consumption and controls* (pp. 201–222). New York. Gardner Press.

Strickland, D. E. (1984). Content and effects of alcohol advertising—Comment on NTIS pub no pb82-123142. *Journal of Studies on Alcohol, 45*(1), 87–93.

Strickland, D. E., & Finn, T. A. (1984). Targeting of magazine alcohol beverage advertisements. *Journal of Drug Issues, 14*(3), 449–467.

Talbot, S., & Crabbe, T. (2008). *Binge drinking, young people's attitudes and behaviour: A report commissioned by Positive Futures.* London, UK: Positive Futures Team, Crime Concern.

Thomsen, S. R., & Rekve, D. (2006). The relationship between viewing US-produced television programs and intentions to drink alcohol among a group of Norwegian adolescents. *Scandinavian Journal of Psychology, 47*(1), 33–41.

Trottman, R., Wyllie, A., & Casswell, S. (1994). *Content analysis of television alcohol advertisements.* Auckland, New Zealand: Alcohol and Public Health Research Unit, University of Auckland.

Unger, J. B., Johnson, C. A., & Rohrbach, L. A. (1995). Recognition and liking of tobacco and alcohol advertisements among adolescents—Relationships with susceptibility to substance use. *Preventive Medicine, 24*(5), 461–466.

Unger, J. B., Schuster, D., Zogg, J., Dent, C. W., & Stacy, A. W. (2003). Alcohol advertising exposure and adolescent alcohol use: A comparison of exposure measures. *Addiction Research & Theory, 11*(3), 177–193.

Van den Bulck, H., Simons, N., & Van Gorp, B. (2008). Let's drink and be merry: The framing of alcohol in the prime-time American youth series the OC. *Journal of Studies on Alcohol and Drugs, 69*(6), 933–940.

Van den Bulck, J., & Beullens, K. (2005). Television and music video exposure and adolescent alcohol use while going out. *Alcohol and Alcoholism, 40*(3), 249–253.

Waiters, E. D., Treno, A. J., & Grube, J. W. (2001). Alcohol advertising and youth: A focus group analysis of what young people find appealing in alcohol advertising. *Contemporary Drug Problems, 28,* 695–718.

Wallack, L., Breed, W., & Cruz, J. (1987). Alcohol on prime-time television. *Journal of Studies on Alcohol, 48*(1), 33–38.

Wallack, L. M., Cassady, D., & Grube, J. (1990). *Beer commercials and children: Exposure, attention, beliefs and expectations about drinking as an adult.* Washington, DC: AAA Foundation for Traffic Safety.

Wells, J. E., Horwood, L. J., & Fergusson, D. M. (2004). Drinking patterns in mid-adolescence and psychosocial outcomes in late adolescence and early adulthood. *Addiction, 99*(12), 1529–1541. doi:10.1111/j.1360-0443.2004.00918.x

Wilks, J., Callan, V. J., & Austin, D. A. (1989). Parent, peer and personal determinants of adolescent drinking. *British Journal of Addiction, 84*(6), 619–630.

Winter, M. V., Donovan, R. J., & Fielder, L. J. (2008). Exposure of children and adolescents to alcohol advertising on television in Australia. *Journal of Studies on Alcohol and Drugs, 69*(5), 676–683.

World Health Organization. (1995). *Global status report: Alcohol policy.* Geneva, Switzerland: Author.

World Health Organization. (2001). *Global status report on alcohol.* Geneva, Switzerland: Author.

World Health Organization. (2004). *Global status report: Alcohol policy.* Geneva, Switzerland: Author.

Wyllie, A., Zhang, J. F., & Casswell, S. (1998). Responses to televised alcohol advertisements associated with drinking behavior of 10-17-year-olds. *Addiction, 93*(3), 361–371.

Zwarun, L., & Farrar, K. M. (2005). Doing what they say, saying what they mean: Self-regulatory compliance and depictions of drinking in alcohol commercials in televised sports. *Mass Communication and Society, 8*(4), 347–371.

14 *Commentary*
Challenging Ourselves
to Advance Scholarship
on Portrayals of Alcohol
in the Media

Lara Zwarun

University of Missouri–St Louis

L ike all good literature reviews, Hansen and Gunter's synthesis of what is known about portrayals of alcohol in the media contributes to our understanding of the topic by giving us perspective. Not only do the authors reference a sizable number of studies, they also include both qualitative and quantitative research, enabling a synthesis often denied to themselves by those entrenched in one methodological camp or the other.

The presentation of such a large body of work requires a coherent organizational scheme, and in providing theirs, Hansen and Gunter are able to make important points about how drinking is portrayed in the media. Thus, we are reminded that promotional messages such as television commercials are not the only place such drinking is shown. There are also frequent depictions of alcohol use in entertainment media, including television shows, movies, and popular songs, that must be considered as well. In summarizing the research on both these types of portrayals, we begin to get a sense of the ubiquitous and cumulative "symbolic environment" through which young people learn about alcohol. By noting this, we are reminded of the similarities between portrayals of alcohol and tobacco use on the silver screen and in television programming: Both activities are most often depicted in the context of pleasant social interactions with little or no portrayal of negative consequences. Indeed the alcohol and tobacco industries have benefited greatly from the legitimization afforded by depictions of their products in films and TV shows designed for large middle-class audiences.

We are also made aware of the wide variety of ways that scholars have examined alcohol in the media; for example, by studying where media portrayals of drinking are found, how often they appear, who is likely exposed to them, and what kind of drinking behavior they actually depict. We are able to see the consistency, over time, of drinking being shown as a positive, attractive, rewarding, social activity.

However, a thorough literature review not only makes clear what we know, but also identifies where there are gaps in knowledge, and Hansen and Gunter's chapter accomplishes this in reviewing the research on what effects media portrayals of alcohol have on young people. It is not that research on this topic has not been conducted; indeed, the chapter takes us through surveys, experiments, and qualitative studies. Rather, what emerges is a problem shared by much media effects research: a difficulty in moving beyond correlational evidence and establishing causation.

We were all trained as scholars to respect the power of causation over correlation, and it seems especially important to achieve this power in the case of portrayals of alcohol in the media. Alcohol abuse, risky drinking, and underage alcohol consumption are all social problems with serious costs, and as Hansen and Gunter note, identifying and implicating causal factors in these problems is an important part of informing policy to address them. Thus, the inability to articulate clearly how media portrayals of drinking affect young people—the inability to even agree on what dependent variable to examine (is it awareness of the portrayals or liking of them? Is it drinking or believing that other people drink? Is it effects on certain at-risk individuals, or attitude formation at a societal level?)—is a shortcoming this chapter helps us to recognize and potentially address.

To that end, I suggest that research on media portrayals of alcohol be looked at through the lens suggested in an article by Potter (2011) on conceptualizing media effects. As Potter points out, most communication scholars operate on the assumption that media messages do have "effects," yet rarely do they define what this concept actually means. Potter identifies nine aspects or "definitional considerations" of the nature of a media effect in an effort to explicate the construct. While Potter's intention is to provide a means by which to organize and synthesize all media effects literature, I propose that we can also use his list to review what is and isn't known specifically about the effects of portrayals of alcohol in the media. In doing so, we can organize extant findings about drinking in the media into a useful landscape, while also building on Hansen and Gunter's suggestions to provide a comprehensive blueprint for future scholarship on the impact of how alcohol is portrayed in the media.

First, Potter asks us to consider the *type of media effect* we are looking for. By type, he means what sort of outcome exposure to media might result in: a behavior, an attitude, a belief? While criticism of media messages about alcohol is common, Hansen and Gunter's review shows there is little consensus among either critics or scholars regarding what the messages are allegedly doing to their audience. This is ironic, considering that by definition, television shows, advertisements, and other media messages are designed to result in specific outcomes on carefully defined audiences. While these outcomes may not always occur, they can surely be articulated by the professionals who paid for and designed the messages. Being mindful of the types of effects sought and the relationship among these effects could stimulate theoretical growth.

Potter also encourages consideration of the *level of media effects*. This consideration is particularly germane to the case at hand because Hansen and Gunter's review makes clear that there is conflation of individual and societal level effects across the research. Most research on alcohol in the media—and by their own admission, all of the research considered in this article by Hansen and Gunter—looks for outcomes that occur at the individual level, despite a suspicion that the real effect of media portrayals of drinking is cumulative and societal. Even phrases like "macrolevel" or "societal" can be too vague, Potter reminds us (2011). If societal-level effects are suspected, does this mean the messages impact a generational cohort, or do they impact a nation, and if so, one defined by geopolitical boundaries or by popular culture? It is not that there will be a single correct answer to these questions, but Hansen and Gunther's review makes it easy to see why simply posing them is a fruitful enterprise: an awareness of how we might answer them in the case of each new study we approach will hone our efforts, make subsequent comparisons and synthesis with other work more fruitful, and lead to more theory-building as opposed to individual studies driven by a "generating-findings perspective" (Potter, 2009).

Hansen and Gunter rightly note in their review that most research on mediated portrayals of alcohol does not reflect the current media environment, specifically the new technologies and platforms that are used both as promotional tools and in ubiquitous interpersonal communication among young people. This reality illustrates the importance of considering the element of *influence,* or whether the effect of media messages is thought to be direct or indirect (Potter, 2011). As this essay is being written, the current media environment is a conglomeration of what was traditionally considered mass versus interpersonal and corporate versus personal communication. Using portable technologies such as Internet-connected cell phones and tablet computers, growing numbers of people, particularly younger adults, remain in nearly constant contact with both institutional media sources and their own personal connections; additionally, largely through social networking, they combine both. As a result, the ways in which media portrayals can affect people have increased, perhaps exponentially. In this environment, along with exposure to the carefully designed messages from institutional sources described above, often comes input from friends, friends of friends, and whatever assortment of celebrities or public figures to which individuals might have opted to make themselves privy. It is almost quaint to think about a study of how a particular television show featuring drinking is interpreted without considering the simultaneous Tweeting that may also be occurring about it, or how it might be discussed later on a celebrity website, or the relationship an audience member might have with the alcohol brand on Facebook. Not only do these represent new methods of media influence, they are extremely intertwined, such that a synergistic effect among them is all but inevitable. The idea of a "pure" direct media effect, if there ever was such a thing, is quickly becoming obsolete. Following the path of influence across this network of connections and technologies is a complicated undertaking beyond the scope of this essay, but it is clear that a necessary first step is an awareness that it must be attempted—an awareness that is gained by considering issues of influence as suggested by Potter. From there, new theories and methods must evolve that keep up with this new reality.

This will also make the element of *timing*, or how long we wait to see if an effect occurs, important to consider. While the media environment described above makes a case for the likelihood of immediate reactions to media messages about alcohol, in terms of effects, many scholars would likely agree that these messages also have an overall, cumulative impression over time. Yet most experimental research is better designed to detect a direct effect of individual ads, campaigns, shows, or movies, suggesting that we will need to rely on survey or qualitative research to richen the search for long-term effects. This need to both tighten and broaden our sense of time will only result if we have asked ourselves about these issues in advance, thereby increasing the likelihood that we will design effective instruments and probe in meaningful ways. There is great promise for naturalistic and positivistic scholarship to work in tandem here, and addressing these issues facilitates this.

In addition to there being value in exploring what sort of outcomes scholars and other interested parties might look for, Potter reminds us there is also value in turning a critical eye to the input, or *type of stimulus itself*. While considering the effects of consistent, repeated media messages about alcohol over time suggests that their "form and nature" (Potter, 2011, p. 898) is relevant, consideration of the type of stimuli under investigation reminds us that there are also fruitful lines of research that have examined specific elements of the messages. In fact, studies of the cumulative effect of messages only make sense if studies of individual messages have already established that there is consistency and commonality across them. This is the sort of broad perspective across bodies of research that is afforded by Potter's suggested exercise.

The issue of *intentionality* is an interesting one because it pertains to media messages about alcohol. Here, Potter is suggesting that researchers consider whether they are interested only in effects that were intended by the producer of a message, or in unintended ones as well. Recent research applying the concept of strategic ambiguity to alcohol advertising provides an example of the type of insight possible when this line of thinking is pursued. Strategic ambiguity refers to designing messages that can create multiple interpretations in multiple audiences in order to accomplish multiple goals (Eisenberg, 1984), and is often used by organizations with diverse stakeholders to satisfy, such as the beer industry, which must contend with consumers, shareholders, critics, and policymakers (Zwarun, 2010). Alcohol advertising is largely unregulated because of First Amendment constraints, but adheres to its own self-regulatory guidelines (Beer Institute, 2007). In some instances, beer commercials are able to demonstrate literal compliance with self-regulatory guidelines (Zwarun & Farrar, 2005), while experimental research has shown that viewers of the ads perceive the exact depiction of drinking that is supposed to be prohibited (Zwarun, 2010; Zwarun, Linz, Metzger, & Kunkel, 2006). As these findings demonstrate, Potter's suggestion that the media stimuli themselves be considered from differing perspectives can yield rich insights.

Potter's list of considerations not only stimulates theoretical advances; it provides valuable challenges to practical and methodological issues as well. For example, he asks scholars to consider *change* as it pertains to media effects, and to define it to include the possibility that a behavior, belief, or attitude can be reinforced rather than altered as the result of exposure to media messages. While this may be a fruitful perspective in terms of advancing knowledge about the impact of alcohol-related media messages, it is not necessarily the best way to get published. In the face of this reality, the importance of Potter's mental exercise is clear.

By asking us to consider the issue of *pervasiveness*, Potter reminds us that even though the study of humans means our research produces statistical laws, not universal ones, this in no way diminishes the importance of what have learned and will continue to understand about who is most likely to be affected by media portrayals of alcohol and under what conditions. Finally, he asks us to consider the issue of *measurability*, in effect as a challenge to ourselves, so that research and instrument design keep pace with change and trends in the mediated world. For example, content analyses of media portrayals of alcohol, long a strong suit of the research literature, must move into new realms so that we first understand all the places and means by which young people encounter images of and information about drinking. As this awareness of what is out there evolves, this should lead to better conceptions of how such exposures might have impact, both individually and in tandem with one another; advances in measurement should follow.

By combining Hansen and Gunter's compilation of the literature on alcohol in the media and Potter's suggestions for conceptualizing what media effects we could and should be looking for, at least two benefits are achieved. For one, a rich landscape of what is known about media portrayals of alcohol is possible, one that expertly synthesizes data and insights produced in fields as diverse as marketing, medicine, public health, and communication. Second, it helps research in this area advance in a systematic, unified way, with proper attention given to conceptual, historical, and methodological considerations. This is the legacy of a good literature review, such as the one we have here, read with an active and curious mind.

References

Beer Institute. (2007). *Beer Institute advertising and marketing code*. Washington, DC: Author.

Eisenberg, E. (1984). Ambiguity as strategy in organizational communication. *Communication Monographs, 51*, 227–242.

Potter, W. J. (2011). Conceptualizing mass media effect. *Journal of Communication, 61*, 896–915.

Potter, W. J. (2009). *Arguing for a general framework for mass media scholarship*. Thousand Oaks, CA: Sage.

Zwarun, L. (2010, August). *Having your beer and drinking it too: Strategic ambiguity and self-regulation in beer commercials.* Paper presented to the Association for Education in Journalism and Mass Communication conference, Denver, CO.

Zwarun, L., & Farrar, K. M. (2005). Doing what they say, saying what they mean: Self-regulatory compliance and depictions of drinking in alcohol commercials in televised sports. *Mass Communication and Society, 8,* 347–371.

Zwarun, L., Linz, D., Metzger, M., & Kunkel, D. (2006). Effects of showing risk in beer commercials to young drinkers. *Journal of Broadcasting and Electronic Media, 50,* 52–77.

CHAPTER CONTENTS

15 Linking Risk Messages to Information Seeking and Processing

Robert J. Griffin

Marquette University

Sharon Dunwoody

University of Wisconsin–Madison

Z. Janet Yang

University at Buffalo

In an effort to better understand the ways in which risk messages can indirectly affect risk-related behaviors, this review explores the links between such messages and information seeking and processing. The narrative first offers a brief look at the literature that shores up salient concepts, and then moves to a model of risk information seeking and processing (RISP), constructed by Griffin, Dunwoody, and Neuwirth (1999), which seeks to organize those factors into a coherent framework. The RISP model, thus, serves as a crossroads for selected concepts synthesized from Eagly and Chaiken's (1993) heuristic-systematic model (HSM) of information processing, Ajzen's (1988) theory of planned behavior (TPB), and other bodies of research in communication and risk perception. Of particular interest is the extent to which the model can accommodate reactions to both personal risks and risks to persons and objects other than oneself. This last domain is particularly important to the development of policy in arenas such as public health and climate change. This review explores the theoretical underpinnings of the RISP model, and then summarizes a decade of studies that have examined a subset of RISP variables most closely related to information seeking and processing: channel beliefs, perceived information gathering capacity, and two motivation variables, information sufficiency and informational subjective norms. Finally, the authors explore the research potential of both the model and efforts to track the role of information in risk perceptions and behavior change.

Research on how best to communicate risk has become something of a cottage industry for federal agencies and for researchers worldwide. Communication scholars understand a great deal now about how experiential, cognitive, and affective factors can influence risk perceptions and risk-related behaviors. But, consistent with much of the literature on information campaigns, risk messages have tended to play only modest roles in behavior change. In many studies, the link between mediated information exposure/ use and behavioral intentions is trumped by other factors, such as personal experience with a risk or a priori beliefs about the risk. Those results, in turn, suggest that information is probably at its most powerful as an indirect rather than direct instigator of behavior change.

Additionally, while much risk communication scholarship that acknowl- edges this indirect path has focused on cognitive or affective reactions to risk as important way stations on the road to behavior change, few studies have tried to "unpack" the processes by which messages can actually influence these variables. Even fewer have sought to turn the tables in order to examine the impacts of risk perceptions on the ways in which individuals seek and utilize risk information.

These issues led us to an interest in information seeking and processing within a risk context. If information use is indeed indirectly (albeit impor- tantly) related to risk behavior change, then developing a more nuanced understanding of what drives more or less effortful use of information is an important goal. This exploration was facilitated by a large body of theory in both psychology and communication studies that focuses on these con- cepts, specifically Petty and Cacioppo's (1981) elaboration likelihood model (ELM) and, more recently, Eagly and Chaiken's (1993) heuristic-systematic model (HSM).

This review, then, examines information seeking and processing in the context of risks to health and the environment, with an eventual focus on the model of risk information seeking and processing (RISP) as first pro- posed by Griffin, Dunwoody, and Neuwirth (1999). Inherent in the model is an assumption that the complicated nature of risk and the potentially serious consequences associated with some health and environmental hazards make it important to understand the conditions that drive individuals to be more or less systematic in their use of risk information. The model also makes the case that variance in seeking and processing will stem from a number of background factors, such as various dimensions of risk perception (e.g., perceived level of risk and its seriousness), affective response to a risk (e.g., worry, anger), and perceived social pressures to stay informed about a risk (Griffin, Dunwoody, & Neuwirth, 1999). These variables have been associ- ated, directly or indirectly, with motivations to achieve sufficient information to deal with a risk (e.g., Griffin, Neuwirth, Dunwoody, & Giese, 2004; Grif- fin, Yang, et al., 2008). The RISP model pays special notice to the ways in which individuals process risk information. Deeper, systematic processing of information is expected to result in longer-lasting attitudes (Eagly & Chai- ken, 1993), an outcome that is particularly important to risk communication efforts designed to encourage individuals to adopt sustained beliefs, attitudes, and behaviors related to health, safety, and environment (Ajzen & Manstead, 2007; Griffin, Dunwoody, & Neuwirth, 1999).

The RISP model introduces few new concepts; instead, it concentrates on forging new linkages among established concepts. It was constructed through a procedure of first isolating factors important to risk behavior change generally, and to information seeking and processing specifically, and then linking those factors together in a coherent way (Griffin, Dunwoody, & Neuwirth, 1999). In that sense, it builds on the wealth of previous risk perception/communication research while seeking to make a contribution via its ability to test a novel *assemblage* of concepts and to allow powerful concepts from other models to compete with one another for variance in the information seeking and processing dependent variables. The RISP model is essentially a work in progress, inviting various researchers to contribute to its evolution and development.

In this narrative, we will first explore the dimensions of risk communication scholarship and theoretical models in both communication and psychology that led us to the RISP model, then we will share evidence to date regarding the model's robustness for human health risks and for risks to things other than self—what Kahlor, Dunwoody, Griffin, and Neuwirth (2006) term *impersonal risk* (p. 163). Finally, we will discuss ways in which scholars can further advance our understanding of linkages among risk messages, information processing and seeking, and behavior change.

Relevant Research Traditions

Although a narrative such as this cannot provide a comprehensive look at the massive literatures that inform the theoretical domains highlighted below, this review seeks to orient the reader with brief reflections on three domains: risk perception and communication, information seeking and processing (with an emphasis on Eagly and Chaiken's heuristic-systematic model), and Ajzen's theory of planned behavior.

Risk Perception and Communication

Early work in this area fell prey to strong effects assumptions, but scholars quickly learned that—as in other message effects domains—risk information influences are mediated by a host of factors, among them personal experiences with risky behaviors, cultural assumptions about risk, and even ideology. A few evolutionary trends have brought us to our current understanding of risk perceptions and the ways in which information informs those perceptions:

Unidimensional to Multidimensional. Initially, scientists and risk managers assumed risk was a unidimensional construct: an estimate of the likelihood of coming to harm. Successful risk communication, then, meant conveying that estimate accurately to audiences and expecting behavior change consonant with the estimate. If audiences reacted in ways contrary to the estimate—if a low risk of harm still sent folks into protective behavior mode, for example— that signaled a bad fit between risk and behavior and the problem was attributed to the inability of audiences to understand the risk (Fischhoff, 1995; Hance, Chess, & Sandman, 1989; National Research Council, 1989). Psychologist

Paul Slovic changed this landscape dramatically with work that suggested individuals' risk perceptions are multidimensional: Perceptions include likelihood of harm but also take into account other factors, such as familiarity with a risk, the extent to which a risk might affect future generations, and the number of people affected at any one time (Slovic, 1987, 1992, 2000).

Cognitive to Affective.   The primacy of "knowing" or of "feeling" has waxed and waned in both the risk perception and communication effects literatures. In health communication, for example, cognitive theories such as the health belief model (Rosenstock, 1966) and social-cognitive models such as the social learning theory (Bandura, 1977) have long competed with fear appeal frameworks such as protection motivation theory and Witte's extended parallel process model (Witte & Allen, 2000; see also Fishbein & Yzer, 2003). Affect took a back seat in the risk perception literature for many years, although Sandman highlighted the role of "outrage" in his work (Sandman, 1987) and Slovic's psychometric paradigm always featured an important factor that he termed *dread*. But today, many risk perception scholars are incorporating affect into their models, principally worry and fear. Slovic himself has been a primary actor in this arena (e.g., see Slovic, 2010)

Psychological to Sociological.   While most risk perception research examines risk and behavior at an individual level, predictors of those beliefs and behaviors have been both individual and aggregate in nature. The bulk of the risk perception literature focuses on individual-level cognitions and affective states, but scholars such as Douglas and Wildavsky (1983), Kasperson (1992) and, most recently, Kahan (Kahan, 2010; Kahan, Braman, Slovic, Gastil, & Cohen, 2009) seek to understand the ways in which societal norms and beliefs drive individual risk judgments.

Personal to Impersonal.   Risk perception and communication studies often focus on health risks to the self. While not surprising, that emphasis has probably contributed to a dearth in the development of theoretical frameworks that predict the ways in which individuals establish and act on perceptions of risk to others or to nonhuman elements in their environments. Individuals do make distinctions between self and other when assessing risk (Klein & Weinstein, 1997; Weinstein, 1989), and scholars have begun to explore the influence of other factors, among them "moral" emotions such as guilt and deeply held values, on behavioral reactions to others who are at risk (e.g., Kollmus & Agyeman, 2002; Massi Lindsey, Yun, & Hill, 2007; O'Keefe, 2000). This "impersonal" risk dimension has become increasingly important as societies struggle with the need to protect threatened ecosystems, maintain public health, or try to mitigate the impacts associated with climate change. Research has come a long way in understanding what motivates behavior change at the level of risk to self, but there is still a long way to go in unpacking the factors that lead individuals to act on behalf of others or in service to the protection of such things as endangered animals and plants.

Information Seeking and Processing

Much of the focus on information seeking and processing in communication scholarship stems from an interest in dual processing theories, which posit that individuals are driven by a variety of factors to engage differently (if dichotomously) with information depending on their needs. Sometimes, these models argue, people utilize information in an effortful, thoughtful way while at other times they move fitfully, even superficially, over the surface of information available to them. People are occasionally moved to seek information purposively but often find themselves in a more passive mode, reacting to information that comes over the transom in the course of a typical day.

Most of the dual processing models establish a normative hierarchy, regarding systematic, effortful processing as better than heuristic, superficial processing. Scholars such as Gigerenzer (1996, 2000) counter such normative assumptions, arguing that heuristic processing has the advantage of being "fast and frugal" and, often, leads to successful outcomes. But in the main, scholars who employ dual processing models privilege systematic processing, arguing that it results in better decision making and more stable belief patterns.

One of the most successful dual processing theories is Eagly and Chaiken's heuristic-systematic model. Structured within a broader framework to probe what constitutes the formation of attitude, Eagly and Chaiken (1993) argue that information processing, which offers cognitive resources to help form judgments, interacts with other affective and experiential factors to shape attitudes. Similar to other dual-processing theories, HSM defines heuristic processing as "a limited mode of information processing that requires less cognitive effort and fewer cognitive resources" (p. 327). Systematic processing, in comparison, is a "relatively analytic and comprehensive treatment of judgment-relevant information" (Chen & Chaiken, 1999, p. 74). These two concepts resemble the "peripheral route" and "central route" described in the elaboration likelihood model (Petty & Cacioppo, 1986). However, as Chaiken and Stangor (1987) pointed out, HSM asserts that "persuasion is often mediated by simple decision rules that associate certain persuasion cues with message validity," whereas ELM specifies motives that produce attitude change without generating active issue-relevant thinking (p. 593).

Even though heuristic processing is viewed as the flawed route in many studies, it has the mental and economic advantage of requiring a minimum of cognitive effort (Chaiken, 1980). Therefore, people tend to engage in heuristic processing unless motivated to adopt the more effortful strategy. However, Chaiken (1980) pointed out that a heuristic approach may be less reliable in judging message validity because an overreliance on simple decision rules may lead recipients to accept conclusions they might otherwise reject had they invested the time and cognitive resources to discover and scrutinize different arguments (p. 753).

Systematic processing, along with its potential to give individuals a better understanding of complex issues such as health and environmental risks, can produce more stable attitudes (Eagly & Chaiken, 1993). Thus, beyond information seeking, the conditions that lead to systematic processing should be of special interest to those who attempt to inform lay audiences about risks (e.g., journalists, public health, and public information professionals) and to those who try to persuade individuals to adopt enduring changes in their behavior, such as eating healthier food.

Although the two processing approaches sound orthogonal, heuristic and systematic processing can occur at the same time (Dijksterhuis, Bos, Nordgren, & Van Baaren, 2006). The bottom line, though, is that one would expect individuals who encounter information about a risk to engage in heuristic information seeking and processing unless one or more mediating factors push them into more systematic mode. Put another way, systematic processing of risk-related information should be rare.

The Theory of Planned Behavior (TPB)

Finding strong linkages between knowledge, attitudes, and behavior has always been challenging in the social sciences, and TPB has emerged as one of the most successful avenues for achieving that. The theory of planned behavior (Figure 15.1) proposes that a person's behavior is anticipated by his or her behavioral intention to perform a specific act. That intention, in turn, is based on three proximate predictors, any of which might be more important than the others from time to time: a favorable or unfavorable evaluation of the behavior (attitude toward the behavior, *AAct*); perceived social pressure to perform or

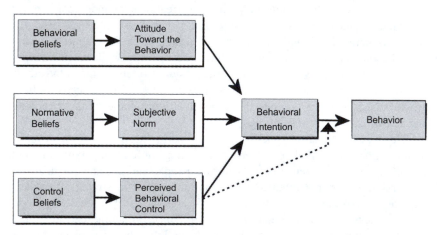

Figure 15.1 Ajzen's (1988, 1991) theory of planned behavior.

not perform the behavior (subjective norm, *SN*); and perceived capacity to perform the behavior (perceived behavioral control, *PBC*) (Ajzen, 1991).

In the TPB model, each of these three elements, in turn, is influenced by a set of specific beliefs measured in expectancy-value scale format. For example, AAct is influenced by a set of behavioral beliefs the individual might have about the likelihood that performing the behavior would lead to various outcomes that he or she might favor or disfavor to various extents. Each outcome belief is measured, on a bipolar scale (unlikely-likely), according to the person's perceived probability of its happening as a result of his or her performing the behavior (e.g., how likely/unlikely it is that a camping trip planned for next week would result in one's exposure to an infectious tick, would result in conversations with fellow campers, would cost a certain amount of money, would mean doing a lot of hiking, etc.). Then, the individual evaluates each potential outcome on a bipolar scale according to how bad or good it would be for him or her. Each outcome belief is multiplied by its evaluation rating and the product terms are summed to represent a cognitive structure of behavioral beliefs, which represents the trade-offs the person perceives in judging the behavior and developing an attitude toward performing it. In the above example, the person effectively weighs the risk of exposure to an infectious tick and the perceived seriousness of that exposure against the benefits (or drawbacks) of the other outcomes associated with the trip. Indeed, recent theoretical development emphasizes individuals' beliefs about the positive and negative consequences of the behavior (Fishbein & Yzer, 2003). In comparison with other popular behavioral theories, these authors concluded that a cost–benefit analysis approach should become an integral part of how one conceptualizes and evaluates attitude.

One benefit that TPB offers for many studies of risk-related behaviors is that fundamental elements of risk perception—perceived susceptibility to a hazard and the potential seriousness of exposure to it (e.g., Rosenstock, 1966)—can be incorporated directly into the measures of behavioral beliefs, as in the camping trip example where the individual considers the likelihood of encountering an infectious tick as well as the potential seriousness (badness) of that outcome. For one individual, that risk may be the one factor that overwhelmingly affects his or her attitude toward going on the camping trip, while for another individual the risk is simply weighed along with all the other perceived costs and benefits of the trip. Thus, TPB invites researchers to consider other beliefs and values that individuals weigh when considering a risky behavior or when thinking about taking steps to avoid or overcome hazards to self, others, or the environment (e.g., weighing the costs and benefits of having a flu shot, quitting smoking, engaging in recycling, buying compact fluorescent lamp bulbs).

Another element of TPB essential to studies of risk-related behavior is perceived behavioral control. Perceived behavioral control deals with the perceived presence of factors that can facilitate or impede one's performance of the behavior. To assess perceived behavioral control, TPB-based research usually focuses on self-efficacy, which refers to one's perceived capacity or confidence to perform the recommended behavior. The TPB suggests that greater perceived control leads to stronger behavioral intention (Ajzen, 1988) and, when it is an accurate perception of actual control, strengthens the link between behavioral intention and actual behavior (Ajzen, in press).

TPB also brings to studies of risk behavior the concept of subjective norms. People who perceive a greater social pressure to perform the behavior are expected to develop stronger behavioral intentions (Ajzen, 1988). These perceived behavioral expectations usually come from one's family and friends, as well as other important referent groups in one's social network (normative beliefs). An individual might perceive that these relevant others think he or she should perform the behavior (injunctive subjective norms) or perceive that the relevant others themselves generally do so (descriptive subjective norms).

Over the past three decades, the theory of planned behavior (TPB) has guided hundreds of empirical tests of its applicability in explaining why people engage in certain behaviors (for a review, see Ajzen & Fishbein, 2005), including a wide array of studies related to health behaviors (Ajzen & Manstead, 2007). TPB has been criticized for not including emotion, an important factor in risk perception and behavior, among the drivers of behavior (e.g., Dutta-Bergman, 2005). Ajzen and Manstead (2007), however, indicate that emotion can be one of the background factors that affect behavioral, control, and normative beliefs in the theory of planned behavior.

A Rationale for Integrating these Three Research Traditions into One Model

The research traditions and models discussed above have been spectacularly successful at illuminating segments of risk perception and decision-making processes. But as scholars have struggled to introduce communication variables into the mix, they have employed messages as something akin to "black boxes," components that may produce effects—albeit often indirect ones—but whose mechanisms are rarely well specified. We felt the theoretical domains discussed above offered a way to explore the mechanisms underlying risk information seeking and processing and, in the next section, detail how we extracted concepts from each in order to build a model that could usefully explore the ways in which individuals utilize information related to both personal and impersonal risks.

Model of Risk Information Seeking and Processing

To rise to the challenge of helping researchers understand how individuals seek and process information about risks, the model of risk information seeking and processing (Griffin, Dunwoody, & Neuwirth, 1999) incorporates elements from the larger risk perception literature and, more specifically, from Eagly and Chaiken's (1993) heuristic-systematic model (HSM) and Ajzen's (1988) theory of planned behavior (TPB). The risk perception literature offers a rich array of potential mediating factors, while the heuristic-systematic model provides the framework with a basic theoretical foundation in which to examine individuals' motivations and information processing capacities associated with risk information they might seek or encounter. The theory of planned behavior, in turn, makes available compatible insights into risk information seeking and processing specifically as communication *behaviors.*

From the risk perception and extant risk communication literature, Griffin, Dunwoody, and Neuwirth (1999) sequestered not only salient demographic characteristics of the audience but also a small set of cognitive and affective factors. On the cognitive side are perceived hazard characteristics, which employ a subset of Slovic's psychometric factors. On the affective side is a set of questions about both positively and negatively valenced reactions to the risk at hand.

The RISP model adopts HSM's proposition of a sufficiency principle, which suggests that "people will exert whatever effort is required to attain a 'sufficient' degree of confidence that they have satisfactorily accomplished their processing goals" (Eagly & Chaiken, 1993, p. 330). This judgmental confidence is closely tied to message validity and is termed, thus, an *accuracy motivation.* In the RISP model, information seeking and systematic processing are motivated by a person's desire for sufficiency and moderated by a person's capacity to do so (Griffin, Neuwirth, et al., 2004). According to Trumbo (2002), this framework is appropriate for communication studies because it effectively links the questions of where people get information about a particular topic to how they deal with this information.

Griffin, Dunwoody, and Neuwirth (1999) related the theory of planned behavior to the RISP model in two different ways. First, they proposed that systematic processing of information about a risk-related behavior would strengthen and stabilize behavioral beliefs and attitudes toward that behavior; to the extent that AAct, among other factors, influences behavior, stable AAct should help stabilize behavior. However, this proposed effect is not directional in terms of promoting risk-reducing beliefs, attitudes, or behaviors. For example, a person might carefully consider some information advising her to exercise to lose weight and then decide, for the long term, that exercising is not for her.

Second, Griffin, Dunwoody, and Neuwirth (1999) incorporated two elements of the theory of planned behavior, perceived behavioral control and subjective norms. Perceived behavioral control is compatible with the concept of capacity in the HSM model, given that risk information seeking and processing are the target behaviors. The upshot in the RISP model is a concept termed *perceived information gathering capacity.* Similarly, subjective norms beget *informational subjective norms* in the RISP model; the latter track an individual's beliefs that relevant others think he or she should stay informed about a given risk (i.e., seek and process information about it), considered an injunctive subjective norm, or that relevant others are themselves seeking and processing such information, a descriptive subjective norm.

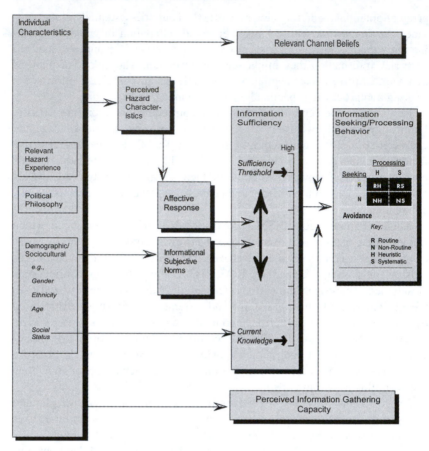

Figure 15.2 Model of risk information seeking and processing (based on Griffin, Dunwoody, & Newirth, 1999).

Figure 15.2 illustrates the model of risk information seeking and processing. While the original model proposed relationships between information seeking/processing and subsequent risk-related behaviors as specified by Ajzen's (1988) theory of planned behavior (see Griffin, Dunwoody, & Neuwirth, 1999), we limit our discussion in this review chapter to the variables shown in Figure 15.2, especially those on the right side of the figure: risk information seeking and processing and their proximate predictors (information insufficiency, perceived information gathering capacity, relevant channel beliefs, and informational subjective norms). These variables have received the most scholarly attention to date among the studies that have employed the RISP model.

Generally, the RISP model proposes that risk information seeking (or avoidance) and processing are affected by three main components, each of which may be more or less influential under different conditions: perceived information gathering capacity, relevant beliefs about the channels of communication that might carry risk-related information (channel beliefs), and information insufficiency, a subjectively perceived "gap" between one's current knowledge about the risk and the level of knowledge needed to deal adequately with the risk in one's life. In the RISP model, information insufficiency is considered a primary motivation for seeking and processing and can be affected by two other factors: informational subjective norms and affective responses to the risk, such as worry or anger. We propose that various risk perceptions, labeled in Figure 15.2 as "Perceived Hazard Characteristics," could trigger such affective responses to the risk.

Demographic and other personal characteristics might influence other RISP model variables, among them risk perceptions and channel beliefs. The capacity to successfully seek and process new risk information can be affected by factors such as social status (especially education) and current knowledge. Although the RISP model does not show feedback loops, we assume that most variables in the model (e.g., current knowledge, capacity, channel beliefs, risk perception, affective responses to risks) represent ongoing, cyclical processes that can be continuously affected by an individual's previous information seeking and processing and other factors, such as their personal experiences with risks.

Generally, if one assumes that audiences are goal-directed in seeking and processing information, then any study of these information-oriented behaviors must also examine variables that lead individuals to opt for some information channels over others. Slater (1997) explores this "active audience" approach in a theoretical article that draws on the existing uses and gratifications literature (e.g., Katz, Blumler, & Gurevitch, 1974; Rosengren, 1974; also see Rubin, 2002) but then posits that different receiver goals should create different information processing strategies. Those strategies, then, would lead an individual to select particular channels to satisfy particular needs, and would also lead an individual to opt into different levels of processing intensity. By way of example, Slater notes that a surveillance goal would lead an individual to the kinds of information channels that emphasize timely, relevant information (e.g., television news), but that goal would also permit a less effortful processing mode.

Thus, the RISP model strives to capture the relationship between processing goals (motivations) and general beliefs about channels of risk information that one might use to reach these goals, and then complements those relationships with measures of the impact of an individual's capacity to seek and process risk information. Consistent with Eagly and Chaiken's (1993) heuristic-systematic model, the perceived information gathering capacity concept in the RISP model reflects an individual's ability (albeit self-reported) to perform the information processing steps necessary for the outcome he or she desires, but expands the concept to include the individual's ability to seek the information as well (Griffin, Dunwoody, & Neuwirth, 1999). As illustrated in Figure 15.2, three factors (capacity, channel beliefs, and information insufficiency motivation) are expected to combine to affect individuals' seeking, avoidance, and processing of risk information.

The Key Components

With this as background, our exploration of the model begins with an explanation of the key variables, emphasizing those more closely related to communication and starting with the dependent variables: risk information processing and seeking. We will then visit studies that explore how well the key communication-related variables in the RISP model—information insufficiency, capacity, channel beliefs, and informational subjective norms—relate to risk information seeking and processing across time and different risks. A brief digest of these communication-related variables, their definitions, and theoretical origins, can be found in Table 15.1.

Information Processing.   Information processing is the keystone of the RISP model, and forms the primary theoretical gateway between communication-related variables and their potential impacts on the structure and stability of risk-related beliefs, attitudes, and behavior.

By default and necessity, according to the HSM model, most people employ the principle of least effort in processing messages, judging their validity and making inferences or decisions to comply through superficial cues such as the length of the message, the use of a trusted spokesperson, or the use of statistical data. This "heuristic processing" of information, Eagly and Chaiken (1993) state, is: "a limited mode of information processing that requires less cognitive effort and fewer cognitive resources" (p. 327) than systematic processing. The latter, by comparison, is a much more comprehensive effort to analyze and understand information. In HSM terms, people tend to adopt the form of processing that they use for a given message based on (a) their *capacity* to process the information in each manner, and (b) their *motivation* to go beyond the more superficial (heuristic) processing to engage in systematic processing. In the absence of sufficient capacity and motivation, individuals will usually default to heuristic processing.

According to the HSM formulation, a person's desire for sufficiency motivates systematic processing. For example, the personal relevance of the message topic to the individual can elevate the amount of confidence people want to have in the validity of the message or the judgmental confidence people tend to want (the "sufficiency threshold") in their own attitudes: Do those attitudes square with relevant facts? (*accuracy motivation*); are they defensible? (*defense motivation*); are they socially acceptable? (*impression motivation*) (Chaiken, Giner-Sorolla, & Chen, 1996; Eagly & Chaiken, 1993).

To help validate the concept and measurement of systematic processing within the RISP model, and to examine the proposed relationship of processing to the structure of subsequent beliefs (Griffin, Dunwoody, & Neuwirth, 1999), Griffin, Neuwirth, Giese, and Dunwoody (2002) examined the relationship between the RISP model and Ajzen's TPB. Consistent with RISP predictions, they found that systematic processing of risk information was positively related to attitude strength, evaluation strength, and the number of strongly

Table 15.1 Theoretical Origins and Definitions of Information Seeking and Processing Variables in the RISP Model, and Their Proximate Predictors

Concept	Definition	Origin

Information Processing	Treatment of information as a chain of responses: attention to the message (presentation, attention); comprehension of its content (comprehension); and acceptance or rejection of its conclusions (yielding, retention, and behavior) (Eagly & Chaiken, 1993, 259–260). The RISP model focuses broadly on cognitive processes related to the selection, encoding, and storage of risk-related information in human memory, and retrieval of relevant knowledge (beliefs) from memory; individuals' motivations, beliefs, and capacity related to seeking and processing; and outcomes, especially in terms of the stability of risk-related beliefs, attitudes, and behaviors.
	
	Systematic processing:
	   Relatively analytic and comprehensive treatment of judgment-relevant risk information.
	Heuristic processing:
	   Limited mode of information treatment that requires less cognitive effort and fewer cognitive resources.
		Heuristic-Systematic Model (HSM), e.g., Eagly & Chaiken (1993); McGuire (1968); Hovland, Janis, & Kelley (1953); Atkinson & Shiffrin (1968)

Information Seeking / Avoidance	Deliberate, intentional pursuit of further knowledge, as well as the more casual skimming of message and accidental observations and encounters.
	
	Information seeking:
	   More or less effortful attempts to gather information through a variety of mediated and interpersonal channels to achieve personal goals, including those representing various cognitive and affective motivations. Seeking might be routine (e.g., fairly passive exposure to risk-related information based on media use habits) or non-routine (e.g., more active efforts to gather risk-related information that go beyond habitual sources).
	Information avoidance:
	   More or less effortful attempts to evade information due to uncertainty management strategies, including avoiding information to reduce negative affect and maintain positive affect.
		Brashers (2001); Gantz, Fitzmaurice, & Fink (1991); Johnson & Meischke (1993); Knobloch-Westerwick (2008) Witte (1994)

(continued)

Table 15.1 Continued

Concept	Definition	Origin
Information (In) Sufficiency	Information sufficiency is a subjectively satisfactory level of judgmental confidence in one's knowledge to cope with a given risk. Information insufficiency, therefore, refers to an individual's subjective sense that one's current knowledge is not sufficient for that purpose. Information in this context refers to knowledge (beliefs) held by an individual, or potentially available to the individual (e.g., that he or she can seek or avoid), subjectively related to coping with a given risk.	HSM
Informational Subjective Norms	Perceived socio-environmental influence on one's subjective evaluation of information held to cope with a given risk and motivation to engage in subsequent information seeking and processing activities. *Descriptive norms:* Beliefs, from perceptions of others, about the extent to which gathering and learning risk information is done by relevant others. *Injunctive norms:* Perceived social normative influence from relevant others on information held about a given risk.	Theory of Planned Behavior (TPB), e.g., Ajzen (1988)
Relevant Channel Beliefs	*Original definition:* Beliefs about channels of information, including their trustworthiness and usefulness. *Newer, recommended approach:* One's beliefs and evaluations about the outcomes of one's seeking and processing risk information from various channels.	Kosicki & McLeod (1990); TPB; Palmgreen & Rayburn (1982)
Perceived Information Gathering Capacity	Perceived ability to perform the information seeking and processing steps necessary for the outcome one desires.	TPB, HSM

held behavioral beliefs across three environmental risks and among residents of two metropolitan areas, results that are consistent with RISP model predictions based on Eagly and Chaiken (1993). Similarly, other studies employing the RISP model have found that systematic processing is associated with attitudes toward clinical trial enrollment (Yang et al., 2010a) and with health-protective behaviors (Hovick, Freimuth, Johnson-Turbes, & Chervin, 2011).

Information Seeking and Avoidance. In an effort to extend the heuristic-systematic model in a way that more closely relates to communication research, the RISP model includes information seeking and avoidance as another set of behaviors for which components of the model could account. The model proposes that a greater need for information sufficiency is likely to motivate active information seeking. On the other hand, people who believe that they already know enough—or even too much—about a given topic might avoid additional information. Besides motivation, information processing capacity also influences information seeking activities because of individuals' differential access to information channels and differences in their abilities to understand the messages those channels convey.

Communication researchers have consistently argued for a distinction between active, purposeful information seeking and incidental exposure to information (Johnson & Meischke, 1993; Kim & Grunig, 2011; Niederdeppe, Frosch, & Hornik, 2008), especially in an information-saturated media environment (Brashers, Goldsmith, & Hsieh, 2002; Romantan, Hornik, Price, Cappella, & Viswanath, 2008). Thus, in addition to examining superficial and effortful processing separately, the RISP model distinguishes between "routine" exposure to risk information, as might occur through a casual encounter with risk information via habitual use of certain media, and the more active seeking of risk information (termed *nonroutine*) in Figure 15.2.[1] Kim and Grunig (2011) draw a similar distinction between *information seeking* and the more passive *information attending* in their situational theory of problem solving. The RISP model also acknowledges that people might devote more or less effort to avoiding information that distresses them (Case, Andrews, Johnson, & Allard, 2005; Witte, 1994) or distracts them from their primary goals for communication (McLeod & Becker, 1974).

The RISP model distinguishes seeking from processing, and emphasizes the latter, primarily because of the effects that processing can have on the stability and structure of beliefs that individuals may hold about a risk. Thus, for validity purposes, it is important to separate processing from seeking. However, the various combinations of seeking (nonroutine/routine) and processing (heuristic/systematic) are worth considering (Griffin, Dunwoody, & Neuwirth, 1999). These would include: (a) routine/heuristic, probably the most common, in which people superficially attend to risk messages they encounter through routine scanning of habitual media (e.g., they come across a health risk story while checking a news website they frequent); (b) routine/systematic, in which people do not alter their seeking patterns, but do process more deeply and critically the risk information they come across through habitualized media use; (c) nonroutine/heuristic, in which people expend extra effort to get information that they would then process heuristically (e.g., calling or seeing the doctor to acquire diagnoses and treatment recommendations that they plan to follow uncritically); and (d) nonroutine/systematic, the most effortful, in which people expend extra effort to go beyond routine sources of information to get information that they plan to examine more deeply and to evaluate critically (e.g., getting second opinions from doctors and complementing that with visits to sources such as WebMD to get further background information).

The outcomes of these admixtures on such things as belief structures would be exploratory. However, following are the various factors that could affect individuals' seeking and processing of risk information, separately or in combination.

Information (In)Sufficiency.   Building on the HSM concepts of accuracy motivation, sufficiency, and judgmental confidence, the RISP model proposes that different people try to reach varying but subjectively satisfactory levels of confidence in the information that they hold about a given topic ("information sufficiency"), especially as the basis for developing their risk-related beliefs, attitudes, and behavioral intentions. Griffin, Dunwoody, and Neuwirth (1999) propose that the drive to overcome information insufficiency (e.g., to gain and hold enough information to deal with a risk in daily life) motivates individuals to process risk-related information more systematically and less heuristically. In two studies applying elements of HSM to risks, Trumbo (1999, 2002) found full or at least partial support for a relationship between information sufficiency motivation and more effortful processing of risk information. Griffin, Dunwoody, and Neuwirth (1999) also propose that the sufficiency drive can similarly motivate more active, nonroutine seeking of information— that is, attempts to gather relevant risk information (e.g., calling the doctor) that go beyond habitual or routine channels a given individual might use for such information (e.g., watching the evening newscast)—and less avoidance.

Based on Eagly and Chaiken's (1993) accuracy motivation factor, the size of the subjective gap between information held (termed *current knowledge* in the RISP model) and that needed (*knowledge sufficiency threshold*)[2] will ultimately affect the information-seeking and processing styles employed by individuals to learn more about the risk. However, information seeking and processing are also seen as dependent upon one's ability to learn more about the risk (based on HSM's concept of capacity), on one's existing knowledge structures, and on the perceived usefulness and credibility of available information. Therefore, seeking (which includes avoidance) and processing are also affected by the variables "perceived information gathering capacity" and "relevant channel beliefs" in the RISP model.

Perceived Information Gathering Capacity.   Because the dependent variables of risk information seeking and processing are essentially communication *behaviors*, one's sense of self-efficacy (e.g., Bandura, 1986) or perceived behavioral control (e.g., Ajzen, 1988) in performing them are considered as important to measure here as in other domains of behavior or behavioral intention. Information-gathering capacity should reflect an individual's perceived ability to perform the information-seeking and processing steps necessary for the outcome he or she desires, especially when an outcome requires more cognitive effort and nonroutine gathering of information.

Although not specified in the original RISP model, current knowledge could enhance one's perceived capacity to seek and process new information about that topic, a proposition consistent with the knowledge gap model (ter Huurne, Griffin, & Gutteling, 2009; Tichenor, Donohue, & Olien, 1970).

In terms of seeking and accessing information, Chaffee (1986) pointed to two concepts that he argued were important predictors of channel use. One, channel accessibility, reflects the ease with which an individual can make use of the channel.[3] The second concept posed is relevance, the likelihood that a channel will actually contain the information sought.[4] In essence, Chaffee's approach posits a cost-benefit analysis in which an individual weighs the likelihood that a channel will deliver the content sought versus the difficulty he or she would have in accessing that channel. In the RISP model, an individual's sense of the cost of access (seeking) and processing is captured by the perceived information gathering capacity variable (i.e., greater capacity would make access easier, less "costly" and, therefore, more likely). Perceived benefits of seeking and processing information from various channels would be assessed by the individual's beliefs about the channels he or she might use to get risk-related information.

Relevant Channel Beliefs. Beliefs about channels of risk information, including their trustworthiness and usefulness, could affect the information seeking and processing strategies people employ. In their study of how audiences relate to general and political news in the mass media, Kosicki and McLeod (1990) observed that people's beliefs about the media (e.g., that the media represent special interests, that they are accurate and responsible) are affected by social structural, political, and cultural factors. Furthermore, their evidence indicates that these images of the media seem to affect the habitual information processing strategies that people develop. Thus, the RISP model suggests that relevant channel beliefs might affect, directly or indirectly, the ways in which people seek and process risk information.

Generally, factors that drive individuals toward purposeful, active seeking of risk-related information might also motivate them to engage in more effortful (i.e., systematic) processing of that information as well. Conversely, those who happen to encounter risk information through habitual, fairly routine monitoring of their various channels of communication may default to less effortful (i.e., heuristic) processing. However, various combinations of channel beliefs, motivations, and capacity could yield the different blends of seeking and processing activity noted previously (e.g., nonroutine/heuristic). Thus, the RISP model suggests that these factors might interact to affect risk information seeking and processing.

For example, a patient worried about the potential side effects from a newly prescribed drug might be highly motivated to reduce her uncertainty by contacting her physician (the "channel," in this case). She may be quite capable of seeking the information but, without a medical diploma, she may not have the capacity to understand and critically assess the technical information her physician could relay to her. Thus, despite her motivation, she might default to heuristically processing what the trusted expert doctor tells her about the drug and just take the doctor's advice. However, given sufficient motivation and a sense that she can indeed find the information that she needs, she might seek out other sources of information, trusted channels that she expects will explain the side-effects in everyday language, in an attempt to triangulate the doctor's advice. Or she might even take steps to improve her own capacity to understand, and thus think critically about the biochemical workings of the vexing pharmaceutical.

Informational Subjective Norms.   Social environments could influence people's judgment about the amount of information that they feel they need to achieve their information processing goals (ter Huurne et al., 2009). For example, family and friends' expectations that people will stay informed about risks related to health and environment could trigger a greater need for relevant information. The RISP model labels this perception of others' expectation about one's information level as informational subjective norms, basing this on Ajzen's (1988) concepts of normative beliefs and subjective norms. Stated more formally, the RISP model suggests that individuals' own beliefs about what others—especially people who are important to them—think they should know about a risk topic, or individuals' perceptions about what relevant others already know about the risk, could motivate them to seek greater information sufficiency and, thus, indirectly drive seeking and processing.

Perceived Hazard Characteristics.   In place of concepts such as personal relevance, salience, or involvement, the RISP model proposes perceived hazard characteristics and affective responses to the risk as effective background predictors of information use and processing. The former are often associated with more effortful processing of information (e.g., Eagly & Chaiken, 1993), but they may be too broad for studies of risk communication and may not provide as much interpretive—and, thus, theoretical and practical—value (Griffin, Dunwoody, & Neuwirth, 1999).

Cognitive evaluations of the nature of a hazard could have a direct impact on people's judgment of information sufficiency about the risk. Elevated risk perception could increase one's need for additional information if the risk issue is unknown. Alternatively, even with some familiarity, people might still want to gather additional information to deal with concerns they have about these health risks and environmental hazards.

Consonant with classic works such as the Health Belief Model (Rosenstock, 1966), which assess risk perception based on perceived susceptibility and severity, the RISP model recognizes risk as a multidimensional concept that could involve other mechanisms. For example, the perceived loci of control and responsibility (e.g., myself? others? everybody? nobody?) for managing a risk could influence the way a person responds cognitively and affectively to a hazard to self, others, or the ecosystem. Thus, a person's perception of hazard characteristics can include one's sense of efficacy; that is, personal control over harm from the hazard (Weinstein, 1993; Rogers, 1985); one's trust in risk management agencies and institutions (Slovic, 1992) to manage harm to individuals or the ecosystem; and one's causal attributions for the occurrence of the hazard (Griffin et al., 2008; McGuire, 1974). Perceived hazard characteristics can also include, among other factors, perceived threat to one's personal values (Earle & Cvetkovich, 1994) and the personal or impersonal nature of the risk.

Affective Responses.   Affective responses resulting from risk perception could also contribute to a sense of information insufficiency related to risk. Negative emotions such as worry, anger, or fear are often associated with risk and hazard, and fear appeals have a fairly lengthy, if mixed, relationship to individuals' responses to health risks (Witte, 1992). Affective responses could increase one's need for information by activating tendencies embedded in these emotions, such as anger's role in urging an individual to reassert control over a situation (Frijda, 1986). Or, based on the dynamics of Witte's (1992) extended parallel process model, an individual's fear of a salient hazard could combine with various components of perceived hazard characteristics in the RISP model (i.e., one's sense of susceptibility to a risk and its severity, and one's sense of efficacy in dealing with it) to affect information seeking or avoidance as well as one's behavior toward the hazard itself.

Positive emotions, such as hope, can arise in risky situations characterized by high uncertainty (Lazarus & Smith, 1988), or a heightened need to maintain positive affect in order to regulate negative affect might also influence judgmental confidence based on risk-related information sufficiency.

Individual Characteristics.   The RISP model in Figure 15.2 also includes a role for demographic variables (e.g., education) and other individual characteristics (e.g., past experience with a hazard, relevant values) in the deep background of risk information seeking and processing. Studies related to environmental risks, for example, might include measures of fundamental environmental beliefs and values (e.g., Dunlap, Van Liere, Mertig, & Jones, 2000; Stern, Dietz, & Kaloff, 1993).

How Robust is RISP?

The main goal of this section is to explore the robustness of that part of the model most closely associated with communication: the relationships of information insufficiency, channel beliefs, perceived information gathering capacity, and informational subjective norms to information seeking and processing. We will do so in two ways. The first approach is based on a report of a comparative analysis across five risks, employing data from two comprehensive, federally funded sample surveys that were guided by the RISP model (Griffin, Powell, et al., 2004). Since these two data sets formed the basis for a variety of published works referred to at the end of the following subsection, we will use the Griffin, Powell, et al. (2004) synthesis as the most efficient and straightforward way to present these results rather than to report the outcomes of each of these studies separately. The second approach is to examine in more detail the findings of literature that has utilized at least some of the RISP model across a number of risks. To be as comprehensive as possible, we conducted a systematic, online search of the relevant literature databases with the assistance of a reference librarian at one of the authors' universities. A brief, graphic overview of the results of these studies can be found in Table 15.2. Our take-home message: Although the behavior of some model components waxes and wanes with type of risk, type of measurement, and other factors, the model itself seems to be surviving these tests reasonably well.

Comparative Analysis

One of the surveys that Griffin, Powell, et al. (2004) utilized in their analysis, the "Great Lakes study," focused on the ways that adult residents of two Great Lakes cities—Milwaukee, WI, on Lake Michigan and Cleveland, OH, on Lake Erie—sought and processed information about risks related to the Great Lakes.[5] Two of the hazards could harm personal health: eating Great Lakes fish and drinking tap water drawn from the Great Lakes. The third hazard involved threats to the ecological integrity (health) of the Great Lakes themselves. The data in the other survey, the "Watershed study," concerned the ways that heads of households in two urban river watersheds in the Milwaukee, WI area dealt with risk information about flood hazards (one watershed) and hazards to the ecological integrity of the streams (both watersheds).[6] The data were from the first wave of each of these multiwave panel surveys (1996–1997 for the Great Lakes study, n = 1,123, and 1999–2000 for the Watershed survey, n = 759). Testing the model by using environmental as well as health risks opened the door to exploring the model's applicability to "impersonal risks"; that is, risks not to the self but, for example, to others or to the ecosystem.

A series of multiple regression analyses showed that information insufficiency was positively associated with risk information seeking and with systematic processing and was negatively related to risk information avoidance and to heuristic processing. These results were consistent with the RISP model. However, the relationships of perceived information gathering capacity and of channel beliefs with risk information seeking and processing were mixed, much of it a function of measurement issues.

In the watershed study, an improved measure of the capacity variable performed generally as expected; that is, it was positively associated with risk information seeking and, to lesser extents, positively with systematic processing and negatively with heuristic processing and with avoidance. (A different measure of capacity had produced null or, in one situation, enigmatically

Table 15.2 Overview of Results from Past Analyses of Proximate Predictors of Risk Information Seeking and Processing in the RISP Model

Key Predictors		Information Insufficiency	Information Seeking	Systematic Processing	Heuristic Processing
Information insufficiency		—	a+ b+ d+ e0 f+ gx h+	a+ b+ c+ e0 i+	a- b- c0 e0
Informational Subjective Norms		a+ b+ d+ f+ j+	a+ b+ d+ e+ fx j+	a+ b+ c0 e+	a- b- c0 e-
Channel Beliefs:	Media distort	a0 b0	a0 b0	a0 b0 c0	ax b+ c0
	Validity cues	a0 b0	a+ b0	a+ b+ c0	a0 b0 c0
Perceived Information Gathering Capacity		a0 b0	ax b+ d0 f+ h+	ax b+ c0	ax b- c-

Notes: The studies (a–j below) that have investigated a given variable relationship are listed in each cell with the following code to indicate the results:
  + Statistically significant positive relationship found.
  – Statistically significant negative relationship found.
  0 No statistically significant relationship found.
  x Mixed results, see text.

The RISP model does not propose that information insufficiency is correlated with channel beliefs or perceived information gathering capacity. They should be independent.
Study codes:
a. Griffin et al. (2004b)
b. Griffin et al. (2008)
c. Kahlor et al. (2003)
d. Kahlor (2007)
e. Yang et al. (2010b)
f. ter Huurne et al. (2009)
g. Fischer & Frewer (2009)
h. Johnson (2005)
i. Horvick et al. (2011)
j. Yang et al. (2010c)

contrary results in the earlier Great Lakes study.) The improved measure (see Griffin, Yang, et al., 2008) has been used successfully in subsequent studies.

In terms of channel beliefs, a person's belief that risk communication channels provided him or her with essential cues to the validity of the information was positively related to systematic processing of the information, consistent with the model. However, this same belief was related only weakly (but positively) to risk information seeking and was generally unrelated to heuristic processing and risk information avoidance. The belief that risk information channels were biased and distorted bore essentially no relationship to risk information seeking and processing. In the wake of these results, the researchers suggested that channel beliefs in the RISP model be reconceptualized: Instead of reflecting broad beliefs about channels of risk information, measures should reflect the individual's expectations about the outcomes (e.g., benefits or drawbacks for the self) of using specific channels for risk information. This approach would be more in line with the conceptualization and measurement commonly used for "behavioral beliefs" in Ajzen's (1988) theory of planned behavior.

Alas, the Griffin, Powell, et al. (2004) analysis did not include informational subjective norms (ISN). However, to provide a comparable basis of results for this review, we conducted subsequent multiple regression analyses with the same data and variables. Results show consistent positive relationships between those norms and risk information seeking (overall beta = .34, $p < .01$) and processing (overall beta = .28, $p < .01$). Similarly, informational subjective norms demonstrated consistently negative relationships with risk information avoidance (overall beta = $-.18$, $p < .001$) and heuristic processing (overall beta = $-.20$, $p < .001$). These results indicate that informational subjective norms might serve as a more direct motivator of risk information seeking and processing, alongside information insufficiency or perhaps as an alternative under some conditions, a possible change to the RISP model.

Expanded descriptions of the tests of the RISP model, using the above data and examining the variable relationships above, can be found in Kahlor et al. (2006), in regard to impersonal risks to the Great Lakes ecosystem, and in Griffin et al. (2008) as related to risks from river flooding. Other analyses of the dynamics of the model using these data can be found in Griffin, Neuwirth, Giese, et al. (2002). Griffin, Neuwirth, Dunwoody, et al. (2004), and in Kahlor, Dunwoody, Griffin, Neuwirth, & Giese (2003).

RISP in the Hands of Other Scholars

In addition to work by the model developers, discussed in some detail above, various studies by other scholars have explored the robustness of the RISP model in terms of relationships among the communication-related variables spotlighted in this report. In some cases, those scholars enlisted the assistance of one of the original model developers, while in other cases the work was independent.

One analysis with strong ties to the original data was conducted by Kahlor et al. (2003). The team employed an "information catalyst"—an alleged magazine article about the ecological health of the Great Lakes—that was mailed to a set of respondents with instructions to read the piece. The individuals were then contacted and asked to respond to questions relevant to the RISP model. The PIs were trying, in this effort, to operationalize heuristic and systematic information processing with reference to an actual piece of information.

Consistent with the predictions of the model, respondents' information processing capacity was negatively related to heuristic processing: The less able someone believed she was to handle the information the more likely she was to have engaged in superficial processing of the article. And the model's predictions about information insufficiency were also borne out: The larger one's perceived information gap the more likely one processed the article systematically. Those who engaged in this effortful processing also reported that they paid more attention to the scientific information in the article, a result consistent with the concept of systematic processing. However, this time informational subjective norms played no significant role in motivating information processing. Channel beliefs were also unrelated to processing. As might be expected, one strong predictor of systematic processing of the article was respondent interest in the topic. While not surprising, this kind of relationship may be a byproduct of efforts to measure information processing strategies in the field with real-world messages.

In another study, Kahlor (2007) supplemented the RISP model with a number of additional variables from the theory of planned behavior (Ajzen & Fishbein, 2005) in order to explore respondent reactions to the ecological risks of global warming. Results supported the role of information insufficiency and, especially, informational subjective norms in encouraging individuals to seek more information about the issue.

In an effort to better understand the ways in which Americans evaluate the possible risks of participating in clinical trials, Yang et al. (2010b, 2010c) employed RISP concepts. Information insufficiency fared badly in this study; the size of the perceived information gap about this risk was not a motivator of information seeking and processing after the analysis controlled for the extant knowledge of the respondents. However, informational subjective norms and affective responses emerged as primary predictors of information seeking, including multichannel information seeking (2010c), and of systematic and heuristic processing (2010b).

A two-country test of the model that focused on industrial risks found support for most of the predicted relationships. Ter Huurne et al. (2009) employed a number of the model's variables in surveys in both the United States and the Netherlands. With a focus on information seeking but not processing, the PIs found that respondents were more motivated to seek information about industrial chemicals if they felt there was a lot they needed to learn (information insufficiency) about these risks and if they felt they could find the information they needed (perceived information gathering capacity). In one interesting cultural difference, those U.S. respondents who indicated they felt pressure from others to learn about the risks (informational subjective norms) were more motivated to seek information while the same relationship did not hold for the Dutch.

Fischer and Frewer (2009) utilized a few variables from the RISP model among a wider set of variables in their experiments on the effects of information about the risks and benefits of foods that were familiar and those that were unfamiliar to their subjects. They found that, for unfamiliar foods, subjects who believed they had received sufficient information to make a decision about risks and benefits from an unfamiliar food (information sufficiency) were less inclined to seek further information, a result consistent with the RISP model.

A study by Johnson (2005) borrowed concepts from the work of three groups of scholars, including the RISP team, to create a model of cognitive processing of risk information. His design focuses on a single potential risk—an industrial factory and the possible hazards it might present to nearby residents—and adds measures of involvement, relevance, and ability to RISP concepts. While both information insufficiency and perceived information gathering capacity were positively associated with information seeking, Johnson's involvement variable also contributed to variance in both information seeking and information avoidance. In contrast, few of the variables in Johnson's model were related to information processing, either systematic or heuristic. Informational subjective norms and channel beliefs were not included in the analysis.

Most recently, Horvic et al. (2011) employed most of the RISP model in a study of risk information processing among poor Whites and African Americans living in the southern United States. Each of the respondents picked one of 10 possible health risks she or he worried about the most. Across risks, results generally supported the relationships among perceived hazard characteristics, worry, information insufficiency, and systematic processing proposed by the RISP model. A self-report measure of health protective behavior was also associated positively with systematic processing. The study did not, however, measure informational subjective norms or channel beliefs.

Across these studies, the size of individuals' perceived knowledge gap about the risks, their perceived capacity to gather the information they need, and their judgment that others expect them to learn more about the risks repeatedly contributed to information seeking and processing. The strength of these contributions varied by study and by risk, which lead us to caution the reader that comparability will be influenced by differences in measurement strategies and in the risks themselves. But the emergence of these factors across both operational differences in study design and in type of risk does suggest that these RISP variables seem indeed to be important precursors to information seeking and processing.

Implications for the Study of Information Seeking and Processing in a Risk Context

The series of studies discussed above suggest that there is merit in a focus on information seeking and processing across different types of risk. Interest in developing valid ways to operationalize seeking and processing in a survey format has grown (Eveland, 2001, 2005; Schemer, Matthes, & Wirth, 2008; Trumbo, 2002), broadening the methodological landscape for those interested in these dependent variables. And models such as RISP suggest that some factors will be more valuable than others in studies seeking to better understand what encourages the types of seeking and processing that underlie stable beliefs about risks. We take a brief look at those factors below.

Motivations for Risk Information Seeking and Processing

Information Insufficiency. To date the RISP model has concentrated on employing, behind the scenes of its information insufficiency concept, the HSM *accuracy* motivation to represent individuals' drives for seeking and processing risk-related information. In tests of the model, the cognitive drive for information sufficiency has performed reasonably well, even when its component variables (current knowledge and sufficiency threshold) have been operationalized differently (e.g., ter Huurne et al., 2009; ter Huurne & Gutteling, 2009) from those used by the original researchers.

Accuracy motivation is based on a person's "desire to hold attitudes and beliefs that are objectively valid" (Chaiken et al., 1996, p. 556), a concept highly appropriate as a centerpiece for studies of communication about health and environmental risks. Information about these risks, after all, is typically couched in exhortations to change one's beliefs, attitudes, or behaviors in response to real-world conditions, but conditions that are nonetheless often hidden (e.g., small particulates as a form of air pollution) or that might occur only in the future (e.g., radiation escaping from failed long-term storage facilities many decades hence). Risk information can be especially challenging for even educated laypersons to examine and process critically because it often includes technical terminology and is expressed in terms of probabilities.

However, other deep-seated motivations (e.g., McGuire, 1974) for seeking/avoiding and processing risk information may also be valuable to explore. These could readily include the pair of complementary motivations from the HSM model (Chaiken et al., 1996) noted previously: *defense* motivation, which originates from a person's desire to form, hold, or defend beliefs or attitudinal positions important to the individual, and *impression* motivation, which is based on a person's desire to have or form socially acceptable beliefs or attitudes that help him or her meet social goals.[7] Of course, individuals may have various admixtures of HSM motivations at any given time. However, defense motivation and, particularly, impression motivation are the most likely to result in biased information processing (Chen & Chaiken, 1999) and seeking. In addition, social roles, such as preparing to tell someone else about a topic or, instead, preparing to learn more from another person or source, might differentially affect the ways in which information is sought, avoided, processed, and structured in long-term memory (Guerin & Innes, 1989; Zajonc, 1960).

Personality traits such as one's need for cognition (Cacioppo & Petty, 1982) also appear to motivate information seeking and systematic processing through information insufficiency (Eagly & Chaiken, 1993, p. 332). That is, these motivational determinants of elaboration could increase people's desired levels of judgmental confidence. As a result, the elevated sufficiency threshold could generate greater amounts of information seeking and systematic processing. Future studies should include need for cognition as part of the individual characteristics block on the left side of the RISP model.

Informational Subjective Norms.   Within the RISP model, subjectively perceived social pressures on seeking and processing risk information are channeled primarily through informational subjective norms, a variable derived from Ajzen's (1988) TPB. Informational subjective norms was originally conceptualized as a background factor that affects risk information seeking and processing only indirectly, via information insufficiency (Griffin, Dunwoody, & Neuwirth, 1999). However, as this review has noted, subsequent research has indicated that informational subjective norms may also be a consistent and fairly strong direct motivational factor in its own right, sometimes working through the cognitive drive for information sufficiency to affect information seeking and processing but sometimes working independently of it (Figure 15.3).

In fact, subjective norms like the ones used here may well be among the most important motivators of effortful information seeking and processing for impersonal risks. In the absence of concern about one's personal welfare, individuals may still be encouraged to develop beliefs and behaviors because they are sensitive to what others think they should do. That is, while you may feel that global warming will not influence you personally, you may become convinced that others think it is important and, as a result, believe you should be informed. Those perceptions, in turn, may jump start more systematic information seeking and processing. Scholars such as Cialdini (2003) have demonstrated the power of subjective norms to generate environmentally sensitive behaviors; the question for us is whether those behaviors may also include effortful information use.

However, informational subjective norms require fuller development in terms of concept, operationalization, antecedents, and outcomes. For example, through most of its history, the concept has been defined and operationalized in terms of injunctive perceived norms (i.e., one's beliefs regarding what relevant others think one should do in terms of possessing or seeking knowledge of a risk). However, it is also valuable to develop concepts and measures related to descriptive informational subjective norms (based on one's perceptions about the seeking and holding of risk knowledge by relevant others), as has been initiated by Kahlor (2007) and Kahlor and Rosenthal (2009), at least in regard to subjective norms for risk information seeking. In applying their measure to a study of knowledge about global warming, Kahlor and Rosenthal (2009) found a slight negative relationship between informational subjective norms related to information seeking and two of their four open-ended measures of knowledge and its structure.[8] Although there may be various explanations for these results, they might reflect biased or selective seeking or processing[9] of global warming information in response to perceived social forces, at least among some individuals.

In terms of antecedents to informational subjective norms, Ajzen (1988) indicates that subjective norms are the byproduct of an individual's beliefs about the norms held by specific referent others (e.g., friends, spouse, cowork-ers) pertinent to the behavior, and the motivation one has to comply with these referents. One could apply the same formulation to informational subjective norms when the risk involves specific others relevant to the individual (e.g., a meal preparer for a household might feel social pressures specifically from his family to stay informed about fatty foods, or a parent might feel that other parents in her neighborhood have already sought important information that she doesn't have about a pesticide the city plans to apply locally).

People who are more inclined toward self-monitoring (e.g., Gangestad & Snyder, 2000; Snyder & Gangestad, 1986) might be more sensitive to infor-mational subjective norms, as might those who perceive themselves in various social roles that involve being informed or providing others with information; for example, in the role of an opinion leader, as proposed by Clarke (2009). Under some circumstances, informational subjective norms might be associ-ated with impression or even defense motivation for information processing (Chaiken et al., 1996). If so, then the kinds of risk information the individual seeks and processes may be highly selective.

Affect.   Although predominantly cognitive, the RISP model does include a set of affective variables ("affective response") as an anticipated driver of a person's perceived information gap. That decision stemmed from an acknowledgment of a large and growing literature that explores the power of emotion generally in catalyzing behavior and the influence of affect more specifically in behaviors related to risks. Items related to negative emotions, especially worry and anger, were indeed related to respondents' information gaps and to information seeking and processing across a range of RISP-related studies (see Table 15.3).

In particular, seven studies found a consistent, positive relationship between negative emotions and risk information insufficiency (Griffin, Neuwirth, et al., 2004; Griffin, Yang, et al., 2008; Hovick, Freimuth, Johnson-Turbes, & Chervin, 2011; Kahlor, 2007; Powell, Dunwoody, Griffin, & Neuwirth, 2007; ter Huurne et al., 2009; Yang et al., 2010c). Two studies looked at the role of positive affect as a potential predictor of risk information insufficiency but

Table 15.3 Relationship of Affective Response with Information Insufficiency, Seeking, and Processing Variables in the RISP Model

Affect	Information Insufficiency	Information Seeking	Systematic Processing	Heuristic Processing
Anger (Griffin et al., 2008)	+	+	+	N.S.
Worry (Griffin et al., 2004a)	+	N/A	N/A	N/A
Worry (Hovick et al., 2011)	+	N/A	+	N/A
Worry (Kahlor et al. (2003)	N/A	N/A	N.S.	N.S.
Worry (Kahlor, 2007)	+	(+)1	N/A	N/A
Negative (Anger, Worry) (Powell et al., 2007)	+	N/A	N/A	N/A
Negative (Anger, Worry, etc.) (ter Huurne et al., 2009)	+	+	N/A	N/A
Negative (Afraid, Worried, Anxious)	+	+	N/A	N/A
Positive (Hope) (Yang et al., 2010c)	N.S.	+	N/A	N/A
Positive (Hope) (Yang et al., 2010b)	N.S.	+	+	–

Notes: 1. Kahlor (2007) reported a zero-order positive correlation in a table.

found no significant relationship (Yang et al., 2010b, 2010c). Thus, the valence of the affect might influence whether people sense a need to know more about a given risk.

Four studies found a direct, positive relationship between affect and information seeking. Two used negative emotions only (Griffin, Yang, et al., 2008; ter Huurne et al., 2009), one used positive emotions only (Yang et al., 2010b), and another included both negative and positive emotions (Yang et al., 2010c).[10] In addition, all four included information insufficiency in the analysis, which meant that affect might not necessarily work through information insufficiency to influence seeking. Some aspect of affect might be a more direct predictor of seeking.

Fewer studies have explored direct relationships between negative emotions and information processing. Two studies showed a positive relationship between negative emotions and systematic processing (Griffin, Yang, et al., 2008; Hovick et al., 2011), but another showed no significant relationship (Kahlor et al., 2003). Yang et al. (2010b) found that a positive emotion, hope, had a positive relationship with systematic processing and a negative relationship with heuristic processing. In the three studies that found significant relationships between affect and information processing, information insufficiency was also included in the analysis. As with seeking, therefore, affect might influence processing in a manner that does not require a need for cognitive closure (information sufficiency).

In sum, existing empirical evidence using the RISP model suggests that affect does not necessarily work through information insufficiency to influence risk information seeking and processing. Future research should continue to explore whether and why the origin and valence of the affect might govern its performance as a motivator in the RISP model.

As we refine the model, we will seek to incorporate affect more substantively and in a more complex fashion. Studies of the ways in which emotion interacts with thinking to drive attitudes and behaviors are flourishing and demonstrate that cognitive and affective systems are not orthogonal to one another; rather, they are often employed in concert, making their relative use in risk judgments important to understand.

The question for our RISP model is not whether to employ affect as a predictor but, rather, what role we would expect that concept to play in risk judgments relative to cognitive elements. Most risks in our world are low level ones; they do not generate high levels of fear and, on the contrary, may be the product of behaviors that are enjoyable. People who catch and eat fish from the Great Lakes, for example, are exposing themselves and their families to contamination that can cause developmental delays in fetuses or cancer in adults. But those risks are relatively low while the enjoyment derived from fishing is often quite high. Affect may be a powerful actor in risk judgments when it comes to catching and eating contaminated fish, but one would need to be able to track not only the interaction between affect and cognition but also possible interactions among affective responses.

This suggests that the role of affect will be highly situational. So while we include affect in our revised RISP model (Figure 15.3), we give it a wide operating berth; it may influence information seeking and processing directly for some risks, be mediated by information sufficiency for others, and it may interact with cognition, with perceptions of information gathering efficacy, with channel beliefs, or with other components of the model.

Capacity and Channel Beliefs

Two essential, but sometimes challenging, components of the RISP model have been *perceived information gathering capacity* and *channel beliefs*. The two are seen as working in tandem as individuals conduct cost-benefit analyses in service to deciding if more effortful information gathering/seeking is worth the trouble.

In many ways, capacity reflects the cost to the individual—in terms of time and effort—of seeking and processing risk information. The individual might, in effect, weigh these subjectively assessed costs against channel beliefs, that is, the perceived benefits (e.g., usefulness) and drawbacks of seeking and

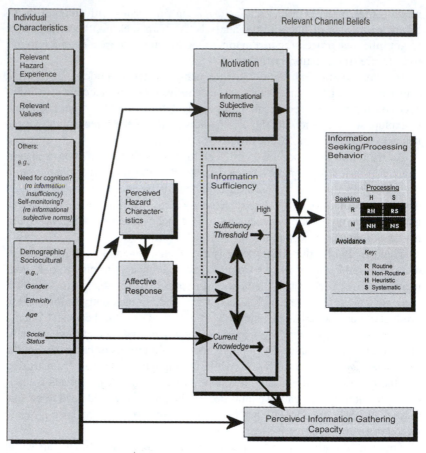

Figure 15.3 Amended RISP model (Based on Griffin, Dunwoody, & Neuwirth, 1999).

processing the information in different ways from different channels. At any given level of motivation, people with higher capacity have more channel and information options open to them; those who have less capacity (e.g., because of constraints on time, channel access, effort, existing knowledge, or cognitive ability) would be more limited in their choices, especially when it comes to nonroutine seeking of risk information and to processing it systematically. In a result consistent with the above scenario, our analyses show that the more knowledge people believe they currently have about a risk, the more capacity they believe they have to seek and process new information about it.

The first attempts to operationalize capacity in the RISP model, as employed in the Great Lakes study and illustrated earlier, were based on one aspect of Ajzen's (1988) perceived behavioral control variable from the theory of planned behavior (TPB), in particular, the expected ease or difficulty the individual would have in performing an action, in this case, getting information about the risk. Kahlor (2007) and Kahlor and Rosenthal (2009) expanded the perceived behavioral control application to include measures of the extent to which the individual has volitional control over seeking the risk information. Unfortunately, these measures did not work out well in any of these applications of the RISP model. Instead, the six-item measure used in the Watershed study (Griffin, Yang, et al., 2008), as noted earlier, operationalized some elements of processing as well as seeking capacity and provided more interpretable results. However, it needs further development in concept and measurement (e.g., reliability).[11]

Individuals' beliefs about the channels of risk information have related only weakly and inconsistently to risk information seeking and processing in studies employing the RISP model.[12] Much of this may be due to channel beliefs being operationalized in terms of individuals' reflections on news media rather generally as sources of risk information. At minimum, the ascendance of the Internet and of social media would make this approach incomplete. In addition, interpersonal channels are essential to include, especially given the apparent role of informational subjective norms as motivation for seeking and processing risk information. The challenge is to operationalize channel beliefs in ways relevant to seeking and to processing, to capture the notion of subjectively perceived benefits vs. costs or drawbacks, and to do so with an appropriate level of channel specificity or generality.

By applying a source-specific operationalization of channel beliefs, Yang et al. (2010b) found that trust in doctors was associated positively with systematic processing of information about enrolling in clinical trials (beta = .22, $p < .05$). However, trust was unrelated to information seeking. In her study of individuals' intentions to seek information about global warming, Kahlor (2007) adopted another of Ajzen's (1988) TPB variables, AAct, and termed it *attitude toward the behavior (seeking)*. Her measure was not source-specific. It was designed to capture at least part of the concept of benefits vs. drawbacks behind channel beliefs as related to risk information seeking, although not necessarily to replace the channel beliefs variable. Consistent with Ajzen's formulation, her measure (alpha = .79) was comprised of four semantic differential scales assessing whether the individual considers the seeking of global warming information to be worthless/valuable, harmful/beneficial, bad/good, more unhelpful/more helpful. Her measure correlated positively with information seeking intention (beta = .22, $p < .001$), the expected direction. The study did not address risk information processing, however.

Perhaps the more promising approach to operationalizing channel beliefs is to employ what Ajzen (1988) considers to be the antecedent to AAct, that is, a set of behavioral beliefs. Applied in this manner, each behavioral belief could be measured in an expectancy-value format that represents the individual's estimated likelihood that an action (e.g., seeking or processing information about a risk from a specific channel or channels) would lead to a particular outcome (e.g., encountering countervailing advice, statistics, technical terminology, reassurance), weighted by the valence (good/bad) the individual puts on that outcome. The advantage of behavioral beliefs is that they tend be more finely grained in their explanation of behavior than the more general AAct variable. They also offer an array of interesting and revealing analytical options (e.g., one individual might default to considering just one behavioral belief, while another's behavior might be affected by many). A similar formulation has been used in the uses and gratifications literature (e.g., Palmgreen & Rayburn, 1982; Rubin, 2002), and has also been suggested by Kahlor and Rosenthal (2009).

Measuring Information Processing

As noted earlier in this section, there is increased interest in devising better ways to measure information seeking and processing, particularly in a survey context. Employing measures used in RISP and other studies, Schemer et al. (2008) conducted an extensive review of the track record of various measures of heuristic and systematic processing of media information. They then developed and tested the validity and reliability of their resulting scales in three separate surveys among German-speaking Swiss residents. More recently, Smerecnik, Mesters, Candel, De Vries, and De Vries (2011) further developed and tested self-report measures of heuristic and systematic processing specifically within a risk context. Overall, the results reinforce the two-dimensional, heuristic-systematic nature of information processing, the value of information processing concepts and measures in communication research, and point the way to much needed further research developing and validating measures of these phenomena.

Reprise

In general, the RISP model suggests that there are ways to identify and configure factors that could affect the ways in which individuals seek and process information about a risk.[13] The set of concepts employed seems to capture both cognitive and affective dimensions of risk experience and judgment, and the model itself offers ways to array those factors in service to identifying individuals' perceptions of their information needs, which in turn are associated with types of information processing and seeking. The model also suggests that subjective norms constitute a means of introducing perceptions of societal pressure on individuals, which in turn may be important catalysts for learning more about risks to others and to the world around us. Our examination of the track record of the RISP model also suggests a "to-do" list for future research:

- Although much more exploration is still needed into the cognitive, affective, and behavioral "so what?" of risk information processing activity, aspects of the RISP model not detailed in this report (e.g., Griffin, Dunwoody, & Neuwirth, 1999; Griffin, Neuwirth, et al., 2002) offer some guidance. In particular, risk information processing and some other variables in the RISP model might affect elements of Ajzen's (1988) theory of planned behavior when the latter is applied to individuals' behavioral responses to a risk. For example, processing activity could influence the structure, strength, and stability of behavioral beliefs which, in TPB, are one of the essential elements that can eventually drive behavior (Griffin, Dunwoody, & Neuwirth, 1999).

- Research is also needed into the interactions among the RISP model predictors of risk information seeking and processing, although improved measurement, especially of seeking, processing, affect, and channel beliefs, should precede these efforts.
- Channel beliefs could be recast in a manner consistent with Ajzen's (1988) concept of behavioral beliefs, for example, as a person's expectations about the outcomes of gathering risk-related information from a given channel or channels of information.
- Future research should delve into the various potential roles of affect in the RISP model. Not covered in this chapter have been the results of analyses of the RISP model that investigate the relationships among affective responses to a risk, perceived hazard characteristics, and individual characteristics. These offer fertile ground for research using the RISP model, including a potential application of the Extended Parallel Process Model (Witte, 1994).
- Other investigations should examine two variables that might be included among individual characteristics in the RISP model: need for cognition (Cacioppo & Petty, 1982) and self-monitoring (Snyder & Gangestad, 1986). The former could influence information insufficiency and systematic processing fairly directly, and the latter could sensitize individuals to informational subjective norms (e.g., they might weigh these perceived norms more heavily).
- Other motives for risk information seeking and processing, such as impression and defense motivations (Chaiken et al., 1996), would be valuable to explore. Although the context is political communication, Neuwirth, Frederick, and Mayo (2010) have developed useful measures of accuracy and defense motives.

Perhaps the most significant outcome of this overview, however, is the appearance of the comparatively strong role of informational subjective norms. It would be valuable to explore the descriptive as well as the injunctive perceived norms of this type. Overall, examining the various motivations for risk information seeking and processing that have powerful underpinnings in social interactions would contribute to new dimensions of research in risk communication. For the most part, research in that field has concentrated on finding cognitive, affective, and behavioral effects on individuals who have been exposed to risk messages. Given the politicization of various risk-related issues (e.g., health care and global climate change), and the explosive growth of social media, the impact of social variables such as informational subjective norms on risk information seeking and processing is especially important and inviting to explore.

Notes

1. Kahlor and Rosenthal (2009), using some variables from the RISP model, found that active seeking of information was associated with more accurate knowledge of global warming.
2. Although information insufficiency is a subjective judgment on the part of the individual, at least one analysis found that it related to actual knowledge in a way consistent with the concept. In a comparison of respondents' perceived information insufficiency with a test of their knowledge about global warming, Kahlor and Rosenthal (2009) found that "the larger one's perceived knowledge deficit … the lower one's actual knowledge" (p. 401).
3. Accessibility will be affected by a variety of costs, from actual dollars (a book that costs $150 may be too expensive to purchase) to expertise (inability to operate a computer may make the World Wide Web unavailable) to cultural costs (we view physicians as channels of last resort for our health questions, despite their obvious expertise on the matter, because they are difficult and costly to schedule).
4. Channels differ dramatically in the kinds and levels of information they offer. While a newspaper story may satisfy a surveillance need, it may be too superficial to provide the level of detail sought by an individual trying to understand an issue fully. Conversely, someone interested in a rapid surveillance function may eschew a book-length treatise on the topic at hand.
5. The research was funded by a grant from the federal Agency for Toxic Substances and Disease Registry (ATSDR).
6. The research was funded by a Science to Achieve Results (STAR) grant from the National Science Foundation, U.S. Environmental Protection Agency, and U.S. Department of Agriculture.
7. Chaiken, Lieberman, and Eagly (1989) propose that both defense motivation and impression motivation could lead to either heuristic or systematic processing, depending on the social contexts in which they function. For instance, when defense-motivated individuals receive information from an authority figure that is in line with their own position, they may employ heuristics such as the belief that expertise and specialized knowledge are always trustworthy. However, when the same defense-motivated individuals receive a similar message from a less-valued source, they may engage in further deliberation to reinforce their own belief. Similarly, even though following a simple decision rule such as *go with the consensus* sounds heuristic in nature, the desire to identify the consensus and reach conformity might generate greater information seeking and more effortful processing.
8. It might be valuable to relate the RISP model, especially variables related to motivations for heuristic and systematic processing, to outcomes on individuals' mental models of risks (e.g., Bostrom & Lashof, 2007; Fischoff, 2009).
9. Although ISN is normally associated with systematic over heuristic processing, it is possible for individuals to seek information actively but process it heuristi-

cally. Unfortunately, their study did not include measures of risk information processing, which would be more closely associated with cognitive structure.

10. Kahlor (2007) showed a positive zero-order relationship between worry and seeking.

11. Kahlor and Rosenthal (2009) used the item "I usually understand what I read or hear when I encounter information about global warming" as a measure of what they term *understanding*. This measure correlated positively with knowledge complexity in their study and might be useful among the newer measures of perceived information gathering capacity.

12. Griffin, Neuwirth, Giese, et al. (2002), however, found that channel beliefs related consistently to the apparent outcomes of processing, including the strength of cognitive structure regarding risk-related behaviors.

13. There is also some initial evidence that the communication-related variables in the RISP model might be applicable to individuals' seeking and processing of information about other issues, such as energy (Griffin, Yang, et al., 2005), that are steeped in technical information and the potential for behavioral change.

References

Ajzen, I. (1988). *Attitudes, personality, and behavior.* Milton Keynes, England: Open University Press.

Ajzen, I. (1991). The theory of planned behavior. *Organizational Behavior and Human Decision Processes, 50*, 179–211.

Ajzen, I. (in press). Perceived behavioral control, self-efficacy, locus of control, and the theory of planned behavior. *Journal of Applied Social Psychology.*

Ajzen, I., & Fishbein, M. (2005). The influence of attitudes on behavior. In D. Albarracin, B. T. Johnson, & M. P. Zanna (Eds.), *The handbook of attitudes* (pp. 173–221). Mahwah, NJ: Erlbaum.

Ajzen, I., & Manstead, A. S. R. (2007). Changing health-related behaviors: An approach based on the theory of planned behavior. In K. van den Bos, M. Hewstone, J. de Wit, H. Schut, & M. Stroebe (Eds.), *The scope of social psychology: Theory and applications* (pp. 43–63). New York: Psychology Press.

Atkinson, R. C., & Shiffrin, R. M. (1968). Human memory: A proposed system and its control processes. In K. W. Spence & J. T. Spence (Eds.), *The psychology of learning and motivation* (Vol. 2, pp. 89–195). New York: Academic Press.

Bandura, A. (1977). *Social learning theory.* Englewood Cliffs, NJ: Prentice Hall.

Bandura, A. (1986). *Social foundations of thought and action.* Englewood Cliffs, NJ: Prentice Hall.

Bostrom, A., & Lashof, D. (2007). Weather or climate change? In S. C. Moser & L. Dilling (Eds.), *Creating a climate for change: Communicating climate change and facilitating social change* (pp. 31–43). Cambridge, England: Cambridge University Press.

Brashers, D. E. (2001). Communication and uncertainty management. *Journal of Communication, 51*(3), 477–497.

Brashers, D. E., Goldsmith, D. J., & Hsieh, E. (2002). Information seeking and avoiding in health contexts. *Human Communication Research, 28*, 258–271.

Cacioppo, J. T., & Petty, R. E. (1982). The need for cognition. *Journal of Personality and Social Psychology, 42*, 116–131.

Case, D. O., Andrews, J. E., Johnson, J. D., & Allard, S. L. (2005). Avoiding versus seeking: The relationship of information seeking to avoidance, blunting, coping, dissonance, and related concepts. *Journal of the Medical Library Association, 93*, 353–362.

Chaffee, S. H. (1986). Mass media and interpersonal channels: Competitive, convergent, or complementary? In G. Gumpert & R. Cathcart (Eds.), *Inter Media* (3rd. ed., pp. 62–80). New York: Oxford University Press.

Chaiken, S., Giner-Sorolla, R., & Chen, S. (1996). Beyond accuracy: Defense and impression motives in heuristic and systematic information processing. In P. M. Gollwitzer & J. A. Bargh (Eds.), *The psychology of action: Linking cognition and motivation to behavior* (pp. 553–578). New York: Guilford.

Chaiken, S., Lieberman, A., & Eagly, A. H. (1989). Heuristic and systematic information processing within and beyond the persuasion context. In J. S. Uleman & J. A. Bargh (Eds.), *Unintended thought* (pp. 212–252). New York: Guilford Press.

Chaiken, S., & Stangor, C. (1987). Attitude and attitude change. *Annual Review of Psychology, 38*, 575–630.

Chen, S., & Chaiken, S. (1999). The heuristic-systematic model in its broader context. In S. Chaiken & Y. Trope (Eds.), *Dual-process theories in social psychology* (pp. 73–96). New York: Guilford.

Cialdini, R. B. (2003). Crafting normative messages to protect the environment. *Current Directions in Psychological Science, 12*, 105–109.

Clarke, C. (2009). Seeking and processing information about zoonotic disease risk: A proposed framework. *Human Dimensions of Wildlife, 14*, 314–325.

Dijksterhuis, A., Bos, M. W., Nordgren, L. F., & Van Baaren, R. B. (2006). On making the right choice: The deliberation-without-attention effect. *Science, 311*, 1005–1007.

Douglas, M., & Wildavsky, A. (1983). *Risk and culture*. Berkeley: University of California Press.

Dunlap, R. E., Van Liere, K. D., Mertig, A. G., & Jones, R. E. (2000). Measuring endorsement of the new ecological paradigm: A revised NEP scale. *Journal of Social Issues, 56*, 425–442.

Dutta-Bergman, M. J. (2005). Theory and practice in health communication campaigns: A critical interrogation. *Health Communication, 18*, 103–122.

Eagly, A. H., & Chaiken, S. (1993). *The psychology of attitudes*. Fort Worth, TX: Harcourt Brace & Jovanovich.

Earle, T. C., & Cvetkovich, G. (1994). Risk communication: The social construction of meaning and trust. In B. Brehmer & N. Sahlin (Eds.), *Future risks and risk management* (pp. 141–181). Dordrecht, the Netherlands: Kluwer Academic.

Epstein, S., & Pacini, R. (1999). *Some basic issues regarding dual-process theories in social pscyhology* (pp. 462–482). New York: Guilford Press.

Eveland, W. P., Jr. (2001). The cognitive mediation model of learning from the news: Evidence from nonelection, off-year election and presidential election contexts. *Communication Research, 28*, 571–601.

Eveland, W. P., Jr. (2005). Information processing strategies in mass communication research. In S. Dunwoody, L. B. Becker, G. Kosicki, & D. McLeod (Eds.), *The evolution of key mass communication concepts: Honoring Jack McLeod* (pp. 217–248). Cresskill, NJ: Hampton Press.

Fischer, A. R. H., & Frewer, L. J. (2009). Consumer familiarity with foods and the perception of risks and benefits. *Food Quality and Preference, 20*, 576–585.

Fischhoff, B. (1995) Risk perception and communication unplugged: Twenty years of progress. *Risk Analysis, 15,* 137–145.

Fischhoff, B. (2009). Risk perception and communication. In R. Detels, R. Beaglehole, M. A. Lansang, & M. Guilliford (Eds.), *Oxford textbook of public health* (5th ed., pp. 940–952). Oxford, England: Oxford University Press.

Fishbein, M., & Yzer, M. C. (2003). Using theory to design effective health behavior interventions. *Communication Theory, 13,* 164–183.

Frijda, N. H. (1986). *The emotions.* Cambridge, England: Cambridge University Press.

Gangestad, S. W., & Snyder, M. (2000). Self-monitoring: Appraisal and reappraisal. *Psychological Bulletin, 126,* 530–555.

Gantz, W., Fitzmaurice, M., & Fink, E. (1991). Assessing the active component in information seeking. *Journalism Quarterly, 68,* 630–637.

Gigerenzer, G. (1996) Reasoning the fast and frugal way: Models of bounded rationality. *Psychological Review, 103,* 650–669.

Gigerenzer, G. (2000). *Adaptive thinking: Rationality in the real world.* New York: Oxford University Press.

Griffin, R. J., Dunwoody, S., & Neuwirth, K. (1999). Proposed model of the relationship of risk information seeking and processing to the development of preventive behaviors. *Environmental Research, 80,* S230–S245.

Griffin, R. J., Neuwirth, K., Dunwoody, S., & Giese, J. (2004). Information sufficiency and risk communication. *Media Psychology, 6,* 23–61.

Griffin, R.J., Neuwirth, K., Giese, J., & Dunwoody, S. (2002). Linking the heuristic–systematic model and depth of processing. *Communication Research, 29,* 705–732.

Griffin, R. J., Powell, M., Dunwoody, S., Neuwirth, K., Clark, D., & Novotny, V. (2004, August). *Testing the robustness of a risk information processing model.* Paper presented at the Association for Education in Journalism and Mass Communication annual convention, Toronto, ONT, Canada.

Griffin, R. J., Yang, Z., Boerner, F., Bourassa, S., Darrah, T., Knurek, S., Ortiz, S., & Dunwoody, S. (2005, August). *Applying an information seeking and processing model to a study of communication about energy.* Paper presented at the Association for Education in Journalism and Mass Communication annual convention, San Antonio, TX.

Griffin, R. J., Yang, Z., ter Huurne, E., Boerner, F., Ortiz, S., & Dunwoody, S. (2008). After the flood: Anger, attribution, and the seeking of information. *Science Communication, 29,* 285–315.

Guerin, B., & Innes, J. M. (1989). Cognitive tuning sets: Anticipating the consequences of communication. *Current Psychology: Research & Reviews, 8,* 234–249.

Hance, B. J., Chess, C., & Sandman, P. M. (1989). Setting a context for explaining risk. *Risk Analysis, 9,* 113–117.

Hovick, S. R., Freimuth, V. S., Johnson-Turbes, A., & Chervin, D. D. (2011). Multiple health risk perception and information processing among African Americans and Whites living in poverty. *Risk Analysis.* Advance online publication. doi: 10.1111/j.1539-6924.2011.01621.x .

Hovland, C. I., Janis, I. L., & Kelley, H. H. (1953). *Communication and persuasion: Psychological studies of opinion change.* New Haven, CT: Yale University Press.

Johnson, B. B. (2005). Testing and expanding a model of cognitive processing of risk information. *Risk Analysis, 25,* 631–650.

Johnson, J. D., & Meischke, H. (1993). A comprehensive model of cancer related information seeking applied to magazines. *Human Communication Research, 19,* 343–367.

Kahan, D. (2010). Fixing the communications failure. *Nature, 463,* 296–297.

Kahan, D. M., Braman, D., Slovic, P., Gastil, J., & Cohen, G. (2009) Cultural cognition of the risks and benefits of nanotechnology. *Nature Nanotechnology, 4,* 87–90.

Kahlor, L. A. (2007). An augmented risk information seeking model: The case of global warming. *Media Psychology, 10,* 414–435.

Kahlor, L. A., Dunwoody, S., Griffin, R. J., & Neuwirth, K. (2006). Seeking and processing information about impersonal risk. *Science Communication, 28,* 163–194.

Kahlor, L. A., Dunwoody, S., Griffin, R. J., Neuwirth, K., & Giese, J. (2003). Studying heuristic–systematic processing of risk communication. *Risk Analysis, 23,* 355–368.

Kahlor, L. A., & Rosenthal, S. (2009). If we seek, do we learn? Predicting knowledge of global warming. *Science Communication, 30,* 380–414.

Kasperson, R. E. (1992). The social amplification of risk: Progress in developing an integrative framework. In S. Krimsky & D. Golding (Eds.), *Social theories of risk* (pp. 153–178). Westport, CT: Praeger.

Katz, E., Blumler, J. C., & Gurevitch, M. (1974). Utilization of mass communication by the individual. In J. G. Blumler & E. Katz (Eds.), *The uses of mass communication* (pp. 19–32). Newbury Park, CA: Sage.

Kim, J.-N., & Grunig, J. E. (2011). Problem solving and communicative action: A situational theory of problem solving. *Journal of Communication 61,* 120–149.

Klein, W. M., & Weinstein, N. D. (1997). Social comparison and unrealistic optimism about personal risk. Health, coping and well-being: Perspectives from social comparison theory. In B. P. Buunk & F. X. Gibbons (Eds.) *Health, coping and well-being: Perspectives from social comparison theory* (pp. 25–61). Mahwah, NJ: Erlbaum.

Knobloch-Westerwick, S. (2008). Information seeking. In W. Donsbach (Ed.), *International encyclopedia of communication* (Vol. 5, pp. 2264–2265). Malden, MA: Wiley-Blackwell.

Kollmuss, A., & Agyeman, J. (2002). Mind the gap: Why do people act environmentally and what are the barriers to pro-environmental behavior? *Environmental Education Research, 8,* 239–260.

Kosicki, G. M., & McLeod, J. M. (1990). Learning from political news: Effects of media images and information processing strategies. In S. Kraus (Ed.), *Mass communication and political information processing* (pp. 69–93). Hillsdale, NJ: Erlbaum.

Lazarus, R. S., & Smith, C. A. (1988). Knowledge and appraisal in the cognition-emotion relationship. *Cognition and Emotion, 2,* 281–300.

Massi Lindsey, L. L., Yun, K. A., & Hill, J. B. (2007) Anticipated guilt as motivation to help unknown others: An examination of empathy as a moderator. *Communication Research, 34,* 468–480.

McGuire, W. J. (1968). Personality and attitude change: An information-processing theory. In A. G. Greenwald, T. C. Brock, & T. M. Ostrom (Eds.), *Psychological foundations of attitudes* (pp. 171–196). San Diego, CA: Academic Press.

McGuire, W. J. (1974). Psychological motives and communication gratification. In J. G. Blumler & E. Katz (Eds.), *The uses of mass communication* (pp. 167–196). Newbury Park, CA: Sage.

McLeod, J. M., & Becker, L. B. (1974). Testing the validity of gratification measures through political effects analysis. In J. G. Blumler & E. Katz (Eds.), *The uses of mass communication* (pp. 137–166). Newbury Park, CA: Sage.

National Research Council. (1989). *Improving risk communication*. Washington, DC: National Academy Press.

Neuman, R., Marcus, G. E., Crigler, A. N., & Mackuen, M. (2007). *The affect effect*. Chicago, IL: University of Chicago Press.

Neuwirth, K., Frederick, E., & Mayo, C. (2010, November). *The role of heuristic-systematic accuracy and defensive information processing during a Congressional election*. Paper presented at the Midwest Association for Public Opinion Research annual conference, Chicago, IL.

Niederdeppe, J., Frosch, D. L., & Hornik, R. C. (2008). Cancer news coverage and information seeking. *Journal of Health Communication 13*, 181–199.

O'Keefe, D. J. (2000). Guilt and social influence. In M. E. Roloff (Ed.), *Communication Yearbook* (Vol. 23, pp. 67–101). Thousand Oaks, CA: Sage.

Palmgreen, P., & Rayburn, J. D., II. (1982). Gratifications sought and media exposure: An expectancy value model. *Communication Research, 9*, 561–580.

Peters, E., Romer, D., Slovíc, P., Jamieson, K. H., Wharfield, L., Mertz, C. K., & Carpenter, S. M. (2007). The impact and acceptibility of Canadian-style cigarette warning labels among US smokers and nonsmokers. *Nicotine & Tobacco Research, 9*, 473–481.

Petty, R. E., & Cacioppo, J. T. (1981). *Attitudes and persuasion: Classic and contemporary approaches*. Dubuque, IA: W. C. Brown.

Petty, R. E., & Cacioppo, J. T. (1986). *Communication and persuasion: Central and peripheral routes to attitude change*. New York: Springer-Verlag.

Rogers, R. W. (1985). Attitude change and information integration in fear appeals. *Psychological Reports, 56*, 179–182.

Romantan, A., Hornik, R., Price, V., Cappella, J. N., & Viswanath, K. (2008). A comparative analysis of the performance of alternative measures of exposure. *Communication Methods and Measures, 2*, 80–99.

Rosengren, K. E. (1974). Uses and gratifications: A paradigm outlined. In J. G. Blumler & E. Katz (Eds.), *The uses of mass communication*. (pp. 269–286). Newbury Park, CA: Sage.

Rosenstock, I. M. (1966). Why people use health services. *Milbank Memorial Fund Quarterly, 44*, 94–124.

Rubin, A. M. (2002). The uses-and-gratifications perspective of media effects. In J. Bryant & D. Zillmann (Eds.), *Media effects* (2nd ed., pp. 525–548). Mahwah, NJ: Erlbaum.

Sandman, P. M. (1987, November). Risk communication: Facing public outrage. *EPA Journal, 9*, 21–22.

Schemer, C., Matthes, J., & Wirth, W. (2008). Toward improving the validity and reliability of media information processing measures in surveys. *Communication Methods and Measures, 2*, 193–225.

Slater, M. D. (1997). Persuasion processes across receiver goals and message genres. *Communication Theory, 7*, 125–148.

Slovic, P. (1987). Perception of risk. *Science, 236*, 280–285.

Slovic, P. (1992). Perceptions of risk: Reflections of the psychometric paradigm. In S. Krimsky & D. Golding (Eds.), *Social theories of risk* (pp. 117–152). Westport, CT: Praeger.

Slovic, P. (2000). *The perception of risk*. London: Earthscan.

Slovic, P. (2010). *The feeling of risk*. London: Earthscan.

Smerecnik, C. M. R., Mesters, I., Candel, M. J. J. M., De Vries, H., & De Vries, N. K. (2011). Risk perception and information processing: The development and validation of a questionnaire to assess self-reported information processing. *Risk Analysis*. Advance online publication. doi: 10.1111/j.1539-6924.2011.01651.x.

Snyder, M., & Gangestad, S. (1986). On the nature of self-monitoring: Matters of assessment, matters of validity. *Journal of Personality and Social Psychology, 51*, 125–139.

Stern, P. C., Dietz, T., & Kalof, L. (1993). Gender orientations, values, and environmental concern. *Environment & Behavior, 25*, 322–348.

ter Huurne, E., Griffin, R. J., & Gutteling, J. (2009). Risk information seeking among U.S. and Dutch residents: An application of the model of risk information seeking and processing. *Science Communication, 31*, 215–237.

ter Huurne, E., & Gutteling, J. (2009). How to trust? The importance of self-efficacy and social trust in public responses to industrial risks. *Journal of Risk Research, 12*, 809–824.

Tichenor, P. J., Donohue, G. A., & Olien, C. N. (1970). Mass media flow and differential growth in knowledge. *Public Opinion Quarterly, 34*, 159–170.

Trumbo, C. W. (1999). Heuristic-systematic information processing and risk judgment. *Risk Analysis, 19*, 391–400.

Trumbo, C. W. (2002). Information processing and risk-perception: An adaptation of the heuristic-systematic model. *Journal of Communication, 52*, 367–382.

Weinstein, N. D. (1989). Optimistic biases about personal risks. *Science, 246*, 1232–1233.

Witte, K. (1992). Putting the fear back into fear appeals: The extended parallel process model. *Communication Monographs 59*, 329–349.

Witte, K. (1994). Fear control and danger control: A test of the extended parallel process model (EPPM). *Communication Monographs, 61*, 113–134.

Witte, K., & Allen, M. (2000). A meta-analysis of fear appeals: Implications for effective public health campaigns. *Health Education & Behavior, 27*, 591–615.

Yang, Z. J., McComas, K., Gay, G., Leonard, J. P., Dannenberg, A. J., & Dillon, H. (2010a). From information processing to behavioral intentions: Exploring cancer patients' motivations for clinical trial enrollment. *Patient Education and Counseling, 79*, 231–238.

Yang, Z. J., McComas, K., Gay, G., Leonard, J. P., Dannenberg, A. J., & Dillon, H. (2010b). Motivation for health information seeking and processing about clinical trial enrollment. *Health Communication, 25*, 423–436.

Yang, Z. J., McComas, K. A., Gay, G., Leonard, J. P., Dannenberg, A. J., & Dillon, H. (2010c). Information seeking related to clinical trial enrollment. *Communication Research*. Advance online publication. doi: 0.1177/0093650210380411.

Zajonc, R. B. (1960). The process of cognitive tuning in communication. *Journal of Abnormal and Social Psychology, 61*, 159–167.

16 *Commentary*
Risk Communication in Context
Theories, Models, Research, and Future Endeavors

Kenzie A. Cameron

Northwestern University

Attempts to understand, explain, and predict individuals' risk percep-tions and risk-related behaviors continue to fascinate scholars both within and outside the communication discipline. Outside of the aca-demic realm, as noted by Griffin, Dunwoody, and Yang, understanding and effectively communicating risk is a critical task for agencies such as the federal government, which has found itself a "spokesperson" of sorts for numerous catastrophic events in the recent past, whether natural disasters, environmen-tal catastrophes, or disasters and events arising from political dissension and unrest.

Risk communication, and understanding the effects of what is communi-cated, remain significant for these large-scale issues, as well as for numerous other events which may affect a smaller number of individuals simultane-ously, yet a relatively large number of individuals when counted as a whole. For example, many patients have a general understanding of various health-related risks, but when the patient is faced with assessing her own risk for breast cancer, the information sought, received, and processed remains likely to be interpreted differently among various individuals. These interpretations are often driven by, as the risk information seeking and processing (RISP) model recognizes (Griffin, Dunwoody, & Neuwirth, 1999; Griffin et al., this volume), individual characteristics such as past experiences (or relevant haz-ard experience) and perceptions of the dangers of the risk (perceived hazard characteristics).

The Risk Information Seeking and Processing Model

In their chapter, "Linking Risk Messages to Information Seeking and Process-ing," Griffin and his colleagues present a brief overview of research traditions relevant to their original (Griffin et al., 1999) and now their revised model, the risk information seeking and processing (RISP) model. The RISP model draws concepts from other extant theories and models, in particular Eagly and Chaiken's (1993) heuristic-systematic model (HSM) and Ajzen's (1985,

1988) theory of planned behavior (TPB). The authors briefly review other research related to risk perception and communication that is relevant to the RISP model, noting how information informs risk perceptions by exploring unidimensional/multidimensional, cognitive/affective, psychological/socio-logical, and personal/impersonal relationships (shifts, structures) that clarify our understanding of how individuals use and assimilate information in their personal risk perceptions. Following a review of the theoretical foundations of the RISP model, the authors discuss RISP-related studies, and discuss how the RISP model, and future refinements to the model, can assist researchers in identifying and understanding how information functions related to individuals' risk perceptions and eventual behavior change.

The Critical Component of Context

Just as the phrase "location, location, location" is consistently brought up when discussing the value and attractiveness of real estate, the phrase "context, context, context" could easily be applied when discussing risk communication, and one's seeking and processing of the (relevant or irrelevant) information attained. Context may include whether or not the risk or hazard is personal and immediate (i.e., a health diagnosis) or something that affects others at some future time (i.e., future harm to the environment brought on by current prac-tices). Previous work by Slovic, Fischhoff, and Lichtenstein (1982) explored the structure of 18 separate risk characteristics, and reported that these charac-teristics could be explained by two or three higher-order factors: (a) the degree to which a risk is understood, (b) the degree to which a risk evokes a feeling of dread, and (c) the number of people expected to be exposed to the risk. The context in which an individual would be exposed to these various types of risk is likely to affect numerous components of the RISP model, such as one's sufficiency threshold, perceived information gathering capacity, and perceived hazard characteristics.

For example, one's intention to or behavior related to seeking and process-ing risk information is likely to be influenced by the timing of the risk, a char-acteristic found on the "dread" factor (effect immediate/effect delayed, Slovic et al., 1982). If an individual recognizes a future risk to herself or an individual she cares about, she may begin to seek and process some information related to that risk over a lengthy period of time. At any given time, if the risk still appears distant to that individual, she may not have taken the personal effort to fully process the information she has uncovered, or, she also may not fully put her efforts into seeking the needed information. Thus, her information suf-ficiency threshold may be rather low. However, once the risk is no longer dis-tant, and the context has changed, the sufficiency threshold for that individual is likely to be much higher. Depending on the time frame in which the context has changed, the available time to gather the needed information to reach the sufficiency threshold is likely also to affect one's perceived information gathering capacity. Thus, the RISP model truly describes what may well be a very fluid, and unstable, process.

Similarly, one's *tolerance* for risk in a health context is likely to vary based upon context (time, place, who is involved, etc.). For example, an individual may avoid elective surgery where the risk of death is listed prominently (or listed at all) on the surgical consent form. However, when the context becomes an adult child donating a kidney for a parent, although the risk of death is still viewed as both significant and serious, the context has changed considerably, to the extent that the adult child may be willing to undertake such an elective surgery (elective for the donor), due to the importance of the perceived benefits and outcomes of the procedure. This fluidity in risk tolerance brings to mind measurements of financial risk tolerance used to assist financial advisors in suggesting alternate investment strategies that will not only serve the client well by increasing her initial investment, but also maintain a necessary comfort level for the client over her many years of investing. Advisors recognize the need to continually reassess their clients' risk tolerance as the context in which the client is investing her money may change from year to year.

Message Framing in Risk Communication

Future applications and refinements of the RISP model may seek to incorporate the work of Tversky and Kahneman, and others who have focused their efforts on prospect theory and understanding how the framing of messages can affect recipients' response to the messages (Kahneman & Tversky, 1979; Rothman, Bartels, Wlaschin, & Salovey, 2006; Rothman & Kiviniemi, 1999; Rothman & Salovey, 1997; Tversky & Kahneman, 1981). Prospect theory focuses on understanding how individuals evaluate either gains or losses that they may face, and suggests that individuals' preferences can be influenced by how information is framed.

Rothman and Salovey (1997) reported that gain framed messages (messages that emphasize the gains or benefits from taking action) were more likely to encourage prevention behaviors than were loss-framed messages (i.e., those focusing on the losses from inaction); a finding consistent with a recent meta-analysis of the persuasive impact of both gain- and loss-framed messages (Gallagher & Updegraff, 2012). Rothman and Salovey (1997) also suggested that loss-framed messages appeared to work better than gain-framed messages when the health behavior in question was related to *screening or early detection*, a finding not consistent with the Gallagher and Updegraff (2012) meta-analysis, which reported no effect of message framing among studies related to detection.

However, regardless of the message frame used, when health information is being relayed at an individual level, as opposed to a public health level, practitioners will do well to remember that any individuals' current understanding of risk may not be the same understanding held by the practitioner. A 20%

likelihood of an event (positive or negative) happening tends to be perceived by an individual based upon the context. For example, if one were told that she had a 20% chance of winning the lottery (a positive event), but an 80% chance of losing her money (a presumably negative event), those odds may appear to be fairly optimistic. However, that same woman being told not to worry about the fact she needs to undergo a breast biopsy because there is a "small" (20%) chance of the biopsy finding breast cancer, and a much larger (80%) chance of the biopsy indicating there is nothing of concern in the breast tissue is very likely to respond quite differently to being provided with the risk estimates. In one case, the risk of the negative event (loss of money) is significantly higher than the risk of the negative event in the other (finding breast cancer, regardless of the stage), yet the context in which the risk is being discussed not surprisingly leads to a very different risk perception for the individual—even if she understands very well the risks and the relationship of the risky event occurring.

Thus, it remains critical for those of us attempting to understand risk perception and risk communication as a scholarly endeavor to recognize that the audience may well understand the risk, but they understand the risk in a way that is not comparable to how we may understand that risk. Indeed, practitioners often forget that a 20% chance of a negative event may not be a small enough risk if you are the person facing that 1 in 5 chance. Although one may be able to cognitively reason that the odds are in one's favor, the affective elements of the situation may color our perceptions significantly. This issue is particularly important when we consider applying risk perception and risk models in the realm of health care, where the ability to cognitively and dispassionately view risks presented to you as a patient, or a family member of a patient, is often colored by the context of the outcome.

The Heuristic Value of the RISP Model and Future Related Research

When evaluating a theory (or in this case, a model), we may be reminded of criteria presented in Littlejohn's *Theories of Human Communication*, criteria which include theoretical scope as well as heuristic value (Littlejohn, 1992). My discussion of the RISP model has been framed in general in the realm of health communication, and often at more of an individual level, although Griffin and his colleagues along with others have applied it to issues affecting the environment (e.g., Kahlor, Dunwoody, Griffin, & Neuwirth, 2006) and broader public health and health policy issues (e.g., Hovick, Freimuth, Johnson-Turbes, & Chervin, 2011). Further applicability of the RISP model remains to be tested, and researchers are encouraged to do so by the RISP model's creators themselves. In consideration of increasing further the theoretical scope of the model an extension of some of the previous applications may be warranted. The majority of the applications of the model appear to be environmental, or health at more of a public health level. The application of the model at an interpersonal level, in differing contexts (to allow for greater exploration of the impersonal/personal dimensions) is an attractive avenue to pursue.

The criterion that resonated the most as I reviewed this manuscript was that of *heuristic value*. The RISP model itself is a demonstration of the continuing heuristic value of other theories and models (most specifically HSM and TPB) through its synthesis and application of concepts of each of those models in its own development. Future research using the RISP will continue the story of the heuristic value of the RISP model itself. As the RISP is described as being "essentially a work in progress," I take the liberty of joining the authors in inviting other researchers to continue to contribute to the development and further evolution of the model. For it is in such fine tuning and replication that we as scholars are able to further science. New models and theories may serve us well to better define, describe, and predict human processes; however, building upon the foundations of effective models already in existence also can lead to significant research accomplishments.

Additional areas of future research return to the idea of the importance of affect when studying risk perceptions. The authors specifically reference the extended parallel process model (Witte, 1992, 1994) and its focus on fear. The authors note their intention to continue to incorporate affect into their existing model, which is identified as being primarily cognitive. Affect is indeed a critical aspect of risk and risk perception; previous scholars such as Slovic et al. (1982) have discussed the emotions of worry and dread. When considering applying the RISP in either a health or environmental context, other relevant emotions to consider may include anxiety, anger, guilt, and hope, among many others.

As Slovic et al. (1982) noted in their manuscript published in one of the early issues of *Risk Analysis*: "Risk means different things to different people. When experts judge risk, their responses correlate highly with technical estimates of annual fatalities. Laypeople can assess annual fatalities if they are asked to (and produce estimates not unlike the technical estimates). However, their judgments of risk are sensitive to other factors as well (e.g., catastrophic potential, threat to future generations) and, as a result, are not closely related to their own (or experts') estimates of annual fatalities." (p. 85). Challenges remain for researchers interested in pursuing risk communication and the ability to predict and explain individual's information seeking and processing behaviors as often individuals themselves are unlikely to be able to accurately predict their own risk perception, or risk response, making the challenge for researchers even more daunting. Human behavior will always retain an element of the unplanned, or the unexpected. However, the acknowledgment of the importance of both the numerous cognitive elements (such as perceived information gathering capacity, need for cognition, and perceived hazard characteristics) as well as affective elements (such as fear and anxiety) that often influence one's risk perceptions, and information seeking and processing behavior, is an encouraging step toward a deeper, more robust understanding of how individuals act and interact when presented with risk information. Risk and risk perception remain in the realm of the individual, steeped in context and highly affected by individual characteristics. We still seek to better understand the context in which risk messages are presented to better understand both information processing and its relation, for example, to future health behaviors (Gallagher & Updegraff, 2011). The RISP model has explored and identified numerous individual characteristics as well as the motivation one has in processing the message. Future research both using and arising from the RISP model will both increase the heuristic value of the RISP model and those upon which it was built as well as increase our understanding of information seeking and processing in the context of risk communication.

References

Ajzen, I. (1985). From intentions to action: A theory of planned behavior. In J. Kuhl & J. Beckman (Eds.), *Action control: From cognitions to behaviors* (pp. 11–39). New York: Springer.

Ajzen, I. (1988). *Attitudes, personality and behavior.* Milton Keynes, England: Open University Press.

Eagly, A. H., & Chaiken, S. (1993). *The psychology of attitudes.* Fort Worth, TX: Harcourt Brace & Jovanovich.

Gallagher, K. M., & Updegraff, J. A. (2012). Health message framing effects on attitdues, intentions, and behavior: A meta-analytic review. *Annals of Behavioral Medicine, 43,* 101–116.

Griffin, R. J., Dunwoody, S., & Neuwirth, K. (1999). Proposed model of the relationship of risk information seeking and processing to the development of preventive behaviors. *Environmental Research, 80,* S230–S245.

Hovick, S. R., Freimuth, V. S., Johnson-Turbes, A., & Chervin, D. D. (2011). Multiple health risk perception and information processing among African Americans and Whites living in poverty. *Risk Analysis, 31,* 1789–1799.

Kahlor, L. A., Dunwoody, S., Griffin, R. J., & Neuwirth, K. (2006). Seeking and processing information about impersonal risk. *Science Communication, 28,* 163–194.

Kahneman, D., & Tversky, A. (1979). Prospect theory: An analysis of decision making under risk. *Econometrica, 6,* 621–630.

Kahneman, D., & Tversky, A. (1982). The psychology of preferences. *Scientific American, 46,* 160–173.

Littlejohn, S. W. (1992). *Theories of human communication* (4th ed.). Belmont, CA: Wadsworth.

Rothman, A. J., Bartels, R. D., Wlaschin, J., & Salovey, P. (2006). The strategic use of gain- and loss-framed messages to promote healthy behavior: How theory can inform practice. *Journal of Communication, 56,* S202–S221.

Rothman, A. J., & Kiviniemi, M. (1999). Treating people with health information: An analysis and review of approaches to communicating health risk information. *Journal of the National Cancer Institute Monographs, 25,* 44–51.

Rothman, A. J., & Salovey, P. (1997). Shaping perceptions to motivate healthy behavior: The role of message framing. *Psychological Bulletin, 121,* 3–19.

Slovic, P., Fischhoff, B., & Lichtenstein, S. (1982). Why study risk perception? *Risk Analysis, 2,* 83–93.

Tversky, A., & Kahneman, D. (1981). The framing of decisions and the rationality of choice. *Science, 221,* 453–458.

Witte, K. (1992). Putting the fear back into fear appeals: The extended parallel process model. *Communication Monographs 59,* 329–349.

Witte, K. (1994). Fear control and danger control: A test of the extended parallel process model (EPPM). *Communication Monographs, 61,* 113–134.

CHAPTER CONTENTS

17 On the Study of Process in Communication Research

Marshall Scott Poole

University of Illinois Urbana-Champaign

One of the defining characteristics of communication is that it is a process. Yet the vast majority of studies of communication do not focus on process, but rather on static models and explanations. This essay develops a conception of process research in the social scientific study of communication that distinguishes it from traditional variance based research approaches. The process approach is based on the development of theoretical narratives that explain how series of events unfold over time. Explanation in process theories is based on formal and final causality as well as on the efficient causality that is the foundation for variance explanations. Four basic types of process explanations are described. Four strategies for process research are explicated and examples of process studies in communication are used to illustrate them.

That communication is a process was one of the foundational assumptions of the modern field of communication.[1] Early influential works such as Schramm's (1954) *Process and Effects of Mass Communication* and Berlo's (1960) *The Process of Communication* enshrined process as a central characteristic of communication. Process figures in most of the more than 100 definitions of communication catalogued by Dance and Larson (1976). It is a staple of basic and advanced communication texts (e.g., Littlejohn, 1996; Miller, 2012).

Definitions of process by communication scholars vary widely, but they generally fall into two types that reflect two general orientations to process. Berlo (1960) wrote:

> If we accept the concept of process, we view the events and relationships as dynamic, on-going, ever-changing, continuous.... We mean that it does not have a beginning, an end, a fixed sequence of events.... The ingredients within a process interact; each affects all of the others. (p. 24)

This encompassing and somewhat formidable definition focuses on the essential features of processes as essential features of communication. Monge, Farace, Eisenberg, Miller, and White (1984) offer an observer-oriented definition of process: "A pattern that is seen in reference to time is called a process" (p. 22). This second type of definition suggests that process is a category of thought on the part of the researcher, a concept that captures aspects of change, such as the transmission of a message from one person to another or the diffusion of an innovation through communication networks.

A number of process theories have been advanced in communication studies. They include:

- Diffusion of innovations theory (Rogers, 2003; Valente, 1995)
- Group decision emergence theory (Fisher, 1970)
- The multiple sequence theory of group decision development (Poole, 1983; Poole & Roth, 1989a)
- The organizational community network evolution model (Bryant & Monge, 2008; Monge, Heiss, & Margolin, 2008)
- Stages of change theory (transtheoretical model) (Prochaska, Redding, & Evers, 2008; Valente & Saba, 1998; Vaughan & Rogers, 2000)
- The interactive health media use model (Street, 2003)
- Action assembly theory (Greene, 1984, 2008)
- The interpersonal relationship dissolution model (Knapp, 1978)
- Relational dialectics theory (Baxter, 1988; Baxter & Montgomery, 1996)
- The relational turbulence model (Solomon & Knobloch, 2004)
- Agenda-setting theory (Dearing & Rogers, 1996; McCombs & Shaw, 1993; McQuail, 2010)
- Spiral of silence theory (McQuail, 2010; Noelle-Neumann, 1984; Scheufle & Moy, 2000)

These theories, summarized in Table 17.1, span most subdisciplines of communication, including group communication, organizational communication, communication and cognition, persuasion, health communication, interpersonal communication, and mass and mediated communication.

In the actual conduct of communication research, however, there has been much less emphasis on communication process per se than one would expect. An important essay on the process of studying communication processes by Monge, Farace et al. (1984) concluded that, as of the early 1980s, actual research on processes was remarkably sparse. In the succeeding 30 plus years a number of process-based theories of communication have been articulated and empirical studies of process are more common. However, process research still represents only a small minority of communication studies. A search of *Communication Abstracts* for the years 2000 to 2011 reveals 760 articles with the term *process* in their titles or abstracts, out of a total of 131, 000 articles; about .5%.

At the time of their writing, Monge, Farace et al. (1984) traced the lack of research on process to three factors: "methodological determinism, the inaccessibility of process techniques, and the perceived scope of effort required from the researcher" (p. 28). They argued that the experimental and survey

Table 17.1 Exemplary Process Theories in Communication

Theory	Unit of Analysis	Description of Process	Process Type	Notes
Diffusion of innovations (Rogers, 2003)	Social system at the macrolevel; individual at the microlevel	Individual adopters make innovation decisions in a process of 5- stages: (a) knowledge; (b) persuasion; (c) decision; (d)implementation; (e) confirmation. At the system levels different types of adopters (innovators, early majority, late majority, laggards) with different motivations adopt sequentially in order listed, resulting in the diffusion curve	Life cycle at individual level; Life cycle at system level	There are also two critical events (a) at the transition between early adopters and (b) at the transition between late adopters and laggards
Decision emergence model of group decision making (Fisher, 1970)	The group	Decisions emerge in a unitary, set 5-stage sequence: (a) orientation; (b) conflict; (c) emergence; (d) reinforcement. Transitions between phases occur due to uncertainty amplification and reduction processes	Life cycle	
Multiple sequence model of group decision making (Poole, 1983; Poole & Roth, 1989a)	The group at the macrolevel; the individual at the microlevel	Members have schemas (logics) that represent norms for effective group decision making. Logics include the ideal sequence (similar to Fisher's), negotiation, and political maneuvering. If members have the same logics, then simple sequences result, but if they disagree or run into problems making the decision more complex sequences result	Teleological model governs group process; individual member logics are life cycles	There are three types of breakpoints (critical events) that might punctuate the decision process
Organizational community network evolutionary model (Bryant & Monge, 2008; Monge et al., 2008;)	The community at the macrolevel; the organization at the microlevel	Evolutionary model of variation-selection-retention governs linkage formation and maintenance at the interorganizational level. Fitness of linkages determines selection and retention. At the community level there is a three stage progression: (a) a few organizations enter the niche; (b) their success attracts additional members; (c) the niche and/or network reach their respective carrying capacities and network/population growth slows and may decay	Life cycle at the macro level; evolutionary at the micro level	

(continued)

Table 17.1 Continued

Theory	Unit of Analysis	Description of Process	Process Type	Notes
Stages of change theory (transtheoretical model) (Prochaska, Redding, & Evers, 2008)	Individual	Individuals undertaking a major life change (e.g. smoking cessation) go through five stages: (a) precontemplation; (b) contemplation; (c) preparation; (d) action; (e) maintenance. Transitions between stages occur due to individual's self-evaluation and group centered support	Life cycle	
Interactive health media use model (Street, 2003)	Individual	Media use by individuals interacting with technology goes through three stages: (a) implementation; (b) use; (c) outcomes	Life cycle	
Action assembly theory (Greene, 1984, 2008)	Individual	In order to achieve interactional outcomes, the individual assembles appropriate units of action at different levels from procedural memory: (a) the interactional representation (objective to be achieved); (b) the ideational representation (ideas to be expressed in the course of achieving the objective; (c) the utterance representation (appropriate language to use in achieving the goal); (d) the sensorimotor representation (neural commands). The hierarchical assembly can be put together in several orders provided they help achieve the objective.	Teleological	
Interpersonal relationship dissolution model (Knapp, 1978)	Dyad	Dissolution follows a five-step sequence: (a) differentiating; (b) circumscribing; (c) stagnating; (d) avoiding; (e) terminating	Life Cycle	

Theory	Level	Description	Type
Relational dialectics theory (Baxter & Montgomery, 1996)	Dyad	Relationships involve three dialectical tensions: (a) integration-separation; (b) stability-change; (c) expression-nonexpression. These are experienced internally within the dyad or externally between the dyad and family/ community. How the relationship develops depends on the relative strength of these dialectics and how the dyad copes with the dialectic. The dialectic is never resolved, but must be dealt with continuously	Dialectical
Relational turbulence model (Solomon & Knobloch, 2004)	Dyad	Members in a relationship respond to conflict based on their intimacy level. There are three sequential intimacy levels: (a) initial (reaction to conflict is not particularly strong and governed by social norms); (b) intermediate (reaction to conflict is strong due to uncertainty and insecurity about relationship); (c) high (reaction to conflict is not strong because parties trust their relationship and one another)	Life Cycle
Agenda setting theory (McCombs & Shaw, 1993)	Society or public	The cycle of political influence on issues passes through three stages: (a) public opinion and the opinions of political elites set the issues; there is competition to determine relative salience of the issues; (b) mass media select issues according to the pressures from publics and elites and frames them for public; (c) media portrayal affects public opinion and evaluation of the situation based on framing	Life Cycle
Spiral of silence theory (Noelle-Neumann, 1984)	Society or public	People constantly assess the current climate of prevailing opinion and compare it to their own. The spiral operates by a three stage process: (a) the media present a particular opinion as predominant; (b) if the individual's opinion is different from the presented predominant opinion, the individual is fearful of expressing opinion; (c) this silences the individual and his or her side of the issue is never presented.	Life Cycle

methods that predominated empirical communication research at the time were ill-suited to process research, that techniques like time series analysis and Markov analysis were not often applied (because they were viewed as esoteric and difficult), and that gathering longitudinal data was sufficiently time-consuming and difficult as to discourage process studies. During the ensuing period, a number of qualitative and quantitative techniques for process research have been developed and time series has been rendered formulaic in statistical packages (Langley, 1999; Miller, Poole, Seibold, & Associates, 2010; Poole, Van de Ven, Dooley, & Holmes, 2000). However, the bulk of quantitative research in communication studies employs designs that do not directly delve into process. Rather than studying process directly, they either measure pre-to-post change, and infer something about the process, or they include variables that attempt to measure characteristics of the process (such as having group members rate the degree to which their discussion was "open"), without actually measuring the process directly. In the same vein, the bulk of qualitative research does not describe or explain processes as they unfold, but provides synoptic accounts that elide temporal or developmental dimensions.

Lack of methods and inculcated habits of research design are likely to be among the causes of the dearth of direct research on communication processes. Just as important, however, has been a lack of guidelines for the development of theories of communication processes and explicit frameworks for conducting process research. In general there has not been much reflection on the conduct of research on communication processes within the communication discipline. Monge, Farace et al. (1984) is the only general review I have been able to locate of process research in communication.

Discussions of process in communication tend toward two extremes. Some are broad and relatively imprecise as to the nature of process. Exemplified in Berlo's definition, these discussions are rather vague as to the nature of processes and portray them as dynamically changing groups of elements in which everything is connected to everything else. This daunting picture has, no doubt, discouraged many scholars, because it does little to describe the various forms that processes might take and seems to invite the researcher into the impossible task of specifying dynamic connections among an endless array of messages, people, variables, or whatever makes up the process. Included in this category are definitions of process in general terms as any sort of change or dynamics that are involved in explanations of communication phenomena, with no specification of the nature of the process per se. Many of the studies delivered by the *Communication Abstracts* search used process in this manner and it is no doubt used in this way in many other articles that did not have "process" in their titles or abstracts.

On the other end of the continuum are narrow definitions of process. Some, like Monge et al.'s (1984) definition, offer a rather narrow view of process that is delimited by analytical methods such as time series analysis. While such views are encouraging to those who are familiar with the methods and whose problems clearly fit them, this review will make the case that they constrain the imagination and hence limit inquiry into communication processes. Others, like Littlejohn (1996), use the word *process* to refer to specific phenomena like message processing. In a similar vein, Barnett (1997) defines process as change in structure over time. These views restrict process theories to particular content areas, whereas this review will contend that they are generally applicable to any area of inquiry in communication.

This review will stake out the middle ground by offering an analysis of process theory and research that applies to a broad range of communication phenomena and that specifies the forms that process theories should take and requirements for developing and conducting empirical research on process theories. It draws together thinking on process from the disciplines of communication, philosophy, organizational studies, and information systems in an attempt to present a holistic picture of process theory that can form a foundation for more systematic inquiry into communication processes (see Poole, Van de Ven, et al., 2000, for an in-depth discussion of process theory and research). The conceptualization of process theories and research developed in this chapter is not simply descriptive, but also normative in the sense that it suggests preferred ways to lay out process theories in communication as well as preferred research strategies. It is also by nature exclusionary in that it suggests that certain theoretical formulations of process are vague or inadequate and that certain research designs offer at best incomplete evidence related to process theories. The goal is to establish that process research is a distinctive approach that differs from many traditional modes of research and requires different modes of thought and analysis.

The next section presents a definition of process and distinguishes variance research—the traditional approach in social science—from process research. A discussion follows of four different forms process theories may take. The final section then articulates four different strategies for studying communication processes based on combinations of variance and process research approaches.

Process Research

Process Defined

What is a process? Nicholas Rescher (1996; see also Teichmann, 1995) offers a succinct and inclusive definition:

> A process is a coordinated group of changes in the complexion of reality, an organized family of occurrences that are systematically linked to one another either causally or functionally.... A process consists in an integrated series of developments unfolding in joint coordination in line with a definite program. Processes are correlated with occurrences or events: Processes always involve various events, and events exist only in and through processes. (p. 38)

This definition implies several characteristics of processes. First and most obvious, they involve change. In a thoroughgoing processual view, even stability should be understood in terms of processes that are maintaining (apparent) stability. Second, processes unfold over time, which necessitates longitudinal research designs. Third, processes are made up of one or more series of events. An event is a "happening, occurrence or episode ... a change ... or composite of changes" (Mackie, 1995, p.253). Teichmann (1995, p. 721) comments that: "'process' is to 'change' or 'event', rather as 'syndrome' is to 'symptom'. So a process is a collection of events or changes "with some sort of unity or unifying principle, to it" (Teichmann, 1995, p. 721).

Fourth, processes maintain coherence through unifying principles, such as causal relationships along the series of events (event A leads to event B, which leads to event C, ...), functional interrelationships among their elements (A changes in order to perform a function for B, which then changes in order to perform a function for C, which then changes to perform a function for A, leading to a change in the entire system), or a self-organizing system (individual components form causal or functional relationships that give rise to a larger systemic unit). There is no single, best way for a process to maintain itself, but rather, as will be discussed, several different motors may drive processes and each generates its own type of coherence.

Process Research: A Contrast between Variance and Process Approaches

Mohr (1982; Poole, Van de Ven, et al., 2000) first distinguished variance and process approaches to social scientific research, and Poole, Van de Ven, et al. (2000) expanded their discussion to incorporate multiple types of process theory. The basic contrast between them is that a *variance theory* explains phenomena in terms of relationships among independent and dependent variables, while a *process theory* explains them in terms of how a sequence of events leads to some outcome. Figure 17.1 provides a pictorial comparison of the two approaches.

A variance theory focuses on variables that represent the important aspects or attributes of the subject under study. Explanations take the form of causal statements or models that incorporate these variables (e.g., X causes Y which causes Z), and an implicit goal of variance research is to establish the conditions necessary and sufficient to bring about an outcome. Variance research employs experimental and survey research designs and is grounded in the general linear model that underlies most common statistical methods, including ANOVA, regression, factor analysis, and structural equation modeling. A key criterion for assessing variance theories is their generality, which refers to the range of cases, phenomena, or situations the causal explanation applies to.

The variance approach is useful in the study of communication processes in two important respects. First, the variance approach is well-suited for testing hypotheses related to the mechanisms that generate processes. For example, spiral of silence theory assumes that a person's perception of support for or

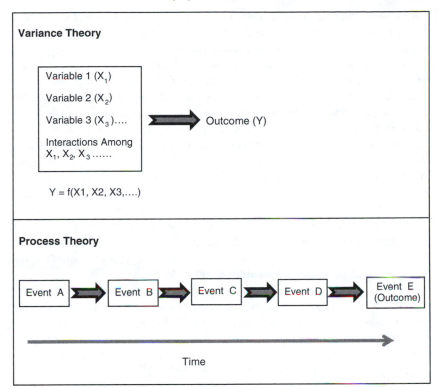

Variance Theory

Variable 1 (X_1)

Variable 2 (X_2)

Variable 3 (X_3)....   Outcome (Y)

Interactions Among
X_1, X_2, X_3 ......

$Y = f(X1, X2, X3,....)$

Process Theory

Event A → Event B → Event C → Event D → Event E (Outcome)

Time

Figure 17.1 Variance and process theories.

against his or her position influences a person's willingness to speak out on a subject. Numerous survey studies have been conducted to test this assumption, and a meta-analysis by Glynn, Hayes, and Shanahan (1997) concluded that overall this effect was weak or nonexistent. The variance approach can also be used to study processes if variables describing the process can be defined. For example, Poole and Roth (1989b) developed a measure of the degree to which a decision-making group's discussion conformed to an ideal model of the phases of group decision making (given the somewhat awkward name *unitariness*). They were then able to test hypotheses concerning the conditions that led groups to conform to or deviate from the ideal model. As will be argued later on in this essay, the variance approach can be used to study processes with good effect.

The variance approach also has limitations, however, when it is applied in the study of processes (Poole, Van de Ven, et al., 2000). It is difficult to study the activities or steps in which change and innovation unfold using variance methods. While some methodologies for the study of processes have been applied in variance research (e.g., Davison, King, Kitchener, & Parker, 1980; Davison, Robbins, & Swanson, 1978; Poole & Roth, 1989a,b), they require researchers to abstract variables such as unitariness from the process data, which forces them to study it at one remove (at least). This focus on variables rather than sequencing of events makes it difficult for variance approaches to shed light on how the process functions over time.

A second limitation of most variance methods and designs is that they are not sufficiently flexible to capture the variability in processes due to the multiple forms the same process may manifest. Different relational dissolution processes, for example, may go through the same stages at very different rates, with the length of different stages varying greatly from relationship to relationship. A longitudinal variance research design that tracked relational dissolution by measuring couples at set intervals is likely to run into difficulties because of this case-to-case variation in the "velocity" of the process (see Poole, 1981 for a similar criticism of empirical tests of phase models of group decision making). At any given point couples are likely to be in different stages of dissolution, resulting in mixed data and in some cases couples may have gone through more than one stage during an interval. While adjustments can be made in variance methods to allow for this variability, they require "improvisations" that go beyond the traditional methodologies.

The statistical methods of variance research assume that causality in the system is "well-behaved"; that is, that causal factors operate homogeneously across cases and on approximately the same time scale (Abbott, 1988). These assumptions do not seem particularly restrictive within the variance framework, but they rule out the influence of some factors and influences that might figure in a process, including critical events; multiple causes operating unevenly in different parts of the system and at different points in time; causes operating across greatly different time scales; and sequences of events that chain together in a contingent fashion to lead up to some outcome. Variance methods are available to study each of these factors and influences (for example, interrupted time series analysis can study the impact of critical events), and mixed methods approaches are promising (Miller et al., 2010). However, processes may include several or all of these influences, and traditional designs for variance research are not sufficiently flexible to capture complex ensembles of these elements. The process research approach attempts to bring a more flexible approach to bear.

The primary focus of a process theory is a series of events that unfold through time to eventuate in some outcome. Explanations in process theories tend to be more complex than variance explanations because events often have multiple implications and multiple effects on the process, because of the need to account for temporal connections among events, and because different time scales may operate simultaneously in the same process. Process theories may incorporate several different types of explanatory elements, including causal and contextual factors that influence the series of events, critical events or "tipping points," and overall formative patterns that shape the pattern of events over the entire series.

The heart of a process explanation should ideally include three elements: (a) a description and explanation of the overall pattern that characterizes the series (e.g., "the process follows four stages, A, B, C, and D, because these stages are logically required to get from the beginning of the process to the end"); (b) a more microlevel account of how one event leads to and influences subsequent events in the series; and (c) an explanation of how event transitions are related to the overall pattern. To this basic generative mechanism may be added causal and contextual factors that intersect with and influence the event series at various points and by critical events and tipping points.

For example, the classical description of the group decision-making process portrays it as a series of phases (orientation, problem analysis, solution development, choice, and confirmation) that unfolds as it does because these are logically necessary steps that must be taken to move from a felt need to a final decision. The events that make up the phases is the series of individual statements made during the decision-making discussion and the relationships among these events depend on norms of relevance and logic (e.g., if the group is currently discussing the nature of the problem, then members should focus their effort on this topic and not introduce suggestions, jokes, or other irrelevant comments). As a result of adherence to this norm, successive comments in the series will tend to have similar functions and a larger unit of interaction that serves this function, a phase, will emerge. Transitions from one phase to another are explained as a result of the group collectively deciding that the current function has been fulfilled and it is time to move on to the next one. For example, the group may verbally agree that it understands the problem and this is a signal to move on to generating solutions to the problem. In addition to this basic account in terms of a logical sequence of phases, the decision process may also be influenced by critical events such as the occurrence of a conflict that divides the group, external influences such as the need to make a decision to meet a certain deadline, and external processes such as prior history of cooperation or competition among various members of the group (Poole, 1983; Tracy & Standerfer, 2004).

Process accounts may also be more complex than the preceding example. There may be several levels between the event level series and the larger pattern, including individual events, local clusters of events, and larger phases or stages (Poole, 1983; Poole, Van de Ven et al., 2000). Relationships between units in each level may be expressed in several forms, including quantitative indices such as transition probabilities and qualitative descriptions of the historical connections among events derived through colligation, "the procedure of explaining an event by tracing its intrinsic relations to other events and locating it in its historical context" (Abbott, 1984, p. 194).

Poole, Van de Ven et al. (2000) argue that process explanations differ from variance explanations because they may incorporate three of Aristotle's four causes. They utilize the efficient causation that is the basis of causal explanation in variance research, but the key to process explanations is formal causation or final causation.

Final causality shapes processes by directing them according to an end or goal that guides the path that the process follows to its conclusion. It is common to assume that human agents pose the goals in question, but final causality can also be driven by natural ends and outcomes of natural processes. Relationship termination, for example, can sometimes be set in motion by the desire (perhaps unconscious) of one or both parties to break free of the relationship, but it may also occur gradually as parties partially disengage, then disengage further, without really recognizing that the relationship is ending until they are in the final stages. Put another way, final causality is any end state that attracts a process to itself. As such, the final cause draws the participants in the process along the path it follows to its end, subject to various diversions posed by external causal and contextual factors and critical incidents. Some of these events and conjunctures function consistently with final cause, while others counteract the pull of the final cause. For example, while our couple is progressing through the stages of relational dissolution, one partner may suffer a major medical emergency which results in the other partner recommitting. This may short-circuit the dissolution, or it may prove to be simply a side-track and eventually the dissolution resumes.

In communication processes formal causation is embodied in templates that govern the unfolding process, such as a normative model or a plan that is followed during the process. In group communication, for example, one important type of form is a procedural agenda, such as a list of requirements that a research team must fulfill when writing and submitting a grant. There are also institutional, cultural, or ritualistic formulas that may enform processes. For example, people commonly look to media for information about political issues and this institutional participation may set the agenda-setting process in motion.

Both final and formal causation engender patterns for the process as a whole. In Mohr's (1982) terminology, process theories incorporate a *"pull-type causality*: X [the precursor] does not imply Y [the outcome], but rather Y implies X" (p. 59). Efficient causality—what Mohr calls "push-type causality"—accounts for immediate impacts of events and for the influence of external factors on the process. For instance, a downturn in the economy may slow the rate of diffusion of an innovation through a social system. While efficient causality plays a role in the explanation of processes, the focus of a process theory, however, is accounting for change over time, and this is primarily done through articulating larger patterns in the events, patterns driven by formal or final causality. Such accounts cannot be framed in terms of efficient causality, which operates only in the immediately and not over the long term.

Process research employs a wide variety designs whose goal is to identify or reconstruct the process through direct observation, archival analysis, or multiple case studies. The analysis of this data requires methods that can identify and test both temporal linkages between events and also overall temporal patterns (Poole, Van de Ven et al., 2000). Variance research is premised on hypothetico-deductive procedures, but process research employs a mixture of approaches due its need for flexibility. A common approach is first to map events and to identify local connections among them, as well as key events, and then to work up to identify more macrolevel patterns. In some cases this is done inductively (e.g., Langley, 1999), but there are also methods for testing hypotheses concerning the basic generative mechanism for the process once an event series has been specified and properly indexed to indicate larger units (e.g., Poole, 1981). Another common pattern is retroduction, whereby theories are used to suggest patterns to look for in observations and analysis of observations is then used to narrow down theoretical possibilities (Poole, Van de Ven et al., 2000, pp. 115–117). As a result, process research employs both qualitative and quantitative approaches and often uses what is now called mixed methods (see Langley, 1999; Poole, Van de Ven et al., 2000 for description of process methods).

As with variance theories, an important criterion for the evaluation of process theories is their generality. For a process theory, however, generality is defined in terms of the theory's *versatility*, "the degree to which it can encompass a broad domain of developmental patterns without modification of its essential character" (Poole, Van de Ven et al., 2000, p. 43; Poole, 2007). A versatile process explanation can be made to "stretch" or "shrink" to fit specific cases that may differ in their length, how rapidly they unfold, or differences in quality or length of stages or other parts of the process. For instance, Knapp's model of relational dissolution is highly versatile because it can be applied to processes of dissolution that take a week and those that take months and to a wide range of relationships. Table 17.2 presents a comparison of variance and process approaches.

Just as with variance studies, process research has its own limitations. Process studies typically require a great deal of time and labor to compile series of events, to extract meaning or variables from events, to draw connections between events, to identify larger scale patterns, and to work out and evaluate the generative mechanisms and other factors that affect the observed process.

Table 17.2 Variance and Process Approaches Contrasted

Attributes of Approach	Variance Approach	Process Approach
Central focus	Variables	Patterns in series of events
What makes a good explanation?	Necessary and sufficient account of causal relationships among variables	Account of necessity in series of events based on patterns generated by final or formal causes, external causal factors, other related processes, and critical events
What contributes to generality?	Ability of causal model to apply uniformly across a broad range of cases and contexts	Versatility of generative mechanism across processes that may differ in their length, how rapidly they unfold, or differences in quality or length of stages or other parts of the process.

Process studies typically involve the collection of large amounts of multifaceted data, so that the researcher is in danger of what Pettigrew (1990) has termed "data asphyxiation." This tends to limit the number of cases that can be collected, which limits confidence in the generalizability of the conclusions of process research.

The variance and process approaches are often regarded as in opposition to each other, and this discussion, which contrasts them, may inadvertently reinforce this idea. However, it is more appropriate to view variance and process approaches as complementary, or at least as mutually reinforcing. Variance studies can explore and test the mechanisms that drive process theories, while process studies can explore and test the narratives that ground both variance and process theories.

Types of Processes

Defining some basic types of processes is essential in order to avoid the "process is a formless everything and everything is process" dilemma. These types should describe the process and identify a basic generative mechanism that produces the longitudinal patterns that the process exhibits. In this section we will distinguish four basic generative mechanisms that—in concert with critical events and external causes and conditions—can be used to explain observed processes.

Table 17.3 lists the four basic types of process theories originally identified in Van de Ven and Poole (1995) and expanded by Poole and Van de Ven (2004). Each portrays the process as unfolding in a fundamentally different progression of change events and as governed by a different generating mechanism or motor. The theories can also be distinguished in terms of whether the end state of the process can be predicted from the outset and whether the path of development is predetermined.

Life Cycle Processes

A life cycle theory conceptualizes a process in terms of a necessary sequence of stages. The function and content of each stage is determined by some natural, logical, or institutional program that predates the cycle and prefigures how it unfolds. Life cycle theories assume that the process always unfolds through the same unitary sequence of stages and that the program can account for both the ordering of stages and transitions between them. There are two possible sources for the set sequential pattern of the life cycle. First, it may be immanent or inherent within the developing entity; a decision, for example, logically requires that the problem first be defined and then solutions can be considered. Alternatively it may be imposed by external institutions; in agenda setting, the institutional role of the media is to identify key issues in the agenda and then broadcast them to the public, and hence there are the three stages shown in Table 17.1.

Table 17.3 Four Types of Processes

Characteristic	Life Cycle	Teleological	Dialectical	Evolutionary
Basic sequence	Set unitary sequence of stages: A→B→C→Etc.	Multiple sequences of stages or activities oriented to goal attainment	Two possible patterns: (1) Classical dialectic: thesis→antithesis→ synthesis; (2) Tension dialectic with polarized terms continuously in tension	Population develops through variation-selection-retention (VSR) sequence at the member level and community ecological processes at the macro level
Process of change (generative mechanism of temporal pattern)	Sequence of stages and transitions between them is dictated by logic, natural process (e.g. human development), or institutionally- defined norms	Unit perceives problem or opportunity, sets goals, acts to achieve goals, monitors outcomes	In classical dialectic the thesis gives rise to the antithesis as part of its operation and synthesis is an emergent; In the tension dialectic, poles are continually in tension and interplay among them and how parties deal with the tension shapes the process	VSR process is influenced by nature of the niche that the population is located in and by competitive and cooperative relationships among members of different populations; VSR introduces the new forms
Number of developing entities	A single unified entity	A single entity or a unified collection of entities	Multiple entities	Multiple entities in populations
Termination point	End of sequence, dissolution, death	Goal attainment and steady state of goal maintenance	In classical dialectic, the synthesis; in tension dialectic there is no end state	Decline and extinction of the population

As Table 17.1 indicates, the life cycle is the most common type of process theory in communication. Examples of life cycle theories include Fisher's (1970) model of decision emergence, the relational turbulence model (Solomon & Knobloch, 2004), and Knapp's (1978) model of relationship dissolution. In these models, the goal and end point of the process is defined at the outset, a decision in one case, relationship development in the second, and an end to a relationship the third.

In Fisher's (1970) decision emergence model the stages are logically required; a group must first orient itself to the problem, and only then can it begin to debate what to do (conflict stage); conflict can only go so far and must be resolved for a decision to be made (emergence), and finally the group must smooth over differences and unify around the decision to confirm it and set the stage for unified action based on the decision (reinforcement). In the decision emergence model the sequence is a natural result of the need of a group to make sense of a problem and reduce its ambiguity concerning a situation through making a decision

Solomon, Knobloch, and colleagues developed the relational turbulence model (Solomon & Knobloch, 2004; Solomon, Weber, & Steuber, 2009) as a three-stage model in which partners' reactions to conflict vary widely across stages. In the initial stage of the relationship and at high levels of intimacy, partners react to conflict much less strongly than they do at intermediate levels of intimacy. The model posits that at low levels of intimacy, couples can rely on scripts to guide their behavior, while at high levels of intimacy they are close enough that they trust each other. In the intermediate intimacy stage, however, couples have a higher degree of relational uncertainty and behavioral disruptions due to having to coordinate routines with the partner increase. The result of this is that cognitions about the other are stronger and more extreme and conflicts and irritations are perceived to be worse than they are. The result is more extreme reactions to slights and problems during this intermediate stage. A clear strength of the relational turbulence model is its exposition of uncertainty and interdependence as factors that advance the relationship through the three stages.

Knapp (1978) advances a stage model of relationship resolution in which couples move through five phases as they dissolve a relationship. Dissolution begins with a differentiating stage in which partners emphasize differences over similarity. This passes into a circumscribing stage in which communication between partners becomes more limited, and then moves to a stagnating stage in which communication nearly comes to a halt, and then to an avoiding stage when partners do their best to avoid social contact. Finally the couple reaches the terminating stage and the relationship ends. Knapp notes that parties can move back and forth through the sequence and that sometimes couples may skip stages, but the progression as described has a logical escalating force that implies it is a unitary sequence.

Transitions between stages or phases in a life cycle model involve a qualitative change in the process. Moving from differentiating to circumscribing, for instance, involves a qualitative shift in the amount and content of communication between partners. As its name implies, a life cycle theory incorporates a cyclic view of time: life cycle models are comprised of repeating milestones that move the process from inception to demise or fulfillment. Once the end of the cycle has been attained, the process may commence anew; a group that has made a decision is likely to be posed with future decisions and it assumed that new cycles will ensue. Particularly important for a completely specified life cycle model is an explanation of what triggers the transition from one stage or phase to the next. Without this explanation, all we have is a series of stages but no motor for the process. In the case of both the decision emergence model and the relational turbulence model, the needs to cope with uncertainty and increase or maintain interdependence motivate the parties in the group or relationship to advance through the stages. Without an explanation of what drives stage transitions, a life cycle model is essentially incomplete.

Teleological Processes

A teleological perspective views processes as a sequence of goal formulation, implementation, evaluation, and modification of actions or of goals based on deviation of expected outcomes from actual outcomes. This sequence depends on the degree of consensus actors have on the envisioned goal state and how to get there.

Examples of teleological models include Poole's multiple sequence model of group decision making (Poole & Baldwin, 1996; Poole & Roth, 1989a) and Baxter, Braithwaite, and Nicholson's (1999) model of blended family development. In a teleological theory setting a goal in response to a perceived problem or opportunity—in these cases making a decision or building a family that feels like a family—puts the process in motion. The unit—the group or the family—is assumed to be purposeful and adaptive; by itself or in interaction with others, it constructs an envisioned end state, takes action to reach it, and monitors its progress. Thus, teleological theories view development as a repetitive sequence of goal formulation, implementation, evaluation, and modification of goals based on what was learned or intended by the unit.

Teleological processes are goal driven and their end depends on achieving the goal. Since there is often more than one way to achieve the same goal, the developmental path followed by the unit is not predetermined, but is generated by activities required to fulfill the goal. Hence, multiple paths through the process are possible and there is no predetermined sequence of stages, as it was for the life cycle. Some of these paths may be more effective in attaining the goal than others. While teleological theories may define steps or stages in a process, the assumption is that actual process may follow multiple paths and so different orderings of stages or steps are expected. A complete teleological process theory specifies the factors that determine which paths occur or influence the choices actors make that determine the observed paths.

The multiple sequence theory of group decision development posits that

members' attempts to fulfill what they believe to be the functional prerequisites of the decision (their decision logics) influence which phases are generated
and their sequencing. For example, if the group is agreed that they understand
the problem from the outset, then members are likely to launch into solutions,
generating a solution-oriented sequence. The complexity of the decision path
is determined by two factors, the degree to which members' decision logics
match actual task requirements and the degree of consensus among members
about decision logics and prerequisites. If members are not accurate about the
demands of the task or if they are in conflict about prerequisites, a more complex path will result.

Factors that influence members' beliefs about prerequisites for decisions
include (a) task characteristics such as goal clarity and task novelty and (b)
internal structural variables such group cohesiveness, concentration of power,
and group size. Members' implicit theories of decision making, such as whether
decisions are best made through rational discussion or political bargaining,
also should influence beliefs about prerequisites (Poole & Baldwin, 1996).

The resulting developmental process does not follow any specific ordering of phases, but evolves as members attempt to fulfill what they see as the
requisites for an effective decision. As a result several different decision processes may be observed. Poole and Baldwin (1996) summarize evidence that
about 25% of observed decision paths resemble the simple sequence posited
by the life cycle models of decision making, about 33% mainly revolve around
generation and evaluation of solutions, and the remainder are complex paths
in which problem-solution cycles occur multiple times and in which the group
often loops back to consider previous work. This implies that groups enact
decision processes designed to attain the specific goals they think they must
satisfy to make an effective decision.

Baxter, Braithwaite, and Nicholson (1999: Braithwaite, Olson, Golish, Soukup, & Turman, 2001) found that blended families with the goal of creating a
unit that "feels like a family" followed five distinct trajectories over a 4-year
period: (a) an accelerated trajectory showed fast and increasing family feelings; (b) the prolonged trajectory built the family feeling more gradually, but
along an increasing path; (c) the declining trajectory began with strong family feeling which decreased to a minimum at the end of the period; (d) the
stagnating trajectory began and ended with low levels of family feeling; and
(e) the high amplitude turbulent trajectory had large increases and decreases
during the 4-year period. The accelerated and prolonged trajectories were
clearly more effective at building the blended family than the other three. Differences between these trajectories were traced by Braithwaite et al. (2001) to
differences in how the families dealt with three issues: boundary management,
solidarity, and adaptation. More effective trajectories were those in which
boundary management was more successful and flexible. More effective trajectories also built solidarity in ways that were genuine for the members rather
than forcing them to be someone they were not. Finally, more effective coping
trajectories occurred when the families felt free to deviate from traditional

family roles and adapt them to the blended situation. Each of the three issues represents prerequisites for an effective family—boundaries between members, closeness, and role differentiation—and how they were attained resulted in different trajectories of blended family development.

Dialectical Processes

Dialectical processes are driven by conflicts or tensions within the developing entity. Contradictions, conflicts, and tensions elicit reactions from actors, groups, or organizations, and these reactions shape how the dialectic unfolds. In some cases, a resolution or synthesis occurs, while in others efforts to deal with contradictions, conflicts, or tensions simply manage them for a while, and they reemerge to drive the process forward.

In dialectical theories the goal or endpoint of the process is not always clear at the beginning, but may emerge from the dialectic. As a result, developmental paths for dialectically driven processes may take multiple sequences. While the basic moments of the dialectical process—for example, thesis, antithesis, synthesis—can be conceptually distinguished, in actual cases they often overlap and interrelate in complex ways. A couple confronting the stability-change tension may immediately converge on a coping strategy (e.g., emphasize one pole over the other) or they may switch among strategies in an attempt to deal with the inevitable negatives that emerge from prolonged pursuit of any specific coping mechanism. The paths that the process follows will differ considerably for different cases and there is no way to predict the nature of the developmental path.

Two variations of dialectical theories can be distinguished: (1) a Hegelian process of thesis, antithesis, and synthesis, and (2) a Bakhtinian process of tension-based dialectics. Hegelian dialectics, the traditional approach, operates through the emergence of an antithesis in response to a thesis and an eventual resolution in a synthesis. The synthesis represents a temporary resolution and has embedded within it a new contradiction, which is likely to give rise to a new cycle of dialectics.

In their discussion of arguments underlying boycotts, Meyers and Garrett (1993) discuss structural contradictions in modern organizations in a way amenable to a Hegelian dialectical process. Meyers and Garrett argue that profitability, the key driver behind modern corporations, depends on membership of the organization in the community and maintenance of its good standing there (i.e., its social responsiveness). Hence, implicit within the profitability drive is an antithesis, social responsibility, which tends to reduce profitability by leading the organization to act in the interest not of itself but of society. The thesis and antithesis stand in contradiction to each other and the potential conflict puts pressure on the organization and society to respond. This response may deny, suppress, or hide the conflict, thereby short-circuiting the move to synthesis. If the organization contributed to local charities that bought its goods, for example, the organization would look socially responsible, but still be guarding its profits. Other responses, such as the boycotts Meyers and Garrett studied, bring the conflict out in the open and generate different communicative responses from the organizations and the boycotters. While the boycotters seek to put pressure on the organization to change, the organization seeks to educate the boycotters about the need to balance profitability and social responsibility. The result, Meyers and Garrett conclude, is reproduction of the existing contradiction, which also prevents the synthesis from emerging. It is also possible, however, that a true synthesis might emerge, for example, public ownership of the corporation and dedication of its profits to social good. The synthesis is comprised of elements from both thesis and antithesis and represents a stable point in the change process (at least temporarily).

Norton (2009) develops a model of the dialectic between control and resistance in organizations as a Hegelian dialectic. In a longitudinal study of a land use conflict, he argues that efforts to control breed resistance as an antithesis, which in turn breeds attempts to control and so on, each term arising from the other.

A second type of dialectical process, the tension-based dialectic (Bakhtin, 1981; Baxter, 1988; Baxter & Montgomery, 1996; Werner & Baxter, 1994), is more common in communication research. The tension based dialectic proposes that rather than developing through a thesis-antithesis-synthesis pattern, the dialectic plays itself out in a recurring series of tensions between dualisms such as integration-separation. There is a constant interplay between the two poles of the dualism. Rather than being resolved, the tension is always operating and the process is shaped by how the individual, couple, group, or organization chooses to respond to the dialectic. Denying one pole and emphasizing the other will result in one outcome (positive or negative), while trying to acknowledge both poles and alternate between them over time will result in a different outcome. Opposing poles in the tension-based dialectic mutually imply each other and function as potential sources of influence on the process.

Baxter and Montgomery's (1996) dialectical model of interpersonal relationships is a prominent exemplar of the Bakhtinian dialectic. They identify three overarching relational dialectics: integration-separation, stability-change, and expression-nonexpression. These dialectical tensions play out both internally, within the relationship, and externally between the couple and their family and community. They posit that relationships develop according to how the couple deals with the dialectic and the problems, challenges, and conflicts it spawns. Baxter and Montgomery (1996; Werner & Baxter, 1994) define seven possible responses to tensions and contradictions, including: (a) denial—ignoring the tension; (b) spiraling inversion—attending to one side of the tension, then to the other, then to the first again, and so on; (c) segmentation—using different parts or aspects of the unit to relate to the two poles of the tension; (d) balance—which attempts to engage both poles, but reduce the pressure from each; (e) integration—which actively engages with both poles; (f) recalibration—reframing the situation so that the poles are no longer in opposition; and (g) reaffirmation—acknowledging both poles and actively incorporating both into the unit. Some of these—integration, recalibration, and reaffirmation—represent more effective responses to the tensions than others, notably denial and spiraling inversion. This dialectical model has been applied to organizational change by Harter and Krone (2001).

Evolutionary Processes

An evolutionary model of the communication process assumes that a population of entities develops through sequences of variation, selection, and retention events. The nature of the entities in these populations may vary widely including individuals, organizations, technologies, arguments, or texts. Moreover, populations do not live in isolation; almost all exist in social communities or ecologies and are interconnected by various relations and networks that constitute a communication infrastructure (Monge & Poole, 2008). Within these communities populations can be in competitive, symbiotic, or commensalistic (cooperative) relationships. The evolutionary motor drives the process through the core sequence of variation-selection-retention (VSR). In this familiar explanation, variations in existing entities occur, and those that are fit for the environment survive while those that are not are selected out.

The evolutionary model assumes that variations occur both by chance and by plan. Some variations are novel, but variations may be also be hybrid products of previous elements. How variation occurs, and which variations are selected and retained cannot be predicted, because of shifting competitive pressures for scarce resources in the environment. Hence, the developmental path for an evolutionary motor is not predetermined: one or more cycles of variation-selection-retention will occur, but how many cycles and the specific activity paths through the cycles cannot be predicted.

Monge, Heiss, and Margolin (2008) developed an evolutionary theory of communication networks. In variation, organizations or individuals within organizations try out linkages to various others, often seeking many sources of information, advice, or exchange. The techniques used to communicate (e-mail, phone contact, face-to-face) may also vary. Over time organizations or individuals will find some linkages more rewarding than others, which results in the less rewarding linkages being selected out. Over time these biases in communication links may become institutionalized into norms for who to contact or preferences for certain types of partners, resulting in retention of the mechanism that drove linking. In this model, links are what evolves and links "display fitness and fitness variations that are similar to those displayed by nodes" (p. 462). Linkage fitness is

> the propensity for a relationship to sustain itself, that is, to survive or reproduce itself.... A link is an interesting evolutionary entity in that it is jeopardized by several selection events. For a link to survive, both of its nodes must survive. The nodes must also conduct themselves in a manner consistent with the link's continuation, either by continuing to actively

maintain it (e.g., in communication links) or by refraining from severing it (e.g., Internet hyperlinks). (pp. 462–463)

Link formation and selection is influenced by characteristics of the organizations (which make them more or less attractive to link to), by other networks external to the network in question that organizations may belong to, and by the member carrying capacity (the number of organizations/individuals that a given system can support) and relational carrying capacity (the density of links the network can support). These factors limit linkage density and influence the nature of the resulting network.

Multiple Motor Processes

Most processes are complex and hence it is often the case that they are driven by more than one motor. Often these motors operate at different levels of analysis. For example, Bryant and Monge (2008) developed a model of the development of the children's television community that posits that linkages develop through an evolutionary process, but that the specific nature of this process varies through four stages of community development—emergence, maintenance, self-sufficiency, and transformation. So the microlevel development of linkages occurs through an evolutionary process, while at the macrolevel the process takes the form of a life cycle.

In the case of multiple motors, it is important to specify how the motors interrelate. Poole and Van de Ven (2004) identified two dimensions of intermotor relationships:

Interlevel Relationships.   Motors may be arranged in a *hierarchy* in which the process at any given level is dependent on changes in units at higher and lower levels. The motors in Bryant and Monge's model of community evolution are hierarchical. Influence in hierarchies may be either strictly downward, with higher levels exerting control over lower ones or influence may be two-way, up and down the hierarchy. A second type of relationship occurs when different levels are *entangled* (Kontopolous, 1993). Entangled motors operate somewhat independently, but still influence each other without being linked into a single, coherent process, as they would be in the hierarchy. Action assembly theory (see Table 17.1) appears to offer an example of entangled motors. Different processes could govern each of the four levels of representation of the action schema (interactional, ideational, utterance, and sensorimotor) and each level operates somewhat independently but is influenced by others, with no particular order in which the representations assemble. The third type, *aggregated* motors, represents the case where a process on a higher level emerges from or is constituted by an aggregation of lower level processes. In this case, a higher-level process is constituted by a collective of interdependent lower-level processes. The multiple sequence model of group decision development is an example of aggregation, because the resulting phase sequence is the result of the interactions among the members' decision making logics (schemas). A simple decision sequence that follows the classical models such as Fisher's would result when members' logics are similar and the group does not run into problems as it attempts to carry out the logic, whereas more complex developmental paths would result when members' logics differ and the group runs into problems.

Directness of Relationship.   Whether within the same or a different level, motors can be related both directly and indirectly. Types of direct relationships include *reinforcing* (positive), *dampening* (negative), and *complex* (nonlinear). There are two types of indirect relationships. *Entrainment* occurs when motors synchronize their operation due to an external pacing factor (an entrainer). For example, a required deadline to make a budget decision may synchronize the pace of decision making among group members. In the case of innovation diffusion, a key event, such as the 9-11 attack, might synchronize the individual municipal adoption decisions related to security technology. The second type of indirect relationship, a *cyclical* relationship, occurs when two or more motors alternate in their impact on the change process. In relational dialectics theory, for example, a couple may move through cycles in which they focus primarily on tensions internal to their relationship and then switch to focus on external tensions between themselves as a couple and their families or job demands or other external community elements.

Identification of Process Types

The preceding discussion suggests certain conditions that are necessary for each type of process to operate. Determination of whether these conditions are met in an observed process can provide some evidence as to whether the motor is in operation.

Specifically, for a life-cycle motor to operate: (a) there should be a single unified entity at the center of the process (an organization, a decision, a family, a network, a collaboration) and it should maintain a degree of coherence throughout the process; (b) the process should exhibit a standard series of stages that are distinguishable in function and form; and (c) there should be a program, routine, institution, or logic that determines the ordering of stages.

For a teleological motor to operate: (a) there should be an individual or group that acts as a singular entity throughout the process and works to maintain coherence and consensus (possibly in the face of pressures toward divergence or breakdown of the coalition); (b) there should be a goal or end state that the entity is working toward (and which sometimes may be implicit); (c) there should be a set of functional prerequisites for attaining the goal and the activities undertaken by the entity should attempt to address them; and (d) there should be discernible stages which differ in form and function, but there is no definitive ordering among them and in study of a set of teleological processes, multiple paths to the goal or end state should be observed.

If a dialectical motor is in operation: (a) at some point in the process there should be conflict or tension, either between two or more discrete entities or between conflicting requirements; (b) symptoms of this conflict or tension should be evident as well as attempts to deal with them; and (c) outcomes of the conflict or tension and of attempts to deal with it should influence the developing process.

For an evolutionary motor to hold: (a) a population of entities should be involved and the population itself should have a degree of unity; (b) entities within the population should be competing for scarce resources within a niche that has limited capacity to support this or other populations (there may also be cooperative relations across populations in the same niche); and (c) identifiable mechanisms should exist for variation, retention, and selection.

These requirements suggest the types of evidence necessary to establish whether a given motor is in play in a process. They are necessary, but possibly not sufficient evidence for a process theory. It should also be noted that not all processes conclude successfully. Many are aborted due to intervening events and other accidents and there may in some cases be only partial evidence for a process in a given case.

Utility of the Process Typology

The typology of processes is useful, first, because it describes process theories in relatively simple, abstract terms, offering a resource for theory building and explication. The four ideal type motors serve as theoretical templates that can be used to describe and to recognize patterns in process theories and relate them to generative mechanisms. In developing several of the descriptions of the process theories in Table 17.1, I had to "rewrite" a theory that was expressed in unique verbal terms using the "language" of the four motors (I hope without butchering any of the theories too much!).

Related to this first function is a second: the four basic process motors and the requirement that relationships among multiple motors be specified can be used as standards to evaluate the form and completeness of communication process theories. Most theories are originally developed within a specific context that includes the original motivations for the research, the theoretical traditions the theory's developers were steeped in and responding to, characteristics of empirical studies involved in the original development and testing of the theory, and other historical accidents. As a result, most process theories are expressed in somewhat idiosyncratic terms and may omit theoretical elements or shortchange issues that the typology suggests are important. For example, some life cycle theories do not clearly specify what motivates or causes stage transitions. However, this is an important component of the generative mechanism for life cycles and should be specified for any life cycle theory to be complete. The four motors delineate the necessary elements in an adequate explanation, providing standards for constructing and evaluating process theories.

The typology suggests ways in which existing theories could be fleshed out. Spiral of silence theory, for example, is somewhat unclear as to the process by which silencing occurs and so I had to construct the life cycle model in Table 17.1 based on Noelle-Neumann's (1984) original statement and McQuail's (2010) account. In so doing, it became evident to me that the theory would be strengthened by an account at the microlevel of the processes by which individuals decided to silence themselves and how these individual decisions combine to yield the silence of a class of opinion-holders (see McQuail, 2010, for a similar observation). The silencing process is discussed, but which of the four process types (or perhaps another type of process altogether) it corresponds to is not clear. Whether this would improve the theory I will leave to the judgment of readers. It is, however, a canon of science that clear exposition of theories is an important prerequisite to effective scientific inquiry (Chaffee, 1992). Other process theories that have been critiqued on grounds of ambiguity include agenda setting theory (Dearing & Rogers, 1996) and cultivation theory (McQuail, 2010).

A third useful aspect of the framework is that it supports inductive study of processes by spelling out the characteristics of the four motors and the conditions under which they are likely to operate. This enables researchers to apply tests for the four motors hold for a given observed process. This helps to provide the flexibility needed to identify processes that are present in the phenomenon under study. These can then be compared to the processes expected on the basis of theory. The ability to identify process characteristics flexibly and inductively can help researchers avoid the self-fulfilling prophecies which may occur when we expect a certain number of stages of development or a certain process. In trying to cut through the complexity of process data, it is all too easy to find evidence in complex processes for whatever we expect, and ignore other motors (Poole, 1981).

Having defined several types of process models, how do we conduct research on processes that enables us to identify or test these motors, as well as other elements of process explanations, such as critical points? As noted previously, although we can distinguish variance and process approaches, methods traditionally associated with variance research can be applied in process studies. The next section describes four strategies for process research that can be employed by communication scholars.

Strategies for Process Research

Process research involves three basic operations: (a) event identification, (b) representation of the meaning of events in the observed sequence, (c) evaluation of which process models characterize the event sequence based on the relationships among the meaningful events and their overall pattern. The third operation can be accomplished through inductive identification of the process from event sequences or through hypothesis testing procedures to establish whether a given model best fits the data. As mentioned previously, process research is eclectic and can employ either qualitative or quantitative methods or mixed methods. Process research often requires multiple studies employing a variety of methods. Procedures for conducting process research have been discussed in detail in Poole, Van de Ven et al. (2000) and Poole and Van de Ven (2009). In this section we will discuss how both variance and process research approaches have been and could be used by communication scholars in the study of communication processes. We will move from variable-centered approaches that represent more or less "pure" variance research strategy to mixed approaches that represent a hybrid of variance and process strategies to strategies that represent more or less "pure" process research. Our argument will be that there is no one best strategy for research on processes, but that several different avenues can generate valid knowledge about communication processes.

Variance Strategies for the Study of Processes

The variance approach is not geared to study processes directly. Its rigorous statistical methods can, however, be used to test assumptions behind process theories and to test hypotheses regarding properties of processes. A good analogy here is atomic physics. According to the precepts of quantum mechanics any atomic entity is both wave and particle. Methods of classical physics can be used to study particles, but they cannot get at waves directly without turning them into particles, because any observation of waves changes them, according to the Heisenberg uncertainty principle. Properties of waves can be measured, however, and this enables physical methods to be used to generate evidence about waves and test wave-related hypotheses. In the same vein, reducing a process to a set of variables provides only synoptic traces of the process, but with careful design and measurement, these traces can be used to shed light on the process.

The most straightforward application is to utilize the variance approach to test the assumptions behind a process theory. Traditional survey and statistical methods have been used, for example, to test the assumption of spiral of silence theory that fear of isolation leads to the silencing of minority opinions (Glynn et al., 1997). Siune and Borre (1975) used a survey panel design to assess the order of effects in agenda setting. They took advantage of the Danish electoral system in which campaigns and media coverage of issues occur over only a few months before election day, to assess media coverage of politicians' positions and public opinion at two points in time. They used panel analysis to test whether the public position affected politicians' agendas (it did not) and whether in turn the politicians' agendas affected the public agenda (it did).

Experimental studies can also be used to test assumptions of process theories. Hirokawa (1985) conducted an experiment designed to test the assumption of both life cycle and more complex models of group decision making that the sequence of stages groups follow as they make a decision is related to the outcome of the decision. The experimental results indicated that the order of decision activities had no impact on outcomes; what was related was the thoroughness with which group members engaged in various communication functions that were prerequisites of effective decision making, no matter the order in which they did so. In a similar vein, Greene (1984) conducted experiments testing assumptions of action assembly theory.

Variance studies offer valuable evidence on process theories by enabling tests of basic assumptions. Their focus on variables, however, means that strict variance strategies study processes "from the outside," and do not give us information about how the process unfolds and the relationship of the process to variables that reflect symptoms, byproducts, or outcomes of the process. For example, if Siune and Borre (1975) had been able to measure public opinion weekly or daily and track politicians' agendas at similar intervals, they might have found different and more complex causal processes. Perhaps the public agenda was more influential on politicians at the outset of the process but its influence declined over time as politicians began to persuade the public regarding their issues. The later zero relationship would "wash out" the impact of the early influence, resulting in the nonsignificant effect of public opinion on politicians. Without a closer look at the process, it is difficult to tell if many tests of basic assumptions are definitive.

Hybrid Variance/Process Strategies

Research strategies that hybridize variance and process approaches directly analyze event sequences, but do so with techniques adapted from variance research that allow systematic coding of the meanings of events and comparative analysis of sizable samples of processes. These studies attempt to characterize communication processes in terms of stages, steps, states, sequences, and properties of sequences that are amenable to "variabilization," and therefore open the way to the application of statistical methods. The latter often requires improvisation and utilization of analytical techniques that are not commonly used.

Hybrid analytical strategies involve at least four steps once an event sequence has been generated: (a) develop hypotheses or research questions regarding patterns that should be observed in the event sequence; (b) classify events in the event sequence into meaningful categories or derive quantitative indices from events; (c) identify or test for patterns in the data derived from the events in step 2; and (d) evaluate whether the results are consistent with the hypothesized process model or use results to identify a process model or respecify a rejected hypothesis. We will discuss two examples that show the range of possibilities for hybrid analytical strategies.

Poole and Roth (1989a,b) sought to test the multiple sequence model of group decision development, which argued that groups should follow multiple types of decision paths and that the nature of developmental paths should be determined by factors such as task difficulty, prior group conflict, and members' level of experience with one another in the group. They applied two different coding systems, the decision functions coding system and the group working relationships coding system to classify decision behavior and conflict management behavior, respectively, in a diverse sample of 47 decision-making groups. Poole and Roth's coding labeled events (statements) in the discussion sequence categorically as serving various decision functions or indicating various levels of conflict.

They then applied a flexible phase mapping procedure developed by Holmes and Poole (1991) which parsed the coded event sequence into phases such as problem analysis, solution development, orientation, solution critique, and integration. This mapping procedure was flexible in that it did not predetermine the number, order, or lengths of phases, but identified them based on local information in the coded sequence. They then applied a procedure for sequence comparison and utilized cluster analysis to identify three major clusters of decision paths (see Poole & Roth, 1989a for details): the classical unitary sequence similar to Fisher's (1970) model (about 25% of the paths), solution-oriented decision paths (about 30% of the paths), and complex cyclic paths (about 45 % of the paths). Additional analysis that combined phases of conflict management with phases of decision development led to further elaboration of subtypes.

Poole and Roth then used regression analysis to test hypotheses regarding causal factors that influenced decision paths. The types served as dependent variables, but Poole and Roth also defined variables that captured properties of the sequences, such as the complexity of the sequence and the degree to which it departed from the unitary sequence (unitariness). These variables were defined through analysis of the decision paths defined by the flexible phase mapping procedure; for example, complexity was defined by counting the number of repeating phases in a decision map and the number of times the discussion cycled back from phases logically later in the sequence to those earlier in the sequence. The results supported the basic framework of the multiple sequence model by showing that there were multiple sequences in decision making, indicated the approximate proportions of decision path types that occurred, and provided some evidence on causal factors—though it was inconsistent with Poole's (1983) original hypotheses.

While Poole and Roth's events were classified into nominal categories, data generated from events can also be quantitative. Watt, Mazza, and Snyder (1993) tested and extended agenda setting theory using a process design. Like many early agenda setting studies they were concerned with the time latency between media coverage and impact on the public agenda, but they framed this in terms of theories of human memory. In order to study decay of agenda effects using a model of memory decay they conducted time series analyses to probe the agenda setting process.

Watt et al. (1993) sampled stories from 1979 to 1983 related to three topics—Iran, inflation, and the Soviet Union, which varied in terms of their maturity in the news cycle—from the Vanderbilt Television News Archives and also public opinion polls from the Roper Poll Archive over the same period.

These constituted two event series that tapped the media agenda and the public agenda. They then developed a quantitative measure of issue prominence for each news story (averaging prominence scores for stories occurring on the same day) and a measure of issue salience in each poll based on the percentage of people rating a topic as "most important" in a given poll. The result was two time series of quantitative data on media reporting and issue salience to the public. Using time series correlation, Watt et al. traced the decay of coverage effects and it paralleled what memory theory would suggest. They also found differences in impact on agendas depending on the salience of the issue and which issues were less advanced in the news cycle. This evidence is consistent with the hypothesis of a life cycle motor driving agenda setting as specified in the original theory.

These studies illustrate how a combination of statistical techniques typically associated with variance approaches and event coding can be used to directly study processes. The pure variance strategy focuses on assumptions or outcomes of processes, unlike hybrid strategies that map and test hypotheses about processes. Both examples in this section illustrate the improvisation necessary to adapt traditional methods to the study of processes. Poole and Roth had to make use of a newly developed algorithm for flexible phase mapping and, although it is not noted in the summary presented here, also had to rely on the optimal matching technique from operations research for sequence comparison and on multidimensional scaling and cluster analysis—neither widely used techniques—to derive their typology of decision paths. Watt et al. had to develop a mathematical formulation of prominence (Watt & Van den Bergh, 1978) to generate their quantitative timeline and their use of time series correlation was unusual at the time (today better methods for testing cross-sequence relationships are available in many econometrics packages).

These two studies also illustrate another key aspect of process research. They make discoveries both through description (through deriving a typology of decision paths and through mapping parallel time series) and through hypothesis testing (through testing for causes of decision paths and through correlating the time series). Processes are sufficiently complex that description in itself is an important moment of inquiry. Watt et al. (1993), for example, also identify critical points in the agenda setting process, and Poole and Roth found that some segments of the event series were "chaotic" periods with no clear function (at least in terms of the functions coded).

Other exemplars of the hybrid strategy in recent research include Bryant and Monge's (2008) study of community evolution and several studies from the special issue of *Small Group Research* on jury decision making (e.g., Meyers, Seibold, & Kang 2010; Poole & Dobosh, 2010). Additional methods for conducting this type of research are described in Poole, Van de Ven, et al. (2000) and include Markov analysis of event relationships (used by Poole & Dobosh, 2010) and complex adaptive systems analysis.

Strengths of the hybrid strategy include that it directly studies the process as it unfolds, as well as that it requires the researchers to explicitly define the elements of the process. By employing statistical methods and systematic analysis and coding, it can handle large samples of processes as well as lengthy processes. Because it traces the process, this approach also facilitates discoveries of unexpected properties or patterns.

The major shortcoming of the hybrid strategy is that by extracting variables from the event series, it is eliminating some meanings of the events. The coding systems employed by Poole and Roth picked up only a small part of the meaning in the discussions they coded. Watt et al. disregarded the content of news stories, capturing only length and other descriptive information. Coding facilitates clean definition of variables and focuses on specific aspects of the process, but at the expense of sacrificing the richness of the event data and potential insights to the process that could be gained through layered qualitative, historical analyses of the process. To gain these types of insights requires investigating processes from a purely processual standpoint.

The Pure Processual Strategy

This strategy for process research focuses on the complexity of processes and operates on the assumption that they must be understood first and foremost in terms of change and emergence. Hence, reduction to variables or relatively static constructs such as stages or curvilinear relations over time is to be avoided. Instead it is important to capture the rich, multilevel nature of the process under study and to describe it in terms of all the "twists and turns" in the particular case at hand, with the full panoply of explanatory elements—critical events, context, external causes, patterns—at hand to employ in explaining the process. Many, though not all, studies that employ this strategy are rooted in social constructionist or critical theories.

As Langley (1999, 2009) argues, studies employing this strategy are primarily qualitative. Many take the form of historical case studies in which the events are arrayed in a historical chronicle that depicts the process. This chronicle takes the form of first this happened, and then this happened, and so on. The chronicle does not capture every detail of the process, but instead represents a selection of significant events. The chronicle and associated records is the basis for a narrative history that tells the story of a process in detail.

Ashcraft and Mumby (2004), for example, provide a rich historical account of the development of the airline pilot's occupational role in terms of a feminist "communicology." They note that in the early years of flying, women were encouraged to fly to show that it was safe and could be done even by a weaker gender. However, this discourse undermined the legitimacy of pilots, which posed problems for the airline industry. As airlines became more accepted, male pilots took over, and the discourse of professionalization of (male) pilots evolved, relegating women to the role of flight attendant, whose job was primarily safety related, but also involved serving pilots and passengers. This evolving discourse "functioned to naturalize men's seat in the cockpit and women's service in the cabin—thus calling for performances of gender relations that became institutionalized for decades to come…these discursive transformations … were communicated into existence by individuals and institutions with concrete interests situated within a specific political economy" (p. 166). Ashcraft and Mumby (2004) portray a politically driven process that resulted in gendered occupational roles. Their account was based on finding continuities, patterns that extend over time, and contingencies, individual critical events, the two ingredients of historical explanation, according to Gaddis (2002).

Other examples of qualitative case studies of communication processes include an account of the structuring of organizational climate in a community organization by Bastien, McPhee, and Bolton (1995) and a dialectical analysis of collaboration within a community mental health initiative (Medved et al., 2001).

A study of the development of relationships in blended (step) families by Braithwaite et al. (2001) illustrates how the pure processual strategy can be applied to multiple cases. Braithwaite and colleagues conducted interviews with members of over 50 blended families in which they reconstructed the development of the families in terms of turning points over the first 4 years of the family's existence. They also had interviewees draw timelines of their family's development indicating on a vertical axis that varied from 0% to 100% the degree to which their family "felt like a family" at various turning points. They asked the interviewees to define what "feeling like a family meant to them," thus letting the interviewee anchor the scale. Interviewees were asked to describe each turning point in as much detail as they could.

In their analysis, Braithwaite et al. sorted the accounts into the five trajectories for blended family development identified in an earlier study by Baxter, Braithwaite, and Nicholson (1999). They then conducted comparative analyses across the five sequences to identify the major concerns as the sequences unfolded and how family members navigated their unfolding. They identified the different narratives that unfolded for each of the five sequences, and both functional and dysfunctional aspects of each. The dynamics of each of the five processes were discussed in terms of boundaries, solidarity, and adaptation.

Visual maps of the process were one useful representation of the process utilized by Braithwaite et al. Langley (1999) commented on the advantages of visual maps in process research:

> They allow the presentation of large quantities of information in relatively little space, and they can be useful tools for the development and verification of theoretical ideas. Visual graphical representations are particularly attractive for the analysis of process data because they allow the simultaneous representation of a large number of dimensions and they can be easily used to show precedence, parallels, and the passage of time. (p. 700)

Mapping the process often generates a complicated representation that records the complex relationships among elements. In this case, the "peaks and valleys" of the five different trajectories were illustrated, highlighting the degree of turbulence in the family relationships. Maps were also used in the hybrid variance-process strategy by Poole and Roth (1989a).

The pure processual strategy is probably the truest to Rescher's (1996) definition of process, which was introduced at the beginning of this essay. Rescher's goal was to develop a "process metaphysics," that conceptualized everything in terms of processes. Tsoukas and Chia (2002) advocate a similar position that everything is change and stability and substance are simply reifications of change. The purely processual strategy is also advantageous because it generates nuanced and flexible descriptions and explanations of the process which operate on multiple levels with a specificity that general methods like those of statistical analysis cannot approach.

The dilemma for this strategy is that it too, like all analysis, is inevitably reductionist. The description and explanation of the process is subject to the judgment of the analyst, who both generates the data by selective use of records or interviews, and makes sense of connections among events and larger patterns.

The Process Modeling Strategy

A fourth strategy for process research constructs a mathematical model or simulation of the process that incorporates its generative mechanisms. The model is used to generate a predicted trajectory or path for the process under various combinations of conditions. This prediction is then compared to actual instances of the process in order to judge the fidelity of the model.

Display of the results of modeling is often in terms of a visualization of the process or an analysis of how it unfolds under different conditions that often go beyond what investigators are capable of thinking through. Models with quite complex relationships can be built and may result in emergent and unexpected effects and outcomes. These often show up in qualitative patterns in the model results that can be compared to qualitative features of actual processes; often qualitative similarities to characteristics of the processes are more important than exact quantitative match to the actual processes.

Corman (2006), for example, used cellular automata, agent based models, to model network linkage formation in networks based on reticulation theory (Corman & Scott, 1994). With sufficient computing power it would be possible to simulate portions of the organizational community evolution model using the agent based reticulation model (there are also numerous other network simulations in the computer science literature, among other sources). These simulations can be run through hundreds of replications with different starting parameters, equivalent to sampling a very large number of networks, and the configuration of the network over time generated. This can be used to shed light on the behavior of the model. If the model yields predictions about network configurations over time, these can be compared to those from the simulation.

Contractor and Whitbred (1997) developed a simulation that incorporated many of the assumptions of the multiple sequence model of group decision development. They developed models predicting statements of individual members corresponding to the various phases based on three contingencies: (a) task type (simple, complex); (b) medium (face-to-face, computer mediated communication); and (c) history of prior interaction (short, long). To determine the order in which statements are made by individual members, they added a social influence network that influences the rate of occurrence of various types of decision statements and priority among members in contributing. This influence network is not stable but develops over time. They proposed simulating decision making discussions in groups under eight combinations of contingencies, with 475 runs per combination. The resulting simulations could be analyzed using flexible phase analysis or Markov analysis to determine whether the results correspond to prior results from decision development studies.

This model, like all simulations, is useful because it extends the original model and renders it more precise. Development of the simulation model requires precise specification of relationships between the likelihood of making certain types of statements and the contingency variables. If these can be plausibly developed, they bring greater rigor to the process model. In the course of building the model Contractor and Whitbred recognized that they also needed to incorporate a model of social influence, something not allowed for in the original multiple sequence model. Modeling thus contributes something new to the theory.

Most models do not fit observed data perfectly and it is a given among modelers that one learns more from failures and lack of fit than from success. Deviations from what would be expected prompt new ideas on the part of the investigator and may stimulate revision of the original formulation and the theory behind it.

One advantage of modeling processes is that it applies rigorous analytical methods to build theory about what generates a given process into our models. Generally these generative mechanisms are more precise than those in verbally specified process theories. Simulation enables researchers to generate much larger samples of processes than could be obtained empirically, and if the simulation is valid, this can yield important information about how the process would occur in a population of cases. Models are also often able to capture complexity and emergence that are difficult to express verbally.

One limitation of modeling is similar to that for any variance related approach: defining the variable and relationships in the model may reduce the complex process to simplistic terms that detract from the richness of the process. Precision comes at the price of oversimplification or misrepresentation of complex relationships. The benefits of modeling processes may be offset by the need to reduce the process in order to represent it in the model.

Discussion

A core assumption of communication research is that communication is a process. As the preceding examples indicate, a number of communication scholars throughout the years have taken this assumption quite seriously and have endeavored to map and to understand the process of communication. However, they have done so largely through improvisation and with only a thin underlying theoretical foundation concerning the nature of processes.

It is often the case that disciplines initially pursue important and significant lines of research without formulating them or differentiating them from existing lines. This essay argues that this is exactly what has happened to process studies in communication research. Many communication scholars have pursued process research without explicitly recognizing it and without thinking about what makes process research unique and how process research should be conducted. However, at a certain point it is important to explicitly consider basic assumptions and what they imply concerning the conduct of research.

This essay has attempted to explicitly formulate process research for the communication discipline. It has attempted to differentiate process research from the variance approach that dominates current quantitative inquiry in communication. The basic argument has been that to study processes one must focus on patterns over time and delineate the generative mechanisms that account for those patterns as well as the contingencies and critical events that drive changes in the direction of the process. Methods for the study of patterns over time are fundamentally different from methods for the explanation of variance, and must be understood as such. To explain a process, the researcher must uncover and explicate a theoretical narrative that depicts the unfolding of the process. Like all stories, this theoretical narrative accounts for the order in which events occur and explains why they had to occur in the particular fashion that they did in order to reach the end of the process and its outcomes.

We have defined four different types of generative mechanisms that can explain processes, when supplemented by critical events and external causes: the life cycle, teleological, dialectical, and evolutionary models. Often more than one of these process motors is in operation in a given case, and a complete process theory will specify the relationships among them. These four basic models may not exhaust the possibilities for process theories, and it is to be hoped that more will be added in the future.

Four strategies for process research were also discussed: a pure variance approach, a hybrid variance-process approach, a pure process approach, and process modeling. They are not meant to be mutually exclusive. Most processes are sufficiently complex that multiple studies employing different strategies must be conducted to identify the process theories that "fit" them and to test process theories.

Some process research is quantitative, though its methods differ from those of traditional variance research. Process research can also be qualitative and employ critical methods, as the example of Ashcraft and Mumby

(2004) shows. However, not all qualitative research is process research. The majority of qualitative studies in communication does not generate narratives that describe how processes unfold over time, but instead present a relatively "timeless" account. Atemporal interpretive studies elide process just as much as variance-based quantitative work does.

This is not to argue that process research is inherently superior to variance or atemporal interpretive inquiry. Rather process studies complement these other types of research. They represent a different perspective on communication phenomena and should be understood as such.

The psychologist Jerome Bruner (1986) distinguished two basic types of human intelligence: the paradigmatic logico-scientific mode and the narrative mode. He contrasted them as follows:

> There are two modes of cognitive functioning, two modes of thought, each providing distinctive ways of ordering experience, of constructing reality. The two (though complementary) are irreducible to one another.... Each of the ways of knowing, moreover has operating principles of its own and its criteria of well-formedness. They differ radically in their procedures for verification. (Bruner, 1986, p. 11)

This essay argues that it is time to develop a more explicit process-based communication scholarship to complement the variance approach. This approach has the potential to unlock a different, more fundamental level of understanding of temporal processes.

Note

1. I would like to express my gratitude to my colleagues in process research over the past 20 years, Andrew Van de Ven, Michael Holmes, Kevin Dooley, Gerry DeSanctis, Peter Monge, Bob McPhee, Steve Corman, and Noshir Contractor. They have all contributed greatly to my understanding of the nature of process research and methods for conducting it. Any misunderstandings or errors in this chapter are mine alone.

References

Abbott, A. (1984). Event sequence and event duration: Colligation and measurement. *Historical Methods, 14,* 192–204.

Abbott, A. (1988). Transcending general linear reality. *Sociological Theory, 6,* 169–186.

Ashcraft, K. L., & Mumby, D. K. (2004). *Reworking gender: A feminist communicology of organization.* Thousand Oaks, CA: Sage.

Bakhtin, M. M. (1981). *The dialogic imagination: Four essays by M. M. Bakhtin* (M. Holquist Ed.; C. Emerson & M. Holquist, Trans.). Austin: University of Texas Press.

Barnett, G. (1997). Organizational communication systems: The traditional perspective. In G. Barnett & L. Thayer (Eds.), *Communication–organization: Emerging perspectives* (Vol. 5; pp. 1–46). Greenwich, CT: Ablex.

Bastien, D. T., McPhee, R. D., & Bolton, K. A. (1995). A study and extended theory of the structuration of climate. *Communication Monographs, 62*, 87–109.

Baxter, L. A. (1988). A dialectical perspective on communication strategies in relationship development. In S. Duck (Ed.), *Handbook of personal relationships* (pp. 257–273). New York: Wiley.

Baxter, L. L., Braithwaite, D. O., & Nicholson, J. (1999). Turning points in the development of blended family relationships. *Journal of Social and Personal Relationships, 16*, 291–313.

Baxter, L., & Montgomery, B. (1996). *Relating: Dialogues and dialectics*. New York: Guilford.

Berlo, D. (1960). *The process of communication*. New York: Holt, Rinehart & Winston.

Braithwaite, D., Olson, L., Golish, T., Soukup, C. & Turman, P. (2010). "Becoming a family": Developmental processes represented in blended family discourse. *Journal of Applied Communication Research, 29*, 221–247.

Bruner, J. (1986). *Actual minds, possible worlds*. Cambridge, MA: Harvard University Press.

Bryant, J. A., & Monge, P. R. (2008). The evolution of the children's television community: 1953–2003. *International Journal of Communication, 2*, 160–192.

Chaffee, S. H. (1992). *Explication*. Newbury Park, CA: Sage.

Contractor, N. S., & Whitbred, R. C. (1997). Decision development in work groups: A comparison of contingency and self-organizing systems perspectives. In G. Barnett & L. Thayer (Eds.), *Communication–organization: Emerging perspectives* (Vol. 5, pp. 83–104). Greenwich, CT: Ablex.

Corman, S. R. (2006). Using activity focus networks to pressure terrorist organizations. *Computational and Mathematical Organization Theory, 12*, 35–49.

Corman, S. R., & Scott, C. R. (1994). Perceived communication relationships, activity foci, and observable communication in organizations. *Communication Theory, 4*, 171–190.

Dance, F. E. X., & Larson, C. E. (1976). *The functions of human communication: A theoretical approach*. New York: Holt, Rinehart & Winston.

Davison, M. L., King, P. M., Kitchener, K. S., & Parker, C. A. (1980). The stage sequence concept in cognitive and social development. *Developmental Psychology, 6*, 121–131.

Davison, M. L., Robbins, S., & Swanson, D. B. (1978). Stage structure in objective moral judgments. *Developmental Psychology, 14*, 137–146.

Dearing, J. W., & Rogers, E. M. (1996). *Agenda-setting*. Thousand Oaks, CA: Sage.

Fisher, B. A. (1970). Decision emergence: Phases in group decision-making. *Speech Monographs, 37*, 53–66.

Gaddis, J. L. (2002). *The landscape of history: How historians map the past*. Oxford, England: Oxford University Press.

Glynn, C. J., Hayes, A. F., & Shanahan, J. (1997). Perceived support for one's opinion and willingness to speak out. *Public Opinion Quarterly, 61*, 452–463.

Greene, J. O. (1984). A cognitive approach to human communication: An action assembly theory. *Communication Monographs, 51*, 289–306

Greene, J. O. (2008). Action assembly theory: Forces of creation. In L. A. Baxter & D. O. Braithwaite (Eds.), *Engaging theories in interpersonal communication: Multiple perspectives* (pp. 23–36). Thousand Oaks, CA: Sage.

Harter, L., & Krone, K. (2001). The boundary spanning role of a cooperative support organization: Managing the paradox of stability and change in non-traditional organizations. *Journal of Applied Communication Research, 29,* 248–277.

Hirokawa, R. Y. (1985). Discussion procedures and decision-making performance: A test of a functional perspective. *Human Communication Research, 12,* 203–222

Holmes, M., & Poole, M. S. (1991). The longitudinal analysis of interaction. In B. Montgomery & S. Duck (Eds.), *Studying interpersonal interaction* (pp. 286–302). New York: Guilford.

Knapp, M. L. (1978). *Social intercourse: From greeting to goodbye.* Boston, MA: Allyn & Bacon.

Kontopoulos, K. (1993). *The logics of social structure.* Cambridge, England: Cambridge University Press.

Langley, A. (1999). Strategies for theorizing from process data. *Academy of Management Review, 24,* 691–710.

Langley, A. (2009). Studying processes in and around organizations. In D. Buchanan & A. Bryman (Eds.), *Sage handbook of organizational research methods* (pp. 409–430). London: Sage.

Littlejohn, S. W. (1996). *Theories of human communication* (5th ed.). Belmont, CA: Wadsworth.

Mackie, P. (1995). Event. In T. Honderichs (Ed.), *The Oxford companion to philosophy* (p. 253). New York: Oxford University Press.

McCombs, M. E., & Shaw, D. L. (1972). The agenda-setting function of the press. *Public Opinion Quarterly, 36,* 176–187.

McQuail, D. (2010). *McQuail's mass communication theory* (6th ed.). London: Sage.

Medved, C., Morrison, K., Dearing, J., Larson, S., Cline, G., & Brummans, B. (2001). Tensions in community health improvement initiatives: Communication and collaboration in a managed care environment. *Journal of Applied Communication Research, 29,* 137–152.

Meyers, R. A., & Garrett, D. E. (1993). Contradictions, values, and organizational argument. In C. Conrad (Ed.) *The ethical nexus* (pp. 149–170). Norwood, NJ: Ablex.

Meyers, R. A., Seibold, D. R., & Kang, P. (2010). Examining argument in a naturally-occurring jury deliberation [Special issue]. *Small Group Research, 41,* 452–473.

Miles, M., & Huberman, A. M. (1994). *Qualitative data analysis.* Newbury Park, CA: Sage.

Miller, K. (2012). *Communication theory: Approaches and processes* (6th ed.). Boston, MA: Wadsworth.

Miller, V., Poole, M. S., Seibold, D. R. & Associates (2010). Advancing research in organizational communication through quantitative methodology. *Management Communication Quarterly, 25,* 4–58.

Mohr, L. (1982). *Explaining organizational behavior.* San Francisco, CA: Jossey-Bass.

Monge, P. R., Farace, R. V., Eisenberg, E. M., Miller, K. I., & White, L. L. (1984). The process of studying process in organizational communication. *Journal of Communication, 22,* 414–427.

Monge, P. R. Heiss, B. M., & Margolin, D. B. (2008). Communication network evolution in organizational communities. *Communication Theory, 18,* 449–477.

Monge, P. R., & Poole, M. S. (2008). The evolution of organizational communication. *Journal of Communication, 58,* 679–692.

Noelle-Neumann, E. (1984). *The spiral of silence.* Chicago, IL: University of Chicago Press.

Norton. T. (2009). Situating organizations in politics: A diachronic view of control-resistance dialectics. *Management Communication Quarterly, 22,* 525–554.

Pettigrew, A. (1990). Longitudinal field research on change: Theory and practice. *Organization Science, 1,* 267–292.

Poole, M. S. (1981). Decision development in small groups. Part I: A test of two models. *Communication Monographs, 48,* 1–24.

Poole, M. S. (1983). Decision development in small groups. Part III: A multiple sequence theory of decision development. *Communication Monographs, 50,* 321–341.

Poole, M. S. (2007). Generalization in process theories of communication. *Communication Methods and Measures, 1,* 181–190.

Poole, M. S., & Baldwin, C. (1996). Developmental processes in group decision-making. In R. Y. Hirokawa & M. S. Poole (Eds.), *Communication and group decision making* (pp. 215–241). Thousand Oaks, CA: Sage.

Poole, M. S., & Dobosh, M. (2010). Exploring conflict management processes in jury deliberations through interaction analysis [Special issue]. *Small Group Research, 41,* 408–426.

Poole, M. S., & Roth, J. (1989a). Decision development in small groups. Part IV: A typology of decision paths. *Human Communication Research, 15,* 323–356.

Poole, M. S., & Roth, J. (1989b). Decision development in small groups. Part V: Test of a contingency model. *Human Communication Research, 15,* 549–589.

Poole, M. S., & Van de Ven, A. H. (2004). Theories of organizational change and innovation processes. In M. S. Poole & A. H. Van de Ven (Eds.), *Handbook of organizational change and innovation* (pp. 374–397). New York: Oxford University Press.

Poole, M. S., & Van de Ven, A. H. (2009). Empirical methods for research on organizational decision processes. In P. Nutt & D. Wilson (Eds.), *The Blackwell handbook of organizational decision-making* (pp. 543–580). Malden, MA: Blackwell.

Poole, M. S., Van de Ven, A. H., Dooley, K., & Holmes, M. E. (2000). *Organizational change and innovation processes: Theory and methods for research.* New York: Oxford University Press.

Prochaska, J. O., Redding, C. A., & Evers, K. E. (2008). The transtheoretical model and stages of change. In K. Glanz, B. K. Rimer, & K. Viswanath (Eds.), *Health behavior and health education: Theory, research, and practice* (4th ed., pp. 97–102). New York: Wiley.

Rescher, N. 1996. *Process metaphysics: An introduction to process philosophy.* Albany, NY: SUNY Press.

Rogers, E. M. (2003). *Diffusion of innovations* (5th ed.). New York: Free Press.

Schramm, W. (1954). *Process and effects of mass communication.* Urbana: University of Illinois Press.

Sheufle, D., & Moy, P. (2000). Twenty-five years of the spiral of silence: A conceptual review and empirical outlook. *International Journal of Public Opinion Research, 12,* 3–28.

Siune, K., & Borre, O. (1975). Setting the agenda for a Danish election. *Journal of Communication, 25,* 65–73.

Solomon, D. H., & Knobloch, L. K. (2004). A model of relational turbulence: The role of intimacy, relational uncertainty, and interference from partners in appraisals of irritations. *Journal of Social and Personal Relationships, 21,* 795–816.

Solomon, D. H., Weber, K. M., & Steuber, K. R. (2010). Turbulence in relational transitions. In S. W. Smith & S. R. Wilson (Eds.), *New directions in interpersonal communication research* (pp.115–134). Thousand Oaks, CA: Sage.

Street, R. L., Jr. (2003). Communication in medical encounters: An ecological perspec-tive. In T. Thompson, A. M. Dorsey, K. I. Miller, & R. Parrott (Eds.), *Handbook of health communication* (pp. 63–93). Mahwah, NJ: Erlbaum.

Teichmann, R. (1995). Process. In T. Honderichs (Ed.), *The Oxford companion to phi-losophy* (p. 721). New York: Oxford University Press.

Tracy, K., & Standerfer, L. (2002). Selecting a school superintendent: Sensitivities in group deliberation. In L. R. Frey (Ed.), *Group communication in context: Studies of bona fide groups* (2nd ed., pp. 109–134). Thousand Oaks, CA: Sage.

Tsoukas, H., & Chia, R. (2002). On organizational becoming: Rethinking organiza-tional change. *Organizational Science, 13* 567–582.

Valente, T. W. (1995). *Network models of the diffusion of innovations.* Cresskill, NJ: Hampton Press.

Valente, T. W., & Saba, W. P. (1998). Mass media and interpersonal influence in a repro-ductive health communication campaign in Bolivia. *Communication Research, 25,* 96–124.

Van de Ven, A. H., & Poole, M. S. (1995). Explaining development and change in orga-nizations. *Academy of Management Review, 20,* 510–540.

Vaughan, P. W., & Rogers, E. M. (2000). A staged model of communication effects: Evidence from an entertainment-education radio soap opera in Tanzania. *Journal of Health Communication, 5,* 203–227.

Watt, J. H., & van den Berg, S. (1978). *Time series analysis of alternative media effects theories.* Retrieved from ERIC database http://www.eric.ed.gov/contentdelivery/servlet/ERICServlet?accno=ED165193

Watt, J. H., Mazza, M., & Snyder, L. (1993). Agenda-setting effects of television news coverage and the effects decay curve. *Communication Research, 20,* 408–435.

Werner, C. M., & Baxter, L. A. (1994). Temporal qualities of relationships: Organis-mic, transactional, and dialectical views. In M. L. Knapp & G. R. Miller (Eds.), *Handbook of interpersonal communication* (2nd ed., pp. 323–397).

18 *Commentary*
Some Reflections on Quantitative Modeling of Communication Processes

W. Wayne Fu

Nanyang Technological University

In a strict sense, all communication activities and their consequences occur in a process. It is only intuitive that it takes a process for a message to be conveyed from a sender to a recipient and for the message and its transmission (or mediation) to yield some sort of influence in the system. Whereas communication is inherently processual in nature and behavior, empirical research that uses process methods in the field of communication is still limited (Monge, Farace, Eisenberg, Miller, & White,1984; Poole, in this volume). The dearth of communication process research is attributable to a number of factors, not the least of which has been the familiar difficulty of collecting longitudinal data, as Scott Poole notes in his chapter. However, the situation is changing with the advent of online communication behaviors that are recorded automatically and traced comprehensively over time. Real-time, automated accounts of activities require little to become reliable and systematic sources of data about communication processes. It is believed that this abundance of Web data will increase interest in communication process studies in the future, as has been seen in the areas of business, marketing, economics, information science, and others.

This commentary expands on Scott Poole's review of communication-as-process and focuses on quantitative aspects of processes. It addresses three main points with the goal of contributing to the methodological robustness of quantitative process research. First, there should be a greater realization that *time* is an underlying reference system for examining a theory that embeds a process in a real-time longitudinal scale, so that temporal properties or behaviors such as pace, acceleration, duration, frequency, trend, and so on, can be studied. Second, the generality of quantitative process research can be enhanced by extending the scope of observing a process to a cross-section of different cases of the same process. The dual operationalization of longitudinal and cross-sectional observations leads to the use of panel analysis. Third, when the time dimension is accounted for consistently, an important and fundamental question to evaluate is this: "What drives the process forward through specific, sequential phases?" This question can be examined by explaining the duration of a phase that occurs in different cross-sectional cases.

Modeling a Process in Terms of Longitudinal Variables

Process method advocates have distinguished "process" research through a dichotomous contrast to "variance" research, following Mohr (1982). This paradigmatic comparison gives a vivid and efficient perspective of what the two apparent polar approaches tend to emphasize in terms of analytical structure. The former focuses on distinct *stages* or *events* that sequentially unfold over time, whereas the latter accounts for relationships among *variables* measured at a given point in time. Yet, the applicability of this binary conceptualization can be related to certain contingencies: first, how a "process" is construed; second, how quantifiable the generative mechanism or behavior of the process is.

Many communication processes are best theorized as stages or phases, because it is conceptually illustrative, practically relevant, and inherently meaningful to accentuate this character of the process. However, if the stages are distinguished by way of, or related to, any underlying construct that is measurable throughout the course of the process, the analysis of such a process should be richer and more precise by treating the process as a continuous progression rather than splicing it into discrete time segments. As a matter of fact, Monge (1990) models processes as cyclic patterns, rather than a sequence of events or stages, when a given pattern can reoccur over time. For example, a study that looks at the process pertaining to how advertising shifts movies' box office attendances must consider seasonal cycles.

Processes can be gradual and progressive without distinct phases or cycles. Examples of such processes abound in communication research, such as: diffusion of innovation (Rogers, 1962), bandwagon behavior (Simon, 1954), cultural globalization (Norris & Inglehart, 2009), and preferential attachment (Barabàsi & Bonabeau, 2003). These processes entail smooth transition or gradual transformation in the workings of a communication system, especially at the aggregate level. In the case of either cyclic or gradual processes, reducing the continuous occurrence to quantumlike states would cause loss of information on the dynamic nuances of the process. Further, even for processes which do have natural stages, the stages are not necessarily distinct and discrete but often have long, blurry overlaps with one another.

In those circumstances, the distinction highlighted in the "variance" and "process" terminology should be relaxed to be more conceptually flexible. To be more specific, *variables* can also exist and operate longitudinally because they represent "longitudinal variance." Here, observations are taken from a process at stretched time points and so offer data variance. From the methodologically functionalist point of view, longitudinal and cross-sectional variations may not be differentiable because both of them are empirically observed differences and thus can be used to test hypotheses or trace patterns. This methodological or technical equivalence is true insofar as any violations of requisite statistical assumptions and conditions are redressed on either side. For example, autocorrelation is a common symptom to address in the time series context, just as *inter*dependence of observations, for example, needs to be addressed in the cross-sectional setting. (Actually, the two problems arise from the same mathematical nature of data.) This discussion suggests that the "variance" ("cross-sectional") and "process" ("time-serial") approaches do not have to be at the two extremes of the methodological continuum, although they can appear to be so conceptually or logistically, as is apparent. This view may further the quantitative understanding of the two major types of methods.

Given a continuous process, its quantitative analysis can derive advantageously from math-based modeling, in order to capitalize fully on all temporal information that is available. Built on explicit formulation, time series analysis is a useful tool for that purpose. By no means can this brief commentary elaborate on time series models and their applications in communication, especially because others have already made elaborate contributions in this area (e.g., Monge, 1990; Monge et al, 1984). Instead, the point to be made here is to review the requirements and needs of quantitative process analysis and then convey certain empirical approaches and strategies that can serve accordingly.

Operationalizing Time and Temporal Variables in Process Research

Where a process is represented as a continual progression, time is the reference axis (such as day, year, decade) along which a phenomenon is tracked. In this sense, time is the index of longitudinal observations. Even for some other communication theories, not only the temporal order but durations of observable phases embody the mechanism and characteristics of a process under consideration. For a process whose discrete phases or gradual progression are supposed to develop in the passing of time, then *time* per se is in practical terms a factor that, independently or in interaction with by other factors, explains the dynamics of the process. Only by accounting for time explicitly as an independent or indexing variable can a process be evaluated meaningfully and precisely. Consider the diffusion (Bass, 1969; Rogers, 1962) and critical mass (Markus, 1987; Oliver, Marwell, & Teixeira, 1985; Oliver & Marwell, 1988) theories: Manifested by the S-shaped curve of diffusion, they predict that a new technology diffuses into a society more rapidly soon after it reaches the critical mass of adopters than when it is just introduced or becomes saturated in the market. However, these intertemporal differences in penetration rate, central to these theories, would not show in an empirical assessment, were the process not timed consistently. That is, diffusion rate can be evinced only by using a consistent temporal yardstick.

Moreover, according to these theories, how fast (and how much) the same technology penetrates into different societies depends on group conditions that include the extent of within-group variations in adoption value (i.e., how unequal the benefit of using the tech is to the individuals in a society). Again, the test of this conjecture hinges on indexing the time when the diffusion is observed.

Sometimes, phases or events named in the course of a process may not be in natural existence (the innovators, early adopter, early majority, late majority, and laggards named along the diffusion curve, for example), but are only an abstraction of the evolution of some underlying longitudinal construct(s). Placing "pegs" on the trajectory as conceptual milestones can help explicate the process. But, zooming in on them instead of tracing the whole trajectory empirically reduces longitudinal information to mere snapshots. This affects the generalizability and power of process research.

Monge (1990) identifies a number of generic temporal patterns and causality structures for longitudinal variables that can work in a process and proposes time-serial models to study them. In terms of methodology, he articulates using temporal variables to model the unfolding of a process without phasic presentation as an analytical basis. One of the advantages of a time series analysis, whenever required data are available, is the maximal use of information with respect to longitudinal variance in detecting time trends and intertemporal causality. Such dynamic modeling is useful in examining the diffusion process, as has been done in Fu (2004) and Fu and Sim (2011).

Panel Analysis for Process Research and its Generalizability

As mentioned earlier, pure time-serial analysis operates with longitudinal variance. Poole (2007) also points out that process research establishes *generality* as to how extrapolate-able and interpolate-able a concluded process pattern can be on the scale of time. I would call the generality that is drawn temporally *longitudinal generality*. Nonetheless, a question of importance is whether or not the process as concluded applies not only for unique observations (individuals or groups) but across some critical set of observations. That is to say, the conclusion should be deemed more robust if it is found true to more cases. This calls for analytical frames that can cross-sectionally generalize the validity of process research.

Panel analysis explains data which are made of both time-serial and cross-sectional observations of an enduring phenomenon. This two-dimensional technique not only traces what an individual case goes through over the timeline of a process under interest, but does so for all cases in a study. When formulated similarly as a time series function, panel regressions can test the temporal prediction or causality of a dependent variable that measures the process over time. On top of that, the panel model evaluates whether the causality or prediction holds true across a lineup of cases that are supposed to undergo the same process.

As such, a given hypothesized process mechanism can be tested statistically on different cases in parallel. Making the cross-sectional extension of generalizability, such models strengthen a quantitative process study with respect to how universal the process is as postulated. But it remains yet to be applied more in communication research.

Duration Analysis of Phasic Processes

Processes can be intrinsically *phasic*; that is, composed of discrete, distinct stages or events in sequence. This is the typical structure of process that has been accentuated by the avant-garde process research methodologists (Abbott, 1990; Langley, 1999; Poole & Van de Ven, 2009; Poole et al., 2000; Van de Ven, 1992). Those forerunners have proposed a wide range of procedures and approaches to identify and analyze phasic processes depending on the sequencing properties and data structure, as process data and research are considered eclectic and inclusive (e.g., Langley, 1999; Poole et al., 2000). Poole's chapter offers a detailed, synthesized review of the process methods proposed and executed so far in the field. Insofar as these emerged methods or analyses present a useful, versatile guide for conducting process research, their goals tend to be deriving process sequencing or predicting and validating the existence and order of stages (events), rather than consider the duration(s) of a process as a whole and its stages in real-time perspective. Hence, if there was anything to add to this line of method development, one meaningful and significant inquiry about a phasic process is to explain why different participants would go through the process from one stage to another in unequal lengths of time.

Consider individuals' adoption of innovation, for instance. According to Rogers (1962), adopters undergo a five-stage process (knowledge, persuasion, decision, implementation, and confirmation). When testing this five-stage transition on adopters of, say, *Twitter*, questions can be asked as, such as: Do older people move more slowly than young people from any particular one of these adoption phases to the next one? Likewise, would the extent of how widely *Twitter* penetrates among a person's friends and contacts at a given time affect how readily he or she passes through the current stage (say, persuasion) to the next (decision)? These questions correspond to data with individuals (cross-sectional cases) engaging varying amounts of time to pass through a given state.

This research situation requires a regression-based procedure that explains the *duration* of an event by way of factors and covariates in individual cases. Duration analysis is the tool package designed to analyze such data. With time consistently accounted for, the analysis tests the effects of the factors on the duration as a dependent variable, which is formulated as some temporal-sensitive probability function. An attractive feature of duration analysis is its dynamic flexibility in identifying causation of the duration. The factors and covariates can be case-specific, time-variant measurements, or even a combination of both. In other words, the procedure in the above example can enter not only the fixed demographics of observed persons but also the changing condition of "social influence" for each individual, both of which are hypothesized as antecedents of the transition from the current stage to the next of the process. And, it is conceivable that, for each stage transition, a duration model can be specified with a unique set of regressors contingent on what should precede *that* particular transition in theory.

Duration analysis can determine what drives the process forward step by step, via observing cross-sectional variance. It is a powerful instrument to make quantitative sense of the transformational or evolutionary dynamics of a phasic process. As with panel analysis, the duration model resonates well with what Poole labels in his chapter as the "hybrid variance/process" strategy to study process research. While extremely rare in communication research, its power has been more realized in economics and information science in examining processes with naturally distinguishable milestones, such as technology adoption (e.g., Kauffman & Techatassanasoontorn, 2005; Saloner & Shepard, 1995).

In summary, although communication has long been defined as a process, communication process research itself is a relatively youthful methodological enterprise. Scott Poole's essay makes great strides in advancing our thinking about process research. In this commentary, I have attempted to provide a brief review of the quantitative side of this ongoing endeavor, with the hope of expanding methodological opportunities and generating ideas for new analytical tools.

References

Abbott, A. (1990). A primer on sequence methods. *Organization Science, 1*(4), 375–392.

Barabàsi, A-L., & Bonabeau, E. (2003). Scale-free networks. *Scientific American, 288*(5), 50–59.

Bass, F. M. (1969). A new product growth model for consumer durables. *Management Science, 15*(5), 215–227.

Fu, W. W. (2004). Termination-discriminatory pricing, subscriber bandwagons, and network traffic patterns: The Taiwanese mobile phone market. *Telecommunications Policy, 28*(1), 5–22.

Fu, W. W., & Sim, C. (2011). Aggregate bandwagon effect on online videos' viewership: Value uncertainty, popularity cues, and heuristics. *Journal of the American Society for Information Science and Technology, 62*(12), 2382–2395.

Kauffman, R. J., & Techatassanasoontorn, A. A. (2005). International diffusion of digital mobile technology: A coupled-hazard state-based approach. *Information Technology and Management, 6,* 253–292.

Langley, A. (1999). Strategies for theorizing from process data. *Academy of Management Review, 24*(4), 691–710.

Markus, M. L. (1987). Toward a "Critical Mass" theory of interactive media: Universal access, interdependence and diffusion. *Communication Research, 14*(5), 491–511.

Mohr, L. B. (1982). *Explaining organizational behavior: The limits and possibilities of theory and research*. San Francisco, CA: Jossey-Bass.

Monge, P. R. (1990). Theoretical and analytical issues in studying organizational processes. *Organization Science, 1*(4), 406–430.

Monge, P. R., Farace, R. V., Eisenberg, E. M., Miller, K. I., & White, L. L. (1984). The process of studying process in organizational communication. *Journal of Communication, 34*(1), 22–43.

Norris, P., & Inglehart, R. (2009). *Cosmopolitan communications: Cultural diversity in a globalized world.* Cambridge, England: Cambridge University Press.

Oliver, P., & Marwell, G. (1988). The paradox of group size in collective action: A theory of the critical mass. Part II. *American Sociological Review, 53*(1), 1–8.

Oliver, P., Marwell, G., & Teixeira, R. (1985). A theory of the critical mass. Part I. Interdependence, group heterogeneity, and the production of collective action. *American Journal of Sociology, 91*(3), 522–556.

Poole, M. S. (2007). Generalization in process theories of communication. *Communication Methods and Measures, 1*(3), 181–190.

Poole, M. S., & Van de Ven, A. H. (2009). Empirical methods for research on organizational decision processes. In P. Nutt & D. Wilson (Eds.) *Handbook of decision-making* (pp. 195–207). Malden, MA: Blackwell

Poole, M. S., Van de Ven, A. H., Dooley, K., & Holmes, M. E. (2000). *Organizational change and innovation processes: Theory and methods for research.* New York: Oxford University Press.

Rogers, E. M. (1962). Diffusion of innovations. New York: Free Press.

Saloner, G., & Shepard, A. (1995). Adoption of technologies with network effects: An empirical examination of the adoption of automated teller machines. *RAND Journal of Economics, 26*(3), 479–501.

Simon, H. A. (1954). Bandwagon and underdog effects and the possibility of election predictions. *Public Opinion Quarterly, 18*(3), 245–253.

Van de Ven, A. H. (1992). Suggestions for studying strategy process: A research note [Special issue]. *Strategic Management Journal, 13,* 169–191.

CHAPTER CONTENTS

19 Assumptions behind Intercoder Reliability Indices

Xinshu Zhao

Fudan University and Hong Kong Baptist University

Jun S. Liu and Ke Deng

Harvard University

Intercoder reliability is the most often used quantitative indicator of measurement quality in content studies. Researchers in psychology, sociology, education, medicine, marketing, and other disciplines also use reliability to evaluate the quality of diagnosis, tests and other assessments. Many indices of reliability have been recommended for general use, and this article analyzes 22 of them, which are organized into 18 chance-adjusted and four nonadjusted indices. The chance-adjusted indices are further organized into three groups, including nine category-based indices, eight distribution-based indices, and one that is double based, on category and distribution.

The main purpose of this work is to examine the assumptions behind each index. Most of the assumptions are unexamined in the literature, and yet these assumptions have implications for assessments of reliability that need to be understood, and that result in paradoxes and abnormalities. This chapter discusses 13 paradoxes and nine abnormalities to illustrate the 24 assumptions. To facilitate understanding, the analysis focuses on categorical scales with two coders, and further focuses on binary scales where appropriate. The discussion is situated mostly in analysis of communication content. The assumptions and patterns that we will discover will also apply to studies, evaluations, and diagnoses in other disciplines with more coders, raters, diagnosticians, or judges using binary or multicategory scales.

We will argue that a new index is needed, but before it can be established, we need guidelines for using the existing indices. This chapter will recommend such guidelines.

Content has always been a central concern of communication research. Wilbur Schramm (1973), whom Tankard (1988) called "the father of communication studies," authored *Men, Messages, and Media: a Look at Human Communication*, where "message" meant content. Harold Lasswell (1948), whom Schramm considered one of the "four founding fathers of the field" (Glander, 2000, Ch. 3), defined the discipline as studying "who says what, through which channels, to whom, and with which effect," where "what" is content. With the explosion of "netted" information from increasingly diversified sources, the need for content research has been rising sharply (Neuendorf, 2002).

Modern *content analysis,* a term no more than 70 years old according to Krippendorff (2004a), focuses on "what *is* the content," as opposed to what *should be* the content. With this empirical emphasis, *validity* and *reliability* have emerged as two methodological pillars. *Validity* addresses whether an instrument measures what it purports to measure. *Reliability* addresses whether the instrument produces consistent results when it is applied repeatedly; that is, test-retest reliability, or by different people; that is, intercoder reliability. While a reliable measure is not necessarily valid, an unreliable measure cannot be valid.

Validity is more difficult to measure numerically. Hence reliability, especially the less costly intercoder reliability, has been the most popular quantitative indicator of measurement quality in content studies. Researchers in education, psychology, sociology, medicine, marketing, and other social science disciplines also use reliability to evaluate the quality of diagnoses, tests, and other assessments.

The main purpose of this chapter is to examine assumptions behind 22 indices of intercoder reliability, most of which are unexamined in the literature. We will report 24 such assumptions, most of which are rarely met in typical research, meaning that the indices have been often used beyond the boundaries for their legitimate use. As a result, paradoxes and abnormalities arise. We will discuss 13 paradoxes and nine abnormalities to illustrate the assumptions. We will argue that a new index is needed and, until such a new index is forthcoming, guidelines are needed for using the existing indices.

Our analysis will focus on categorical scales with two coders and further focus on binary scales where appropriate. The discussion will be mostly situated in analyzing communication content. But the assumptions, patterns, and recommendations that we will discuss also apply to studies, evaluations, or diagnoses in other disciplines with more coders, raters, diagnosticians, or judges using two or more categories.

The calculations and derivations presented in this chapter were done by the first author initially by hand and then verified by MS Excel programming. All formulae, calculations, interpretations, and proofs were then independently replicated or verified by the third author under the supervision of the second author. Guangchao Charles Feng, a doctoral candidate at Hong Kong Baptist University, conducted a final round of verifications using R programming (2011, v 2.14). Large portions of this manuscript, especially those related to π, κ, and α, were previously presented in two conference papers (Zhao, 2011a, 2011b).

An Overview of the Intercoder Reliability Concept

Reliability and Related Concepts

Krippendorff (2004b) and Lombard, Snyder-Duch, and Bracken (2002) see *agreement* as the indicator of *reliability,* and consider *association* to be a separate concept. Tinsley and Weiss (1975, 2000) use *correlation* as the indicator of *reliability* and consider *agreement* as separate. Neuendorf (2002) considers *agreement* and *covariation* as two indicators of *reliability*.

We follow Krippendorff and Lombard et al. to use agreement as the indicator of intercoder or test-retest reliability, and we define *agreement* as proximity between measures. On a categorical scale, if both coders choose the same category for the same case, that is an agreement. If they choose different categories, that is a disagreement. On a numerical scale, the closer the scores are to each other, the higher the agreement. *Correlation* refers to the *covariation* between measures on numerical scales. For instance, on a 0–10 scale, if Coder 2 chooses 0 whenever Coder 1 chooses 9, and chooses 1 whenever Coder 1 chooses 10, there is a very high correlation but a very low agreement.

Association refers to *covariation* between measures on categorical scales. It is typically used when the concept of "intervariable agreement" is not appropriate, helpful, or sufficient, while agreement is typically used when the concept of "intervariable association" is not appropriate, helpful, or sufficient. Suppose, of 200 respondents, all 100 Whites are urban, and all 100 non-Whites are rural. We say the association between ethnicity and residence is at the highest possible, while it does not help as much to talk about agreement. Suppose the data of 200 cases come from a content analysis, in which Coder 1 reports seeing an urban resident whenever Coder 2 does so, and reports seeing a rural resident whenever Coder 2 does so. This signifies complete agreement. Here it is not as informative to talk about association. Suppose the opposite happens: all 100 Whites are rural, while all 100 non-Whites are urban. The association is equally high. But if the same data are from the two coders, they would indicate that Coder 1 reports seeing urban residents whenever Coder 2 reports seeing rural residents, and reports seeing rural residents whenever Coder 2 reports seeing urban residents. That would be a complete disagreement.

Association and agreement also differ when distributions are even; for example, when each ethnic group is half urban and half rural, or when two coders agree with each other half the time. Here association is at the lowest possible, while agreement is 50%, halfway between the lowest and the highest possible. Further, when there is no variation within a variable, for example, when all respondents are of one ethnicity, or they all live in one locale, association is undefined. Association is covariation, which is impossible when there is no variation. If the same data come from two coders, which means one or both coders chooses only one category, agreement should and can still be calculated. If both coders agree that all respondents are urban, there is 100% agreement. Later we will show that three popular indices of reliability, that is, π, κ, and α, become uncalculable, hence undefined, when coders agree all cases fall into one category. We will argue that should not have happened if the indices were to measure general agreement.

Table 19.1 summarizes the relationship between the key concepts. This chapter will focus on agreement/reliability indices for categorical scales, and further focus on binary scales where appropriate. We will not deal with association measures such as χ^2, or correlational measures such as Pearson's r or r^2.

Table 19.1 Reliability and Related Concepts

		Concepts of Consistency	
		Multimeasure reliability	*Intercoder & test-retest reliability*
Scales	Categorical	Association /Covariation e.g., χ^2	Agreement /Proximity e.g., %-agreement
	Numerical	Correlation/Covariation. e.g., Pearson r & r^2	Agreement /Proximity e.g., closeness measure*

* Correlation indices, such as Pearson r or r^2, is at present the most often used indicator of inter-coder or test-retest reliability for numerical scales. Closeness measure would be a more appropriate measure, which we will discuss in another paper.

Reliability vs. Reliabilities

Popping (1988) identified no less than 39 reliability indices, although some of them are association measures or correlational measures, and some are the same indices under different names. This chapter will review 22 indices of intercoder reliability. Many of the 22 are mathematically equivalent, giving us 11 unique indices.

It is assumed that the various indices are indicators of the same concept of intercoder reliability. Yet the indices produce different—often drastically different—results for the same underlying agreements. As reliability means agreement (Riffe, Lacy, & Fico, 1998), these indices of reliability do not appear reliable themselves.

Under the premise of "various indicators for one reliability," methodologists debate which indicator is the best, whether to use this, that, or several of them in a study, and how to fix or cope when some indices, especially Cohen's κ, behave paradoxically (e.g., Brennan & Prediger, 1981; Krippendorff, 2004b; Lombard et al., 2002; Zwick, 1988). This review takes a different approach. As the indices produce different results, we suspect there may be multiple reliability concepts, each having one indicator. No more than one index can be the general indicator, while others are for special conditions. Like mediation researchers (e.g., Hayes, 2009; Zhao, Lynch, & Chen, 2010) who examined the dominant approach to reveal its hidden premises, this chapter analyzes each index of intercoder reliability to uncover its assumptions, which defines the boundaries for its legitimate use and may explain the paradoxes and abnormalities that arise when it is used beyond the boundaries.

A Typology of 22 Indices

The 22 indices we will review fall into two groups. The first group, called nonadjusted indices, includes *%-agreement* (a_o, pre-1901), *Holsti's CR* (1969), *Osgood's coefficient* (1959), and Rogot and Goldberg's A_1. The first three are mathematically equivalent to each other. The four indices assume that all coding behavior is honest, observed agreements contain no random chance coding, hence there is no need to adjust for chance. *Chance-adjusted* indices belong in the second group of indices. These 18 indices assume that coders deliberately maximize random chance coding, and limit honest coding to occasions dictated by chance, so the chance agreement that results must be estimated and removed.

The chance-adjusted group includes three subgroups. The first subgroup of nine indices estimates chance agreement as a function of category in a measurement scale. The second subgroup of eight indices estimates chance agreement as a function of observed distribution. Here "distribution" refers to the pattern by which cases fall into categories. Distribution can be extremely even; for example, 50% of the advertisements coded have endorsers and 50% do not; or extremely uneven; for example, 100% have endorsers and 0% do not; or anywhere between the two extremes. In reliability literature, this important

Table 19.2 A Typology of 22 Intercoder Reliability Indices

		Adjusted for chance agreement?	
		Yes	No
On what basis is chance agreement estimated?	Category	ρ, S, $(G, RE, C, kn, PABAK, rdf\text{-}Pi)^*$, I_r	a_o, (Osgood's, Holsti's CR)* A_1
	Distribution	β, λr, π, $(Rev\text{-}K, BAK)^*$, κ, (A_2), α	
	Category & Distribution	AC_1	

* Index(es) in parentheses is a mathematical equivalent(s) of the preceding index

	Index symbol	Author, Year	Other known name of the index
1	α	Krippendorff (1970, 1980)	
2	A_1	Rogot & Goldberg (1966)	
3	A_2	Rogot & Goldberg (1966)	
4	AC_1	Gwet (2008, 2010)	
5	a_o	unknown author, pre-1901.	*%-Agreement*
6	β	Benini (1901)	
7	*BAK*	Byrt et al. (1993)	
8	*C*	Jason & Vegelius (1979)	
9	*CR*	Holsti (1969)	*Holsti's*
10	*G*	Guilford (1961), (Holley & Guilford, 1964)	
11	I_r	Perreault & Leigh (1989)	
12	κ	Cohen (1960)	
13	*kn*	Brennan & Prediger (1981)	
14	λ_r	Goodman & Kruskal (1954)	
15	*Osgood's*	Osgood (1959)	
16	π	Scott (1955)	
17	*PABAK*	Byrt et al. (1993)	
18	*Rdf-Pi*	Potter & Levine-Donnerstein (1999)	*Redefined Pi*
19	*Rev-K*	Siegel & Castellan (1988)	*Revised K*
20	ρ	Guttman (1946)	
21	*RE*	Maxwell (1977)	
22	*S*	Bennett et al. (1954)	

concept has also been referred to as "frequency" (Gwet, 2008), "base rate" (Grove, Andreasen, McDonald-Scott, Keller, & Shapiro, 1981; Kraemer, 1979; Spitznagel & Helzer, 1985), or "prevalence" (Gwet, 2010; Shrout, Spitzer, & Fleiss 1987; Spitznagel & Helzer, 1985). We will follow Cohen (1960), Perreault and Leigh (1989), and Gwet (2010) to call it *distribution*. The third subgroup has just one index, which uses both category and distribution as the main factors. Table 19.2 summarizes this typology.

Six indices, namely ρ, I_r, and four nonadjusted indices range from 0 to 1. The maximum of λ_r is also 1, but it can get far below -1, according to one interpretation. The other 15 indices all range from -1 to 1. All 22 indices consider 1 as indicating maximum reliability, 0 as indicating no reliability, and a below-zero score as a random variation from 0. An important question is where the threshold for acceptable reliability is. This chapter will focus on estimation of reliability, and leave the threshold issue to future research.

Nonadjusted Indices

Our search found four indices that are not adjusted for chance agreement, including *%- agreement*, two equivalents, and Rogot and Goldberg's A_1.

%-Agreement and Two Equivalents

The most intuitive indicator of reliability is *%-agreement*; that is, the number of cases coders agree (*A*) divided by the total number of targets analyzed (*N*). Krippendorff (2004b) and Neuendorf (2002) denote this as a_o:

$$a_o = \frac{A}{N} \tag{1}$$

Scott (1955, p. 322) observed that a_o was "commonly used." Perhaps because it was so common and intuitive, its early users or critics like Benini (1901) did not mention who invented it. As Osgood (1959) and Holsti (1969) advocated essentially the same index, many researchers referred to it as *Holsti's CR* while a few called it *Osgood's coefficient* (Krippendorff, 2004b). Bennett, Alpert, and Goldstein (1954) pointed out that a_o contains chance agreements from random guessing, and hence inflates reliability. Experts on reliability (e.g., Lombard et al., 2002; Tinsley & Weiss, 1975) often concurred, revealing an important assumption:

Basic Assumption 1:   Zero chance agreement.

%-agreement (a_o) assumes no chance agreement in any situation, no matter how difficult the task is, or how tired, bored, or unprepared the coders are. This assumption leads to an important paradox:

Paradox 1:   **Random guessing can be reliable.**

Suppose two coders watch television programs to see if they contain sub-liminal advertisements, which are flashed quickly to avoid conscious perception. Although the coders try to be accurate, the task is so difficult that their coding amounts to nothing but random guessing. Probability theory expects an a_o=50%, which is the midpoint between 0% for no reliability and 100% for perfect reliability.

Because *%-agreement* fails to take into account chance agreements, it is often considered "the most primitive" (Cohen, 1960, p. 38) and "flawed" (Hayes & Krippendorff, 2007, p. 80) indicator of reliability, leading to decades-long efforts to "account for" and "remove" chance agreements (Krippendorff, 1980, pp. 133–134; Riffe, Lacy, & Fico, 1998, pp. 129–130).

Critics of a_o argued that "flipping a...coin" or "throwing dice" would have produced some "chance agreements" (Goodman & Kruskal, 1954, p. 757; Krippendorff, 2004a, p. 114, 226; 2004b, p. 413). A coin only has two sides and a die always has six. Drawing marbles may be a closer analogy, because colors and marbles per color can vary like categories and cases per category can vary in typical content studies (Zhao, 2011a, 2011b). Hereafter we will use "marble" to refer to any physical or virtual element of equal probability; "urn" to refer to a real or conceptual collection of the elements; and "drawing" to refer to a behavioral or mental process of randomly selecting from the elements. Defined as such, marbles, urns, and drawing turn out to be a set of useful analytical tools. They help to expose assumptions and explain paradoxes and abnormalities that otherwise would be more difficult to uncover or understand.

The no-chance-agreement assumption does not necessarily make %-agreement a bad index, but perhaps a special-purpose index. Some authors argued that, for easy cases or "textbook" cases, all agreements could be from a well-developed protocol (Grove et al., 1981, p. 411; Riffe, Lacy, & Fico, 2005, p.151). In such situations, no chance agreement should be expected; hence %-agreement would be an accurate index. %-agreement cannot be a general-purpose index because all cases are not easy, and all protocols are not well developed.

Rogot & Goldberg's A_1

Rogot and Goldberg (1966) noted that, when calculating %-agreement on a binary scale, each positive agreement, for example, two diagnosticians agree a patient has an abnormality, is given an equal weight as a negative agreement, for example, diagnosticians agree there is no abnormality. Because abnormality is far less frequent than normality, negative agreements as a group are given more weights than positive agreements. To give the two groups equal weights, Rogot and Goldberg (1966) proposed A_1:

$$A_1 = \frac{1}{4}\left(\frac{a}{a+b} + \frac{a}{a+c} + \frac{d}{c+d} + \frac{d}{b+d}\right) \qquad (2)$$

Here a and d are respectively positive and negative agreements, and b and c are two types of disagreements, all in percentages. $A_1=a_o$ when $a=d$ and $b=c$, that is, when two types of agreements are evenly distributed and the two types of disagreements are also evenly distributed. When $a \neq d$, that is, when agreements are unevenly distributed, A_1 decreases from a_o, and more uneven distributions bring larger decreases. When $b \neq c$, that is, when disagreements are unevenly distributed, A_1 increases from a_o, and more uneven distributions bring larger increases. Because the decreases and the increases are at the equal rate, the average of A_1 should be close to the average of a_o when each is averaged across many studies and data. As A_1 is just a reweighted a_o, they share the same assumption and paradox as discussed above. In general A_1 is not an improvement over *%-agreement*. Especially, it still does not take into account chance agreement.

An Overview of Chance-Adjusted Indices

To "account for" and "remove" chance agreement (a_c) from *%-agreement* (a_o), Equation 3 was introduced to calculate reliability index (r_i). The equation was implied in Guttman (1946) and Bennett et al. (1954) and made explicit by Scott (1955):

$$r_i = \frac{a_o - a_c}{1 - a_c} \qquad (3)$$

The subtraction in the numerator appears intuitive. Chance agreement (a_c) needs to be removed from the observed agreement (a_o). The subtraction deflates the otherwise inflated index. The subtraction in the denominator, however, is not as intuitive. Reliability index (r_i) is a percentage, of which the denominator serves as the reference. The full length of the reference is 1 for 100%. The subtraction shrinks the reference, making r_i look larger.

There is a behavioral assumption behind the shrinking. To understand the assumption, we may analyze Equation 4, which was implied in Guttman's ρ (1946), Bennett, Alpert, and Goldstein's S (1954), Scott's π (1955), and Cohen's κ (1960), and made explicit by Cohen (1968, p. 215):

$$1 = a_c + d_c \qquad (4)$$

With a_c representing chance agreement (%) and d_c representing chance disagreement (%), Equation 4 says chance coding constitutes 100% of all coding. Some may argue that "1" here represents "all chance coding." That is true. But all major reliability indices from Guttman's ρ (1946) to Gwet's AC_1 (2008) all state or imply $a_o + d_o = 1$, where a_o is observed agreement and d_o is observed disagreement, hence $a_o + d_o = a_c + d_c$, which means "all coding equals all chance coding," or "all coding is chance."

But *chance coding allows and includes honest coding* in a two-stage process, according to Equations 3 and 4. In the first stage, coders code all cases completely randomly by drawing marbles. If they draw a certain pattern, for example, the same color, they report findings according to a predetermined color-category matching scheme. For example, if the marbles are white they would say that an advertisement has an endorser while if the marbles are black they would say there is no endorser, without looking at the advertisement under coding. If and only if the coders draw another pattern, for example, different colors, they would go to the second stage, during which they would code honestly. Hence honest coding (h) equals chance disagreement (d_c):

$$d_c = h \qquad (5)$$

Here honest coding (h) is defined as percent of cases that coders code by actually examining the objects and categorizing objectively following the instructions during training. Chance coding thus precedes, permits, confines, and constrains honest coding. Since honest coding is limited within chance disagreement, it is the chance disagreement, but not all coding, that should be the baseline for percentage calculation. This is why the denominator in Equation 3 should be shrunk from 1 to $1-a_c = d_c = h$.

Replacing a_o with $1-d_o$ and replacing a_c with $1-d_c$ in Equation 3, we obtain an alternative expression of r_i (Krippendorff, 1980, p.138; 2004a, p. 417):

$$r_i = 1 - \frac{d_o}{d_c} \qquad (6)$$

Most of the chance-adjusted indices share Equations 3 through 6 as they are. Benini's β (1901) and Perreault and Leigh's I_r (1989) modify the two equations, which we will discuss later.

The marble drawing scenario was implicit in Guttman's ρ (1946), Bennett et al.'s S (1954), Scott's π (1955), and all other chance-adjusted indices that followed. Goodman and Kruskal (1954) discussed flipping a coin, and Krippendorff (1980) discussed throwing dice, making the scenario explicit. Zhao (2011a, 2011b) rephrased it as drawing marble to allow more accurate analysis of various indices. This Guttman-Goodman Scenario has been widely accepted because it was told as hypothetical stories. Few believe that coders regularly maximize chance coding in actual research. Yet few realize that, by applying Equations 3 through 6, which are key components of S and all other chance-adjusted indices, we are treating maximum randomness as real occurrences. Riffe et al. (2005) did realize this, pointing out "that agreement can take place by chance does not mean it does…. All agreements could easily be the result of a well-developed protocol" (p. 151). Grove and colleagues (1981) had the same view: "chance agreement means the agreement would be observed if two raters assigned diagnoses to cases at random. Now this is not what diagnosticians do. They assign the easy cases, or 'textbook' cases, to diagnoses with little or no error, they may guess or diagnose randomly on the others" (p. 411).

If we accept this Grove-Riffe Scenario, we may argue that Equations 3 and 6 are inappropriate, as they are based on a behavior that should never happen and probably never did. Even if deliberate and systematic random coding does happen, the data should be thrown out and no reliability should be calculated. Deliberate random coding would be a type of cheating. A simpler cheating would be that two coders always agree with each other, without looking at any cases, throwing any dice, or drawing any marbles. They would have gotten 100% agreement. The fabricated agreements cannot and need not be removed from the data. The data should be thrown away, not analyzed.

So we need to lay bare the assumptions behind Equations 3~6, which are shared by all chance-adjusted indices reviewed in this chapter:

Basic Assumption 2:   Maximum random.

By removing chance agreement using Equation 3 or 6, these reliability indices assume that deliberate and systematic chance coding is not hypothetical, but real—no empirical research should "remove" or "correct for" anything that's not real.

Basic Assumption 3:   Limited honesty.

By estimating reliability using Equation 3 or 6, theses indices assume that honest coding is confined to a portion of the cases defined and confined by random chance.

Assumption 4:   Specified random.

There is an infinite number of ways to be random. Coders may flip a fair coin, throw a biased die, or draw marbles of various numbers of various colors without replacement. Each method produces a different estimate of chance agreements. Because maximum randomness is hypothetical, there is no empirical justification to pick one method over another. Each index picks one way, analogous to a man picking a favorite tie from a large selection. Scott's π assumes drawing from a shared urn with replacement. Cohen's κ assumes drawing from separate urns with replacement. Krippendorff's α assumes drawing from a shared urn without replacement. And so on. Each index treats its way as the only way of being random.

This assumption is not as fundamental as the previous ones. We will not attach the word *basic* to such assumptions so as to draw more attention to the more important ones.

These assumptions entail that the chance-adjusted indices operate under a Guttman-Goodman Scenario, yet each index has been recommended for typical coding, which follows a Grove-Riffe Scenario. The mismatch between the assumption and the reality creates paradoxes:

Paradox 2:   *Nothing but chance.*

Equation 4, which says $1=a_c+d_c$, represents a critical assumption in all chance-adjusted reliability indices reviewed in this chapter: chance coding, which includes chance agreements (a_c) and chance disagreements (d_c), covers 100% of the cases coded.

We found this paradoxical because we believed, under the Grove-Riffe Scenario, coders code objectively at least sometimes, *before and beyond* random chance. Assumptions 2 and 3, under the Guttman-Goodman Scenario, stipulate that coders maximize random coding, and code honestly only when marbles' colors mismatch. "Nothing but chance in the first stage" is an operating boundary for these indices, beyond which paradoxes arise. If coder behavior follows the Grove-Riffe rather than Guttman-Goodman Scenario, Equation 4 is incorrect, and therefore these indices are all incorrect.

Paradox 3:   *Apples compared with oranges.*

In Equation 3, the numerator represents "honest agreements," while the denominator represents "chance disagreements." The division compares the numerator as a part with the denominator as the whole to produce a percentage figure. But why compare *honest agreements* with *chance disagreements*? Are we comparing apples with oranges? Why not compare some apples with all apples; for example, *honest agreements* with *all coding*? We found this paradoxical because we did not realize chance disagreement *is* honest coding under Assumptions 2 and 3—coders code honestly when and *only* when marbles disagree.

Under the Grove-Riffe Scenairo, all coding can be honest, not just those confined to chance disagreement (Riffe et al., 2005). We should replace *maximum-randomness* and *limited-honesty* assumptions with *variable-randomness* and *complete-honesty* assumptions.

Paradox 4:   *Humans are a subgroup of men.*

When we mathematically divide men by humans, we are asking "what percent of humans are men?" assuming men are a subgroup of humans. When we divide d_o by d_c (Equation 6), we are asking "what percent of *chance* disagreements is *observed* disagreements?" assuming observed disagreements are a subgroup of chance disagreements. But should not chance disagreements and honest disagreements be two subgroups of observed disagreements? Shouldn't we divide chance disagreements by observed disagreements, but not vice versa? Dividing d_o by d_c is analogous to saying "humans are a subgroup of men."

Paradox 5:   ***Pandas are a subgroup of men.***

Equations 3~6 imply $a_o - a_c + d_o = d_c$, which implies that *honest agreements* ($a_o - a_c$) and *observed disagreements* (d_o) are two subgroups of *chance disagreements* (d_c), which is analogous to saying that "pandas and humans are two subgroups of men."

This appears paradoxical because we thought, under a Grove-Riffe Scenario that chance disagreement is a subgroup of observed disagreement. Nevertheless, under the Guttman-Goodman Scenario and especially Assumption 2, coders disagree (observed disagreement) when and *only* when marbles disagree (chance disagreement). Therefore observed disagreement should be a subgroup of chance disagreement.

Unfortunately, the major chance-adjusted indices all share Equations 3, 4, and 6 under the Guttman-Goodman Scenario, which we will call *maximum-randomness* equations. No index has been built under the Grove-Riffe Scenario.

Category-Based Indices

Accurately estimating chance agreement may be as important as properly removing it (Equations 3, 4, and 6). How to estimate chance agreement is where major indices differ. Guttman (1946), a pioneer in social psychology and social science methodology, calculated chance agreement (a_c) as the inverse of the number of categories (K) available to the coders:

$$a_c = \frac{1}{K} \tag{7}$$

Equation 7 assumes maximum randomness just as Equations 3 and 6 do. But this is a particular type of randomness: drawing randomly from marbles equally distributed among K colors, which correspond to K categories, each coder has $1/K$ probability of choosing one particular category; two coders have $(1/K)*(1/K)$ probability of agreeing on the category. Multiplying this product by K categories, we see a probability of $(1/K)*(1/K)*K=1/K$ that the two coders would agree by chance. This equation and the rationale are the foundation of the category-based indices discussed below.

Bennett et al.'s S and Six Equivalents

Bennett et al. (1954) recommended a reliability index, S:

$$S = \frac{K}{K-1}\left(a_o - \frac{1}{K}\right) \tag{8}$$

Equation 8 can be derived by inserting the right side of Equation 7 into Equation 3. In other words, S implies directly Equations 1, 3, and 7, and indirectly Equations 4 through 6. So, S assumes maximum randomness not only when chance agreement is removed (Equations 3 and 6), but also when chance agreement is calculated (Equations 7 and 8).

By removing chance agreement, S aims to avoid Assumption 1 and Paradox 1. Nevertheless, by using Equations 3 and 6 to execute the removal, S adopts maximum-randomness and limited-honesty assumptions. Adding Equations 7 and 8, S assumes the following *Bennett Scenario* for two coders:

1. The coders place K sets of marbles into an urn, where K equals the number of coding categories. Each set has an equal number of marbles and has its own color. The coders agree on which color represents which category. Again, in this chapter "marble" refers to any physical or virtual element of equal probability, and "urn" refers to any real or conceptual collection of the elements.
2. They take a target to be coded. Here *target* is anything under coding, such as an advertisement, a news story, or a patient.
3. One coder draws a marble randomly from the urn, notes the marble's color, and puts it back. The other coder does the same.
4. If both draw the same color, each reports that the target belongs to the corresponding category according to the predetermined color-category pairings, without looking at the target. Only if they draw different colors would they code objectively, at which point they may honestly agree or disagree, and report accordingly.
5. The coders repeat Step 2 and the subsequent steps, and end the coding session when they have thus "coded" all targets.

Note that the Bennett Scenario is a special case of the broader Guttman-Goodman Scenario discussed earlier. The Bennett Scenario reveals several additional assumptions of S:

Basic Assumption 5:   *Categories equal marble colors.*

There is an infinite number of ways to be random. The coders could use any number of urns, any number of marbles, any number of marble colors, and choose any distribution pattern of the colors; they could draw with or without replacement; and they could decide on different color-category matching. Each of these parameters may affect chance agreement. To estimate *the* chance agreement, S made several assumptions, one of which is that coders set the number of marble colors equal to the number of categories in the coding scheme.

Assumption 6:   *Equal number per color.*

Coders put in the urn an equal number of marbles per color.

    Assumption 7:   *Drawing with replacement.*

While maximizing random coding, coders draw marbles with replacement. All other chance-adjusted indices assume the same, except Krippendorff's α (1970, 1980), which assumes drawing without replacement.

    Assumption 8:   *Color mismatch equals honesty.*

Coders code honestly when marbles' colors mismatch. Most of the chance-adjusted indices assume the same, except Gwet's AC_1 (2008) and Goodman and Kruskal's λ_r (1954), which we will discuss later.

    Basic Assumption 9:   *Categories reduce chance agreements.*

Equation 7 assumes that category is the *only* parameter affecting chance agreement. Nothing else, including the distribution pattern of the cases coded, affects chance agreement. More categories mean less chance agreement. Two categories imply 50% chance agreement, while 10 categories imply 10% chance agreement. As categories approach infinity, chance agreement approaches 0%. Accordingly, we say the indices sharing Equation 7 are *category based.*

    Bennett et al. (1954) compared S with a_o and a_c. They appeared to be aware that their chance agreements (Equation 7) were only hypothetical, so they used S only as convenient references complementing other information, including a_o, a_c, and K. Between the lines of Bennett et al. (1954), we do not sense that S is the only or better indicator of reliability, but instead one more piece of information added to the overall picture. This nuanced understanding is not often seen in the writings of some later authors of various indices of intercoder reliability.

    Since 1954, S has been independently reinvented at least six times. Some of the reinventions have minor variations or more restricted applications. They are usually based on different reasoning and always bear different labels: Guilford's G (Guilford, 1961; Holley & Guilford, 1964), Maxwell's RE (1977), Jason and Vegelius's C (1979), Brennan and Prediger's k_n (1981), Byrt, Bishop, and Carlin's $PABAK$ (1993), and Potter and Levine-Donnerstein's *redefined Pi* (1999).

Guttman's ρ

About 8 years before Bennett et al. (1954), Guttman (1946) proposed the same Equation 8 and implied the same Equation 7. But Guttman calculates a_o in a unique way:

$$a_o = \frac{1}{2}\left(\frac{N_{l1}}{N} + \frac{N_{l2}}{N}\right) \qquad (9)$$

N_{11} and N_{12} are, respectively, the mode frequency reported by each coder. Suppose on a binary scale Coder 1 reports 85 cases in Category 1 and 15 cases in Category 2, while Coder 2 reports 55 cases in Category 1 and 45 cases in Category 2, N_{11}=85 and N_{12}=55. When the right sides of Equations 7 and 9 replace respectively a_c and a_o in Equation 3, R_i is Guttman's ρ. By contrast, all other indices reviewed in this chapter use Equation 1 to calculate a_o. Except for the calculation of a_o, ρ is identical to S. So ρ shares all assumptions of S that have been discussed, and one paradox that will be discussed below.

Guttman's overriding concern appears to be keeping reliability scores between 0 and 1. Equation 9 achieves that objective, making Guttman's ρ one of the few chance-adjusted indices that never fall below zero. A side effect is that Guttman's a_o only crudely approximates %-agreement, leading to the following assumption:

Assumption 10:   *%-agreement needs to be approximated but not calculated.*

Mode is not %-agreement. But the two are correlated. When distributions are skewed at the same direction, for example, both coders report 90% positive, the more skewed is the distribution, the closer Guttman's a_o is toward %-agreement; when distributions are skewed at the opposite directions, the more skewed is the distribution, the farther away Guttman's a_o is from %-agreement. At one extreme, if both coders report that 100% cases fall into the same category, %-agreement and Guttman's a_o are both 1. At the other extreme, when one coder reports 100% positive and another 100% negative, %-agreement is 0% while Guttman's a_o is 1. If both coders report 50 & 50% distributions, Guttman's a_o is 0.5 while %-agreement can be anywhere between 0 and 100%. As distributions are far more likely to skew at the same direction than opposite directions in actual coding, Guttman's a_o may be seen as a crude approximation of %-agreement.

But it is so crude that we hesitate to call Guttman's a_o an estimation of agreement. This may look more detrimental today as we now define reliability in terms of agreement. So we are not surprised that ρ has rarely been used. Bennett et al. (1954) copied Equation 7 entirely from Guttman (1946) without mentioning ρ, and introduced S by changing only one thing, the calculation of a_o. Scott (1955) cited S but not ρ while developing π. And it was π that served as an inspiration for Cohen's κ (1960) and Krippendorff's α (1970).

We also would not recommend ρ, as ρ has all the defects but not all the benefits of S.

Guttman (1946) was, however, the first we know to introduce Equation 7, which implies Equations 3~6 that contain the basic concepts and premises for reliability calculation in the past six decades. Today, when researchers calculate chance-adjusted reliability, few calculate ρ, yet almost all use Equations 3~6, thereby adopt the assumptions behind.

Perreault and Leigh's I_r

Hayes and Krippendorff (2007, p. 80) and Krippendorff (2004b, p. 417) considered Perreault and Leigh's I_r (1989) a simple modification of S. The modification was to take the square root of S when S is zero or above, and otherwise define reliability as zero:

$$I_r = \sqrt{S} \quad (S \geq 0) \tag{10a}$$

$$I_r = 0 \quad (S < 0) \tag{10b}$$

The two equal each other at two key spots: I_r=1 when S=1, and I_r=0 when S=0. Everywhere else, I_r is larger than S, with the largest difference at S=-1 and I_r=0, and the largest above-zero difference at S=0.5 and I_r≈0.71. So I_r is an elevated version of S, implying an interesting assumption:

Assumption 11: **Reliability index needs to be elevated across scale.**

Perreault and Leigh's I_r (1989) assumes that a reliability index needs to be elevated numerically across the scale, after adjusting for chance using Equation 3 or 6. The only other index that makes the same assumption is Benini's β. Taking the square root of a 0~1 variable produces little change in the pattern of its behavior other than elevating it numerically. Consequently, I_r adopts all assumptions and paradoxes of S, one of which we discuss below.

A Paradox Shared by Nine Category-Based Indices

Users treat ρ, I_r, S and its six equivalents as general indicators for typical studies. As typical studies do not follow Assumptions 2~9, paradoxes arise. The shared equations (3~6) lead to shared Paradoxes 6~7, while Equation 7 leads to another classic paradox:

Paradox 6: **Empty Categories Increase Reliability.**

Scott (1955) observed "given a two-category sex dimension and a P_o (our a_o) of 60 per cent, the S ... would be 0.20. But a whimsical researcher might add two more categories, "hermaphrodite" and "indeterminate," thereby increasing S to 0.47, though the two additional categories are not used at all." The same paradox can be replicated for Guttman's ρ with identical numbers (a_o=.6, ρ = .2 increased to ρ = .47), assuming each coder reports 60% for one gender and 40% for another. The same paradox also shows for Perreault and Leigh's I_r, if we take the square roots of 0.2 and 0.47, which would approximate 0.45 and 0.69 respectively. Now that we know the assumptions behind S, ρ and I_r, there are two ways to interpret Paradox 6:

1. The coding followed a Guttman Scenario in accordance to Assumptions 2~9. Assumption 5, which equates categories with marble colors, requires the coding in Paradox 6 be separated into two sessions. In the first session the coders draw from two colors, while in the second they draw from four colors. With four colors, there are more chances of color mismatch, therefore more chances of honest coding, therefore higher reliability. There is no paradox if coders indeed coded this way.

2. The coding followed a Grove-Riffe Scenario in accordance with the variable-random and complete-honesty assumptions. Coders did not use any urns or marbles to decide when to code honestly or randomly. Assumptions 2~9 have been violated; therefore S, ρ, or I_r should not have been calculated. Paradox 6 is not a real paradox. It is only the symptom of special-purpose indices applied beyond their boundaries.

Scott's (1955) interpretation was: "The index (S) is based on the assumption that all categories in the dimension have equal probability of use $1/K$ by both coders. This is an unwarranted assumption for most behavioral and attitudinal research. Even though K categories may be available to the observers, the phenomena being coded are likely to be distributed unevenly, and in many cases will cluster heavily in only two or three of them ... S would appear to be an unsatisfactory measure of coding reliability" (pp. 321–322).

Scott was right to reject one assumption of S that "categories...have equal probability of use" which is implied in the categories-equal-colors and equal-number-per-color assumptions. Scott however accepted, possibly unknowingly, the more detrimental assumptions of S, namely maximum-randomness and limited-honesty. Consequently, while Scott's π eliminates one symptom of S, it causes other symptoms that are arguably more problematic, which we will discuss below.

Distribution-Based Indices

The eight indices reviewed in this section all assume that distribution is the most important factor affecting chance agreement. They differ with each other in other details.

Scott's π and Two Equivalents, Revised K and BAK

Of the chance-adjusted intercoder reliability indices, Scott's π is second only to Cohen's κ (1960) in popularity. In Communication and Mass Media Complete (CMMC), citations for "Scott's Pi" rose from 11 in 1994 to 61 in 2009, totaling 597 for the period. It has been also recommended later under two different names, Siegel and Castellan's *Revised K* (1988) and Byrt et al.'s *BAK* (1993). Because they are mathematically equivalent to each other, our discussions and findings hereafter about π also apply to *Revised K* and *BAK*.

Like other major chance-adjusted indices, Scott's π shares the same chance-removing procedure (Equations 3, 4, and 6) while adopting its own chance-estimating procedure. For a binary scale, Scott (1955) estimates chance agreement (a_c) using the average of two coders' positive answers (N_p) and the average of their negative answers (N_n):

$$a_c = \left(\frac{N_p}{N}\right)\left(\frac{N_p}{N}\right) + \left(\frac{N_n}{N}\right)\left(\frac{N_n}{N}\right) \qquad (11)$$

Here N_p is from the two coders' (*1* and *2*) positive decisions (N_{p1} & N_{p2}):

$$N_p = \frac{N_{p1} + N_{p2}}{2} \qquad (12)$$

And N_n is from the coders' negative decisions (N_{n1} & N_{n2}):

$$N_n = \frac{N_{n1} + N_{n2}}{2} \qquad (13)$$

When the right side of Equation 11 is inserted into Equation 3, r_i is Scott's π. Like S, π assumes maximum randomness. Two coders draw with replacement from the same urn of N marbles, N_p black and N_n white. The probability of one coder getting black is N_p/N, both getting black is (N_p/N)* (N_p/N), both getting white is (N_n/N)* (N_n/N). The probability of their agreeing through marble drawing is the sum of the two products, hence Equation 11.

Although Scott's π accepts the categories-equal-colors assumption, it rejects the equal-number-per-color assumption, allowing the number of marbles for each color to vary between 0 and N. Hence it succeeds in excluding category (K) per se as a parameter and avoids the categories-increase-reliability paradox. By sharing Equations 3, 4 and, 6, however, π shares maximum-randomness and limited-honesty assumptions. Further, π adopts average distribution as a parameter (Equation 11), hence adopts more consequential assumptions:

Basic Assumption 12: Conspired quota.

To calculate chance agreement under the maximum randomness assumption, we need to know the marble distribution. S assumes even distribution across all colors, making category a parameter. Scott's π rejects this assumption. So what is the distribution? No one knows, because marble drawing is only hypothetical. Even if marble drawing had happened, marble distribution can be anywhere between 0% & 100% and 100% & 0%. Scott's π assumes that average of the "observed distributions" reported by the coders is also the marble distribution. That means that π mathematically equates marble distribution with observed target distribution.

But there is no natural linkage between the two. Coders may draw from an urn of 40% and 60% marbles while coding a pile of 90% and 10% commercials. If the research is done reasonably well, its observed distribution should be related to the targeted commercials but normally unrelated to the marbles.

Under a Guttman-Goodman Scenario, marble distribution must be set before drawing, which has to take place before the coding that produces the observed distributions. There is only one way marble distributions could equal observed distributions regularly and precisely—if someone sets a quota that is accurately executed. While ordinary marble drawing contains sampling errors, Equation 11 leaves no room for error, implying that π assumes a strict quota—the two coders execute the quota so faithfully that the average distribution they report is identical to the marble distribution in the urn.

Equation 11 uses the average of two coders' observed distributions, implying that the two coders set one quota, share one urn, and work together to deliver the quota, hence "conspired quota," or "collectively strict quota."

To justify using observed distribution, it is often argued that the observed distribution is a reasonable estimate of the population distribution (Cohen, 1960, p. 40; Krippendorff, 2004b, p. 418; Scott, 1955, p. 324). This reasoning mixed two populations, *target population* under study, such as news and ads, and *marble population* in the urn, from which coders hypothetically draw. Observed distribution can be a reasonable estimate of target distribution, but normally not a legitimate estimate of marble distribution.

Equation 11 needs a marble distribution, and employs observed distribution as a surrogate. The equation does not need the distribution of the target population. The sample-population linkage does not justify Equation 11 or π, while a conspired quota does. This also implies the following assumptions behind Scott's π, which were later also adopted by κ, α, and AC_j:

Assumption 13:   *Trinity distribution.*

This is a group of three assumptions. (a) Observed sample distribution equals target population distribution; (b) observed sample distribution equals marble distribution; hence (c) target population distribution equals marble distribution. The first assumption may find support in probability theory assuming a probability sample. The latter two are inventions implied in π, which cannot be justified by probability theory or empirical evidences.

Gwet (2010) commented: "Scott's π is...very sensitive to trait prevalence" (p. 40). This is because distribution (prevalence) is a main factor in π, even though the index is supposed to measure agreement but not prevalence. We will discuss later that distribution also affects Gwet's AC_j, although inversely.

By sharing maximum-randomness equations (3, 4, and 6), π also shares the underlying assumptions of *maximum-randomness* and *limited-honesty* (2 and 3). By adopting Equation 11, π also shares *replacement-drawing* and *mismatch-equals-honesty* assumptions (7 & 8), and three additional assumptions below:

Assumption 14:   *Constrained task*

A study is not to investigate how many targets are in what category, which has been predecided by the quotas, but to place targets into appropriate categories under the quotas.

Assumption 15:   *Predetermined distribution.*

Executing a quota implies that distribution is determined before coding. Therefore the observed distribution must remain unchanged within a study when the coders improve their work, as their "work" is not to assess distribution between categories.

Assumption 16:   *Quota and distribution affect chance agreement.*

Chance agreement a_c is a function of marble distributions, which is predetermined by the quotas. This assumption is implied in the maximum-randomness and conspired-quota assumptions. If all marbles in the urn are of one color, the coders have no chance to code honestly; they have to agree all the time, by chance. If the marbles are 50% black and 50% white, the coders have a 50% chance of agreeing randomly and 50% chance coding honestly.

As quota determines both observed distribution and chance agreement, the latter two also correlate with each other. Table 19.3 displays Scott's chance agreement as a function of observed distributions. According to Equations 3 and 6, chance agreement a_c is a bar that %-agreement must pass to produce a positive index, and pass by margins to produce a good-looking index. Higher a_c means a higher bar and lower looking reliability. So an important pattern emerged: a more skewed observed distribution produces a higher bar, which produces a lower π.

These assumptions, as summarized in Table 19.4, portray the following *Scott Scenario* for a binary scale, which is another case of the broader Guttman-Goodman Scenario:

1. Two coders set a quota for the black and white marbles, and fill the urn accordingly. They also agree on which color represents positive and which negative. We will assume black-positive and white-negative pairings hereafter.
2. They take a target to be coded.
3. One coder draws a marble randomly from the urn, notes the marble's color, and puts it back. The other coder does the same.
4. If both draw black, each reports positive; if both draw white, each reports negative; in either case they do not look at the target being coded. Only if one draws a black and the other draws a white would they code objectively, at which point they may honestly agree or disagree, and report accordingly.

Table 19.3 Scott's Chance Agreement (a_c) as a Function of Two Distributions*

Distribution 2: Percent of Positive Findings by Coder 2 (N_{p2}/N)**	Distribution 1: Percent of Positive Findings by Coder 1 (N_{p1}/N)**										
	0	10	20	30	40	50	60	70	80	90	100
100	50.0	50.5	52.0	54.5	58.0	62.5	68.0	74.5	82.0	90.5	100.0
90	50.5	50.0	50.5	52.0	54.5	58.0	62.5	68.0	74.5	82.0	90.5
80	52.0	50.5	50.0	50.5	52.0	54.5	58.0	62.5	68.0	74.5	82.0
70	54.5	52.0	50.5	50.0	50.5	52.0	54.5	58.0	62.5	68.0	74.5
60	58.0	54.5	52.0	50.5	50.0	50.5	52.0	54.5	58.0	62.5	68.0
50	62.5	58.0	54.5	52.0	50.5	50.0	50.5	52.0	54.5	58.0	62.5
40	68.0	62.5	58.0	54.5	52.0	50.5	50.0	50.5	52.0	54.5	58.0
30	74.5	68.0	62.5	58.0	54.5	52.0	50.5	50.0	50.5	52.0	54.5
20	82.0	74.5	68.0	62.5	58.0	54.5	52.0	50.5	50.0	50.5	52.0
10	90.5	82.0	74.5	68.0	62.5	58.0	54.5	52.0	50.5	50.0	50.5
0	100.0	90.5	82.0	74.5	68.0	62.5	58.0	54.5	52.0	50.5	50.0

*:   Main cell entries are Scott's Chance Agreement (a_c) in %.

**: N_{p1} is the number of positive answers by Coder 1, N_{p2} is the number of positive answers by Coder 2, and N is the total number of cases analyzed. See also Table 19.4 for various assumptions behind Scott's π.

Table 19.4 Assumptions of 22 Intercoder Reliability Indices

Down: Assumption name (assumption #)	%-Agreement a_o (Osgood, Holsti's CR), Rogot & Goldberg's A_1	Benini's β	Guttman's ρ	Bennett et al.'s S (C, G, k_n, PABAK, rdf-Pi, RE)	Goodman & Kruskal's λr	Scott's π (Rev-K, BAK)	Cohen's κ(A_2)	Krippendorff's α	Perreault & Leigh's I_r	Gwet's AC_1
Random chance agreement (1, 2)	zero	maximum	maximum	maximum	maximum	maximum	maximum	maximum	maximum	maximum
Honesty (3)	complete	limited	limited	limited	limited	limited	limited	limited	limited	limited
Specified random (4)	no	yes	yes	yes	yes	yes	yes	yes	yes	yes
Rounds of marble drawing (23)	zero	one	one	one	one	one	one	one	one	two
Drawing with replacement (7, 18)	N/A	yes	yes	yes	yes	yes	yes	no	yes	yes
What marble pattern=honesty? (8, 22, 24)	N/A	mismatch	mismatch	mismatch	mode color	mismatch	mismatch	mismatch	mismatch	mismatch or 2 matches
Categories = colors (5)	no	yes	yes	yes	yes	yes	yes	yes	yes	yes
Equal number per color (6)	no	no	yes	yes	no	no	no	no	yes	yes

Categories reduce chance agreements a_c (9)	no	no	yes	yes	no	no	no	no	yes	yes
Agreement observed or approximated (10)	observed	observed	approximated	observed	observed	observed	observed	observed	observed	observed
Elevated index (11)	no	yes	no	no	no	no	no	no	yes	no
Quota (12, 17)	no	individual	no	no	individual	conspired	individual	conspired	no	conspired
Trinity distribution (13)	no	yes	no	no	yes	yes	yes	yes	no	yes
Constrained task (14)	no	yes	no	no	yes	yes	yes	yes	no	yes
Predetermined distribution (15)	no	yes	no	no	yes	yes	yes	yes	no	yes
Quota & Distribution affects a_c (16)	no	yes	no	no	yes	yes	yes	yes	no	yes
Trinity size (19)	no	no	no	no	no	no	no	yes	no	no
Predetermined target size (20)	no	no	no	no	no	no	no	yes	no	no
Larger samples increase a_c (21)	no	no	no	no	no	no	no	yes	no	no

5. The two coders calculate the average of positive cases and the average of negative cases they have reported. If one average reaches the quota, they stop drawing, report the remaining targets according to the quota, then end the coding session. If neither average reaches the quota, they repeat Step 2 and the subsequent steps.

The *Scott Assumptions* (2~4, 7, 8, 12~16), as illustrated in the *Scott Scenario*, constitute the boundaries beyond which Scott's π should normally not be used. Scott's π, however, has been used as a general indicator of reliability for typical coding. As typical coding is closer to a Grove-Riffe Scenario than a Scott Scenario, paradoxes and abnormalities arise, which we will discuss after analyzing two closely related indices, κ and α.

Cohen's κ and an Equivalent, A₂

Cohen's κ (1960) has been the most often used chance-adjusted index of reliability. In Social Sciences Citation Index (SSCI), Cohen (1960) was cited 203 times in 1994 and 306 times in 2010, totaling 3,624 during the period. Rogot and Goldberg (1966) proposed A_2, which Fleiss (1975) pointed out is equivalent to κ; so all our discussion about κ also applies to A_2.

Cohen (1960) disagreed with Scott's estimation of chance agreement, a_c, arguing: "(Scott) assumes...the distribution...is...equal for the judges ... (which) may be questioned" (pp. 40–41) because "the judges operate independently" (p. 38). So he replaced two coders' *average* positive (N_p) and negative answers (N_n) in Equation 11 with each coder's (*1 and 2*) *individual* positive (N_{p1} & N_{p2}) and negative (N_{n1} & N_{n2}) answers:

$$a_c = \left(\frac{N_{p1}}{N}\right)\left(\frac{N_{p2}}{N}\right) + \left(\frac{N_{n1}}{N}\right)\left(\frac{N_{n2}}{N}\right) \tag{14}$$

When the right side of Equation 14 is inserted into Equation 3, r_i is Cohen's κ. Cohen (1960) agreed with Scott (1955) on one important point: "the distribution of proportions over the categories for the *population* is known." Here, like Scott (1955), Cohen (1960) conceptually mixed the target population with the marble population, treating the two as one. He injected into κ the observed distribution as if it was the marble distribution, but justified the injection in terms of the target distribution. In other words, κ shares the *trinity distribution* assumption, making distribution a major parameter like π does. Consequently, κ adopts a quota assumption similar to π's, and κ behaves quite similarly to π. By adopting maximum-randomness equations (3, 4, and 6), κ also shares maximum-randomness and limited-honesty assumptions with S and π. The only difference among them is how to estimate chance agreement a_c and the only difference between π and κ is how to set and execute the quota. While π assumes that two coders set one quota, and work together to execute it, κ assumes differently:

Basic Assumption 17: Individual quotas.

Cohen's κ uses observed *individual* distributions, implying that each coder sets his own quota, places marbles accordingly into his own urn, and works individually to assure that the distribution he reports meets his own quota, hence "individual quotas."

Cohen (1960, Table 1) adapted "agreement matrix of proportions" from the χ^2 procedure to justify and explain κ. While χ^2 multiplies margins of an association matrix to calculate the probabilities expected under the no-association hypothesis, Cohen's κ (1960, p. 38) multiplies margins of an agreement matrix to calculate a_c.

There is, however, a crucial difference between the two matrices, as we alluded to in the Overview at the beginning of this chapter. The variables of an association matrix, such as race and locale, may be independent of each other, while the variables of an agreement matrix are coders' observations of the *same* targets, and hence normally cannot be independent of each other. By multiplying the distributions of race and locale, χ^2 assumes that each is independent. Likewise, by multiplying individual distributions of the coder observations, κ assumes that each is independent. If each is independent, they cannot come from objective observations of the same targets. We have to find another source to justify the presumed independence, which we found in two independently predetermined quotas. This analysis does not apply to π, α or AC_1, each of which uses average rather than individual distributions, hence assumes a conspired rather than individual quota.

Table 19.5 for Cohen's a_c is to be compared with Table 19.3 for Scott's a_c. The comparison reveals that Cohen's a_c is usually lower and never higher than Scott's a_c, which means that κ is usually higher and never lower than π. The most striking difference occurs when the two observed distributions are skewed in the opposite directions, where Cohen's a_c approaches 0%, while Scott's a_c approaches 50%.

Feinstein and Cicchetti (1990) observed "The reasoning (of κ) makes the assumption that each observer has a relatively fixed probability of making positive or negative responses. The assumption does not seem appropriate, however for most clinical observers. If unbiased, the observers will usually respond to whatever is presented in each particular instance of challenge" (p. 548). "Fixed probability" is quota. Feinstein and Cicchetti (1990) recognized κ's individual quota assumption more than 20 years ago without naming it so. As discussed earlier it is a strict quota, not "relative."

The *Cohen Assumptions* (2~4, 7, 8, 14~17), which are also summarized in Table 19.4, portray the following *Cohen Scenario*, which is another special case of the Guttman-Goodman Scenario:

1. Each coder sets a quota for the black and white marbles, and fills his or her urn accordingly.
2. They take a target to be coded.

Table 19.5 Cohen's Chance Agreement (a_c) as a Function of Two Distributions*

| | | | | | Distribution 1: Positive Findings by Coder 1 (N_{p1}/N) in %** | | | | | | |
	0	10	20	30	40	50	60	70	80	90	100
100	0.0	10.0	20.0	30.0	40.0	50.0	60.0	70.0	80.0	90.0	100.0
90	10.0	18.0	26.0	34.0	42.0	50.0	58.0	66.0	74.0	82.0	90.0
80	20.0	26.0	32.0	38.0	44.0	50.0	56.0	62.0	68.0	74.0	80.0
70	30.0	34.0	38.0	42.0	46.0	50.0	54.0	58.0	62.0	66.0	70.0
60	40.0	42.0	44.0	46.0	48.0	50.0	52.0	54.0	56.0	58.0	60.0
50	50.0	50.0	50.0	50.0	50.0	50.0	50.0	50.0	50.0	50.0	50.0
40	60.0	58.0	56.0	54.0	52.0	50.0	48.0	46.0	44.0	42.0	40.0
30	70.0	66.0	62.0	58.0	54.0	50.0	46.0	42.0	38.0	34.0	30.0
20	80.0	74.0	68.0	62.0	56.0	50.0	44.0	38.0	32.0	26.0	20.0
10	90.0	82.0	74.0	66.0	58.0	50.0	42.0	34.0	26.0	18.0	10.0
0	100.0	90.0	80.0	70.0	60.0	50.0	40.0	30.0	20.0	10.0	0.0

Distribution 2: Positive Findings by Coder 2 (N_{p2}/N) in %**

*: Main cell entries are Cohen's Chance Agreement (a_c) in %.
**: N_{p1} is the number of positive answers by Coder 1, N_{p2} is the number of positive answers by Coder 2, and N is the total number of cases analyzed. See also Table 19.4 for various assumptions behind Cohen's κ.

3. One coder draws a marble randomly from his urn, notes the marble's color, and puts it back. The other coder does the same from her urn.

4. If both draw black, each reports positive; if both draw white, each reports negative; in either case they do not look at the target being coded. Only if one draws a black and another draws a white would they code objectively, at which point they may honestly agree or disagree, and report accordingly.

5. Each coder calculates the positive and negative cases that he or she has reported. If either reaches the quota, he or she stops drawing, reports the remaining targets according to the quota, then ends the coding. If neither reaches the quota, he or she repeats Step 2 and the subsequent steps.

If a study conforms to the Cohen Scenario and Cohen Assumptions, κ would be an appropriate index of intercoder reliability, otherwise κ would be inappropriate. When κ is applied in violation of the Scenario and the assumptions, paradoxes arise, which κ shares with π and Krippendorff's α. We will discuss these paradoxes after analyzing α.

Krippendorff's α

Krippendorff's α (1970, 1980) may not be as often cited as Scott's π or Cohen's κ. But it is among the most often recommended (Hayes & Krippendorff, 2007; Krippendorff, 2004b). Like Scott (1955) and Cohen (1960), Krippendorff (1980) also adopted Equations 3, 4, and 6. But Krippendorff believed that Cohen made a mistake by using individual distributions, and Scott made a mistake by assuming marble drawing with replacement, which fails to correct for sample size (cf. Krippendorff, 2004b). So Krippendorff's estimation for chance agreement retains Scott's average distributions but assumes no replacement:

$$a_c = \left(\frac{2N_p}{2N}\right)\left(\frac{2N_p - 1}{2N - 1}\right) + \left(\frac{2N_n}{2N}\right)\left(\frac{2N_n - 1}{2N - 1}\right) \tag{15}$$

In Equation 11, Scott gave the first and second drawing the same probability, assuming replacement. In Equation 15, Krippendorff subtracted one for the second drawing, assuming no replacement. With two coders, this is the only mathematical difference between α and π. When the sample gets larger, the relative impact of subtracting one gets smaller, Krippendorff's a_c approaches Scott's a_c, and α approaches π. This can be seen by comparing Table 19.6 with Table 19.3. When the sample is smaller than 50, however, Krippendorff's a_c can be noticeably smaller than Scott's. Table 19.7 shows Krippendorff's a_c as a function of target sample.

When the right side of Equation 15 is inserted into Equation 3, r_i is Krippendorff's α.

By adopting the *maximum-randomness equations* (3, 4, and 6), Krippendorff's α adopts the maximum-randomness and limited-honesty assumptions

(2 and 3) and other related assumptions summarized in Table 19.4. By retaining average distribution (Equation 15), α also adopts Scott's assumptions of conspired quota (12) and trinity distributions (13). To reject the replacement assumption (7), however, α adds several unique assumptions.

Basic Assumption 18: Drawing without replacement.

All other chance-adjusted indices assume drawing with replacement. Krippendorff's α (1970, 1980) is the only one that assumes no replacement, which implies other unique assumptions explained below.

Assumption 19:   *Trinity size.*

When drawing without replacement, the size of the marble population, N_m, becomes important. Assuming half black and half white, if two coders draw from an urn containing only two marbles ($N_m=2$), the probability of getting the same color is zero; if N_m rises to four, the probability rises to nearly 0.167; if N_m rises further, the probability rises further; if N_m approaches infinity, the probability approaches 0.5. We need N_m to calculate Krippendorff's a_c and α. But N_m is usually not known. Under a Grove-Riffe Scenario, coders don't draw marbles to determine which cases to be coded randomly or honestly. Even if they do, N_m could be anything above zero. Krippendorff's α assumes each coder puts one marble in the urn for each target; so, with two coders, N_m is twice the target sample, N:

$$N_m = 2N \tag{16}$$

Krippendorff's α also assumes all marbles in the urn are drawn, so marble population equals marble sample. Therefore a *trinity-size* assumption: *marble sample* and *marble population* equal each other, and each doubles the *target sample*.

Krippendorff (1970, 1980, 2004a) argues that the nonreplacement assumption "corrects for" sample sizes. But which sample—target or marble? Krippendorff's nonreplacement argument would make sense if he means targets; that is, coders do not put every news story or advertisement back for recoding. Krippendorff's calculation in Equation 15 would make sense if he means marbles; that is, if coders indeed draw marbles without replacement, the subtraction by one would be necessary. But normally the argument does not justify the calculation because normally the targets and marbles are not linked. Coders may code targets with no replacement while drawing marbles with replacement; under a Grove-Riffe Scenario, coders code targets without first drawing marbles. To justify the calculation, α needs a special link between marble size and target size. Trinity-size assumption provides that link, by requiring that coders set the number of marbles according to the size of the target sample.

Table 19.6 Krippendorff's Chance Agreement (a_c) as a Function of Two Distributions (N = 100)*

Distribution 2: Percent of Positive Findings by Coder 2 (N_{p2}/N)**	Distribution 1: Percent of Positive Findings by Coder 1 (N_{p1}/N)**										
		0	10	20	30	40	50	60	70	80	90	100
100	49.7	50.3	51.8	54.3	57.8	62.3	67.8	74.4	81.9	90.5	100.0
90	50.3	49.7	50.3	51.8	54.3	57.8	62.3	67.8	74.4	81.9	90.5
80	51.8	50.3	49.7	50.3	51.8	54.3	57.8	62.3	67.8	74.4	81.9
70	54.3	51.8	50.3	49.7	50.3	51.8	54.3	57.8	62.3	67.8	74.4
60	57.8	54.3	51.8	50.3	49.7	50.3	51.8	54.3	57.8	62.3	67.8
50	62.3	57.8	54.3	51.8	50.3	49.7	50.3	51.8	54.3	57.8	62.3
40	67.8	62.3	57.8	54.3	51.8	50.3	49.7	50.3	51.8	54.3	57.8
30	74.4	67.8	62.3	57.8	54.3	51.8	50.3	49.7	50.3	51.8	54.3
20	81.9	74.4	67.8	62.3	57.8	54.3	51.8	50.3	49.7	50.3	51.8
10	90.5	81.9	74.4	67.8	62.3	57.8	54.3	51.8	50.3	49.7	50.3
0	100.0	90.5	81.9	74.4	67.8	62.3	57.8	54.3	51.8	50.3	49.7

*:   Main cell entries are Krippendorff's Chance Agreement (a_c) in %.

**: N_{p1} is the number of positive answers by Coder 1, N_{p2} is the number of positive answers by Coder 2, and N is the total number of cases analyzed. See also Table 19.4 for various assumptions behind Krippendorff's α.

Table 19.7 Krippendorff's Chance Agreement Rate (a_c) as a Function of Coded Targets (N) and Average Distribution (Np/N)

Number of Coded Targets (N)	Average Distribution of Positive Cases (N_p/N in %)										
	0	10	20	30	40	50	60	70	80	90	100
1	100.00	64.00	36.00	16.00	4.00	0.00	4.00	16.00	36.00	64.00	100.00
2	100.00	76.00	57.33	44.00	36.00	33.33	36.00	44.00	57.33	76.00	100.00
3	100.00	78.40	61.60	49.60	42.40	40.00	42.40	49.60	61.60	78.40	100.00
4	100.00	79.43	63.43	52.00	45.14	42.86	45.14	52.00	63.43	79.43	100.00
5	100.00	80.00	64.44	53.33	46.67	44.44	46.67	53.33	64.44	80.00	100.00
6	100.00	80.36	65.09	54.18	47.64	45.45	47.64	54.18	65.09	80.36	100.00
7	100.00	80.62	65.54	54.77	48.31	46.15	48.31	54.77	65.54	80.62	100.00
8	100.00	80.80	65.87	55.20	48.80	46.67	48.80	55.20	65.87	80.80	100.00
9	100.00	80.94	66.12	55.53	49.18	47.06	49.18	55.53	66.12	80.94	100.00
10	100.00	81.05	66.32	55.79	49.47	47.37	49.47	55.79	66.32	81.05	100.00
11	100.00	81.14	66.48	56.00	49.71	47.62	49.71	56.00	66.48	81.14	100.00
12	100.00	81.22	66.61	56.17	49.91	47.83	49.91	56.17	66.61	81.22	100.00
13	100.00	81.28	66.72	56.32	50.08	48.00	50.08	56.32	66.72	81.28	100.00
14	100.00	81.33	66.81	56.44	50.22	48.15	50.22	56.44	66.81	81.33	100.00
15	100.00	81.38	66.90	56.55	50.34	48.28	50.34	56.55	66.90	81.38	100.00

16	100.00	81.42	66.97	56.65	50.45	48.39	50.45	56.65	66.97	81.42	100.00
17	100.00	81.45	67.03	56.73	50.55	48.48	50.55	56.73	67.03	81.45	100.00
18	100.00	81.49	67.09	56.80	50.63	48.57	50.63	56.80	67.09	81.49	100.00
19	100.00	81.51	67.14	56.86	50.70	48.65	50.70	56.86	67.14	81.51	100.00
20	100.00	81.54	67.18	56.92	50.77	48.72	50.77	56.92	67.18	81.54	100.00
21	100.00	81.56	67.22	56.98	50.83	48.78	50.83	56.98	67.22	81.56	100.00
22	100.00	81.58	67.26	57.02	50.88	48.84	50.88	57.02	67.26	81.58	100.00
23	100.00	81.60	67.29	57.07	50.93	48.89	50.93	57.07	67.29	81.60	100.00
24	100.00	81.62	67.32	57.11	50.98	48.94	50.98	57.11	67.32	81.62	100.00
25	100.00	81.63	67.35	57.14	51.02	48.98	51.02	57.14	67.35	81.63	100.00
26	100.00	81.65	67.37	57.18	51.06	49.02	51.06	57.18	67.37	81.65	100.00
27	100.00	81.66	67.40	57.21	51.09	49.06	51.09	57.21	67.40	81.66	100.00
28	100.00	81.67	67.42	57.24	51.13	49.09	51.13	57.24	67.42	81.67	100.00
29	100.00	81.68	67.44	57.26	51.16	49.12	51.16	57.26	67.44	81.68	100.00
30	100.00	81.69	67.46	57.29	51.19	49.15	51.19	57.29	67.46	81.69	100.00

Main cell entries are Krippendorff's Chance Agreement (a_c) in %.

Also, mathematically Equation 15 needs marble *population*, not target *sample* that the equation actually uses, or marble (die) *sample* that Krippendorff could be referring to. The trinity-size assumption also closes this gap, by making the three essentially one.

The trinity-distribution assumption (13) also links marbles to targets. But the trinity-distribution assumption is shared by α, π, κ, and AC_1, while the trinity-size assumption is unique to α. AC_1, π or κ makes no assumption about the size of a population or sample, of marbles or targets, as their replacement assumption makes size irrelevant.

Assumption 20:   *Predetermined target size.*

Krippendorff's α assumes that the sizes of marble population, marble sample, and target sample are decided before a study and remain unchanged within the study. To test and improve their protocol, content researchers sometimes expand target samples in the middle of a study. For example, a researcher may test her protocol on a sample of 20 targets, calculate reliability, and then apply the protocol to 80 additional targets and calculate the reliability for the 100 targets combined. Krippendorff's α assumes such adjustment of sample size can never happen within a study. Instead, α assumes the coders treat the 20 cases and the 100 cases as two separate studies, meaning (a) the coders draw from 40 marbles to code the 20 cases, and (b) the coders draw from 200 marbles to code the 100 cases, including recoding the 20 cases already coded. When α is applied to situations where coders expand their sample without drawing marbles, abnormalities arise, which we will show below.

Other indices like S, π, κ and AC_1, all assume replacement, so they do not assume a fixed N_m or N within a study. If two coders draw from an equal number of black and white marbles with replacement, the probability of getting the same color is 50% regardless of N_m or N.

Assumption 21:   *Larger samples increase chance agreements.*

It is often said that α is superior to π and all other indices in part because "α … is corrected for small sample sizes" (Krippendorff, 2004a, p. 250). This is appealing, as we are accustomed to statistical indicators that reward larger samples. For example, everything else being equal, statistical significance is more likely with a larger sample of respondents, and Cronbach's alpha is larger with a larger sample of measures.

Krippendorff's "correction," however, does the opposite. It systematically rewards smaller samples. As shown in Table 19.7, everything else being equal, a smaller sample produces a smaller a_c, hence a higher α. This is a consequence of the trinity-size and nonreplacement assumptions (18, 19): a smaller target sample means a smaller marble population, which means lower a_c and higher α.

In typical studies under a Grove-Riffe Scenario, such a correction is not needed for marble sample or target sample, because marbles were actually not drawn to determine when to code randomly or honestly, and targets were not drawn for deliberate random coding. As the correction is not needed, α is not needed. When α is applied in such a study, sample-size related paradoxes arise, which we will discuss shortly.

Equations 3, 4, 6, and 15 constitute Krippendorff's α for binary scale with two coders. With multiple coders and multiple categories, Krippendorff's α takes more complex forms (Hayes & Krippendorff, 2007; Krippendorff 2004a, 2004b). While the above analysis uses binary scales with two coders, these boundaries also apply to more categories and more coders.

The 13 Krippendorff Assumptions (2~4, 8, 12~16, 18~21), again summarized in Table 19.4, portray the following Krippendorff Scenario, which is another case of the broader Guttman-Goodman Scenario:

1. Two coders set a quota for the black and white marbles. They also set the number of marbles to be twice the target sample. They fill the urn accordingly.
2. They take a target to be coded.
3. One coder draws a marble randomly from the urn, notes the marble's color, and puts it aside without placing it back into the urn. The other coder does the same from the same urn.
4. If both draw black, each reports positive; if both draw white, each reports negative; in either case they do not look at the target being coded. Only if one draws a black and the other draws a white would they code the target objectively, at which point they may honestly agree or disagree, and report accordingly.
5. The two coders calculate the average of positive cases and the average of negative cases they've reported. If one of the two averages reaches the predetermined quota, they report the remaining targets according to the quota, and end the coding session. If neither average reaches the quota, they repeat Step 2 and the subsequent steps.

When α is applied beyond the boundaries defined by the assumptions and illustrated in the Scenario, it creates abnormalities and paradoxes. Here we discuss three that are unique for α:

Paradox 7:   ***Punishing larger sample and replicability.***

Suppose two coders code 40 online news stories to see if they were commentaries in disguise. With $N=40$, they generate 20 positive agreements, 10 negative agreements, and 10 disagreements. This means a 62.5% & 37.5% distribution, $a_o=75\%$, and Krippendorff's $\alpha = 0.4733$, which may appear improvable given the relatively small N. Suppose the researcher expands the target sample 10 fold by coding 360 more stories. For the 400 targets combined, the coders produce 200 positive agreements, 100 negative agreements, and 100 disagreements, replicating the 62.5% & 37.5% distribution and 75% a_o. The only difference is Krippendorff's α, which is decreased to 0.4673. It's not a huge decrease. But for 10 times as much work of the same quality and the same agreement rate, we would not have expected *any* decrease.

This unexpected phenomenon will appear more dramatic if N is smaller. Suppose the coders take four stories out of their original 40, including two positive agreements, one negative agreement, and one disagreement. With the same distribution and the same agreement rate but a dramatically smaller N, one would not expect any improvement in the reliability score. Instead, Krippendorff's α improves to 0.5333, which is a 12.68% increase for one tenth of the work of the same quality. While calculating reliability on four items is not a good practice, α rewards it with a higher reliability score.

When the decrease in α caused by an increased N is large enough, it could offset or even overcome an increase in a_o, producing a "larger sample, higher agreement, but lower α." Suppose the researcher expands N from 4 to 1,000, producing 501 positive agreements, 251 negative agreements, and 248 disagreements. This would produce a much larger N and a slightly improved a_o (from 75.0% to 75.2%) while the distribution remains unchanged. Yet α still decreases, from 0.5333 to 0.4712. This phenomenon is limited to situations when the increase in a_o is small relative to the larger increase in sample size, and the resulted drop in α is usually not large. It however adds another dimension to the paradox.

Reliability is often understood as replicability. But in these cases α punishes replicability. The same phenomena do not exist for π, κ or other major indices, none of which is affected by N. In the three examples of N=4, 40, or 400, the other indices all remain the same. They report larger reliability in the example of N=1,000, because a_o is higher.

Two examples from Krippendorff (1980, pp. 133–135; 2007, pp. 2–3) can be adapted to illustrate the same phenomenon. Both have $N = 10$, distribution 70% and 30%, $a_o = 0.6$ and α = 0.09524. If N increases to 100 while distribution and a_o remain the same, one might expect α to improve or at least remain the same, but instead, α drops to 0.05238.

We found this paradoxical because we assumed normal studies in which researchers pretest 10 cases, calculate reliability, add 90, and test reliability again, all in full honesty. In this Grove-Riffe Scenario, more of the same quality deserves no punishments, and more of the better quality deserves rewards. Krippendorff's α, however, assumes that coders maximize random coding by drawing marbles *without replacement*. They don't simply "add cases." Instead they draw from 10 marbles each to code the 10 messages, then draw from 100 marbles each to code the 100 messages, including redrawing to recode the 10. More coding means more marbles, which mean more chance agreements, which have to be punished.

These phenomena are not isolated. They are a part of the paradoxical pattern of Krippendorff's a_c. Table 19.7 shows that Krippendorff's a_c is positively correlated with N: larger N leads to higher a_c, at any level of distribution! Higher a_c means lower reliability. Under a Grove-Riffe Scenario, larger N

means more cases coded hence higher replicability, which Krippendorff's α punishes systematically. When we see a larger N, we see more honest coding, for which the bar should *not* be raised. But when α sees a larger N, it sees more marbles drawn, hence more chance agreements, hence a raised bar.

Paradox 8:	***Purely random guessing can be somewhat reliable.***

Suppose two coders coded four television stories to see if they contain subliminal advertisements. The task was so difficult that the coders end up guessing randomly. As probability theory would predict, each of them reported two positives, two negatives, with a 50% agreement rate (a_o = .5, N = 4), as if they had flipped four coins each. As one might expect, most of the reliability indicators, including Scott's π and Cohen's κ, are exactly 0.00. Krippendorff's α, however, stands out at 0.125. It's a tiny sample and it is not a spectacular α. But why is it not zero?

In Krippendorff's α, only "drawing with quota and without replacement" qualifies as random (Assumptions 4, 12, and 18). Random guessing or flipping coins does not qualify, because neither allows quota and both have replacement. Guessing with coins generated more agreement than drawing with quota without replacement. We attribute the difference to "another kind of randomness," and do not believe it deserves a higher reliability score. Krippendorff's α attributes the difference to honest coding, and rewards it with a higher α.

Paradox 9:	***Random guessing may be more reliable than honest coding.***

Extending the above example, this α = 0.125, from a_o = .5, N = 4, from totally random guessing, is better than α = 0.095 from two Krippendorff examples, each having a_o = 0.6, N = 10, from totally honest coding (Krippendorff, 1980, pp. 133–135; 2007, pp. 2-3). So, according to α, more agreement from an objective process can be less reliable than less agreement from a random process. There are two reasons for this phenomenon. First, α assumes some of our random guessing is honest coding. Second, Krippendorff's examples have a larger N (10) than our coin flipping (4), and α assumes that larger N generates more chance agreements, which have to be "corrected for," meaning punished.

Paradoxes 7~9 offer some evidences that Krippendorff's α should not be used beyond the highly restrictive boundaries defined by the Krippendorff Scenario and the Krippendorff Assumptions.

Paradoxes and Abnormalities Shared by π, κ, α and Equivalents

Paradoxes are unexpected qualitative features of an index that seem to defy logic or intuition. There are also unexpected numerical outcomes of an index when it is used in typical research, which we will call abnormalities. Paradoxes and abnormalities are closely linked, we will number them consecutively. The purpose of the discussion is to further illustrate the assumptions.

In addition to its unique sample-size-related paradoxes, α shares paradoxes 2~5 with all other chance-adjusted indices. Further, π, κ and α also share a few of their own paradoxes and abnormalities, which we discuss below.

We will first discuss three abnormalities that have been better known for κ. We will show that π and α suffer from the same abnormalities. We will then discuss other abnormalities and paradoxes not yet in the literature. As noted earlier, all findings about π also apply to Siegel and Castellan's *Revised K* (1988) and Byrt's et al.'s *BAK* (1993), and findings about κ also apply to Rogot and Goldberg's A_2.

Abnormality 10:   High agreement, low reliability.

Feinstein and Cicchetti (1990) called this a paradox for Cohen's κ (1960). Lombard et al. (2002) and Krippendorff (2004b, p. 426) debated over the same phenomenon for κ and π. Here is a more dramatic example. Suppose two coders code 1,000 magazine advertisements for cigarettes in the United States, to see whether the Surgeon General's warning has been inserted. Suppose each coder finds 999 "yes" and one "no," with 998 positive agreements and two disagreements, generating a 99.8% agreement rate. But π, κ, and α are all below zero (-.001 or -.0005). Zero indicates a totally unreliable instrument. Given the near-perfect agreement, it's difficult to understand why the instrument is that bad.

Some authors found this paradoxical because they assumed the coders code honestly. The three indices, however, assume that all observed agreement (a_o=99.8%) is due to chance because each coder draws from 999 or 998 black marbles and one or two white marbles. The marbles show different colors only twice, which are the only opportunities for honest coding (Assumption 8). The coders disagrees both times, hence the low π, κ, and α.

Abnormality 11:   Undefined reliability.

When two coders agree that the distribution of one category is 100% and another is 0%, π, κ, and α is undefined. 0% and 100% and 100% and 0% are the two ends of all possible distributions, like the two ends of a ruler that define its length and scope. If a ruler is completely broken at both ends, it is probably not accurate in between.

Many found this paradoxical because we expected perfect agreement to be credited with a decent reliability score, and because we believed some agreements must be honest, no matter how skewed a distribution is. But π, κ, and α assume that a 0% and 100% target distribution means that all marbles are of one color, hence there is no chance for color mismatch and honest coding, hence π , κ , and α should not be calculated. In defense of the undefined π and α , Krippendorff (2004b) explained:

> Such data can be obtained by broken instruments or by coders who fell asleep or agreed in advance of the coding effort to make their task easy.... appropriate indices of reliability cannot stop at measuring agreement but must infer the reproducibility of a population of data; one cannot talk about reproducibility without evidence that it could be otherwise. When all coders use only one category, there is no variation and hence no evidence of reliability. (p. 425)

To those who assume coders intend to be honest, the explanation is still puzzling. Suppose 100% of the target population of magazine ads under study had the Surgeon General's warning. Suppose coders agreed that 100% of the target sample had the warning. Suppose there was no broken instrument, no falling asleep or agreeing in advance, but only honest and diligent coding, as evidenced in the perfect agreements between the coders, and between the sample and the population. Why is this not an "evidence" that reliability is good, or at least calculable?

Now that we know π , κ , and α is to be used only under assumptions of strict quota, maximum randomness, and trinity distribution within the Guttman-Goodman Scenario, Krippendorff's (2004b, p. 425) explanation could be sensible, if we think of his "population" as "marble population." Under strict-quota and trinity-distribution assumptions, zero variation in the observed targets is evidence for zero variation in the marbles. Coders *are assumed* to "agree in advance" to make the marbles all one color, and to code honestly *only* when the marbles mismatch. There is no chance for color mismatch, hence no chance for honest coding, hence no "evidence that it (the observation) could be otherwise.... [H]ence no evidence of reliability." Krippendorff's defense in effect provides support for our observation that π , κ , and α assume maximum randomness, strict quota, and trinity distribution.

Abnormality 12:   *Zero change in a_o causing radical drop in reliability.*

These indices are supposed to measure agreement. Feinstein and Cicchetti (1990) argued that Cohen's κ should rise and fall with agreement rate, a_o . So should all other reliability indices. Kraemer (1979) pointed out that, with no change in a_o , κ changes with "base rate," which we call "distribution." Uneven distribution generates lower κ than even distribution. Grove et al. (1981) and Spitznagel and Helzer (1985) called it the "base rate problem" for κ . Feinstein and Cicchetti (1990) called it a paradox for κ . It is not as widely known that π and α can produce the same abnormality.

Here is a stronger example for all three indices. Revising Abnormality 10, suppose two coders initially agree on 998 "yes" and one "no," plus one disagreement, producing a_o=99.9%, π=.6662, and κ=.6662, α=.6663. Suppose both coders flip an erroneous negative decision, resulting in 999 agreed positives and one disagreement, and increasing the average of the positives from 99.85% to 99.95%. While a_o remains 99.9%, π, κ, and α each drops from .666 to .0000 or -.0005, which covers two thirds of the distance between "perfectly reliable" and "totally unreliable."

This happens because the coders code honestly without quota, violating π, κ, and α's strict quota assumption. Distributions changed as the coders improved their work, violating the predetermined-distribution assumption. The violation of the same two assumptions also causes the next four abnormalities (13–16).

Abnormality 13:   Eliminating disagreements doesn't improve reliability.

Extending Abnormality 10: Suppose one coder finds his only negative finding erroneous and flips, reducing disagreements by half, and increasing agreements to 99.9%: One might expect π, κ, and α to improve half way toward 1, to be around 0.5. Instead, κ and α barely move, to be 0, and π remains negative, at -.0005. Suppose the other coder also flips his only negative finding, improving agreement to 100%. One might expect π, κ, and α jump to 1. Instead, none of the three can be calculated, repeating Abnormality 11.

Abnormality 14:   Tiny rise in a_o causing radical rise in reliability.

Again starting from Abnormality 10, with 998 agreements on "yes," suppose one coder flips his positive decision in one of the two disagreements. Now disagreements decrease to one and agreements increase to 999. a_o improves slightly from 99.8% to 99.9%. Given what we have seen in Abnormality 13, one might expect the three indices to change little. Instead, π and κ jump from −.001 to .6662, while α jumps from -.0005 to .6663, each covering two-thirds of the distance between "totally unreliable" and "perfectly reliable."

Abnormality 15:   Rise in a_o causing radical drop in reliability.

Suppose two coders initially had two disagreements and 998 agreements, with 997 positive and one negative, producing an a_o = 99.8%, π = .499, κ =. 4993, and α = .4992. Suppose one coder finds all his three negative decisions erroneous, and flips each, resulted in 999 positive agreements and one disagreement. While a_o increases to 99.9%, κ and α drop drastically to 0, and π drops even more, to -.0005.

Abnormality 16:   Honest work as bad as coin flipping.

Suppose we show at normal speed 60 television segments, 50 of which contain subliminal advertisements that are barely recognizable. One coder finds the ads in all 60 segments, making 10 false alarms, while the other recognizes only 40, calling 10 false negatives. The 40 positive agreements and 20 disagreements produce a 66.667% a_o and an 83.333% average distribution, which matches the target distribution. While the instrument may seem adequate, especially considering the difficult task, $\pi = -.2$, $\kappa = 0$, and $\alpha = -.2$.

Now suppose we ask the coders to flip coins *without looking at any television segments*. Their a_o is expectedly 50%, 16.667% lower than honest coding. Their average distribution is also expected to be around 50%, 33.333% lower than the target distribution. This, however, produces $\pi = 0$, $\kappa = 0$ and $\alpha = 0.0083$. So, honest coding that produces more accuracy and more agreement is no better or even worse than dishonest coding that produces less accuracy and agreement, according to π, κ, and α.

This appeared puzzling because we assumed all of the 67% agreements were honest under a Grove-Riffe Scenario. But π and α presume the coders draw from 50 black and 10 marbles. Without a single glance at the targets, they should generate 72% agreement, much higher than the 67% they actually report, leading to a justifiable $\pi = -.2$ and $\alpha = -.2$.

Under the Cohen Scenario, κ presumes one coder draws from 40 black and 20 white while the other from 60 black and no white. Without a glance at the TV, they should obtain 67% agreements, implying that they have not produced any honest agreement. So κ should be zero.

Paradox 17: Punishing Improved Coding.

Abnormality 15 is a case of improved coding causing a drastic drop in π, κ, and α, from halfway reliable (0.5) to not at all reliable (0)! Of all the symptoms of π, κ, and α, this one may be among the most troublesome. Abnormality 12 is another example. After the errors are corrected, π, κ, and α drop even more drastically.

Paradox 18: Punishing agreement.

The three a_c not only move significantly, they also move to punish the good and reward the bad. Table 19.3 shows that, when one coder's distribution N_{p2}/N is 100%, Scott's a_c is positively linked to the other coder's distribution N_{p1}/N; an increase in N_{p1}/N brings it closer to N_{p2}/N, producing a higher agreement a_o and a higher a_c, which means a higher bar. The same pattern exists when N_{p1}/N = 100%, N_{p2}/N = 0%, or N_{p1}/N = 0%. The maximum agreement at the lower left and upper right corners of Table 19.3 makes a_c=100%, which is impossible to pass. As agreement rate decreases from either corner along any of the four sides, a_c decreases at an averaged half rate, until maximum disagreement at the upper left or lower right corner where a_c = 50%, which is the lowest possible bar in Scott's π.

Tables 19.6 and 19.7 show that when the sample is large enough Krippendorff's a_c behaves almost exactly the same as Scott's a_c. Cohen's a_c behaves in the same pattern, except the paradox is twice as dramatic: as a_o decreases from either corner along any of the four sides of Table 19.5, a_c decreases at the same (rather than half) rate, until it reaches maximum disagreement at the upper left or lower right corner where a_c=0% (rather than 50%). Again, higher agreement brings a higher bar, and the lower agreement brings a lower bar.

While the paradoxical pattern is strongest in the four sides encompassing Tables 19.3, 19.5, and 19.6, it also manifests itself inside although in less dramatic rates. The three indices are advertised as general indices of reliability, which is defined as agreement. Why do they *systematically* punish agreement and reward disagreement?

We found this paradoxical because we compared across different distributions, violating the quota and predetermined-distribution assumptions. Each of the three indices would reward higher agreement, but only within a predetermined distribution decided by the quota(s). If the distribution changes, a different study including a different round of marble drawing is assumed. More skewed distribution in a different marble population produces higher chance agreement, hence less honest coding, which π, κ, and α punish according to Assumption 16.

Paradox 19:   *Radically and erratically moving bar.*

To highlight the dramatic paradoxes and abnormalities, the above examples used extremely uneven distributions, such as 99.8% & 0.2%. More even distribution such as 60% and 40% would produce the same pattern, although less dramatic symptoms. Scott's, Cohen's, and Krippendorff's chance agreements (a_c) are all functions of distribution. Uneven distribution produces higher a_c, which is *the* bar that a_o must pass in order to produce an above-zero index. Both a_c and a_o have100% as the maximum: The closer is a_c to100%, the less room above it, the less chance for a high index. When distribution reaches 0% or 100%, a_c reaches 100%, leaving *no* chance for a_o to pass a_c, which is the technical reason why π, κ, and α are all undefined there.

Tables 19.3, 19.5, and 19.6 show how a_c changes with two distributions. Chance agreement a_c can reach as high as 100%, but it moves gradually with no gap or abrupt jump, starting from 0% (Cohen), 49.7% (Krippendorff when N=100), or 50% (Scott). This demonstrates that the undefined π, κ, and α are not isolated incidents under extreme circumstances. They are symptoms of intrinsic defects of the three supposedly general indicators. The moving bars also explain why π, κ, and α change with distribution.

We found the phenomenon paradoxical because we didn't think the bar, as a part of the general indicator for typical studies, should move with distribution. But π, κ, and α are not general indicators. Each is to be used only when all of its assumptions are met. Under these assumptions, especially Assumptions 12, 15, 16, and 17 the bar should move.

Paradox 20:   *Circular logic.*

The three indices are functions of coder's observation of distribution, whose quality depends on the quality of the coding instrument. But that is the very instrument that the indices evaluate. The three indices depend on an instrument's reliability to assess the instrument's reliability! We found this circular because we thought the reported distributions embedded in π, κ, and α came from coders' observations. We were wrong. The distributions came from pre-determined quotas independent of the observations, according to Assumptions 12, 14, 15, and 17. The logic would not be circular if coders behave under a Scott, Cohen, or Krippendorff Scenario.

These paradoxes and abnormalities show tha π, κ, and α cannot be general indicators of reliability. They might be useful within highly restrictive boundaries defined by various assumptions and scenarios, beyond which the paradoxes and abnormalities arise.

Benini's β

Nearly 60 years before Cohen (1960), Italian sociologist Benini (1901) designed a chance-estimating formula that is identical to Cohen's Equation 14. Benini's chance removing formula is also similar to Cohen's (Equation 3), except it subtracts an extra $n_{pn} - n_{np}$ from the denominator:

$$\beta = \frac{a_o - a_c}{1 - a_c - |\, n_{pn} - n_{np}\,|} \tag{17}$$

Here n_{pn} is percent of cases Coder 1 judges as positive while Coder 2 judges as negative, and n_{np} is % of cases Coder 1 judges as negative while Coder 2 judges as positive. They are two components of between-coder disagreements. If all disagreements are strictly random, $n_{pn} = n_{np}$, hence $|n_{pn} - n_{np}| = 0$. So some may see $|n_{pn} - n_{np}|$ as nonrandom disagreements.

The denominator of Equation 3 is a reference scale. Benini's β (Equation 17) has a shorter reference scale than κ, which means β tends to be higher than κ across a scale when κ is above zero. So Benini's β is an elevated κ in the important 0–1 range, like I_r is an elevated ρ. So β adopts all assumptions, paradoxes, and abnormalities of κ, and adopts Assumption 8 of I_r.

Goodman and Kruskal's λ_r

Goodman and Kruskal (1954) proposed an agreement index, λ_r, based on a_c that behaves in some ways similarly to Cohen's (1960):

$$a_c = \frac{1}{2}\left(\frac{N_{l1}}{N} + \frac{N_{l2}}{N}\right) \tag{18}$$

One may interpret N_{11} and N_{12} as, respectively, individual modal frequency reported by each coder. Suppose on a binary scale Coder 1 reports 85 cases in Category 1 and 15 cases in Category 2, while Coder 2 reports 45 cases in Category 1 and 55 cases in Category 2, N_{11}=85, N_{12}=55, and a_c=(.85+.55)/2=0.7. Goodman and Kruskal's λ_r shares Equations 1, 3, 4, and 6 with other chance-adjusted indices. Replacing a_c in Equation 3 with the right side of Equation 18, we have Goodman and Kruskal's λ_r.

An alternative interpretation appears equally plausible, according to Fleiss (1975). $(N_{11}+N_{12})/2$ may be the modal average frequency reported by two coders, which in the above example would instead produce an a_c=(.85+.45)/2=.65. As Goodman and Kruskal did not provide a numerical example, we are unable to decide with certainty which interpretation they meant. The differences between the two interpretations would be analogous to the differences between κ and π, one assuming individual behaviors while the other presuming collective action. Given the limited space we will assume individual modal interpretation in the following discussion, and analyze the modal average interpretation in more details in a future study.

As N_{11} and N_{12} are a part of two coders' individual distributions, λ_r shares almost all assumptions and paradoxes we have discussed of Cohen's κ. Most notably, λ_r shares with κ the individual quota assumption (17). Goodman and Kruskal (1954) were the first we know to make Equation 3 explicit. Their λ_r also started the practice of sharing the chance-removing procedure while creating a unique chance-estimating formula.

Goodman and Kruskal's λ_r makes a set of unique assumptions, which we will put under one title, "modal color assumption." We analyze the assumption using κ as a reference:

Basic Assumption 22:   ***Coders code randomly when they draw the modal color.***

While κ assumes that coders code randomly every time marbles' colors match, λ_r assumes that coders code randomly some of the time when one or both coders draw a certain color. Specifically, λ_r assumes: (a) In addition to placing marbles into the urns according to individual quotas, each coder also notes which color has the largest number of marbles, which we call "mode color," in his or her urn. (b) The coders would code randomly every time both draw the modal color(s). (c) The coders would code randomly half the time when one draws his or her modal color but the other does not.

Equation 18 of λ_r uses addition to estimate chance agreement, while Equation 14 of κ uses multiplication. Consequently, Goodman and Kruskal's chance agreement is equal to or larger, often much larger, than Cohen's, which can be seen by comparing Table 19.8 with Table 19.5. Further comparison of Table 19.8 with Tables 19.3 and 19.6 and other estimates by other indices show that Goodman and Kruskal provide the highest estimation for chance agreement, which makes λ_r the most conservative estimation among the 22 indices reviewed in this chapter.

A Double-Based Index—Gwet's AC_1

Gwet's (2008, 2010) theory about coder behavior differs from the stated theories behind all other indices reviewed in this chapter. Gwet separated difficult cases from easy cases, in a way that appears much closer to the Grove-Riffe Scenario than the Guttman-Goodman Scenario. By adopting Equations 3, 4, and 6, however, Gwet's index, AC_1, adopts the maximum randomness assumption and the related paradoxes just like other chance-adjusted indices. Gwet's chance-estimating formulas are unique. While all other chance-adjusted indices use either category or distribution to estimate chance agreement, AC_1 uses both, hence "double-based." For a binary scale with two coders, Gwet's Equation 19 looks similar to Scott's Equation 11, except it switches one positive distribution rate (N_p/N) with a negative one (N_n/N):

$$a_c = \left(\frac{N_p}{N}\right)\left(\frac{N_n}{N}\right) + \left(\frac{N_p}{N}\right)\left(\frac{N_n}{N}\right) \tag{19}$$

All chance-adjusted indices before Gwet assume coders code randomly when marbles match, and code honestly when marbles mismatch. Accordingly, Scott's Equation 11 multiplies the positive rate by itself, and the negative rate by itself. In contrast, Gwet's Equation 19 multiplies the positive rate by the negative rate, implying a unique assumption: coders code randomly when marbles mismatch, and code honestly when marbles match.

The multiplication is done twice because the mismatches include black-white and white-black. A practical implication is that Gwet's coders have to agree on which color of which coder represents which category when the marbles mismatch, in a similar fashion that Scott's coders agree on which color represents which category when the marbles match. The choice of color-category pairing does not affect probability calculation.

While Scott had extended Equation 11 to three or more categories, Gwet also needed to extend Equation 19. But Gwet could not do a simple extension like Scott had done. More categories mean more marble colors hence more mismatches, which mean more random coding under Gwet's unique assumption discussed above. A simple extension of Equation 19 would lead to intolerably high a_c and intolerably low AC_1, especially when number of categories is large. To counter the effect, Gwet reintroduced categories (K) as a main parameter:

$$a_c = \frac{1}{(K-1)} \sum_{q=1}^{K} \left(\frac{N_q}{N} * \frac{N - N_q}{N}\right) \tag{20}$$

Table 19.8 Goodman and Kruskal's Chance Agreement (a_c) as a Function of Two Distributions*

		Distribution 1: Positive Findings by Coder 1 (N_{p1}/N) in %**										
		0	10	20	30	40	50	60	70	80	90	100
Distribution 2: Positive Findings by Coder 2 (N_{p2}/N) in %	100	100.0	95.0	90.0	85.0	80.0	75.0	80.0	85.0	90.0	95.0	100.0
	90	95.0	90.0	85.0	80.0	75.0	70.0	75.0	80.0	85.0	90.0	95.0
	80	90.0	85.0	80.0	75.0	70.0	65.0	70.0	75.0	80.0	85.0	90.0
	70	85.0	80.0	75.0	70.0	65.0	60.0	65.0	70.0	75.0	80.0	85.0
	60	80.0	75.0	70.0	65.0	60.0	55.0	60.0	65.0	70.0	75.0	80.0
	50	75.0	70.0	65.0	60.0	55.0	50.0	55.0	60.0	65.0	70.0	75.0
	40	80.0	75.0	70.0	65.0	60.0	55.0	60.0	65.0	70.0	75.0	80.0
	30	85.0	80.0	75.0	70.0	65.0	60.0	65.0	70.0	75.0	80.0	85.0
	20	90.0	85.0	80.0	75.0	70.0	65.0	70.0	75.0	80.0	85.0	90.0
	10	95.0	90.0	85.0	80.0	75.0	70.0	75.0	80.0	85.0	90.0	95.0
	0	100.0	95.0	90.0	85.0	80.0	75.0	80.0	85.0	90.0	95.0	100.0

*: Main cell entries are Goodman and Kruskal's Chance Agreement (a_c) in %.
**: N_{p1} is the number of positive answers by Coder 1, N_{p2} is the number of positive answers by Coder 2, and N is the total number of cases analyzed. See also Table 19.4 for various assumptions behind Cohen's κ and Goodman and Kruskal's λ_r.

In Equation 20, the part after the summation sign (Σ) is a simple extension of Equation 19 from two to K categories. N_q/N represents percent of targets in the qth category while $(N-N_q)/N$ represents percent of other targets. With a binary scale, N_q/N and $(N-N_q)/N$ become respectively N_p/N and N_n/N in Equation 19. The part before the summation sign is at least equally important. Multiplying by $1/(K-1)$ effectively lowers the estimated chance agreement, but it also implies another unique assumption:

Basic Assumption 23: Double drawing.

While other chance-adjusted indices all assume one round of marble drawing in the first stage of the two-stage coding (see "Overview of Chance-Adjusted Indices" above), Gwet's AC_1 assumes two rounds of marble drawing from two urns during the first stage. Two coders first draw with replacement from the first urn, which has K minus one colors and an equal number of marbles per color. If colors differ, they go to the second stage to code honestly. If the colors match, they draw with replacement from the second urn that has K colors and a distribution that equals the observed target distribution. Coders go to the second stage after this second drawing, and they code honestly if the colors match, and code by chance if the colors mismatch. This implies another unique assumption:

Basic Assumption 24: Marble mismatch or double-match equals honesty.

Gwet's AC_1 assumes that color mismatch in the first round or color matches in both rounds leads to honest coding, while color match in the first round followed by mismatch in the second round leads to chance coding.

By adopting the maximum random equations and using average distribution as a parameter in Equations 19 and 20, Gwet's AC_1 adopts all of Scott's assumptions except replacing Scott's Assumption 8, which is about color mismatch and honest coding, with Assumptions 23 and 24.

The Gwet assumptions lead to the following *Gwet Scenario,* which is another case of the broader Guttman-Goodman Scenario, for two coders and K categories:

1. Two coders prepare two urns.
2. They place marbles of $(K-1)$ colors into the first urn. Each color has an equal number of marbles.
3. They set a quota for the marble distribution in the second urn, and fill the second urn accordingly. They also agree on which color of which coder represents which category, which we will call *color-category scheme.*
4. They take a target to be coded.

5. One coder draws a marble randomly from the first urn, notes the marble's color, and puts it back. The other coder does the same from the same urn.
6. If the two colors differ, each coder codes and reports objectively, then skips to Step 9. If the colors match, they go to the next step.
7. One coder draws a marble randomly from the second urn, notes the color, and puts it back. The other coder does the same from the same urn.
8. If the two colors differ, each reports the results according to the predetermined color-category scheme, without looking at the target under coding. If the two colors match, each codes and reports objectively.
9. The two coders calculate the averages of the positive and negative cases they've reported. If one of the two averages reaches the predetermined quota, they stop drawing, report the remaining targets according to the quota, and end all coding. If neither average reaches the quota, they repeat Step 4 and the subsequent steps.

Which is right, one round or two rounds, color match or mismatch? If coders code as AC_1 assumes they do, two rounds and mismatch-or-double-match make the right estimation for honest coding. If coders code like π, κ, and α assume they do, one round and mismatch are right. But if coders code like the Grove-Riffe Scenario assumes they do, none of them is right.

With a binary scale, $K-1=1$, which means all marbles in the first urn are of the same color, so the colors always match, and the coders always go to the second urn for the second drawing. So the mismatch-or-2-matches-equals-honesty assumption can be simplified as match-equals-honesty assumption, as we discovered while analyzing Equation 19 above.

Comparing Table 19.9 with Table 19.3, we see that, with a binary scale, Gwet's chance agreement is a mirror image of Scott's, with the "mirror" positioned at the 50% and 50% distribution line. When each individual distribution is exactly 50% and 50%, Gwet's a_c is identical to Scott's, because here the probabilities of color match and mismatch are equal. When average distribution deviates from 50% and 50%, Scott's a_c increases while Gwet's a_c decreases at the same rate. When distribution becomes more uneven, Scott's a_c continues to increase toward 100%, while Gwet's a_c continues to decrease toward 0%. As Krippendorff's a_c and Cohen's a_c behave in the same pattern as Scott's, Gwet's a_c also behaves in opposite directions of Krippendorff's or Cohen's, as can be seen by comparing Table 19.9 with Table 19.6 or 19.5.

With a binary scale, Gwet's a_c assumes that color mismatch equals random coding while Scott, Cohen and Krippendorff's a_c assume the opposite, and Bennett et al.'s a_c is a constant at 0.5. So Gwet's a_c tends to be lower than the other four, hence Gwet's AC_1 tends to be higher than S, π, κ, and α. One extreme is when distribution is 0% or 100%, where π, κ, and α cannot be calculated because they all assume 100% chance coding and 0% honest coding, while, in contrast, AC_1 assumes 0% chance coding and 100% honest coding, producing a perfect $AC_1=1$.

Table 19.9 Gwet's Chance Agreement (a_c) as a Function of Two Distributions*

| | | Distribution 1: Percent of Positive Findings by Coder 1 (N_{p1}/N)** | | | | | | | | | | |
		0	10	20	30	40	50	60	70	80	90	100
Distribution 2: Percent of Positive Findings by Coder 2 (N_{p2}/N)**	100	50.0	49.5	48.0	45.5	42.0	37.5	32.0	25.5	18.0	9.5	0.0
	90	49.5	50.0	49.5	48.0	45.5	42.0	37.5	32.0	25.5	18.0	9.5
	80	48.0	49.5	50.0	49.5	48.0	45.5	42.0	37.5	32.0	25.5	18.0
	70	45.5	48.0	49.5	50.0	49.5	48.0	45.5	42.0	37.5	32.0	25.5
	60	42.0	45.5	48.0	49.5	50.0	49.5	48.0	45.5	42.0	37.5	32.0
	50	37.5	42.0	45.5	48.0	49.5	50.0	49.5	48.0	45.5	42.0	37.5
	40	32.0	37.5	42.0	45.5	48.0	49.5	50.0	49.5	48.0	45.5	42.0
	30	25.5	32.0	37.5	42.0	45.5	48.0	49.5	50.0	49.5	48.0	45.5
	20	18.0	25.5	32.0	37.5	42.0	45.5	48.0	49.5	50.0	49.5	48.0
	10	9.5	18.0	25.5	32.0	37.5	42.0	45.5	48.0	49.5	50.0	49.5
	0	0.0	9.5	18.0	25.5	32.0	37.5	42.0	45.5	48.0	49.5	50.0

*: Main cell entries are Gwet's Chance Agreement (a_c) in %.
**: N_{p1} is the number of positive answers by Coder 1, N_{p2} is the number of positive answers by Coder 2, and $_N$ is the total number of cases analyzed. See also Table 19.4 for various assumptions behind Gwet's AC_1.

There are a few exceptions to this general pattern. The first exception is when individual distributions are 50% and 50% where Gwet's a_c and the other four all equal 0.5, assuming a large enough sample for α. With a large enough sample, Gwet's a_c also equals Scott's and Krippendorff's when average distribution is 50% and 50%, even when individual distribution is not even. The second exception is when N is very small, leading to very low a_c by Krippendorff hence higher α than AC_I. The third exception is when two coders give highly uneven distributions at the opposite directions, which could lead to very low a_c by Cohen hence higher κ than AC_I.

When categories increase to three, Bennett et al.'s a_c is 1/3, while Gwet's a_c ranges from 0, when the coders report that all targets fall into one category, to $(2/9+2/9+2/9)/2=1/3$, when the targets distribute evenly into three categories. So Gwet's a_c is usually smaller and never larger than Bennett et al.'s a_c, hence AC_I is usually larger and never smaller than S. As categories increase further, the margins of AC_I over S increase further. That means that AC_I is more liberal than S and the equivalents.

Comparing AC_I with I_r is more complicated. With even distribution and a_o=0.5, I_r may be higher than AC_I. With uneven distribution and a_o closer to 0 or 1, AC_I may be higher than I_r. A simulation by Guangchao Charles Feng, a doctoral student at Hong Kong Baptist University School of Communication, shows I_r is more often higher than AC_I, and the difference is statistically significant (Zhao, Deng, Feng, Zhu, & Chan, 2012).

Low estimate of a_c means that AC_I assumes less chance agreement and more honest coding. So even though AC_I still assumes maximum randomness, its specific type of randomness is closer to complete honesty under a Grove-Riffe Scenario. Consequently, even though AC_I shares most of its assumptions with π, κ, and α (see Table 19.4), AC_I does not generate as many or as dramatic paradoxes or abnormalities (see Table 19.10) when used under a Grove-Riffe Scenario.

But there are still paradoxes and abnormalities. Most notably, by reintroducing category as a major parameter, AC_I brought back the classic paradox that Scott (1955), Cohen (1960) and Krippendorff (1970) worked hard to avoid, which is that empty categories increase reliability. In Scott's example (see Paradox 6) that originally had "male" and "female," by adding "hermaphrodite" and "indeterminant," S increases from .2 to .47, while AC_I increases from .2 to .52. The larger increase means an even more dramatic paradox. Gwet's AC_I also shares Paradoxes 2~5 with other chance-adjusted indices, and shares Paradoxes 19 and 20 with π, κ, and α. It also suffers a couple abnormalities of its own:

Abnormality 21:   *Same quality, same agreement, higher reliability.*

Suppose, as a way of testing our instrument, we give two coders 100 news stories, and ask the coders to judge whether the stories contain commentary opinions. We put in 80 easy cases, 40 of them having obvious commentaries, and other 40 obviously not. We put in 20 difficult cases that even experienced teachers can't judge with certainty. As expected, the two coders agree on 40 clearly positive cases, 40 clearly negative cases, and disagree on 20 difficult cases. Also as expected, of the 20 disagreements, each coder reports half positive and half negative. This generates an a_o=0.8 and AC_I=0.6.

Now we delete the commentaries from the 40 clearly positive cases, so they become clearly negative. With no other changes, we give the 100 stories to the same coders to be coded again. The two coders again agree on 80 easy cases and disagree on 20 difficult cases. Of the 20, each coder again reports half positive and half negative. The only change is that all 80 easy cases are now negative. Again a_o=0.8. But AC_I jumps from 0.6 to 0.7561.

The same coders, the same procedure, the same targets, the same quality of work, and the same agreement rate: Why the jump?

> ### *Abnormality 22:*   *Lower quality, less agreement, higher reliability.*

Suppose, instead of switching all 40 easily positive to easily negative, we switch only 36, and switch the other four to be difficult by making the commentaries ambiguous: Now we have 76 obviously positive and 24 difficult cases. As expected, the same two coders agree on 76 and disagree on 24, and each reports half and half for the difficult 24. As the task is more difficult, the quality of the coding and the agreement rate is understandably lower, a_o=0.76. Gwet's AC_I, however, is 0.69574, higher than the original 0.6 by nearly 1/6. Why?

We found the results "abnormal" because, again, we assumed the coders code honestly under the Grove-Riffe Scenario. AC_I assumes that the coders conspire to set quotas, place marbles into the second urn according to the quotas, and draw from it. They code randomly when marbles mismatch. In both abnormalities, target distribution moves from even to uneven, which means uneven marble distribution, less chance for color mismatches, less random agreement, lower bar, and therefore higher AC_I. The results would have seemed "normal" had coders indeed followed the Gwet Scenario.

When to Use Which Index?

Tables 19.4, 19.10, and 19.11 summarize our findings from various angles. A contrast emerges in Tables 19.4 and 19.10—the long list of assumptions, paradoxes, and abnormalities for what we believed to be the sophisticated and rigorous measures, such as α, and the much shorter list, just one unreasonable assumption and one paradox, for the supposedly primitive and flawed %-agreement a_o. To avoid this one assumption and one paradox, we adopted more and stronger assumptions, which created more and stagier paradoxes and abnormalities. Are the medicines worse than the disease?

The "medicines" cause not only more symptoms, but also more severe symptoms. Under a Grove-Riffe Scenario, the zero-chance-agreement assumption underlying a_o may hold sometimes, namely for "easy" and "textbook" cases with "well-developed protocols," while the maximum-randomness and other assumptions of the chance-adjusted indices may never hold.

Methodologists talk about chance agreement (a_o) as what *would* have happened, as a reference for comparison, but not what really happens in typical research. Following this thinking, each methodologist could have selected several hypothetical scenarios, such as flipping coins or throwing dice, drawing marbles of 60% or 90% distribution, from one or multiple urns, with or without replacement, in one, two, or more rounds, and code randomly with color match or mismatch, and so on. Each scenario can produce a unique chance agreement. There is an unlimited number of ways for "random coding," so we could have an unlimited number of chance agreements, as reference lines for comparison with just one index, which is %-agreement. Had we done that, we would not have assumed so many whimsical coders, and we would not have had so many paradoxes and abnormalities.

The methodologists, instead, used maximum-randomness equations (3, 4, and 6) to "remove" and "correct for" chance agreement. Each of them chose one hypothetical scenario of randomness, yet each believed his index applied to all real studies. This created a gap between theoretical understanding, which sees maximum randomness as hypothetical, and the actual computation, which treats maximum randomness as real, leading to the paradoxes, abnormalities, and confusions. We need to close this gap by developing a reliability index based on *complete honesty* and *variable randomness* assumptions under a Grove-Riffe Scenario.

Table 19.11 shows 18 cells under Column 1 titled "maximum random," seven of which occupied and 11 empty. Each empty cell represents an opportunity to propose a new index, and spend years advocating it. There are even more opportunities for creativity outside the table – e.g. rounds of drawing or number of urns could increase to three or more; marble colors could be any positive constant or variable; and marble distribution could be any percentage.

What we really need, however, is to fill the empty Column 2 titled "variable random," representing typical studies under a Grove-Riffe Scenario. We need reliability formulas based on empirical facts, rather than hypothetical imagination.

Liberal vs. Conservative Estimates of Reliabilities

Do some indices regularly give higher scores than others? Earlier, by comparing chance agreements estimated by Scott (Table 19.3) and Cohen (Table 19.5), we established that Scott's π is more conservative than Cohen's κ. By comparing Goodman and Kruskal's Table 19.8 with other counterpart estimates, we found that λ_r is more conservative than all others.

Lombard et al. (2002) used the "liberal" vs. "conservative" concepts. Krip-

Table 19.10 Paradoxes and Abnormalities of 22 Intercoder Reliability Indices

Paradox or Abnormality #	Paradox or Abnormality	%-Agreement a_o (Osgood, Holsti's CR), Rogot & Goldberg's A_1	Bennett et al.'s S, Guttman's ρ, Perreault & Leigh's I_r (C, G, k_n, PABAK, rdf-Pi, RE)*	Scott's π, (Rev-K, BAK)	Cohen's κ, (Rogot & Goldberg's A_2), Benini's β, Goodman & Kruskal's λ_r	Krippen-dorff's α	Gwet's AC_1
Prdx 1	Random guessing is reliable	yes					
Prdx 2	Nothing but chance		yes	yes	yes	yes	yes
Prdx 3	Apples compared with oranges		yes	yes	yes	yes	yes
Prdx 4	Humans are subgroup of men		yes	yes	yes	yes	yes
Prdx 5	Pandas are subgroup of men		yes	yes	yes	yes	yes
Prdx 6	Categories increase reliability		yes				yes
Prdx 7	Punishing larger sample & replicability					yes	
Prdx 8	Purely random coding is reliable					yes	
Prdx 9	Randomness more reliable than honesty					yes	
Abn 10	High agreement, low reliability			yes	yes	yes	
Abn 11	Undefined reliability			yes	yes	yes	
Abn 12	No change in a_o, large drop in reliability			yes	yes	yes	
Abn 13	Zero disagreement, no improvement in r_i			yes	yes	yes	
Abn 14	Tiny rise in a_o, huge rise in r_i			yes	yes	yes	

(continued)

Table 19.10 Continued

Paradox or Abnormality #	Paradox or Abnormality	%-Agreement a_o (Osgood, Holsti's CR), Rogot & Goldberg's A_1	Bennett et al.'s S, Guttman's ρ, Perreault & Leigh's I_r, (C, G, k_n, PABAK, rdf-Pi, RE)*	Scott's π, (Rev-K, BAK)	Cohen's κ, (Rogot & Goldberg's A_2), Berini's β, Goodman & Kruskal's $λ_r$	Krippen-dorff's α	Gwet's AC_1
Abn 15	Rise in a_o, huge drop in r_i			yes	yes	yes	
Abn 16	Honest coding as bad as coin flipping			yes	yes	yes	
Prdx 17	Punishing improved coding			yes	yes	yes	
Prdx 18	Punishing agreement			yes	yes	yes	
Prdx 19	Moving bar			yes	yes	yes	yes
Prdx 20	Circular logic			yes	yes	yes	yes
Abn 21	Same quality, same a_o, higher r_i						yes
Abn 22	Lower quality, lower a_o, higher r_i						yes

Table 19.11 What's Missing in the Map of Reliabilities?

	1. Maximum Random			2. Variable Random	3. Zero Random
	Observed Distribution = Marble Distribution		Categories = Colors		&-Agreement (a_o) Osgood's coefficient, Holsti's CR, Rogot & Goldberg's A1
	Individual Quota	Conspired Quota			
Color Mismatch = Honesty	Replacement drawing κ, A_2, β	π, Rev-K, BAK	ρ, S, G, RE, C, k_n I, PABAK, rdf-Pi.		
	Nonreplacement drawing	α			
Mismatch or Double Match = Honesty	Replacement Drawing	AC_1*	AC_1*		
	Nonreplacement drawing				
Largest Color = Honesty	Replacement Drawing λ_r				
	Nonreplacement drawing				

* AC_1 occupies two cells because it is double based, on category and distribution.

pendorff (2004b) objected, arguing that "trying to understand diverse agreement coefficients by their numerical results alone, conceptually placing them on a conservative-liberal continuum, is seriously misleading" (p. 412). We contend that patterns of numerical results can be helpful if they are grounded on an analysis of the underlying concepts and assumptions. Suppose we know that, with a large sample, λ_r is always lower than or equal to α, which is always lower than or equal to I_r, which is always lower than or equal to a_o, then if a researcher gets a very low λ_r, low α, high I_r, and very high a_o, she may look into the possibility that this is an artifact of the four indices, rather than focusing exclusively on possible deficiencies in her data, calculation, or coding instrument.

The key is that this pattern or continuum must be based on a systematic and comprehensive comparison, rather than anecdotal observations of isolated cases. Such a comparison is now feasible for three reasons.

First, of the 11 unique indices, the only difference between seven (%-agreement and equivalents, S and equivalents, λ_r, π and two equivalents, κ and an equivalent, α, and AC_I) is in chance agreement a_c. The other four are more complicated but still comparable, as β is an elevated κ, I_r is an elevated S, ρ is an approximate of S, and A_I is a reweighted a_o.

Second, there is an inverse relation between chance agreement a_c and agreement index r_i. This can be proven by assuming $a_{c1} \geq a_{c2}$, replacing a_o in Equation 3 with a_{c1} and a_{c2} to obtain $r_{i1} = (a_o - a_{c1})/(1 - a_{c1})$ and $r_{i2} = (a_o - a_{c2})/(1 - a_{c2})$. Rearranging the equalities and inequalities, we have $a_{c1} \geq a_{c2} \rightarrow r_{i1} \leq r_{i2}$. So if Index A's a_c is often larger and never smaller than Index B's a_c, we may conclude with confidence that A is more conservative than B.

Third, chance agreement a_c for all indices have been calculated for binary scale with two coders. Five of them are in Tables 19.3, 19.5, 19.6, 19.8, and 19.9. We also know $a_c = 0$ for a_o and A_I, $a_c = 0.5$ for S, I_r is an elevated S with the same a_c, β is an elevated κ with the same a_c, and ρ is an approximate of S with the same a_c.

So we can and should compare these a_c. If a hierarchy emerges for the nine a_c, it implies a reversed hierarchy for the nine groups of indices listed in Table 19.4.

The result of this comparison is in Table 19.12, which shows two hierarchies. The relative positions of any two indices in two different hierarchies are also meaningful, e.g., ρ is *generally* more liberal than β because ρ is in a higher cell in one hierarchy than β is in another hierarchy. They are in two different hierarchies because strict mathematical comparison between them does not yield stable results; that is, in less frequent or less important situations, an index in a lower cell in one hierarchy could produce a higher number than another index in a higher cell in another hierarchy. We assume two coders, binary scale, and reasonably large samples. When categories increase to three or more, category and double-based indices can be very liberal. When a sample reduces to 20 or below, Krippendorff's α can be very liberal.

To the extent that these indices have to be used, the liberal-conservative hierarchies in Table 19.12 may be helpful. If a researcher gets high scores from

Table 19.12 Liberal vs Conservative Estimates of Reliability for Binary Scale, Two Coders, and Sufficiently Large Sample

	Hierarchy 1	Hierarchy 2
More *liberal* estimates of reliability. ↕	%-Agreement (a_o) (pre 1901), Osgood's (1959), Holsti's *CR* (1969), Rogot & Goldberg's A_1 (1966)	%-Agreement (a_o) (pre 1901), Osgood's (1959), Holsti's *CR* (1969), Rogot & Goldberg's A_1 (1966)
	— Perreault & Leigh's I_r (1989) —	
	— Gwet's AC_1 (2008, 2010) —	
	Guttman's ρ (1946), Bennett et al.'s *S* (1954), Guilford's G (1961), Maxwell's *RE* (1977), Jason & Vegelius C (1979), Brennan & Prediger's k_n (1981), Byrt et al.'s *PABAK* (1993), Potter & Levine-Donnerstein's *rdf-Pi* (1999).	Benini's β (1901)
		Cohen's κ (1960), Rogot & Goldberg's A_2 (1966)
	Krippendorff's α (1970, 1980)	Krippendorff's α (1970, 1980)
	Scott's π (1955), Siegel & Castellan's *Rev-K* (1988), Byrt et al.'s BAK (1993)	Scott's π (1955), Siegel & Castellan's *Rev-K* (1988), Byrt et al.'s BAK (1993)
More *conservative* estimates of reliability.	Goodman & Kruskal's $λ_r$ (1954)	Goodman & Kruskal's $λ_r$ (1954)

Comparisons across the dotted lines are between the general patterns in situations that are more frequent and more important for typical research, e.g., when indices are zero or above, and when the distribution estimates of two coders are not extremely skewed in opposite directions. Comparisons involving Bennett et al.'s *S* and equivalents, its eight equivalents, and Perreault and Leigh's I_r assume binary scale. Comparisons involving Krippendorff's α assume sufficiently large sample.

the most liberal indices, she should not assume everything is fine. If she gets low scores from the most conservative indices, she should not immediately abandon the study. In both cases, check what other indices say. Researchers might pay more attention to the more liberal indices at early stages of a study when the protocols are formulated and coders are trained, and pay more attention to the more conservative indices in the later stages, so as to be cautious before publication. We developed software to assist researchers to calculate the various indices. The software is available at http://reliability.hkbu.edu.hk.

Discussions and Recommendations

Reliability assesses the empirical foundation of research. Ironically, the foundation of intercoder reliability calculation is more imaginative than empirical. Scientists and scholars tend to be skeptical that our findings are sound. We tend to guard against Type I errors more than Type II errors. We want to be rigorous, which often means conservative. This usually helpful tendency may have contributed to the development of some intercoder reliability indices. But can we be too conservative? Are we overcorrecting?

Perhaps some designers of the indices wanted to estimate and remove the occasional dishonesty, and used maximum randomness as a surrogate. They probably did not realize their formulas assume that all coders maximize randomness, hence were all dishonest, in every study. We know dishonesty does not exist in large amounts in all data. Even if it exists, it has no consistent patterns that can be modeled or estimated mathematically.

We need an index of intercoder reliability to accommodate typical research where coders try to be accurate but sometimes involuntarily allow some randomness. The existing indices do not meet this need. They assume either no or maximum randomness. The maximum-randomness assumption also entails other whimsical behaviors, such as setting quota or matching categories with marble colors. The chance-adjusted indices assume category, distribution or both as the factors affecting chance agreement, causing various paradoxes and abnormalities.

While a zero-random assumption likely overestimates reliability, we do not know when it overestimates or by how much. While maximum-random assumption may underestimate reliability in many situations, it may also overestimate in other situations, and, again, we do not know when it errs, in which direction, or by how much. We do know that some indices are more liberal than others, and the differences can be drastic.

When agreement is 100% and distribution is not 0% or 100%, major indices produce the same result—$r_i=1$. The indices start to differ when a_o is lower than 100%. This implies that researchers can help to overcome deficiencies of the indices by perfecting their protocols, assuming their distributions are not too skewed. The difficulty is that researchers cannot always expect perfect agreement or even distribution.

Researchers want the appearance of high reliability. The various indices and easy software allow shopping around until hitting the highest number. The two newer indices, I_r and AC_l, are more liberal than other chance-adjusted indices and are gaining in popularity. It should worry those striving to maintain high standards in academic publications. On the other hand, we should not equate low estimates with rigor, or complex calculations with sophistication. We should not require π or λ_r just for their low estimates. Given its unusual assumptions, we also should not require universal application of α, especially when the distribution is highly uneven or the sample is very small. We should not condemn research just because the observed distribution is uneven, presuming that the coders have fallen asleep, agreed in advance, or had a broken instrument. We also should not reward small sample sizes.

The frequent use of π, κ, and α may have had an undesired effect. All three favor more even distributions. Since the three have been applied by so many for so long, it may have reduced the publication of more uneven distributions of communication content and other things coded, rated, assessed, or diagnosed, making the world appear a bit more even than it actually is.

Our century-old concern over the zero-randomness assumption is legitimate. Our century-long search for a remedy assuming maximum-randomness and dishonest coders needs to stop. We need an index based on assumptions of variable-randomness and honest coders that uses degree of difficulty, rather than category or distribution, as the main factor.

Before such an index is established, researchers have to choose from the existing indices. We hope the practical recommendations in Table 19.13 can be of some help. As the table recommends various indices for various situations, we developed software (available at http://reliability.hkbu.edu.hk) to help researchers to calculate the indices. It is not a long-term solution. If and when the better index(es) is established, we should stop using Table 19.13 and the existing indices.

A major difference between indices is in their assumptions about coder behavior: %-agreement indices assume coders never do any random coding, while chance-adjusted indices assume coders maximize random coding. Category-based indices assume coders draw from marbles of equal distribution, while distribution-based indices assume quotas. This chapter derived these assumptions through mathematical analysis. Social scientists may be more receptive of empirical evidences. Future research may test these assumptions as empirical hypotheses, through simulations and controlled experiments. For instance, a researcher may assign some participants to code according to a Bennett Scenario, and others to follow a Scott Scenario, yet others follow other scenarios. We may consider derived assumptions supported if the observed "wrong" agreements produced by a scenario (e.g., Cohen Scenario), are closest to or best correlated with the predictions of the corresponding index; e.g., κ.

Table 19.13 When to Use or Not Use Which Index of Reliability

Down: Observed Condition	Indices that Tend to Produce **Unfairly Low** Reliability Scores	Indices that Tend to Produce Unfairly High Reliability Scores	Indices **Not Obviously Unfair** due to the Observed Condition at the Left, Hence may be Considered for Temporary Use until a More Reasonable Index isa Available [iv, v, vi]
Low agreement		&-Agreement a_o, Osgood's, Holsti's CR, Rogot and Goldberg's A_1	Gwet's AC_1, Perreault & Leigh's I_r, Bennett et al.'s S, Cohen's κ, Scott's π, Krippendorff's α
Highly uneven individual distribution	Benini's β [i], Goodman & Kruskal's λ_r, Scott's π, Cohen's κ[i], Rogot & Goldberg's A_2, Krippendorff's α, Byrt et al.'s *BAK*, Siegel and Castellan's *Rev-K* (1988)	Benini's β [i], Cohen's κ [i], Rogot & Goldberg's A_2, Gwet's AC_1	%-Agreement a_o, Perreault & Leigh's I_r, Bennett et al.'s S
Highly uneven average distribution	Benini's β, Goodman & Kruskal's λ_r, Scott's π, Byrt et al.'s *BAK*, Siegel and Castellan's *Rev-K* (1988), Cohen's κ, Rogot & Goldberg's A_2, Krippendorff's α	Gwet's AC_1	%-Agreement a_o, Perreault & Leigh's I_r, Bennett et al.'s S
$\rho \approx 0.5$		Perreault & Leigh's I_r	%-Agreement a_o, Gwet's AC_1, Bennett et al.'s S, Cohen's κ, Scott's π, Krippendorff's α
$N < 20$ [ii]		Krippendorff's α	%-Agreement a_o, Gwet's AC_1, Perreault & Leigh's I_r, Bennett et al.'s S, Cohen's κ, Scott's π

Down: Observed Condition	*Indices that Tend to Produce **Unfairly Low** Reliability Scores*	*Indices that Tend to Produce Unfairly High Reliability Scores*	*Indices **Not Obviously Unfair** due to the Observed Condition at the Left, Hence may be Considered for Temporary Use until a More Reasonable Index isa Available [iv, v, vi]*
$K \geq 3$ [iii]		Guttman's ρ, Perreault & Leigh's I_r, Bennett et al.'s S, Guilford's G, Maxwell's RE, Jason & Vegelius' C, Brennan & Prediger's k_n, , Byrt et al.'s *PABAK*, Potter & Levine-Donnerstein's redefined *Pi*, Gwet's AC_1	%-Agreement a_o, Cohen's κ, Scott's π Krippendorff's α

i   When individual distributions are highly uneven, Benini's β and Cohen's κ can be unfairly high when the two distributions are highly skewed at the opposite directions, e.g., one coder reports 95% positive while the other 95% negative; the two can be unfairly low when the two distributions are skewed at the same direction, e.g., both coders report 95% positive.

ii N is number of target cases analyzed.

iii K is number of categories in the nominal coding scale.

iv   Use with caution! While the indices in the extreme right cells are not necessarily unfair due to the observed condition in the extreme left cells of the same row, they may be unfair due to other condition(s) present in a study. For example, when a study uses three or more categories (last row), it does not make Scott's π unfair. But the same study may also have highly uneven distribution (second and third rows), which makes π unfairly low, so the researcher may have to use %-Agreement. Combination of conditions could make all available indices unfair for a given study, which is one of the reasons that a better index is needed.

v   In each cell of this column, the indices are listed according to their positions in the liberal-conservative hierarchies shown in Table 19.12. The information may be useful for meta analysts and other content analysts who wish to better evaluate their reliability level.

vi   We excluded all "equivalents" from this "not obviously unfair" column, as credits should go to the first designer(s).

Acknowledgments

This study was supported in part by HKBU Faculty Research Grant (2008 & 2009, Zhao PI), HKBU Strategic Development Fund (2009 & 2011, Zhao PI), and grants from Panmedia Institute (2010, Zhao PI) and ENICHD (R24 HD056670, Henderson PI). The authors acknowledge with gratitude the substantial contributions of Guangchao Charles Feng, and thank Jane Brown, Visne K.C. Chan, Timothy F. Hamlett, Sri Kalyanaraman, Juntao Kenneth He, Jing Lucille Li, Colin Sparks, and Ning Mena Wang for their support and assistance. The authors also thank the editor and reviewers of *Communication Yearbook 36*, whose questions, criticism, and suggestions helped to significantly improve this chapter.

References

Benini, R. (1901). *Principii di Demongraphia: Manuali Barbera Di Scienze Giuridiche Sociali e Politiche* (No. 29) [Principles of demographics (Barbera Manuals of Jurisprudence and Social Policy)]. Firenze, Italy: G. Barbera.

Bennett, E. M., Alpert, R., & Goldstein, A. C. (1954). Communication through limited response questioning. *Public Opinion Quarterly, 18,* 303–308.

Brennan, R. L., & Prediger, D. J. (1981). Coefficient kappa: Some uses, misuses, and alternatives. *Educational and Psychological Measurement, 41,* 687–699.

Byrt, T., Bishop, J., & Carlin, J. B. (1993). Bias, prevalence and kappa. *Journal of Clinical Epidemiology, 46,* 423–429.

Cohen, J. (1960). A coefficient of agreement for nominal scales. *Educational and Psychological Measurement, 20,* 37–46.

Cohen, J. (1968). Nominal scale agreement with provision for scaled disagreement or partial credit. *Psychological Bulletin, 70,* 213–220.

Feinstein, A. R., & Cicchetti, D. V. (1990). High agreement but low kappa: I. The problems of two paradoxes. *Journal of Clinical Epidemiology, 43,* 543–549.

Fleiss, J. L. (1975). Measuring agreement between two judges on the presence or absence of a trait. *Biometrics, 31,* 651–659.

Glander, T. (2000). *Origins of mass communications research during the American cold war: Educational effects and contemporary implications.* Mahwah, NJ: Erlbaum.

Goodman, L. A., & Kruskal, W. H. (1954). Measures of association for cross classification. *Journal of the American Statistical Association, 49,* 732–764.

Grove, W. M., Andreasen, N. C., McDonald-Scott, P., Keller, M. B., & Shapiro, R. W. (1981). Reliability studies of psychiatric diagnosis: Theory and practice. *Archives of General Psychiatry, 38,* 408–413.

Guilford, J. P. (1961, November). *Preparation of item scores for correlation between individuals in a Q factor analysis.* Paper presented at the annual convention of the Society of Multivariate Experimental Psychologists.

Guttman, L. (1946). The test-retest reliability of qualitative data. *Psychometrika, 11,* 81–95.

Gwet, K. L. (2008). Computing inter-rater reliability and its variance in the presence of high agreement. *British Journal of Mathematical and Statistical Psychology, 61,* 29–48.

Gwet, K. L. (2010). *Handbook of inter-rater reliability: The definitive guide to measuring the extent of agreement among multiple raters* (2nd ed.). Gaithersburg, MD: Advanced Analytics.

Hayes, A. F. (2009). Beyond Baron and Kenny: Statistical mediation analysis in the new millennium. *Communication Monographs, 76,* 408–420.

Hayes, A. F., & Krippendorff, K. (2007). Answering the call for a standard reliability measure for coding data. *Communication Methods and Measures, 1,* 77–89.

Holley, W., & Guilford, J. P. (1964). A note on the *G*-index of agreement. *Educational and Psychological Measurement, 24,* 749–753.

Holsti, O. R. (1969). *Content analysis for the social sciences and humanities.* Reading, MA: Addison-Wesley.

Jason, S., & Vegelius, J. (1979). On generalizations of the G index and the phi coefficient to nominal scales. *Multivariate Behavioral Research, 14,* 255–269.

Kraemer, H. C. (1979). Ramifications of a population model for kappa as a coefficient of reliability. *Psychometrika, 44,* 461–472.

Krippendorff, K. (1970). Bivariate agreement coefficients for reliability of data. *Sociological Methodology, 2,* 139–150.

Krippendorff, K. (1980). *Content analysis: An introduction to its methodology.* Newbury Park, CA: Sage.

Krippendorff, K. (2004a). *Content analysis: An introduction to its methodology* (2nd ed.). Thousand Oaks, CA: Sage.

Krippendorff, K. (2004b). Reliability in content analysis: Some common misconceptions and recommendations. *Human Communication Research, 30,* 411–433.

Krippendorff, K. (2007). *Computing Krippendorff's alpha reliability.* Philadelphia, PA: University of Pennsylvania Scholarly Commons. Retrieved from http://repository.upenn.edu/asc_papers/43

Lasswell, H. D. (1948). The structure and function of communication in society. In L. Bryson (Ed.), *The communication of ideas* (pp. 215–228). New York: The Institute for Religious and Social Studies.

Lombard, M., Snyder-Duch, J., & Bracken, C. C. (2002). Content analysis in mass communication research: An assessment and reporting of intercoder reliability. *Human Communication Research, 28,* 587–604.

Maxwell, A. E. (1977). Coefficients of agreement between observers and their interpretation. *British Journal of Psychiatry, 130,* 79–83.

Neuendorf, K. (2002). *The content analysis guidebook.* Thousand Oaks, CA: Sage.

Osgood, C. E. (1959). The representational model and relevant research methods. In I. de Sola Pool (Ed.), *Trends in content analysis* (pp. 33–88). Urbana: University of Illinois Press.

Perreault, W. D., & Leigh, L. E. (1989). Reliability of nominal data based on qualitative judgments. *Journal of Marketing Research, 26,* 135–148.

Popping, R. (1988). On agreement indices for nominal data. In W. E. Saris & I. N. Gallhofer (Eds.), *Sociometric research: Vol. 1. Data collection and scaling* (pp. 90–105). New York: St. Martin's.

Potter, W. J., &. Levine-Donnerstein, D. (1999). Rethinking validity and reliability in content analysis. *Journal of Applied Communication Research, 27,* 258–284.

R Development Core Team (2011). R: A language and environment for statistical computing. Vienna, Austria. Retrieved from http://www.R-project.org

Riffe, D., Lacy, S., & Fico, F. G. (1998). *Analyzing media messages: Using quantitative content analysis in research.* Mahwah, NJ: Erlbaum.

Riffe, D., Lacy, S., & Fico, F. G. (2005). *Analyzing media messages: Using quantitative content analysis in research* (2nd ed.). Mahwah, NJ: Erlbaum.

Rogot, E., & Goldberg I. D. (1966). A proposed index for measuring agreement in test-retest studies. *Journal of Chronic Diseases, 19*(9), 991–1006

Schramm, W. L. (1973). *Men, messages, and media: A look at human communication.* New York: Harper & Row.

Scott, W. A. (1955). Reliability of content analysis: The case of nominal scale coding. *Public Opinion Quarterly, 19,* 321–325.

Shrout, P. E., Spitzer, R. L., & Fleiss, J. L. (1987). Quantification of agreement in psychiatric diagnosis revisited. *Archives of General Psychiatry, 44,* 172–177.

Siegel, S., & Castellan, N. J. (1988). *Nonparametric statistics for the behavioral sciences.* New York: McGraw-Hill.

Spitznagel, E. L., & Helzer, J. E. (1985). A proposed solution to the base rate problem in the kappa statistic. *Archives of General Psychiatry, 42,* 725–728.

Tankard, J. W., Jr. (1988). Wilbur Schramm: Definer of a field. *Journalism Educator, 43*(3), 11–16.

Tinsley, H. E. A., & Weiss, D. J. (1975). Interrater reliability and agreement of subjective judgments. *Journal of Counseling Psychology, 22,* 358–376.

Tinsley, H. E. A., & Weiss, D. J. (2000). Interrater reliability and agreement. In H. E. A. Tinsley & S. D. Brown (Eds.), *Handbook of applied multivariate statistics and mathematical modeling* (pp. 95–124). San Diego, CA: Academic Press.

Zhao, X. (2011a). *When to use Cohen's κ, if ever?* Paper presented at the 61st annual conference of International Communication Association, Boston.

Zhao, X. (2011b). *When to use Scott's π or Krippendorff's α, if ever?* Paper presented at the annual conference of the Association for Education in Journalism and Mass Communication, St. Louis.

Zhao, X., Deng, K., Feng, G., Zhu, L., & Chan, V. K. C. (2012, May). *Liberal-conservative hierarchies for indices of inter-coder reliability.* Paper presented at the 62nd annual conference of International Communication Association, Phoenix, Arizona.

Zhao, X, Lynch, J. G., & Chen, Q. (2010). Reconsidering Baron and Kenny: Myths and truths about mediation analysis. *Journal of Consumer Research, 37,* 197–206.

Zwick, R. (1988). Another look at inter-rater agreement. *Psychological Bulletin, 103,* 374–378.

20 *Commentary*
A Dissenting View on So-Called Paradoxes of Reliability Coefficients

Klaus Krippendorff

University of Pennsylvania

In their preceding chapter on "Assumptions behind Intercoder Reliability Indices" Zhao, Liu, and Deng claim to have discovered numerous paradoxes and abnormalities. In logic, paradoxes can be resolved from a meta-perspective. So, in my comments on their chapter, I shall take a larger and more technical perspective of the issues these authors raise and will end with radically different recommendations. The reader will have to decide the merits of my critique. I contend that most of the authors' discoveries are the artifacts of being led astray by strange, almost conspiratorial uses of language.

To begin with the most basic question: Why testing reliability and what should its results tell us? Linguistically, reliability means the ability to rely on something. In much of the social sciences, reliability concerns the quality of data and of the process of generating them in pursuit of a particular research question. *Data* is the plural of *datum*; hence, data must always be numerous and varied. Data need to represent some real phenomena, be analyzable by available techniques, and provide information about the research questions concerning these phenomena. A measure that informs us of whether data can be relied upon has to correlate with the extent to which one can trust their roots in reality.

In pursuit of the assurances that reliability is to provide, content analysts typically ask:

1. What counts as proper reliability data to start
2. What can available reliability coefficients do. Can they accommodate
   - Unitizing or coding
   - Assignments of more than one coding category
   - Various levels of measurement: nominal, ordinal, interval, ratio, and other metrics
   - More than two observers, coders, or judges
   - Observers who contribute unequal amounts of data, causing data to be missing
   - Different sample sizes?

3. How to interpret the values obtained by a chosen reliability coefficient.
4. Where to find available software, what it does and does not do.

The authors of the chapter under review limit themselves to reliability coefficients for the binary coding of given units of analysis by two coders. This is the most reduced situation that content analysts might face. It does not mention processes of unitizing, and multiple descriptions of unitized matter, which are not as simple to assess. It also omits the assessment of reliability involving more than two coders, missing and ordered data. Since the latter is where most content analysts need advice, I will briefly discuss them at the end of this commentary.

Reliability Basics

One needs to be clear about the epistemological difference between agreement and reliability. Agreement is measurable among observers, coders, or judges. Reliability needs to be inferred from several conditions. Reliability is an attribute of data or of the coding process generating them, which enables researchers to decide whether they can proceed with their analysis. The relationship between agreement and reliability is not one-to-one, however, as the authors suppose. Let me state with Equation 1 what it takes to infer reliability, briefly discuss each requirement, and then continue where the authors' conceptions fail.

$$\left\{ \begin{array}{c} \text{Preparatory} \\ \text{conditions} \end{array} \right\} \text{ and } \left\{ \begin{array}{c} \textbf{Information} \text{ in} \\ \text{data or instrument} \end{array} \right\} \times \left\{ \begin{array}{c} \textbf{Agreement} \\ > \text{baseline} \end{array} \right\} \Rightarrow \left\{ \begin{array}{c} \textbf{Reliability} \text{ of} \\ \text{data or instrument} \end{array} \right\} \quad (1)$$

The preparatory conditions are

- There have to be a number of observers, coders, or judges, as many as possible but at least two.
- For the coding process to be replicable in principle, their qualifications need to be explicit and found elsewhere as well.
- They must be given the same explicit instructions and training for replication elsewhere.
- They must be given the same set of phenomena to observe, read, or judge and record or code.
- They must work independently of each other, not communicate about the specific phenomena they face, not discuss how they coded particular phenomena, and not deliberate on the reasons for the judgments they end up recording, or revising what they have done after discussions.

Failing to meet any one of these conditions renders agreement coefficients not interpretable in terms of reliability.

The Baseline that Agreement Needs to Exceed Is the Condition of Statistical Independence of the Data Generated and the Phenomena of Interest

Data are always analyzed in view of the phenomena they represent. Whereas the phenomena of interest may be of fleeting existence, too difficult to be measured physically, or symbolic, requiring reading by qualified individuals, data are expected to endure formal analysis, be re-searchable. In the absence of evidence about what observers, coders, or judges saw and recorded as data, consensus among them is the only epistemologically available indication that distinct phenomena are represented in differences among data. The idiosyncrasies of the coders and the circumstances in which data are made may influence reliability but must not be given credit. Hence observers and circumstances must be treated as interchangeable.

Because consensus may not be perfect, agreement coefficients suitable for inferring the reliability of data or of the instrument generating them must define a scale with two reference points:

- The condition of perfect consensus among all observers, coders, or judges involved;
- The condition for data to be statistically unrelated to the phenomena they are intended to represent.

To claim reliability, the observed agreement must deviate little from perfect consensus and be significantly larger than the agreement expected under conditions of statistical independence of data and the phenomena of interest.

By these criteria, not all coefficients discussed by the authors are suitable for assessing the reliability of data or the instruments generating them. Being called reliability indices does not make them so. Agreement well above the stated baseline is essential, but not sufficient, however; hence the following two informational requirements.

Informational Requirements: Any One of Two Apply (Krippendorff, 2011a)

1. When the *reliability of an instrument* is to be assessed all possible decisions that observers, coders, or judges could be making, all categories an instrument makes available for coding, and all points on a given scale must have occurred with adequate frequencies. One could not talk about the reliability of an instrument if only a part of that instrument, say 2 out of 20 categories, were actually used. In such a situation, the reliability test is not generalizable to the 18 unused categories. In other words, the variety in reliability data must cover all available coding options. Let me give two ordinary examples.
   - Fire extinguishers tend to have a pressure gauge. Usually the pointer on the dial does not change. Their owners have no ability to vary the

gauge and therefore no clue whether it indicates hydrostatic pressure or is stuck and dysfunctional. Therefore, by law, fire extinguishers need to be checked by professionals who can de- and repressurize the extinguisher. Without demonstrable variability, there is no evidence of the reliability of the gauge.

- Nurses, measuring the temperature of patients, would start distrusting their thermometer if the second patient had the same temperature as the first. To check whether it works, they would measure something known to have another temperature and discard the thermometer if it does not respond accordingly. Variability or information is an essential requirement of the reliability of any device.

2. When the *reliability of data* is to be assessed, the actual number of ≥ 2 categories which an instrument makes available is unimportant, but data need to have enough information to answer the research questions under consideration. This requirement may be less obvious and benefits from two examples.

- Suppose a researcher wants to test whether two phenomena correlate. She will have to record at least two variables that must show some variation, provide information about the distinctions among the phenomena in question. If one or both variables do not vary, correlations cannot be established conceptually and cannot be calculated either. Such data exhibit no evidence about distinctions within the phenomena of interest and no information about the research question. In the absence of variability, a reliability test cannot provide the researcher with the desired assurances that the data are reliable.

- Let me use the second example to illustrate the authors' first conceptual problem.

First Conceptual Problem

Ignoring the informational context in which questions of the trustworthiness of data making processes arise and confusing the numerical values of so-called agreement coefficients with the reliability to be inferred.

Suppose an instrument manufacturer claims to have developed a test to diagnose a rare disease. Rare means that the probability of that disease in a population is small and to have enough cases in the sample, a large number of individuals need to be tested. Let us use the authors' numerical example: Suppose two separate doctors administer the test to the same 1,000 individuals. Suppose each doctor finds one in 1,000 to have the disease and they agree in 998 cases on the outcome of the test. The authors note that Cohen's (1960) κ, Scott's (1955) π, and Krippendorff's (1980, 2004a, 2012) α are all below zero ($-.001$ or $-.0005$). They are aware that "zero indicates a totally unreliable instrument," but continue: "Given the near-perfect agreement (of 99.8%), it is difficult to understand why this instrument is that bad." Echoing Feinstein and Cicchetti (1990), Lombard, Snyder-Duch, and Bracken (2002), and Gwet's (2002) arguments, they proclaim that chance-adjusted indices entail the paradox (their abnormality 10) of "high agreement but low reliability" as sure proof of the inadequacy of these coefficients.

Dissenting from their conclusion, I contend that a test which produces 99.8% negatives, 2% disagreements, and not a single case of an agreement on the presence of the disease is totally unreliable indeed. Nobody in her right mind should trust a doctor who would treat patients based on such test results. The inference of zero reliability is perfectly justifiable. The paradox of "high agreement but low reliability" does not characterize any of the reliability indices cited but resides entirely in the authors' conceptual limitations.

How could the authors be so wrong? I suggest that it is due to being sidetracked by talking of %-agreements rather than focusing on the distinctions among subjects to which the test is applied. In fact, in their example there is not a single distinction on which the test results agree. The paradox is resolved by reference to the informational context of the reliability data (Krippendorff, 2011a). Note that in Equation 1, the amount of information (distinctions or variation) and the agreement above the baseline are products. Accordingly, inferences from high agreement coefficients to the reliability of data or of measuring instruments is compromised by low amounts of information in the data; just as large amounts of information would become meaningless in the face of low agreement coefficients. In the authors' example, not only is variation extremely low, agreement is near chance as well. Even if there were perfect agreement on the presence of the disease in one out of 1,000 cases, agreement would be measured as perfect, but the informational requirement would not be met, raising doubts about the significance of the inference. And if nobody turns out to have the disease and agreement on the absence of the disease is 100%, the test does not prove to be discriminating, reliability would be mathematically indeterminate but zero by the complete absence of information in the data. Increasing the sample size is one remedial response to this situation. Finding a pretest of the subjects that would increase the probability of the disease's occurrence in the sample would be another.

Second Conceptual Problem

Deriving abnormalities and paradoxes of reliability coefficients, from privileging %-agreement as an honest path to reliability and ignoring the need for consensual distinctions.

I suppose here language has taken the authors for a ride. We speak of "chance-corrected" or "chance-adjusted agreement measures" as if agreement were the primary measure and its correction a minor modification of it. With this conception, it would not make sense indeed how, in the previous example, an agreement coefficient could "ignore the fact" of observing 99.8% agreement and yielding near zero reliability. If one observes a coefficient to behave so "unimaginably," I could understand how one would be led to look for abnormalities or declare paradoxes, and it does not seem farfetched to dismiss such coefficients for their apparent flaws. I contend this is the result of privileging %-agreement over the ability of relying on data within which differences relate to distinctions among the phenomena made by coders.

The authors' conceptual problem is compounded by their introduction of "honesty" into the discussion. The authors conceive of %-agreement measures as assuming "that all observed agreements are honest and 'true,' that is, there is no chance agreement." They contrast four %-agreements with 18 mostly chance-adjusted agreement measures and claim from the start that the latter "assume that coders are largely dishonest. They (the coders) code deliberately randomly without looking at the targets under coding. They maximize such chance coding, and they limit honest coding to occasions dictated by random chance."

How wrong can one be? Yes, %-agreement is a scale that ranges from 0 = maximum disagreement to 1 = maximum agreement. Both extremes tend to deviate from what would happen by chance but in unequal degrees. The point on this scale at which one would have to conclude that data are totally unreliable is variable and not determinable without reference to knowledge of circumstances that are extraneous to the %-agreement scale. For example, knowing that we are flipping a coin leads us to expect 50% agreement and throwing a six-sided dice yields 16.667%. Its mathematical blindness for chance disqualifies %-agreement as a reliability measure. The authors' paradox number 1, that in %-agreement, "random guessing is reliable," does not follow from its mere blindness for chance. Random guessing is never reliable. Again, the authors' confusion of a quantitative coefficient with the reliability that can be inferred only when other conditions are met, here burdened by their conception of honest coding, gets in the way of a clear interpretation of the mathematics of %-agreement. There also is absolutely no basis for claiming that chance-adjusted agreement coefficients assume dishonesty on the part of coders.

Third Conceptual Problem

> Confusing what coders do with the hypothetical condition under which data are considered unrelated to the phenomena they are intended to represent

Coders tend to be given instructions to examine something and record what they have found, mostly in predefined categories or scale values. They are generally unaware about the statistics by which their reliability is assessed although they usually know that achieving high reliability is the ideal and therefore tend to do their best in attaining it. Coders might not achieve perfect agreement because of ambiguous coding instructions, badly defined units of analysis, phenomena that are hard to distinguish or do not fit available categories, or experiencing stress. However, the point at which data are totally unreliable, the hypothetical condition of statistical independence of data and the phenomena they are meant to distinguish, is neither meaningful to coders nor reproducible by them.

It is a leap of logic when the authors say that: "By removing chance agreement (from the % of agreement observed between coders)...these (chance-adjusted) reliability indices assume that deliberate and systematic chance coding is not hypothetical, but real—no empirical research should 'remove' or 'correct for' anything that's not real." And then proceed to develop step-by-step index-specific scenarios for how "coders maximize random coding and code honestly only when marbles' colors mismatch: Nothing but chance in the first stage" of the coding process.

Unlike what the authors claim, there is absolutely no assumption in any of the indices reviewed that coders are dishonest or code randomly. Coders do not role dice or draw marbles from urns, and coefficients do not predefine quotas for coders' use of categories. The scenarios described by the authors contradict textbook accounts for coding data (e.g., Krippendorff, 1980, 2004a, 2012; Krippendorff & Bock, 2009; Neuendorf, 2002; Potter & Levine-Donnerstein, 1999) and all of my experiences with conducting content analyses. Drawing marbles from urns is a metaphor that may be useful to explain what is meant by chance, but none of the coefficients assume that coders actually do code randomly, nor do they employ randomness in their calculations (see the authors' sixth conceptual problem). I consider all assumptions and paradoxes based on the metaphorical scenarios that the authors have constructed to be flawed.

Fourth Conceptual Problem

> Creating paradoxes from strange if not illogical interpretations of mathematically unambiguous expressions related to %-agreement.

The authors examine the role of two separate %-agreement scales:

- The observed agreement a_o and its complement, the observed disagreement d_o: $a_o + d_o = 1$
- The chance agreement a_c and its complement, the chance disagreement d_c: $a_c + d_c = 1$

The equations $a_o + d_o = 1$ and $a_c + d_c = 1$ are a mathematical consequence of nominal scale coding by two coders involving the distinction between agreement and disagreement, between matching and nonmatching categories, or between same and different codes chosen for characterizing given units of analysis. They are not questionable assumptions as the authors claim. Observed and chance (dis)agreements characterize two different distributions, the first observed and the second hypothetical.

From the equation $a_c + d_c = 1$ the authors conclude that "chance coding constitutes 100% of all coding." And because "all major reliability indices ... state or imply $a_o + d_o = 1$, ... hence $a_o + d_o = a_c + d_c$, which means 'all coding equals all chance coding,' or 'all coding is chance'." Here again, the authors confuse what coders do with the statistical reference point for totally unreliable data that coders never experience. Approvingly quoting Riffe, Lacy, and Fico (2005, p. 151), who write, quite agreeably, "that agreement can take place by chance does not mean it does," the authors feel the need to ask "is there at least some honest coding?" Finding no place for "honesty" in the equation $a_c + d_c = 1$, they conclude that this equation is incorrect and therefore chance-adjusted "indices are all incorrect," and come to their paradox 2: "Nothing but chance," or everything is assumed to be chance to begin with. There is no basis for this conclusion.

Equation 2 shows the most common forms of chance-adjusted indices:

$$r_i = \frac{a_o - a_c}{a_{max} - a_c} = \frac{a_o - a_c}{d_c} = \frac{(a_o - a_c)}{(a_o - a_c) + d_o} = 1 - \frac{d_o}{d_c} \qquad (2)$$

In the first form, r_i is the proportion of the observed above chance agreement, $a_o - a_c$, and the largest possible above chance agreement, $a_{max} - a_c$. It relates what is observed to what could be observed. To most users of statistics, coefficients with this interpretation are common and make perfect sense. Moreover and for this form, when a coding task becomes complex and chance agreement a_c becomes very small, the proportion r_i asymptotically converges to a_o.

However, the authors note that $a_{max} = 1$ and $a_c + d_c = 1$ imply $a_{max} - a_c = d_c$, so that in the second form of Equation 2 this proportion reads: agreement above chance/ chance disagreement. This reading prompts the authors to claim their paradox 3 that chance-adjusted indices compare "apples with oranges." This simple substitution does not change the proportion r_i, however, or reveal anything outstandingly wrong.

Similarly, from the two equivalent ways of expressing chance agreement: $a_o - a_c = d_c - d_o$, the authors come to their paradox 5, claiming that $(a_o - a_c) + d_c = d_c$ "is analogous to saying that 'pandas and humans are two subgroups of men'." Yet, the third form of Equation 2 is familiar in measurement theory as the proportion of true score, $a_o - a_c$ /true score $a_o - a_c$ + the measurement error d_o – a perfectly meaningful proportion and hardly paradoxical.

The fourth form of Equation 2 can be obtained by replacing a_o with $1 - d_o$ and a_c with $1 - d_c$. It is the general form of Krippendorff's α, see Equations 4 and 5. This form expresses r_i not as deviating from a_c (at which point $r_i = 0$) but from the other end, as deviating from perfect agreement, $a_{max} = 1$ (at which point $r_i = 1$). d_o / d_c is the proportion of observed disagreement and the disagreement that could be observed if data were totally unreliable. Again, to me, this form makes perfect sense. However, the authors see it as paradoxical as well. Their paradox 4 reads: "Dividing d_o by d_c is analogous to saying 'humans are a subgroup of men'."

I see absolutely no benefit in characterizing chance-adjusted agreement coefficients with groundless paradoxes and abnormalities. They say nothing about these coefficients but much about the authors' conspiratorial conceptions. Their Table 19.10 lists 22 similar paradoxes and abnormalities. Space does not permit me to critically examine them one by one.

Fifth Conceptual Problem

> Ordering reliability coefficients in terms of a liberal/conservative dimension according to their numerical values hides their mathematical differences and misleads researchers regarding the choices available to them.

In the authors' Table 19.12, %-agreement, including Osgood's (1959) and Holsti's (1969) *CR*, are listed as the most liberal reliability indices and Goodman and Kruskal's (1954) λ_r the most conservative with all others falling somewhere between these two extremes—as if this were their essential differences. The basis of their scaling is the numerical values these coefficients achieve relative to each other. Table 19.13 groups these differences in terms of "unfairly high" or "unfairly low."

Arranging available reliability coefficients on a scale of the achievable magnitudes suggests that researchers have choices among these coefficients and interpreting this scale as liberal vs. conservative moreover suggests that researchers can choose among them according to their attitude toward the unreliability of their data. If they can tolerate unreliability, a liberal index would do, and if their research results have important consequences, a more conservative index might be appropriate. The authors mention but do not condemn shopping around for coefficients yielding the highest numbers. They cite my earlier objection to this scale (Krippendorff, 2004b, p. 412) but counter it with the belief that an understanding of their paradoxes and assumptions would be helpful in making appropriate choices. I continue to maintain that constructing such a continuum not only hides the mathematical structures of these coefficients that cause them to differ numerically, but also undermines the whole idea of testing the reliability of data. For once, the authors' indiscriminate list includes many coefficients that by Equation 1 could not possibly serve as indicators of reliability.

I already mentioned the %-agreement scale, the proportion of agreements a_o, which is blind to any indication of the point at which data would have to be considered totally unreliable. This disqualifies %-agreement as a reliability index, notwithstanding its frequent use by statistically naïve researchers.

The same can be said about Maxwell's (1977) $RE = 2a_o - 1$, which linearly transforms %-agreement to range between −1 and +1. It is zero at 50% but this midpoint does not indicate the condition at which data would be totally unreliable either. Incidentally RE is mathematically equivalent to Guilford's G (Holley & Guilford, 1964) and Byrt, Bishop, and Carlin's (1993) PABAK.

Rogot and Goldberg's (1966) two coefficients mentioned by the authors as reliability coefficients range between 0 and 1, merely altering the intervals of %-agreement a_o, also without a reliability-appropriate baseline.

Gwet's (2002) AC_1, intended to overcome the paradox of "high agreement but low reliability," has to be disqualified as well. For binary data, it replaces the chance agreement a_c in the first form of Equation 2 by its complement the chance disagreement d_c: $AC_1 = \dfrac{a_o - d_c}{1 - d_c}$. Besides its odd behavior, its zero-value occurs when all coincidences are equal, much as for S, which is a highly specialized case of a reliability-adequate baseline. I have no idea why Zhao et al. do not recognize that here "apples are subtracted from oranges."

The other extreme on the authors' liberal/conservative scale is occupied by Goodman and Kruskal's (1954) λ_r. Goodman and Kruskal motivate λ_r in terms of its ability to predict the probability of agreement as one goes from no information about either coder's categorizations to knowing the other coder's categorizations. Putting the average of the two modal probabilities of categories in place of a_c in Equation 2 acknowledges the inequality of marginal distributions, much as in κ, has the advantage of yielding an index that varies between −1 and +1, but does not provide a reference at which data can be said to be totally unreliable. $\lambda_r = 0$ is unrelated to reliability and so is the part of the λ_r-scale between 0 and 1.

Regarding the so-called chance-adjusted agreement coefficients the authors face a sixth conceptual problem:

Sixth Conceptual Problem

> Noticing but failing to appreciate the reliability implications of different conceptions of chance.

The authors label any a_c in the first form of Equation 2 "chance-agreement" and suspect that there are a large number of them but then distinguish between only two kinds: category based and distribution based chance-adjusted indices. This distinction does not isolate proper reliability coefficients from those that do not qualify. The literature contains at least three chance concepts:

- The logical conception of chance which defines the probability of the elements in a product set as the algebraic product of the inverse of the number of elements in each component set.
- The association-statistical conception of chance equates chance with that probability distribution in cross tabulations of two or more variables for which associations or correlations among these variables is absent. Applied to coding, coders take the place of variables, and chance equals the statistical independence of the two coders' individual uses of categories. Chance exists when one coder's use of categories is not predictable from those of the other.

- In reliability tests, coders are treated as interchangeable, rendering the reliability-statistical conception of chance as that probability distribution of value coincidences which exhibits no statistical relationship between units coded and values used by all observers, coders, or judges (see the above definition of the baseline that agreements need to exceed).

Only the latter is appropriate in coefficients with valid reliability interpretations, as will be seen in the following.

Let me visualize with Figure 20.1 the chance agreements for Bennett, Alpert, and Goldstein's (1954) S, standing for all other coefficients based on the logical conception of chance, Cohen's (1960) κ and Benini's (1901) β representing the association-statistical conception of chance, and Scott's (1955) p and Krippendorff's (1970, 1980, 2004a, 2012) α, manifesting reliability statistical conceptions of chance.

Evidently, the logical conception of chance depends entirely on the number of categories available for coding: a_c is the inverse of that number. The limitations of this chance conception are correctly discussed by the authors. However, what the authors summarily describe as distribution based, apparently involves three very different conceptions of chance.

In the case of Cohen's κ and Benini's β, two coders A and B judge N units of analysis. Unequal use of categories 0 or 1 is reflected in unequal marginal distributions. In a footnote, the authors assert that when the two coders' individual distributions are uneven, κ and β can be "unfairly high." True, but as already stated, the choice of coefficients should not be a matter of fairness or of one's liberal/conservative attitude toward data, but of the adequacy of their mathematical structure. One can see that a_c for κ and β, represented by the two shaded areas in their cross-tabulation of both coders' values, are not symmetrical around its diagonal, as would be required for representing observed as well as chance agreements, visually demonstrating the association-statistical conception of chance at work. This disqualifies κ and β as proper reliability coefficients for not treating coders interchangeably, giving their individual idiosyncrasies credit in the calculation of a_c.

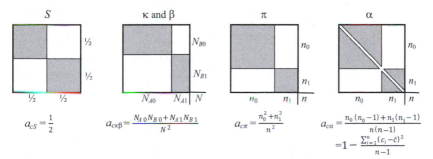

Figure 20.1 Expected agreements a_c for S, κ, β, π, and α and binary data.

There are two quantitative consequences of this chance conception. The first, recognized in the authors' footnote as "unfair," is their increase when marginal distributions disagree. As noted by Brennan and Prediger (1981), "judges who independently, and with no a priori knowledge, produce similar marginal distributions must obtain a much higher agreement rate to obtain a given value of kappa, than two judges who produce radically different marginals. Cohen's kappa gives the former judges no credit for producing agreement in marginals. Indeed, they are in a sense penalized" (p. 692). Actually, κ *adds* a correlate of this disagreement to its agreement value.

The second is that marginal disagreements prevent κ but not β from reaching 1.000. This property is less recognized in the literature because at its maximum, κ seems to account for marginal disagreements without clear indication of how. This is where β enters. Unlike in κ where with reference to the first form of Equation 2: $a_{max} = 1$, β's a_{max} is the largest agreement possible within the constraints of unequal margins, reaching 1.000 when the observed agreement equals that maximum. But $\beta = 1.000$ is then far removed from perfect reliability, disqualifying β as a reliability coefficient on this additional ground. Widespread use of κ notwithstanding, it is a mistake to list κ and β as optional agreement coefficients without qualifications.

Now to the chance agreements for Scott's π and Krippendorff's α in Figure 20.1: Several observations can shed light on their properties:

First, unlike in κ and β, the a_c's of π and α are defined from the joint distribution of n values used by all coders in categorizing N units of analysis. For two coders, $n = 2N$. The authors seem to privilege the individual distributions in κ and β when calling the joint distribution in π and α dismissively "conspired," not realizing that proper reliability coefficients must relate the latter to the phenomena of interest.

Second, unlike for κ and β, one may appreciate the symmetry of the frequency-dependent shaded areas that represent the chance agreement of π and α.

Third, the two square matrices consist of a cross-tabulation of all n values collectively contributed by all coders, that is, they contain all pairs of values that could be formed from the values in the joint distribution. Pairs of matching values are shaded and a_c is the proportion of pairs of matching values and all possible pairs. Although one can expect that Monte Carlo simulations or other randomization devices would approximate a_c as well, the definitions and computations of a_c for κ, β, π, and α are deterministic. The authors references to "randomness," "random guessing," "random coding," or "randomly drawing marbles from an urn," are completely metaphorical, unrelated to how a_c is obtained in fact, certainly not describing coders' behavior, and in effect misleading the authors' findings.

Fourth, the authors do not like how α corrects for small sample sizes and point out that α is the only coefficient that does that—as if majority opinions mattered. They consider it counterintuitive that under conditions of a constant a_o, α becomes larger when sample sizes become smaller. I am suggesting that this intuition is due to the confusion, discussed in the authors' first conceptual problem, of the role of the amount of information (variation and sample size) and of the agreement coefficients involved, and moreover, not recognizing what π and α differentially count as chance agreement.

For the latter, let me start with π. It assumes infinite sample sizes owing to the fact that its chance agreement is computed from probabilities $\Sigma_c p_c^2$ where c is a category or value. To account for small sample sizes, one has to take finite numbers into consideration. With the sample size $n = \Sigma_c n_c$, the whole matrix, cross-tabulating all n^2 pairs of values, can be decomposed into three numbers:

$$n^2 = \underbrace{\sum_c \sum_{k \neq c} n_c n_k + \sum_c n_c (n_c - 1) + n}_{n(n-1)}$$

(3)

The double sum in Equation 3 enumerates all pairs of mismatching values. The single sum enumerates all pairs of matching values. The remaining n is the number of values that n^2 pairs with themselves. Comparing the matrix for π with that for α in Figure 20.1, one may see the difference. The shaded area $\Sigma_c p_c^2$ for π includes the number of values paired with themselves, the shaded area $\sum_c \dfrac{n_c (n_c - 1)}{n(n-1)}$ for α excludes this number. The latter is consistent with variance notions which underlie α. $\sum_{i=1}^n (c_i - \bar{c})^2$ does not double count any of the n values c_i. Pairs of identical values are the artifact of multiplication, not enumeration, agree by definition, inflate a_c, and introduce a bias that has the effect of undervaluing π. The authors are plainly wrong in judging α to be too large when samples are small. It is π that is too small by including in its chance agreement n self-matching value pairs. Consequently, Scott's π is not free of that bias when sample sizes are too small.

The authors also claim that κ, β, π, and α assume that sample sizes and probability distributions are decided before a reliability study and cannot be changed as more reliability data are added. There is no evidence for this assertion. Usually, the categories of a coding instrument are fixed. Coders are confronted with uncategorized recording units, examine them one at a time, and are given complete freedom to choose among available categories whichever they deem appropriate. As the number of coded units grows the joint distributions of values may change with it. Reliabilities may be checked as the data making process advances.

Since the authors have looked for paradoxes in these coefficients, I might mention a true epistemological dilemma, which has motivated Bennett et al.'s S to be reinvented several times. This concerns the probability distribution in the population of phenomena, unknown before coding a sample of them, but used to estimate chance agreement from potentially unreliable coding processes. Because that distribution is unknown independent of the coding process, some proponents of S prefer not to estimate this distribution and instead resort to what is known: the logical probability of their coding categories, notwithstanding the known biases of S (Krippendorff, 2012, p. 303). By contrast, users of chance-corrected coefficients π, κ, α, r_{ii}, and ρ_c, take the collective judgments of all coders as the only and best estimate of these population proportions. Perreault and Leigh (1989) had the interesting idea of estimating population distributions only from values on which coders agree, but did not develop it further. My approach to this dilemma is to use as many coders as possible so that their collective distribution has a better chance to sideline individual differences.

The Scope of and Mathematical Relations between Available Reliability Coefficients

After my critique of the authors' chapter, I can be brief and address some of the initially mentioned questions that content analysts tend to pose.

To be clear, coefficients that correct %-agreement a_o, are limited to where %-agreement can be obtained. This is why S, κ, β, and π are restricted to two coders and nominal data. The binary data that the authors discuss are the smallest subset of these situations, easily analyzed, rare in practice, and far removed from what happens in content analysis and other forms of generating data. To be of practical value, I want to address the range of options available, starting with the form of reliability data.

Because coders need to be interchangeable in all reliability considerations, references to them are redundant and can be omitted. This allows all reliability data to be represented in terms of the frequencies with which available values are assigned to a given set of recording units, that is, in the form of the values-by-units matrix in Table 20.1. If data cannot be represented in this form, they do not qualify as reliability data for coding.

Incidentally, for two coders and no missing data in Table 20.1, all frequencies $n_u. = 2$. And for binary data, there would be only two rows of values, say

Table 20.1 The Values-by-Units Representation of Reliability Data

Units:		1	2	.	.	.	u	.	.	.	.	.	N	
Values:	1	n_{11}	n_{21}	.	.	.	n_{u1}	.	.	.	.	.	n_{N1}	$n._1$
	.	.	.				.						.	
	c	n_{1c}	n_{2c}	.	.	.	n_{uc}	.	.	.	.	.	n_{Nc}	$n._c$
	.	.	.				.						.	.
	m	.	.	.			.						.	
Totals:		$n_1.$	$n_2.$	.	.	.	$n_u.$	.	.	.	.	.	$n_N.$	$n..$

Where n_{uc} = the number of values c assigned to unit u. $n_{uc} \leq m$ observers. n_{uk} by analogy

$n_u. = \Sigma_c\, n_{uc}$ = the number of values assigned to unit u

$n._c = \Sigma_{u|n_u.\geq 2}\, n_{uc}$ = the number of pairable values c occurring in the reliability data (omitting all units with lone or no values: $n_u. \leq 1$)

$n.. = \Sigma_{u|n_u.\geq 2}\, n_u.$ = the total number of all pairable values in the reliability data (omitting all units with lone or no values: $n_u. \leq 1$); $n.. \leq mN$

for $c = 0$ and 1. Having limited themselves to these kinds of data, the authors could not appreciate the scope of Krippendorff's α, which is depicted in Figure 20.2. Because different levels of measurement impose unlike weights of mismatching values, not of agreements, references to agreements in Equation 2 cannot serve generalizations to metrics other than the nominal metric, which is why α takes the fourth form in Equation 2, $\alpha = 1 - \frac{D_o}{D_e}$:

$$\alpha_{metric} = 1 - \frac{D_o}{D_e} = 1 - (n.. - 1)\frac{\sum_u \frac{1}{n_{u.} - 1} \sum_c n_{uc} \sum_{k>c} n_{uk\ metric}\delta^2_{ck}}{\sum_c n_{.c} \sum_{k>c} n_{.k\ metric}\delta^2_{ck}} \tag{4}$$

Where $_{metric}\delta^2_k$ is a difference function available for nominal, ordinal, interval, ratio, and other kinds of data (Krippendorff, 1980, 2011b, 2012). For binary data and two coders, α_{metric} reduces to:

$$\alpha_{binary} = 1 - \frac{D_o}{D_e} = 1 - (n.. - 1)\frac{\sum_u n_{u0}n_{u1}}{n_{.0}n_{.1}} \tag{5}$$

Most computations of α, including of its distribution, can be performed with SPSS or SAS macros written by Andrew Hayes, available at http://www.afhayes.com: $\Rightarrow$ SPSS and SAS Macros $\Rightarrow$ KALPHA.

By focusing on mere numerical differences among a variety of coefficients, the authors failed to realize the mathematical relationships between these coefficients and the conditions under which one is a special case of the other. Figure 20.2 depicts the scope of α as the most general coefficients and where the other coefficient fit.

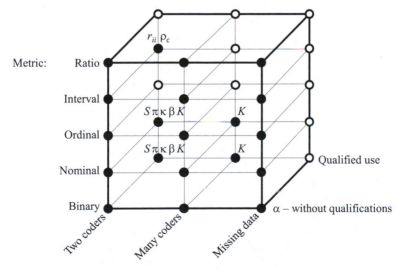

Figure 20.2 Cube of available reliability coefficients.

Missing in Figure 20.2 are statements of the conditions under which the available coefficients qualify for use as reliability coefficients. These can be found in Table 20.2.

To give some substance to these qualifications, let me explore just one coefficient, Fleiss's (1971) kappa, renamed K by Siegel and Castellan (1988). K is a generalization of π to a fixed number $m \geq 2$ of coders and equals π when $m = 2$. Thus, the conclusion drawn from an examination of K applies to π as well. In terms of Table 20.1, Fleiss's K is defined as:

$$K = \frac{P(A) - P(E)}{1 - P(E)}, \quad \text{where} \quad \begin{cases} P(A) = \dfrac{1}{N} \sum_{u=1}^{N} \sum_{c} \dfrac{n_{uc}(n_{uc} - 1)}{m(m - 1)} \\[2ex] P(E) = \sum_{c} \left(\dfrac{n_{.c}}{mN} \right)^2 = \sum_{c} p_c^2 \end{cases} \tag{6}$$

The resemblance to the first form in equation 2 is apparent. According to Equation 3, $n_{uc}(n_{uc} - 1)$ is the number of matching values c in unit u. $\dfrac{n_{uc}(n_{uc} - 1)}{m(m - 1)}$ is the proportion of that number and the number of possible pairs of values in unit u, so that $P(A)$ is the average number of pairs of values found matching within all units.

The form of $P(E)$, although enumerating pairs of values as well, is surprisingly different. It is the average number of pairs of matching values in the data as a whole, according to Equation 3, also including $n.. = mN$ values paired with themselves, agreeing by definition, not by pairing all given values of the same kind.

What does this difference mean? First, K and π reveal themselves as inconsistent measures. $P(A)$ excludes all pairs of identical values, but $P(E)$ includes these pairs. Second, by including pairs of identical values that agree *a priori*, $P(E)$ exaggerates the expected or chance agreement and introduces a bias into K that causes it to be smaller than what it should be. The only consolation is that the effect of this inconsistency becomes asymptotically less effective when sample sizes become large. Third, suppose $P(E)$ would be defined consistent with $P(A)$, that is: $P(E)' = \sum_{c} \dfrac{n_{.c}(n_{.c} - 1)}{n_{..}(n_{..} - 1)}$, then K and π would equal α when each unit is categorized by all of a fixed number m of coders. Thus, when sample sizes grow to infinity, K and π asymptotically approximate α_{nominal} but remain merely special cases of α. When samples are small, K and π undervalue reliability. To approximate α_{nominal} with K within a desired precision, the number of units coded needs to be $N > 2(1-K)/m \cdot \text{Precision}$. So, when $K = 0.800$, obtained by $m = 5$ coders, and the desirable Precision is 0.001, these coders need to code at least $2(1-0.8)/5 \cdot 0.001 = 80$ units of analysis in order to overcome K's bias. The sample size is the only difference between K and π and α_{nominal}. Table 20.2 lists these requirements for the other chance-corrected coefficients discussed here.

Table 20.2 A Comparison of the Scope and Adequacy of Reliability Coefficients

Coefficient	Limited to	Qualifying Conditions
Bennett et al's (1954) S and its relatives	• Two coders • Nominal data	• All available categories are used • Marginal distributions are uniform • Sample size $N > (1–S)/2 \cdot$ Precision
Scott's (1955) π	• Two coders • Nominal data	• Sample size $N > (1–\pi)/2 \cdot$ Precision
Cohen's (1960) κ Benini's (1901) β	• Two coders • Nominal data	• Marginal distribution are identical • Sample size $N > (1–\kappa)/2 \cdot$ Precision $\quad\quad N > (1–\beta)/2 \cdot$ Precision
Fleiss' (1971) K	• m coders • Each unit coded • Nominal data	• Sample size $N > (1–K)/m \cdot$ Precision
Pearson's (1901) intraclass correlation r_{ii} Lin's (1989) ρ_c	• Two coders • Interval data	• Sample size $N > (1–r_{ii})/2 \cdot$ Precision $\quad\quad N > (1–\rho_c)/2 \cdot$ Precision

κ, β, and π are all numerically equal when the two coders' marginal frequencies show no disagreement. Zwick (1988) proposed a test for marginal equality as a condition of κ's applicability as a reliability coefficient. I am including κ and β in Table 20.2 with this qualification but find it impractical to have to test for κ's applicability when α is available directly and without that bias.

I did not mention Pearson's (1901) intraclass correlation coefficient r_{ii}. His original proposal was to apply the product-moment correlation coefficient to a coincidence matrix, which consists of an initial contingency matrix plus its inverse (Tildesley, 1921), resulting in a symmetrical matrix with $2N$ entries and marginal frequencies that agree. There is also Lin's (1989) concordance correlation coefficient ρ_c, a near reinvention of Krippendorff's (1970) α. Both asymptotically approximate α for interval data when sample sizes are large.

Comparing the mathematical structures of these reliability coefficients confirms the generality and scope of Krippendorff's α. Figure 20.2 shows α not only to be in good company, but also providing researchers with uniform standards for accepting or rejecting the reliabilities of a diversity of data and/ or the processes that generate them. I am afraid, the authors' paradoxes and abnormalities do not reveal anything of interest to content analysts.

References

Benini, R. (1901). *Principii di Demografia* (Manuali Barbera Di Scienze Giuridiche Sociali e Politiche) [Principles of demographics (Barbera manuals of jurisprudence and social policy, No. 29)]. Florence, Italy: G. Barbera.

Bennett, E. M., Alpert, R., & Goldstein, A. C. (1954). Communication through limited response questioning. *Public Opinion Quarterly, 18,* 303–308.

Brennan, R. L., & Prediger, D. J. (1981). Coefficient kappa: Some uses, misuses, and alternatives. *Educational and Psychological Measurement, 41,* 687–699.

Byrt, T., Bishop, J., & Carlin, J. B. (1993). Bias, prevalence and kappa. *Journal of Clinical Epidemiology, 46,* 423–429.

Cohen, J. A. (1960). A coefficient of agreement for nominal scales. *Educational and Psychological Measurement, 20,* 37–46.

Feinstein, A. R., & Cicchetti, D. V. (1990). High agreement but low kappa: I. The problems of two paradoxes. *Journal of Clinical Epidemiology, 43,* 543–549.

Fleiss, J. L. (1971). Measuring nominal scale agreement among many raters. *Psychological Bulletin, 76,* 378–382.

Goodman, L. A., & Kruskal, W. H. (1954). Measures of association for cross classification. *Journal of the American Statistical Association, 49,* 732–764.

Gwet, K. L. (2002). Kappa statistic is not satisfactory for assessing the extent of agreement between raters. *Statistical Methods 1.* Retrieved from http://agreestat.com/research_papers/kappa_statistic_is_not_satisfactory.pdf

Holley, W., & Guilford, J. P. (1964). A note on the *G*-index of agreement. *Educational and Psychological Measurement, 24,* 749–753.

Holsti, O. R. (1969). *Content analysis for the social sciences and humanities.* Reading, MA: Addison-Wesley.

Krippendorff, K. (1970). Estimating the reliability, systematic error, and random error of interval data. *Educational and Psychological Measurement, 30,* 61–70.

Krippendorff, K. (1980). *Content Analysis: An Introduction to its Methodology.* Thousand Oaks, CA: Sage.

Krippendorff, K. (2004a). *Content analysis: An introduction to its methodology* (2nd ed.). Thousand Oaks, CA: Sage.

Krippendorff, K. (2004b). Reliability in content analysis: Some common misconceptions and recommendations. *Human Communication Research 30*(3), 411–433. Retrieved from http://repository.upenn.edu/asc_papers/242

Krippendorff, K. (2011a). Agreement and information in the reliability of coding. *Communication Measures and Methods 5*(2), 93–112. Retrieved from http://repository.upenn.edu/asc_papers/278

Krippendorff, K. (2011b). Computing Krippendorff's alpha-reliability (rev. ed). Retrieved from http://repository.upenn.edu/asc_papers/43 (Original work published 2007)

Krippendorff, K. (2012). *Content analysis: An introduction to its methodology* (3rd ed.). Thousand Oaks, CA: Sage.

Krippendorff, K., & Bock, M. A. (2009). *The content analysis reader.* Thousand Oaks, CA: Sage.

Lin, L. I. (1989). A concordance correlation coefficient to evaluate reproducibility. *Biometrics, 45,*1, 255–268.

Lombard, M., Snyder-Duch, J., & Bracken, C. C. (2002). Content analysis in mass communication research: An assessment and reporting of intercoder reliability. *Human Communication Research, 28,* 587–604.

Maxwell, A. E. (1977). Coefficients of agreement between observers and their interpretation. *British Journal of Psychiatry, 130,* 79–83.

Neuendorf, K. (2002). *The content analysis guidebook.* Thousand Oaks, CA: Sage.

Osgood, C. E. (1959). The representational model and relevant research methods. In I. de Sola Pool (Ed.), *Trends in content analysis* (pp. 33–88). Urbana: University of Illinois Press.

Pearson, K. et al. (1901). Mathematical contributions to the theory of evolution: IX. On the principle of homotyposis and its relation to heredity, to variability of the individual, and to that of race. Part I: Homotyposis in the vegetable kingdom. *Philosophical Transactions of the Royal Society, 197*(Series A), 285–379.

Perreault, W. D., & Leigh, L. E. (1989). Reliability of nominal data based on qualitative judgments. *Journal of Marketing Research, 26,* 135–148.

Potter, W. J., & Levine-Donnerstein, D. (1999). Rethinking reliability and validity in content analysis. *Journal of Applied Communication Research, 27,* 258–284.

Riffe, D., Lacy, S., & Fico, F. G. (2005). *Analyzing media messages: Using quantitative content analysis in research* (2nd ed.). Mahwah, NJ: Erlbaum.

Rogot, E., & Goldberg I. D. (1966). A proposed index for measuring agreement in test-retest studies. *Journal of Chronic Diseases, 19*(9), 991–1006.

Scott, W. A. (1955). Reliability of content analysis: The case of nominal scale coding. *Public Opinion Quarterly, 19,* 321–325.

Siegel, S., & Castellan, N. J. (1988). *Non-parametric statistics for the behavioral sciences* (2nd ed.). New York: McGraw-Hill.

Tildesley, M. L. (1921). A first study of the Burmese Skull. *Biometrika 13*(2–3), 176–262. Retrieved from http://www.jstor.org/pss/2331753

Zwick, R. (1988). Another look at inter-rater agreement. *Psychological Bulletin, 103,* 374–378.

About the Editor

Charles T. Salmon is Professor of Communication at Nanyang Technological University, Singapore. He previously held the Ellis N. Brandt Chair in Public Relations and is Past Dean of the College of Communications at the Michigan State University. Previous positions include the University of Wisconsin–Madison and Emory University; Fulbright Fellow at Tel Aviv University; Visiting Professor at the Norwegian School of Management and the University of Iowa; Visiting Scientist at the U.S. Centers for Disease Control and Prevention; and social marketing consultant and trainer for UNICEF in Kazakhstan. His research focuses on the intersection of public information, public health, and public opinion.

About the Associate Editors

Cindy Gallois is an Emeritus Professor in Psychology and Communication at the University of Queensland. She is a Fellow of the Academy of the Social Sciences in Australia, International Communication Association, Society of Experimental Social Psychology, and International Academy of Intercultural Relations. She is a past president of the International Communication Association, the International Association of Language and Social Psychology, and the Society of Australasian Social Psychologists. Her research interests encompass intergroup communication in health, intercultural, and organisational contexts, most recently involving the impact of communication on quality of patient care.

Christina Holtz-Bacha is Professor of Communication at the University of Erlangen-Nürnberg, Germany. Prior to her current position she taught at universities in Mainz, Bochum, and Munich. She was a Visiting Scholar at the University of Minnesota, and a Research Fellow at the Joan Shorenstein Center on the Press, Politics and Public Policy at the John F. Kennedy School of Government, Harvard University and a guest researcher at the University of Gothenburg, Sweden. She is Coeditor of the German journal *Publizistik* and has served as Chair of the Political Communication Division of ICA. She has published widely in the area of political communication and media policy. Among her most recent publications is the two-volume *Encyclopedia of Political Communication*, coedited with Lynda L. Kaid.

Joseph B. Walther is Professor of Communication and of Telecommunication, Information Studies and Media at Michigan State University. The author of several original theories and numerous empirical studies on computer-mediated communication, he has held regular or visiting appointments in Psychology, Information Science, and Education at Northwestern, Rensselaer Polytechnic, Cornell, Kent State, the University of Manchester, and elsewhere. He is associate editor at *Human Communication Research* and the *Journal of Media Psychology*, was an officer in the Academy of Management and ICA. He has twice received the National Communication Association's Woolbert Research Award for articles that offered new conceptualizations of communication that influenced thinking in the discipline for more than 10 years.

About the Contributors

Yair Amichai-Hamburger is Director of the Research Center for Internet Psychology at The Sammy Ofer School of Communications, The Interdisciplinary Center, Herzliya, Israel. He has received awards from the Academy of Management and the American Library Association. His research interests include Internet use and well-being, intergroup contact on the Internet, and virtual teams. He is the editor of *The Social Net, Human Behavior in Cyberspace;* and *Technology and Psychological Well-being.*

Joel Best is Professor of Sociology and Criminal Justice at the University of Delaware. He is a past president of the Society for the Study of Social Problems, and a former editor of the society's journal, *Social Problems.* His books on social problems include *Threatened Children, Random Violence, Damned Lies and Statistics, More Damned Lies and Statistics, Social Problems, Stat-Spotting, The Stupidity Epidemic, Images of Issues, The Satanism Scare,* and *How Claims Spread.*

Isabel C. Botero is a Visiting Scholar in the Center for Corporate Communication at Aarhus University, Denmark. Her research interests include communication in and about family firms, influence processes in organizations, information sharing in groups, and crisis communication. Her work has appeared in *Communication Monographs, Management Communication Quarterly, Corporate Communications: An International Journal, Journal of Management Studies,* and *Journal of Cross-Cultural Psychology.*

Kenzie A. Cameron is a Research Associate Professor in the Division of General Internal Medicine and Geriatrics in the Department of Medicine at Northwestern University Feinberg School of Medicine. She applies her background in social influence, message design, and health literacy to research on racial and ethnic health disparities, and develops, evaluates and implements theoretically based multimedia messages for health promotion.

Ke Deng is a Research Associate in the Department of Statistics, Harvard University. His research interests include statistical modeling, statistical computation and applications in bioinformatics, text mining and sociology.

Wolfgang Donsbach is Professor of Communication and Director of the Department of Media and Communication at Dresden University of Technology, Germany. A former president of the World Association for Public Opinion Research and the International Communication Association, he is an ICA Fellow and recipient of the Helen-Dinerman and David Swanson Awards. He is the general editor of the 12-volume *International Encyclopedia of Communication.*

Sharon Dunwoody is Evjue-Bascom Professor of Journalism and Mass Communication at the University of Wisconsin–Madison. She is a Fellow of the Society for Risk Analysis, as well as of the American Association for the Advancement of Science and the Midwest Association for Public Opinion Research. She has published extensively on risk communication processes for 20 years.

W. Wayne Fu is Associate Professor in the Wee Kim Wee School of Communication and Information at Nanyang Technological University. His research focuses on the socioeconomic dynamics of media systems and includes building econometric or statistical models to study communication issues and problems. He also examines online network behaviors and formation of collective attention.

Bernadette M. Gailliard is Assistant Professor of Communication at University of California, Santa Barbara. Her research examines the intersections of race, gender, and class in relation to identity and membership negotiation. She is particularly concerned with the ways that members of underrepresented and marginalized groups navigate increasingly complex organizational environments. Her current work examines communication and identity negotiation processes among professionals in health care organizations.

Cindy Gallois is an Emeritus Professor in Psychology and Communication at the University of Queensland. She is a Fellow of the Academy of the Social Sciences in Australia, International Communication Association, Society of Experimental Social Psychology, and International Academy of Intercultural Relations. She is a past president of the International Communication Association, the International Association of Language and Social Psychology, and the Society of Australasian Social Psychologists.

Robert J. Griffin is a Professor in the Diederich College of Communication at Marquette University. He is a Fellow of the American Association for the Advancement of Science. He has been principal investigator or co-PI on various federally funded research projects on environmental risk, and served for 5 years on a National Research Council standing committee concerned with emerging issues in environmental contamination.

Barrie Gunter is Professor of Mass Communications and Head of the Department of Media and Communication, University of Leicester, England. He has published 50 books and more than 250 articles, papers, and reports on media, marketing, management, and psychology. His research interests include advertising and young people, the social impact of television, and the use of the Internet across generations. He is an Academician of the UK Academy of Social Sciences.

Anders Hansen is Senior Lecturer in the Department of Media and Communication, University of Leicester. His research focuses on media roles in relation to health, science, environment and risk communication. He is Chair of IAMCR's Environment, Science and Risk Communication Group and a Member of the Executive Board of the International Environmental Communication Association. He has published widely on media and alcohol.

Jake Harwood is Professor of Communication at the University of Arizona. He is author of *Understanding Communication and Aging* and coeditor of *Intergroup Communication: Multiple Perspectives* and *The Dynamics of Intergroup Communication.* He is a recipient of the National Communication Association's Giles/Nussbaum Distinguished Scholar Award for outstanding teaching, scholarship, and service to the field of communication and aging.

Miles Hewstone is Professor of Social Psychology and Fellow of New College, University of Oxford. His awards include the Kurt Lewin Award for Distinguished Research Achievement from the European Association for Social Psychology; the Gordon Allport Intergroup Relations Prize; and the Robert B. Cialdini Award. He is a Fellow of the British Academy and an Honorary Fellow of the British Psychological Society.

Hans Hoeken is Professor of Persuasive Communication at the Centre for Language Studies, Radboud University Nijmegen, the Netherlands. His research focuses on language and persuasion. He has published on the use of rhetorical figures in advertising and health communication, the persuasive impact of exemplars and narratives, and the question of what distinguishes strong from weak arguments.

Klaus Krippendorff is Emeritus Professor in the Annenberg School for Communication, University of Pennsylvania. His recent books include *Content Analysis: An Introduction to its Methodology* (3rd ed.); *On Communicating, Otherness, Meaning and Information*; and *The Semantic Turn: A New Foundation for Design.* He is a Fellow of the American Association for the

Advancement of Science, the International Communication Association, and Past President of the International Communication Association.

Paul M. Leonardi holds the Allen K. and Johnnie Cordell Breed Junior Chair in Design and is Assistant Professor of Communication Studies and Industrial Engineering and Management Sciences at Northwestern University. His research and teaching focus on how organizations employ advanced information technologies to more effectively create and share knowledge. He is particularly interested in how computationally sophisticated technologies enable new ways to manage information.

Jun S. Liu is Professor of Statistics and Biostatistics at Harvard University. He is an elected Fellow of the Institute of Mathematical Statistics and of the American Statistical Association. He has won the NSF Career Award, the COPSS Presidents' Award, and the Morningside Gold Medal. He has served as associate editor and coeditor for the *Journal of the American Statistical Association,* and is author of *Monte Carlo Strategies in Scientific Computing.*

Cornelia Mothes is a doctoral student in the Department of Media and Communication at Dresden University of Technology, Germany. She was a research fellow at the Rino Snaidero Scientific Foundation, Majano, Italy, and a scholarship holder of the Studienstiftung des deutschen Volkes (German National Academic Foundation). Her current research focuses on political communication, journalism, and the psychology of news production and consumption.

Karen K. Myers is an Associate Professor in the Department of Communication at the University of California, Santa Barbara. Her primary areas of research are membership negotiation; vocational socialization; organizational identification; organizational knowledge; emotion management; and workplace relationships. Her work has appeared in such venues as *Human Communication Research, Communication Monographs, Communication Theory,* and *Journal of Applied Communication Research.*

Matthew C. Nisbet is Associate Professor of Communication and Director of the Climate Shift Project at American University, Washington, DC. His research investigates the role of communication and media in policymaking and public affairs, focusing on issues related to science, technology and sustainability.

Daniel J. O'Keefe is the Owen L. Coon Professor in the Department of Communication Studies at Northwestern University. His awards include the National Communication Association's Charles Woolbert Research Award; the International Communication Association's John E. Hunter Meta-Analysis Award; the American Forensic Association's Daniel Rohrer Memorial

Research Award; and the International Society for the Study of Argumentation's Distinguished Research Award.

Marshall Scott Poole is Professor of Communication and Director of the Institute for Computing in the Humanities, Arts, and Social Science at the University of Illinois at Urbana-Champaign. He has authored over 150 articles, chapters, and proceedings, and coauthored or edited 11 books including *Organizational Change and Innovation Processes: Theory and Methods for Research*, and *The Handbook of Organizational Change and Innovation*.

Linda L. Putnam is a Professor in the Department of Communication at the University of California, Santa Barbara. She is the coeditor of eight books, including *Building Theories of Organization: The Constitutive Role of Communication*. She is a Distinguished Scholar of the National Communication Association, a Fellow of the International Communication Association, and a recipient of the Lifetime Achievement Award from the International Association for Conflict Management.

Dietram A. Scheufele is the John E. Ross Chaired Professor and Director of Graduate Studies in the Department of Life Sciences Communication at the University of Wisconsin–Madison. His research deals with public opinion on emerging technologies and the political effects of mass communication.

Nicole Tausch is a Lecturer in Social Psychology at the University of St. Andrews and a former British Academy Postdoctoral Fellow at Cardiff University. Her research interests lie in the areas of social identity, intergroup relations, prejudice, and collective action. She is recipient of the British Psychological Society's Award for Outstanding Doctoral Research Contributions to Psychology.

Jeffrey W. Treem is a doctoral student in Media, Technology, and Society in the School of Communication at Northwestern University. His research focuses on the relationship between technology use and social perceptions of expertise, primarily in organizational contexts. His work explores whether changes in information processing associated with technology result in shifts in social structures and attributions of knowledge.

Joseph Turow is the Robert Lewis Shayon Professor of Communication at the University of Pennsylvania's Annenberg School for Communication. He is a Fellow of the International Communication Association and a recipient of the National Communication Association's Distinguished Scholar Award. His most recent book is *The Daily You: How the New Advertising Industry is Defining Your Identity and Your Worth*.

Joseph B. Walther is Professor of Communication and of Telecommunication, Information Studies and Media at Michigan State University. He is associate editor at *Human Communication Research* and the *Journal of Media Psychology*, a former officer in the Academy of Management and ICA, and a two-time recipient of the National Communication Association's Woolbert Research Award.

Z. Janet Yang is Assistant Professor of Communication at the University at Buffalo, State University of New York. Her recent projects include identifying pathways to improve patient accrual for cancer clinical trials, public communication about the H1N1 vaccine, and exploring agenda-setting effects of climate change news coverage on public perception.

Xinshu Zhao is Cheung Kong Chair Professor of Journalism, Fudan University, Shanghai. He is also Chair Professor of Communication and a Codirector of the Carter Center Initiative at Hong Kong Baptist University. He has over 100 publications, including a book in Chinese, *Plight of Elections—A Critique of the World's Election Systems and Constitutional Reforms.*

Lara Zwarun is Associate Professor in the Department of Communication at the University of Missouri–St. Louis. Her research examines the content, regulation, and effects of "sensitive" media messages, such as alcohol and tobacco marketing and television violence. Her most recent work uses media literacy education to increase awareness of how risky products and behaviors are portrayed in the media.

Author Index

Subject Index